Routledge History of Philosophy, Volume VIII

D0209717

Continental philosophy, as it has emerged in the twentieth century, is less a seamless fabric than a patchwork of diverse strands. Phenomenology, hermeneutics, existentialism, structuralism, critical theory, deconstruction – these are some of the salient movements which have developed in continental Europe between 1900 and the 1990s, though their influence is by no means confined to geographical location. Continental thought has proved highly exportable, circulating far beyond the frontiers of Europe to provoke strong responses in the intellectual world at large.

The fourteen articles in this volume outline and assess some of the issues and experiments of continental philosophy. The first five span the twin movements of phenomenology and existentialism, running from Husserl and Heidegger to Sartre, Merleau-Ponty and Levinas. Subsequent essays deal with specific currents of continental thought in such areas as science, Marxism, linguistics, politics, aesthetics, feminism and hermeneutics. A final chapter on postmodernism highlights the manner in which so many concerns of continental thought culminate in a radical anti-foundationalism.

This volume provides a broad, scholarly introduction to this period for students of philosophy and related disciplines, as well as some original interpretations of these authors. It includes a glossary of technical terms and a chronological table of philosophical, scientific and other cultural events.

Richard Kearney is a Professor of Philosophy at University College, Dublin and a Visiting Professor at Boston College. He is the author of *Poetics of Modernity* (1994), *Poetics of Imagining* (1991), *The Wake of Imagination* (1988), *Modern Movements in European Philosophy* (1986) and *Dialogues with Contemporary Continental Thinkers* (1984).

Routledge History of Philosophy

General editors – G.H.R. Parkinson and S.G. Shanker

The *Routledge History of Philosophy* provides a chronological survey of the history of Western philosophy, from its beginnings in the sixth century BC to the present time. It discusses all major philosophical developments in depth. Most space is allocated to those individuals who, by common consent, are regarded as great philosophers. But lesser figures have not been neglected, and together the ten volumes of the *History* include basic and critical information about every significant philosophy of the past and present. These philosophers are clearly situated within the cultural and, in particular, the scientific context of their time.

The *History* is intended not only for the specialist, but also for the student and the general reader. Each chapter is by an acknowledged authority in the field. The chapters are written in an accessible style and a glossary of technical terms is provided in each volume.

Routledge History of Philosophy
Volume VIII

Twentieth-Century Continental Philosophy

EDITED BY
Richard Kearney

London and New York

First published 1994
by Routledge
11 New Fetter Lane, London EC4P 4EE

Simultaneously published in the USA and Canada
by Routledge
29 West 35th Street, New York, NY 10001

© 1994 Richard Kearney and individual contributors

Typeset in 10½/12pt Garamond by Intype, London

Printed and bound in Great Britain by
T.J. Press (Padstow) Ltd, Padstow, Cornwall

British Library Cataloguing in Publication Data

Twentieth-Century Continental Philosophy – Routledge History of Philosophy
Series;
Vol. 8
I. Kearney, Richard
190.9
A catalogue record for this book is available from the British Library

Library of Congress Cataloging-in-Publication Data
Twentieth-century Continental philosophy / edited by Richard Kearney.
p. cm. – (Routledge history of philosophy : v. 8)
Includes bibliographical references and index.
1. Philosophy, Modern–20th century. 2. Philosophy, European.
I. Kearney, Richard. II. Series.
B804.T884 1994
190'.9'04–dc20
93–15763

ISBN 0-415-05629-2

Contents

General editors' preface

The history of philosophy, as its name implies, represents a union of two very different disciplines, each of which imposes severe constraints upon the other. As an exercise in the history of ideas, it demands that one acquire a 'period eye': a thorough understanding of how the thinkers whom it studies viewed the problems which they sought to resolve, the conceptual frameworks in which they addressed these issues, their assumptions and objectives, their blind spots and miscues. But as an exercise in philosophy, we are engaged in much more than simply a descriptive task. There is a crucial aspect to our efforts: we are looking for the cogency as much as the development of an argument, for its bearing on questions which continue to preoccupy us as much as the impact which it may have had on the evolution of philosophical thought.

The history of philosophy thus requires a delicate balancing act from its practitioners. We read these writings with the full benefit of hindsight. We can see why the minor contributions remained minor and where the grand systems broke down: sometimes as a result of internal pressures, sometimes because of a failure to overcome an insuperable obstacle, sometimes because of a dramatic technological or sociological change, and, quite often, because of nothing more than a shift in intellectual fashion or interests. Yet, because of our continuing philosophical concern with many of the same problems, we cannot afford to look dispassionately at these works. We want to know what lessons are to be learnt from the inconsequential or the glorious failures; many times we want to plead for a contemporary relevance in the overlooked theory or to reconsider whether the 'glorious failure' was indeed such or simply ahead of its time: perhaps even ahead of its author.

We find ourselves, therefore, much like the mythical 'radical translator' who has so fascinated modern philosophers, trying to understand author's ideas in their and their culture's eyes, and at the same time, in our own. It can be a formidable task. Many times we fail in the historical undertaking because our philosophical interests are so strong, or lose sight of the latter because we are so enthralled by the former. But the nature of philosophy is such that we are compelled to master both techniques. For learning about the history of philosophy is not just a challenging and engaging pastime: it is an essential element in learning about the nature of philosophy – in grasping how philosophy is intimately connected with and yet distinct from both history and science.

The *Routledge History of Philosophy* provides a chronological survey of the history of Western philosophy, from its beginnings up to the present time. Its aim is to discuss all major philosophical developments in depth, and, with this in mind, most space has been allocated to those individuals who, by common consent, are regarded as great philosophers. But lesser figures have not been neglected, and it is hoped that the reader will be able to find, in the ten volumes of the *History*, at least basic information about any significant philosopher of the past or present.

Philosophical thinking does not occur in isolation from other human activities, and this *History* tries to situate philosophers within the cultural, and in particular the scientific, context of their time. Some philosophers, indeed, would regard philosophy as merely ancillary to the natural sciences; but even if this view is rejected, it can hardly be denied that the sciences have had a great influence on what is now regarded as philosophy, and it is important that this influence should be set forth clearly. Not that these volumes are intended to provide a mere record of the factors that influenced philosophical thinking; philosophy is a discipline with its own standards of argument, and the presentation of the ways in which these arguments have developed is the main concern of this *History*.

In speaking of 'what is now regarded as philosophy', we may have given the impression that there now exists a single view of what philosophy is. This is certainly not the case; on the contrary, there exist serious differences of opinion, among those who call themselves philosophers, about the nature of their subject. These differences are reflected in the existence at the present time of two main schools of thought, usually described as 'analytic' and 'continental' philosophy respectively. It is not our intention, as general editors of this *History*, to take sides in this dispute. Our attitude is one of tolerance, and our hope is that these volumes will contribute to an understanding of how philosophers have reached the positions which they now occupy.

One final comment. Philosophy has long been a highly technical subject, with its own specialized vocabulary. This *History* is intended not only for the specialist but also for the general reader. To this end, we have tried to ensure that each chapter is written in an accessible style; and since technicalities are unavoidable, a glossary of technical terms is provided in each volume. In this way these volumes will, we hope, contribute to a wider understanding of a subject which is of the highest importance to all thinking people.

G.H.R. Parkinson
S.G. Shanker

Notes on contributors

Alison Ainley is Lecturer in Philosophy at Anglia Polytechnic University, Cambridge, and author of a forthcoming book on Luce Irigaray.

Babette Babich is Professor of Philosophy at Fordham University, New York, and author of several studies on continental thought.

Richard Cobb-Stevens is Head of the Philosophy Department at Boston College and author of *James and Husserl* (1974) and *Husserl and Analytic Philosophy* (1989).

Simon Critchley is Lecturer in Philosophy at the University of Essex and author of *The Ethics of Deconstruction* (1992) and co-editor of *Re-Reading Levinas* (1991).

Bernard Cullen is a Professor of Philosophy at Queen's University, Belfast, editor of the *Irish Philosophical Journal* and author of *Hegel and Political Theory*.

William Desmond is Chair of Philosophy at Loyola College, Baltimore, visiting professor at Louvain University and author of *Desire, Dialectic and Otherness* (1988), *Art and the Absolute* (1986) and *Philosophy and its Others* (1991).

Thomas Docherty is Chair of the Department of English at Trinity College, Dublin and author of *On Modern Authority* (1987), *Reading (Absent) Character* (1983), *John Donne, Undone* (1986) and *After Theory* (1991).

Thomas R. Flynn is Professor of Philosophy at Emory University and author of several studies of modern continental thought.

Michael Kelly is Professor of French at the University of Southhampton, and author of several books including *Modern French Marxism* (1982).

Gary Madison is Professor of Philosophy at McMaster University, Canada and founder-director of the Canadian Society of Hermeneutics and Postmodern Thought. He is the author of *Phénoménologie de Merleau-Ponty* (1973), *Understanding* (1982), *Logic of Liberty* (1986) and *Hermeneutics of Postmodernity* (1988).

Timothy Mooney is a Lecturer in Philosophy at University College, Dublin, and author of several studies of modern European thought.

Mara Rainwater is a Lecturer in Philosophy at University College, Dublin. Her special areas of interest include Critical Theory, Nietzsche, and Communicative Ethics.

David Rasmussen is Professor of Philosophy at Boston College, founder-editor of the journal *Philosophy and Social Criticism* and author of *Reading Habermas* (1991).

Giacomo Rinaldi is Professor of Philosophy at the University of Urbino and an expert in German and Italian idealist philosophy.

Hugh J. Silverman is Professor of Philosophy and Comparative Literature at the State University of New York at Stony Brook and author of *Inscriptions: Between Phenomenology and Structuralism* (1987), editor of *Philosophy and Non-Philosophy since Merleau-Ponty* (1988) and Executive Director of the International Association for Philosophy and Literature.

Jacques Taminiaux is Professor of Philosophy at the University of Louvain and Boston College, Director of the Centre d'études phénoménologiques at Louvain University, and author of many books on continental philosophy including *Dialectic and Difference* (1985), *Heidegger's Project of Fundamental Ontology* (1991) and *Poetics, Speculations and Judgment* (1994).

Chronology
Mara Rainwater, University College Dublin

Unless otherwise specified, the dates assigned to books or articles are the dates of publication, and the dates assigned to musical or stage works are those of first performance. The titles of works not written in English have been translated, unless they are better known in their original form.

	Continental philosophy: roots and dialogue	The arts
1755	Rousseau, *Discourse on the Origin of Inequality*	
1756		Voltaire, 'Poem on the Disaster at Lisbon' (1755 earthquake)
1759	Hamann, *Socratic Memorabilia*	Sterne, *Tristram Shandy* Voltaire, *Candide*
1762	Rousseau, *Emile* Rousseau, *The Social Contract*	Diderot, *Rameau's Nephew*
1764		Voltaire, *Philosophical Dictionary*
1765		
1766		Lessing, *Laöcoon* 'Sturm und Drang' Movement to 1787 (Goethe, Schiller, Herder)
1772	Herder, *On the Origin of Language*	
1774		Goethe, *The Sorrows of Young Werther*
1779		Lessing, *Nathan the Wise*
1781	Kant, *Critique of Pure Reason* ('A' edition)	Schiller, *The Robbers*
1783	Kant, *Prolegomena to any Future Metaphysics*	
1784	Herder, *Outlines of the Philosophy of the History of Mankind* (4 vols, 1784–91) Kant, 'Idea for a Universal History'	Beaumarchais, *The Marriage of Figaro*
1785	Kant, *Foundations of the Metaphysics of Morals*	
1787	Jacobi, 'On the Transcendental Idealism' Kant, *Critique of Pure Reason* ('B' edition)	Mozart, *Don Giovanni* Schiller, *Don Carlos*

Science and technology	Politics	
Magnesium discovered (Davy)	War between French and British in North America Lisbon earthquake kills 35,000	1755
	Seven Years War in Europe (1756–63)	1756
	French defeated in Quebec by British	1759
	Catherine II (The Great); Tsarina 1762–96	1762
Spinning jenny (Hargreaves)		1764
Condensing steam engine (Watt)	Joseph II of Austria; Holy Roman Emperor until 1790	1765
Hydrogen discovered (Cavendish)		1766
Nitrogen discovered (Rutherford)	Poland partitioned among Russia, Prussia, and Austria	1772
Oxygen (Priestly and Scheele)	Louis XVI; King of France (to 1792)	1774
First cast-iron bridge at Coalbrookdale, Shropshire	Spain joins French and Americans against Britain	1779
	British surrender to French and American forces at Yorktown, Virginia	1781
First successful hot-air balloon (Montgolfier brothers)	Treaty of Paris ending American War of Independence	1783
		1784
Power loom (Cartwright)	Frederick the Great establishes League of German Princes against Joseph II of Austria	1785
	French Assembly dismissed for refusal to introduce financial reforms	1787

	Continental philosophy: roots and dialogue	The arts
1788	Kant, *Critique of Practical Reason*	Goethe, *Egmont*
1789		Blake, *Songs of Innocence*
1790	Kant, *Critique of Judgment*	
1791		Mozart, *The Magic Flute*
1792	Fichte, *Attempt at a Critique of All Revelation* Wollstonecraft, *Vindication of the Rights of Women*	
1793		
1794	Condorcet, *Sketch for a Historical Picture of the Human Mind* Fichte, Jena *Wissenschaftslehre*	Blake, *Songs of Experience*
1795	Schelling, *Philosophical Letters on Dogmatism and Criticism* von Humboldt, *On Thought and Language*	Goethe, *Wilhelm Meister's Apprenticeship* Schiller, *On the Aesthetic Education of Mankind*
1796		
1797	Kant, *Metaphysics of Morals* Schelling, *Ideas for a Philosophy of Nature*	Goethe and Schiller, *Ballads* Hölderlin, *Hyperion*
1798		Wordsworth and Coleridge, *Lyrical Ballads*
1799	Schleiermacher, 'On Religion' von Humboldt, *Aesthetic Essays*	Goya, *Los Caprichos* Schiller, *Wallenstein's Death* Schlegel, *Lucinde*
1800	Fichte, *The Vocation of Man* Schelling, *System of Transcendental Idealism* Schleiermacher translates Plato into German (1800–28)	Beethoven, *First Symphony* Novalis, *Hymn to the Night*
1802		Mme. de Stael, *Delphine* Novalis, *Heinrich von Ofterdingen*
1804		Schiller, *Wilhelm Tell*
1807	Hegel, *Phenomenology of Spirit* (Jena)	Beethoven, *Fourth Symphony*

Science and technology	Politics	
	First convicts shipped from Britain to Australia	1788
Theory of Combustion (Lavoisier)	Storming of the Bastille, Paris; the French Revolution begins	1789
		1790
Metric system proposed by France	Louis XVI and family captured; he affirms new French Constitution	1791
	France declared a Republic; Austria and Prussia unite against France	1792
Cotton gin (Whitney)	Louis XVI and Marie Antoinette executed; Reign of Terror under Robespierre	1793
	Danton and Robespierre executed; ends Reign of Terror	1794
	France makes peace with Spain and Prussia	1795
Lithography invented (Senefelder) Laplace, *System of the World*	Napoleon Bonaparte leads French army to conquer Italy	1796
		1797
Malthus, *Essay on the Principle of Population*	French occupy Rome, Switzerland, Egypt; Vinegar Hill Rebellion in Ireland for separation from Britain	1798
	Napoleon rules France as Consulate until 1804	1799
First electric battery (Volta)		1800
	Bonaparte created First Consul for life	1802
Steam locomotive (Trevithick)	Napoleon crowns self Emperor 'Napoleon I' and the First Empire begins	1804
The *Clermont*, first steamship (Fulton)	British abolish slave trade throughout their empire	1807

	Continental philosophy: roots and dialogue	The arts
1808		Goethe, *Faust* (Pt I)
1809	Schelling, *Philosophical Inquiries into the Nature of Human Freedom*	Chateaubriand, *Les Martyrs*
1811		
1812	Hegel, *Science of Logic* (3 vols, 1812–16)	
1813	Schopenhauer, *On the Fourfold Root of the Principle of Sufficient Reason*	
1814		Goya, *Executions of 3rd May*
1815	de Tracy, *Elements of Ideology* (4 vols, 1801–15) Schopenhauer, *On Vision and Colours*	
1817	Hegel, *Encyclopedia of the Philosophical Sciences*	
1818	Schopenhauer, *The World as Will and Representation*	Grillparzer, *Sappho*
1820		Lamartine, *Meditations*
1821	Hegel, *Philosophy of Right* Schleiermacher, *The Christian Faith* (2 vols)	De Quincey, *Confessions of an Opium Eater* Heine, *Poems*
1822		
1825	Saint-Simon, *The New Christianity*	
1826		Hölderlin, *Lyrical Poems*
1827		
1830	Comte, *Positive Philosophy* (6 vols, 1830–42) Feuerbach, *Thoughts Concerning Death and Immortality*	Berlioz, *Symphonie Fantastique* Stendhal, *The Red and the Black*
1831		
1832		Goethe, *Faust* (Pt II)
1837	Bolzano, *Scientific Writings* (4 vols)	Balzac, *Lost Illusions* (1837–43)

Science and technology	Politics	
	French occupy Spain; Joseph Bonaparte becomes King of Spain	1808
		1809
Avogadro's Molecular Hypothesis	Luddite riots in England against mechanization in the textile industry	1811
	500,000 of Napoleon's army die in retreat from Moscow	1812
	Coalition of Austria, Prussia, Russia, Britain and Sweden invades France	1813
Laplace, *A Philosophical Essay on Probabilities*	Treaty of Paris ends Napoleonic Wars; Napoleon abdicates and is exiled to Elba; Congress of Vienna	1814
	Napoleon escapes Elba; marches on Paris; Battle of Waterloo; Napoleon exiled to St Helena	1815
Kaleidoscope (Brewster)		1817
	Aix-la-Chapelle: France joins great powers in Quintuple Alliance	1818
Electromagnetism (Oersted)	Liberal revolutions in Spain, Portugal, and Italy	1820
		1821
Camera (Niepce)		1822
Electromagnet (Sturgeon)	In Russia, Decembrist Rising against Tsar	1825
Laws of Electromagnetism (Ampère) First permanent photograph (Niepce)		1826
Ohm's Law of Electromagnetic Conduction		1827
Lyell, *Principles of Geology* (3 vols)	Paris July Revolution Charles X overthrown; Louis-Philippe King (to 1848)	1830
Electromagnetic induction (Faraday and Henry)	Mazzini forms 'Young Italy' movement; Polish revolution crushed by Russians	1831
	Reform Act passed in Britain	1832
Telegraph (Morse)	Victoria Queen of England (to 1901)	1837

	Continental philosophy: roots and dialogue	The arts
1839	Feuerbach, *Towards a Critique of Hegelian Philosophy*	
1841	Feuerbach, *The Essence of Christianity* Proudhon, *What Is Property?*	Emerson, *Essays* (1841–4) Turner, *Snowstorm – Steamboat off a Harbour's Mouth*
1842		Gogol, *Dead Souls* G. Sand, *Consuelo*
1843	Feuerbach, *Provisional Theses* Kierkegaard, *Fear and Trembling* Kierkegaard, *Repetition* Kierkegaard, *Either/Or* Marx, *Critique of Hegel's Philosophy of Right*	Ruskin, *Modern Painters*
1844	Kierkegaard, *The Concept of Dread* Marx, *The Paris Manuscripts* Stirner, *The Ego and Its Own*	Chateaubriand, *Life of Rancé*
1845	Marx, *Theses on Feuerbach* Marx and Engels, *The Holy Family*	Gautier, *España*
1846	Kierkegaard, *Concluding Unscientific Postscript* Marx and Engels, *The German Ideology*	Michelet, *The People*
1848	Marx and Engels, *Communist Manifesto*	
1851	Proudhon, *General Idea of the Revolution in the 19th Century*	Sainte-Beuve, *Lundis*
1852		Grimm, German Dictionary (vol. 1, 1852–4)
1854		Nerval, *Aurélia*
1855		Transformation of Paris by Haussmann
1857	Marx, drafts *Grundrisse*	Flaubert, *Madame Bovary* Baudelaire, *Les Fleurs du mal*
1859		
1862	Brentano, *On the Manifold Sense of Being in Aristotle*	Hugo, *Les Misérables* Turgenev, *Fathers and Sons*
1863	Proudhon, *On the Federal Principle*	Salon des Refusés – Paris Tolstoy, *War and Peace* (1863–9)

Science and technology	Politics	
Vulcanized rubber (Goodyear) Ozone discovered (Schönbein)	Opium War between China and Britain	1839
		1841
'Doppler Effect' predicted the apparent change in wavelength when the observer and wave source are in relative motion (C. Doppler)	Hong Kong ceded to Britain	1842
	Natal becomes British colony	1843
		1844
		1845
Planet Neptune discovered (Galle) Sewing machine (Howe)	Potato famine in Ireland (a million dead by 1851)	1846
	Revolutions throughout Europe Louis-Philippe abdicates in Paris	1848
	Bakunin imprisoned by Tsar (1851-7)	1851
Gyroscope (L. Foucault)		1852
	Crimean War: France, Britain, and Turkey against Russia (to 1856)	1854
Celluloid (Parkes) Conversion process for steel (Bessemer)		1855
	Indian mutiny (Lucknow) against Britain	1857
Darwin, *The Origin of Species* Internal combustion engine (Lenoir)		1859
Rapid repeat-fire gun (Gatling)	Bismarck becomes Prime Minister in Prussia	1862
	French occupation of Mexico City Lincoln emancipates slaves	1863

	Continental philosophy: roots and dialogue	The arts
1864		Dostoyevsky, *Notes from Underground*
1865	Taine, *Philosophy of Art*	Wagner, *Tristan and Isolde*
1866		Dostoyevsky, *Crime and Punishment*
1867	Marx, *Das Kapital*	Ibsen, *Peer Gynt*
1869		Wagner, *Ring Series* produced 1869–76
1870	Dilthey, *The Life of Schleiermacher*	Rosetti, *Poems*
1871		Zola, *Rougon-Macquart Series*
1873	Nietzsche, *Untimely Meditations* Stumpf, *On the Psychological Origin of the Idea of Space*	Rimbaud, *A Season in Hell*
1874	Brentano, *Psychology from an Empirical Standpoint*	First Impressionist Exhibition in Paris
1876		Turgenev, *Virgin Soil*
1877		Rodin, *Age of Bronze*
1879	Frege, *The Foundations of Arithmetic*	Ibsen, *A Doll's House*
1880		French Symbolist Movement (1880–95) Mallarmé, Verlaine
1882	Nietzsche, *The Gay Science*	Wagner, *Parsifal*
1883	Dilthey, *Introduction to the Human Sciences* Mach, *The Science of Mechanics*	
1885		Cézanne, *Mont S. Victoire* Van Gogh, *The Potato-Eaters* Van Gogh, *The Sunflowers*
1886	Nietzsche, *Beyond Good and Evil*	Pointillism (Seurat, Signac, Luce)
1887	Husserl, *On the Concept of Number: A Psychological Analysis* Nietzsche, *On the Genealogy of Morals*	Strindberg, *The Father*

Science and technology	Politics	
Maxwell's Electromagnetic Theory of Light	Marx founds First International in London; Bakunin challenges his leadership	1864
	End of American Civil War; Lincoln assassinated	1865
Dynamite invented (Nobel)	Treaty of Paris ends Austro-Prussian War	1866
Typewriter (Scholes)	Prussian leadership of North German Confederation	1867
Periodic arrangement of elements (Mendeleev)		1869
	Kingdom of Italy annexes Papal States French Third Republic begins	1870
Darwin, 'The Descent of Man'	Paris Commune crushed German Empire declared by Wilhelm I	1871
	First Republic of Spain (to 1874)	1873
		1874
Telephone (Bell)	Britain and France take joint control of Egypt's finances	1876
Phonograph (Edison)	Queen Victoria as Empress of India	1877
Incandescent lamp (Edison)	Irish Land League under Parnell	1879
	Boers revolt against British control in South Africa	1880
	Triple Alliance: Germany, Austria, Italy (to 1914)	1882
	Health insurance introduced in Germany	1883
First rabies innoculation (Pasteur) Electric transformer (Stanley)	French protectorate over Indochina	1885
Electromagnetic waves discovered (Hertz)	Gladstone's Irish Home Rule Bill defeated in Parliament	1886
Gramophone (Berliner) Motor car engine (Daimler and Benz)	Italy and Ethiopia at war	1887

	Continental philosophy: roots and dialogue	The arts
1888	Natorp, *Introduction to the Psychology of Critical Method*	
1889	Bergson, *Time and Free Will*	Hauptmann, *Before Sunrise*
1890	Frazer, *The Golden Bough* Guyau, *The Origin of the Idea of Time*	Van Gogh, *Road with Cypress Trees*
1891	Husserl, *Philosophy of Arithmetic*	Gauguin leaves France for Tahiti
1893	Durkheim, *The Division of Labour in Society* Mach, *Popular Scientific Lectures*	*Art Nouveau* in architecture: Horta's 'Tassel House' (Brussels)
1894	Husserl, *Psychological Studies on Elementary Logic*	Monet, *Rouen Cathedral Series* Wilde, *Salomé*, with Beardsley illustrations
1895	Freud, *Studies on Hysteria*	Munch, *The Cry*
1896	Bergson, *Matter and Memory* Santayana, *The Sense of Beauty*	
1897	Durkheim, *Suicide*	
1898		
1899		Tolstoy, *Resurrection*
1900	Freud, *The Interpretation of Dreams* Husserl, *Logical Investigations* (vol. 1)	Chekhov, *Uncle Vanya* Mahler, *Fourth Symphony* Sibelius, *Finlandia*
1901	Husserl, *Logical Investigations* (vol. 2)	T. Mann, *Buddenbrooks* Strindberg, *The Dance of Death*
1902	Croce, *Aesthetics as a Science of Expression and General Linguistics* Poincaré, *Science and Hypothesis*	Gide, *The Immoralist* Monet, *Waterloo Bridge*
1903		Schoenberg begins teaching in Vienna Salon d'Automne in Paris
1904	Duhem, *The Aim and Structure of Physical Theory* (1904–6) Meinong, *On the Theory of the Object*	Isadora Duncan performs in Berlin Puccini, *Madame Butterfly*

Science and technology	Politics	
Kodak camera (Eastman) Pneumatic tyre (Boyd)	Wilhelm II German Emperor (to 1918)	1888
	French collapse of Panama Canal Company in financial scandal	1889
Rotogravure process (Klic)		1890
Cinema history: Edison patents the Kinetoscope and Kinetograph		1891
	French protectorate over Ivory Coast	1893
	Dreyfus Affair in France Nicholas II last Russian Tsar (to 1918)	1894
Marconi's wireless (radio) Discovery of X-Ray (Roentgen) Edison patents Kinetophone for sound		1895
Radioactivity discovered (Becquerel) 'Cinematographie' in France (Lumière)	France annexes Madagascar Boundaries of Siam (Thailand) settled by British and French	1896
Diesel engine (Diesel) Discovery of electron (Thomson)		1897
Radium discovered (P. & M. Curie)	Treaty of Paris: Cuban independence from Spain	1898
Tape recorder (Poulsen)	First Hague Peace Conference to settle international disputes	1899
Max Planck's Quantum Theory	German Navy Law begins arms increase with Britain Boxer Rebellion in China	1900
	Increasing terrorist activity in Russia	1901
Radio-Telephone invented (Fessenden)		1902
Wright Brothers first aeroplane flight	Bolshevik–Menshevik split Emmeline Pankhurst forms Women's Social and Political Union	1903
Diode (Fleming)	Entente-Cordiale between France and Britain	1904

	Continental philosophy: roots and dialogue	The arts
1905	Mach, *Knowledge and Error* Weber, *The Protestant Ethic and the Spirit of Capitalism*	Matisse, *Woman with a Hat* (Fauvism) German artists (Kirchner, Bleyl) form *Die Brücke* (The Bridge) Debussy, *La Mer*
1906	Santayana, *The Life of Reason*	
1907	Bergson, *Creative Evolution* Husserl, *The Idea of Phenomenology* W. James, *Pragmatism*	Picasso, *Les Demoiselles d'Avignon* Stefan George, *The Seventh Ring*
1908	Poincaré, *Science and Method*	Brancusi's sculpture, *The Kiss*
1909	Croce, *Pragmatic Philosophy* W. James, *A Pluralistic Universe*	Diaghilev and Fokine, *Ballets Russes* in Paris Marinetti, *Futurist Manifesto*
1910	Husserl, *Philosophy as a Rigorous Science* (1910–11) Russell and Whitehead, *Principia Mathematica* (3 vols, 1910–13)	Rilke, *The Notebooks of Malte Laurids Brigge* Stravinsky, *The Firebird* for Diaghilev
1911	Bergson, 'Philosophical Intuition'	German Expressionism: *Der Blaue Reiter* (Blue Rider) group, 1911–14 (Klee, Marc, Kandinsky)
1912	Durkheim, *The Elementary Forms of Religious Life*	Duchamp, *Nude Descending a Staircase* Nijinsky performs *Afternoon of a Fawn* for Diaghilev's company
1913	Husserl, *Ideas, General Introduction to Pure Phenomenology* Jung, *Psychology of the Unconscious* R. Luxemburg, *The Accumulation of Capital* Unamuno, *The Tragic Sense of Life*	Apollinaire, *Alcools* Proust, *Remembrance of Things Past* Stravinsky, *Rites of Spring*
1914	Ortega y Gasset, *Meditations on Quijote*	Joyce, *Dubliners*
1915		D.W. Griffith, *Birth of a Nation* Kafka, *The Metamorphosis* Pound begins *Cantos*
1916	Gentile, *General Theory of Spirit as Pure Act* Saussure, *Course in General Linguistics* Scheler, *Formalism in Ethics*	Dada Movement in Zurich (Arp, Tzara)
1917	Lenin, *State and Revolution*	Satie, *Parade* for *Ballets Russes* Picasso, designs costumes for *Parade*
1918	Masaryk, *The New Europe*	Tzara, *Dada Manifesto* Malevich, *White Square on a White Background*

Science and technology	Politics	
Einstein's Special Theory of Relativity	St Petersburg 'Bloody Sunday': troops fire on crowd resulting in general strike and revolt	1905
Triode (DeForest)	First Russian Duma meets but is dissolved	1906
	Second Hague Peace Conference	1907
	Austria annexes Bosnia-Herzogovina	1908
Henry Ford begins 'Assembly-Line' production Peary reaches North Pole	Old-age pensions introduced in Britain	1909
	Suffragette movement increases demands	1910
Combine harvester (Holt) Amundsen reaches South Pole	German–French confrontation in Morocco Manchu Dynasty falls to Sun Yat-sen	1911
	French protectorate in Morocco	1912
Atomic Number (Moseley) Bohr's Model of the Atom	Third Irish Home Rule Bill defeated	1913
Tank (Swinton)	Archduke Franz Ferdinand of Austria assassinated in Sarajevo First World War begins	1914
Einstein publishes *General Theory of Relativity*	Sinking of the *Lusitania*	1915
	Easter Rising in Ireland suppressed German offensive on Western Front	1916
	October Revolution in Russia; Bolsheviks victorious	1917
Automatic rifle (Browning)	Armistice ending First World War	1918

	Continental philosophy: roots and dialogue	The arts
1919	Wittgenstein, *Tractatus Logico-Philosophicus*	*Bauhaus* Architecture and Design (1919–33): Kandinsky, Albers, Klee; Wieve, *The Cabinet of Dr. Caligari*; German Expressionist films (1919–30)
1920	Freud, *Beyond the Pleasure Principle*	
1921	Mach, *The Principles of Physical Optics* Rosenzweig, *The Star of Redemption*	Pirandello, *Six Characters in Search of an Author* Man Ray, *Rayographs*
1922	Bergson, *Duration and Simultaneity*	Eliot, *The Waste Land* Joyce, *Ulysses*
1923	Buber, *I and Thou* Cassirer, *The Philosophy of Symbolic Forms* (3 vols, 1923–9) Korsch, *Marxism and Philosophy* Lukács, *History and Class Consciousness*	Le Corbusier, *Vers une architecture* Rilke, *Duino Elegies* Yeats receives Nobel Prize
1924	N. Hartmann, *Ethics*	A. Breton, *Surrealist Manifesto* T. Mann, *The Magic Mountain* Schoenberg, 12-tone *Suite for Piano*
1925		Eisenstein, *Battleship Potemkin*
1926	Scheler, *Forms of Knowledge*	Lang, *Metropolis*
1927	Heidegger, *Being and Time* Santayana, *Realms of Being* (4 vols, 1927–40)	Artaud & Vitrac, Théâtre Alfred Jarry V. Woolf, *To the Lighthouse*
1928	Bachelard, *The New Scientific Spirit*	Brecht & Weill, *The Threepenny Opera*
1929	Dewey, *Experience and Nature* Heidegger, *What is Metaphysics?* Heidegger, *Kant and the Problem of Metaphysics* Husserl, *Formal and Transcendental Logic* Mannheim, *Ideology and Utopia* Piaget, *The Child's Concept of the World* Volosinov, *Marxism and the Philosophy of Language*	Bakhtin, *Problems of Dostoyevsky's Poetics* Rivera, *Workers of the Revolution* Vertov, *Man with a Movie Camera*
1930	Freud, *Civilization and Its Discontents* Ortega y Gasset, *The Revolt of the Masses*	Buñuel & Dali, Surrealist film, *L'Age d'or* Empson, *Seven Types of Ambiguity*

Science and technology	Politics	
Discovery of proton (Rutherford)	Treaty of Versailles sets reparations Rosa Luxemburg murdered in Germany Mussolini's fascist movement in Italy League of Nations founded	1919
	Weimar Republic in Germany Civil War in Ireland	1920
	Irish Free State established	1921
	March on Rome by Mussolini	1922
	Hitler imprisoned after abortive Munich 'putsch'	1923
Wave nature of electron (de Broglie)	Lenin dies; succeeded by Stalin	1924
First working television (Baird)		1925
Rocket (liquid) fuel (Goddard) Schrödinger's Wave Mechanics	Germany admitted to League of Nations	1926
Heisenberg's 'Uncertainty Principle' that position and momentum of a body cannot be simultaneously determined; First transatlantic flight (Lindbergh)	Civil War in China: Communists against Nationalists	1927
	Kellogg–Briand Pact: Major powers renounce war	1928
Zworykin's electronic television system adopted as standard	Collapse of Wall Street leads to world- wide economic depression	1929
Jet engine (Whittle)	London Naval Conference: failure to agree on arms limitation	1930

	Continental philosophy: roots and dialogue	The arts
1931	Husserl, *Cartesian Meditations* Jaspers, *Man in the Modern Age*	Gide, *Oedipus* Ravel, *Piano Concerto for the Left Hand*
1932	Bergson, *Two Sources of Morality and Religion* Maritain, *The Degrees of Knowledge*	Céline, *Journey to the End of Night*
1933	Kojève, Paris Seminars on Hegel's *Phenomenology* (1933–9)	Malraux, *The Human Condition*
1934		René Char, *The Hammer without a Master* H. Miller, *Tropic of Cancer* Webern, *Concerto for Nine Instruments*
1935	Berdyaev, *The Fate of Man in the Modern World* Marcel, *Being and Having*	Canetti, *Auto-da-Fé*
1936	W. Benjamin, 'The Work of Art in the Age of Mechanical Reproduction' Husserl, *Crisis of European Sciences and Transcendental Phenomenology*	International Surrealist Exhibition
1937	C. Caudwell, *Illusion and Reality*	Picasso, *Guernica* J. Renoir, *The Grand Illusion*
1938	Bachelard, *The Psychoanalysis of Fire* Husserl Archives established at Louvain	Artaud, *The Theatre and Its Double* Beckett, *Murphy* Brecht, *Mother Courage* Sartre, *Nausea*
1939	Sartre, *Sketch for a Theory of Emotions*	Joyce, *Finnegans Wake* Saurraute, *Tropisms*
1940	Marcel, *Creative Fidelity* Sartre, *Psychology of Imagination*	Picasso, *Woman Dressing Her Hair*
1941	Bultmann, *The New Testament and Mythology* Marcuse, *Reason and Revolution* Whorf, *Language, Thought and Reality* (1941–56)	*Maltese Falcon*; cinematic style (*film noir*) influenced by Cain, Hammett, Chandler
1942	Merleau-Ponty, *The Structure of Comportment*	Anouilh, *Antigone* Camus, *Myth of Sisyphus* Camus, *The Outsider*
1943	Hjelmslev, *Prolegomena to a Theory of Language* Sartre, *Being and Nothingness*	Musil, *The Man Without Qualities* Sartre, *The Flies*

Science and technology	Politics	
Pauli's predicts massless neutrino Gödel's Incompleteness Theorum claiming the unprovability of mathematical first principles	Britain abandons gold standard Japanese aggression in Manchuria	1931
Neutron discovered (Chadwick)	Geneva Disarmament Conference	1932
	Hitler appointed Chancellor by von Hindenburg; Reichstag burned; Germany withdraws from League of Nations	1933
	Hitler becomes Führer Stalin purges Communist Party	1934
Radar discovered (Watson-Watt)	Hitler renounces Treaty of Versailles Mao Tse-tung: The Long March	1935
	Spanish Civil War (1936–9) Germany reoccupies Rhineland	1936
		1937
	Anschluss: Hitler annexes Austria Munich Pact: Germany, Italy, Britain, and France	1938
Electron microscope (Zworykin)	Second World War begins Germany invades Poland	1939
Plutonium discovered (Seaborg)	Nazi occupation of Paris Trotsky assassinated in Mexico Japan joins Axis Powers	1940
	Germany invades Russia; Leningrad siege Pearl Harbor bombed by Japan; American entry into Second World War	1941
	Battle of Stalingrad; Germany defeated Rommel defeated by Allies in North Africa	1942
	Italian government surrenders	1943

	Continental philosophy: roots and dialogue	The arts
1944	Adorno and Horkheimer, *Dialectic of Enlightenment* Marcel, *Homo Viator*	Bartok, *Violin Concerto* Eliot, *Four Quartets* Sartre, *No Exit*
1945	Bataille, *On Nietzsche* Merleau-Ponty, *Phenomenology of Perception*	Broch, *The Death of Virgil* Sartre, *Roads to Freedom*; vol. 1 – *The Age of Reason*; vol. 2 – *The Reprieve*
1946	Collingwood, *The Idea of History* Sartre, *Existentialism and Humanism*	Italian Neo-Realism in film (1946–54) De Sica, Fellini, Rossellini, Visconti Rossellini, *Rome Open City*
1947	de Beauvoir, *Ethics of Ambiguity* Gramsci, *Letters from Prison* Heidegger, 'Letter on Humanism' Horkheimer, *Eclipse of Reason* Levinas, *Existence and Existents*	Pollock, *Full Fathom Five* Camus, *The Plague*
1948	Adorno, *Philosophy of Modern Music* Gramsci, *Prison Notebooks* (6 vols, 1948–51) Merleau-Ponty, *Sense and Non-Sense*	René Char, *Fury and Mystery* De Sica, *Bicycle Thieves* Orwell, *1984* R. Strauss, *Four Last Songs*
1949	de Beauvoir, *The Second Sex* S. Weil, *The Need for Roots*	Genet, *Deathwatch* Sartre, *Iron in the Soul* (vol. 3 of trilogy *Roads to Freedom*)
1950	Austin, *How to Do Things with Words* Marcel, *The Mystery of Being*	Blanchot, *The Space of Literature* Ionesco, *The Bald Soprano*
1951	Adorno, *Minima Moralia* Arendt, *The Origins of Totalitarianism* Camus, *The Rebel*	Beckett, *Molloy*; *Malone Dies* Dali, *Christ of St. John of the Cross*
1952	Goldmann, *The Human Sciences and Philosophy*	Boulez, *Structures* Buñuel, *El*
1953	Barthes, *Writing Degree Zero* Dufrenne, *The Phenomenology of Aesthetic Experience* Heidegger, *Introduction to Metaphysics* Lacan, 'Rome Discourse' ('Function of Language in Psychoanalysis') Lacan, *Seminar I* (1953–78: XXVI Seminars) Wittgenstein, *Philosophical Investigations*	Beckett, *Waiting for Godot* Milosz, *The Usurpers*
1954	Heidegger, *Discourse on Thinking*	Balthus, *Nude Playing with a Cat* Fellini, *La Strada*

Science and technology	Politics	
Automatic digital computer (Aikin)	Allied Normandy Landing Paris and Brussels liberated	1944
	Atomic Bomb on Hiroshima and Nagasaki Mussolini assassinated Hitler suicide Yalta Conference	1945
Electronic computer (Eckert & Mauchly)	UN replaces League of Nations Nuremburg trials French Indo-China War begins	1946
Polaroid camera (Land)	Marshall Aid Program for Europe UN approves partition of Palestine	1947
Xerography invented (Carlson) Long-playing record (Goldmark) Transistor (Bardeen, Brattain, Schockley)	Soviet blockage of West Berlin State of Israel declared	1948
von Neumann, 'Recent Theories of Turbulence'	Germany divided: Federal Republic and German Democratic Republic Mao Tse-tung Communist victory in China	1949
Einstein's Unified Field Theory Turing, 'Computing Machinery and Intelligence'	Korean War begins	1950
	West Germany admitted to the Council of Europe Schuman Plan proposes Coal and Steel Community	1951
	European Coal and Steel Community implemented	1952
Crick & Watson's Double Helix Theory for DNA	Stalin dies	1953
Solar battery (Fuller, Pearson)	French defeat at Dien Bien Phu	1954

	Continental philosophy: roots and dialogue	The arts
1955	Canguilhem, *The Formation of the Concept of Reflex in the XVII and XVIII Centuries* de Chardin, *The Phenomenon of Man* Lévi-Strauss, *Tristes Tropiques* Marcuse, *Eros and Civilization* Merleau-Ponty, *Adventures of the Dialectic*	Béjart choreography, *Symphony for a Lone Man*
1956		Durrenmatt, *The Visit* Camus, *The Fall*
1957	Barthes, *Mythologies* Bataille, *Eroticism* Chomsky, *Syntactic Structures*	Stockhausen, *Gruppen* (for three spatially arranged orchestras) Bergman, *The Seventh Seal*
1958	Arendt, *The Human Condition* Lévi-Strauss, *Structural Anthropology* Winch, *The Idea of a Social Science and Its Relationship to Philosophy*	Beckett, *Krapp's Last Tape* Primo Levi, *If This Is a Man*
1959	Bloch, *The Principle of Hope*	French 'New Wave' (*Nouvelle Vague*) in film, 1959–64 Goddard, *Breathless* Truffaut, *The 400 Blows* Duras, *Hiroshima Mon Amour*
1960	Gadamer, *Truth and Method* Ingarden, *The Literary Work of Art* Merleau-Ponty, *Signs* Ricoeur, *The Symbolism of Evil*	Fellini, *La Dolce Vita* Penderecki, *Threnody to the Victims of Hiroshima*
1961	Fanon, *The Wretched of the Earth* Heidegger, *Neitzsche* (2 vols) Levinas, *Totality and Infinity*	Miró, *Blue II* Robbe-Grillet, *Last Year in Marienbad*
1962	S. Breton, *Essence and Existence* Deleuze, *Neitzsche and Philosophy* Derrida, *Husserl's* Origin of Geometry	Fellini, *8½* Solzhenitsyn, *One Day in the Life of Ivan Denisovitch* Warhol, *Campbells Soup Cans 200*
1963	Arendt, *On Revolution* Habermas, *Theory and Praxis* Richardson, *Through Phenomenology to Thought*	Paul Celan, *Die Niemandsrose* (*The No One's Rose*) G. Grass, *Dog Years*
1964	Barthes, *Elements of Semiology* Lacan, *Seminar XI; The Four Fundamental Concepts of Psychoanalysis* Lévi-Strauss, *The Raw and the Cooked* Marcuse, *One-Dimensional Man*	Pasolini, *The Gospel According to St. Matthew*

Science and technology	Politics	
The Contraceptive Pill (Pincus) Antiproton (Segré, Chamberlain)	Warsaw Pact for Eastern Bloc	1955
Discovery of neutrino predicted by Pauli in 1931 Videotape recording (Poniatoff)	Hungarian uprising crushed by Soviets	1956
Sputnik launched (USSR)	Treaty of Rome establishes Common Market (EEC)	1957
Radiation belts surrounding the earth (Van Allen) Space race escalates with launch of *Explorer 1* (US)	De Gaulle elected first President of French Fifth Republic	1958
Luna space probes (USSR) enter solar orbit; photograph far side of the moon	Fidel Castro overthrows Batista government in Cuba	1959
Laser (Maiman) *Pioneer 5* (US): first deep-space probe	EFTA (European Free Trade Assn)	1960
First 'Cosmonaut' in space *Vostok 1* (USSR)	Berlin Wall constructed	1961
Mariner 2 (US): first successful flybys of Venus	Algeria gains independence from France Cuban Missile Crisis	1962
Quasars discovered (Matthews & Sandage)	John F. Kennedy assassinated	1963
Mariner 4 (US): first successful flybys of Mars	US enters Vietnam War in support of South Vietnam	1964

	Continental philosophy: roots and dialogue	The arts
1965	Althusser, *For Marx* Bachelard, *The Poetics of Space* Foucault, *Discipline and Punish* Foucault, *Madness and Civilization* Ricoeur, *Freud and Philosophy: An Essay on Interpretation*	Postmodernist architecture (1965–85) Venturi, Jencks H. Miller, *The Rosy Crucifixion* S. Plath, *Ariel*
1966	Adorno, *Negative Dialectics* Beneviste, *Problems in General Linguistics* Chomsky, *Cartesian Linguistics* Foucault, *The Order of Things* Greimas, *Structural Semantics* Lacan, *Ecrits* Macherey, *A Theory of Literary Production*	China's Cultural Revolution; Red Guard formed Moravia, *The Lie*
1967	Derrida, *Speech and Phenomena* Derrida, *Of Grammatology* Derrida, *Writing and Difference* Horkheimer, *Critique of Instrumental Reason* Jauss, *Toward an Aesthetic of Reception*	Garcia-Marquez, *One Hundred Years of Solitude* Kundera, *The Joke*
1968	Althusser and Balibar, *Reading Capital* Dumézil, *Myth and Epic* (2 vols, 1968–71) Habermas, *Knowledge and Human Interests*	Berio, *Sinfonia* C. Metz, *Film Language: Semiotics of the Cinema* (1968–72) Solzhenitsyn, *Cancer Ward*
1969	Blanchot, *Infinite Conversation* S. Breton, *Philosophy and Mathematics in Proclus* Foucault, *The Archaeology of Knowledge* Kristeva, *Semeiotiké* Ricoeur, *The Conflict of Interpretations: Essays in Hermeneutics* Serres, *Hermès* (vols 1–5, 1969–80)	Beckett receives the Nobel Prize
1970	Barthes, *S/Z* Kuhn, *The Structure of Scientific Revolutions*	
1971	de Man, *Blindness and Insight* Habermas, *Legitimation Crisis* Hassan, *The Postmodern Turn* Lefort, *Elements of a Critique of Bureaucracy* Rawls, *A Theory of Justice*	Tarkovsky, *Solaris*

Science and technology	Politics	
Gabor's Holography using laser	Malcolm X assassinated	1965
Surveyor 1 (US): probe returns with detailed photographs of lunar surface	UN imposes economic sanctions on Rhodesia	1966
Pulsars discovered (Cambridge) *Venera 4* (USSR): first successful entry of Venus atmosphere	Six-Day Arab–Israeli War France vetoes British application to enter Common Market	1967
	Paris Riots N. Ireland Civil Rights Movement Soviet troops to Czechoslovakia to halt reforms (Prague Spring)	1968
Astronauts land on moon (US)	British troops to Northern Ireland	1969
Venera 7 (USSR): first probe to survive Venusian surface	US announces invasion of Cambodia	1970
EMI Scanner (Hounsfield)	Independence of East Pakistan as Bangladesh Communist China joins UN – Taiwan expelled	1971

	Continental philosophy: roots and dialogue	The arts
1972	Baudrillard, *For a Critique of the Political Economy of the Sign* Bourdieu, *Outline of a Theory of Practice* Deleuze and Guattari, *Anti-Oedipus* Derrida, *Dissemination* Genette, *Figures III: Narrative Discourse* Girard, *Violence and the Sacred* S. Kofman, *Nietzsche and Metaphor* Marcuse, *Counter-revolution and Revolt*	Bertolucci, *Last Tango in Paris* Heinrich Böll receives Nobel Prize
1973	Apel, *Towards a Transformation of Philosophy* Bataille, *Inner Experiences* Bloom, *The Anxiety of Influence* Geertz, *The Interpretation of Cultures* Jay, *The Dialectical Imagination*	Calvino, *The Castle of Crossed Destinies* Solzhenitsyn, *Gulag Archipelago* (3 vols, 1973–8)
1974	Derrida, *Glas* Irigaray, *Speculum of the Other Woman* Kristeva, *Revolution in Poetic Language*	D. Lessing, *The Memoirs of a Survivor*
1975	Barthes, *The Pleasure of the Text* Castoriadis, *The Social Imaginary* Cixous and Clément, *The Newly Born Woman* Feyerabend, *Against Method* G. Hartman, *The Fate of Reading* Patočka, *Heretical Essays* Ricoeur, *The Rule of Metaphor* Steiner, *After Babel*	Havel, *Audience*
1976	Dufrenne, *Aesthetics and Philosophy* (2 vols) Eco, *A Theory of Semiotics* Foucault, *The History of Sexuality* (3 vols, 1976–84) Gadamer, *Philosophical Hermeneutics* Iser, *The Act of Reading: A Theory of Aesthetic Response*	Twyla Tharp choreographs *Push Comes to Shove* for Baryshnikov
1977	Derrida, *Limited, Inc.* Irigaray, *This Sex Which Is Not One*	*Nouveaux Philosophes* Movement (Levy, Benoist, and Glucksmann) Stockhausen, *Licht* Cycle
1978	Castoriadis, *Crossroads in the Labyrinth* Derrida, *Truth in Painting* Lefort, *The Forms of History* Marcuse, *The Aesthetic Dimension*	

Science and technology	Politics	
Apollo Lunar Rover used on lunar surface (US)	Britain takes over direct rule in Northern Ireland	1972
Mars 6 (USSR): first probe to enter Martian atmosphere	Britain, Ireland, and Denmark join EC Paris Peace Settlement ending Vietnam War Oil crisis – OPEC Nations restrict supply	1973
	Former Portuguese colonies gain independence (Angola, Mozambique) Watergate Scandal	1974
First international docking in space: *Apollo 18* (US) and *Soyuz 19* (USSR)	General Franco dies in Spain S. Vietnam surrenders to N. Vietnam	1975
Mandelbrot's Fractal Geometry claims mathematical order exists in apparently random phenomena	Mao Tse-tung dies	1976
Prigogine awarded Nobel Prize	Czech 'Charta 77' Movement	1977
Feigenbaum, 'Quantitative Universality for a Class of Non-Linear Transformations'	UN Peace Force to Lebanon	1978

	Continental philosophy: roots and dialogue	The arts
1979	Baudrillard, *Seduction* de Man, *Allegories of Reading* Lyotard, *The Postmodern Condition* Lyotard, *Just Gaming (Au Juste)*	Fassbinder, *Lili Marlene*
1980	Kristeva, *Powers of Horror* Le Doeuff, *The Philosophical Imaginary* Olsen, *Silences* Rorty, *Philosophy and the Mirror of Nature* Vattimo, *Adventure of Difference* R. Williams, *Problems in Culture and Materialism*	Balthus, *Sleeping Nude* Eco, *The Name of the Rose* Kundera, *The Book of Laughter and Forgetting*
1981	Baudrillard, *Simulations* Habermas, *Theory of Communicative Action* (2 vols) Jameson, *The Political Unconscious: Narrative as a Socially Symbolic Act* MacIntyre, *After Virtue*	Rushdie, *Midnight's Children*
1982	Girard, *The Scapegoat (Le Bouc-émissaire)* Rorty, *The Consequences of Pragmatism*	Herzog, *Fitzcarraldo* Garcia-Marquez receives Nobel Prize
1983	Habermas, *Moral Consciousness and Communicative Action* Lyotard, *The Differend* Ricoeur, *Time and Narrative* (3 vols, 1983–5) Said, *The World, the Text, and the Critic*	Murdoch, *The Philosopher's Pupil* Rushdie, *Shame*
1984	Eco, *Semiotics and the Philosophy of Language* Giddens, *The Constitution of Society: Outline of a Theory of Structuration* Parfit, *Reasons and Persons* Prigogine and Staengers, *Order out of Chaos*	Kundera, *The Unbearable Lightness of Being*
1985	Benhabib, *Critique, Norm and Utopia* Habermas, *The Philosphical Discourse of Modernity* Havel, *The Power of the Powerless* Honneth, *The Critique of Power* Taminiaux, *Dialectic and Difference* Vattimo, *The End of Modernity*	
1986	de Certeau, *Heterologies* Dworkin, *Law's Empire*	Eco, *Foucault's Pendulum* Magris, *Danube*

Science and technology	Politics	
	First direct elections for European Parliament held in all nine member states	1979
Voyager Spacecraft flies by Saturn	Lech Walesa: Solidarity trade union confronts Communist government in Poland	1980
First US Space Shuttle flight	Greece accepted as tenth member of Common Market	1981
	British force reoccupies Falklands	1982
	Indira Ghandi assassinated	1983
Hao Bai-Lin, *Chaos* (first attempt to collect the scientific literature on chaos and complexity)	Chernenko becomes leader of Soviet Communist Party Reagan re-elected by landslide in US elections	1984
	Gorbachev succeeds Chernenko in Soviet Union Spain and Portugal join Common Market	1985
Challenger (US) Space Shuttle explodes on take-off Chernobyl nuclear disaster in USSR	Philippine President Marcos overthrown	1986

	Continental philosophy: roots and dialogue	The arts
1987	Derrida, *Psyché: Inventions of the Other* Derrida, *The Post Card* Derrida, *Schibboleth*	Calvino, *The Literature Machine* Vargas-Llosa, *The Storyteller*
1988	S. Breton, *Poetics of the Sensible* Habermas, *Postmetaphysical Thinking* Lyotard, *The Inhuman* Vattimo, *The Transparent Society*	
1989	C. Taylor, *Sources of the Self*	C.J. Cela receives Nobel Prize
1990	Nussbaum, *Love's Knowledge: Essays on Philosophy and Literature* Ricoeur, *Oneself as Another*	Kristeva, *Les Samuraïs*
1991	Derrida, *Given Time/Counterfeit Money* Jameson, *Postmodernism, or the Cultural Logic of Late Capitalism* Kristeva, *Strangers to Ourselves* Rorty, *Philosophical Papers* Said, *Musical Elaborations*	Enzensberger, *Europe in Ruins* Murdoch, *Message to the Planet*
1992	Benhabib, *Situating the Self* Habermas, *Facticity and Validity* Honneth, *The Struggle for Recognition* Murdoch, *Metaphysics as a Guide to Morals* Ricoeur, *Lectures I and II* (1991–2)	Jordan, *The Crying Game* Koslowski, *Imagine Europe* Schmidt/Cohn-Bendit, *Heimat Babylon*
1993	Derrida, *Spectres of Marx* Derrida, *Khôra* S. Kofman, *Explosion 2* Lyotard, *The Postmodern Contradiction* J.-L. Nancy, *The Sense of the World* Levinas, *God, Death and Time*	G. Grass, *Novemberland*

Science and technology	Politics	
Minsky's 'Mental Kollectivs': *The Society of Mind*	USSR and US agree to cut nuclear arsenals and reduce nuclear missiles	1987
Neurocomputing (Anderson and Rosenfeld)	Lockerbie: Terrorist sabotage of a jumbo jet kills 270	1988
Prigogine/Grégoire, *Exploring Complexity*	Fall of Berlin Wall Havel elected Czech President	1989
Santa Fe Institute studies on chaos, entropy and complexity	Nelson Mandela freed after 27 years imprisoned in South Africa Saddam Hussein annexes Kuwait	1990
	Soviet Union dissolved Gulf War drives Iraq from Kuwait	1991
S. Kauffman, *Origins of Order: Self-Organization and Selection in Evolution*	Break-up of Yugoslavia Croats, Serbs, Bosnians at war	1992
	Ratification of Maastricht Treaty on European Union	1993

Introduction
Richard Kearney

Continental philosophy, as it has emerged in the twentieth century, is less a seamless fabric than a patchwork of diverse strands. Phenomenology, hermeneutics, existentialism, structuralism, critical theory, deconstruction – these are some of the salient movements which have developed in continental Europe between 1900 and the 1990s, though their influence is by no means confined to their area of origin. Continental thought has proved highly exportable, circulating far beyond the frontiers of Europe to provoke strong responses in the intellectual world at large.

It is worth recalling at the outset that the term 'continental' philosophy was coined not by European thinkers themselves but by academic philosophy departments in the Anglo-American world eager to differentiate it from 'analytic' thought. It was initially more a label of convention than a category corresponding to a given essence of thought. But whatever the origin or accuracy of the distinction, what became known as 'continental philosophy' has managed to exert a decisive impact on contemporary thought over the decades – an impact which exceeds the specialized discipline of academic philosophy and embraces such diverse fields as sociology, political science, literary theory, theology, art history, feminism and a variety of cultural studies.

Some view this protean character of continental thought as a defect – a sign that it cannot be rigorous or reliable. If it can be applied to anything in general it must be saying nothing in particular! More an art (*Kunst*) than a science (*Wissenschaft*)! More an exercise in poetic intuition than ratiocinative inquiry! What these objections tend to ignore, however, is that most founding fathers of continental thought were committed to a view of philosophy as science and saw themselves as guided by a basic notion of critical reason. Edmund Husserl, for instance, spoke of phenomenology as a 'rigorous science', while his disciple Heidegger regarded it as a transcendental science of the

I

categories of Being. Even Sartre, the combative pioneer of French existentialism, sought to apply phenomenology to an historical 'critique of dialectical reason'.

Similar scruples operate in other major currents of continental thought. Ferdinand de Saussure, founder of structuralism, spoke of semiology as a 'science of signs'; and the works of such disciples as Lévi-Strauss, Foucault, Althusser, Lacan or the early Barthes were each marked by a determination to apply the structural model of language to a variety of disciplines (anthropology, historiography, historical materialism, psychoanalysis, sociology). One even finds critical theory and hermeneutics combining philosophical inquiry with other human sciences – with Paul Ricoeur calling for a creative dialogue between a historical 'understanding' (*Verstehen*) alert to the contingencies of human circumstance, and scientific 'explanation' (*Erklären*) committed to goals of universal objectivity. Many continental thinkers have sought to redefine and reinterpret reason, but few would claim to jettison it altogether.

Perhaps the most persistent feature of continental philosophy, through all its multiple mutations, is a commitment to the *questioning of foundations*. From phenomenology to deconstruction, one encounters the persuasion that the old foundationalist arguments no longer suffice. Meaning is not some metaphysical essence or substance; it is a task of intersubjective and intertextual relations. Truth cannot be grounded on a given system of being (realism) or mind (idealism); it must be radically rethought as an interplay of differences (perspectives, *Abschattungen*, intentionalities, situations, structures, signifiers, etc.). Continental philosophy thus finds itself renouncing the metaphysical quest for absolute grounds, even if some of its proponents – Husserl in particular – found this renunciation vexed and regrettable. Kant's claim to 'lay the foundation of knowledge', Hegel's appeal to Absolute Spirit, Kierkegaard's recourse to a Transcendent Deity, Marx's call for a Total Science, are largely superseded (albeit often reinterpreted) by continental thinkers in the twentieth century.

But if metaphysical foundationalism is one adversary, positivism is another. Reductionist attempts to explain away *meaning* in terms of *facts* are invariably resisted by phenomenologists, existentialists, critical theorists and postmodernists. Philosophical questioning, they argue, requires the specific methodology of a human science (*Geisteswissenschaft*); and while remaining in critical dialogue with the empirico-metric procedures of natural sciences (*Naturwissenschaft*), it must not be *reduced* to the latter. Both methods are valid. It is the effort to confound or conflate them that leads to misunderstanding.

This is not to suggest that the critique of positivism is an exclusively continental concern. Analytic thinkers inspired by the later

Wittgenstein, Ryle, Davidson or Dummett, show equal resolve in disentangling such category mistakes. But the reasons for doing so are different in each case. Generally speaking, analytic thinkers seek to avoid such error in the interests of clarity, evidence, verification and coherence; continentals appear more impelled by ontological scruples to keep thought open to 'irreducibles' and 'undecidables' – that is, to questions which surpass the limits of 'pure reason' – questions of being and nothing, of transcendence and difference, of alterity and historicity.

The reference to Kant here is perhaps useful. Continental philosophers have often tended to privilege the moral and aesthetic questioning of the Second and Third *Critiques* over the strictly epistemological reading of the First. This is not to say that they ignore the First but that they read it in a particular way. For example, while both analytic and continental thinkers share a common commitment to Kant's *transcendental aesthetic* (the origination of all experience in sensible time and space), the former tend to show preference for the *transcendental analytic* (dealing with objective categories of understanding), whereas the latter incline more towards the 'limit ideas' of World, Soul and Freedom contained in the *transcendental dialectic*. To put this more succinctly, continental thought is on balance more likely than analytic thought to bypass the confines of pure reason, venturing into the liminal areas of noumenal experience and dialectic. Indeed Husserl's repudiation of the Kantian distinction between phenomenal and noumenal in his *Logical Investigations* (1900–1) already signalled this direction. Continental philosophy, it could be said, favours dialectical and practical reason over 'pure' reason. It holds that *being* is ultimately irreducible to *verification*, *meaning* to *evidence*, *truth* to *coherence*, *time* to *measurement*, *paradox* to *problem*.

This raises the controversial subject of style. Continental philosophy is marked by distinctive signatures of thinking and writing. Its practitioners would claim, for instance, that extraordinary questions of experience cannot always be expressed in ordinary language. Ideas of 'dialectical' reason (as both Kant and Hegel realized in their different ways) cannot be translated into categories of 'pure' reason. And the attendant *surplus of meaning* requires that standard criteria of correspondence and coherence have to be occasionally transgressed. This is by no means unprecedented in philosophy. As Heidegger points out in his introduction to *Being and Time*, Aristotle's innovative use of language to express his discovery of being was far from transparent to his original Greek readers. This line of reasoning could be construed as an 'anything goes' argument; but there is more to it than that. A certain experimental *style de pensée* is the risk certain philosophers are prepared to take in order to say the unsayable (or, in Beckett's ludic phrase, to 'eff the ineffable'). Adorno, Heidegger, Merleau-Ponty,

Lacan, Levinas, Derrida, Kristeva – each has his or her own inimitable voices.

Finally, it must be acknowledged that continental philosophy does not arise in a vacuum. True to its conviction that thought is always *situated*, the predominant mood of such philosophy, from existentialism to postmodernism, is one deeply committed to moral and political questions. Thinking is no longer regarded as some neutral exercise in cognition but an intervention in the 'lived world' of history and society. This responsiveness of ideas to the *Lebenswelt* was, in the case of modern continental thought, radically informed by the experience of two world wars on European soil – and the corresponding horrors of Auschwitz and the Gulag. Husserl was one of the first to register this sense of breakdown and disorientation when, fleeing from Nazi Germany, he called for a fundamental rethinking of the western intellectual tradition. And most continental philosophers after him have shared this persuasion, advancing forms of inquiry that are increasingly exploratory, tentative, iconoclastic, *engagé*. Critical theorists from Horkheimer to Habermas, existentialists from Merleau-Ponty to de Beauvoir, structuralists from Barthes to Foucault, not to mention postmodernist thinkers like Lyotard and Vattimo, all demonstrate a keen preoccupation with social and political issues. The common challenge is to start all over again, seeking alternative modes of questioning. Totalizing Archimedean principles are renounced. Meaning and value are to be reinterpreted from first to last. Recurrent crises call for perpetual revision. And it is perhaps this urgency to respond to the trauma of historical change that has compelled so many continentals to abandon the metaphysical obsession with foundations in favour of post-metaphysical experiments of thought.

The fourteen essays in this volume outline and assess some of these experiments. The first five span the twin movements of phenomenology and existentialism, running from Husserl and Heidegger to Sartre, Merleau-Ponty and Levinas. Subsequent essays deal with specific currents of continental thought in such areas as science, Marxism, linguistics, politics, aesthetics, feminism and hermeneutics, while a final essay on postmodernism highlights the manner in which so many concerns of continental thought culminate in a radical anti-foundationalism. Each study speaks for itself; but I wish to thank the contributors, drawn from six different countries, for their co-operation and collegiality in putting this volume together. It has been a gratifying reminder that for all the controversies surrounding continental philosophy, it remains a forum of debate where critical intelligence, scholarly expertise and a passionate commitment to the burning issues of our time are still alive and well.

CHAPTER 1

The beginnings of phenomenology

Husserl and his predecessors

Richard Cobb-Stevens

Edmund Husserl was the founder of phenomenology, one of the principal movements of twentieth-century philosophy. His principal contribution to philosophy was his development of the concept of intentionality. He reasserted and revitalized the premodern thesis that our cognitional acts are intentional, i.e., that they reach out beyond sensa to things in the world. When we think or speak about things, and when we perceive them, we deal with those things and not with mental intermediaries. Intentionality is our openness to the world, our transcending mode of being. Husserl also developed the implications of this fundamental thesis. He repudiated Locke's interpretation of 'mind' as an inner space set off from the rest of nature, and he rejected Kant's distinction between phenomena and things-in-themselves. He also rejected the view that the task of philosophy is to guarantee that our concepts and theories somehow mirror the world.

These themes brought a sense of liberation to many philosophers who by the early decades of the twentieth century had become weary of the insoluble problems generated by the modern account of cognition. Husserl's analysis of signs and semantic systems had a similar effect in the fields of linguistics and logic which had been dominated by associationist and psychologistic accounts of the production of meaning. His interpretation of the complementarity of pre-scientific and scientific modes of rationality contributed to the demise of positivism and inspired new and fruitful approaches in the social sciences. His theories of time and ego-identity provided much-needed correctives to reductionist tendencies in psychology. Finally, his balanced interpretation of the interplay between historical horizons and the drive for truth offers a reasonable alternative to the contemporary tendency to regard all truths as relativized by their historical conditions.

It is unfortunate that Husserl's writings had little influence on the development of the tradition of analytic philosophy, the other major movement of twentieth-century philosophy. Husserl himself engaged in spirited but amicable debate with Gottlob Frege, who is generally considered to be the proximate founder of analytic philosophy. However, such exchanges became increasingly rare among their followers who have tended on the whole to ignore one another's works. This breakdown of communication was due in part to an early misunderstanding. Frege thought that Husserl was a proponent of psychologism, i.e., the view that numbers, propositions and logical laws are reducible to mental states. Frege's critique of Husserl's alleged psychologism was decisive for a whole generation of analytic philosophers whose goal was to defend rationality from relativism by detaching logic and semantics from all dependence on what they took to be irremediably subjective intuitions. On the other hand, Frege's decision to divorce logical analysis entirely from cognitive intuition alienated philosophers within the phenomenological tradition who saw in this strategy only a revival of Hobbes's preference for an exclusively calculative rationality. Ironically, Husserl's critique of psychologism was in fact more coherent and more complete than that of Frege and his followers, for he showed how propositions are grounded in cognitive intuitions without thereby being reduced to merely subjective phenomena. In recent years both phenomenological and analytic traditions have found themselves increasingly vulnerable to contemporary forms of historicism and relativism. This situation has had the felicitous effect of encouraging within both traditions a reappraisal of the reasons for their mutual distrust. Considerable progress has been made of late in restoring a climate conducive to renewed dialogue.

In the judgment of many, the originality of Husserl's thought and the rigour of his analyses guarantee him a place among the greatest of philosophers. However, his writings tend to be excessively abstruse and technical. As a result, his readership has generally been limited to professional philosophers. By contrast, Martin Heidegger's more evocative philosophical style and Jean-Paul Sartre's literary brilliance assured for the subsequent phenomenological tradition a wider audience and an unusually immediate cultural influence. This is not to say that these thinkers were merely commentators on Husserl (indeed, many regard Heidegger as a more profound and original thinker), but only that they often succeeded in communicating the basic insights of Husserl's phenomenology more clearly and forcefully than did Husserl himself. There is another reason why Husserl's writings often failed to convey to his readers the full force of his criticism of the modern epistemological perspective. It seems clear, in retrospect, that he was not sufficiently sensitive to the gravitational pull that the language of modern philosophy exercised on his thought. He explicitly modified the senses of such key modern terms as 'presentation', 'content', 'immanence', 'subjectivity', 'phenomenon', but he never completely jettisoned the lexicon of modern philosophy. Indeed, he always maintained a conservative stance with regard to innovative philosophic language, preferring to take familiar terms to their limits rather than to introduce unusual metaphors and neologisms. He therefore failed to appreciate the extent to which the familiar linguistic matrix of modern philosophy conceals a long history of accumulated premises which determine the kinds of questions that readers would bring to his texts. His goal was to call those premises into question, but his philosophical vocabulary tended too often to reinforce them. It is unfortunate, too, that Husserl seems to have had little first-hand familiarity with ancient and medieval philosophic texts. He was always more at home with the traditions of British empiricism and Kantian criticism. Had he been more attuned to the weight of words in the development of philosophic concepts, and better informed about the ancient and medieval traditions, his breakthrough would no doubt have been less plagued by ambiguities and less subject to misinterpretations.

Husserl was born in Prossnitz, a town then located in Austria. He took courses in mathematics at the universities of Leipzig, Berlin and Vienna. In Berlin, he studied with the renowned mathematicians Leopold Kronecker and Karl Weierstrauss, and also attended occasional lectures in philosophy by Wilhelm Wundt. He received his Ph.D. in 1882 from the University of Vienna for a dissertation entitled 'Contributions to the Theory of the Calculus of Variations'. After a year in Berlin as assistant to Weierstrauss, he returned to Vienna to study philosophy with Franz Brentano, who had recently resigned his chair of philosophy. In 1886, on Brentano's recommendation, Husserl went to Halle to work with Karl Stumpf, who supervised the thesis submitted for his *Habilitation*, a study of the concept of number. From 1887 to 1928, Husserl held teaching positions at Halle, Göttingen, and Freiburg im Breisgau.

As a Jew, Husserl was increasingly the subject of harassment during his retirement years in Freiburg. It must have been an especially cruel blow to have found himself denied access to the library of the university he had served so well. After his death in 1938, Husserl's unpublished manuscripts were saved from destruction by Hermann Van Breda, a Belgian priest and philosopher, who also arranged for Husserl's wife and daughter to be sheltered in a Belgian convent during the occupation. Van Breda subsequently founded the Husserl Archives at Louvain.

Husserl was a person of high moral character and of impeccable intellectual integrity. He looked upon philosophy as a vocation, and felt personally called upon to defend reason against the various forms of relativism prevalent in his day. However, his was never a merely defensive or narrowly conservative project. Indeed, he often expressed admiration for the sceptical tradition in philosophy, and thought that Hume's radical critique of presuppositions made him the greatest of modern philosophers. He also rejected the arrogance and chauvinism of those who claimed that philosophy had achieved its culmination in German thought and expression. Philosophy, he argued, cannot be the exclusive property of any single culture or language, for the emergence of the philosophic spirit introduced a new mode of teleology character-ized by the complementary traits of universality and infinity. The telos of philosophy is universal in that it strives to attain an identical truth which is valid for all who are no longer blinded by traditions, and infinite in that this goal of truth can never be fully realized and thus remains always a regulative idea. By reason of its universality, therefore, philosophy cannot be limited to a particular period or people, and by reason of its infinity philosophy remains always an unending process ([1.33], 286; [1.89], 151–60).

During his lifetime Husserl published several books and also left an extraordinary number of manuscripts, lecture notes and working papers. Both the published works and the unpublished materials contain many repetitive passages, tantalizingly unfinished descriptions, and agonizing reappraisals of earlier positions. As a result, it is often diffi-cult to co-ordinate earlier and later works, or even to be sure of the direction ultimately taken by his thought. Husserl would not be entirely displeased by this situation, for he concluded finally that there can be no totalizing syntheses. We must strive for objectivity, and hope for progress towards that goal, but we must also acknowledge all the while that the goal of truth functions always as 'the idea of an infinite task' ([1.33], 291).

❧ EARLY WORKS: INFLUENCE OF FREGE, ❧ BRENTANO, HERBART, STUMPF AND LOTZE

Husserl's first published work, *Philosophy of Arithmetic* (1891), was a revised version of his earlier analysis of the concept of number. Adopt-ing a distinction first made by Brentano, Husserl distinguishes between intuitive presentation and symbolic intention of numbers. He describes how our primitive intuitions about numbers and their interrelationships are based upon the experiences of counting, comparing and collecting, and how we think in symbols of more complex numbers for which there can be no such authenticating intuitions. Unfortunately, he makes several remarks which give the impression that he conflated numbers and their presentations. For example, he refers to the unity of a number as a psychic relation, and claims that understanding the concept of a number requires reflection on its presentation in relevant acts of collective combination. In 1894, Frege called attention to these compromising remarks in a critical review of Husserl's book. He objected that Husserl's analysis blurs the distinction between subjective and objective domains, and concluded that his work was a typical example of psychologism ([1.65], 200–1). While Frege's critique finds some justification in Husserl's text, this extreme conclusion is unwarranted. Frege was inclined to regard as psychologistic any attempt to relate the status of numbers to the activities of counting and collecting. Hence, he was not likely to be attuned to the nuances of Husserl's intention which was surely not to collapse the objectivity of numbers into their acts of presentation but rather to describe just how their objectivity manifests itself to us. At any rate, Husserl later distinguished clearly between numbers and their presentations, and between the concept of number and the concept of collective combination ([1.35], 784; [1.86], 24). Frege also criticized Husserl for holding the view that numbers are totalities (determinate multitudes) comprised of mere 'somethings' having no specific content and yet somehow differing from one another. However, this is a caricature of Husserl's position, for he clearly maintains that objects are always identified by way of their features. His point is simply that, once we have identified objects to be counted, we prescind from the determinate content of those objects in the instance numbering them.

It took some time, however, for Husserl to clarify the ambiguities generated by his continued dependence on the linguistic and conceptual framework of the empiricist tradition, which was the remote forerunner of late nineteenth-century psychologism. In his essay 'Psychological Studies in the Elements of Logic' (1894), he makes the unequivocal claim that our cognitive intuitions truly present the things intended by our speech acts. Moreover, he distinguishes clearly between mental acts and their contents, a distinction that had been blurred by the empiricist notion of a mental 'process', which in effect reduces cognitive acts to the mere having of associatively modified impressions. Nevertheless, he constantly uses the term 'contents' in an ambiguous fashion, sometimes to refer to ill-defined mental representations and sometimes to refer to things in the world in so far as they are known. Hence he does not yet make it clear that the intended objects of both our signitive and intuitive acts are, ordinarily at least, things in the world rather than mental substitutes ([1.40], 126–42; [1.122], 34–8).

These ambiguities testify to the influence of Brentano on the early

Husserl. Brentano rejected the empiricists' reduction of mental acts to associative reactions, reaffirmed at least vaguely the medieval distinction between acts and contents, and retrieved in part the ancient thesis that cognitive acts reach out to the intended objects themselves. He is therefore rightly celebrated for having revived the theory of intentionality. However, his interpretation of this notion intermingled modern and premodern themes. His early writings described intentional contents in ways that evoke the modern notion that impressions and ideas function as intra-mental substitutes for inaccessible real objects of reference. He said, for example, that every intentional experience 'contains something as its object within itself', and referred also to this 'immanent objectivity' as the 'intentional in-existence of an object' ([1.45], 88–9).

Although Brentano explicitly related his account of intentionality to the scholastic tradition, and traced its origin to Aristotle's books on the soul, he unfortunately tended to read the modern interpretation of immanence into the medieval theme of *esse intentionale*. It is true that the Scholastics used the term 'intentional' (and more frequently the term 'objective') to refer to the mode of being had by things known, in so far as they are present in the knower. The point of the medieval distinction between intentional (objective) being and real being was to clarify Aristotle's claim that the knower 'is somehow' the form of the thing known, without thereby entering into physical identity with the thing. It was thought that the intentional object ('inner word', 'formal concept', 'expressed species') functions as a unique sort of intermediary, i.e., as a transparent sign through which the mind is related to reality ([1.101], 62 n. 3). Although this emphasis on the mediating function of formal concepts may well have prepared the way for the modern thesis that to know is to have a representation of something (its 'idea' or 'concept') within the mind's interiority, the medieval thinkers themselves clearly maintained that the intentional object is the very thing itself, considered as known (Aquinas, *De Veritate*, iv, 2 ad 3).

Aristotle does not seem to have thought it necessary to postulate any intermediary, however special, between intellect and thing known. Indeed, he suggests that the intellect must itself be free of formal structure, and hence empty of content, so that it can become the forms of all things. The intellect, says Aristotle, possesses the same sort of adaptability as the human hand. It takes on the forms of things in the way that the human hand grasps tools (Aristotle, *De Anima*, 423a 1–3; [1.90], 132–7). Thus, the intellect operates within the realm of nature itself rather than within some subjective enclosure. Its mode of being is its transcending function. Aristotle further describes a thing's form as its sortal feature, its 'look' (*eidos*). The look is *what* we know when we know *this* particular thing. Although there is a difference between intuiting an individual *qua* individual (the primary substance), and intuiting its species-look (the secondary substance), these modes of intuition are complementary and interdependent. We grasp the species-look both as a surplus whose sense exceeds the particularity of this instance and as a condition for the manifestation of the particular (Aristotle, *Metaphysics*, 1042a 17–49). Aristotle also emphasizes the continuity between perception and predication. Predicative discourse gives syntactical articulation to the inarticulate nuances of intuition (Aristotle, *On Interpretation*, 16b 25–6). Judging is therefore directed primarily upon things and their perceived features, not upon propositions as such.

Brentano revived the Aristotelian notion that the intellect's intentional targets are things in the world, but he imagined the intellect's grasp of forms as taking place within the mind's inner space. He therefore concluded that the intellect could never effectively reach those targets. Brentano also subscribed wholeheartedly to the modern interpretation of perception. He claimed that our perceptions yield merely subjective appearances, and he appealed to physical causality alone in order to account for the relationship between these appearances and real objects. Corresponding to perceived colours, he claimed, there are only the 'vibrations' which emanate from the interaction of atoms, molecules and forces. A thing's true being, therefore, is its hidden quantifiable reality accessible only to the methods of the natural sciences. Perceived objects do not exist really outside of us; they are *mere* phenomena ([1.45], 9–10). In his later works, Brentano nevertheless claimed that linguistic references are ordinarily directed upon transcendent real entities, rather than upon mental contents. However, there is no indication that this new position entailed a critique of the empiricist account of intuition. Everything suggests a compromise: we refer to real things, but we see only phenomena. Moreover, Brentano adopted the modern interpretation of the relationship between assertive and predicative moments of judgment. Judgment, he says, is an act of acceptance or denial directed upon some presentation. This definition implies that judging is not primarily directed upon things and their perceived features, but upon intra-mental or ideal contents ([1.45], 198–9).

Dallas Willard's historical research has demonstrated how the influence of Johann Friedrich Herbart, Karl Stumpf and Hermann Lotze helped Husserl to make a more decisive break with the empiricist tradition than that achieved by Brentano ([1.122], 30–4). Herbart defined 'apperception' as the 'awareness of what is going on in us', and subsequently distinguished clearly between awareness of the activity of thinking and awareness of its content ([1.72], v, 43). Stumpf, to whom Husserl dedicated his *Logical Investigations*, held that second-order representations (such as the idea of a causal nexus) may arise out of first-order representations, and that the former are not reducible to associative manipulations of the latter. In short, he held that we some-how perceive causal connections ([1.112], 5). Lotze broke away even more completely from the empiricist position. Whereas Hume had claimed that the impression of the mind's transition (which accounts for the idea of necessary connection) is reducible to the process of transition itself, Lotze asserted unequivocally that ideas of relations depend on a reflexive awareness of the mind's transitions. Moreover, he drew a distinction between the object of the reflexive act (a second-order mental content) and the relationship represented as obtaining between the transcendent objects of the first-order impressions ([1.78], 537–8). Willard points out that these distinctions are unthinkable within the context of the usual empiricist account of cognition. There is no way, for example, of reducing Lotze's relating activities to the mere having of automatic transitional processes, or of reducing his second-order contents to faded and less forceful copies of impressions. On the other hand, these authors continue to interpret mental activities as purely inner psychological happenings, and they do not explicitly call into question the empiricist description of mind as a theatre of represen-tations. Hence, their modifications of the Humean account do not constitute a full fledged revival of the premodern notion of cognition. None the less, once the distinction between activity and content had been re-established, and once the notion of irreducible second-order operations and contents had been elaborated, the stage was set for a comprehensive reappraisal of the modern thesis that the terminus of our knowing is located within the mind's inner space.

～ LOGICAL INVESTIGATIONS ～

Husserl was the first to challenge the modern position squarely. During the period from 1894 to 1900, further reflection on the incoherence of psychologism and on the need for a new foundation for logic led him to make a more decisive break with the modern epistemological model for mind. There is no evidence that he engaged during these years in any prolonged study of medieval or later scholastic literature on the topic of cognition, or that he was markedly influenced by a reading of the relevant texts of Aristotle. Yet he was able to achieve what amounts to a reconstruction of the premodern notion of the intentional con-tinuity between mind and nature. His reflections during this period culminated in the publication of his greatest work, *Logical Investi-gations* (1900–1). This book begins with a series of prolegomena which make a powerful critique of the tenets of psychologism. The rest of the work develops a more positive account of how our cognitive acts have the capacity to yield access to objective truths. Its six investi-

gations are devoted to the following related topics: signs and signification, universals and particulars, parts and wholes, logical grammar,
intentionality, evidence and truth.

In the prolegomena, Husserl demonstrates the incoherence of
trying to reduce the objectivity of numbers, propositions, and truth
itself to subjective states or activities. Like Frege, he calls attention to
the self-contradiction involved in every attempt to defend the thesis
that truth is reducible to our acceptance of it. One cannot coherently
propose a theory that subjectivizes truth and then go on to make
objective claims for that theory. To make any statement whatsoever,
including a statement in defence of relativism, is to make a claim that
something is the case independently of one's making that claim. Like
Frege, Husserl also contends that the principles of logic cannot be
regarded as provisional generalizations because inductively derived laws
could never serve as standards for adjudicating between valid and
invalid arguments. It would make no sense to criticize some individual's
thinking as illogical or inconsistent on the basis of inductive generalizations about how thinking occurs. The idiosyncratic thinking in question
might legitimately be characterized as unusual, but not as invalid.
Husserl holds that psychologism also fails to account for the kind of
evidence belonging to principles of logic, such as the laws of the
syllogism. He criticizes John Stuart Mill's description of logical laws
as inductive generalizations on the grounds that the evidence for logical
laws is absolutely certain rather than merely probable and provisional
([1.35], 187–96). This sort of argument would be unacceptable to Frege,
who insisted that any appeal to evidence blurs the distinction between
a proposition's truth and its being recognized as true. According to
Frege, a proposition is simply true or false in itself. He argued that
genetic accounts of how people come to think of propositions as true
are irrelevant to the issue of truth ([1.64], vi; [1.66], 133; [1.86], 32–8).
Husserl contends, on the contrary, that there is no reason why an
appeal to evidence should entail the reduction of truth to its recognition. When the objective truth of a proposition makes itself manifest
to the seeker of truth, it does not thereby become subjective.

The first investigation opens with a discussion of two kinds of
signs: indications and expressions. Indications either stand for what
they signify (a flag as the sign of a nation) or point to the existence of
some absent reality (smoke as a sign of fire). In both cases, association
provides the link between sign and signified. As opposed to indications,
linguistic expressions introduce a stratum of meaning. Their use
requires acts of interpretation on the part of speakers and listeners. A
speaker's words ordinarily accomplish three functions: they express
meanings, refer to objects, and 'intimate' to a listener the intellectual
activity of the speaker. Husserl observes that the 'intimating' function

of expression is a kind of indication, in the sense that spoken or written words are indices of the existence of the speaker's hidden and therefore 'absent' thoughts. He adds that many philosophical errors arise from the failure to distinguish properly between indication and expression. He takes Mill's account of naming as an example. Mill held that proper names denote but do not connote. They point to an object without in any way presenting or conveying information about the object. Proper names, he added, are like the distinctive chalk-marks made by the robber (of a popular tale) on a house that he intended to plunder at a later hour. Husserl observes that this comparison unfortunately suggests that proper names function only as indications. It is true that when the robber later sees the chalk-marks, he recalls by association his earlier thought 'This is the house I must rob'. But in relation to its object a name does not function as an indication or signal. An indication always motivates belief in the existence of whatever it indicates. However, a names does not similarly entail the existence of the object named ([1.35], 295–8). Named objects may be real, ideal, imaginary or even impossible. Thus, meaningful reference to an object does not perforce entail the existence of the object. The context of its use determines the kind of ontological commitment entailed by a linguistic expression. Husserl thus elegantly avoids the paradoxes that Bertrand Russell later discovered were implicit in Mill's view that names are like purely indexical signs.

The second investigation makes a convincing critique of the empiricist reduction of universals to blurred particulars. Husserl contends that recognition of some particular feature requires a grasp of the primitive relationship between species and instances. We could not discern a distinctive particular feature as such (e.g., this particular red) if we did not also intuit the corresponding universal (the species, Red). The two modes of intuition are interdependent. We grasp the particular feature as an instance of a range of similar instances in which the species is realized, and we grasp the identity of the species as the condition for the possibility of identifying the particular as such an instance.

The third investigation deals with the relationships between parts and wholes. Husserl first distinguishes between independent parts, or 'pieces', and non-independent parts, or 'moments'. Pieces are parts that are separable from their wholes. Moments are parts that are so interrelated with one another, or with their wholes, that they cannot be given separately. We learn to recognize the various relationships between parts and wholes by attempting successfully or unsuccessfully to vary these relationships in imagination. For example, we may conclude that the colour of a thing is inseparable from its surface (or extension) because we cannot successfully imagine eliminating one without also eliminating the other.

The fourth investigation discusses the relationship between grammar and logic. Husserl contends that grammatical laws governing distinctions between complete and incomplete expressions, and senseless and absurd expressions, are grounded in ontological structures. Laws governing the compounding of meanings are also similarly grounded in the way things are. All such rules have their origins in the interplay of parts and wholes given in perception. Husserl acknowledges that various languages may organize perceptual part–whole complexes differently. He suggests, however, that a study of the different ways in which various languages accomplish this task will reveal common categorial structures concealed by empirical differences ([1.35], 526; [1.100], 206).

In the fifth investigation, Husserl objects to the above-mentioned expressions that Brentano had used to describe the status of intentional objects ('immanent objectivity', 'intentional in-existence'). He points out that these phrases suggest that the intentional object enters into consciousness as a component of the flux of experience and that it functions within the enclosure of the mind as a substitute for the object of reference. Husserl insists, on the contrary, that the intentional object and the object of reference are one and the same: 'It need only be said to be acknowledged that the intentional object of a presentation is the same as its actual object . . . it is absurd to distinguish between them' ([1.35], 595). He thus affirms unequivocally that our intentional acts target things in the world. Husserl also clarifies the relationship between intentional contents and intentional objects. He says that the term 'intentional content' may legitimately be interpreted in the following ways: (1) as the intentional object (either the object *tout court*, or the object considered as it is intended); (2) as that feature (the act's 'matter') in virtue of which the act achieves determinate reference; (3) as the 'intentional essence' of the act, i.e., the 'matter' combined with its 'quality'. The term 'quality' refers in this context to the type of intentional act, e.g., question, wish, statement, etc. ([1.35], 578–80, 589, 657; [1.54], 26–36). These distinctions are consistent with Husserl's claim, in the first investigation, that propositions are related to the acts in which they are expressed in a manner comparable to the way in which species are related to their instances. Considered as an intentional essence, the intentional content (matter and quality) is an ideal proposition that is independent of particular intentional acts. Taken as instantiated, the matter and quality are non-independent 'moments' of a particular act ([1.35], 330).

Many commentators have rejected this thesis on the grounds that it seems to commit Husserl to the questionable view that ideal propositions may somehow be particularized as moments of individual intentional acts. John Drummond has called attention to two passages that suggest that Husserl eventually modified his position. A note in the second edition (1913) strongly implies that the intentional content should not be regarded as a particularized feature of the intentional act ([1.35], 576; [1.54], 26–36, 39–42). Moreover, in *Ideas Pertaining to a Pure Phenomenology and to a Phenomenological Philosophy* (1913), Husserl adds that what he had formerly taken to be a property of acts was really a property of the 'meant as such' ([1.41], 308; [1.54], 41). In other words, Husserl finally identifies intentional matter and intentional object (in the sense of the 'object considered as it is intended'). This is an important statement, for it effectively eliminates any residue of the medieval notion that we must postulate some sort of intermediary content in between intentional acts and their objects.

Husserl agrees with Brentano that we must distinguish between predication and judgmental assent. However, he disagrees with Brentano's view that judgment is the acceptance or rejection of a neutralized presentation. According to Husserl, judgment is an assertive attitude which pervades the achievement of predication. This attitude is determined by anticipated or concomitantly experienced intuitions of things and their features, rather than by some sort of appraisal of the sense of the sentence. Husserl also agrees with Frege, as opposed to Brentano, that judgment is always a positive attitude, even when the content to which it assents includes a negation. In the context of discourse, assertoric statements make truth claims by reason of their form, not by reason of their predicative content as such, nor by reason of some tacit prefixed existential proposition ([1.35], 612–16). He thus firmly rejects the modern view that judgments are appraisals of nominalized propositional contents. In our straightforward dealings with the world, we are ordinarily preoccupied with things and their properties, rather than with what we are saying. Our speech is guided not by a scan of meanings but rather by anticipated or achieved intuitions of the essential structures of things. It follows that we need not postulate mediating structures (ideas or concepts) between words and things, nor do we need to speculate about a 'place' in which they dwell. To know something is simply to possess its form, to intuit it through its essence, i.e., its intelligible structure. Speech acts express meanings as ideal objects, but meanings are not grasped as such in the instance of articulation.

Husserl also develops more in detail the guiding metaphor of his account of intentionality. He contrasts the 'emptiness' of symbolic intentions with the 'fullness' of intuitive presentations. An empty act is directed toward an object in its absence. A fulfilling act registers its presence. Symbolic intentions may be either nominal (simple) or propositional (complex). A nominal act is single-rayed and directed towards a whole. A propositional act is multi-rayed, since it articulates discrete parts within a complex object. Intuitive presentations may be either perceptual or categorial.

These distinctions prepare the way for a discussion of truth in the sixth investigation. According to Husserl, the experience of truth occurs when we recognize the identity of an object in the transition from empty intention to fulfilling intuition ([1.35], 621–4, 765–70). This description displaces the problem of truth from its traditional locus in the judgment, since the identity-synthesis may occur both in nominal and propositional contexts. Truth is achieved on the pre-predicative level in the identity-synthesis of an empty nominal intention and its correlative perceptual intuition. If judgments achieve truth in a comparable sense, it is not by reason of their propositional structure but by reason of a parallel intuitive fulfillment of their emptily intended objects ([1.76], 68).

The sixth investigation also offers a more extensive critique of the restrictive account of intuition proposed by British empiricism. Husserl approaches this issue indirectly by first criticizing the interpretation that the empiricist tradition had given to the role of those components of a proposition that belong to its categorial form, e.g., prepositions, conjunctions, cases and the copula. According to Locke and Hume, these syntactical operators refer to intra-mental processes rather than to aspects of the world. Husserl dismisses this thesis on the grounds that, when we use such expressions, we are directed towards things rather than towards inner processes. For example, if we say 'This paper is white', it is because we find that the property 'white' belongs to the paper. Hence we surely use the term 'is' in such a sentence to refer to the objective situation rather than to some inner psychological happening. Besides syntactical terms, he adds, there are other formal components of propositions that cannot find their fulfillment in ordinary simple intuitions. Nouns, verbs and even adjectival expressions introduce senses which cannot be fulfilled by simple intuitions: 'The intention of the word "white" only partially coincides with the colour-aspect of the appearing object; a surplus of meaning remains over, a form which finds nothing in the appearance itself to confirm it' ([1.35], 775). Husserl concludes that we must acknowledge the role of non-sensuous or 'categorial' intuitions which function in conjunction with simple perceptions and which bring the formal components of predication to intuitive fulfillment. The fulfilling intuition of any expression describing a particular thus involves the intuition of formal senses that exceed what is intuited in the simple perception of the particular. These expressions refer to particular things by way of accidental or essential descriptive features whose surplus senses function as conditions for the manifestation of the particulars as such ([1.114], 70–1). Categorial intuition is therefore the first step in the process of discernment of essences, for to grasp the essence of some thing or situation is first of all to grasp its sortal property, i.e., its specific form. Translated into Aristotelian terms, intuition of the looks of things (secondary substances) is the condition for the presentation of particulars (primary substances).

⤔ THE TRANSCENDENTAL TURN ⤔

During the period from 1900 to 1913, Husserl developed more fully his criticism of the modern account of cognition. He spelled out his new position in a series of five lectures which introduce the theme of transcendental phenomenology for the first time. Given in Göttingen in 1907 and later published as *The Idea of Phenomenology*, these lectures are devoted to a clarification of the notions of immanence and transcendence. According to Husserl, modern descriptions of the relationship between immanence and transcendence tend to invoke two complementary themes: inside versus outside and accessibility versus inaccessibility. When immanence is described as an enclosure containing mental processes and impressions, transcendence is correspondingly defined as whatever remains outside of that enclosure. When immanence is described as a region of indubitable givenness, transcendence is defined as a region populated by unknowable things-in-themselves. Most epistemologies combine these two senses of the relationship between immanence and transcendence. They first conflate mental acts and their contents by describing both as 'contained' within the mind's psychic processes. They then construe the enigma of cognition as a problem of how to establish a connection between intra-mental representations and extra-mental things. The 'unspoken assumption' of these theories is that our cognitive processes are devoid of intentional import. This, according to Husserl, is the 'fatal mistake' of modern philosophy. Husserl praises Hume for acknowledging that this way of formulating the problem would in the end lead only to scepticism, but he adds that Hume's scepticism is itself riddled with contradictions. On the one hand, Hume degrades to the status of fictions everything that transcends impressions and ideas. On the other hand, he ascribes to the processes of mind the same sort of reality as the transcendent things that we would reach if we could somehow break out of the circle of immanence. Husserl concludes that whenever philosophers ask about the possibility of cognition in a way that implies that 'cognition is a thing apart from its object', or that 'cognition is given but the object of cognition is not given', they introduce an inappropriate notion of transcendence, which in turn entails an inappropriate interpretation of immanence ([1.34], 27–30).

According to Husserl, philosophy needs to adopt a new way of thinking and a new critique of reason: 'philosophy lies in a wholly new dimension. It needs an entirely new point of departure and an entirely new method distinguishing it in principle from any "natural" science' ([1.34], 19). He therefore proposes a new and radical method which requires the bracketing (*epoche*) or suspension of natural convictions: 'At the outset of the critique of cognition the entire world of nature, physical and psychological, as well as one's own human self together with all the sciences which have to do with these objective matters, are *put into question*' ([1.34], 22). Husserl immediately distinguishes his new method from Descartes' doubt. Descartes' goal was to establish certitude about the existence of the thinking self and transcendent things. Husserl has no interest in such a project. His goal is simply to uncover the essence of cognition. He points out that Descartes failed to grasp the essence of cognition because he defined himself, *qua* inquirer, as a 'thinking thing' having the same status as the transcendent *things* whose existence he had called into doubt ([1.34], 5–7). The purpose of the new method is to free us from this incoherent interpretation of transcendence, and consequently to enable us to redefine both transcendence and immanence. When we bracket everything within the realm of transcendence (as it is understood by Descartes and Hume), we in fact exclude nothing more than the incoherent interpretation of transcendent being as a region situated beyond the range of our knowledge. In so far as the mind's 'inside' is interpreted as having the same sort of ontological status, it too must be bracketed. This approach permits us to redefine immanence, in a broader sense, as the zone of all manifestation, wherein both immanent objects (considered now, in a narrower sense, as reflectively intuited experiences) and their intentional correlates (transcendent things) appear to us. Immanent and transcendent objects are now distinguished in terms of their different styles of appearing, rather than by appeal to the difference between intra-mental appearance and extra-mental being.

In the first volume of *Ideas*, Husserl describes this broader field of immanence as a realm of transcendental consciousness. He distinguishes in this work between the 'natural attitude', in which we are preoccupied by things in the world, and the 'phenomenological attitude', in which we reflect on the intentions at work in the natural attitude and on the objective correlates of those intentions. We achieve the latter transcendental point of view by suspending our natural attitude of belief in the reality of things and the world. Husserl emphasizes once again that the purpose of this procedure is not to call natural convictions into doubt but rather to achieve a distance that will enable us to reflect upon them. He adds that the method may also be called 'reduction', for it 'leads back' from lived acts and attitudes to reflective consideration of those acts and attitudes. After the reduction, we no longer live in our intentions. We step back from them in order to reflect on them in their full concreteness. For example, we step back from our participation in the positing of things as real, but continue to maintain that positing as something upon which we reflect. We also maintain our contact with things. The same things in the world are still there for our consideration, but the change in focus initiated by the reduction now permits us to appreciate them precisely *as* intended objects. We now notice them as perceived, as judged, as posited, as doubted, as imagined. Husserl calls any object so considered a *noema*, and he calls the correlative intention a *noesis* ([1.41], 214; [1.54], 46–56, 256–7).

Many commentators equate the phenomenological reduction with the reflective turn of consciousness away from things and facts towards concepts and propositions. They contend that the purpose of the reduction is to orient philosophical analysis towards semantic issues. Proponents of this view find striking similarities between Husserl's concept of the *noema* and Frege's concept of 'sense' (*Sinn*). They hold that both Fregean senses and Husserlian noemata ordinarily serve as intermediaries between our linguistic expressions and their referents ([1.61], 680–7). Frege claimed that the sense conveyed by an expression shapes or determines its reference. Certain passages from *Ideas* seem to assign an analogous role to the noema. For example, in one passage Husserl speaks enigmatically of a 'determinable X' that functions as a centre for the noematic contents which present an object in diverse ways ([1.41], 313–14, 320–2). Proponents of the Fregean interpretation of the noema suggest that Husserl meant to say that the noematic 'X' functions like the sense conveyed by a demonstrative pronoun. It identifies the object of reference not through its properties but as the bearer of properties ([1.95], 195–219). On this interpretation, the role of the phenomenological reduction is to disclose the semantic entities through which intentional direction to objects is achieved.

Robert Sokolowski points out that this interpretation fails to take into account the later Husserl's remarks, in *Formal and Transcendental Logic* (1929), on the difference between the kind of reflection that yields access to propositions and the properly philosophical reflection made possible by the reduction ([1.31], 110–27; [1.100], 45–7). Husserl makes it clear in this work that there is nothing specifically philosophical about propositional reflection, i.e., the reflective turn away from the 'ontological' realms of things and facts towards the 'apophantic' realm of concepts and propositions. This shift in focus occurs quite naturally whenever we reflect on what we ourselves or others have said, in such a way as to take what has been said as a mere supposition or proposal, i.e., as a proposition. It also occurs regularly in the context of scientific inquiry. Scientific verification requires a constant oscillation between investigation of facts and reflection on propositions. Both ordinary and scientific forms of propositional reflection take place within the natural attitude, and therefore do not require the phenomenological reduction as their condition.

What then is the difference between propositional reflection and philosophical reflection? Propositional reflection turns our attention from things and facts to concepts and propositions. Philosophical reflection focuses on the correlation between intentional acts and attitudes (*noeses*) and the ways in which things are presented (*noemata*). It considers things and facts as the correlates of the attitude of straightforward involvement in the world, and it considers propositions as the correlates of the intentional attitude of propositional reflection. We may therefore conclude that, for Husserl, the noema is simply the object itself, considered under the reduction *as* presented. It follows that the 'determinable X' is not a semantic entity that functions as a medium of reference. It is the intentional object itself considered as an identity genuinely given in each of its presentations ([1.54], 181–91).

Husserl's description of the relationship between the ontological and apophantic domains reinforces his thesis that concepts and propositions do not function as mental intermediaries. Concepts and propositions emerge only when we shift from an ontological to an apophantic focus. Hence, they do not serve as mediating entities that somehow link speech acts to their intentional referents. As we have seen, Husserl explicitly rejected Locke's view that concepts are mental representations, and implicitly rejected the medieval view that concepts are transparent media of reference. Moreover, he never claimed, as does Frege, that concepts and propositions belong to a 'third realm' (the first realm is the outer world of physical things; the second realm is the inner world of psychic processes) that functions as a non-subjective medium of reference. Robert Sokolowski suggests that the tendency to regard concepts and propositions as reified intermediaries is probably due to a confusion between object-oriented and reflective stances of consciousness. We enjoy a marginal awareness of what we are saying in the process of saying it. However, we do not at that moment objectify what we are saying as a proposition, for our consciousness remains directed towards the world. We can, none the less, easily shift back and forth between ontological and propositional attitudes. The very mobility of our consciousness inculcates a forgetfulness of the change in attitude requisite for the manifestation of concepts and propositions. Concepts and propositions then easily come to be thought of as having a status analogous to things and facts. We thus come to think of them as separate entities situated in some psychic or semantic realm. For those who are looking for a solution to the modern epistemological problem of establishing a link between our speech acts and their targets, it is then perfectly natural to assign this mediating role to concepts and propositions. According to Husserl, however, there is no such need for mediation. Our consciousness is intentional by its very nature ([1.101], 110–11; [1.106], 451–63).

This does not mean, of course, that there is no mediating role for language. Husserl draws a distinction between genuinely thoughtful speech and routine linguistic performances. He observes that when we speak, we ordinarily focus upon what we see, or anticipate seeing, and only marginally upon what we are saying. Though marginal, our consciousness of the meanings of linguistic expressions testifies to a familiarity with a vast network of culturally established distinctions and nuances whose ultimate justification lies in the intuitive disclosure of the looks of things. Once in command of the standardized senses of words, we need no longer focus on those senses. When we speak about things, we let ourselves be guided only by our categorial intuitions. Our choice of words is governed directly by the looks of the things we struggle to describe. Sometimes we simply repeat standard formulae. We then fail to exercise the potential for clarity or distinctness provided by the linguistic code. Sometimes we are more conscious of making linguistic choices. At such moments, we shift our focus away from things towards the senses of words ([1.31], 56–60). Husserl thus suggests that our ability to shift back and forth easily between these orientations accounts for the interdependence of intuitive and linguistic discriminations. Finding the appropriate word, therefore, is not just a matter of familiarity with the rules of a language-game. An exclusively pragmatic account of linguistic use amounts to a nominalism that rejects any link between predicates and the intuited forms of things. Thoughtful speech is the product of an artful integration of seeing and saying. Mastery of an extensive linguistic repertoire makes for more nuanced perceptions, which in turn call for more nuanced linguistic options.

In the first volume of *Ideas*, Husserl takes up again the effort to redefine the notions of immanence and transcendence. He attempts to bring the reader gradually to the realization that the new dimension revealed by the reduction is not a region comparable to other regions of being. He first defines a region of being as a specific domain of objects (e.g., the regions 'material thing' and 'culture') whose unity is determined by some maximally broad genus. He notes that empirical sciences which deal with a given region of being ought to be grounded in a corresponding science of essences which he calls a 'regional ontology'. The task of a regional ontology is to specify the essences that structure all objects in its domain, and to spell out the hierarchically ordered relationships between them. In addition to the various regional ontologies, Husserl proposes that there should be a new science, called 'formal ontology', devoted to the study of the fundamental categories that govern the relations and arrangements between objects in any region whatsoever. He then criticizes the thesis, common to most epistemological accounts, that consciousness is confined within a psychic region, opposed to the region of things. Whenever consciousness is described in this manner, there is a tendency, he argues, to reduce intentionality to representation within the enclosure of the mind. Repeating the themes developed earlier in *The Idea of Phenomenology*, he then describes the transcendence of things as a mode of givenness within immanence, now more broadly understood as the range of intentionality's transcending power. He again stresses that the reduction does not exclude anything that is genuinely given. Finally, he points out that this new dimension of immanence cannot coherently be understood as situated within the co-ordinates of a pre-given world. Even the horizon of the world is given as such within the sphere of immanence. Unlike all other regions, therefore, the transcendental domain is absolute and all-inclusive. It has no perimeters, no outside. Husserl thus takes the metaphor of 'region' to its limits, in order to demonstrate that it is, in fact, incoherent to think of immanence as a sector within a broader whole. Any attempt to conceive of a dimension of being beyond the zone of possible consciousness is nonsensical. Consciousness and being belong together. Their ranges are co-extensive. There can be no outside for a being whose mode of being is to be open to all things.

❧ EGO AND WORLD ❧

One of the most controversial theses of Husserl's transcendental phenomenology is his claim that both ego and world may be considered as noemata by the transcendental inquirer. He frequently distinguishes between the ego considered as part of the world and the transcendental ego for whom the world itself is a *noema*. He contends that our capacity to function as transcendental subjects permits us to achieve a reflective distance from our own natural way of being in the world, and therefore to understand that way of being more fully. Husserl develops these themes in *Ideas II, Cartesian Meditations*, and in a manuscript published posthumously under the title *The Crisis of European Sciences and Transcendental Phenomenology*.

Ideas II introduces the theme of the human ego in an oblique fashion by first describing the role of corporeal orientation and intellectual perspective in the presentation of things. Things appear to us in quite different ways, depending on the condition of our sense organs, on variations in our kinesthetic orientation, and especially on whether we take a pragmatic or theoretical attitude towards them. Husserl situates his analysis within the context of an understanding of nature that has been substantially affected by modern science. The contemporary sense of nature, he contends, is the intentional correlate of an attitude which he describes as both 'doxic' and 'theoretical'. It is doxic because it is permeated by an unthematic belief in the existence of its objects; it is theoretical because it prescinds from the practical, aesthetic and ethical features of its objects. While ordinary experience does not constantly maintain an exclusively theoretical stance, none the less the influence of science has generated the everyday conviction that the true sense of the thing is what remains when we bracket the useful, the beautiful and the good ([1.5], 1–11; [1.89], 39–40). Further analysis of the presentation of things reveals that the full sense of their objectivity is dependent upon a recognition of intersubjectivity. For example, a sense of relatively fixed spatial positions is essential to our sense of objectivity. It would surely be difficult to develop this notion from an exclusively private perspective. We manage eventually to locate ourselves within a public system of co-ordinates by first recognizing that one individual's 'here' may be another's 'there', and then agreeing upon some convention for relating all positions to a stable network of places. This is a typical example of phenomenological analysis. Husserl's goal is always to unpack the layers of meaning sedimented in the senses of various types of objects, and thus to reveal the intentional acts and attitudes tacitly at work in the presentation of these objects.

In *Cartesian Meditations* (1931), Husserl continues his analysis of intersubjectivity by introducing a modification of the bracketing technique that he calls 'reduction to the sphere of ownness'. He proposes to abstract from everything in our experience that testifies to the presence of others. The purpose of this strategy is not to describe the production of meaning by a subjectivity actually cut off from others and the world, or to assure us that we are really in contact with other people. Despite its title, *Cartesian Meditations* is not motivated by any such epistemological concern. On the contrary, Husserl's purpose is simply to uncover the contribution of the sense that there are other selves to the individual's sense of self and of world. Phenomenological analysis is a reconstruction, not a creation of meaning.

In his *Lectures on the Phenomenology of Inner Time-Consciousness* (1928), Husserl claims that a second-order reflection reveals a level of time-consciousness that accounts for the identity of the transcendental ego. He first distinguishes between transcendent temporal objects, such as musical performances or public lectures, and immanent temporal objects, such as our perceptions of these events. He then points out that the perception of a temporal object may itself be taken as temporal object. Whenever we perceive the elapsing of a speaker's words into the past, we also experience the fading of our perceptions of those words into the past. We thus learn to situate transcendent happenings within the context of objective time, and also to locate our perceptions of those events within the horizon of immanent time. Finally, he claims that reflection on the correlation between the flux of immanent temporal objects and our experience of that flux reveals that we are conscious of a deeper level of time which accounts for our sense of the temporal flow of our intentional acts. We experience this primal flux as the basic form within which all experience occurs. This form is composed not of the basic temporal phases (past, present and future), but of the conditions for their possibility, i.e., a primal impression, 'retention' of the just-past, and 'protention' of the just-about-to-be. Awareness of the concatenation of these components makes it possible for us to experience our own intentional life as temporal, and to grasp intentional objects as the same again throughout their successive presentations ([1.14], 378–82; [1.46], 298–326; [1.100], 138–68).

<h2>~ ESSENCES ~</h2>

Husserl claims that we are sometimes able to discern the essential structures of things. In *Experience and Judgment*, he distinguishes between the grasp of empirical universals and the fully-fledged intuition of essences. A preliminary awareness of empirical universals occurs when we make the transition from merely associative judgments, which express perceived likenesses among things, to those judgments which explicitly identify particulars as instances of some category. Once we have discerned what is the same among many individuals, we may then thematize the universal itself and begin to make scientific judgments about it. The goal of science is to specify ever more completely the characteristics of such empirical universals. According to Husserl, however, science never fully realizes this ideal, for it is impossible to achieve a truly exhaustive and definitive determination of all of the features of any empirical universal. The determination of every empirical concept is 'always in progress, always being further fashioned, and also re-fashioned' ([1.35], 116; [1.36], nos 80–98; [1.100], 58–62).

We make the transition from the grasp of an empirical universal to the intuition of an essence when we move from the perceptual to the imaginary mode of consciousness by submitting the universal to a process of 'free variation' designed to reveal an invariant structure. Husserl describes this technique as follows. We attempt to imagine successively the subtraction of one after another of the various features of the object under consideration. In this way we eventually isolate those invariant features without which the object in question would cease to be what it is. We need not consider every conceivable variation. Indeed, in most cases it would be impossible to carry out an exhaustive survey of every possibility. What matters is that the manner of variation should be such that not only do we have the sense that the process could go on indefinitely, but also that it would in fact be fruitless to continue. As Husserl puts it, the process of variation should have a character of 'exemplary arbitrariness' ([1.36], no. 87b). Eidetic intuition is therefore a product of method. As Husserl puts it: 'The inward evidence on which all knowledge ultimately reposes is no gift of nature, appearing together with the idea of states of affairs without any methodically artful set-up' ([1.35], 63; [1.110].

Husserl does not, like some contemporary philosophers, extend the method of free variation to the consideration of improbable scenarios imagined as taking place within possible worlds. His imaginative variations, like Aristotle's, are generally guided and limited by our ordinary intuitions of things in this world. Moreover, he never attempts to provide anything like a clear-cut rule for deciding when the process of 'free variation' ought to come to an end. He tells us only that there comes a point in any enquiry when it is reasonable to conclude that there are no further pertinent questions to be asked. It is then imprudent or even pathological to consider additional alternative possibilities. In short, discernment of essences requires both method and judgment. A sense of the mean between extremes is as necessary in intellectual enquiry as it is in practical affairs.

Husserl claims, moreover, that the kind of certainty that we should assign to the results of this procedure varies in proportion to the type of access that we have to the objects under investigation. Our apperceptive access to the basic structures of consciousness yields a different sort of evidence than is available in our perceptions of things in the world. Ordinary perceptions are perspectival and therefore necessarily incomplete. However, the philosophic recognition that all such perceptions are perspectival is not itself perspectival or incomplete in the same fashion. Ordinary perceptions are perspectives in the sense that they present only one side of their objects at a time. Philosophic descriptions of the structure of perception are 'perspectives' in the sense that they are influenced by historically conditioned questions and methods. Husserl suggests that it is just as inappropriate to blur these differences by asserting that all forms of cognition are similarly perspectival, as it is to look for mathematical certitudes in the ethical and political domains.

Husserl at first held that the relative immediacy of access to the structures of cognition provided by our tacit awareness of intentional performances makes for apodictic certainty. He eventually acknowledged, however, that even the privileged access of consciousness to its own structures does not guarantee the perfect accuracy of reflective descriptions of those structures. Given the oblique and unthematic character of our tacit awareness of intentional acts and attitudes, and given the distorting influence of prevalent philosophic categories, our reflective descriptions are often vague and confused. Indeed, the history of philosophy testifies convincingly to the fact that no philosophic reflection can dissipate all vagueness. In any case, Husserl adds, philosophic differences are never settled by sweeping refutations, but rather by the elaboration of strategic distinctions that reveal the partial, vague or confused character of opposing positions. This is why philosophy must be a co-operative effort of a community of investigators.

∾ LIFE-WORLD AND HISTORY ∾

Husserl's later works are largely devoted to the themes of life-world and history. He hoped that his phenomenological analyses of these topics would serve as correctives to the naturalism and historicism which he recognized as two of the most powerful themes of modernity. Naturalism is a philosophic position consequent upon the mathematization of nature achieved by the new scientific method at the beginning of the modern era. Its thesis is that the entire realm of nature, including human nature, is comprised only of entities and processes susceptible of such quantitative analysis. Historicism may be defined as the tendency to regard the conceptual systems of both the natural and the human sciences as world views whose presuppositions are determined by contingent historical transformations.

Husserl traces the drift of modern science towards reductionism to Galileo's failure to relate scientific truths adequately to their sources in the life-world, the pre-scientific world in which we live. He calls attention, in particular, to the ambiguous implications of Galileo's bold decision to overcome the obstacle which perceived qualities presented to calculative rationality by treating them as subjective indices of objective quantities. This decision had the effect of concealing the priority of perceived over mathematical objects. Husserl contends that two factors contributed to this concealment ([1.33], 21–60; [1.89], 162–7).

In the first place, he observes, we must not forget that Galileo was heir to a relatively advanced tradition of 'pure geometry', which by reason of its very advances had already lost contact with the fundamental insights on which it was first constructed. Geometry most likely had its origins in the invention of practical techniques of surveying and measuring. Its ideal figures were thus first derived by abstraction and progressive idealization from the perceived forms of things. Once having acquired the notion of a field of pure 'limit-shapes', mathematical praxis was able to achieve an exactness and a freedom that is denied to us in empirical praxis. This ideal geometry was subsequently translated into applied geometry in the field of astronomy, where it became possible to calculate 'with compelling necessity' the relative positions and even the existence of events that were never accessible to direct empirical measurement. This achievement constituted a partial fulfillment of the dream of the ancient Pythagoreans who had observed the functional dependency of the pitch of a tone on the length of a vibrating string which produced it, and had therefore evoked the possibility of a generalized theory of correlations between perceived properties and measurable changes in geometrical properties. All of this, Husserl speculates, inclined Galileo to bracket the problem of the original derivation of geometry from the perceived qualities of things, and to interpret such qualities as merely subjective indicators of the true quantitative being of the world ([1.33], 29).

In the second place, Husserl continues, we must take into account the 'portentous' influence on Galileo's thinking of the new algebraic formalization of geometry. The development of algebra in effect liberated geometry from all intuited actuality and even from the concept of number. Although it was only with Descartes' invention of analytic geometry that the full implications of this move would be realized, Galileo had already clearly understood that Euclid's geometry could now be interpreted as a general logic of discovery rather than as a theory limited to the realm of pure shapes ([1.33], 44–6). Husserl's argument may be confirmed by considering the role of Galileo's diagrams for his theorems about uniformly accelerated bodies. It is clear that the lines and angles of these diagrams no longer refer literally to spatial shapes created by geometric relations between linear magnitudes but rather to a sequence of ratios between time and velocity. Galileo therefore implicitly considered such 'geometric' diagrams as expressive of relationships among any magnitudes whatever. Although this realization contributed significantly to the advance of modern physics, it also initiated a process of further alienation of scientific method from its roots in the perceived world. Unlike traditional geometry, which requires insight into the reasons for every step in its demonstrations, algebra lends itself to the development of techniques of calculation which no longer demand such comprehension but require instead only the blind implementation of procedural rules.

Galileo himself continued to employ the more traditional geometrical style of demonstration, and hence demanded of his readers conscious insight into the point of each transition. Nevertheless, his method took modernity further along the road towards the reductionist interpretation of reason as an adaptive power whose operations are mechanistic processes devoid of intuitive insight. Husserl cites as an example of this account of reason the tendency of some twentieth-century logicians to conflate computing procedures with authentic deductions, and even to interpret the rules governing such procedures as a genuine logic ([1.37], 117). He concludes that the great discovery of modernity, i.e., the emancipation of mathematics from the constraints imposed by the intuition of Euclidean shapes, was both an advance and a setback. On the one hand, freedom from servitude to intuited forms would give to the geometer a greater potential for mastery over nature. On the other hand, it also further promoted the modern forgetfulness of the priority of insight into perceived structures over technical virtuosity. This forgetfulness would eventually lead to a bracketing of those acts and attitudes of the human spirit that render scientific and other modes of cognition possible. Naturalism forgets the role of the inquiring subject whose intentional acts remain inaccessible to empirical observation.

Husserl calls attention to the irony implicit in this history of modernity. He observes that it is unlikely that Galileo was ever aware of the hidden 'motivation' of his project. The seeds of reductionism and even of scepticism were, of course, already present in Hobbes's rationalistic exaltation of the power of reckoning. Hobbes had dismissed the whole sphere of pre-scientific experience and discourse. Whatever cannot be quantified he assigned to the realm of illusion. Moreover, Hobbes clearly regarded reason's calculus as an outgrowth of our biological drives and needs. For a long time, however, the success of the new sciences obscured the implications of this naturalism. Hobbes thought that calculative procedures could succeed where the ancient and medieval quest for essences had failed. Reckoning would reveal the hidden structures of reality. It required a genius such as Hume, says Husserl, to take the naturalism initiated by Hobbes to its logical conclusions. Hume realized that if cognitive intuition cannot break out of the circle of impressions and ideas, there is no justification for supposing that reckoning can yield any less fanciful results. The fundamental categories requisite for a mathematicized version of nature must somehow be derivable from information provided by the manifold of impressions. According to Hobbes, however, sensory impressions yield only illusions. It follows that scientific theories too are productions of fancy. This realization is the key to Hume's scepticism: 'Hume goes on to the end. All categories of objectivity – the scientific ones through which an objective extra-psychic world is thought in scientific life, and the pre-scientific ones through which it is thought in everyday life – are fictions' ([1.33], no. 23). Scientific descriptions are useful fictions, but they nevertheless remain fictions. The high hopes of modernity thus culminated finally in a thoroughgoing pragmatism. It seems clear in retrospect that the hidden intent of Galileo's fateful decision, and indeed of the entire project of modernity, was to give up on truth and settle for power.

Husserl therefore thought that the most urgent task of philosophy was to restore confidence in the rationality of our ordinary intuitions about the life-world. We must demonstrate how scientific accounts of nature are always dependent upon the evidences of ordinary experience, and show how the success of Galileo's method in some areas does not justify an unlimited application in all fields of enquiry. Phenomenological analysis reveals, for example, that human acts have a conscious dimension that cannot be reduced to quantifiable processes, or explained as a product of causal sequences. This is especially true of the procedures of scientific discovery which require a disciplined detachment from biological needs and environmental stimuli. In short, the acts prerequisite for the emergence of things as empirical objects cannot coherently be taken as exclusively empirical processes.

Husserl also makes some interesting remarks on the implications of his own method of historical interpretation, as exemplified in the above analysis of the unintended project concealed by Galileo's manifest intentions and accomplishments. He observes that whenever we engage in an historical analysis of this type we always find ourselves in a sort of circle. We can only understand the past in the light of the present, and yet the present has meaning only in the light of the past. 'Relative clarification' in one direction brings about 'some elucidation' in the other, and vice versa. There is no tone of pessimism in Husserl's description of this methodological predicament ([1.33], 58). He suggests that his 'zigzag' method of historical interpretation makes it possible to achieve ever more comprehensive historical understanding, but he never claims that it will yield definitive truths. He does not lament this situation. He simply calls attention to the kind of truth that is available to historical interpretation.

These remarks suggest that, in his later works at least, Husserl was sensitive to the hermeneutic circle implicit in all human enquiry. His comments on the historicity of the life-world confirm this impression. Although he sometimes describes the life-world as a horizon of experience common to human beings in every historical epoch, at other times he speaks of multiple life-worlds and hints that every life-world is conditioned by layered sedimentations of meaning produced by forgotten cultural achievements. He even goes so far as to say that we must look for truth 'not as falsely absolutized, but rather, in each case, as within its horizons' ([1.20], 279). This passage suggests that all evidence is subject to correction by further evidence. Husserl adds, moreover, that it is in accordance with the nature of a horizon that 'it leaves open the possibility that conflicting experiences may supervene and lead to corrections in the form of a determining as otherwise or else in the form of a complete striking out (as illusion)' ([1.20], 281; [1.110], 50).

Husserl's reflections on these issues did not cause him to repudiate the original project of phenomenology. Indeed, in the same passages which call attention to the role of intentional horizons he constantly reaffirms the phenomenological goal of uncovering and 'explicating' the sedimented senses of these horizons. Husserl therefore apparently saw no conflict between this goal and his properly hermeneutic discovery that all inquiry takes place within an historical context. Jacques Derrida contends that this attitude indicates that the entire enterprise of phenomenology was founded on an uncontrolled presupposition. Husserl tacitly took for granted the trans-historical validity of the ideal of universal truth, even though his own historical interpretation established that commitment to this ideal is an historically conditioned attitude. His description of this ideal as a regulative idea effectively exempted him from the task of justifying it ([1.51], 154). It seems more likely, however, that Husserl always understood that the ideal of universal truth functions more as a moral imperative than as a demonstrable or self-evident principle. He was convinced that our experience of the world yields enough intelligibility and direction to encourage the expectation that further investigation will yield further progress in truth. However, his choice of the Kantian notion of a regulative idea to describe the telos of philosophy suggests that he regarded the expectation of progress in truth as a postulate of rationality rather than as a metaphysical principle.

❧ SELECT BIBLIOGRAPHY ❧

Primary texts

Where pertinent, references are to the more recent critical editions (the 'Husserliana' series published by the Husserl Archives at Louvain) rather than to the original German editions.

1.1 'Besprechung: E. Schröder, *Vorlesungen über die Algebra der Logik, I*', *Göttingische gelehrte Anzeigen* (1891): 243–78.

1.2 'Die Folgerungskalkül und die Inhaltslogik', *Vierteljahrsschrift für wissenschaftliche Philosophie*, 15 (1891): 168–89, 351–6.

1.3 'Psychologische Studien zur elementaren Logik', *Philosophische Monatshefte*, 30 (1894): 159–91.

1.4 *Die Idee der Phänomenologie*, ed. W. Biemel (Husserliana II), The Hague: Nijhoff, 1950.

1.5 *Ideen zu einer reinen Phänomenologie und phänomenologischen Philosophie*, Buch II, ed. M. Biemel (Husserliana IV), The Hague: Nijhoff, 1952.

1.6   *Ideen zu einer reinen Phänomenologie und phänomenologischen Philosophie*, Buch III, ed. M. Biemel (Husserliana V), The Hague: Nijhoff, 1952.

1.7   *Erfahrung und Urteil*, ed. L. Landgrebe, Hamburg: Claassen, 1954.

1.8   *Die Krisis der europäischen Wissenschaften und die transzendentale Phänomenologie*, ed. W. Biemel (Husserliana VI), The Hague: Nijhoff, 1954.

1.9   *Erste Philosophie, Band I, Kritische Ideengeschichte*, ed. R. Boehm (Husserliana VII), The Hague: Nijhoff, 1956.

1.10   *Cartesianische Meditationen*, ed. S. Strasser (Husserliana I), The Hague: Nijhoff, 1959.

1.11   *Erste Philosophie*, Band II, ed. R. Boehm (Husserliana VIII), The Hague: Nijhoff, 1959.

1.12   *Phänomenologische Psychologie*, ed. W. Biemel (Husserliana IX), The Hague: Nijhoff, 1962.

1.13   *Cartesianische Meditationen*, 2nd edn. S. Strasser (Husserliana I), The Hague, Nijhoff, 1963.

1.14   *Analysen zur passiven Synthesis: Aus Vorlesungs und Forschungsmanuskripten (1918–1926)*, ed. M. Fleischer (Husserliana XI), The Hague: Nijhoff, 1966.

1.15   *Phänomenologische Psychologie: Vorlesungen Sommersemester 1925*, ed. W. Biemel (Husserliana IX), The Hague: Nijhoff, 1968.

1.16   *Philosophie der Arithmetik*, 2nd edn, ed. L. Eley (Husserliana XII), The Hague: Nijhoff, 1970.

1.17   *Erfahrung und Urteil: Untersuchungen zur Genealogie der Logik*, ed. L. Landgrebe, Hamburg: Felix Meiner, 1972.

1.18   *Die Idee der Phänomenologie: Fünf Vorlesungen*, ed. U. Melle (Husserliana II), The Hague: Nijhoff, 1973.

1.19   *Ding und Raum: Vorlesungen 1907*, ed. U. Claesges (Husserliana XVI), The Hague: Nijhoff, 1973.

1.20   *Formale und transzendentale Logik*, ed. P. Janssen (Husserliana XVII), The Hague: Nijhoff, 1974.

1.21   *Logische Untersuchungen*, Band I, ed. E. Hollenstein (Husserliana XVIII), The Hague: Nijhoff, 1975.

1.22   *Ideen zu einer reinen Phänomenologie und phänomenologischen Philosophie*, Buch I, ed. K. Schumann (Husserliana III/1 and III/2), The Hague: Nijhoff, 1976.

1.23   *Aufsätze und Rezensionen (1890–1910)*, ed. B. Rang (Husserliana XXII), The Hague: Nijhoff, 1979.

1.24   *Studien zur Arithmetik und Geometrie: Texte aus dem Nachlass (1886–1901)*, ed. I. Strohmeyer (Husserliana XXI), The Hague: Nijhoff, 1983.

1.25   *Einleitung in der Logik und Erkenntnistheorie: Vorlesungen 1906–7*, ed. U. Melle (Husserliana XIV), Dordrecht: Nijhoff, 1984.

1.26   *Logische Untersuchungen*, Band II, ed. U. Panzer (Husserliana XIX/1), The Hague: Nijhoff, 1984.

1.27   *Logische Untersuchungen*, Band III, ed. U. Panzer (Husserliana XIX/2), The Hague: Nijhoff, 1984.

1.28   'Philosophie als strenge Wissenschaft, in *Aufsätze und Vorträge (1911–21)*', ed. T. Nenon and H. R. Sepp (Husserliana XXV), Dordrecht: Nijhoff, 1987.

Translations

1.29 On the Phenomenology of the Consciousness of Internal Time (1893–1917), trans. J. B. Brough, Holland: Dordrecht Kluwer, 1990.

1.30 'Philosophy as a Rigorous Science', trans. Q. Lauer, in Phenomenology and the Crisis of Philosophy, New York: Harper & Row, 1965, pp. 71–147.

1.31 Formal and Transcendental Logic, trans. D. Cairns, The Hague: Nijhoff, 1969.

1.32 Cartesian Meditations, trans. D. Cairns, The Hague: Nijhoff, 1970.

1.33 The Crisis of European Sciences and Transcendental Phenomenology, trans. D. Carr, Evanston: Northwestern University Press, 1970.

1.34 The Idea of Phenomenology, trans. W. Alston and G. Nakhnikian, The Hague: Nijhoff, 1970.

1.35 Logical Investigations, 2 volumes, rev. edn, trans. J. N. Findlay, London: Routledge & Kegan Paul, 1970.

1.36 Experience and Judgment, trans. J. Churchill and K. Americks, Evanston: Northwestern University Press, 1970.

1.37 'A Review of Volume I of Ernst Schröder's Vorlesungen über die Algebra der Logik', trans. D. Willard, The Personalist, 59 (1978): 115–43.

1.38 'The Deductive Calculus and the Logic of Contents', trans. D. Willard, The Personalist, 60 (1979): 7–25.

1.39 Ideas Pertaining to a Pure Phenomenology and to a Phenomenological Philosophy, Book III, trans. T. Klein and W. Pohl, The Hague: Nijhoff, 1980.

1.40 'Psychological Studies for Elementary Logic', in P. McCormick and F. Elliston (eds), Husserl: Shorter Works, South Bend: Notre Dame University Press, 1981, pp. 126–42.

1.41 Ideas Pertaining to a Pure Phenomenology and to a Phenomenological Philosophy, Book I, trans. F. Kersten, The Hague: Nijhoff, 1983.

Other works and criticism

1.42 Aristotle, Aristotelis Opera, ed. I. Bekker, Berlin: Reimer, 1860–70.

1.43 Bell, D. Husserl, London and New York: Routledge, 1990.

1.44 Boehm, R. 'Immanenz und Transzendenz', in Vom Gesichtspunkt der Phänomenologie: Husserl-Studien, The Hague: Nijhoff, 1968.

1.45 Brentano, F. Psychology from an Empirical Standpoint, trans. A. C. Rancurello, D. B. Terrell and L. L. McAlister, London: Routledge & Kegan Paul, 1973.

1.46 Brough, J. 'The Emergence of an Absolute Consciousness in Husserl's Early Writings on Time-Consciousness', Man and World, 5 (1972): 298–326.

1.47 Carr, D. Interpreting Husserl: Critical and Comparative Studies, The Hague: Nijhoff, 1987.

1.48 Cobb-Stevens, R. 'Logical Analysis and Cognitive Intuition', Etudes phénoménologiques, 7 (1988): 3–32.

1.49 Cobb-Stevens, R. Husserl and Analytic Philosophy, Dordrecht: Kluwer, 1990.

1.50   de Boer, T. *The Development of Husserl's Thought*, trans. T. Plantinga, The Hague: Nijhoff, 1978.

1.51   Derrida, J. *Speech and Phenomena, and Other Essays on Husserl's Theory of Signs*, trans. D. Allison, Evanston: Northwestern University Press, 1973.

1.52   Derrida, J. *Edmund Husserl's Origin of Geometry: An Introduction*, trans. J. Leavey, Stony Brook: Nicholas Hays, 1978.

1.53   Dreyfus, H. 'Husserl's Perceptual Noema', in H. Dreyfus and H. Hall (eds), *Husserl: Intentionality and Cognitive Science*, Cambridge, Mass.: MIT Press, 1982.

1.54   Drummond, J. *Husserlian Intentionality and Non-Foundational Realism: Noema and Object*, Dordrecht: Kluwer, 1990.

1.55   Dummett, M. A. E. *Frege: Philosophy of Language*, London: Duckworth, 1973.

1.56   Dummett, M. A. E. *The Interpretation of Frege's Philosophy*, London: Duckworth, 1981.

1.57   Elliston, F., and McCormick, P. (eds) *Husserl: Expositions and Appraisals*, South Bend: Notre Dame University Press, 1977.

1.58   Fink, E. 'Operative Begriffe in Husserl's Phänomenologie', *Zeitschrift für philosophische Forschung*, 2 (1957): 321–37.

1.59   Fink, E. 'The Phenomenological Philosophy of Edmund Husserl and Contemporary Criticism', in R. O. Elverton (ed.) *The Phenomenology of Edmund Husserl: Selected Critical Readings*, Chicago: Quadrangle Books, 1970, pp. 73–147.

1.60   Føllesdal, D. *Husserl and Frege*, Oslo: Aschehoug Press, 1958.

1.61   Føllesdal, D. 'Husserl's Notion of the Noema', *The Journal of Philosophy*, 66 (1969): 680–7.

1.62   Føllesdal, D. 'Brentano and Husserl on Intentional Objects of Perception', *Grazer Philosophische Studien*, 5 (1978): 83–94.

1.63   Frege, G. 'Rezension von E. Husserl, *Philosophie der Arithmetik*', *Zeitschrift für Philosophie und philosophische Kritik*, 103 (1894): 313–32.

1.64   Frege, G. *The Foundations of Arithmetic: A Logico-Mathematical Enquiry into the Concept of Number*, trans. J. L. Austin, Oxford: Basil Blackwell, 1959.

1.65   Frege, G. 'Review of Dr. E. Husserl's Philosophy of Arithmetic', trans. E. W. Kluge, in J. N. Mohanty (ed.) *Readings on Husserl's Logical Investigations*, The Hague: Nijhoff, 1977.

1.66   Frege, G. *Posthumous Writings*, trans. P. Lang and R. White, Chicago: University of Chicago Press, 1979.

1.67   Frege, G. *Collected Papers on Mathematics, Logic, and Philosophy*, ed. B. McGuinness, trans. M. Black *et al.*, Oxford: Basil Blackwell, 1984.

1.68   Gadamer, H. G. 'The Science of the Life-World', in *Philosophical Hermeneutics*, trans. D. Linge, Berkeley: University of California Press, 1972.

1.69   Hall, H. 'Was Husserl a Realist or an Idealist?', in H. L. Dreyfus (ed.) *Husserl, Intentionality and Cognitive Science*, Cambridge, Mass.: MIT Press, 1984.

1.70   Heelan, P. 'Natural Science and Being-in-the-World', *Man and World*, 16 (1983): 207–19.

1.71 Heelan, P. *Space-Perception and the Philosophy of Science*, Berkeley: University of California Press, 1983.

1.72 Herbart, J. F. *Sammtliche Werke*, Leipzig: Leopold Voss, 1850.

1.73 Hintikka, J. *The Intentions of Intentionality and Other New Models for Modalities*, Dordrecht: Reidel, 1975.

1.74 Holmes, R. 'An Explication of Husserl's Theory of the Noema', *Research in Phenomenology*, 5 (1975): 143–53.

1.75 Langsdorf, L. 'The Noema as Intentional Entity: A Critique of Føllesdal', *Review of Metaphysics*, 37 (1984): 757–84.

1.76 Levinas, E. *The Theory of Intuition in Husserl's Phenomenology*, trans. A. Orianne, Evanston: Northwestern University Press, 1973.

1.77 Lotze, H. *Logic*, trans. B. Bosanquet, Oxford: Clarendon Press, 1888.

1.78 Lotze, H. *Metaphysik*, Leipzig: Hirzel, 1897.

1.79 McKenna, W. 'The "Inadequacy" of Perceptual Experience', *Journal of the British Society for Phenomenology*, 12 (1981): 125–39.

1.80 Mill, J. S. *A System of Logic*, London: Longmans, Green, 1843.

1.81 Miller, J. P. *Numbers in Presence and Absence: A Study of Husserl's Philosophy of Mathematics*, The Hague: Nijhoff, 1982.

1.82 Mohanty, J. N. 'On Husserl's Theory of Meaning', *The Southwestern Journal of Philosophy*, 5 (1974): 240.

1.83 Mohanty, J. N. 'Husserl's Theory of Meaning', in F. Elliston and P. McCormick (eds) *Husserl: Expositions and Appraisals*, South Bend: Notre Dame University Press, 1977, pp. 18–37.

1.84 Mohanty, J. N. *Readings on E. Husserl's Logical Investigations*, The Hague: Nijhoff, 1977.

1.85 Mohanty, J. N. 'Intentionality and the Noema', *The Journal of Philosophy*, 78 (1981): 706–17.

1.86 Mohanty, J. N. *Frege and Husserl*, Bloomington: Indiana University Press, 1982.

1.87 Mohanty, J. N. *Transcendental Phenomenology*, Oxford: Basil Blackwell, 1989.

1.88 Natanson, M. *Edmund Husserl: Philosopher of Infinite Tasks*, Evanston: Northwestern University Press, 1966.

1.89 Ricoeur, P. *Husserl: An Analysis of his Phenomenology*, trans. G. Ballard and L. Embree: Evanston, Northwestern University Press, 1967.

1.90 Rosen, S. 'Thought and Touch: A Note on Aristotle's *De Anima*', *Phronesis*, 6 (1961): 127–37.

1.91 Rosen, S. *The Limits of Analysis*, New York: Basic Books, 1984.

1.92 Schröder, E. *Vorlesungen über die Algebra der Logik*, Leipzig: Teubner, 1890.

1.93 Schutz, A. 'Type and Eidos in Husserl's Late Philosophy', *Philosophy and Phenomenological Research*, 20 (1959): 154.

1.94 Smith, D. W. and McIntyre, R. 'Intentionality via Intensions', *Journal of Philosophy*, 68 (1971): 541–61.

1.95 Smith, D. W. and McIntyre, R. *Husserl and Intentionality: A Study of Mind, Meaning and Language*, The Hague: Nijhoff, 1983.

1.96 Smith, Q. 'On Husserl's Theory of Consciousness in the Fifth Logical

Investigation', *Philosophy and Phenomenological Research*, 37 (1977): 356–67.

1.97 Sokolowski, R. 'The Logic of Parts and Wholes in Husserl's *Investigations*', *Philosophy and Phenomenological Research*, 38 (1968): 537–53.

1.98 Sokolowski, R. *The Formation of Husserl's Concept of Constitution*, The Hague: Nijhoff, 1970.

1.99 Sokolowski, R. 'The Structure and Content of Husserl's *Logical Investigations*', *Inquiry*, 14 (1971): 318–47.

1.100 Sokolowski, R. *Husserlian Meditations: How Words Present Things*, Evanston: Northwestern University Press, 1974.

1.101 Sokolowski, R. *Presence and Absence: A Philosophical Investigation of Language and Being*, Bloomington: Indiana University Press, 1978.

1.102 Sokolowski, R. 'Husserl's Concept of Categorial Intuition', *Phenomenology and the Human Sciences* (formerly *Philosophical Topics*), 12 (1981): 127–41.

1.103 Sokolowski, R. 'Intentional Analysis and the Noema', *Dialectica*, 38 (1984): 113–29.

1.104 Sokolowski, R. 'Quotation', *Review of Metaphysics*, 37 (1984): 699–723.

1.105 Sokolowski, R. 'Exorcising Concepts', *Review of Metaphysics*, 60 (1987): 451–63.

1.106 Sokolowski, R. 'Husserl and Frege', *The Journal of Philosophy*, 84 (1987): 521–8.

1.107 Sokolowski, R. 'Natural and Artificial Intelligence', *Daedalus*, 142 (1988): 45–64.

1.108 Sokolowski, R. 'Referring', *Review of Metaphysics*, 42 (1988): 27–49.

1.109 Spiegelberg, H. *The Phenomenological Movement: A Historical Introduction*, 2 vols, The Hague: Nijhoff, 1971.

1.110 Ströker, E. 'Husserl's Principle of Evidence', in *The Husserlian Foundations of Science*, Washington, DC: University Press of America, 1987.

1.111 Ströker, E. *Husserls transzendentale Phänomenologie*, Frankfurt am Main: Vittorio Klostermann, 1987.

1.112 Stumpf, K. *Über den psychologischen Ursprung der Raumvorstellung*, Leipzig: Hirzel, 1873.

1.113 Taminiaux, J. *Le Regard et l'excédent*, The Hague: Nijhoff, 1977.

1.114 Taminiaux, J. 'Heidegger and Husserl's *Logical Investigations*: In Remembrance of Heidegger's Last Seminar (Zähringen, 1973)', in *Dialectic and Difference: Finitude in Modern Thought*, trans. R. Crease and J. Decker, Atlantic Highlands: Humanities Press, 1985, pp. 91–114.

1.115 Taminiaux, J. 'Immanence, Transcendence, and Being in Husserl's *Idea of Phenomenology*, in J. Sallis, G. Moneta and J. Taminiaux (eds), *The Collegium Phaenomenologicum: the First Ten Years*, Dordrecht: Kluwer, 1989, pp. 47–75.

1.116 Taminiaux, J. *Heidegger and the Project of Fundamental Ontology*, trans M. Gendre, Albany: SUNY Press, 1991.

1.117 Tragesser, R. *Husserl and Realism in Logic and Mathematics*, Cambridge: Cambridge University Press, 1984.

1.118 Welton, D. *The Origins of Meaning: A Critical Study of the Thresholds of Husserlian Phenomenology*, The Hague: Nijhoff, 1983.

1.119 Willard, D. 'The Paradox of Logical Psychologism: Husserl's Way Out', *American Philosophical Quarterly*, (1972): 94–100.

1.120 Willard, D. 'Concerning Husserl's View of Number', *The Southwestern Journal of Philosophy*, 5 (1974): 97–109.

1.121 Willard, D. 'Husserl's Critique of Extensionalist Logic: A Logic that Does not Understand Itself, *Idealistic Studies*, 9 (1979): 143–64.

1.122 Willard, D. *Logic and the Objectivity of Knowledge*, Athens: Ohio University Press, 1984.

CHAPTER 2

Philosophy of existence 1
Heidegger
Jacques Taminiaux

❧⸙❧

At the very outset and up to the end, the long philosophical journey of Martin Heidegger (1889–1976) remained oriented by a single question, the question of Being, the *Seinsfrage*. This does not mean, however, that the question preserved the same meaning or ruled an identical field of investigation throughout the whole journey. Indeed, Heidegger himself repeatedly claimed that at some point a turn (*Kehre*) occurred in his thought. Moreover, thanks to the current publication of his entire *corpus* (*Gesamtausgabe*), it is now possible to draw a fair picture of the vicissitudes of the journey. For the purpose of this chapter, I propose to divide Heidegger's work into two phases. The first covers publications and lecture courses devoted to setting out the project of what Heidegger, at that time, called 'fundamental ontology'. The later phase covers writings which are all characterized by a meditation on the history of Being. Whereas the project of fundamental ontology aimed at completing metaphysics as the science of Being, the later meditation consistently aimed at overcoming metaphysics.

❧ FUNDAMENTAL ONTOLOGY ❧

After a few years of study in theology the young Heidegger, who first wanted to become a Catholic priest, had decided for reasons both personal and theoretical to dedicate his life to philosophy.

At the turn of the century, the burning area for philosophical research in Germany was logic. Two major trends were in conflict as far as the approach to the basic problems of epistemology and the philosophy of science is concerned. On the one hand under the influence of British empiricism, John Stuart Mill predominantly, many

German scholars in those fields were convinced that the foundations of knowledge in general were strictly empirical. Accordingly they were looking for the roots of all cognitive principles in observable facts such as those which are investigated by psychology taken as an empirical science. On the other hand, in a reaction against empiricism, several scholars were attempting to revive in the disciplines at stake the transcendental orientation of Kant's criticism. In the history of ideas this conflict is known as the quarrel about *psychologism* between empiricism and transcendentalism. Whereas the former claims that thinking and knowing are a matter of facts occuring in the mind, the latter claims that thought and knowledge, however much they may depend on facts, could not exist without the help of a transcendental *cogito*. In 1900–1 a book appeared which had a decisive influence in the quarrel: Edmund Husserl's *Logical Investigations*. Like neo-Kantianism, the book was a refutation of all empiricist reductionism. But unlike neo-Kantianism it vindicated a new and original method which was altogether intuitive and a priori: phenomenology.

Heidegger's early writings were contributions to the new phenomenological trend. His doctoral dissertation (1914) was entitled *The Doctrine of Judgment in Psychologism*. His *Habilitationsschrift* (1916), *The Theory of Categories and Meaning in Duns Scotus* was inspired by Husserl's idea of a pure a priori grammar. Heidegger's genuine project emerged after these academic exercises, when he came to realize that he was less interested in logic for its own sake than in the link between logic and ontology or even in the ontological foundation of the logical. Indeed he repeatedly claimed that the influence on him of the *Logical Investigations* was at that time on a footing with the impact of a book by one of Husserl's masters, Brentano's dissertation *On the Manifold Meaning of Being in Aristotle* (1862). Brentano showed that in Aristotle the Being of beings is expressed in at least four basic ways: as substance (*ousia*), as potentiality (*dunamis*) and actuality (*energeia*), as truth (*alētheia*), according to the categories such as quality, quantity, relation and so on. While meditating upon this manifoldness in the meanings of Being, Heidegger raised the following question: is there a unique focus of intelligibility which illuminates these various meanings, a common source for understanding them, and how and where is it to be found? Such is the *Seinsfrage*, the question of Being.

The reappropriation of Husserl and Aristotle

On the basis of his early dissertations, Heidegger was already convinced that the phenomenological method was to be his way to address the question. When he became Husserl's personal assistant at the University of Freiburg-im-Breisgau, thereby gaining the opportunity to become familiar with all aspects of phenomenological research, he came to realize that the work of his master provided him not only with a method but also with basic discoveries thanks to which he was able to transform his ontological question into a genuine field of investigation. On the basis of the posthumous publication of several drafts and lecture courses, it is now possible to draw a fair picture of Heidegger's early attempts to articulate his own field of ontological investigations thanks to a peculiar retrieval or reappropriation of both Aristotle and Husserl. It could even be demonstrated that Heidegger's project of fundamental ontology is the outcome of an overlapping of what he considered to be the basic discoveries of Husserl with what he took to be the basic discoveries of Aristotle. This means that, with the help of Husserl's teaching, Heidegger was able to find in Aristotle's teaching an authentic phenomenology while, with the help of Aristotle's teaching, he discovered the possibility of transforming phenomenology into a field of ontological investigation. This ontological overlapping of Aristotle and Husserl is already noticeable in the short manuscript *Phenomenological Interpretations of Aristotle* [2.27] that Heidegger wrote in the autumn of 1922 at the request of P. Natorp in order to support his application for a teaching position at the University of Marburg. The overlapping pervades the teaching of Heidegger from the time of his appointment at Marburg until the publication of *Being and Time*.

Heidegger credited Husserl with three basic discoveries useful for articulating his own field of investigation. The first discovery is *intentionality*. According to Husserl, intentionality is the very structure of consciousness in all its modes (perception, imagination, conceptualization, judgment, reasoning and so on). In every form of consciousness there is a specific relatedness between a specific way of intending and a specific correlate which has its way of appearing *qua* intended. Already in the 1922 manuscript, Heidegger makes clear that for him this structural relatedness is much more than a basic feature of consciousness. It is the fundamental character of the very life of each human being. *De facto*, or factically, the life of an existing human being is essentially *related*. In Heidegger's language of that time, this means that such relatedness is an ontological character of 'factical life'. This is why he writes:

> the complete intentionality (the relatedness to, that towards which there is a relation, the accomplishment of the self-relating, the temporalism of it, the preservation of temporalisation) is nothing but the intentionality of the object which has the ontological character of factical life. Intentionality, merely taken as relatedness

to, is the first phenomenal character, proximally noticeable of the fundamental mobility of life, that is of care.([2.27], 17)

Whereas Husserl's discovery of intentionality was confined within the limits of a theory of consciousness, i.e., within the framework of a theory of knowledge, Heidegger's peculiar retrieval of the discovery results very early in another philosophical project aiming at an ontology of factical life, or of facticity. Along with this alteration, the new philosophical project entails an alteration in the very notion of logic. In Husserl, logic was another name for the theory of knowledge, i.e., of the basic categories making cognition possible. As a result of the shift from consciousness to factical life, logic becomes a name for the investigation of the ways in which factical life expresses and understands itself as a result of specific categories.

This second shift is at the core of Heidegger's reinterpretation of what he viewed as the second major discovery of Husserl, i.e., the doctrine of *categorial intuition*. According to this doctrine, the meaning of human discourse (*Rede*) depends on a complex set of structures, forms and basic concepts which are all of an ideal nature. In spite of the fact that, precisely because they are ideal, these idealities are in a position of excess or surplus *vis-à-vis* any sensuous content given to sensible perception, they are none the less, claims Husserl in the sixth *Logical Investigation*, offered to an intuition or insight that is no longer sensible, but ideal: the so-called *categorial intuition*.

Among the categorial intuitions mentioned by Husserl, one stood out as having a decisive relevance for the project to which Heidegger had subscribed from the outset: the problem of the *meaning of Being*. Indeed in the context of the sixth *Logical Investigation* Husserl was developing a twofold thesis about Being. First, he stated, in agreement with Kant, that 'Being is not a real predicate'. Second, he maintained, in contradistinction to Kant, that 'Being' is given to categorial intuition. Heidegger took advantage of this double thesis and transformed it for his own ontological purpose. 'Being is not a real predicate' meant for both Kant and Husserl that it is not to be found among the predicates which define the quiddity or *realitas* of beings: what they are. This thesis turned out to mean for Heidegger that Being is not in any sense a being. In other words the thesis amounted to stating a difference between beings and Being, an ontico-ontological difference. Likewise, the thesis according to which 'Being' is given to a categorial intuition, which in Husserl was an element of his transcendental logic, turned out to mean for Heidegger that in its factical life the human being has an understanding of Being. In other words, factical life interprets itself in terms of Being. This is to say that the ontology of those factical beings who understand Being is an hermeneutics, or a theory of interpretation.

But, by the same token, Husserl's twofold thesis about Being, thus reappropriated in an ontological framework, induced Heidegger to search in the *de facto* life of the human being for the unique ground for an intelligibility of the various meanings of Being. It induced him to search for the focus of intelligibility within what he was to call, a little later, the human *Dasein*.

In this search, Heidegger availed himself of a third discovery made by Husserl: the discovery of the a priori, a word with an obvious temporal connotation. Husserl often claimed that time consciousness was the most fundamental consideration of his phenomenology. In order for consciousness to be intentional at all, it has to be temporal. This means for Husserl that in order to be able to intend any intentional correlate, consciousness has to be a 'living present', a present which constantly articulates the 'retention' of what is just past with the anticipation (or 'protention') of what is going to happen. Heidegger, who was to edit in 1928 Husserl's *The Phenomenology of Internal Time-consciousness*, took advantage of this third discovery. His ontology of human *Dasein* aims at demonstrating that temporality is the only horizon within which we understand the meanings of Being. This is condensed in the very title of his masterwork of 1927, *Being and Time* [2.2, 2.45], a book in which the three Husserlian discoveries operate in a peculiar way along with an Aristotelian inspiration. The link between this inspiration and Husserl's legacy is already noticeable in the fact that Heidegger, in his Introduction, characterizes the phenomenological method at work in the book by using the very language of Aristotle.

What Heidegger discovered very early, as he puts it in a later survey of his 'way to phenomenology' is that 'what occurs for the phenomenology of the acts of consciousness is thought more originally by Aristotle and in all Greek thinking and existence as *alētheia*' (*On Time and Being* [2.70], 78). In its traditional definition, truth is an adequation between the mind and the real, and it occurs in a specific place: the predicative judgment. In one way, Husserl's phenomenology contributed to overcoming the classical notion of truth. For Husserl indeed, prior to the so-called *adequatio intellectus ad rem* (of the mind to the thing), the touchstone of truth is *evidence*, i.e., the self-manifestation of the object *qua* phenomenon to intentionality. Moreover, Husserl claimed that the locus of truth is in no way restricted to the predicative judgment: it is intentionality itself, or consciousness in all its forms. Heidegger took advantage of this breakthrough in his phenomenological interpretation of Aristotle. As far as truth is concerned, the Greek philosopher, he claims, is more original than Husserl on two accounts: first because he understands truth as the unconcealment of beings for an unconcealing being, the human being; second because this unconcealing, instead of being restricted to consciousness, is attributed by him to the human comportment as such, more precisely to the human way of being. In other words, for Aristotle, claims Heidegger, *alētheia*, or truth, is a matter of *bios*, of life or of existence. It is in the context of this phenomenological reading of Aristotle that Heidegger was led to replace the words 'factical life' by the key word *Dasein* in order to characterize the human way of being. In German the word is both a verb meaning 'to be present', or to exist, and a noun meaning 'presence', or existence. Moreover, *da* the prefix of the word, means both *there* and *then*; it points to a place and time for something to happen. Heidegger's use of the word to characterize the human way of being is an attempt to suggest that the concrete existence of a human being is a phenomenon which is *there*, thrown into a place and a time in which an unconcealment happens.

But in addition to a concept of truth in terms of existence, Heidegger also discovered in Aristotle a concrete analysis of human existence as an unconcealing way of being. The ontological reappropriation of Husserl's discovery of intentionality taught him that human existence as such is a *relatedness to*. The reappropriation of Husserl's discovery of categorial intuition taught him that human existence, in its relatedness to, understands Being. Likewise, the appropriation of Husserl's discovery of the a priori taught him that time is at the core of the understanding of Being. Since those three ontological reappropriations were oriented by a single question – where is the source for the understanding of Being to be found? – they all required an analysis of *Dasein* as the being who understands Being. In other words they required an analysis of *Dasein*'s way of being, i.e., for an ontology of *Dasein*. And here Heidegger discovered very early that Aristotle's description of human comportment paved the way to the ontology of *Dasein* that he was attempting to articulate. His lecture courses of the Marburg period demonstrate that, in his view, the *Nicomachean Ethics* was such an ontology. It is in such terms that Heidegger deals with Aristotle's *Ethics* in the introduction to his celebrated lecture course of 1924–5 on Plato's *Sophist* [2.29], which had a deep influence on those who originally heard it, including Hannah Arendt, Hans-Georg Gadamer and Hans Jonas.

The *Nicomachean Ethics* scrutinizes the dianoetic excellences or intellectual virtues and establishes them in a hierarchy. According to Aristotle these virtues have two levels: the lower are the deliberative excellences, the higher are the epistemic excellences. At the lower level two deliberative virtues take place: *technē* and *phronēsis*. In Greek *technē* means art, in the sense of knowhow. Heidegger insists that in Aristotle *technē* is an intellectual excellence because it is a matter of truth, of *alētheia* as unconcealment. It is a peculiar way of disclosing, or discovering, what is required for a specific comportment: the productive comportment called *poiēsis*. In other words, it is a way of knowing truth, or even of being in truth, linked with a peculiar way of being: the production of such and such a work or result. However, claims Heidegger, the reason why Aristotle puts *technē* on the lowest rank among the deliberative excellences is to be understood in terms of an ontology of *Dasein*. Indeed, in the productive way of being which is ruled by *technē*, *Dasein* is busy with, and concerned by, products or results out there. To that extent the pair *technē–poiēsis* suffers an ontological deficiency. To be sure, the principle for the productive activity informed by an unconcealing knowhow is *within* the agent, hence within the *Dasein* and of the same nature as *Dasein* itself: it is the model conceived by the agent and held in view by him. But the telos or end of productive activity is in no way within *Dasein* or of its nature: it occurs *outside* of *Dasein*.

This ontological deficiency, claims Heidegger, is no longer the case in the second deliberative excellence, namely *phronēsis*, also conceived by Aristotle as a peculiar way of disclosing, or of being in truth, adjusted to a specific comportment or active way of being. This active way of being is no longer *poiēsis* but *praxis*, i.e., action in the sense of the conduct by an individual of his or her own life. *Phronēsis* discloses to *Dasein* the potentiality of its own existence. Here again, according to Heidegger, the reason why Aristotle puts *phronēsis* on the highest level among the deliberative excellences is to be understood in terms of an ontology of *Dasein*. Indeed neither the principle of *phronēsis* nor its goal falls outside the human being. The principle here is a prior option of the *Dasein* for well-doing, while the end is the very way of being of *Dasein*, its own *praxis*. *Phronēsis* is nothing but the resoluteness to exist in the highest possible manner.

Thus understood in ontological terms, Aristotle's distinction between the *technē–poiēsis* and the *phronēsis–praxis* distinctions allowed Heidegger to set up the framework of his own ontology of *Dasein*, as a being who understands Being. This ontology, which was to be developed in *Being and Time*, describes the existence of *Dasein* in terms of a tension between an everyday way of Being in which the *Dasein* is not authentically who it is, and an authentic way of Being in which *Dasein* is properly itself. The description shows that in everydayness *Dasein* cannot be its ownmost Being, because it lives in a condition of preoccupation or concern for ends to be attained by a variety of means or tools, a condition which is enlightened by a specific circumspection about surroundings. To that extent everydayness is ruled by *Das Man*, the 'They'. In it everybody is nobody, because such a condition never confronts *Dasein*'s own existence. This description is the outcome of a peculiar reappropriation of Aristotle's doctrine concerning *technē* and *poiēsis*. On the other hand, the analytic of *Dasein* shows that *Dasein* authentically becomes a Self by confronting its ownmost potentiality for Being. It does so by accepting existence in its finitude, as a Being-unto-death. This description, with the exception of the emphasis put on anxiety, is again the result of a peculiar reappropriation of Aristotle's analysis of *phronēsis* and *praxis*. Aristotle indeed insists that *phronēsis*, as a dianoetic virtue, has its proper realm in the perishable. On the other hand, Heidegger occasionally suggested when he was teaching Aristotle that the latter's concept of *phronēsis* somehow anticipates the notion of conscience (*Gewissen*). And conscience in Heidegger's analytic of *Dasein* is the phenomenon in which *Dasein* listens to a call from it own depths summoning it to confront its finitude.

But the Aristotelian inspiration in Heidegger's ontology of *Dasein* is not restricted to *technē* and *phronēsis*. It also includes a peculiar reappropriation of Aristotle's doctrine of the epistemic virtues. In the *Nicomachean Ethics* these virtues are *epistēmē* (science) and *sophia* (wisdom). Both are adjusted to *theoria*, i.e., to a purely contemplative attitude, which bears upon a realm which is no longer perishable, a realm which is forever what it is and how it is. For Aristotle that realm is higher than the realm of human affairs precisely because it is not perishable as they are. And in his view it is at this level only, specifically at the level of *sophia*, that a true concern with Being can take place, as a contemplation of the ontological structure of the totality of beings and of the prime mover which is the principle for all movements of *physis* (nature). Heidegger insists, in his Marburg lectures, that, according to Aristotle, the contemplation of that immutable realm is the most authentic way of being that a mortal can attain, because as long as such contemplation lasts, the mortal spectator lives in the proximity of the divine.

According to Heidegger's teaching in the Marburg period, there is in the Aristotelian concept of *sophia* an equivocation between ontology as the science of the Being of beings and theology as the science of the divine. There is also an indeterminacy, because for Aristotle the only meaning of Being is limited to what he calls *ousia*, i.e., in Heidegger's interpretation, presence in the sense of presence-at-hand (*Vorhandenheit*). This meaning of Being, Heidegger says, is adjusted to nature, but it is not relevant as far as the Being of *Dasein* is concerned. Moreover, considering presence as the only meaning of Being amounts to understanding Being in the light of a temporality in which only the present is important. This temporality, considered as a succession of present moments, is in fact the concept of time that Aristotle develops in his *Physics*. Heidegger raised objections to the predominance of this concept. In the case of the Being of *Dasein*, putting the emphasis only on the present is one-sided and misleading. In order for *Dasein* to be authentically present, it has to retrieve who it was as thrown in its own Being as well as to anticipate its own end. Whereas the temporality of nature is ruled by the exclusive privilege of the present, the temporality of *Dasein* not only is determined by a triad, in which three *ec-stasis* – past, present, and future – co-operate, but also is ruled by the privilege of the future.

Accordingly, Heidegger, who agrees with Aristotle in considering the contemplation (*theoria*) of Being as the authentic accomplishment of *Dasein*, reorients that contemplation exclusively towards the finite being of *Dasein* and its finite temporality. As a result, fundamental ontology claims to be able to overcome both the onto-theological equivocation and the ontological indeterminacy which characterized the ancient ontology and its legacy. The overcoming includes a deconstruction (*Destruktion*) of the ancient concepts along with a reversal of the old hierarchy between the perishable and the immutable. This deconstruction aims at demonstrating that for the most part the basic concepts of ancient philosophy and consequently of the entire western tradition of metaphysics – concepts such as matter (*hulē*) and form (*morphē*), potentiality (*dunamis*) and actuality (*energeia*), idea (*eidos*), substance (*hupokeimenon*), and so on – find their phenomenal origin in the activity of production, an activity which in order to be possible at all presupposes the permanence of nature, and liberates its products from their link to the producer to bestow on them a permanence similar to the natural one. Consequently these ontological concepts, instead of being coined after the authentic ontological experience that *Dasein* has of its own Being, were coined in the inauthentic framework of everydayness. In such a framework *Dasein*, while coping with entities which are ready-to-hand, pays attention to a meaning of Being – presence-at-hand (*Vorhandenheit*) – which is not adjusted to finite existence as its own way of Being. In other words, the genealogy carried out by deconstruction aims at showing that Greek ontology, in its concern for the eternal features of nature, was mistaken in believing that the contemplation of those features allowed the philosopher to go beyond the finitude and reach the proximity of the divine. Quite the contrary; it remained trapped within everydayness. Here appears the *reversal*: the so-called overcoming of finitude was a falling away from it. The falling away from the authentic towards the inauthentic explains the predominance of the notion of presence-at-hand in traditional ontology.

As a result of this reversal, the notion of transcendence, which traditionally defined the position of the divine above the lower realm of immanence, was transformed by Heidegger to designate the process through which the *Dasein* goes beyond beings towards Being: only the *Dasein* properly transcends, and it transcends beings towards Being.

The articulation of the project

Heidegger's project, inspired by a singular appropriation of Husserl and Aristotle, of fundamental ontology, designed as a reply to the question of the meaning of Being, included two tasks which provide the structure of *Being and Time* [2.2; 2.45].

The first part of the treatise was supposed to be devoted to 'the interpretation of *Dasein* in terms of temporality, and the explication of time as the transcendental horizon for the question of Being' (pp. 39; 63). The book, which came out in 1927, announced three divisions of Part One: (1) 'the preparatory fundamental analysis of *Dasein*'; (2) '*Dasein* and temporality' (*Zeitlichkeit*); (3) 'time and Being' (pp. 39; 64). The third division never appeared.

Part Two of the treatise was supposed to deal with the 'basic features of a phenomenological destruction of the history of ontology, with the problematic of Temporality [*Temporalität*] as our clue' (pp. 39; 63). This part, which also never appeared, was designed to have three divisions: the first one dealing with Kant's doctrine of schematism, the second with the ontological foundation of Descartes' *cogito sum*, the third with Aristotle's essay on time.

The published portion of Part One (which made Heidegger instantly famous) proceeded in two steps, corresponding to divisions one and two. If Part One starts with an analysis of *Dasein*, it is because the leading question of the meaning of Being rebounds as it were on the one who poses it. Indeed *Dasein* is the only being for whom Being is a question or an issue. If such analysis has to be fundamental, it is because, instead of restricting itself to the teachings of disciplines such as anthropology, psychology or biology, it must treat *Dasein* as a being for whom Being itself is the question, and not 'what is man?', 'what is mind?' or 'what is life?' If such analysis is preparatory, however, it is because it is carried out not for its own sake but in order to provide an answer to the question of the meaning of Being.

But even leaving aside the problem of what is prepared by it, the analysis of *Dasein* is not governed at all by the traditional question 'what?' Instead of addressing the question 'what is *Dasein*?' the analysis has to address the question 'who is *Dasein*?' Indeed the question 'what?' is not adjusted to *Dasein* for the reason that, in its *de facto* existence, *Dasein* is such that its very essence lies in its 'to be' (*Zusein*), or in its 'existence', a word which indicates an openness to a task, a possibility, and which is allotted by Heidegger solely to *Dasein* in order to avoid any confusion with the traditional use of *existentia* as equally valid for designating the Being of any entity whatsoever. In Heidegger's terminology the meaning of the word *existentia*, in its traditional use, is 'presence-at-hand', and is appropriate only to entities which are precisely *not* of *Dasein*'s character. *Dasein* is thus the only entity in which existence has a priority over essence. Moreover if the question 'what?' has to be replaced by the question 'who?', it is because there is no *Dasein* in general, because an individual *Dasein* is not a special instance of some genus. *Dasein* as an entity for which Being is an issue in its very Being, is 'in each case mine' (pp. 42; 67–8). As an entity which is its own possibility or existence and which is in each case mine, *Dasein*, in its very Being, can win or lose itself. 'Mineness' grounds either *authenticity* or *inauthenticity*. The German words, *Eigentlichkeit* and *Uneigentlichkeit*, have no moral connotation. *Eigentlichkeit* designates a condition in which someone is its own Being; *Uneigentlichkeit* refers to a condition in which someone is not properly its own Being.

As a result of the priority of existence over essence, the fundamental analysis of *Dasein* has to treat it from the existentiality of its existence. The access to the basic characters of that existentiality is given in the condition in which *Dasein* is 'proximally and for the most part' – everydayness. These basic characters of existentiality are called *existentialia*.

Because mineness grounds either authenticity or inauthenticity, all existentialia have an authentic and inauthentic modality. They all have a transcendental status, which means that they are a priori conditions of possibility for *Dasein*'s existence. They are factors or items of a constitutive state of *Dasein* that Heidegger calls 'being-in-the-world'.

Being-in-the-world is the primordial phenomenon which has to be analysed in order to uncover the *existentialia*. Though the phenomenon is unitary, it is possible to look at it in three ways, by putting the emphasis on the 'world' as such, or on the 'being-in' as such, or on the one 'who' is in the world.

The world is neither the total amount of entities composing what is usually called the universe nor a framework for those entities. It is neither a global container nor an addition of contents. It is not nature. In order for nature to appear, a world is presupposed. The world must be understood a priori in terms of existentiality. Properly speaking, only *Dasein* is in the world, and there would be no world without *Dasein* intimately open to it. And since *Dasein* is not present-at-hand but existing, the world is not a global presence-at-hand that constantly encircles *Dasein*. Because *Dasein*'s existence is its own 'can be' or possibility, the world which is at issue in the phrase 'being-in-the-world' must be described in terms of possibility, but a possibility which is already given. It is an *existentiale*.

If we take as clue our everyday way of Being, we must admit that our comportment is characterized as a concern with an environment. Within that concern we do not merely observe things present-at-hand. Instead we are constantly busy dealing with entities of a pragmatic nature endowed with a pragmatic meaning that we understand. Each of these entities is essentially 'something in-order-to', it is an instrument adjusted to this or that purpose. None of those entities is isolated. They are all interrelated, and in order for them to appear as 'in-order-to', they all presuppose as backdrop a context of involvement, with which we are familar. Such involvement is that 'wherein' we understand our ways and that 'for which' we let entities be encountered and used. But the involvement presupposed by our everyday concern itself refers to a deeper a priori which is the very relatedness of *Dasein* to its own potentiality for Being. This ultimate 'for the sake of which' is not a possibility within the world, it is the world itself as *Dasein*'s own potentiality. World is another name for Being as that for the sake of which *Dasein* is transcending.

Similarly 'Being-in' has to be understood in terms of existentiality. And since existence as such is a disclosing process, the 'Being-in' is better captured as a lighting or as an openness than as an insertion. Three existentialia constitute the 'Being-in': disposition, comprehension and discourse.

Disposition (*Befindlichkeit*) is the state in which *Dasein* finds itself. That *Dasein* essentially finds itself in some state is revealed by the moods or humours making manifest how one is. In terms of existentiality, moods reveal that *Dasein* has been delivered over to the Being is has to be. Heidegger calls 'thrownness' the facticity of being delivered over to Being. Hence disposition discloses *Dasein* in its thrownness.

Comprehension (*Verstehen*) is also to be conceived in terms of existentiality. In order to comprehend or understand the significance of the utensils it deals with in everydayness, *Dasein* has to project itself upon this or that possibility. In any act of understanding, there is some projection. But the *de facto* projections pervading *Dasein*'s ordinary comportment have their ontological foundation in *Dasein*'s projection upon its own 'can be'. As an *existentiale*, comprehension discloses *Dasein* itself in its own potentiality-for-Being.

'Discourse is existentially equiprimordial with disposition and comprehension' (161). The German word for discourse is *Rede*, which is Heidegger's translation of the Greek *logos*. In terms of existentiality, discourse is the disclosing articulation of the intelligibility of Being-in-the-world.

The reply to the question ' "who" is in the world?' shows that *Dasein* in its everyday mode of Being is not properly a Self. Most of the time it loses itself in what it is busy with. In other words it understands itself in terms of what is ready-to-hand within the world. On the other hand it essentially belongs to *Dasein* to be with other *Daseins*. But here again the everyday mode of Being-with-one-another is such that *Dasein* is absorbed in the neutrality of the 'They' (*das Man*), instead of confronting its own *Dasein*. In both cases the inauthentic prevails over the authentic. Heidegger calls 'fallenness' the tendency *Dasein* has to forget its own Self or to move away from it. Fallenness is an *existentiale*. As a result of such a tendency, all the *existentialia* have two modalities: an authentic and an inauthentic one. For example, discourse in its inauthentic form is idle talk. Likewise comprehension in its inauthentic form is curiosity.

We can readily see that a temporal connotation is involved in the description of all these items. Already pre-given as a 'wherein', the world is a past. But as constantly anticipated as a 'for which', it is a future as well.

A temporal dimension is also involved in the three interconnected modes of disclosure which constitute 'Being-in'. Since disposition discloses the facticity of *Dasein*'s thrownness, it reveals that it belongs to existence to have already been. It is also obvious in the case of comprehension as a project: if *Dasein* itself is a project, this means that structurally it throws itself forwards in the direction of a future. Discourse as an *existentiale* also shows a temporal dimension. By articulating 'Being-in-the-world' it expresses both the thrownness and the self-projection of *Dasein*.

Likewise, if the ontological answer to the question 'who?' has to be expressed in terms of a tension between authenticity and inauthenticity, the answer itself either emphasizes a future or, concerning the rule of the 'They' and of the everyday equipment, the predominance of what is currently the case.

Once Being-in-the-world is analysed in its constitutive items, there must be a synthetic return to the unitary character of the phenomenon. Heidegger characterizes the ontological unity of *Dasein*'s Being-in-the-world with a single word, *Sorge*, usually translated by the word 'care'. Care is the transcendental structure at the root of all the existential features mentioned so far. Care, as the ontological unifying structure of *Dasein*, is revealed in the fundamental disposition of anxiety, thanks to which *Dasein* realizes that it is already thrown in the world, that it has to be its own Being, and that it is thus thrown and projecting itself in a condition of proximity to inner-worldly beings whose Being is not its own Being. In the experience of anxiety the three interconnected dimensions of care are disclosed: facticity, possibility, fallenness among other beings.

This is a turning point in the existential analytic: it opens the way to the second division of Part One: *Dasein* and temporality.

The phenomenon of care is now manifest in its unity. However, the question remains: what about its totality? A phenomenon appears as a whole when its limits are made visible. Hence the problem is: what are the limits of care as the basic structure of existence? Clearly the limits of existence are birth and death. If we consider both limits as terms of a process which is not intrinsically determined by them, then we might say that, as soon as we exist, birth is over and that until we cease to exist, death is not there. But this view does not fit with *Dasein*'s mode of Being: a project which is thrown. Precisely because *Dasein*'s project is thrown, birth is not a mere moment which is over as soon as *Dasein* exists. *Dasein* cannot be who it is without having been thrown in the world with the limited possibilities which from the outset condition its Being. Likewise death is not the other external limit of existence. Existence as a project includes in itself, i.e., in its potentiality, its own end. This means that *Dasein*'s death is not restricted to its Being-at-the-end. It is rather a manner of Being that *Dasein* takes over as soon as it is. It thoroughly permeates existence. It makes *Dasein*'s project essentially finite and turns it into a Being-towards-the-end.

Because of such finitude, a negative feature, a negativity determines care in relation to both thrownness and project. What about the third dimension of care, i.e., the proximity with other beings? Is it also determined by negativity? The answer is ambiguous. It can be if and only if *Dasein* resolutely takes over its own mortality. But for the most part, because the proximity with other beings entails a predominance of pragmatic preoccupation over care, *Dasein* covers up its own finitude and thinks of death as a contingent event occurring to everybody and to nobody. They die, I don't.

This description allows us to understand how temporality is the ground of the ontological constitution of *Dasein*. According to ordinary views and a philosophical tradition going back to Aristotle, time is an unlimited sequence of moments, including the moments which once were but no longer are, those which are not yet and the one which is now. The sequence is considered to be irreversible and measurable. Heidegger claims that such a concept of time was shaped not on the basis of a phenomenal analysis of *Dasein* but on the basis of the experience of nature. Instead, the original concept of time has to be articulated in conformity with the ontological constitution of *Dasein*. A clue for the articulation is provided by the structure of care: Being-ahead-of-itself and already-being-in-a-world as well as falling and

Being-alongside entities within-the-world. This structure points to the originary time. The 'Being-ahead-of-itself' indicates an anticipatory dimension. Since such anticipation is already there, it includes a retrieval of what and who the *Dasein* already is or has been. The anticipation is *Dasein*'s future. It is the existential future, whereas the retrieval is *Dasein*'s existential past. Finally, the proximity with other beings points towards *Dasein*'s present. Since that proximity is properly finite if and only if *Dasein* resolutely takes over its own Being-towards-the-end, the existential present can only be the instantaneous vision (*Augenblick*) by *Dasein* of the situation of its finite existence. Such vision includes a glimpse of the difference between the mode of Being called existence and modes of Being such as readiness-to-hand and presence-at-hand.

Heidegger claims that the foundation of care on the triadic structure of existential time is not at all a philosophical construct. It is ontically or pre-ontologically revealed to each one in the phenomenon of conscience (*Gewissen*), a phenomenon which is not itself moral in the first place, and demands a description in terms of existentiality. A specific call belongs to the phenomenon of conscience. The structure of such a call reveals a temporal foundation. The call is addressed to a fallen *Dasein* currently captivated by entities in-the-world. The call comes from *Dasein* itself in its facticity, a condition in which *Dasein* as thrown is in the mode of having been. And the message of the call is addressed to *Dasein* again in its ownmost potentiality-for-Being, i.e., in the mode of a future.

Heidegger insists that 'the primordial meaning of existentiality is the future' (324). However, neither the existential future (anticipation) nor the existential past (retrieval) nor the existential present (instant of vision) has the traditional character of a discrete entity. Because the existential future is a coming-to-oneself, it is a dimension and not at all a not-yet-present moment nor a sequence of not-yet-present moments. In Heidegger's language it is an *ecstasis*. Likewise the existential past and the existential present. The word *ecstasis*, which in Greek means 'standing outside', is used by Heidegger in order to emphasize a connotation of stretching towards, or openness to. With this Heidegger associates the notion of horizon. The horizon is that to which each *ecstasis* is open in a specific way. Existential temporality is ecstatico-horizontal. Now, because the *ecstases* are interconnected under the primacy of the future, because they belong together intrinsically, temporality is an ecstatic unity of future, past and present. Such unity has itself a horizon which is the condition of possibility of the world as existential and of *Dasein*'s transcendence.

Because of its existentiality, temporality is essentially finite, instead of being an infinite sequence wherein existence would take place. It is the very process through which an intrinsically finite mode of Being opens itself to its own potentiality for Being and to other modes of Being. For the same reason, it is not enough to say that *Dasein*'s existence is temporal. Rather, *Dasein temporalizes*. Genuine time is temporalization and even self-temporalization. In its ownmost Being, *Dasein* exists in such a way that it runs ahead towards its own end (*Vorlaufen*), retrieves its own thrownness (*Wiederholung*), and renders present its own situation (*Gegenwärtigung*).

In the light of all this, it turns out that common time, as an infinite sequence, is derived from existential time. According to the common concept of it, time is a sequence of now-moments revealing itself in counting, a counting done in reference to a motion (the sun or the hands of a clock). In fact, Heidegger says, this reckoning of time is guided by and based upon a reckoning with time: time is already disclosed to us *before* we use a clock. The disclosure occurs in our daily comportment. Hence our daily reckoning with time is what deserves analysis, if we want to define common time fully. As soon as we approach common time in these terms, we realize that the 'now' we check on the clock every day is never a naked and discrete entity given as an object at hand (*vorhanden*). Now is always 'now that' I am doing this or that. When I say now, in daily life, I am always expressing myself as attending to something, as *presentifying* it. Likewise, when I say 'at that time', I display myself as *retaining* something bygone, either in the mode of recollecting it or in the mode of forgetting it. Similarly, when I say 'then', I show that I am *expecting* something to happen, on its own or by reason of my own deeds. Hence counting time leads back to a reckoning-with-time articulated according to presentification, retention and expectation. But this triad presupposes the existential triad mentioned above. While presupposing the original temporality, however, it also covers it up because of the falling character of everydayness, in which inner-worldly entities tend to prevail upon the existential world. As a result of our fallenness, time becomes an infinite sequence, whereas the original temporality is essentially finite. For the same reason, time becomes irreversible whereas authentic temporality is an ever-renewed encroachment of the past upon the future and vice versa. For the same reason, time gets bound to the *motion* of things whereas authentic temporality is the ownmost mobility of *Dasein*.

The entire analysis involves an explicit criticism of Aristotle, whose concept of time is indeed a free-floating sequence of nows, and an implicit criticism of Husserl's notion of time-consciousness which, as an articulation of retentions, living impressions and protentions, does not go beyond the level of everyday preoccupation.

The deconstructive reappropriation of the history of ontology

As far as Greek philosophy is concerned, there are in fundamental ontology several traces of a 'deconstructive' retrieval of Plato. Heidegger agrees with Plato that human beings are naturally philosophers although most of the time people do not care about philosophy. He also agrees with Plato's characterization of philosophy as a way of Being, a form of existence: the *bios theoretikos*. The distinction between the 'They' (*Das Man*) and the authentic Self owes much to Plato's demarcation between the multitude (the *polloi*) and the philosopher. The description of everydayness in terms of a productive preoccupation owes much to Plato's condescending characterization of active life in terms of *poiēsis*. The description of everyday language as empty talk is obviously indebted to Plato's contempt for *doxa* (opinion) and sophistry. Above all the Heideggerian hierarchy between three levels of seeing – the immediate intuition (*Anschauung*) of entities merely present-at-hand; the awareness that the mere presence of those entities is an abstraction deriving from a loss and fall in relation to their readiness-to-hand (*Zuhandenheit*) open to a practical circumspection; and finally the awareness, reached in the silence of conscience, that the everyday surrounding world (*Umwelt*) is in a position of falling away from one's authentic world, a world transparent (*durchsichtig*) to conscience only – that hierarchy is obviously an echo to the levels of seeing mentioned by Plato in the parable of the cave.

As far as medieval thought, with which Heidegger became acquainted during his early theological studies, is concerned, it is possible to recognize in his analytic of *Dasein* a discreet reappropriation of the scholastic concept of *analogia entis* (analogy of being). Just as the medieval theologians determined what they called the degrees of Being in terms of an analogy between the kinds of beings and the *summum ens* (highest being), a divine being whose actuality is devoid of any potentiality and whose essence is identical with its existence, Heidegger determines analogically an hierarchy of the ways of Being, in reference to the *Dasein*. Thus he characterizes the being of the stone as 'world-less' and the being of the animal as 'poor in world' on the basis of a unique analogy with *Dasein*, whose essence, once it is thrown in its Being, is to exist, or to be in the world.

Likewise the very distinction between an everyday world in which the *Dasein* feels at home, and an authentic world in which it is homeless is not without a secularized reminiscence of Augustine's notion that the world is an exile, and that the Christians do not belong to it.

For modern philosophy, fundamental ontology includes a reappropriation and deconstruction of several major authors, such as Leibniz, Kant and Hegel.

In Leibniz the 'principle of ground' (*Satz vom Grund*), also formulated as the principle of Sufficient Reason which is supposed to provide an ultimate answer to the question 'why?', is based on the nature of truth. For Leibniz truth is to be found primarily in judgment, and judgment ultimately consists in an identity between subject and predicate, an identity such that it can be demonstrated that any *P* is analytically derived from *S*. But for Leibniz this analytical concept of truth is not simply a matter of logic. It has an ontological basis. Ultimately all the logical propositions '*S is P*' have their ontological foundation in the monads that harmoniously compose reality, each of them having in itself the reason or ground for what happens to it. At the time of fundamental ontology, Heidegger discussed Leibniz in the published essay *The Essence of Reasons (Vom Wesen des Grundes* [2.4]), but also in posthumously edited lecture courses such as *The Metaphysical Foundations of Logic* [2.34, 2.48]. Though rejecting the traditional privilege of judgment shared by Leibniz, he agrees with him that the problem of ground has to be dealt with in terms of the problem of truth. He also agrees that any ontic truth presupposes an ontological foundation of a monadic nature. But whereas Leibniz inserts such a foundation into an onto-theological framework, Heidegger attributes it to the transcending process through which the *Dasein*, as a Self, overcomes beings towards Being. That process of transcendence which is the ontico-ontological difference itself is the foundational coming-to-pass of truth as unconcealment.

Kant's philosophy was also the topic of a deconstructive appropriation. The major proof of this is offered by Heidegger's book *Kant and the Problem of Metaphysics* [2.3, 2.47]. The book is an attempt to demonstrate that the *Critique of Pure Reason*, at least in its first edition, somehow anticipates the project of fundamental ontology in its reply to the question 'How are synthetic judgments possible?' Heidegger insists that according to Kant the question makes sense only if it stems from a knowing being which is essentially finite. Kant finds the sign of that finitude in the fundamental receptivity of sensibility. Sensible receptivity means that we, human beings, can know only beings that we do not create. However the ontic knowledge of those beings, which for Kant takes place in the experience of natural entities, requires an a priori synthesis which has, Heidegger claims, the nature of an ontological knowledge, i.e., of an a priori comprehension of the Being of those beings. In Kant, that a priori synthesis is the union of pure intuition (the a priori forms of space and time) with the pure categories of the understanding, a union carried out by transcendental imagination through the protection of transcendental schemata characterized as transcendental determinations of time. By recognizing the decisive role of time – more precisely of a temporalizing process performed in the depths of the knowing subject, at the core of a synthetic or ontological knowledge enabling ontic access to beings as objects – Kant would have anticipated Heidegger's own attempt to show that our openness to beings presupposes a comprehension of their Being, i.e., a transcendence happening in the horizon of temporality. However, in its deconstructive aspect, this reappropriation of Kant also emphasizes the limitations of his endeavour: (1) a framework which is the legacy of Christian metaphysics with its distinction between *metaphysica generalis* and *metaphysica specialis* (psychology, cosmology, theology); (2) a one-sided concept of Being as presence-at-hand, therefore a one-sided concept of time, as a sequence of present moments, although Kant's notion of self-affection partially overcomes this one-sidedness; and (3) also the fact that Kant himself, as evinced by the second edition of the *Critique of Pure Reason*, seems to have withdrawn from his own discovery of finite transcendence in the operation of transcendental imagination.

Heidegger in *Being and Time* is entirely critical of Hegel, and at several places in the book he carefully discards any semblance of a proximity between the Hegelian conceptions and his own position. He claims, for example, that the Hegelian definition of time merely maintains traditional views leading back to Aristotle's *Physics*, and is one-sidedly focused on presence-at-hand. Moreover, he insists on the abstraction and formalism of Hegel, compared to the concreteness of his own fundamental ontology. And against the Hegelian thesis according to which Spirit falls into time, he objects that the very meaning of a 'fall' is left in the dark by Hegel. Instead of claiming that Spirit falls *into* time, the meaningful thesis about the fall should be expressed in this way: 'factical existence "falls" as falling *from* primordial, authentic temporality' ([2.2] 486; [2.45], 435–6). In spite of this apparent discarding of Hegel, readers of *Being and Time* are allowed to suspect, in relation to the history of ideas, that Heidegger's analysis of anxiety as a crucial experience which is not to be confused with ordinary fear, and the characterization of Being in terms of 'no being' or Nothingness, are not without some relation to Hegelian topics. One is inclined to suspect that there is indeed some reappropriation of Hegel in fundamental ontology.

Such a reappropriation comes to the fore in Heidegger's essay of 1929, *What is Metaphysics?* [2.5, 2.50], the text of his inaugural lecture at the University of Freiburg on the occasion of his accession to the Chair of Philosophy left vacant by the retirement of Husserl. At the outset of this essay, Heidegger states that he is in accord with Hegel's comment that 'from the point of view of sound common sense, philosophy is the "inverted world"' (p. 95). And further on, he reveals a second point of agreement. After a description of anxiety as a metaphysical experience in which nothingness manifests itself, he quotes Hegel's *Science of Logic*: 'Pure Being and pure Nothing are therefore the same' (*Wissenschaft der logik*, vol. 1, 111, p. 74). This proposition, Heidegger says, is correct, 'Being and nothing do belong together' (*Basic Writings*, p. 110). To be sure, these two points of agreement are rather formal and Heidegger adds that his own emphasis on the finitude of Being revealing itself in the transcendence of *Dasein* marks a fundamental divergence in spite of a formal proximity. But a lecture course of 1930–1 devoted to an interpretation of Hegel's *Phenomenology of Spirit* shows that there was much more than a formal convergence, and that Heidegger's fundamental ontology really crossed the Hegelian path. Focusing on the transition from consciousness to self-consciousness, the lecture course claims that Hegel's notion of 'life' in the *Phenomenology of Spirit* unfolds a concept of Being which is no longer caught in the traditional notion of presence-at-hand. Moreover, Heidegger in the lecture course expresses admiration for the Hegelian description of the movement by which absolute knowledge absolves itself from natural knowledge. That description, he suggests, has to be considered as a transposition in an absolute framework of the very movement of finite transcendence.

Finally, fundamental ontology involves a reappropriation of Nietzsche on one point at least: historicality. In *Being and Time* ([2.45], section 76), Heidegger attempts to demonstrate that historiology (*Historie*) has its existential source in *Dasein*'s historicality. *Dasein*'s Being is essentially historical 'in so far as by reason of its ecstatico-horizontal temporality it is open in its character of "having been" ' ([2.45], 445). In the context of the demonstration, Heidegger insists that 'Nietzsche recognized what was essential as to the "use and abuse of historiology for life" in the second of his studies "out of season" (1874), and said it unequivocally and penetratingly' ([2.45, 448]). For both Heidegger and Nietzsche the so-called objectivity of historical sciences, instead of being primordial, is a falling away from an active movement of uncovering directed towards the future. For both, that active movement is essentially interpretative or hermeneutical. For both, it is also circular because it creates an overlapping of the future and the past.

In other words, Heidegger suggests that by saying that only master builders of the future who know the present will understand the past, Nietzsche anticipates the Heideggerian topic of the 'hermeneutic circle'.

⚬ THE HISTORY OF BEING ⚬

Paroxysm and interruption of fundamental ontology

The basic principle of the analytic of *Dasein*, worked out in *Being and Time*, was: *Das Dasein existiert umwillen seiner* ('*Dasein* exists for the sake of itself'). In the light of this principle, the project of fundamental ontology intended to demonstrate under the heading 'Time and Being' how the various meanings of Being – such as life, actuality, reality, permanence and so on – had to be understood as deriving from the self-projecting existence of *Dasein*. But the principle itself was restricted to the way of Being of individuals.

That restriction vanished in 1933 when Heidegger decided to support Hitler and became the first National Socialist rector of the University of Freiburg. The focus of his Rectoral Address is no longer the individual *Dasein* but the *Dasein* of the German people. As a result of that shift many concepts of *Dasein*'s analytic undergo a significant metamorphosis.

The early version of fundamental ontology had reappropriated the Aristotelian *praxis* in the direction of *Dasein*'s solitary insight (*theoria*) into the finiteness of its own Being, therefore in the direction of *Dasein*'s *bios theoretikos*. Heidegger in 1933 once again claims that the intention of the Greeks was to understand *theoria*, in its relation to Being, as the highest form of *praxis*. But he adds that *theoria*, thus understood as the science of the Being of beings, is 'the very medium that determines, in its ownmost Being, the *Dasein* of a people and of the State' (*The Self-assertion of the German University (Die Selbstbehauptung der deutschen Universität)* [2.7], 12). Accordingly, no longer the individual *Dasein* but the very existence of a people organized in a state seems to become the authentic location for the unconcealment of beings in their totality and in their Being. Now the organization of a people is obviously not a matter of pure *theoria*, but a matter of *technē*, of knowhow and of *poiēsis*. Consequently as a result of the shift from individual *Dasein* to the *Dasein* of a people-in-a-state, *technē* is no longer confined within the inauthentic realm of everydayness. To be sure, there is an ordinary *technē* which is still restricted to those limits, but, in addition to it, there is now place for an authentic *technē*, a knowhow which, instead of being fascinated by what is merely present-at-hand, is ontologically creative. In this context, Heidegger recalls an old Greek legend according to which Prometheus would have been the first philosopher, and he quotes the words of Prometheus in Aeschylus' tragedy: '*technē* however is much weaker than necessity.' Necessity is here interpreted by him as the 'overpower' of destiny. In such 'overpower' a concealment of being is involved which challenges knowledge and demands a metaphysical reply, in terms of a creative *technē*.

Along with the transposition of the notion of *Dasein* to a people, and the introduction of a creative *technē*, the Rectoral Address also introduces the idea that Being itself, and not only *Dasein*, is intrinsically polemical and historical; and that *Dasein* – either as an individual or as a people – is the 'there' of Being.

But in spite of all these modifications, the Rectoral Address maintains the project of a fundamental ontology, as a task including a metaphysics of *Dasein* articulated according to the opposition between a fallen everydayness, fascinated by presence-at-hand, and a resolute authenticity dedicated to unconcealing Being by transcending beings.

The two lecture courses offered by Heidegger after the rectorate period – a lecture course on Hölderlin [2.37] given in the winter term 1934–5, and a lecture course on the *Introduction to Metaphysics* [2.8, 2.53] given in the summer term 1935 – introduce developments of topics treated in the Rectoral Address, but they also maintain the framework of fundamental ontology.

The lecture course on Hölderlin starts by discarding, in order to listen to the poet, all the forms of fallen everydayness already described in *Being and Time* as obstructing the question: Who is *Dasein*? The *Dasein* at stake here, however, is no longer the individual but 'the authentic gathering of individuals in a community' ([2.45], 8). Hölderlin's poetry, in the poems '*Germania*' and '*Am Rhein*', is supposed to raise the question: 'Who are we, the German people?' The question demands a withdrawal from everydayness and a resolute attitude of racial questioning opposed to the 'They'. In continuity with *Being and Time*, Heidegger characterizes everydayness in terms of *technē*, i.e., circumspection dedicated to the management of surroundings, to production, usefulness and the general progress of culture. That inauthentic comportment encompasses the everyday life of the Nazi regime: cultural activism, subordination of thought and the fine arts to immediate political needs, biologism, and the rule of bureaucrats. But on the level of authenticity there is a place for a quite different *technē*, adjusted to the historical *Dasein* of the German people. Only a few individuals are aware of the innermost historiality of that people. These few are the creators: the poet, the thinker and the founder of the state. The co-operation of these three creative types is described by Heidegger in his interpretation of what he calls the *Grundstimmung*, the basic mood of the two poems, i.e., Hölderlin's holy mourning in the face of the flight of the gods. The poet institutes (*stiftet*) the truth of the *Dasein* of the people. The thinker elucidates and articulates the Being of beings thus disclosed by the poet. But the co-operation of the two requires the people to be led to itself as a people. This can only occur through the creation by the state-creator of a state adjusted to the essence of that people. That triad embodies the Promethean *technē* mentioned in the Rectoral Address. The three of them rise to the level of demigods preparing the conditions for a return of the divine.

The same Promethean trend is to be found in Heidegger's dialogue with pre-Socratic thought in the *Introduction to Metaphysics*. As a result of the elevation of a creative *technē* to the highest ontological level, Heidegger now detects between Parmenides, Heraclitus and Sophocles convergences pointing to an ontological assignment to setting-into-work what the creative *technē* sees or knows. The assignment is required by the polemical essence of what the early Greek thinkers called *physis*, an appellation which, like the word *alētheia*, is taken to be another name for Being. Being is polemical because, on the one hand, it is an unconcealment which retains itself in itself while disclosing itself in beings; and because, on the other hand, it is again and again threatened, in its very disclosure, by sheer semblance, deception, illusion. Therefore it is an 'overpowering' calling for a creative self-assertion defined as a decision (*Entscheidung*) to provide a 'separation in the togetherness of Being, unconcealment; appearance, and Non-Being' ([2.8], 84; [2.53], 92). And since there is a violence in the 'overpowering' of Being such decision has to be disrupting and violent. This violent response to the 'overpowering' of Being is what characterizes *technē* in its essential meaning. *Technē* provides the basic trait of the Greek *deinon* (uncanny) evoked in a famous chorus of Sophocles' *Antigone*. So understood, *technē* is both a knowledge and a creative power. As a knowledge, it is a sight looking beyond what is present-at-hand; as a creative power, it is the capacity to set-into-work within being the historical unconcealment of Being. In this context, Heidegger claims that unconcealment takes place only when it is achieved by work: 'the work of word in poetry, the work of stone in temple and statue, the work of the word in thought, the work of the *polis* as the historical place in which all this is grounded and preserved' (pp. 146; 160). In this context, Heidegger celebrates what he calls 'the inner truth and greatness' of the National-Socialist movement versus the ideology (racism) and everyday practice of the Nazi Party.

In these two lecture courses the introduction of a distinction between a petty *technē* trapped in everydayness or presence-at-hand and a lofty *technē* able to set-in-work Being itself in its unconcealment not only leaves untouched but even reinforces the articulation of fundamental ontology – i.e., the opposition between ordinary time and authentic temporality. The fact that the *Dasein* at stake is now understood as the *Dasein* of a people, either Greek or German, simply widens the basic principle of *Being and Time* according to which the *Dasein* exists for its own sake and by willing itself. It could even be said that the

Promethean connotation of these texts brings fundamental ontology to a sort of metaphysical climax. Heidegger suggests, indeed, that it is because of its foundational role towards his people that his own work deserved the heading of fundamental ontology (pp. 113; 146). And he quotes with admiration Hegel's words in the *Logic* of 1812: 'A people without a metaphysics is like a temple without a Holy of Holies.' Metaphysics is thus the privilege of Germany, whereas western democracies, particularly the United States, on the one hand, and the USSR on the other hand, are said to be absorbed in the frenetic development of the petty *technē*.

However, this paroxysm was soon going to bring fundamental ontology to an end, and to open the way to a 'turn' (*Kehre*) in Heidegger's thought. A comparison between the successive versions of his essay *The Origin of the Work of Art* bears witness to such a turn, or at least to a shift in Heidegger's treatment of the question of Being. Indeed the two early versions of the essay preserve the Promethean tendency which characterized the *Introduction to Metaphysics*; whereas the third and final version is no longer Promethean at all. All the topics tackled by the *Introduction to Metaphysics* – the people and its gods, the greatness of a creative *technē*, decision, the ontological *polemos* (conflict) – are still mentioned in the final version, but they lose their previous hardness thanks to an overall tonality which is more meditative and open to enigmas than voluntarist and proclamatory.

In the three versions, Heidegger insists that there is a circle in the investigation into the origin of the work of art. Indeed, if it is true that the artist is the origin of the work, it is also true that the work is the origin of the artist since neither is without the other. However, both are what they are by virtue of art itself. But if it is true that the essence of art should be inferred from the work, it is no less true that we could not recognize a work of art as such without referring to the essence of art. Hence the interrogation into the origin of the work of art moves in a circle. In the two early versions of the essay the topic of the circle operates as a device for signifying the circular character of *Dasein* as a being which projects its own Self by retrieving its thrownness, in such a way that project is a retrieval, and retrieval is a project. But in the final version that emphasis on *Dasein*'s existence for its own sake is replaced by an emphasis on Being itself inasmuch as Being is neither limited to beings nor without them, and neither encapsulated in *Dasein* nor without it.

Moreover, whereas the early versions insisted on the contrast between everydayness and creative self-assertion, the final version is almost without sign of a contempt for everydayness and its pettiness. It is significant in this regard that the first section of the final version of the essay is entirely devoted to the question: what is a thing in its thingly character? In the framework of fundamental ontology, as well as in the early versions of the essay, that question was clearly not an important issue for the task of thinking, and there was nothing enigmatic in the question. Indeed, there was an easy answer to it, in terms of everydayness: the Being of things is either presence-at-hand (natural things) or readiness-to-hand (equipment). By contrast, the final version of the essay states the following: 'The unpretentious thing evades thought most stubbornly. Can it be that this self-refusal of the mere thing, this self-contained independence, belongs precisely to the nature of the thing? Must not this strange feature of the nature of the thing become what a thought that has to think the thing confides in? If so, then we should not force our way to its thingly character' ([2.55], 32). In other words, everydayness, instead of being the familiar realm that resoluteness has to overcome in order to face the homelessness of existence, now becomes strange and deserves meditation in its familiar outlook. Dwelling among things no longer obstructs thought, quite the contrary. It is also significant that the reliability of equipment previously defined by its readiness-to-hand, hence in relation to *Dasein* only, now turns out to bear testimony to an enigmatic interplay of unconcealment and concealment in Being itself. This is what Heidegger tries to suggest in his meditation on one of Van Gogh's paintings of a pair of shoes.

The second section of the final version of the essay also marks a change regarding the notion of truth. Heidegger's point in the three versions is that in the work of art truth sets itself to work. Truth, here once again understood as *alētheia* or unconcealment, is of an essentially ambiguous and polemical nature, for it is a mixture of disclosedness and withdrawal. This polemical nature of truth is revealed by the conflictual nature of the work of art. While setting up a world, the artwork sets forth the earth, but whereas the world is an opening of paths, the earth is a self-seclusion. Hence there is in the work of art a strife between world and earth. Such strife characterizes truth itself as unconcealment. But whereas the early versions of the essay maintain the priority of *Dasein* regarding truth by making the *Dasein* of a people the locus of truth, the final version characterizes unconcealment as a clearing (*Lichtung*) to which human beings belong and are exposed. Consequently the meaning of resoluteness also changes: it is no longer the project to be a Self but an exposure to the secret withdrawal at the core of the clearing.

Finally, the last section of the final version is an attempt to define creation without reference to Promethean self-assertion. What is now considered to be fundamental in the work, inasmuch as it is created, is no longer its ability to anticipate in a leap what a people decides to be.

What is decisive in it, as created, is this: 'that such work is at all rather than is not' ([2.55], 65). In other words, the enigma of a coming-to-presence now overcomes the previous privilege of future self-projection. The creator is no longer a violent struggler but someone receptive to the clearing.

The turn and the overcoming of metaphysics

Why did Heidegger give up his project of fundamental ontology? The question raises an extremely complex issue and there are at least three ways of approaching it. From a strictly systematic point of view, it is possible to notice a paradox at the core of the project. Indeed if fundamental ontology – the science of the meaning of Being – is identified with the ontological analysis or metaphysics of *Dasein* (as seemed to be the case up to the *Introduction to Metaphysics*), then, as Heidegger himself said at the time, 'ontology has an ontical foundation' (*Basic Problems*, p. 26). But how is it possible to avoid then the reduction of Being to characteristics of a being, more precisely to *Dasein*'s way of Being? If, on the other hand, the metaphysics of *Dasein* is only the provisional preparation of a systematic ontology, then a distinction has to be made between the temporality of *Dasein* and the temporality of Being itself; and, consequently, the provisional character of the analytic of *Dasein* contradicts its allegedly fundamental function. In both cases, the attempt made in *Being and Time* (and later extended to surpass the limits of individual *Dasein*) turns out paradoxically to be itself a manner of oblivion of Being to the benefit of a being.

A second way of approaching the issue would be a close chronological investigation of the variations, appearing during the 1930s and early 1940s, in Heidegger's use of the notions coined in *Being and Time*. Such investigation remains to be done on a twofold basis: the lecture courses already published or in the process of being edited in the *Gesamtausgabe*, particularly those on Nietzsche (1936–41), and the long text written by Heidegger for his own use under the heading *Contributions to Philosophy* (*Beiträge zur Philosophie* 1936–8) [2.38].

A third approach is offered by Heidegger's own explanations of what he called the 'turn' which, at some point, occurred in his thought. The first among these self-interpretations is Heidegger's *Letter on Humanism*, written in 1946 in reply to questions raised by Jean Beaufret.

It is not certain, however, that the results of the three approaches could ever coincide, mainly because of Heidegger's tendency to justify retrospectively each step of his philosophical development. Despite these difficulties there is no doubt that several topics which had no place whatsoever in fundamental ontology came to the fore during the second half of the 1930s. The lecture courses on Nietzsche are extremely significant in this regard.

It has been noticed by several readers of the *Nietzschebuch* (Mehta; Arendt) that in the first lecture courses (1936–9) Heidegger interprets Nietzsche in terms of the analytic of *Dasein* and shows a basic agreement with Nietzsche, whereas the courses of 1939–41 are polemical. This is why Hannah Arendt claimed that initially the 'turn' was a biographical event, by which she meant that, underneath a polemical debate with Nietzsche, it was an explanation of Heidegger to himself, and an attempt to discard his own voluntarist inclinations during his activist period.

At any rate, what comes to the fore in the polemic against Nietzsche is a new way of considering the history of metaphysics. In fundamental ontology, the point was to deconstruct the biases and confusions inherent in past philosophies in order to liberate metaphysics and complete it as the science of the meaning of Being. Now, the point is to consider its development as a fatal destiny and to prepare its overcoming. That destiny is characterized as an increasing oblivion of Being culminating in Nietzsche's philosophy of the will-to-power and of the eternal return of the same, interpreted by Heidegger as nihilism.

At the dawn of western thought, the key words of the pre-Socratic thinkers, above all the word *alētheia*, all signalled the process through which beings are brought to the 'open' in tension between a reserve and an appearing. This means that Being was experienced as fully differentiated in the manner of an offering which withholds itself in what it gives. This differentiation indicates a finiteness of Being to which corresponds thinking as a receptivity to the secret of Being. The first erasing of this differentiated correspondence and mutual belonging starts with Plato. Plato's dialogues demonstrate a tendency to transform a mere consequence of the ambiguous process of *alētheia* into the essence of truth. In Plato beings reveal their beingness through ideas. The word initially meant the outlook offered by things as they emerge out of *physis*. Therefore it meant a consequence of the process of unconcealment. But Plato's ideas come to the forefront and get split off from the unconcealing process. Moreover, they acquire a normative status in relation to *physis*. Unconcealment then becomes a result of the clarity of the ideas which themselves refract the clarity of a supreme idea, the Good. This is the birth of metaphysics as onto-theology. The task of metaphysics from now on is to develop a theory of the essence of beings, a logic of their beingness, i.e., an ontology, and simultaneously to develop a theology by relating their beingness to a primordial being. *Alētheia* is thus obliterated by an ontical hierarchy, and truth becomes a matter of correctly seeing the ideas. Accordingly, the mutual belonging of Being in its ambiguity and of thinking in its receptivity to the same is levelled down to a contemplative conformity of the mind to essences.

A second stage in the metaphysical oblivion of Being took place in the Middle Ages. In medieval thought the Platonic concept of truth as conformity of the intellect to the beingness of beings, coupled with the founding role of a supreme being, was retrieved within the Christian speculations about creation and the dependence of the created on the creator. Truth in the scholastic sense of *adaequatio intellectus ad rem* (adequacy of the mind to the thing) is now grounded upon the deeper *adaequatio rei Dei intellectus* (adequacy of the thing to the mind of God).

A third stage occurred at the beginning of the modern age with the invention of subjectivity. When Galileo Galilei introduces, in still approximate terms, the first formulation of what Newton, a few decades later, was to call the principle of inertia, he uses the words 'mente concipio' (conceive in my mind). What is significant here, for Heidegger, is not the replacement of the sensible outlook of natural phenomena (the cornerstone of Aristotelian physics) by a purely intellectual approach of nature, but the fact that inertia, in order to appear at all, requires the human mind to give itself a preconception of what motion is and thus projects in advance the condition for phenomenality. In the conformity of adequation between intellect and thing, the stress is now put on the intellect in such a way that the thing manifests its truth inasmuch as it fits with a project emanating from the *mens*. Deeper than the modern use of mathematics in physics, there is what Descartes called *mathēsis* – a project by which the *cogito* ascertains itself on its own and acquires a position of mastery. In Descartes' philosophy, with the restriction of the dependence of the finite human mind on the divine infinity, the *cogito* posits itself as the unique basis upon which beings reveal their beingness. The word for basis in Greek was *hupokeimenon*, in Latin *subjectum*. The *cogito* becomes the only *subjectum*. The rule of subjectivity begins. The modern object–subject correlation means that beings are what they are to the extent that they submit themselves to the rule of the human *cogito*.

Such is the birth of the reckoning and evaluating reason which determines modernity. All its features appear at the outset. The *mathēsis* is *universalis*, which means that it is planning for the totality of beings. It is both a subjectivation of all beings referring them to the *cogito* and an objectivation making them all equally calculable and controllable. Earlier than the current reign of technology, right at the beginning of the modern era, nature as a whole was conceived as one huge mechanism in relation to a technological way of looking.

Between Descartes and Nietzsche, Heidegger does not notice a fundamental discontinuity. Nietzsche's notion of the will-to-power was in several ways anticipated by Descartes and subsequent thinkers: Leibniz's notion of the monad as a conjunction of perception and appetite in addition to his principle of Sufficient Reason; Kant's concept of reason as a condition of possibility; Fichte's reinterpretation of Kant in terms of practical reason; Schelling's conviction that there is no other Being than the Will; Hegel's concept of the Absolute, willing its self-identity throughout differentiation. So while claiming to be liberated from metaphysics, Nietzsche was merely bringing it to its accomplishment and carrying modern subjectivity to an onto-theological climax. Heidegger indeed interprets the will-to-power in ontological terms as the beingness of all beings, and the eternal return of the same in theological terms as the ultimate ground of beingness and being. Defined as the beingness of all beings, the will-to-power pushes to an extreme limit the project of objectivation and subjectivation inherent in *mathēsis*. Objectivation is brought to an extreme because the will not only treats every being as an object (*Gegenstand*) but also compels any object to become a storage (*Bestand*) available to all kinds of assignment and manipulation. Subjectivation is brought to an extreme as well, for all things are reduced to the values that the will bestows on them in order to intensify its power. On the other hand, the eternal return of the same, defined as the ultimate form of being, signifies an endless, circular, repetitive machination which is the metaphysical essence of modern technology. The abyssal thought of the eternal return means that the will aiming to intensify itself is itself willed and challenged to will itself infinitely. On both counts, Being has definitely lost the enigmatic ambiguity which was experienced by the early Greeks. Being is like nothing. Nihilism rules.

It is significant of the 'turn' at work in this meditation on modernity that Heidegger's description of what he calls 'European nihilism' in a 1940 lecture course on Nietzsche includes the following remarks about *Being and Time*: 'The path followed in it is interrupted at a decisive place. The interruption is explainable by the fact that, all the same, the attempt made on that path was running the risk, against its own intention, to reinforce furthermore subjectivity' (*Gesamtausgabe* vol. 48, p. 261).

The main result of the above description of the history of metaphysics is the claim that modern technology is the last accomplishment of a long process of oblivion of Being inherent in metaphysics since Plato. Heidegger uses the word *Gestell* to characterize the nature of modern technology. *Gestell* is a global 'enframing' wherein beings are entirely available to all sorts of arbitrary evaluations and manipulations, and in which Being counts for nothing. To that global enframing

Heidegger opposes what he calls *Ereignis*, often translated as 'event of appropriation', a term already used in his *Beiträge* of 1936–8. Within the global enframing, thinking is replaced by calculation. It is only by meditating *Ereignis* that thinking can remain alive. Thinking the *Ereignis* is a counter-current to nihilism.

That opposition pervades the writings of Heidegger after the Second World War. In all of them the voluntarist tonality of *Being and Time* and of the *Introduction to Metaphysics* has vanished. Significantly the word *Dasein* is now spelled *Da-sein*: there-being. The mortals are the 'there' of Being. They are exposed to the secret granting of Being. Significantly, also, a topic such as the 'call', which was restricted in *Being and Time* to *Dasein*'s listening to its ownmost potentiality, now emanates from Being itself. Whereas in fundamental ontology the human *Dasein* was the lieutenant of nothingness, it is now the shepherd of Being. Whereas fundamental ontology somehow conflated thinking and willing, thinking is now a matter of not-willing, of letting-be (*Gelassenheit*), and even of thanking. Whereas fundamental ontology conceived of dwelling in terms of a preoccupation of inauthentic everydayness, dwelling now deserves profound meditation. Likewise for the 'thing', a topic to which Heidegger devoted several essays in the late period. Likewise for speech, formerly taken as a capacity of *Dasein*, and now characterized in terms of a call emanating from Being, of a gathering of Being and of a corresponding to it. That shift from *Dasein* to Being explains why Heidegger criticized humanism as an aspect of metaphysics.

The shift of emphasis also generates a change in Heidegger's thought about time. While maintaining the notion of *ecstasis*, Heidegger no longer understands ecstatical temporalization in terms of an existential self-project, but in terms of a belonging of *Dasein* to the ambiguous unconcealing process of Being allegedly covered up by the entire tradition of metaphysics. This becomes apparent in a lecture given by Heidegger more than thirty years after *Being and Time*, under the significant title *Time and Being* (1962). This is the title which had been announced in 1927 as the heading of the third division of the book, a division which never appeared. The lecture of 1962, however, is not to be considered as the completion of the project of 1927.

It is a significant feature of the 'turn' that the topic is presented in neutral terms, in which *Dasein* no longer plays a central role. Heidegger indeed announces that his meditation is oriented by the sentence 'Es gibt Sein, Es gibt Zeit', which literally means: 'It gives Being, It gives time.' This neutral phrasing clearly suggests that the issue is no longer Dasein's temporalization. In both sentences, the phrase 'Es gibt' invites the audience to hear an offering which is not itself reducible to what it is offering. Hence the sentence 'It gives time' points to an offering which keeps withdrawing itself within what is offered. Already in the word 'present' there is more than the now; what is also meant by the word is a gift bestowed upon man. Open to the presence of the present, mortals welcome the granting. The emphasis is no longer on the project of the self but on receptivity to the granting.

In this context, the prior concept of *ecstasis* is modified. Each *ecstasis*, as well as the unity of the three *ecstases*, is now understood as a granting extended to human beings. Instead of saying that the past is what we retrieve in the light of our finite project, Heidegger now says that it happens to us, extending itself to us and soliciting us. The past is an *ecstasis* in the sense of the coming towards ourselves of an absence which concerns us while it is granted to us. Absence is itself a mode of presence if we think of presence in the sense of a granting. But in each there is an interplay of granting and withholding. The same holds true for the unity of the *ecstases*. Heidegger now calls each *ecstasis* a dimension, and he calls the unity of the *ecstaseis* the fourth dimension of time.

About such unity, Heidegger no longer evokes a privilege of the future. The emphasis is now on the coming-to-presence. Moreover, instead of evoking *Dasein*'s temporalization, he suggests that time temporalizes from itself. The unifying fourth dimension of time is characterized as a disclosed interplay of the three *ecstases*, a clearing extension, an opening. However it is also characterized by a denial, a withholding. Time nears and holds back. It is radically ambiguous. The granting, effective in it, is also a denial.

This new apprehension of time is at the core of Heidegger's notion of *Ereignis* which he opposes to *Gestell* – the technological enframing for which there is no secret whatsoever. In German *Ereignis* means 'event'. In Heidegger's terminology it designates the co-belonging of Being and man. He insists on both etymological roots of the word. They are *er-eignen*, 'appropriating', and *'er-äugen'*, bringing to visibility. There is no doubt that the use of the word in this twofold meaning signifies a contrast with the use of words such as *eigen* ('own'), and *Eigentlichkeit* ('authentic selfhood') in *Being and Time*. The *Ereignis* is not to be conceived of in terms of the Self at issue in the work of 1927. What is at stake in it is no longer a project but a *Schicken*, a sending or a destining. The event of co-belonging between Being and man is the manner in which Being destines itself to us, by opening the playspace (*Spielraum*) of time wherein beings appear. But destiny withholds itself in order for its granting to occur. The history of Being is that destiny. In it each epoch is an *epokhē*, a withholding of Being within its donation. In each case the *Ereignis* witholds (*enteignet*) itself. Consequently the task of thinking is no longer to be defined by the phrase 'Being and time' but by the phrase *Lichtung und Anwesenheit*, 'clearing and coming-to-presence', both understood in terms of a granting and a denial.

The trouble with this history of Being is that, in spite of the above signals of a significant shift in Heidegger's thought, it reproduces in a new way the previous contrast between the 'They' and the Self. Indeed only a few German poets (Hölderlin, Trakl, George) and Heidegger himself – but not the plurality of human beings interacting in a common world of appearances and events – seem able to properly respond to the ambiguity of the destiny of Being.

Moreover, the previous privilege of Dasein's bios theoretikos reapppears in a new manner: thinking is the only activity able to prepare a new beginning in the history of Being.

❧ SELECT BIBLIOGRAPHY ❧

Major books published by Heidegger himself

2.1 *Frühe Schriften* (1912–16), ed. F.-W. von Hermann, Frankfurt: Klostermann, 1978.

2.2 *Sein und Zeit* (1927), Tübingen: Niemeyer, 1953.

2.3 *Kant und das Problem der Metaphysik* (1927), Frankfurt: Klostermann, 1951.

2.4 *Vom Wesen des Grundes*, Frankfurt: Klostermann, 1928.

2.5 *Was ist Metaphysik?* (1929), Frankfurt: Klostermann, 1955.

2.6 *Vom Wesen der Wahrheit* (1930, 1943), Frankfurt: Klostermann, 1961.

2.7 *Die Selbstbehauptung der deutschen Universität*, Breslau: Korn, 1933. Later reprinted in *Das Rektorat 1933/34: Tatsachen und Gedanken*, Frankfurt: Klostermann, 1983.

2.8 *Einführung in die Metaphysik* (1935), Tübingen: Niemeyer, 1953.

2.9 *Erläuterungen zu Hölderlins Dichtung* (1936, 1944), Frankfurt: Klostermann, 1953.

2.10 *Holzwege* (1936–46). Frankfurt: Klostermann, 1950.

2.11 *Nietzsche* (1936–46), 2 vols, Pfullingen: Neske, 1961.

2.12 *Vorträge und Aufsätze* (1943–54). Pfullingen: Neske, 1961. Contains eleven essays, including 'Die Frage nach der Technik' and 'Bauen, Wohnen, Denken'.

2.13 *Platons Lehre von der Wahrheit* (1942). *Mit einem Brief über den 'Humanismus'* (1946), Bern: Francke, 1947.

2.14 *Was heisst Denken?* (1951–52), Tübingen: Niemeyer, 1954.

2.15 *Was ist das – die Philosophie?* (1955), Pfullingen: Neske, 1956.

2.16 *Zur Seinsfrage* (1955), Frankfurt: Klostermann, 1956.

2.17 *Der Satz vom Grund* (1955–6), Pfullingen: Neske, 1957.

2.18 *Identität und Differenz*, Pfullingen: Neske, 1957.

2.19 *Unterwegs zur Sprache* (1950–9), Pfullingen: Neske, 1957.

2.20 *Gelassenheit*, Pfullingen: Neske, 1959.

2.21 *Die Frage nach dem Ding* (1936, 1962), Pfullingen: Neske, 1962.

2.22 *Die Technik und die Kehre*, Pfullingen: Neske, 1962.
2.23 *Wegmarken* (1967), Frankfurt: Klostermann, 1978.
2.24 *Zur Sache des Denkens*, Tübingen: Niemeyer, 1969.
2.25 *Schellings Abhandlung über das Wesen der menschlichen Freiheit* (1936), ed. H. Feieck, Tübingen: Niemeyer, 1971.
2.26 *Phänomenologie und Theologie* (1927, 1954), Frankfurt: Klostermann, 1972.

Major lecture courses and manuscripts

Published in Heidegger's *Gesamtausgabe* (*Collected Edition*), Frankfurt: Klostermann:

2.27 *Phänomenologische Interpretationen zu Aristoteles* (1921–2), ed. W. Bröcker and K. Bröcker-Oltmanns, *GA* 61, 1985.
2.28 *Ontologie: Hermeneutik der Faktizität* (1923), ed. K. Bröcker-Oltmanns, *GA* 63, 1988.
2.29 *Platon: Sophistes* (1924–5), ed. I. Schüssler, *GA* 19, 1992.
2.30 *Prolegomena zur Geschichte des Zeitbegriffs* (1925), ed. P. Jaeger, *GA* 20, 1979.
2.31 *Logik: Die Frage nach der Wahrheit* (1925–6), ed. W. Biemel, *GA* 21, 1976.
2.32 *Die Grundprobleme der Phänomenologie* (1927), ed. F. W. von Hermann, *GA* 24, 1975.
2.33 *Phänomenologische Interpretation von Kants Kritik der reinen Vernunft* (1927–8), ed. I. Görland, *GA* 25, 1977.
2.34 *Metaphysische Anfangsgründe der Logik* (1928), ed. K. Held, *GA* 26, 1978.
2.35 *Die Grundbegriffe der Metaphysik: Welt, Endlichkeit, Einsamkeit* (1929–30), ed F.-W. von Hermann, *GA* 29/30, 1983.
2.36 *Vom Wesen der menschlichen Freiheit* (1930), ed. H. Tietgen, *GA* 31, 1982.
2.37 *Hölderlins Hymnen 'Germanien' und 'Der Rhein'* (1934–5), ed. S. Ziegler, *GA* 39, 1980.
2.38 *Beiträge zur Philosophie: Vom Ereignis* (1936–8), ed. F.-W. von Hermann, *GA* 65, 1989.
2.39 *Grundfragen der Philosophie* (1937–8), ed. F.-W. von Hermann, *GA* 45, 1984.
2.40 *Grundbegriffe* (1941), ed. P. Jaeger, *GA* 51, 1981.
2.41 *Hölderlins Hymne 'Andenken'* (1941–2), ed. C. Ochwaldt, *GA* 52, 1982.
2.42 *Hölderlins Hymne 'Der Ister'* (1942), ed. W. Biemel, *GA* 53, 1984.
2.43 *Parmenides* (1942–3), ed. M. S. Frings, *GA* 54, 1982.

Translations

2.44 *History of the Concept of Time*, trans. T. Kisiel, Bloomington: Indiana University Press, 1985.
2.45 *Being and Time*, trans. J. Macquarrie and E. Robinson, London: SCM Press, 1962.
2.46 *The Basic Problems of Phenomenology*, trans. A. Hofstadter, Bloomington: Indiana University Press, 1982.

2.47 *Kant and the Problem of Metaphysics*, trans. S. Churchill, Bloomington: Indiana University Press, 1962.

2.48 *The Metaphysical Foundations of Logic*, trans. M. Heim, Bloomington: Indiana University Press, 1984.

2.49 *The Essence of Reasons*, trans. T. Malich, Evanston: Northwestern University Press, 1969.

2.50 *What is Metaphysics?*, trans. D. F. Krell, in M. Heidegger, *Basic Writings*, ed. D. F. Krell, New York: Harper & Row, 1977, pp. 95–116.

2.51 *On the Essence of Truth*, trans. J. Sallis, in *Basic Writings*, pp. 117–41.

2.52 'The Rectorate 1933/34: Facts and Thoughts', trans. K. Harries, *Review of Metaphysics*, 38 (March 1985): 467–502.

2.53 *An Introduction to Metaphysics*, trans. R. Manheim, New Haven: Yale University Press, 1959.

2.54 *Nietzsche*, trans. and ed. D. F. Krell in 4 vols, New York: Harper & Row, 1979.

2.55 'The Origin of the Work of Art', third version, from *Holzwege*, trans. A. Hofstadter in M. Heidegger, *Poetry, Language, Thought*, New York: Harper & Row, 1971, pp. 7–87.

2.56 *The Question Concerning Technology and Other Essays*, trans. W. Lovitt, New York: Harper & Row, 1977, pp. 3–35.

2.57 'Building, Dwelling, Thinking', trans. A. Hofstadter, in *Basic Writings*, pp. 323–39.

2.58 Three essays on Heraclitus and Parmenides, trans. D. F. Krell and F. A. Capuzzi, in M. Heidegger, *Early Greek Thinking*, New York: Harper & Row, 1975.

2.59 'Plato's Doctrine of Truth', trans. J. Barlow in W. Barrett *et al.* (eds), *Philosophy in the Twentieth Century II*, New York: Random House, 1962, pp. 251–70.

2.60 'Letter on Humanism', trans. F. A. Capuzzi and J. G. Gray, in *Basic Writings*, pp. 193–242.

2.61 *What is Called Thinking?*, trans. F. D. Wieck and J. G. Gray, New York: Harper & Row, 1968.

2.62 *What is Philosophy?*, trans. J. R. Wilde and W. Klubach, New Haven: College and University Press, 1968.

2.63 *The Question of Being*, trans. W. Klubach and J. T. Wilde, New York: Twayne, 1958.

2.64 *The Principle of Reason*, trans. R. Lilly, Bloomington and Indianapolis: Indiana University Press, 1991.

2.65 *Identity and Difference*, trans. J. Stambaugh, New York: Harper & Row, 1969.

2.66 *On the Way to Language*, trans. P. D. Hertz and J. Stambaugh, New York: Harper & Row, 1966.

2.67 *Discourse on Thinking*, trans. J. M. Anderson and E. H. Freund, New York: Harper & Row, 1966.

2.68 *What is a Thing?*, trans. W. Barton and V. Deutsch, Chicago: Regnery, 1969.

2.69 'The Turning', trans. W. Lovitt in [2.56], 36–49.

2.70 *On Time and Being*, trans. J. Stambaugh, New York: Harper & Row, 1972.

2.71 *The Piety of Thinking*, trans. J. G. Hart and J. C. Maraldo, Bloomington: Indiana University Press, 1976.

Criticism

2.72 Arendt, H. *The Life of the Mind*, 2 vols, New York: Harcourt Brace Jovanovich, 1977–8.

2.73 Beaufret, J. *Dialogue avec Heidegger*, 3 vols, Paris: Minuit, 1973–4.

2.74 Biemel, W. *Le Concept de monde chez Heidegger*, Louvain and Paris: Nauwelaerts, 1950.

2.75 Birault, H. *Heidegger et l'expérience de la pensée*, Paris: Gallimard, 1978.

2.76 Dastur, F. *Heidegger et la question du temps*, Paris: Presses Universitaires de France, 1990.

2.77 De Waelhens, A. *La Philosophie de Martin Heidegger*, Louvain and Paris: Nauwelaerts, 1942.

2.78 Derrida, J. *De l'esprit: Heidegger et la question*, Paris: Galilée, 1987.

2.79 Haar, M. (ed.) *Martin Heidegger*, Paris: Cahiers de l'Herne, 1983.

2.80 Haar, M. *Heidegger et l'essence de l'homme*, Grenoble: Jérôme Millon, 1990.

2.81 Hermann, F.-W. von, *Die Selbstinterpretation Martin Heideggers*, Meisenheim am Glan: A. Hain, 1964.

2.82 Janicaud, D. *L'Ombre de cette pensée: Heidegger et la question politique*, Grenoble: Jérôme Millon, 1990.

2.83 Kockelmans, J. J. *On the Truth of Being: Reflections on Heidegger's Later Philosophy*, Bloomington: Indiana University Press, 1984.

2.84 Lacoue-Labarthe, P. *La Fiction du politique*, Paris: Christian Bourgeois, 1987.

2.85 Marx, W. *Heidegger and the Tradition*, trans. T. J. Kisiel and M. Greene, Evanston: Northwestern University Press, 1971.

2.86 Mehta, J. L. *The Philosophy of Martin Heidegger*, New York: Harper & Row, 1971.

2.87 Ott, H. *Martin Heidegger: Unterwegs zu seiner Biographie*, Frankfurt: Campus, 1988.

2.88 Pöggeler, O. *Martin Heidegger's Path of Thinking* (1963) trans. D. Magurshak and S. Barber, Atlantic Highlands: Humanities Press, 1987.

2.89 Pöggeler, O. *Philosophie und Politik bei Heidegger*, Freiburg: Alber, 1972.

2.90 Richardson W. *Heidegger: Through Phenomenology to Thought*, The Hague, Nijhoff, 1963.

2.91 Rockmore, T. and Margolin, J. (eds), *The Heidegger Case*, Philadelphia: Temple University Press, 1992.

2.92 Sallis, J. (ed.), *Reading Heidegger: Commemorations*, Bloomington: Indiana University Press, 1993.

2.93 Schürmann R. *Le Principe d'anarchie: Heidegger et la question de l'agir*, Paris: Seuil, 1982.

2.94 Sheehan, T. (ed.) *Heidegger: The Man and the Thinker*, Chicago: Precedent Publishing, Inc., 1981.

2.95 Taminiaux, J. *Heidegger and the Project of Fundamental Ontology* (1989), trans. M. Gendre, Albany: State University of New York Press, 1991.

2.96 Taminiaux, J. *La fille de Thrace et le penseur professionnel: Arendt et Heidegger*, Paris: Payot, 1992.

2.97 Zimmerman, M. *Heidegger's Confrontation with Modernity*, Bloomington: Indiana University Press, 1990.

CHAPTER 3

Philosophy of existence 2
Sartre
Thomas R. Flynn

Born 21 June 1905, in Thiviers (Dordogne), Jean-Paul Sartre was raised in the Parisian home of his widowed mother's parents. After his mother's remarriage, he spent several years with her and his stepfather in La Rochelle but returned to the capital to continue his education, first at the prestigious lycées Henri IV and Louis-le-Grand, and then at the renowned Ecole Normale Supérieure. After several years of teaching in various lycées, interspersed with a year of research at the French Institute in Berlin (1933–4), mobilization during the Phoney War (1939–40), and internment in a prisoner of war camp (1940–1), Sartre abandoned teaching for a career as an author and critic. He founded the review *Les Temps modernes* with Merleau-Ponty, Simone de Beauvoir and others (1944), refused the Legion of Honour (1945) and the Nobel Prize for Literature (1962), and became increasingly involved in the politics of the left in the second half of his life. Sartre adopted a former student, Arlette Elkaïm (1965), who had become his literary heir. He died in Paris on 15 April 1980.

Perhaps no one in the twentieth century better exemplifies the union and creative tension among philosophy, literature and public life than Jean-Paul Sartre. His novel *Nausea* and play *No Exit* emerged in the 1940s as paradigmatic 'existentialist' pieces, for which his masterwork, *Being and Nothingness*, served as the theoretical underpinning. This last, like Darwin's *Origin of Species*, was more mentioned than read during the halcyon days of café existentialism. But its basic insights and powerful phenomenological descriptions have continued to attract a number of contemporary philosophers as well as the general reading public. Several of these themes and theses continued to direct Sartre's philosophy throughout the shifts and adjustments of the next thirty-seven years of his career. So we cannot refer to a rejection of, or a 'turning' from, his earlier thought in his later work as is often done in the cases of Wittgenstein and Heidegger respectively.

The present chapter will survey Sartre's philosophical development, analyse the fundamental concepts and principles that constitute his contribution to philosophy in eight standard fields of inquiry, and conclude with reflections on Sartre's relationship to four movements in the recent history of philosophy, namely, existential phenomenology, Marxism, structuralism and postmodernism.

◆◆ PHILOSOPHICAL DEVELOPMENT ◆◆

Sartre once admitted that his inspiration to write philosophy came from reading Bergson's *Time and Free Will*. The Bergsonian influence on his thought, both positive and by way of reaction, has yet to be studied in depth. But the presence of this formidable French theorist is obvious from the centrality of time and temporalizing consciousness in Sartre's published philosophical writings from the very start. These works of the 1930s, culminating in *Psychology of Imagination* (1940), exhibit both a keen sensitivity to lived experience as distinct from the mechanical or quantified phenomena of positive science (a well-known Bergsonian theme) as well as a profound opposition to the philosophical idealism of his neo-Kantian professors at the Sorbonne. His early writings also tended to take imaging consciousness as paradigmatic of consciousness in general. In fact, if Sartre is known as *the* philosopher of freedom in our times, he could with equal justification be considered *the* philosopher of imagination. We shall observe various forms of imaging consciousness emerge in the course of our essay.

Sartre's long-time companion, Simone de Beauvoir, relates the story of their meeting with Raymond Aron after the latter's return from a year in Berlin. At Aron's account of the new philosophy of Edmund Husserl that could describe 'phenomenologically' an individual object such as the cocktail glass before them, she recounts, Sartre 'turned pale with emotion'. As they left the café, she recalls, Sartre had to find a bookstore open at night in order to purchase a copy of Levinas's *The Theory of Intuition in Husserl's Phenomenology*.

If phenomenology enabled Sartre to philosophize about concrete, individual reality, its central concept of intentionality allowed him to escape the 'principle of immanence' that entangled idealist philosophers in a mind-referring world. Philosophical idealism claims that reality is essentially mental or mind-referring. Berkeley's famous maxim 'To be is to perceive or be perceived' illustrates this view. Sartre published an essay in 1939 that countered this idealist claim with the principle of *intentionality*, namely, that consciousness is essentially *other*-referring:

'All consciousness is consciousness *of* another.' He applied this Husserlian principle with characteristic rigour, even directing it against Husserl himself, whom he accused of sliding into idealism by appeal to a 'transcendental' ego.

Sartre's robust realism continued to shape his epistemological claims over the years. He always insisted that we can know the real world in itself, that historical facts are not the result of our individual or collective creation, and that the harsh facticity of every situation must be dealt with, indeed, that failure to do so is simply 'bad faith'. It made him an apt, if initially reluctant, convert to philosophical materialism in the 1950s. Of course, mechanistic materialism was never a temptation. He had consistently opposed its claims from the start. But once he could separate the emergent features of dialectical materialism from its quasi-mechanical use by Marxist 'economism', he appealed to the 'material conditions of history' that Marxists of all shades respected and undertook to incorporate these socio-historical considerations into his philosophy of individual freedom-responsibility.

The Second World War was the dividing point between the phenomenological existentialist Sartre and his Marxist existentialist avatar. As he said in one of his many interviews, his 'experience of society' during those years forced him to shift from a philosophy of consciousness to one of *praxis*, understood roughly as human action in its material, socio-historical environment. If it is a mistake to see the early Sartre as an unqualified phenomenologist, witness his rejection of a basic Husserlian concept in *The Transcendence of the Ego* (1937), it is equally erroneous to read him as a Marxist *sans phrase*. In fact, in his final decade he explicitly denied he was a Marxist, insisting that 'existentialist' would be a more appropriate label if one had to make such designations. In *Search for a Method* (1958) and the *Critique of Dialectical Reason*, vol. 1 (1960), he makes ample use of historical materialist categories and arguments. Even in his massive Flaubert study, *The Family Idiot* (1971–2), where existentialist and Marxist terms are intertwined, he seems to regard physical labour and human need as the touchstones of reality. Still, his association with *les maos* (ultra-leftists) after the student uprising of 1968, and his unpublished collaborative effort with Benny Lévy on yet another ethic, confirms the judgment that Sartre was and remained a *moralist*. For it was the desire to retain a place for moral assessment within social critique that attracted him to these young radicals. As he noted, in obvious disgust, 'The Communists don't give a damn about justice. All they want is power' [3.28], 76. It is his moralist tendencies more than his so-called 'Cartesianism' that locate him squarely in the French philosophical tradition.

Sartre's final interviews with Lévy are much controverted. Simone de Beauvoir and Raymond Aron claim that the young man took advantage of Sartre's age and ill health to project a false image, a Sartre without critical bite, a domesticated warrior. Indeed, these conversations do read like Platonic dialogues, with Lévy assuming the controlling role of Socrates. Though it would be a mistake to read these pages without reference to the development of Sartre's thought as a whole, comparison of several disputed passages with claims made in posthumously published material from different stages of Sartre's career indicates that at least some of Sartre's so-called revisions of his well-known positions were actually ideas he had defended in these other works quite independent of Lévy's purported influence. Thus his remarks about love and 'fraternity' are anticipated and developed at length in his *Notebooks for an Ethics* (written 1948–9), as we shall see. Again, this does not mean that Sartre 'renounced' his existentialist philosophy in his final years. Nothing could be farther from the truth. But it does reveal Sartre as a living, evolving thinker, responding to the ever-changing challenges of his day. For Sartre, to philosophize was his way of being-in-the-world.

✐ PHILOSOPHICAL CONTRIBUTIONS ✐

Existentialists have been portrayed as non- or even anti-systematic thinkers. No doubt this stems from Kierkegaard's notorious animus against Hegel's 'System' and Nietzsche's strictures against academic philosophy in general. But, unless by 'systematic' one means 'axiomatic deductive', classical existentialist thinkers like Sartre, Merleau-Ponty, Heidegger (who rejected the association) and others were rigorous and consistent theorists, who applied fundamental principles and concepts according to a clear method. Given the interlinking and cumulative nature of Sartre's thought, it is best to order our exposition according to the standard philosophical sub-disciplines. Not only will this facilitate our consideration of his massive *oeuvre*, it will also exhibit the unity and coherence of his theoretical work.

Methodology and epistemology

Sartre had a remarkable talent for psychological description. His novels, plays and short stories were replete with arresting, insightful accounts of both typical and dramatic moments in the human condition. So it is small wonder that he was taken by Husserl's phenomenological method of 'eidetic reduction'. By a 'free, imaginative variation of examples', Husserl proposed to focus on the essence, *eidos*, or intelligible contour of any 'object' whatsoever. Not only physical nature, mathematical abstractions or metaphysical categories but acts of ingratitude and artistic events were likely objects for the phenomenologist's eye. Like the forensic artist's composite photograph, these reductive descriptions serve to reveal the form, figure or essence of an object, whether this be an abstract entity, like 'material object', an emotion, like 'resentment', or a particular phenomenon, like 'this glass'. At its best, such descriptive analysis reveals the essential features of the object in question, that is, those that withstand the imaginative variations to which they are subject by the describer. Descriptive phenomenology is a 'science' of what Aristotle called 'formal', not 'efficient' causes. As Husserl noted, 'phenomenology does not try to explain . . . but simply to get us to see'. When it is unable to generate what Husserl termed the 'intuition of essences' (*Wesensschau*), the phenomenological method must be satisfied with possible or probable opinions about the matter in question. So the first two parts of Sartre's *Psychology of Imagination* are entitled the 'certain' and the 'probable' respectively.

What we may call an epistemology of 'vision', the Husserlian legacy, remains a constant feature of Sartre's method. It accounts for some of the most arresting passages in his philosophical writings, and serves to 'concretize' some of the most abstract sections of his theoretical works. The presuppositions of Husserl's method are Cartesian, however, and Sartre's writings up to and including *Being and Nothingness* refer to a form of the *cogito* as essential to any method that would move beyond mere probability to certainty in its basic claims. The insight of individual reflective consciousness in this approach is taken as the final court of appeal in philosophical argument. Although Sartre seemed to modify this view in his later years, he never abandoned it, as is clear from his retention of the language of *Being and Nothingness* in his final work on Flaubert. A tension between this epistemology of vision and an overlapping epistemology of *praxis* renders Sartre's later philosophy problematic.

After the war, Sartre adopted a form of the dialectical method, which he had been studying in the works of Hegel and Marx during that period. Central to this approach, as he saw it, were the notions of 'finality', 'negativity' and 'time'. It is a feature of dialectical reasoning, he insists, to acknowledge 'a certain action of the future as such'. Explanation in terms of Aristotle's 'final' causality had been philosophically unpopular since Descartes. But Sartre argues that our comprehension of human activity (*praxis*) as distinct from mechanical behaviour depends on the purposes that guided the agents themselves.

He criticized philosophers since Descartes for 'failing to conceive negativity as productive', an oversight that he certainly avoided in *Being and Nothingness*, where negativity assumes pride of place as an essential feature of consciousness as such. Sartre's dialectic differs most from Hegel's by its insistence on the primacy of individual activity in dialectical advance and in its denial of any 'end' to the dialectical process so long as consciousness/*praxis* sustains it. A pivotal claim, and the undoing of any totalitarian theory, is Sartre's thesis that a 'totalizing' consciousness/*praxis* cannot totalize itself, that is, it cannot be completely absorbed in a social whole of which its totalizing activity is a part. This 'nihilating' character of consciousness in the early Sartre remains in the *praxis* of the later one to preclude any 'organicist' or totalitarian tendencies in his social thought.

The later, dialectical thinker prefers 'notions' to 'concepts' as the vehicles for expressing historical intelligibility. Sartre argues that developmental thinking alone can render comprehensible a fluid reality and that notions as dynamic are superior to static concepts in performing this task. Like Aristotle's and Kant's categories, concepts as such are atemporal whereas notions include an essential reference to temporality in their very meaning. We should see 'notion' as a 'dialectical concept' and read Sartre's writings after *Being and Nothingness* as abounding in them.

Sartre's discourse on method is the essay *Search for a Method*, published first as an article and later as a kind of preface to the *Critique of Dialectical Reason*. It combines the phenomenological and dialectical moments in an approach that develops the 'method of understanding' (*Verstehen*) of German social theory at the turn of the century. The method entails three stages or dimensions. The first is a phenomenological description of the subject matter to be studied. The terminus of eidetic reduction, it now forms the beginning of Sartre's approach. The second step is a 'regressive' move from the object of investigation to the conditions of its possibility. These may be purely 'formal', such as the structures of social relations that Sartre uncovers in the *Critique of Dialectical Reason*, vol. I, or they may include a specific content, like the intrafamilial relations of the young Flaubert that conditioned his psychosocial development. The third move in what Sartre calls his 'progressive–regressive' method is the progressive spiral of interiorization/exteriorization of these material and formal conditions by the agent whose meaning-direction (*sens*) we are attempting to uncover. If successful, the progressive–regressive method enables us to 'understand' (not 'conceptualize') an agent as well or even better than he or she understood himself or herself, the ideal of hermeneutical investigation since Kant.

Psychology

Sartre's first published philosophical books were in psychology: *Imagination* (1936), *Sketch for a Theory of Emotions* (1939), and *The Psychology of Imagination* (1940). Not coincidentally, they emphasize the role of the imagination in our psychic life and pursue in depth Husserl's thesis that intentionality is the defining characteristic of the mental. Both these remain influential in Sartre's subsequent writings.

His phenomenological analysis of the imagination reveals three characteristics of its structure: the imagination is a *consciousness*; like all consciousness, it is *intentional*; and it differs from perceptual consciousness in the way it 'intends' its object, namely, as absent, non-existent or *unreal*.

It is better, he argues, to speak of 'imaging consciousness' than of 'imagination' with its corresponding 'images'. The latter form of expression tends to hypostatize consciousness and to turn images into *simulacra*, 'inner' icons of some 'exterior' object. Such discourse succumbs to what Sartre calls the 'illusion of immanence' shared by realists and idealists alike. Rather, imaging consciousness should be conceived as a manner of being-in-the-world, a Heideggerian term that Sartre adopts. Intentionality avoids the paradoxes of traditional inside–outside epistemology and accounts for the relational character of consciousness. Imaging consciousness 'derealizes' the perceptual or recollected object, relating to it in the properly imaginary mode. This derealizing activity employs physical or psychic material (for example, painted surfaces or phosphenes in the case of aesthetic or oneiric objects respectively), to serve as an *analogue* for the imagined object. Sartre's concept of 'representative analogue' figures in much that is original and interesting in his aesthetic theory. It is integral to his existential 'biographies' of such 'lords of the imaginary' as Baudelaire, Genet, Flaubert and Mallarmé. For each in his own way will be portrayed as 'derealizing' the bourgeois world of his contemporaries and enticing others with his art to do likewise. A conceptual flaw that weakens Sartre's usage is his failure to explain in detail what he means by these cardinal terms, 'analogy' and 'analogue'.

These features of imaging consciousness are summarized in the following definition: 'The image is an act which intends [literally, "aims at" (*vise*)] an absent or non-existent object in its corporality by means of a physical or psychical content which is given not for its own sake but only as an "analogical representative" of the intended object' ([3.30], 25; in the French text, p. 45). It is remarkable that Sartre speaks of imaging consciousness in this first period of his writings as the locus of possibility, negativity and lack, and insists that only in the imagining act is the 'nihilation' of objects revealed (see [3.30], 243–5; French, pp. 360–1), because, in *Being and Nothingness* and thereafter, these emerge as the proper features of consciousness in general. To the extent that Sartre's early philosophy by his own admission is a 'philosophy of consciousness', it is likewise a philosophy of the imagination. Our survey of his thought and works will justify considering him *the* philosopher of the imagination as much as *the* philosopher of freedom – the title by which he is commonly designated.

His analysis of the emotions is in direct parallel with that of the image. Like images, emotions are not 'inner states' that somehow correspond to external stimuli. Neither are they reducible to their physiological expression, as some have argued. Emotional consciousness is another way of being-in-the-world. In this case, it is one that entails a physiological change as a means of relating to the world in a 'magical' manner. Emotional consciousness is 'failure behaviour' (*la conduite d'échec*), an expression that will play an important role in Sartre's biography of Flaubert. The agent, unable to change the world through rational activity, changes himself or herself in order to conjure up a world that is no longer frustrating. Thus, the golfer gets red in the face before his/her failure to escape a sand trap. Sartre reads this as conscious, that is, 'intentional', behaviour. Its purpose is to generate another world as if by magic via one's bodily changes: perspiration, increased blood pressure, agitated motions and the like – these are 'intended' to help whisk the ball on to the green. Again, Sartre's phenomenological descriptions are aimed at escaping the 'inner life' and underscoring the correlativity of consciousness and world, psychology and ontology.

Ontology

If Sartre is a moralist, he is likewise basically an ontologist. The close relation between ethics and ontology in his thought lends it a 'traditional' flavour quite foreign to that of recent French intellectuals. His masterwork, *Being and Nothingness*, subtitled 'An Essay in Phenomenological Ontology', develops the basic categories of his theory of being (ontology) and concludes with the promise of an ethics, which never appeared in Sartre's lifetime.

Inspired by the divisions of Hegel's *Phenomenology of Spirit* but always relying on the 'apodictic' evidence of Husserl's eidetic reduction, Sartre undertakes a description of the fundamental forms of being. He calls these 'being-in-itself' (*l'être-en-soi*), 'being-for-itself' (*l'être-pour-soi*) and 'being-for-others' (*l'être-pour-autrui*). Each has distinctive characteristics and is irreducible to the others. Exploiting the proximity of phenomenology to psychology, ontology and literary 'argument',

Sartre relies on powerful examples and tropes to convey his insights. In fact, his first literary success, *Nausea* (1938), both anticipates and 'works through' imaginatively the themes and theses of *Being and Nothingness*, published five years later.

Being-in-itself or the non-conscious is the inert plenum. It is self-identical and without the features commonly ascribed to being in realist ontologies. For example, it is neither active nor passive, is beyond negation and affirmation (other than the judgment that it is and is self-identical), knows no otherness, is not subject to temporality and is neither derived from the possible nor reduced to the necessary. 'Uncreated, without reason for being, without any connection with another being, being-in-itself is *de trop* (superfluous) for eternity' ([3.2] lxvi). Sartre derives these characteristics from an initial phenomenological investigation of the being of any phenomenon. He confirms them by appeal to certain experiences like nausea and boredom that he believes are revelatory of its ontological nature.

Being-for-itself or consciousness is the counter-concept to being-in-itself and is its internal negation. It brings 'otherness' into play, is precisely *non*-self-identical, and is characterized as a 'pure spontaneous upsurge', a feature Sartre's concept shares with the concept of mind in classical German idealism. The for-itself 'temporalizes' the 'world' that it constitutes by its intentional relations. As we noted above, consciousness is the locus of possibility, negativity and lack. Early in *Being and Nothingness*, Sartre undertakes an analysis of our act of questioning, a tactic doubtless learned from Heidegger's *Being and Time*, with which his book has several affinities. His descriptive analysis concludes that the negativity which permeates our lives from the fragility of objects to the absence of friends is not dependent on the act of judging – the standard view – but conversely. We have 'a certain prejudicative comprehension of non-being' ([3.2], 7), and it is this that grounds the negative judgments and realities (*négativités*) that populate our world. Sartre proceeds to argue that this 'nihilating' relation of consciousness to the world is possible only because consciousness (the for-itself) is of its very nature a *no*-thingness (*néant*), an 'othering' relation that holds the in-itself ('thingness') at bay even as it conspires with being-in-itself to constitute the existential 'situation'.

The essence of consciousness as the internal negation or no-thingness of being-in-itself accounts for many of the paradoxes that abound in Sartre's ontology. Chief among these is the claim that 'human reality' (his translation of Heidegger's *Dasein*), 'is not what it is . . . and is what it is not' ([3.2], 123). Human reality 'is' its ego, its past, its 'facticity', in the manner of not-being these givens of its situation, that is, as the internal negation of being-in-itself. Metaphorically, the for-itself 'secretes' nothingness (*le néant*) or otherness between itself and whatever predicate one might wish to ascribe to it. These verbal twists are meant to capture the ephemerality of the for-itself, a transitivity which echoes that of temporality, which the for-itself constitutes.

Following Heidegger, Sartre distinguishes lived or *ekstatic* temporality from the 'universal time' measured by chronometers. The latter is quantitative and homogeneous; the former, qualitative and heterogeneous. Being-for-itself is not 'in' time the way a hand is in a glove, or even the way the glove is 'in' time. Rather, it 'temporalizes' the world which it constitutes. The for-itself 'exists' in three temporal *ekstases*: the past as facticity or 'already', the future as possibility or 'not yet', and the present as 'presence to' or the 'othering' relation that at once unites and distinguishes the for-itself from being. These are three structured moments of an original synthesis. Sartre insists that it is better to accent the present *ekstasis* rather than the future as Heidegger does, because presence-to best exemplifies the internal negation of being-in-itself, which is the total synthetic form of temporality ([3.2], 142).

When one moves from the abstractions of the in-itself and the for-itself to the concrete individual agent, these functional concepts, being-in-itself and being-for-itself, assume the roles of 'facticity' and 'transcendence' respectively. Every individual is a being-in-situation and 'situation' is a vague, indeterminate mix of the givens, including one's physical and cultural environment as well as one's previous choices, on the one hand, and the project that moves beyond them, on the other. These givens must be reckoned with, but, Sartre insists, they are not determining. 'One can always make something out of what one has been made into' is the maxim of Sartrean humanism. The first half of his career was spent explaining the first portion of that remark; the remainder was devoted to articulating how society and history have limited our choices without removing them entirely.

Although Sartre insists that being-for-others is as fundamental as the in-itself and the for-itself, it is clearly dependent on them ontologically. In one of the most famous passages of *Being and Nothingness*, he offers his 'proof' for the existence of other minds in the form of an eidetic reduction of shame-consciousness. After criticizing the adequacy of traditional arguments from analogy to account for the certainty with which we believe in the existence of other minds, he performs an 'imaginative reconstruction' of an example to reveal how such certainty figures essentially in our experience of shame.

He imagines someone looking through a keyhole at a couple. Like all Sartrean consciousness, the couple's consciousnesses are objectifying one another in a reciprocal gaze. The voyeur is a 'pure' consciousness, seeing but unseen, objectifying but unobjectified, whereas they are in a mutual relation of looking/looked at, unaware of the third party. Suddenly, the interloper hears a noise from behind. In one and the same reaction of shame, one experiences the *other as subject* and oneself objectified. In other words, one's experience of shame is analysable into the condition of its possibility, namely, one's embodiedness-as-perceived by another consciousness. One cannot be objectified except by another subject, nor is it possible to feel shame except as an embodied being. Even if the noise turns out to have been a false alarm, the mere rustling of the curtains, for example, the agent has had an immediate experience of another *as subject*; it is written in the blush on his/her face. This 'proof' of other minds is experiential. Rather than the probability of some weak analogy, it yields the certainty of the *Wesensschau*.

After establishing the existence of other minds, albeit in a general, 'pre-numerical' manner that renders my being for-others the precondition of my being objectified by any subject in particular (see [3.2], 280–1), Sartre directs his ontological investigation to each of the conditions for that experience, namely, the body and the other subject.

There are three dimensions to bodily being-in-the-world, namely, the body as for-itself, as for-others, and as what Sartre calls the way I 'exist for myself as a body known by the Other' ([3.2], 351). The absurdities of the mind–body problem, Sartre believes, stem from failure to respect these ontological levels regarding the body and in particular from beginning our analysis with the body-for-others. The latter approach sees body as a thing among things and hence as externally related to consciousness and to other bodies. Sartre begins, on the contrary, with body as being-for-itself, that is, as my way of being-in-the-world. As such, body is 'lived' (pre-reflectively) and not 'known' (reflectively), it is the absolute centre of instrumentality that I am, rather than an instrument that I employ, and it is at once my point of view and my point of departure for acting in the world. Hence Sartre can claim that 'being-for-itself must be wholly body and it must be wholly consciousness; it can not be *united* with a body' ([3.2], 305). Sartre's peculiar kind of 'materialism' depends on defending a body that is likewise wholly intentional, that is, that is not simply externally related to the projects by which an agent is individuated. Accordingly, body is integral to the existential 'situation' and is the vehicle by which other 'necessary contingencies' of our situation such as our race, our class and our very past figure in the mix. In other words, body as being-for-itself is the basic form of our facticity.

Once we have phenomenologically described our way of 'existing' our body, there is no temptation to misread the body-for-others as a thing among things. The latter now appears as the Other's *flesh*, a term elaborated by Merleau-Ponty and designating for Sartre 'the pure contingency of [the Other's] presence' ([3.2], 343). What he calls 'the pure intuition of the flesh' is especially evident in the Other's face (a claim that invites comparison with that of Levinas regarding the primacy of the Other and the ethical significance of the face in this revelation). The body is thus revealed as a 'synthetic totality of *life* and *action*' ([3.2], 346, emphasis his).

The third ontological dimension of the body, for Sartre, is 'my body as known by the Other'. This denotes that real but uncontrollable aspect of our being-in-the-world before others – the poet's 'as others see us'. If shame-consciousness reveals the existence of other subjects, affective structures such as shyness indicate a vivid awareness of my body not as it is for me but as it is 'for the Other'. Significantly, Sartre insists that language shows us abstractly the principal structures of our body-for-others. We shall observe him subsequently locate language among the 'practico-inert'. This relation between language and body-for-others is a suggestive dimension of Sartre's ontology yet to be fully explored.

The social dimension of Sartre's vintage existentialism elaborates our being-for-others as well as the facticity of our being-in-situation. His famous analysis of our basic relations to each other as an attempt to 'assimilate the Other's freedom' through sadistic or masochistic manoeuvres scandalized the public and contributed to his reputation for pessimism in the late 1940s. This was reinforced by the well-known line from his play *No Exit* (1944), that 'Hell is other people' (*l'enfer, c'est les autres*).

Although he later contextualized these remarks, along with the passages in *Being and Nothingness* on which they form a gloss, as referring to interpersonal relations 'in an alienated society' such as ours, the source of the difficulty and the obstacle to a more satisfactory social theory is ontological, not historical: his looking/looked-at model for interpersonal relations. Until this is surpassed in the *Critique of Dialectical Reason*, Sartre can offer us at best a theory of the other writ large, but not a social philosophy properly speaking.

Ethics

It is now common to divide Sartre's ethical thought into three phases: the ethics of authenticity of his vintage existentialist years, the dialectical ethics that he began to formulate in the 1950s and 1960s, and the 'ethic of the we' that he was fashioning with Benny Lévy toward the end of his life. Since the first is his best known and most fully articulated theory, we shall concentrate on the ethics of authenticity.

If there is any existentialist 'virtue', it has been remarked, it is authenticity. The basis for this concept is appropriately ontological: 'man is free because he is not a self but a presence-to-self' ([3.2], 440).

In other words, human reality is a 'being of distances' – whatever it is, it is in the manner of *not*-being that property, that is, as being other-than-*that*. So the male homosexual's friend who urges him to 'come out' and admit what he is, in Sartre's example, is really asking him to be inauthentic, to be a homosexual 'the way a stone is a stone', that is, in the manner of the self-identity of being-in-itself. But, of course, that is precisely what he cannot do – since, as conscious, he is 'in situation' as a homosexual. He is homosexual, French, courageous, or whatever, in the manner of transcending that facticity. Still, it is *that facticity* which he transcends, 'nihilates', 'others'. The 'moral' challenge, if that word is appropriate, is to live that tension from day to day. One can no more resign oneself to complete identity as a homosexual than the reformed gambler or alcoholic can rest secure in his or her 'sobriety' after years of success. What others see as pessimism Sartre proclaims as hope: we are not condemned by our upbringing, our characters or our past behaviour; we are freed from determinisms of every kind; we can always make something out of what we have been made into.

Perhaps Sartre's best description of 'authenticity' published in his lifetime is found in *Anti-Semite and Jew* (1946): 'Authenticity consists in having a true and lucid consciousness of the situation, in assuming the responsibilities and risks it involves, in accepting it in pride or humiliation, sometimes in horror and hate' ([3.1], 90). What emerges from existentialism in general and from Sartre in particular is authenticity as an ethical *style*. Its elements are: first, a heightened awareness of *facticity* and *possibility*, that is, of the existential situation; second, the exercise of creative *choice* of self within this situation; and finally, *owning* or appropriating the consequences of this choice, that is, of the altered situation, the altered self. As he remarks in his posthumously published *Notebooks for an Ethics* (1992), 'It is this double, simultaneous aspect of the human project, gratuitous at its core and consecrated by a reflective reprise, that makes it into *authentic existence*' ([3.26], 481). This is not *amor fati*. Simply to resign oneself to one's facticity is a lie, for it denies that other dimension of the existential situation, transcendence or consciousness, which must sustain the resignation and thereby leave rebellion a constant possibility. Rather, authenticity is the challenge to 'have the courage to go to the limits of ourselves in both directions at once' ([3.32], 599). This is the moral Sartre draws from the biography of his 'hero' of authenticity, Jean Genet.

The ambiguity of 'situation', its indeterminate mélange of facticity and transcendence, reflects the *non*-self-coincidence of human reality. It makes ontologically possible 'bad faith', the best known of Sartrean moral categories. There are two basic forms of bad faith, depending on whether the individual flees the anguish of his or her freedom-possibility for identification with facticity (for example, the alcoholic who is 'cured' once and for all) or denies the force of circumstances to float in the realm of pure possibility (like James Thurber's Walter Mitty). Each is a kind of 'lie to oneself', which, of course, is impossible unless one introduces another kind of otherness or inner distance into human reality, namely, one that affects consciousness itself.

Sartre discovers a twofold duality in the human way of being: ontological (presence-to-self) and psychological (levels of consciousness). The former accounts for the otherness that infects our very being; the latter divides our awareness such that we can be conscious without 'knowing' it. The former constitutes the split; the latter renders possible the self-deception. In *Being and Nothingness*, he speaks of 'pre-reflective' and 'reflective' consciousness. The former is our immediate experience of the other, our being-in-the-world. It is *ekstatic* and pre-personal in the sense that it is not closed in on itself but is 'already in the world' when reflection intervenes. With reflection comes the self (as quasi-object of reflection), the concepts of 'knowledge' as distinct from the notions of 'understanding', which are rooted in the pre-reflective, and the objects of deliberation to which one turns when 'making up one's mind'.

Significantly, the pre-reflective enjoys both an epistemic and an ontological primacy. It is the level of 'fundamental project' that orients our reflective moments as well as the locus of that comprehension which accompanies every conscious act. In fact, pre-reflective comprehension functions in Sartre's thought in a manner not unlike Freud's 'unconscious', to which Sartre was notoriously opposed. The chief and crucial difference is that appeal to the pre-reflective enhances rather than diminishes responsibility for Sartre. The extreme responsibility to which Sartre holds us in his polemical writings is an application of this far-reaching concept of pre-reflective comprehension: we all understand what we are about, even if we do not reflectively know it. Awareness and responsibility are coextensive.

This virtual identification of consciousness and responsibility will strike many as hyperbolic, given the traditional conditions for moral responsibility, namely, some degree of control in addition to an element of knowledge. In the brief compass of a sub-section, it is impossible to pursue this at length, but it should be noted that Sartre is concerned with 'responsibility' in the sense of being the 'incontestable author of an event or of an object' ([3.2], 553). What we might call *noetic* responsibility, that is, our appropriation of the meanings that constitute 'our world', is the ground of the other forms of responsibility that Sartre acknowledges. And here it does not seem incredible to claim that awareness and responsibility are extentionally equivalent. Sartre confirms this interpretation when he occasionally responds as a trump card: 'Well, he or she could always commit suicide.' The point is that, if they did not do so, they have 'chosen' in the existential sense the 'world' in which they live.

Fundamental 'choice' or project is both the individuating feature of existential ontology, the factor that distinguishes consciousnesses among themselves, and the totalizing aspect of human reality that renders it thoroughly responsible for its situation. Problematic as the concept is – Sartre once likened it to what psychologists mean by 'selective attention' (see [3.2], 462) – it is consistent with his claim that being-in-itself cannot act upon consciousness, that the for-itself is a 'pure spontaneous upsurge', and that consciousness is what makes motives motivate. Some have compared basic choice to R. M. Hare's 'decisions of principle' in that both are prior to the principles to which one appeals in settling arguments. As Sartre puts it, when one pauses to decide, the 'chips are [already] down' ([3.2], 451). Fundamental choice is constitutive, not selective. It is coterminous with pre-reflective consciousness. It is a 'choice' which we 'are/were', to paraphrase a barbarism that Sartre introduces to express the transitivity and harsh facticity of lived time.

Because consciousness, choice, freedom, responsibility are roughly extentionally equivalent terms in what Iris Murdoch called Sartre's 'great inexact equations', the challenge to authenticity and the consequences of inauthenticity are all-encompassing. There is a *'Weltanschauung* of bad faith', for example; it constitutes a manner of being-in-the-world ([3.2], 68).

In a set of unpublished manuscripts for lectures in the 1960s, Sartre begins to elaborate another, dialectical ethic. This is more socially minded than his characteristically individualist stance of twenty years earlier. It builds on his concepts of situation and the exemplarity of moral choices as well as the thesis that no one can be free if anyone is enslaved – themes addressed briefly in his earlier works. His ontological categories are those of the *Critique of Dialectical Reason* and his discussions, for the most part inchoate and sketchy, are phenomenological descriptions of moral experience, especially the following of moral norms and their violation in moments of moral crisis and creativity. The ideal is no longer the 'authentic' individual but 'integral man', understood *grosso modo* as the person who has entered into relations of positive reciprocity with others whose basic animal and human needs have likewise been met such that they are liberated from the alienating tyranny of material scarcity and the violence it engenders. These are necessarily vague notions, Sartre admits, because they gain their precision from that which they oppose, namely, what he calls 'sub-man' or the oppressed and oppressing individuals of contemporary society.

The most that can be said of integral man in the present state of our social existence is that he or she is made possible by the continuous refusal to live as sub-man. Although Sartre cites the colonist–native relationship to exemplify the notion of sub-humanity, he has always considered this an instance of more general relations of oppressive practice and structural exploitation that characterize bourgeois society.

Clearly, Sartre was dissatisfied with this second attempt and so in his last years undertook a third ethic in discussion with Benny Lévy. Characterized by Sartre as an 'ethics of the WE', this third version remains buried in the tape-recordings in Lévy's possession. From Sartre's somewhat exaggerated accounts, we learn that this product of a *livre à deux* was to leave uncriticized not a single major thesis of his earlier philosophy. As we noted earlier, the published interviews indicate that this is not the case, though they do reveal the revival of some more 'positive' theses from earlier works such as *Notebooks for an Ethics*. In any case, these tapes, if they are ever published, will almost certainly be chiefly of biographical value and are not likely to warrant our rejecting the systematic thought of Sartre at his prime.

Existential psychoanalysis

Although it has 'not yet found its Freud' ([3.2], 575), this approach to understanding the fundamental project of an agent is followed in increasing detail in Sartre's 'biographies' of Baudelaire, Genet and Flaubert as well as in his Nobel-Prize-winning autobiography, *The Words*.

The method is an application of the ontology of *Being and Nothingness*, although it does not rely on the latter's discredited social theory. It assumes that human reality is a totalization, not a totality, and that this ongoing unity is forged by the existential project. If human reality is the 'useless passion' to coincide consciously with itself, to be in-itself-for-itself, that is, if each of us exemplifies the famous futile desire to be God, then psychoanalysis exercises an hermeneutic on the signs of an individual's life that indicate its distinctive manner of living this futile desire – whether authentically, for example, or inauthentically. Because pre-reflective consciousness has replaced the Freudian unconscious, Sartre considers it possible in principle to understand an individual completely, that is, to uncover his or her self-defining project in complete transparency. Like so many of the claims enunciated at the height of existentialist enthusiasm, the ideal of total transparency is qualified in Sartre's later works, where force of circumstance ('what we have been made into') modifies absolute freedom and ideology clouds individual awareness. But he remained true to the

Rousseauian concept of personal and social transparency, at least as an ideal.

The details of Sartre's love–hate relationship with Freud have yet to be recounted. On the one hand, he rejected the Freudian concept of the unconscious as being deterministic, and criticized Freud's 'censor' for being in bad faith (it both knows and does not know what is acceptable to consciousness). And yet he employs the concept of pre-reflective consciousness in a manner that imitates Freudian unconscious in important ways and allows the analyst to reveal to the analys- and meanings which he or she had hitherto not known (in a reflective sense). Preparing the never-to-be-filmed script for a John Houston movie, later published as *The Freud Scenario*, forced Sartre to rethink his ideas about the unconscious. He acknowledged finding Lacan's theory of the unconscious structured as a language less troublesome but did not go so far as to embrace the idea. As always, the concept of individual freedom-responsibility remained a non-negotiable.

Sartre's most ambitious exercise in existential psychoanalysis and most thorough use of the progressive–regressive method is his massive study of the life and work of Gustave Flaubert, *The Family Idiot* (1971–2). Numbering over three thousand pages in the original, it constitutes a kind of *summa* of Sartre's intellectual endeavours, embracing everything from ontology and psychoanalysis to literary and social criticism. It addresses the question, 'What at this point in time, can we know about a human being?' ([3.15], French, vol. 1, p. ix). A synthesis of existential psychoanalysis and historical materialism, the progressive –regressive method seeks to uncover Flaubert's basic project, namely, his 'choice' of the unreal-imaginary through adopting the 'neurotic' lifestyle that bourgeois society thrust upon any would-be artist of Flaubert's generation. As becomes usual in the second phase of Sartre's career, biography has broadened into social critique. What is both banal and profound in Sartre's undertaking is his attempt to comprehend Flaubert's life and times through the dialectical relationship between his progressive 'personalization' and the production and public reception of *Madame Bovary*. It is a commonplace to study the 'life and times' of a historical figure in mutual clarification. But there is something boldly 'rationalistic' about Sartre's attempt to understand why Flaubert had to write *Bovary* and how he could finally claim, 'I am Madame Bovary.'

Philosophy and literature

No thinker in our century more adequately brokers the marriage of these two disciplines than Sartre. His novels, short stories and plays gave him an audience denied to most philosophers, and his criticism, gathered with occasional pieces in the ten volumes of *Situations*, established him as a major voice in that domain. This was furthered by the journal of opinion and criticism, *Les Temps modernes*, which he founded at the end of the war. In a collection of articles published first in that journal and later as a book, *What is Literature?* (1947), Sartre defends his concept of 'committed literature' (*littérature engagée*). Given his ontological theses of the fundamental project and the possibility of bad faith, Sartre examines literary art in terms of the authenticity and inauthenticity, not merely of its content (which would smell of socialist critiques) but of its very form.

He distinguishes prose from what he calls generically 'poetry' and insists that the latter cannot be committed. Poetry employs its 'analogues' (words, musical sounds, painted surfaces and the like) as ends in themselves. They do not point beyond themselves to our being-in-the-world but undertake to short-circuit that outward movement by rendering the aesthetic object present-absent, that is, imaginatively present, for its own sake. We might say that, for Sartre, where prose looks beyond the pointed finger to the object indicated, 'poetry' focuses on the fingertip. If not precisely escapist, such art avoids the challenges of a period of crisis. Sartre believes that the postwar years form such a period. Hence his recommendation that artists should address social concerns and do so in a manner that 'gives the bourgeoisie a bad conscience'. Once he appropriates this advice himself, ironically about the time the Nobel Committee is preparing to award him the prize for literature, he all but abandons imaginative literature except for an adaptation of Euripides' *The Trojan Women* (1965) and his 'novel that is true' about Flaubert. And yet this very move to committed literature reveals that the distinction between poetry and prose is functional rather than substantive in the final analysis and that imaginative 'derealization' can constitute a form of social action even in genres that Sartre seemed to have dismissed as 'poetic'. In fact his early (1948) praise of black poetry in French as 'the only great revolutionary poetry of our time' ([3.36], vol. 3, p. 233) indicates that he had understood his original distinction in a functional manner from the start.

At this point we should summarize the elements of Sartre's aesthetic theory. Its foundation is the theory of imaging consciousness developed in *Psychology of Imagination*. It applies intentionality to the constitution of an 'aesthetic object' for which the physical artefact serves as *analogon*. Both cognitive and affective 'intentions' conspire to 'presentify', that is, to render imaginatively present-absent the object in an aesthetic mode. In the case of non-figurative art, the artefact serves as analogon for itself. Words or their grammatical and syntactical configuration form the analogue of the literary object, a 'world' with its proper space and time that is a 'derealization' of our real world of *praxis.* Given both the paradigmatic nature of imaging consciousness for Sartre and the extensional equivalence of 'consciousness' and 'freedom', it is not surprising to find him discussing the work of art as an 'invitation from one freedom to another' and interpreting artistic creativity as an act of generosity. In fact, invitation–response replaces command–obedience as the model for ideal social relations in Sartre's 'city of ends', as we shall now see.

Social philosophy

In his 'biography' of Jean Genet, Sartre avows: 'For a long time we believed in the social atomism bequeathed to us by the eighteenth century . . . . The truth is that "human reality" "is-in-society" as it "is-in-the-world"; it is neither a nature nor a state; it is made' ([3.32], 590). As we noted earlier, the possibility of developing an adequate social theory was hampered by Sartre's looking/looked-at model of interpersonal relations. At best, this ontology warranted the methodological individualism that his erstwhile friend Raymond Aron ascribed to him in the social realm. But by subsuming his philosophy of consciousness into one of praxis, Sartre increases qualitatively the social potential of his thought. Whereas there is no such thing as a plural look, except as a merely psychological experience (a basic claim of methodological individualists), there is a 'synthetic enrichment' of my action when it is incorporated into that of a group. 'We' can do many things that remain impossible for me alone.

Sartre's major contribution to social philosophy is made at the level of social ontology, the theory of individual and group identity and action. It takes the form of two concepts, the *practico-inert* and the *mediating third*. But to explain each we must first elucidate the notion of *praxis*, which is the pivot on which his social theory turns.

Praxis denotes purposive human activity in its cultural environment. It is distinct from human action *sans phrase* in being historical; its 'world' is a horizon of meanings that are already 'there', yet liable to interpretation in light of the ongoing project. But whereas the Husserlian discourse of intentions, meanings and noetic responsibility dominated the landscape of *Being and Nothingness*, Sartre displays a marked preference for the language of historical materialism in the *Critique of Dialectical Reason*. The basic form of praxis is *labour* as a response to material need. This original relationship overcomes whatever lingering idealism Sartre's theory may have been liable to and generates a dialectic of negation, negation of negation, and transcendence (*dépassement*) adapted from the Hegelio-Marxist tradition. If the early Sartre left the impression that one could simply change oneself rather than change the world, since the terms were correlative in any case, such 'Stoic' freedom is strongly opposed by the later Sartre, and the factical component of one's situation is finally given its due.

Functional heir to being-in-itself, the 'practico-inert' refers to the facticity of our social situation in its otherness, especially the material dimension of our cultural environment, as well as to those sedimented past *praxes* that return to haunt us. If the act of speaking is an instance of *praxis*, language is a form of the practico-inert. This is the category of 'counterfinality' whereby intended ends entail unintended consequences. Sartre's classic example is the deforestation by Chinese peasants that resulted in the very erosion from floods of the land they hoped to cultivate. Similarly, he employs this concept in his account of the impoverishment of the Spanish state through inflation caused by its hoarding of gold from its newly exploited American mines. Practico-inert 'mediation' is alienating, it steals one's activity the way the 'look' of the Other robs one of one's freedom in *Being and Nothingness*. And when qualified by material scarcity, practico-inert mediation renders human relations violent. Sartre describes violence as 'interiorized scarcity'. The fact that there is not enough of the goods of the world to go around colours human history as a tale of violence and terror. Towards the end of his life, Sartre admitted to Benny Lévy that he had never reconciled these fundamental features of social life, fraternity and violence. Both are essential to his social thought.

'Fraternity' is Sartre's term for the mutuality and positive reciprocity that constitute his social ideal and which are achieved, albeit temporarily, in the spontaneously formed action group. Most relations are 'serial' because they are mediated by the practico-inert. Most of the individuals who populate our world, from the television-viewing public to the people waiting for the same bus, are rendered serial by the 'false' or 'external' unity imposed on them by such collective objects as a television announcer or an expected bus. They are related among themselves as 'other' to 'other' – as competitors for scarce space, for example, or as fashioning their opinions as the newscaster dictates. Sartre notes that such 'serial impotence' is cultivated by dictators who wish to maintain an illusion of power on the part of their subjects in the midst of the latter's profound malleability.

In the 'apocalyptic' moment when people realize in a practical manner through a common project that they are 'the same', not 'other', and that each is performing the task which the other would do were he or she required to do so at this point, the 'We' emerges in a fusing group. Sartre's idealized example of such a genesis is the famous storming of the Bastille. Under threat from an external source, the crowd changes from serial dispersion to practical unity, from a mob to a group. By a performative utterance that effects what it describes, the cry 'We are a hundred strong!' in Sartre's imaginative reconstruction of the event creates a new entity: the fused group. The *mediating Third* is the ontological vehicle for this transformation. Unlike the objectifying voyeur of *Being and Nothingness*, the third party in group formation performs a mediating, not an alienating function. By subordinating purely personal or divisive concerns to general interest, he or she emerges as the 'common individual'. Mediation is exercised no longer via the practico-inert but by means of the *praxes* of 'common' individuals. Complete organic integration is impossible, Sartre continues to insist; some otherness always remains. But it is 'discounted', not fostered. He calls it 'free alterity' of the group in *praxis* as opposed to the serial otherness of the impotent collective.

A threefold primacy of *praxis* emerges in Sartre's later thought. At the ground is an *ontological* primacy. Even at the highest moment of social integration, the group-in-fusion, it is organic *praxes* who create and sustain the group. The entire 'inner life' of the group is a revolving circle of practical relations whereby each *praxis* 'interiorizes' the multiplicity of the rest. (Any member could have cried 'We are a hundred strong!') Even the practico-inert is not an autonomous force that renders us powerless. It is, after all, *practico*-inert; the *praxes* that it absorbs or deflects are still operative, though in alienated fashion. Sartre explicitly adopts the Marxist thesis that 'there are only individuals and real relations among them' ([3.35], 76). If Sartre's early work was a relentless rejection of idealism, his later, social theory is intent on avoiding organicism. The ontological primacy of *praxis* is his chief weapon in that campaign.

On this original primacy Sartre founds an *epistemological* and an *ethical* primacy as well. The epistemological primacy of *praxis* stems from the fact that comprehension is the consciousness of *praxis* and that we can comprehend the other's comprehension through the progressive–regressive method. This is an elaboration of the *Verstehende* sociology of Dilthey, Weber and others, placed in service of an historical materialist conception of social change. But unlike Marxist 'economism', the comprehension Sartre seeks comes to rest in the *praxis*-project of the organic individual. Sartre summarized the difference in a memorable line: 'Valéry is a petit bourgeois intellectual. . . . But not every petit bourgeois intellectual is Valéry' ([3.35], 56).

Because individual *praxis* sustains the most impersonal economic laws, like the 'iron law of wages', and the most 'necessary' practico-inert processes, such as the colonialist system, one can ascribe existential-moral responsibility to the serialized 'agents' whose passive activity carries them out. In other words, one cannot escape responsibility by appeal to facticity. For Sartre the moralist, the spark of human freedom-responsibility is unquenchable: you can always make something out of what you have been made into.

Philosophy of history

A glance at the posthumously published *War Diaries* which Sartre kept during the Phoney War of 1939–40 reveals that his interest in the topic was not the result of his so-called conversion to Marxism after the war. But he does set the matter aside in *Being and Nothingness*, reserving a lengthy discussion of morality and history for his *Notebooks for an Ethics*, again not published in his lifetime. In the *Diaries*, his dialogue is primarily with Raymond Aron, whose two volumes on the philosophy of history had just been published. In criticism of Aron, Sartre enunciates a thesis that will be formative of his existential approach to history ever after: the only way to achieve historical *unity* is by studying the lived appropriation of historical events by an individual agent. What is being sketched at this early stage is the rationale of his existential psychoanalyses of the next decades. If history is to be more than the positivist concatenation of facts and dates, it must come to life in the projects of the historical agent. This is more than psychohistory, to which it exhibits a marked resemblance, because of Sartre's characteristic moral concerns as well as the historical materialist dimension which he will introduce after the war.

In the *Notebooks* Sartre indicates that an existentialist theory of history will have to respect the paradox of moral responsibility. At this stage the dialogue is with Hegel and the French Hegelians, Kojève and Hyppolite. The existentialist individual makes an 'end' to history inconceivable: any totality of which consciousness is part will be a 'detotalized' totality. Although he speaks of positive reciprocity, the generosity–gift relationship and good faith in ways that correct the one-sided, pessimistic view of interpersonal relations conveyed in *Being and Nothingness*, these notes remain in thrall to the looking/looked-at model of the social. Accordingly, the theory of history is faced with seemingly insurmountable difficulties as it attempts to interrelate the individual and the social, morality and history.

It is in the two volumes of the *Critique of Dialectical Reason*, where the dialogue is now with Merleau-Ponty's criticism of his social thought in the latter's *The Adventures of Dialectic*, that Sartre formulates the philosophy of *praxis* and its attendant social ontology that enable him to construct a theory of history that accounts for collective action and counterfinalities, recognizes the specificity of the socio-historical, and reserves pride of place for existential-moral responsibility on the part of organic individuals. Since his *War Diaries*, it has been clear that the root problem for an existentialist theory is the relationship between biography and history. He treats this matter apropos of Joseph Stalin and the Soviet Union in the 1930s in his posthumously published notes for volume 2 of the *Critique*, but the relation of biography to history receives its most extended consideration in *The Family Idiot* (especially in volume 3 of the French edition).

❧ SARTRE AND TWENTIETH-CENTURY ❧ CONTINENTAL PHILOSOPHY

Although one of the few major twentieth-century philosophers not to be associated with academe for most of his career, Sartre was professionally trained and remained in dialogue with academic philosophy all of his life. Any assessment of his thought should address his relationship to the leading philosophical movements of his time.

Existential phenomenology

It was Gabriel Marcel who first called Sartre an 'existentialist'. By the time of his famous public lecture, *Existentialism is a Humanism* (1945), his name had become synonymous with the movement. Indeed, it was in part to separate himself from association with Sartrean existentialism that Heidegger denied he was an existentialist and wrote his groundbreaking *Letter on Humanism* (1947) to explain why. We have noted Sartre's debt to Husserlian phenomenology throughout this chapter. In *Being and Nothingness* he criticizes Hegel, Husserl and Heidegger at several junctures but clearly has adopted numerous concepts from each. While it is a gross exaggeration to characterize Sartre's masterwork as '*Being and Time* translated into French', the similarities as well as the profound differences between each thinker are underscored by comparing the two works. As soon as a French translation of Heidegger's 1930 lecture *The Essence of Truth* appeared (1948), Sartre wrote a lengthy response. It was published posthumously as *Truth and Existence* (1989).

Sartre was a close collaborator with Simone de Beauvoir in the sense that they read each other's work prior to publication, and she completed several of the lacunae in his social ethic in the mid-1940s with her *The Ethics of Ambiguity*. Despite its obvious originality, Merleau-Ponty's *The Phenomenology of Perception* shows numerous signs of Sartrean influence, even as it takes Sartre to task for his 'Cartesianism'. But we noted that the *Critique* seems to be a response to the trenchant criticism levelled by Merleau-Ponty in his *Adventures of the Dialectic* against a Sartrean social philosophy. Sartre's indebtedness both to Merleau-Ponty and to Kierkegaard is recounted in memorial essays he penned in honour of each ('Merleau-Ponty Alive' (1961) and 'Kierkegaard: The Singular Universal' (1966)).

The 'existential turn' that Husserl's phenomenological movement took, if initiated by Heidegger, was completed by Sartre. To the extent that such phenomenology grew increasingly anthropological and ethical, it became associated with its French practitioners. The phenomenological method was enriched and its limitations as an approach to history were compensated for by the progressive–regressive method. This last, as we noted, is a synthesis of existential psychoanalysis and historical materialism. The former places it in direct line with the hermeneutic tradition of interpreting symbolic action; the latter relates Sartre's method to more 'scientific' (in the Hegelian sense) approaches to historical intelligibility.

Marxism

Sartre's 'Marxism' was always adjectival to his existentialism. In the late 1940s, he advised the workers to support the Communist Party *faute de mieux*, while refusing to join it himself. In *Search for a Method*, he declares Marxism 'the philosophy of our times' and even makes it synonymous with 'knowledge' (*savoir*). But he described the *Critique of Dialectical Reason*, to which *Search* served as a kind of preface, as an 'anti-communist book' and in his last years explicitly denied he was a Marxist. Still, historical materialism (the Marxist theory of history) is operative in *The Family Idiot* as well as in his other writings after the late 1950s.

Sartre joins that group of Marxists known as 'revisionists' in that they question or reject totally the Marxist dialectic of nature (DIAMAT) and emphasize the humanistic dimension of Marx's writings. In *Search for a Method*, Sartre announces that his mission in this regard is 'to conquer man within Marxism' ([3.35], 83). It is because of their failure to respect the moral dimension of human action, that Sartre abandoned even fellow-travelling in favour of *les maos* after the events in Paris of 1968. This odyssey is recounted in his discussion with two members of that group, published as *On a raison de se révolter* (1974).

Structuralism

The structuralist movement in France as exemplified by the work of Althusser, Lacan, Lévi-Strauss, Barthes and others in the 1960s is commonly credited with having replaced existentialism as the reigning Parisian 'philosophy'. This is true to a large extent, though that school of thought was subsequently eclipsed by poststructuralist writers. Sartre occasionally criticized the structuralists for ignoring history in general and human agency in particular – essential existentialist concerns. But even a cursory reading of the *Critique of Dialectical Reason* will reveal the important role that Sartre reserves for structural factors in his account. The 'formal conditions' revealed by the regressive movement of the progressive–regressive method are arguably structural. In fact, the major portion of volume 1 of the *Critique* is synchronic and structural. Whether it is thereby 'structuralist' depends on the meaning of the term. Clearly, Sartre opposed it as a system because of its inadequacy to existential experience. And its binary relations, he would accept only as complementing the dialectical, totalizing 'Reason' that he was elucidating in the *Critique*.

The ontological locus of structural relations in his social ontology is the practico-inert. Recall that language as such, for him, is practico-inert. So too is analytical, as distinct from dialectical, reason. Sartre speaks of the practico-inert and hence of structure as non-historical and even 'anti-dialectical'. But this must be taken in the context of the totalizing activity of *praxis*, which renders these structures historically relevant. The 'platonizing' tendencies of structuralist thought are tempered by Sartre's 'dialectical nominalism', an approach to ontology and epistemology that respects the qualitative difference between individual and collective phenomena as well as the irreducibility of the latter to the former, while insisting on the threefold primacy of free organic praxis. Dialectical nominalism is a middle ground between holism and individualism in the methodology of the social sciences.

Postmodernism

Foucault once referred to Sartre as the last of the nineteenth-century philosophers. It was not only his interest in History with a Hegelian 'H' and his seeming fixation on Flaubert that generated this remark. It was equally Sartre's philosophy of the subject, of freedom and of moral indignation that lay behind Foucault's words. And yet one can find several strikingly 'postmodern' theses in Sartre's work. These would make valuable contributions to the current philosophical conversation and deserve closer scrutiny by contemporary thinkers. By way of conclusion let us consider three.

Postmodern thinking is noted for its 'evacuation of the subject' from current discourse. In so far as the 'subject' in question is the Cartesian *res cogitans*, Sartre never held that position. His concept of 'presence to self' instead of a substantial self or ego, with its attendant 'circuit of selfness' rather than an outer spatio-temporal plane, leaves Sartre free to consider the fluidity of subjectivist discourse and speak of the self as an achievement rather than an origin. The constitution of a moral 'self', to which Foucault devoted his last years, could have been the topic of a Sartrean treatise.

There is an aesthetic strain in Sartre's thought, owing to the paradigmatic role that he accords imaging consciousness. Postmodern critics from Lyotard to Foucault have shown a marked preference for aesthetic categories as well, even to the point of advocating the Nietz-schean aestheticist injunction to 'make one's life a work of art'. Not that Sartre should ever be accused of aestheticism. But his reading of history is certainly 'poetic', and his existential biographies as 'novels that are true' suggest a fruitful field of future inquiry and dialogue with postmodern writers.

The Nietzschean inspiration of Sartre's thought has not received the attention it deserves, especially since the 'postmodern' Nietzsche has emerged. Sartre's early essay 'The Legend of Truth', written in 1929, is profoundly Nietzschean in content and tone. The general problem of contingency and chance, which Foucault wished to reintro-duce into postmodern historiography, was an abiding theme of Sartre's existentialist thought. It surfaces again in the posthumous *Notebooks for an Ethics*. The career of Nietzschean interpretation forms another link between Sartre and postmodern thinkers.

And yet it would be excessive to refer to Sartre as a 'postmodern'. He was a thinker of *unities*, not of fragments. His emphasis on inten-tional consciousness and later on totalizing *praxis* was meant to counter the historical pluralism of Raymond Aron as well as the brute facts of the positivists. And his corresponding commitments aimed at effecting socio-economic changes that would make it possible for 'freedoms' to recognize one another. He shared the neo-Stoic belief of postmoderns that one should try to maximize freedom even though there is no hope of complete emancipation. But he persevered in the hope that such a 'city of ends' might be possible and urged people to work to realize its advent. Again, we encounter the integral role of the imagination in effecting a meaning-direction (*sens*) to history.

If Sartre is to be remembered as an important and influential philosopher of the twentieth century, it will be as much for the consist-ency of his commitment to individual freedom as for the insights of his phenomenological descriptions and the force of his categories (bad faith, authenticity, practico-inert, and the like). When he died, the press likened him to Voltaire and noted that we had lost the conscience of our age. It is as moralist, philosopher of freedom and philosopher of the imagination that he made his most memorable contributions. Despite the Teutonic length of his sentences, especially in the later works, he was a quintessential Gallic philosopher.

❧ SELECT BIBLIOGRAPHY ❧

References to the original French texts are given below only in cases where the translations in the text of the chapter are by the author and not from the published versions.

Translations

3.1 *Anti-Semite and Jew*, trans. G. J. Becker, New York: Schocken, 1948.

3.2 *Being and Nothingness*, trans. H. E. Barnes, New York: Philosophical Library, 1956.

3.3 *Between Existentialism and Marxism*, trans. J. Mathews, New York: William Morrow, 1974.

3.4 'Cartesian Freedom', in [3.18], 180–97.

3.5 *The Communists and Peace* with *A Reply to Claude Lefort*, trans. M. H. Fletcher and P. R. Berk respectively, New York: Braziller, 1968.

3.6 *The Condemned of Altona*, trans. S. and G. Leeson, New York: Random House, Vintage Books, 1961.

3.7 'Consciousness of Self and Knowledge of Self', in N. Lawrence and D. O'Connor (eds), *Readings in Existential Phenomenology*, Englewood Cliffs: Prentice-Hall, 1967.

3.8 *Critique of Dialectical Reason*, 2 vols: vol. 1 *Theory of Practical Ensembles*, trans. A. Sheridan-Smith, London: NLB, 1976; vol 2, *The Intelligibility of History*, trans. Q. Hoare, London: Verso, 1991. An emended edition of vol. 1 was produced by A. Elkam-Sartre, *Critique de la raison dialectique* précédé de *Questions de méthode*, vol. 1, *Théorie des ensembles pratiques*, Paris: Gallimard, 1985.

3.9 *The Devil and the Good Lord*, trans. K. Black, New York: Random House, Vintage Books, 1960.

3.10 *Ecrits de Jeunesse*, ed. M. Contat and M. Rybalka, Paris: Gallimard, 1990.

3.11 *The Emotions: Outline of a Theory*, trans. B. Frechtman, New York: Philosophical Library, 1948.

3.12 *Entretiens sur la politique*, with D. Rousset and G. Rosenthal, Paris: Gallimard, 1949.

3.13 'Existentialism is a Humanism', in *Existentialism from Dostoevsky to Sartre*, selected and intro. W. Kaufmann, Cleveland: World Publishing, Meridian Books, 1956.

3.14 'Hope, Now . . . Sartre's Last Interview', *Dissent*, 27 (1980): 397–422.

3.15 *L'Idiot de la famille*, 3 vols, Paris: Gallimard, 1971–2, vol. 3 revised edn, 1988; vols 1 and 2 trans. C. Cosman as *The Family Idiot*, 4 vols, Chicago: University of Chicago Press, 1981–91.

3.16 'Intentionality: A Fundamental Idea of Husserl's Phenomenology', *Journal of the British Society for Phenomenology*, 1:2 (1970): 4–5.

3.17 'Introducing *Les Temps modernes*, in [3.41], 247–67.

3.18 *Life/Situations: Essays Written and Spoken*, trans. P. Auster and L. Davis, New York: Pantheon, 1977.

3.19 *Literary and Philosophical Essays*, trans. A. Michelson, New York: Crowell-Collier, Collier Books, 1962.

3.20 'A Long, Bitter, Sweet Madness', *Encounter*, 22 (1964): 61–3.

3.21 *Marxisme et existentialisme: Controverse sur la dialectique*, with R. Garaudy, J. Hyppolite, J. P. Vigier, and J. Orcel, Paris: Plon, 1962.

3.22 'Materialism and Revolution', in [3.18], pp. 198–256.

3.23 'Merleau-Ponty', in [3.36], vol. 4, pp. 189–287.

3.24 *Nausea*, trans. L. Alexander, New York: New Directions, 1959.

3.25 *'No Exit' and Three Other Plays*, trans. L. Abel, New York: Random House, Vintage Books, 1955.

3.26 *Notebooks for an Ethics*, trans. D. Pellauer, Chicago: University of Chicago Press, 1992.

3.27 *Oeuvres Romanesques*, ed. M. Contat and M. Rybalka with G. Idt and G. H. Bauer, Paris: Gallimard, 1981.

3.28 *On a raison de se révolter*, with P. Gavi and P. Victor, Paris: Gallimard, 1974.

3.29 *On Genocide*, intro. A. Elkaïm-Sartre, Boston: Beacon, 1968.

3.30 *The Psychology of Imagination*, trans. B. Frechtman, New York: Washington Square Press, 1966; *L'Imaginaire*, Paris: Gallimard, 1940.

3.31 'The Responsibility of the Writer', in *Reflections on Our Age*, intro. D. Hardiman, New York: Columbia University Press, 1949.

3.32 *Saint Genet, Actor and Martyr*, trans. B. Frechtman, New York: Braziller, 1963.

3.33 *Sartre on Theater*, ed. M. Contat and M. Rybalka, trans. F. Jellinek, New York: Pantheon, 1976.

3.34 *Sartre, un film*, produced by A. Astruc and M. Contat, Paris: Gallimard, 1977.

3.35 *Search for a Method*, trans. H. E. Barnes, New York: Random House, Vintage Books, 1968.

3.36 *Situations*, 10 vols, Paris: Gallimard, 1947–6.

3.37 *The Transcendence of the Ego*, trans. F. Williams and R. Kirkpatrick, New York: Noonday Press, 1957.

3.38 *Truth and Existence*, trans. A. van den Hoven, Chicago: University of Chicago Press, 1992.

3.39 'L'Universel singulier', in [3.36], vol. 9, pp. 152–90; 'Kierkegaard: The Singular Universal', in [3.2], pp. 141–69.

3.40 *War Crimes in Vietnam*, with V. Dedier, Nottingham: The Bertrand Russell Peace Foundation, 1971.

3.41 *The War Diaries*, trans Q. Hoare, New York: Pantheon, 1984.

3.42 *What is Literature? and Other Essays*, trans. B. Frechtman *et al.*, intro. S. Ungar, Cambridge, Mass.: Harvard University Press, 1988.

3.43 *The Words*, trans. B. Frechtman, New York: Braziller, 1964.

3.44 Preface to *The Wretched of the Earth* by F. Fanon, trans. C. Farrington, New York: Grove Press, 1968.

Bibliographies

3.45 Contat, M. and Rybalka, M. *The Writings of Jean-Paul Sartre*, 2 vols, Evanston: Northwestern University Press, 1974. Updated in *Magazine littéraire*, no. 103–4 (1975): 9–49; and in *Obliques*, 18–19 (1979): 331–47.

3.46 Contat, M. and Rybalka, M. *Sartre: Bibliographie 1980–1992*, Paris: CNRS, 1993.

3.47 Lapoint, F. and C. *Jean-Paul Sartre and His Critics: An International Bibliography (1938–1980)*, 2nd edn, rev., Bowling Green: Philosophy Documentation Center, 1981.

3.48 Wilcocks, R. *Jean-Paul Sartre: A Bibliography of International Criticism*, Edmonton: University of Alberta Press, 1975.

Criticism

3.49 Anderson, T. C. *The Foundation and Structure of Sartrean Ethics*, Lawrence: Regents Press of Kansas, 1979.

3.50 Aron, R. *History and the Dialectic of Violence*, trans. B. Cooper, Oxford: Basil Blackwell, 1975.

3.51 Aronson, R. *Jean-Paul Sartre*, New York: New Left Books, 1980.

3.52 Aronson, R. *Sartre's Second Critique*, Chicago: University of Chicago Press, 1987.

3.53 Aronson, R. and van den Hoven, A. (eds), *Sartre Alive*, Detroit: Wayne State University Press, 1991.

3.54 Barnes, H. E. *Sartre*, New York: Lippincott, 1973.

3.55 Barnes, H. E. *Sartre and Flaubert*, Chicago: University of Chicago Press, 1981.

3.56 Bell, L. A. *Sartre's Ethics of Authenticity*, Tuscaloosa: University of Alabama Press, 1989.

3.57 Burnier, M. A. *Choice of Action*, trans. B. Murchland, New York: Random House, 1968.

3.58 Busch, T. W. *The Power of Consciousness and the Force of Circumstances in Sartre's Philosophy*, Bloomington: Indiana University Press, 1990.

3.59 Cannon, B. *Sartre and Psychoanalysis*, Lawrence: University Press of Kansas, 1991.

3.60 Catalano, J. S. *A Commentary on Jean-Paul Sartre's 'Being and Nothingness'*, Chicago: University of Chicago Press, 1980.

3.61 Catalano, J. S. *A Commentary on Jean-Paul Sartre's 'Critique of Dialectical Reason,' Volume 1*, Chicago: University of Chicago Press, 1986.

3.62 Caws, P. *Sartre*, London: Routledge, 1979.

3.63 Collins, D. *Sartre as Biographer*, Cambridge, Mass.: Harvard University Press, 1980.

3.64 Danto, A. C. *Jean-Paul Sartre*, New York: Viking Press, 1975.

3.65 de Beauvoir, S. *Adieux: A Farewell to Sartre*, trans. P. O'Brian, New York: Pantheon, 1984.

3.66 de Beauvoir, S. *Letters to Sartre*, trans. and ed. Q. Hoare, New York: Arcade, 1991.

3.67 Desan, W. *The Marxism of Jean-Paul Sartre*, Garden City: Doubleday Anchor Books, 1965.

3.68 Detmer, D. *Freedom as Value*, La Salle: Open Court, 1986.

3.69 Fell, J. *Emotion in the Thought of Sartre*, New York: Columbia University Press, 1965.

3.70 Fell, J. *Heidegger and Sartre: An Essay on Being and Place*, New York: Columbia University Press, 1979.

3.71 Flynn, T. R. *L'Imagination au Pouvoir*: The Evolution of Sartre's Political and Social Thought', *Political Theory*, 7:2 (1979): 175–80.

3.72 Flynn, T. R. 'Mediated Reciprocity and the Genius of the Third', in [3.83], 345–70.

3.73 Flynn, T. R., *Sartre and Marxist Existentialism: The Test Case of Collective Responsibility*, Chicago: University of Chicago Press, 1984.

3.74 Hollier, D. *The Politics of Prose*, trans. J. Mehlman, Minneapolis: University of Minnesota Press, 1986.

3.75 Howells, C. (ed.), *The Cambridge Companion to Sartre*, Cambridge: Cambridge University Press, 1992.

3.76 Jameson, F. *Marxism and Form*, Princeton: Princeton University Press, 1971.

3.77 Jeanson, F. *Sartre and the Problem of Morality*, trans. and intro. R. V. Stone, Bloomington: Indiana University Press, 1981.

3.78 McBride, W. L. *Fundamental Change in Law and Society: Hart and Sartre on Revolution*, The Hague: Mouton, 1970.

3.79 McBride, W. L. *Sartre's Political Theory*, Bloomington: Indiana University Press, 1991.

3.80 Merleau-Ponty, M. *Adventures of the Dialectic*, trans J. Bien, Evanston: Northwestern University Press, 1973.

3.81 Murdoch, I. *Sartre, Romantic Rationalist*, New Haven: Yale University Press, 1953.

3.82 Poster, Mark, *Sartre's Marxism*, London: Pluto Press, 1979.

3.83 Schilpp, P. A. (ed.) *The Philosophy of Jean-Paul Sartre*, La Salle: Open Court, 1981.

3.84 Silverman, H. J. *Inscriptions: Between Phenomenology and Structuralism*, London: Routledge, 1987.

3.85 Silverman, H. J. and Elliston, F. A. (eds) *Jean-Paul Sartre: Contemporary Approaches to his Philosophy*, Pittsburgh: Duquesne University Press, 1980.

3.86 Verstraaten, P. *et al. Sur les écrits posthumes de Sartre*, Bruxelles: Editions de l'université de Bruxelles, 1987.

Journal issues devoted to Sartre

3.87 *L'Arc*, 30 (1966).
3.88 *Journal of the British Society for Phenomenology*, 12 (1970).
3.89 *Magazine Littéraire*, 55–6 (1971) and 103–4 (1975).
3.90 *Obliques*, 18–19 (1979) and 24–5 (1981).
3.91 *Les Temps modernes*, 2 vols, nos 531–3 (1990).

CHAPTER 4

Philosophy of existence 3
Merleau-Ponty
Bernard Cullen

à Henri Godin

❧❦❧

❧❦ LIFE AND WORKS ❦❧

Maurice Merleau-Ponty was born on 14 March 1908 into a petty bour-geois Catholic family in Rochefort-sur-Mer on the west coast of France. When he died suddenly, at his desk, on 3 May 1961, he was widely regarded as France's most brilliant and most profound philosopher.

After his father, an artillery officer, died in 1913, the young Maurice grew up in Paris, in the company of his mother, a brother and a sister. He told Jean-Paul Sartre, in 1947, that he had never recovered from an incomparably happy childhood ([4.99], 230). Schooled, as were all philosophy students of his generation, in a distinctively French philo-sophical tradition dominated by Cartesianism, he entered the most elite establishment for the study of philosophy in France, the Ecole Normale Supérieure in Paris, in 1926. It was there he first made the acquaintance of Sartre, in circumstances he was to recount twenty years later in the course of an affectionate defence of that 'scandalous author' against his detractors on the right and on the left: 'the Ecole Normale unleashed its fury against one of my schoolmates and myself for having hissed the traditional songs, too vulgar to suit us. He slipped between us and our persecutors and contrived a way for us to get out of our heroic and ridiculous situation without concessions or damages' ([4.22], 41). Simone de Beauvoir describes in her autobiographical novel *Memoirs of a Duti-ful Daughter*, under the fictitious name Pradelle, her friend and fellow student Merleau-Ponty, a rather serious but optimistic young searcher after truth who still attended mass.

At the Ecole Normale, Merleau-Ponty's main teacher was the

idealist Léon Brunschvicg. In the academic year 1928–9, he prepared a dissertation on Plotinus, under the supervision of Emile Bréhier. Between 1928 and 1930, he attended a series of lectures given at the Sorbonne by Georges Gurvitch on contemporary German phenomenology, especially the writings of Husserl, Scheler and Heidegger; and in February 1929, he attended the lectures given at the Sorbonne by Husserl himself, which were revised and published two years later as the *Cartesian Meditations*. One phrase from those lectures recurs as a leitmotiv throughout Merleau-Ponty's work: 'It is "pure and, in a way, still mute experience which it is a question of bringing to the pure expression of its own significance" ' ([4.18], 219; cf. [4.24], 129 and [4.21], 188). The growing interest in German philosophy within Parisian philosophical circles was not confined to phenomenology. The year 1929 also saw the publication of Jean Wahl's pioneering book *Le Malheur de la conscience dans la philosophie de Hegel (The Unhappy Consciousness in the Philosophy of Hegel)*.

After graduating in second place in the 1930 examinations for the *agrégation en philosophie* (the qualification required to prepare candidates for the *baccalauréat*) and carrying out a year's compulsory military service, Merleau-Ponty taught philosophy in *lycées* in Beauvais and Chartres. He taught himself German. (For his own account of his researches at this time into the nature of perception, together with a list of the works he read in 1933–4, see [4.60], 188–99.) In 1935, he was appointed as a tutor at the Ecole Normale, where he remained until mobilization in 1939. His first two published works, in the Catholic journal *La Vie intellectuelle*, were sympathetic critical notices of the French translation of Max Scheler's book on *'ressentiment'* (1935) and *Etre et avoir* by Gabriel Marcel (1936). (For a summary of these articles, see [4.60], 13–24.)

In the mid-1930s, he began to deepen his study of Marx, especially the writings of the young Marx. From 1935, he attended the influential lectures by Alexandre Kojève at the Ecole Pratique des Hautes Etudes on Hegel's *Phenomenology of Spirit* – a reading of Hegel deeply influenced by the writings of the young Marx, subsequently published under the title *Introduction à la lecture de Hegel*. But around this time (and until the end of 1937), he was still closely associated with the left-leaning Catholic journals *Esprit* and *Sept*. The closure of *Sept*, on instructions from the Vatican, was probably the final blow to his religious faith. In the same way, the publication in 1939 of the reports of the Moscow trials of Bukharin and twenty others the previous year must have influenced his decision not to commit himself to membership of the French Communist Party.

His minor doctoral thesis, *The Structure of Behavior*, was completed in 1938 (though not published in book form until 1942). In early 1939, Merleau-Ponty became acquainted with a special issue of the *Revue internationale de philosophie* devoted to Husserl (who had died in April 1938). The references therein, especially by Eugen Fink, to Husserl's last book, *The Crisis of the European Sciences and Transcendental Phenomenology*, whetted his appetite to learn more about this work, only the first part of which had been published. At the beginning of April, he was the very first visitor to the Husserl Archive at Louvain in Belgium (whence the Husserl papers had been hurriedly moved), where he read the entirety of *The Crisis, Ideas II*, and a number of other unpublished pieces. (See [4.110].) These brief encounters undoubtedly had a decisive influence on the way in which Merleau-Ponty appropriated the later thought of Husserl and incorporated it into the heart of his own philosophy.

The outbreak of war forced Merleau-Ponty to interrupt his research. After a year as a second lieutenant, he was appointed to a post in the Lycée Carnot, where he remained until 1944, when he took over from Sartre as senior philosophy teacher at the Lycée Condorcet. In the meantime, in 1941, he had encountered Sartre again, when he joined Socialism and Liberty, one of the many groups, as Sartre put it, 'which claimed to be resisting the conquering enemy' ([4.99], 231). As Sartre tells it in his remarkably moving extended obituary, the two men immediately recognized their common interests: 'The key words were spoken: phenomenology, existentialism. We discovered our real concern. Too individualist to ever pool our research, we became reciprocal while remaining separate. . . . Husserl became our bond and our division, at one and the same time' ([4.99], 231).

Throughout this period, Merleau-Ponty continued to work on his principal doctoral thesis and philosophical masterpiece, the *Phenomenology of Perception*, which was accepted and published in 1945. Appointed lecturer in philosophy at the University of Lyons, he was made professor in 1948. He combined these duties with editing the left-wing, anti-colonialist journal *Les Temps modernes*, which with Sartre and Simone de Beauvoir he had founded shortly after the Liberation. (See [4.99], 247–53.) He was the journal's (anonymous) political editor and editor-in-chief, writing most of the editorials (unsigned) and many lengthy articles (signed), several of them later gathered in his book *Humanism and Terror: an Essay on the Communist Problem*, published in 1947. Others were gathered in the collection *Sense and Non-Sense*, published in 1948. According to Sartre's reminiscences, 'the review belonged to him. He had defined its political orientation, and I had followed him' ([4.99], 283). From 1949 to 1952, he occupied the chair of child psychology and pedagogy at the Sorbonne; and in 1952, at the unusually early age of 44, he was appointed to the most prestigious position for an academic philosopher in France, the chair of philosophy at the Collège de France. He gave his inaugural lecture, entitled *In Praise of Philosophy*, at the Collège on 15 January 1953.

Relations with Sartre had been cooling for some time: they disagreed deeply over the role of the Communist Party and the actions of the Soviet Union before and during the Korean War, and Merleau-Ponty resigned as editor-in-chief of *Les Temps modernes* in 1952. Almost half of the book in which, in 1955, Merleau-Ponty renounced his adherence to Marxism, *Adventures of the Dialectic*, was devoted to a merciless critique of 'Sartre and ultrabolshevism'. A further collection of essays was published under the title *Signs* in 1960. His last published work, *Eye and Mind*, had just appeared in the journal *Art de France* when Merleau-Ponty died suddenly on 3 May 1961, from a stroke, aged 53. The divisions between him and Sartre had been gradually healing. Merleau-Ponty had taken the opportunity of his Introduction to *Signs* to record in print his affectionate admiration for Sartre. He counters Sartre's harsh self-criticism (in his Preface to *Aden Arabie*, by their mutual friend Paul Nizan) with the observation that 'his accursed lucidity, in lighting up the labyrinths of rebellion and revolution, has recorded in spite of himself all we need to absolve him' ([4.23], 24). Sartre, for his part, records his surprise and delight when Merleau-Ponty unexpectedly turned up, shortly before his death, at a lecture Sartre gave at the Ecole Normale. Among his many posthumous publications, the two most important are *The Prose of the World* (notes dating from 1950–2) and the unfinished manuscript of the book on which he was working at the time of his death, *The Visible and the Invisible*.

❧ THE PRIMACY OF PERCEPTION ❧

In a paper he wrote in 1952 to support his candidacy for the chair of philosophy at the Collège de France, Merleau-Ponty offers a brief summary of the themes of his work thus far, before proceeding to outline his plans for future research. He begins by referring to 'the perceived world which is simply there before us, beneath the level of the verified true and the false'. His first two works, he goes on, 'sought to restore the world of perception' ([4.21], 3). Beginning with the insight that the mind that perceives is an incarnated mind, his writings have tried to establish and illustrate the inadequacy of both behaviourism and idealism and to overcome this dualism by recourse to the fundamental reality of the perceiving body-subject.

He had already announced this programme of work in the opening sentence of his Introduction to *The Structure of Behavior*: 'Our goal is to understand the relations between consciousness and nature.'

Rejecting philosophical approaches that emphasize either the 'pure exteriority' of the objects of perception or the 'pure interiority' of the perceiving subject, Merleau-Ponty insists that the world as perceived is not a sum of objects of our perception; and our relation to the world is not that of a disembodied thinker to an object of thought. What must not be forgotten is 'the insertion of the mind in corporeality, the ambiguous relation which we entertain with our body and, correlatively, with perceived things' ([4.21], 4).

This means that the classical Aristotelian/Kantian distinction between form and matter is misleading. We cannot conceptualize the world to be perceived as disordered 'matter' on which the perceiving mind (or consciousness), through the use of reason, imposes 'form' or in which it deciphers 'meaning'. 'Matter is "pregnant" with its form, which is to say that in the final analysis every perception takes place within a certain horizon and ultimately in the "world" '([4.21], 12). Perception, for Merleau-Ponty, is not a conscious activity of the mind: perception is the mode of existence of the body-subject at a pre-conscious level, the dialogue between the body-subject and its world at a level that is presupposed by consciousness. At the same time, 'the perceived world is the always presupposed foundation of all rationality, all value and all existence' ([4.21], 13).

In *The Structure of Behavior*, his first published book, Merleau-Ponty considers this theme of the relations between perceiving persons and the world in which they live and perceive through an examination of certain physiological and psychological theories, principally behaviourism and *Gestalt* psychology. He exposes the inadequacy of behaviourism by showing that we cannot explain the facts of perceptual life by conceptualizing the relation between the perceiving organism and its milieu in terms of an automatic machine whose pre-established mechanisms are brought to life by reaction to external stimuli. 'The true stimulus is not the one defined by physics and chemistry; the reaction is not this or that particular series of movements; and the connection between the two is not the simple coincidence of two successive events' ([4.20], 99). Behaviourism, in other words, is false as a model of perceptual behaviour.

So is idealism. It is not a question of superimposing a pure, thinking consciousness on a brute, thinglike body. Within the realms of physics or mechanics, a body can legitimately be seen as a thing among things. But the scientific point of view is itself an abstraction. 'In the conditions of life . . . the organism is less sensitive to certain isolated physical and chemical agents than to the constellation which they form and to the whole situation which they define' ([4.21], 4). Furthermore, the behaving organism displays a kind of 'prospective activity', as if it were oriented towards the meaning of certain elementary situations, 'as if it entertained familiar relations with them, as if there were "an *a priori* of the organism", privileged conducts and laws of internal equilibrium which predisposed the organism to certain relations with its milieu' ([4.21], 4). Higher-order behaviours bring out new forms or shapes of the milieu, in correlation with the meaning-conferring activity of the behaving subject. Perceptual behaviour emerges from these relations to a situation and to an environment which are not the working of a pure, knowing subject.

In the *Phenomenology of Perception*, his major published work, Merleau-Ponty takes for granted the emergence of perceptual behaviour and installs himself in it 'in order to pursue the analysis of this exceptional relation between the subject and its body and its world'. The book seeks to illustrate how the body is not 'an object in the world, under the purview of a separated spirit. . . . It is our point of view on the world, the place where the spirit takes on a certain physical and historical situation' ([4.21], 4–5). Although space does not permit any more than a cursory glance at this long and densely textured treatise, it is worth lingering on its Preface, one of the classic texts in the history of phenomenology.

This is Merleau-Ponty's phenomenological manifesto, one that is clearly indebted to the unpublished works of Husserl which he had first inspected in 1939 in Louvain. This is the Husserl who emphasized the *Lebenswelt*, the life-world in which all thinking, perceiving and acting takes place. According to Merleau-Ponty, phenomenology is

> a philosophy which puts essences back into existence, and does not expect to arrive at an understanding of man and the world from any starting point other than that of their 'facticity'. . . . It is also a philosophy for which the world is always 'already there' before reflection begins – as an unalienable presence; and all its efforts are concentrated upon re-achieving a direct and primitive contact with the world, and endowing that contact with a philosophical status.
>
> ([4.18], vii)

The first feature of this phenomenology is that it is a rejection of science: 'I am not the outcome or the meeting-point of numerous causal agencies which determine my bodily or psychological make-up.' I cannot conceive of myself as 'a mere object of biological, psychological or sociological investigation. . . . The whole universe of science is built upon the world as directly experienced, and if we want to subject science itself to rigorous scrutiny and arrive at a precise assessment of its meaning and scope, we must begin by reawakening the basic experience of the world of which science is the second-order expression' ([4.18], viii). If the world as understood by phenomenology is 'always already there', it is not the 'objective' world of zoology, social anatomy or inductive psychology, since 'I am the absolute source, my existence does not stem from my antecedents, from my physical and social environment; instead it moves out towards them and sustains them, for I alone bring into being for myself . . . the tradition which I elect to carry on' ([4.18], ix). To return 'to the things themselves' (an earlier rallying cry of Husserlian phenomenology) is to return to 'the world that precedes knowledge', the world of which science always speaks. In relation to this primordial world, science is an abstract and derivative sign-language, as is geography in relation to the countryside in which we already recognize a forest, a meadow or a river. The purpose of phenomenology is to analyse these perceptual foundations which precede knowledge and upon which our knowledge is built ([4.18], ix).

Also in the Preface to the *Phenomenology of Perception*, Merleau-Ponty offers a revised version of Husserl's 'phenomenological reduction', a way of looking at the world which enables us to see just how embedded in it we actually are. 'It is because we are through and through compounded of relationships with the world that for us the only way to become aware of the fact is to suspend the resultant activity, to refuse it our complicity.' It is because the certainties of common sense and the 'natural attitude' to things are the presupposed basis of any thought that they are taken for granted and go unnoticed. Only by applying the phenomenological reduction, by suspending for the time being our recognition of them, can we bring them into view. Reflection 'steps back [from the world] to watch the forms of transcendence fly up like sparks from a fire; it slackens the intentional threads which attach us to the world and thus brings them to our notice; it alone is consciousness of the world because it reveals that world as strange and paradoxical'. Not only is the philosopher a perpetual beginner, but 'philosophy consists wholly in the description of its own beginning'. It is in this sense that phenomenology 'belongs to existential philosophy', the philosophy that interrogates Heidegger's 'being-in-the-world' ([4.18], xiii).

In the course of this personal restatement of phenomenological principles, Merleau-Ponty considers the notion of intentionality, at the same time sketching out his own understanding of history. Unlike the Kantian relation to a possible object, phenomenological intentionality assumes that the unified world that is already there is the world that is 'lived' by me. What Husserl calls 'operative intentionality' is the way in which consciousness knows itself to be a project of the world, 'meant for a world which it neither embraces nor possesses, but towards which it is perpetually directed'. Operative intentionality 'produces the natural and antepredicative unity of the world and of our life, being apparent in our desires, our evaluations, and in the landscape we see, more clearly than in objective knowledge, and furnishing the text which our knowledge tries to translate into precise language' ([4.18], xviii).

These are the dimensions of history, the events that are never without meaning. In seeking to understand a doctrine, it must be examined from the point of view of ideology, politics, religion, economics and psychology – all at the same time! 'All these views are true provided that they are not isolated, that we delve deeply into history and reach the unique core of existential meaning which emerges in each perspective. It is true, as Marx says, that history does not walk on its head, but it is also true that it does not think with its feet.' Neither head nor feet are paramount, of course: all aspects of a life are captured in 'the body'. In an obvious reference to Sartre's famous claim that 'we are condemned to freedom', Merleau-Ponty concludes this discussion of intentionality and history with the thought that 'because we are in the world, we are condemned to meaning, and we cannot do or say anything without its acquiring a name in history' ([4.18], xix).

The above discussion leads naturally into a discussion of the individual's relations with other people. To the extent that phenomenology unites extreme subjectivism and extreme objectivism in its notion of rationality, it discloses the way in which 'perspectives blend, perceptions confirm each other, a meaning emerges'. Phenomenological rationality exists neither in an ideal world proper to absolute spirit nor in the real world of scientific investigation and knowledge. The phenomenological world is the sense or meaning (*sens*) revealed where the paths of the individual's various experiences intersect; and also 'where my own and other people's intersect and engage each other like gears'. With this image of the meshing of gears (*l'engrenage*), Merleau-Ponty seeks to capture both subjectivity and intersubjectivity, 'which find their unity when I either take up my past experiences in those of the present, or other people's in my own' ([4.18], xx).

THE PHENOMENOLOGY OF SPEECH, LANGUAGE AND ART

The *Phenomenology of Perception* largely consists of a series of studies on the role of the body and perception in various aspects of social and cultural experience: speech and language, expression, sexuality, art and literature, time, freedom and history. Space limitations preclude here more than a few cursory glances in this direction. When I perceive in my world cultural artefacts as varied as roads and churches, or implements such as a bell, a spoon or a pipe, 'I feel the close presence of others beneath a veil of anonymity'. The challenge is: how can the word 'I' be put into the plural? When it comes to 'other selves', contact is established through my perception of other bodies. 'It is precisely my body which perceives the body of another, and discovers in that other body a miraculous prolongation of my own intentions, a familiar way of dealing with the world. Henceforth, as the parts of my body together comprise a system, so my body and the other's are one whole, two sides of one and the same phenomenon' ([4.18], 354).

But bodies only establish initial (mostly visual) contacts. The most important cultural phenomenon in the perception of other people as people (as distinct from simply living beings) is language (*le langage*). In the experience of dialogue, a common ground is constituted between the other person and myself. 'My thought and the thought of the other are interwoven into a single fabric.' Neither my interlocuter nor I invented the language that enables us to communicate: 'our words are inserted into a shared operation of which neither of us is the creator. . . . Our perspectives merge into each other, and we coexist through a common world' ([4.18], 354). Coexistence does not remove the fact of solitude, but solitude and communication are 'two "moments" of one phenomenon, since in fact other people do exist for me' ([4.18], 359). Indeed, I would not even be in a position to speak of solitude, much less declare others inaccessible to me, if I did not have the experience of other people.

Language, then, is discovered by me in my phenomenal field and used by me for expression and communication with others in that shared antepredicative world. One of the uses to which language is put, of course, is literature; and literature, for Merleau-Ponty, is firmly embedded in the lived world of politics and economics. In a long note on the existential interpretation of historical materialism, tagged on to the end of the chapter of the *Phenomenology of Perception* devoted to 'the body in its sexual being' ([4.18], 171–3), Merleau-Ponty writes that 'the existential conception of history' rejects the idea that our actions are *determined* by socio-economic factors in our situation. It does not, however, deny that our actions are *motivated* by such factors. 'If existence is the permanent act by which man takes up, for his own purposes, and makes his own a certain *de facto* situation, none of his thoughts will be able to be quite detached from the historical context in which he lives, and particularly from his economic situation.'

This applies to the philosopher, to the revolutionary and to the artist. It would be ridiculous, writes Merleau-Ponty, to see Paul Valéry's poetry as simply the product of his economic circumstances. But it would not be absurd 'to seek, in the social and economic drama, in the world of our *Mitsein*, the motive of this coming to awareness'. The act of the artist (or the philosopher) is a free act, but it is not motiveless. The freedom of the artist is not exercised in a vacuum, completely divorced from the world of shared experience; 'it consists in appropriating a *de facto* situation by endowing it with a figurative meaning beyond its real one'.

Every aspect of our life 'breathes a sexual atmosphere' (as Freud showed), without our ever being able to identify a single content of consciousness that is either 'purely sexual' or without any sexual content whatsoever. In the same way, all our lives are suffused with 'the social and economic drama' which provides each one of us (the artists as well as everyone else) with an inescapable element of the stuff of our existence, which we set about deciphering and reappropriating in our own distinctive way.

> Thus does Valéry transmute into pure poetry a disquiet and solitude of which others would have made nothing. Thought is the life of human relationships as it understands and interprets itself. In this voluntary act of carrying forward, this passing from objective to subjective, it is impossible to say just where historical forces end and ours begin, and strictly speaking the question is meaningless, since there is history only for a subject who lives through it, and there is a subject only in so far as he is historically situated.
>
> ([4.18], 172–3)

We have barely touched on Merleau-Ponty's impressive, but scattered, phenomenology of expression. Most of his more important studies on language, literature, culture and art – which he defined as 'the progressive awareness of our multiple relations with other people and the world' ([4.22], 152) – are gathered in the collections *Sense and Non-Sense* and (especially) *Signs*, which he prefaced with an Introduction (1960) that helps to situate these studies within his evolving philosophical project. *Eye and Mind* ([4.21], 159–90) is his important late essay on painting. The unfinished manuscript abandoned in 1952 and published posthumously as *The Prose of the World* was conceived, in inspiration at least, as a response to Sartre's *What is Literature?* It could be said that the phenomenon of language became, in one way or another, the main focus for all of Merleau-Ponty's subsequent work. In this respect, he is at one with the other great philosophers of the twentieth century, in both the continental and analytic traditions – one thinks of figures such as Heidegger and Wittgenstein, Gadamer, Ricoeur, Austin and Searle. In Merleau-Ponty's case, language is the entry point for a more profound understanding of human interrelations – which, he writes in 1952, 'will be the major topic of my later studies' ([4.21], 9). The meaning of language consists in 'the common intention' of its constituent elements; 'and the spoken phrase is understood only if the hearer, following the "verbal chain", goes beyond each of its links in the direction that they all designate together' ([4.21], 8). In that direction (as we shall see below) lies Being. (For an excellent summary of Merleau-Ponty's views on these topics, see [4.74], 78–86. For a more extended discussion of his theory of existential expression and communication, see [4.82].)

❧ EXISTENTIAL FREEDOM, HISTORY ❧ AND POLITICS

In the immediate aftermath of the Liberation, taking stock of what had been learned in the experience of the war and the occupation, Merleau-Ponty declared that in the course of the war 'we have learned history, and we claim that it must not be forgotten' ([4.22], 150). Not surprisingly, his conception of history, and the role of the individual in history, was forged in the crucible of his wartime experience. The final chapter of the *Phenomenology of Perception* (written at this time) is devoted to a dialectical encounter with Sartre's notorious theory of 'absolute freedom' (with its obvious implications for our understanding of history and historical *praxis*), as presented to the world only a year or two earlier in *Being and Nothingness*.

The first three pages of this final chapter outline, roughly, the Sartrean position. However, Merleau-Ponty points out that the problem with Sartre's radical opposition between the determinism of the brute in-itself ('scientism's conception of causality') and the absolute freedom of the conscious for-itself ('divorced from the outside') is that it would appear to rule out the possibility of freedom altogether. If it is true that our freedom is the same in everything we do, if the slave who continues to live in fear is as free as the one who breaks his or her chains (or anyone else, indeed), then there can be no free action, since freedom obviously, as in this example, has nothing to do with actions. Furthermore, 'free action, in order to be discernible, has to stand out against a background of life from which it is entirely, or almost entirely, absent' ([4.18], 437). If freedom is everywhere (since it is simply the mark of human being, or being for-itself), then, says Merleau-Ponty, it is nowhere. The very idea of action, the very idea of choice, disappears, 'for to choose is to choose *something* in which freedom sees, at least for a moment, a symbol of itself'. Freedom implies a struggle, freedom must be striven for; freedom must make a decision. If freedom is already achieved without free actions, as it would be in a Sartrean world, then free actions become redundant (ibid.). What is required instead is a theory of freedom that 'allows it something without giving it everything' ([4.22], 77).

Merleau-Ponty works out what this 'something' is by resuming his analysis of *Sinngebung*: that is, interpretation, or, literally, the bestowal of significance on situations. If we accept that there is 'no freedom without a field', and if we reject as non-phenomenological the Kantian idea (which Sartre often seems to adopt) of a consciousness which 'finds in things only what it has put into them', then our understanding of *Sinngebung* must involve the intermeshing of both the conditions of possibility of perception (the body-subject) and the conditions of reality of perception (the world of situations in which I find myself).

To say that a particular rock is unclimbable makes sense only if I entertain the project of climbing it; the attribute 'unclimbable' (like all attributes) can be conferred upon the rock only by 'a human presence'. 'It is therefore freedom which brings into being the obstacle to freedom, so that the latter can be set over against it as its bounds' ([4.18], 439). But given that I have the project to get from A to B, not every rock will appear to me as unclimbable. My freedom does not contrive it that this way there is an obstacle to my progress and that way there is a way through, but it does arrange it for there to be obstacles and ways through in general. Without my 'human presence' there would be neither obstacles nor ways through. But it is crucially important to distinguish: my freedom 'does not draw the particular outline of the world, but merely lays down its general structures' (ibid.).

The general structures of the world, which dictate that some mountains are climbable while others are not, are to be found not out there, in an in-itself, but within me. Irrespective of my 'express intentions' (for example, my plan to climb those mountains next week), my 'general intentions' evaluate the potentialities of my environment: for example, the fact that they exceed my body's power to take them in its stride. This brings us back to Merleau-Ponty's fundamental insight involving the body-subject's 'insertion in the world': underlying myself as a thinking and deciding subject there is 'as it were a natural self which does not budge from its terrestrial situation' ([4.18], 440). All the 'free' choices in the world will not obviate this fundamental relationship: 'in so far as I have hands, feet, a body, I sustain around me intentions which are not dependent upon my decisions and which affect my surroundings in a way which I do not choose' (ibid.).

To use Merleau-Ponty's terminology (borrowed from the *Gestalt* psychologists), these 'general intentions' are the ever-present 'ground' against which my decisions are 'figures'. This ground is 'general' in the sense that it constitutes a system in which all possible objects are simultaneously included; and also in the sense that it is not simply mine but something I share with 'all psycho-physical subjects organized as I am'. For we are all indeed 'intermingled with things'. While it is true that none of those things constitutes an obstacle unless we ordain it so, the self which qualifies them as such is not some acosmic subject. . . . There is an autochthonous significance of the world which is constituted in the dealings which our incarnate existence has with it, and which provides the ground of every deliberate *Sinngebung*.

([4.18], 441)

In the same way as the mountain that constitutes an obstacle is 'my obstacle', the pain that makes me 'say what I ought to have kept to myself' is 'my pain', and the fatigue that makes me break my journey is 'my fatigue'. According to Sartre, I am always free to transform my being in the world, including my chosen tolerance of pain or fatigue. But Merleau-Ponty draws attention to the fact that this transforming for-itself does not operate as if I had no yesterdays. Rejecting Sartre's famous contention that 'existence precedes essence', he insists that a theory of freedom must recognize 'a sort of sedimentation of our life: an attitude towards the world, when it has received frequent confirmation, acquires a favoured status for us' (ibid.). While it's all very well to claim that the self is always free to change the habits of a lifetime, Merleau-Ponty insists that 'having built our life upon an inferiority complex which has been operative for twenty years, it is not *probable* that we shall change' ([4.18], 442).

To the objection of the rationalist (such as Sartre) that my freedom to change is either total or non-existent, that just as there are no degrees of possibility there are no degrees of freedom, Merleau-Ponty retorts that 'generality and probability are not fictions, but phenomena; we must therefore find a phenomenological basis for statistical thought' (ibid.). Statistical thought simply addresses the fact that I have a past which, 'though not a fate' (since my past does not totally determine my future), 'has at least a specific weight and is not a set of events over there, at a distance from me, but the atmosphere of my present'. Drawing once again on the image of *l'engrenage*, Merleau-Ponty concludes that 'our freedom does not destroy our situation, but gears itself to it' (ibid.). (Cf. Merleau-Ponty's application of the Freudian concepts of repression and fixation to 'personal time' and 'the ambiguity of being in the world', [4.18], 83–5. For a discussion, see [4.49].)

The past, therefore, does not determine my future, but neither is my history irrelevant. History – my own personal history and the history of the wider community within which I live – provides the context within which I make my choices. And Merleau-Ponty illustrates this conception of conditioned freedom by reference to the question of the development of class consciousness and the decision to be a revolutionary. He again seeks to discover a third way between the two traditional abstractions. Objective (Marxist) thought derives class consciousness from the objective material conditions; and idealist reflection reduces the condition of being a proletarian to the individual's awareness of it. But 'in each case we are in the realm of abstraction, because we remain torn between the *in itself* and the *for itself*'. What is necessary is a return to the phenomena, 'to the things themselves': instead of abstractions, we must apply 'a genuinely existential method'.

A person's objective position in the production process will never in itself issue in class consciousness; rather, it is the decision of individuals to become revolutionaries that prompts them to see themselves as proletarians. 'What makes me a proletarian is not the economic system or society considered as systems of impersonal forces, but these institutions as I carry them within me and experience them; nor is it an intellectual operation devoid of motive, but my way of being in the world within this institutional framework' ([4.18], 443). The transition from individual self-description to class solidarity with others takes place through a growing awareness that 'all share a common lot' ([4.18], 444). 'Social space begins to acquire a magnetic field, and a region of the exploited is seen to appear' ([4.18], 445). Neither the status quo nor the free revolutionary action that might overturn it is an abstraction; 'they are lived through in ambiguity' (ibid.). To be a member of a social class is not only to be intellectually aware of the fact; it is to identify oneself with a group 'through an implicit or existentialist project which merges into our way of patterning the world and co-existing with other people' ([4.18], 447).

This is not to say that one cannot at any moment amend one's existential project. What one cannot do is pretend to be a nothingness (*néant*) and choose oneself out of nothing. 'My actual freedom is not on the hither side of my being, but before me, in things.' It is misleading to say (as Sartre does) that I continually choose myself; and that to choose not to choose is still to choose. 'Not to refuse is not the same thing as to choose' ([4.18], 452). In the lived world, there is never determinism and never absolute choice; I am never either a 'being' or a 'nothingness'. We are involved in the world and with others 'in an inextricable tangle' ([4.18], 454). This significant life, this certain significance of nature and history that makes me what I am, far from cutting me off from the rest of the world, makes it possible for me to remain in communication with the rest of the world. Philosophy, which teaches us to see things in the world and in history in all their clarity and in all their ambiguity, best performs its role by ceasing to be (intellectualizing) philosophy. In the words of Saint-Exupéry with which Merleau-Ponty closes the *Phenomenology of Perception*: 'Man is but a network of relationships, and these alone matter to him' ([4.18], 456).

(Merleau-Ponty published a wide range of articles on the role of the individual in history and politics, varieties of Marxism, the role of the Communist Party, and the Soviet Union. Most of these were collected in *Sense and Non-Sense, Signs, Humanism and Terror* (a polemical riposte to Arthur Koestler's *Darkness at Noon*), and *Adventures of the Dialectic*. For the best extended discussions of Merleau-Ponty's philosophical politics, see 4.119 and 4.130.)

THE HYPERDIALECTIC OF THE FLESH

In the prospectus of his future work written in 1952, Merleau-Ponty writes: 'my first two works sought to restore the world of perception.' As we have seen, all aspects of our life are underpinned by antepredicative perception, the specifically human mode of inherence in the world in which we all live. Looking to the future, he goes on: 'my works in preparation aim to show how communication with others, and thought, take up and go beyond the realm of perception which initiated us to the truth' ([4.21], 3). He wishes to go beyond the 'bad ambiguity' of his works already published and articulate a 'good ambiguity', 'a spontaneity which gathers together the plurality of monads, the past and the present, nature and culture into a single whole. To establish this wonder would be metaphysics itself' ([4.21], 11). He himself saw the enormous philosophical achievement represented by the works we have been examining thus far in this chapter as furnishing only the groundwork for the ontology that was to be the work of his mature years. His elaboration of this ontology of 'the flesh' is contained in a number of works published posthumously, but especially in the incomplete manuscript entitled *The Visible and the Invisible*.

It is impossible to exaggerate just how ambitious Merleau-Ponty's mature project really is. He proposed to go beyond (or below, for he frequently returns to the metaphor of archaeology) the traditional philosophical categories of realism and idealism, subject and object, consciousness and world, in-itself and for-itself, being and nothingness, the knower and the known, and discover in that scarcely penetrable region what he called 'the flesh of the world', the primordial stuff in which we all inhere and which is the ultimate ground of all human experience. It is also impossible to give any more than a flavour of this dense and enigmatic text, available to us in the form of 160 pages of an apparently finished methodological introduction, followed by a remarkable chapter entitled 'The intertwining – the chiasm' (*L'entrelacs – le chiasme*) and about 110 pages of working notes. I shall do no more here than draw attention to a few key terms introduced by Merleau-Ponty in these pages: the notion of 'hyperdialectic', and the related concepts of 'the flesh' and 'the chiasm'.

When Merleau-Ponty addresses the theory of dialectic in *The*

Visible and the Invisible, he has in his sights the dialectic of Sartre's *Being and Nothingness*. Sartre's dialectic is a 'bad dialectic'. It is a fixed opposition, presented in terms of theses, where reflection imposes an external law and framework upon the content of experience.

> It is with this intuition of Being as absolute plenitude and absolute positivity, and with a view of nothingness purified of all the being we mix into it, that Sartre expects to account for our primordial access to the things.... From the moment that I conceive of myself as negativity and the world as positivity, there is no longer any interaction.... We are and remain strictly opposed.
>
> ([4.24], 52)

The only 'good dialectic', on the other hand, is what he calls 'the hyperdialectic'. A good dialectic is a 'dialectic without synthesis' which must be constantly aware that every thesis is but an idealization, an abstraction from the lived world of experience. 'What we call hyperdialectic is a thought that ... is capable of reaching truth because it envisages without restriction the plurality of the relationships and what has been called ambiguity' ([4.24], 94). What Merleau-Ponty is working towards is 'a dialectical definition of being that can be neither the being for itself nor the being in itself ... that must rediscover the being that lies before the cleavage operated by reflection, about it, on its horizon, not outside of us and not in us, but there where the two movements cross, there where "there is" something' ([4.24], 95).

Where the two movements cross, of course, is the body. The body is simultaneously part of the world of things and the thing that sees and feels things. The body (which is itself visible) can see things not because they are objects of consciousness, at a distance from it, but precisely because those things are the environment in which the seeing body exists. These two aspects of the body (seen and seer, visible and invisible) are inseparably intertwined: 'the experience of my body and the experience of the other are themselves the two sides of one same being' ([4.24], 225). This intertwining at the most fundamental and primordial level, this anonymous generality of the visible and myself, is what Merleau-Ponty calls 'the flesh' (*la chair*).

'There is no name in traditional philosophy to designate it' ([4.24], 139). The flesh is not matter and it is not mind. It is not substance. In a manner that recalls Heidegger, Merleau-Ponty goes back to the pre-Socratic thinkers to try to express what he means:

> to designate it, we should need the old term 'element', in the sense it was used to speak of water, air, earth, and fire, that is, in the sense of a *general thing*, midway between the spatio-temporal individual and the idea, a sort of incarnate principle that brings a

style of being wherever there is a fragment of being. The flesh is in this sense an 'element' of Being.

(ibid.)

To underline the oneness of this primordial element of Being, Merleau-Ponty names it the 'flesh of the world': 'My body is made of the same flesh as the world, . . . this flesh of my body is shared by the world, the world *reflects* it, encroaches upon it and it encroaches upon the world, . . . they are in a relation of transgression or of overlapping' ([4.24], 248). Merleau-Ponty's overriding concern, as it has been throughout his philosophical career, is to offer a phenomenological description of reality that gets beneath the spurious distinction between extension and thought, between the visible and the invisible. He is not suggesting an identity of thought and extension; the key image is that 'they are the obverse and the reverse of one another' ([4.24], 152). But we are all part of the same 'flesh of the world'. We situate ourselves in ourselves *and* in the things, in ourselves *and* in the other, 'at the point where, by a sort of *chiasm*, we become the others and we become world' ([4.24], 160). The word 'chiasm' (*le chiasme*) recalls the intersection of lines in the manner of the Greek letter *chi* (χ), emphasizing the inextricable interlocking of the various aspects of Being, of the perceived and the perceiver, of the visible and the invisible.

One final theme must be mentioned in this brief examination of *The Visible and the Invisible* and that is the important strategic role of language. 'Language is a life, is our life and the life of the things' ([4.24], 125). Parallel to the reverse/obverse relation of the visible and the invisible, language is always considered by Merleau-Ponty against the background of silence: 'language lives only from silence; everything we cast to the others has germinated in this great mute land which we never leave' ([4.24], 126). Because they have experienced within themselves 'the birth of speech [*la parole*] as bubbling up at the bottom of [their] mute experience', no one knows better than philosophers 'that what is lived is lived-spoken (*vécu-parlé*)'.

Language is 'the most valuable witness to Being' (ibid.). Furthermore, language is a witness to Being that does not disrupt the unity of Being, since 'the vision itself, the thought itself, are, as has been said [by Lacan], "structured as a language", are *articulation* before the letter, apparition of something where there was nothing or something else' (ibid.). The speaking word (*la parole parlante*), which brings to the surface all the deep-rooted relations of the lived experience wherein it takes form, the language of life and of action, and also the language of literature and of poetry, is the very theme of philosophy. Of course, philosophy itself is 'that language that can be known only from within, through its exercise, is open upon the things, called forth by the voices of silence, and continues an effort of articulation which is the Being of every being' (ibid.).

❧ CONCLUDING REMARKS ❧

As we come to the close of this brief survey of Merleau-Ponty's *œuvre*, we must take stock. In my view, Merleau-Ponty is one of the great figures of twentieth-century philosophy, a pivotal figure in mid-century: drawing deeply on and creatively reappropriating earlier masters such as Saussure, Husserl and Heidegger, while his formidable presence is evident (albeit indirectly) in the structuralist, poststructuralist and deconstructionist thinkers in the generation that came immediately behind him.

Merleau-Ponty himself always loudly proclaimed his allegiance to Husserl, especially the Husserl of the *Crisis* and the theme of the life-world. Now, Merleau-Ponty's phenomenology was undoubtedly originally inspired by Husserl. And Husserl (as uniquely and creatively interpreted by Merleau-Ponty) remained a living presence throughout his work. But it is arguable that there is more Heidegger than Husserl in Merleau-Ponty's philosophy. First, there is the centrality of time: for Merleau-Ponty as for Heidegger, human existence is essentially temporal existence. Second, there is the privileging of language in both cases, as was illustrated in the last section. In the famous saying in *The Letter on Humanism*, Heidegger proclaims that 'language is the house of Being' ('die Sprache ist das Haus des Seins'). In *The Visible and the Invisible*, Merleau-Ponty writes that language is 'the most valuable witness to Being' ([4.24], 126). Third, there is Merleau-Ponty's intention – like Heidegger – to offer a comprehensive description of Being. It has to be said, however, that while Heidegger's Being (*Sein*) is ontologically distinct from beings (*Seiendes*), Merleau-Ponty's Being is inclusive of both *Sein* and *Seiendes*.

Some of Merleau-Ponty's recurring themes also prefigure subsequent dominant trends in continental philosophy. It is not incidental that his first book was entitled *The Structure of Behavior*. He carried out a detailed study of both the *Gestalt* psychologists and Saussure's structural linguistics and lectured on Saussure in 1949. To the last book he published he gave the title *Signs*. Merleau-Ponty was clearly at the centre of the emerging philosophical schools known as structuralism and semiotics. His continual and deepening polemic against Sartre's privileging of the choosing subject reflected the growing decentring of the subject in his own work, a theme which in turn becomes central to the later deconstructionist approach to philosophy. (For an interesting discussion of Merleau-Ponty's move 'from philosophy to non-philosophy', see [4.103], 123–51).

So what was Merleau-Ponty's main contribution to the continental philosophy of this century? Perhaps more than any other philosopher, Merleau-Ponty was determined to overcome the dualism between mind and matter, between subject and object, which had dominated European philosophy since Descartes. The contemporary representative *par excellence* of the Cartesian tradition was, of course, Merleau-Ponty's friend/foe Sartre. We have seen above how Merleau-Ponty constantly pitched his own philosophical approach against Sartre's radical dualism between the thinking and choosing for-itself and the in-itself that is the object of thought. Merleau-Ponty was always a phenomenologist. His fundamental philosophical impulse was always to describe 'the things themselves'; and he opposed dualism simply because it did not offer an adequate description of the phenomena.

It has been suggested that Merleau-Ponty's late philosophy represents a radical break with his earlier phenomenology of perception. I do not agree with this view. Despite the new terminology he developed in the 1950s, his philosophical work is all of a piece; and his later search for a new fundamental ontology can be seen in germ (and sometimes in more than germ) in the *Phenomenology of Perception*, for example in the chapter on the *cogito*. While it is true that he was concerned in his final years that the basic terminology of the *Phenomenology of Perception* (perceiver and perceived) retained remnants of the old dualism, the fact that he was determined to go further and ground the phenomenology of perception in 'the flesh of the world' in no way implies a rejection of the basic thrust and the achievement (as far as it goes) of the earlier work.

Rather, as he expressed it in a working note of January 1959, Merleau-Ponty's concern was to 'deepen' his first two books within the perspective of an ontology which would finally dissolve the subject/object polarity. This implies only that those first two books constitute the indispensable starting point of his philosophical project and not its terminus. His abiding concern was to provide a full description of the world. His new ontology would go beyond his earlier phenomenology and provide the radical new foundations for such a description. He makes it clear in *The Visible and the Invisible* that the basic philosophical stance is one of 'interrogation'. Merleau-Ponty's profound philosophical questions have not yet received an adequate answer.

❧ SELECT BIBLIOGRAPHY ❧

Primary texts

4.1 *La Structure du comportement*, Paris: Presses Universitaires de France, 1942.

4.2 *Phénoménologie de la perception*, Paris: Gallimard, 1945.

4.3 *Humanisme et terreur: Essai sur le problème communiste*, Paris: Gallimard, 1947.

4.4 'Le Primat de la perception et ses conséquences philosophiques', *Bulletin de la Société Française de Philosophie*, 41 (1947): 119–135 and discussion 135–53.

4.5 *Sens et non-sens*, Paris: Nagel, 1948.

4.6 *Eloge de la philosophie*, Paris: Gallimard, 1953.

4.7 *Les Aventures de la dialectique*, Paris: Gallimard, 1955.

4.8 *Signes*, Paris: Gallimard, 1960.

4.9 'Préface' to A. Hesnard, *L'Œuvre de Freud et son importance pour le monde moderne*, Paris: Payot, 1960, 5–10.

4.10 'Un Inédit de Maurice Merleau-Ponty' [1952], *Revue de métaphysique et de morale*, 67 (1962): 401–9.

4.11 *Le Visible et l'Invisible, suivi de notes de travail* [1959–61], ed. C. Lefort, Paris, Gallimard, 1964.

4.12 *L'Œil et l'esprit* [1961], Paris, Gallimard, 1964.

4.13 'Pages d' "Introduction à la prose du monde" ' [1950–1], ed. C. Lefort, *Revue de métaphysique et de morale*, 72 (1967): 137–53.

4.14 *Résumés de cours, Collège de France, 1952–1960*, ed. C. Lefort, Paris: Gallimard, 1968.

4.15 *L'Union de l'âme et du corps chez Malebranche, Biran et Bergson: prises au cours à l'Ecole Normale Supérieure (1947–48)*, ed. J. Deprun, Paris: Vrin, 1968.

4.16 *La Prose du monde* [1950–1], ed. C. Lefort, Paris: Gallimard, 1969.

4.17 'Philosophie et non-philosophie depuis Hegel' [spring 1961], ed. C. Lefort, *Textures*, 8–9 (1974): 83–129 and 10–11 (1975): 145–73.

Translations

4.18 *Phenomenology of Perception*, trans. C. Smith, London: Routledge & Kegan Paul and Atlantic Highlands: Humanities Press, 1962.

4.19 *In Praise of Philosophy*, trans. J. Wild and J. M. Edie, Evanston: Northwestern University Press, 1963.

4.20 *The Structure of Behavior*, trans. A. L. Fisher, Boston: Beacon Press, 1963.

4.21 *The Primacy of Perception and Other Essays on Phenomenological Psychology, the Philosophy of Art, History and Politics*, ed. J. M. Edie, Evanston: Northwestern University Press, 1964. Includes (pp. 3–11) 'An Unpublished Text by Maurice Merleau-Ponty: A Prospectus of his Work', trans. A. B. Dallery, a translation of [4.10] above; and (pp.

159–90) 'Eye and Mind', trans. C. Dallery, a translation of [4.12] above.

4.22 *Sense and Non-Sense*, trans. H. L. Dreyfus and P. Allen Dreyfus, Evanston: Northwestern University Press, 1964.

4.23 *Signs*, trans. R. C. McCleary, Evanston: Northwestern University Press, 1964.

4.24 *The Visible and the Invisible, followed by Working Notes*, ed. C. Lefort, trans. A. Lingis, Evanston: Northwestern University Press, 1968.

4.25 'Phenomenology and Psychoanalysis: Preface to Hesnard's *L'Œuvre de Freud*', trans. A. L. Fisher, in A. L. Fisher (ed.), *The Essential Writings of Merleau-Ponty*, New York: Harcourt, Brace & World, 1969, pp. 81–7.

4.26 *Humanism and Terror: An Essay on the Communist Problem*, trans. with notes by J. O'Neill, Boston: Beacon Press, 1969.

4.27 *Themes from the Lectures at the Collège de France 1952–1960*, trans. J. O'Neill, Evanston: Northwestern University Press, 1970.

4.28 *The Prose of the World*, trans. J. O'Neill, Evanston: Northwestern University Press, 1973.

4.29 *Adventures of the Dialectic*, trans. J. Bien, Evanston: Northwestern University Press, 1973.

4.30 *Consciousness and the Acquisition of Language*, trans. H. J. Silverman, Evanston: Northwestern University Press, 1973.

4.31 *Phenomenology, Language and Sociology: Selected essays of Maurice Merleau-Ponty*, ed. J. O'Neill, London: Heinemann, 1974. (Contains articles already available elsewhere.)

4.32 'Philosophy and Non-Philosophy since Hegel', trans. H. J. Silverman, *Telos*, 29 (1976): 39–105; reprinted in H. J. Silverman (ed.), *Philosophy and Non-Philosophy since Merleau-Ponty*, New York and London: Routledge, 1988, pp. 9–83.

Bibliographies

4.33 Lanigan, R. L. 'Maurice Merleau-Ponty Bibliography', *Man and World*, 3 (1970): 289–319.

4.34 Métraux, A. 'Bibliographie de Maurice Merleau-Ponty', in X. Tilliette [4.109 below], 173–86.

4.35 Geraets, T. F. [4.60 below], 200–9.

4.36 Lanigan, R. L. 'Bibliography' [annotated], in [4.82 below], 210–43.

4.37 Lapointe, F. H. 'The Phenomenological Psychology of Sartre and Merleau-Ponty: A Bibliographical Essay', *Dialogos*, 8 (1972): 161–82.

4.38 Lapointe, F. and Lapointe, C. C. *Maurice Merleau-Ponty and his Critics: An International Bibliography (1942–1976)*, New York: Garland, 1976.

4.39 Whiteside, K. 'The Merleau-Ponty Bibliography: Additions and Corrections', *Journal of the History of Philosophy*, 21 (1983): 195–201.

Criticism: General studies

4.40 Alquié, F. 'Une philosophie de l'ambiguïté: L'existentialisme de Maurice Merleau-Ponty', *Fontaine*, 59 (1947): 47–70.

4.41 Ballard, E. G. 'The Philosophy of Merleau-Ponty', *Tulane Studies in Philosophy*, 9 (1960): 165–87.

4.42 Bannan, J. F. 'The "Later" Thought of Merleau-Ponty', *Dialogue*, 5 (1966): 383–403.

4.43 Bannan, J. F. 'Merleau-Ponty on God', *International Philosophical Quarterly*, 6 (1966): 341–65.

4.44 Bannan, J. F. *The Philosophy of Merleau-Ponty*, New York: Harcourt, Brace & World, 1967.

4.45 Barral, M. R. *Merleau-Ponty: The Role of the Body-Subject in Interpersonal Relations*, Pittsburgh: Duquesne University Press, 1965.

4.46 Bayer, R. *Merleau-Ponty's Existentialism*, Buffalo: University of Buffalo Press, 1951.

4.47 Caillois, R. 'De la perception à l'histoire: la philosophie de Maurice Merleau-Ponty', *Deucalion*, 2 (1947): 57–85.

4.48 Carr, D. 'Maurice Merleau-Ponty: Incarnate Consciousness', in G. A. Schrader, Jr (ed.) *Existential Philosophers: Kierkegaard to Merleau-Ponty*, New York: McGraw-Hill, 1967, pp. 369–429.

4.49 Cullen, B. ' "Repression" and "Fixation" in Merleau-Ponty's Account of Time', *Journal of the British Society for Phenomenology*, forthcoming.

4.50 Daly, J. 'Merleau-Ponty's Concept of Phenomenology', *Philosophical Studies (Ireland)*, 16 (1967): 137–64.

4.51 Daly, J. 'Merleau-Ponty: A Bridge between Phenomenology and Structuralism', *Journal of the British Society for Phenomenology*, 2 (1971): 53–8.

4.52 de Waehlens, A. *Une philosophie de l'ambiguïté: L'existentialisme de Maurice Merleau-Ponty*, Louvain: Publications Universitaires de Louvain, 1951.

4.53 Dillon, M. C. *Merleau-Ponty's Ontology*, Bloomington: Indiana University Press, 1988.

4.54 Dufrenne, M. 'Maurice Merleau-Ponty', *Les études philosophiques*, 36 (1962): 81–92.

4.55 Edie, J. M. *Merleau-Ponty's Philosophy of Language: Structuralism and Dialectics*, Lanham: University Press of America, 1987.

4.56 Fressin, A. *La Perception chez Bergson et chez Merleau-Ponty*, Paris: Société d'éditions d'enseignement supérieur, 1967.

4.57 Friedman, R. M. 'The Formation of Merleau-Ponty's Philosophy', *Philosophy Today*, 17 (1973): 272–8.

4.58 Friedman, R. M. 'Merleau-Ponty's Theory of Intersubjectivity', *Philosophy Today*, 19 (1975): 228–42.

4.59 Gans, S. 'Schematism and Embodiment', *Journal of the British Society for Phenomenology*, 13 (1982): 237–45.

4.60 Geraets, T. F. *Vers une nouvelle philosophie transcendantale: La Genèse de la philosophie de Maurice Merleau-Ponty jusqu'à la Phénoménologie de la perception*, The Hague: Martinus Nijhoff, 1971.

4.61 Gerber, R. J. 'Merleau-Ponty: The Dialectic of Consciousness and World', *Man and World*, 2 (1969): 83–107.

4.62 Gill, J. H. *Merleau-Ponty and Metaphor*, Atlantic Highlands: Humanities Press, 1991.

4.63 Gillan, G. (ed.) *The Horizons of the Flesh: Critical Perspectives on the Thought of Merleau-Ponty*, Carbondale and Edwardsville: Southern Illinois University Press, 1973.

4.64 Grene, M. 'Merleau-Ponty and the Renewal of Ontology', *Review of Metaphysics*, 29 (1976): 605–25.

4.65 Hadreas, P. J. *In Place of the Flawed Diamond: An Investigation of Merleau-Ponty's Philosophy*, New York: Lang, 1986.

4.66 Halda, B. *Merleau-Ponty ou la philosophie de l'ambiguïté*, Paris: Les Lettres Modernes, 1966.

4.67 Hall, H. 'The Continuity of Merleau-Ponty's Philosophy of Perception', *Man and World*, 10 (1977): 435–47.

4.68 Heidsieck, F. *L'Ontologie de Merleau-Ponty*, Paris: Presses Universitaires de France, 1971.

4.69 Hyppolite, J. *Sens et existence dans la philosophie de Maurice Merleau-Ponty*, Oxford: The Clarendon Press, 1963.

4.70 Johnson, G. A. (ed.) *Ontology and Alterity in Merleau-Ponty*, Evanston: Northwestern University Press, 1991.

4.71 Jolivet, R. 'The Problem of God in the Philosophy of Merleau-Ponty', *Philosophy Today*, 7 (1963): 150–64.

4.72 Kaelin, E. F. *An Existential Aesthetic: The Theories of Sartre and Merleau-Ponty*, Madison: The University of Wisconsin Press, 1962.

4.73 Kaelin, E. F. 'Merleau-Ponty, Fundamental Ontologist', *Man and World*, 3 (1970): 102–15.

4.74 Kearney, R. 'Maurice Merleau-Ponty', in *Modern Movements in European Philosophy*, Manchester and Dover, NH: Manchester University Press, 1986, pp. 73–90.

4.75 Kockelmans, J. J. 'Merleau-Ponty on Sexuality', *Journal of Existentialism*, 6 (1965): 9–30.

4.76 Krell, D. F. 'Merleau-Ponty on "eros" and "logos" ', *Man and World*, 7 (1974): 37–51.

4.77 Kwant, R. C. *The Phenomenological Philosophy of Merleau-Ponty*, Pittsburgh: Duquesne University Press, 1963.

4.78 Kwant, R. C. *From Phenomenology to Metaphysics: An Inquiry into the Last Period of Merleau-Ponty's Philosophical Life*, Pittsburgh: Duquesne University Press, 1966.

4.79 Lacan, J. 'Maurice Merleau-Ponty', *Les Temps modernes*, 184–85 (October 1961): 245–54.

4.80 Langan, T. *Merleau-Ponty's Critique of Reason*, New Haven and London: Yale University Press, 1966.

4.81 Langer, M. M. *Merleau-Ponty's Phenomenology of Perception: A Guide and Commentary*, Basingstoke: Macmillan, 1989.

4.82 Lanigan, R. L. *Speaking and Semiology: Maurice Merleau-Ponty's Phenomenological Theory of Existential Communication*, The Hague and Paris: Mouton, 1972.

4.83 Lefort, C. 'Maurice Merleau-Ponty', in R. Klibansky (ed.), *Contemporary Philosophy: A Survey*, vol. 3, *Metaphysics, Phenomenology, Language and Structure*, Firenze: La Nuova Italia Editrice, 1969, pp. 206–14.

4.84 Levine, S. K. 'Merleau-Ponty's Philosophy of Art', *Man and World*, 2 (1969): 438–52.

4.85 Lévi-Strauss, C. 'On Merleau-Ponty', trans. C. Gross, *Graduate Faculty Philosophy Journal*, 7 (1978): 179–88.

4.86 Madison, G. B. *The Phenomenology of Merleau-Ponty: A Search for the Limits of Consciousness*, Athens: Ohio University Press, 1981.

4.87 Mallin, S. B. *Merleau-Ponty's Philosophy*, New Haven and London: Yale University Press, 1979.

4.88 Natanson, M. 'The Fabric of Expression', *Review of Metaphysics*, 21 (1968): 491–505.

4.89 O'Neill, J. *The Communicative Body: Studies in Communicative Philosophy, Politics, and Sociology*, Evanston: Northwestern University Press, 1989.

4.90 Rabil, A. *Merleau-Ponty: Existentialist of the Social World*, New York: Columbia University Press, 1967.

4.91 Rauch, L. 'Sartre, Merleau-Ponty and the Hole in Being', *Philosophical Studies (Ireland)*, 18 (1969): 119–32.

4.92 *Review of Existential Psychology and Psychiatry*, 18 (1982–3), a special issue devoted to Merleau-Ponty, including translations of several short pieces by Merleau-Ponty on phenomenological psychology, sexuality and the relations between phenomenology and psychoanalysis.

4.93 Ricoeur, P. 'Hommage à Merleau-Ponty', *Esprit*, 29 (1961): 1115–20.

4.94 Robinet, A. *Merleau-Ponty, sa vie, son œuvre, avec un exposé de sa philosophie*, Paris: Presses Universitaires de France, 1963.

4.95 Roman, J. 'Une amitié existentialiste: Sartre et Merleau-Ponty', *Revue internationale de philosophie*, 39 (1985): 30–55.

4.96 Sallis, J. 'Time, Subjectivity, and *The Phenomenology of Perception*', *Modern Schoolman*, 48 (1971): 343–58.

4.97 Sallis, J. *Phenomenology and the Return to Beginnings*, Pittsburgh: Duquesne University Press, 1973.

4.98 Sallis, J. (ed.) *Merleau-Ponty: Perception, Structure, Language*, Atlantic Highlands: Humanities Press, 1981.

4.99 Sartre, J.-P. 'Merleau-Ponty vivant', *Les Temps modernes*, 184–5 (1961): 304–76; translated as 'Merleau-Ponty', in J.-P. Sartre, *Situations*, trans. B. Eisler, London: Hamish Hamilton, 1965, pp. 225–326.

4.100 Sartre, J.-P. 'Merleau-Ponty [1]', trans. W. Hamrick, *Journal of the British Society for Phenomenology*, 15 (1984): 128–54. [An earlier version of the previous entry.]

4.101 Schmidt, J. *Maurice Merleau-Ponty: Between Phenomenology and Structuralism*, New York: St Martin's Press, 1985.

4.102 Silverman, H. J. 'Re-reading Merleau-Ponty', *Telos*, 29 (1976): 106–29; reprinted, with several other chapters on the philosophy of Merleau-Ponty, in [4.103].

4.103 Silverman, H. J. *Inscriptions: Between Phenomenology and Structuralism*, New York and London: Routledge & Kegan Paul, 1987.

4.104 Silverman, H. J. *et al.* (eds) *The Horizons of Continental Philosophy: Essays on Husserl, Heidegger, and Merleau-Ponty*, Dordrecht: Kluwer, 1988.

4.105 Smith, C. 'Sartre and Merleau-Ponty: The Case for a Modified Essentialism', *Journal of the British Society for Phenomenology*, 1 (1970): 73–9.

4.106 Smyth, D. P. 'Merleau-Ponty's Late Ontology: New Nature and the Hyperdialectic', unpublished Ph.D. thesis, The Queen's University of Belfast, 1988.

4.107 Taminiaux, J. 'Merleau-Ponty: de la dialectique à l'hyperdialectique', *Tijdschrift voor Filosofie*, 40 (1978): 34–55.

4.108 Tilliette, X. *Merleau-Ponty ou la mesure de l'homme*, Paris: Seghers, 1970.

4.109 Thévenaz, P. *De Husserl à Merleau-Ponty: Qu'est-ce que la phénoménologie*, Neuchâtel: Editions de la Baconnière, 1966.

4.110 Van Breda, H. L. 'Maurice Merleau-Ponty et les Archives-Husserl à Louvain', *Revue de métaphysique et de morale*, 67 (1962): 410–30.

4.111 Waldenfels, B. 'Das Problem der Leiblichkeit bei Merleau-Ponty', *Philosophisches Jahrbuch*, 75 (1967–8): 345–65.

Criticism: Freedom, history and politics

4.112 Archard, D. *Marxism and Existentialism: The Political Philosophy of Sartre and Merleau-Ponty*, Belfast: Blackstaff Press, 1980.

4.113 Aron, R. *Marxism and the Existentialists*, New York: Harper & Row, 1969.

4.114 Bien, J. 'Man and the Economic: Merleau-Ponty's Interpretation of Historical Materialism', *Southwestern Journal of Philosophy*, 3 (1972): 121–7.

4.115 Borg, J. L. 'Le Marxisme dans la philosophie socio-politique de Merleau-Ponty', *Revue philosophique de Louvain*, 73 (1975): 481–510.

4.116 Capalbo, C. 'L'historicité chez Merleau-Ponty', *Revue philosophique de Louvain*, 73 (1975): 511–35.

4.117 Compton, J. 'Sartre, Merleau-Ponty, and Human Freedom', *Journal of Philosophy*, 79 (1982): 577–88.

4.118 Coole, D. 'Phenomenology and Ideology in the Work of Merleau-Ponty', in N. O'Sullivan (ed.), *The Structure of Modern Ideology*, Cheltenham: Elgar, 1989, 122–50.

4.119 Cooper, B. *Merleau-Ponty and Marxism: From Terror to Reform*, Toronto: University of Toronto Press, 1979.

4.120 Dauenhauer, B. P. *The Politics of Hope*, London: Routledge, 1986.

4.121 de Beauvoir, S. 'Merleau-Ponty et le pseudo-Sartrisme', *Les Temps modernes*, 10 (1955): 2072–122.

4.122 de Beauvoir, S. *J. -P. Sartre versus Merleau-Ponty (Merleau-Ponty ou l'antisartrisme)*, trans. A. Leal, Buenos Aires: Siglo Veints, 1963.

4.123 Kruks, S. *The Political Philosophy of Merleau-Ponty*, Brighton: Harvester and Atlantic Highlands: Humanities Press, 1981.

4.124 Miller, J. 'Merleau-Ponty's Marxism: Between Phenomenology and the Hegelian Absolute', *History and Theory*, 15 (1976): 109–32.

4.125 O'Neill, J. *Perception, Expression, and History: The Social Phenomenology of Maurice Merleau-Ponty*, Evanston: Northwestern University Press, 1970.

4.126 Pax, C. 'Merleau-Ponty and the Truth of History', *Man and World*, 6 (1973): 270–9.

4.127 Ricoeur, P. 'La Pensée engagée: Merleau-Ponty', *Esprit*, 16 (1948): 911–16.

4.128 Schmidt, J. 'Maurice Merleau-Ponty: Politics, Phenomenology, and Ontology', *Human Studies*, 6 (1983): 295–308.

4.129 Spurling, L. *Phenomenology and the Social World: The Philosophy of Merleau-Ponty and its Relation to the Social Sciences*, London: Routledge & Kegan Paul, 1972.

4.130 Whiteside, K. H. *Merleau-Ponty and the Foundation of an Existential Politics*, Princeton: Princeton University Press, 1988.

4.131 Whiteside, K. H. 'Universality and Violence: Merleau-Ponty, Malraux, and the Moral Logic of Liberalism', *Philosophy Today*, 35 (1991): 372–389.

4.132 Wiggins, O. P. 'Political Responsibility in Merleau-Ponty's *Humanism and Terror*', *Man and World*, 19 (1986): 275–91.

4.133 Wolin, R. 'Merleau-Ponty and the Birth of Weberian Marxism', *Praxis International*, 5 (1985): 115–30.

CHAPTER 5

Philosophies of religion
Marcel, Jaspers, Levinas
William Desmond

❧

Gabriel Marcel (1889–1973), Karl Jaspers (1883–1969) and Emmanuel Levinas (1906–) seem like a mere aggregate of thinkers. Jaspers, a German thinker who coined the phrase *Existenz Philosophie*, was influential in making known Kierkegaard's importance. Marcel was a French dramatist with a love of music who came to philosophy from a background in idealism, against which he struggled. Yet the influence, for instance, of Royce, the first person on whom he wrote, was strong. Bergson, now a too neglected thinker, was always in the background. Marcel's Catholicism was extremely significant, yet he bridled at the label 'Christian Existentialist'. He was a philosopher who happened to be a Catholic. Levinas was instrumental in introducing phenomenology to France. In 1930 he published a book on Husserl's theory of intuition that was to excite Sartre to say: That is the way I want to philosophize! Yet Levinas always thought in tension with this phenomenological heritage, and most especially its transformation in Heidegger's fundamental ontology.

These three thinkers have received mixed attention. Jaspers laboured in Heidegger's shadow, as he himself seemed to recognize. Heidegger and he were once friends and Heidegger alone he recognized as being on a par with him. Still Heidegger's enormous influence has tended to eclipse a proper appreciation of Jaspers' achievement. Jaspers was opposed to Nazism, as Heidegger was not. This did not prevent him from acknowledging Heidegger's stature. Indeed Jaspers was more concerned with Heidegger than Heidegger was with Jaspers. Also Jaspers respected the tradition of philosophy, as well as the achievements of science. He did not set himself in contestation with the millennia to hoist himself to unprecedented originality. This, coupled with his restorative efforts *vis-à-vis* perennial philosophy, meant that no cult formed around his thought. This is not to deny that he was and is deeply admired.

Marcel is an insightful existential thinker, but existentialism has been identified widely with its atheistic brands, especially that of Sartre. Because of Marcel's unashamed refusal to silence his own search for God, there has been a failure to listen properly to him by professional philosophers who too easily become embarrassed with the religious. They fail to listen attentively enough to his sometimes elusive themes – the body, the family, the sense of mystery as eluding all objectifications, meditations on what I would call the intimacy of being.

Marcel is difficult to package, though there are recurrent themes which have been packaged as identifiably Marcellian: being and having, problem and mystery, intersubjectivity and embodiment. His style of philosophizing, out of respect for the subject matter itself, refuses to be packaged, even systematically stated in any simple survey. Though he sometimes has a diffuse style of writing, in the very peregrinations of his thinking he *hits* on some absolutely essential insights. Thus the intimacy of being is always other to technical thinking, eludes complete systematic ordering, is on the edge of completely transparent conceptualization. Philosophy tends to home in on themes that are manageable in a more neutral, public, generalized language. We need that language, but it must be counteracted and complemented with modes of thinking that learn from art, and indeed that allow themselves to be shaped by a certain music of being.

Levinas was not widely known in English-speaking philosophy until recently. His work presupposes familiarity with phenomenology, both Husserlian and Heideggerian, and also the currents of intellectual debates that have swept France from the 1930s onwards, over which the shadow of Hegel has hovered in various interpretations and appropriations. Levinas himself distinguishes his own more strictly philosophical writings from his religious studies, but there is little doubt that religion and philosophy cannot be finally insulated from each other. Many of the themes of his major work, *Totality and Infinity*, are incomprehensible without the sense of the presence/absence of God. Levinas's stature is now being more widely recognized outside France, partly owing to the impact of deconstruction, and its high priest Derrida, who learned a thing or two from Levinas. The service to Levinas is ambiguous. Levinas has always exhibited a spiritual seriousness that is ill repaid by the postmodern frivolity to which deconstruction is frequently prone.

Each thinker is deserving of an entire study. Each has been prolific, Levinas less so, but Marcel and Jaspers have been voluminous. To bring some manageable order to the matter, I will concentrate on three major themes, and as the matter dictates I will mention related ideas, without dwelling on them in the detail they might deserve in another study. These three themes will be: the nature of philosophy; the question of the other; the question of transcendence or God.

❧ GABRIEL MARCEL ❧

Marcel's understanding of philosophical thought is determined by a reaction to the idealism of the late nineteenth century. He did some early work on Royce and Schelling. Their themes were to influence him throughout his writing. Thus the theme of loyalty in Royce is transformed into an ontology of intersubjectivity with distinctive emphasis on the notion of what Marcel calls creative fidelity. I mention the struggle of Schelling to break free of the logicism of his own early thought and Hegel's idealism. The struggle led to Schelling's positive philosophy that is the progenitor of all existential thought, including that of Kierkegaard. Schelling tried to think evil as radically other to reason. Marcel has later occasion to mention Schelling and Kant on this score, but the point is more generally relevant to the conception of philosophy at issue. Evil as a philosophical perplexity takes idealistic reason to its limit where the philosopher has to think otherwise of what lies on the other side of reason, as idealistically conceived.

The desideratum of philosophy as system was bequeathed through Kant, Fichte, Hegel to the whole subsequent history of idealistic and post-idealistic philosophizing. Marcel did intend at an early point to couch his thoughts in a systematic form. He discovered he could not bring it off without forcing his thoughts into a form that went against their grain. Eventually he published his *Metaphysical Journal* (1927), breaking ground here not only in terms of content but in terms of a different sense of literary form.

Marcel's commitment to what is other to system is forged in deep tension with the sense that thought ought to have some systematic character, certainly an appropriate order in its development and presentation. His Gifford lectures, published as *The Mystery of Being* (1950), are presented as his most systematic work, but there he disclaims anything like a system. Primarily philosophy is a matter of venture and exploration. System, such as it is, comes *after*; it ought not to dictate to the matter what it should be. Thinking is open to the matter at issue, even when the matter offers insurmountable resistance to the encroachments of our categories. The drift of his thinking is not forced into a form that betrays, so to say, its improvisatory nature. This sense of philosophy shares a lot with Kierkegaard and Nietzsche, though Marcel does not list these as early influences. One thinks too of the plurality of literary forms used by Kierkegaard and Nietzsche, though one could also mention the non-systematic forms developed by Shestov and the later Wittgenstein.

Marcel's philosophy has a phenomenological as well as an existential side. In no sense was he a disciple of Husserl. But his philosophizing is phenomenological in holding that thinking ought to start by an act of attention to what appears to us. As best as possible we allow the matter to make its appearance, according to its own form and requirements. The first act of philosophical intelligence demands a kind of mindful attention to phenomena, appearing, happenings, in all their nuance and surprise. This requirement is continuous with his rejection of idealism. The stress in idealism on purely autonomous thought tempts the philosopher to impose his categories on being as appearing, hence to see there only what thought has itself put there. Kant himself talked about the mind as only seeing in nature what it has itself put there. Kant was no absolute idealist but the equivocities of some of his pronouncements, like the one just cited, led to the more uncompromising, hence more coherent, idealism of his successors.

But the full coherence of idealism is also its undoing in that what is other to thought always gets finally reduced to the construction of a category. Marcel rejects this, for at a critical point the emptiness of the categorial construction makes itself felt. Hence Marcel's desire for phenomenological fidelity entails the reassertion of a realism which asks the thinker to let things take their own shape without interference from the dictating intellect. Marcel does not deny a critical dimension to philosophy. On the contrary, the appearing of things is shot through with ambiguities that have to be interpreted and evaluated. Letting ambiguity come to appearance is part of the phenomenological requirement of philosophy. Mindless surrender to ambiguity is not. The ambiguities of being have to be sifted.

This is especially relevant to the existential side of his thinking. Marcel is an existentialist to the extent that he lays a primary focus on human being and the perplexities that burden it about being and most especially its own being. He used the term 'existential' before it became fashionable through Sartre. As finding itself in the ambiguous middle of things, the human being is in quest of the truth of things and most especially its own truth. It is tempted by possibilities that veil or distort or destroy its own truth and the truth of things. Hence the existential philosopher is again involved in a quest or journey. Not surprisingly, Marcel lays great emphasis on *homo viator*, man the wayfarer, (the title of one of his books).

We are on the way, to where we do not exactly know, from where we know not, in a middle often clouded with uncertainty and sorrow. Marcel does not have quite the intense concentrated passion of Pascal, but they share a similar sense of the enigma of existential contingency. Nor can we stand outside the middle and survey our way of passage as a whole. The deficiency of systematic idealism is the false imputation that we have such an Archimedean point whence we can construct the system of categories to make all being transparently intelligible. Such a system is false to our participation in being, and not least to the singularity of the journeying philosopher. We need a different kind of thinking, which acknowledges our intimacy with being, even in our sense of metaphysical homelessness. The great struggle of philosophy is to get some reflective distance on our being thus in the middle, a distance that does not distort our intimacy with being in the middle. Thinking must be shown in its genesis and process, with all its falterings and flights, its matured fruits and undelivered suggestions.

Here Marcel makes a distinction between what he calls primary and secondary reflection. Primary reflection shows a tendency to objectify being and the human being. It tries to survey the object from outside, or penetrate it as if it were an alien thing to be mastered or overcome. Such a thinking has one of its major sources in Cartesian dualism where knower and known, mind and nature, self and other are posited as antithetical opposites. It is a mode of thinking that attenuates the thinker's participation in being. This kind of thinking corresponds to treating being as a problem.

Secondary reflection is such that the matter being thought unavoidably encroaches on the one doing the thinking. The thinker cannot escape involvement with the matter that is being thought. A thinking that objectifies and fosters the self-forgetfulness of the thinker will not do. It is not that the thinker now collapses into a mushy subjectivism, softly surrendering to the inarticulate, having given up the stiff precisions of articulate objectivism. Secondary reflection, Marcel says, is a recuperative thinking. Once having lived or been caught up or carried along by a process of living, one struggles to get a thoughtful distance on one's course, all the more to interiorize mindfully its possible significance.

In human existence secondary reflection in some form goes on always, but not necessarily in the accentuated form the existential philosopher cultivates. As Kierkegaard says: life has to be lived forward, but thought backward. Secondary reflection is thus recollective. As such it is not a nostalgic thinking; for to gain a mindful sense of one's present and past may open a truer orientation to what is to come. Secondary reflection is bound up with the possibility of hope. Hope is a major theme for Marcel. Indeed one can say that Marcel takes very seriously Kant's question: For what may we hope?

The difference of primary and secondary reflection is relevant to Marcel's treatment of the notions of problem and mystery, and these in turn influence his critique of the spiritual devastations wrought by the modern hegemony of unrestrained technicism, indeed the idolatry of technique. Like many other thinkers, Marcel recognizes the modern dominance of scientific method and its way of conceiving the world. He does not deny the benefits that come from this way, but is disturbed at the accompanying neglect of issues that fall outside its purview. Scientific method treats of all questions as problematic matters: difficulties that can be solved by means of techniques of objective experimentation and calculation. The hegemony of this approach can lead to the atrophy of human perplexity before the metaphysical enigmas of existence.

Consider questions of despair and salvation. These become a matter of psychological adaptation as the singular self becomes a case of maladjustment. The promise of our despair is betrayed, not even guessed. With issues like suffering, the pervasiveness of evil and the inevitability of death we deal with mysteries or meta-problematic themes. These are perplexities that involve us and shake us and make us sleepless. We are threatened and challenged and put on trial. They never yield a univocal answer; indeed they cannot properly be formulated as univocal problems. A constitutive openness and ambiguity remains. We have to return to such perplexities again and again. We never conclusively master them.

Marcel does not advocate the abandonment of reason, as if these mysteries were absurdities. They do demand a thoughtfulness not reducible to scientific knowledge, moving the philosopher closer to the poet and the religious. The hegemony of the problem makes us take for granted the existence of things and our own. By contrast, the philosopher for Marcel is stunned into thought by just that fact of existence, astonished at the marvel that things are. That the world is at all is the wonder. This mystery is all around and within us, though to it we are heedless. We look but overlook; we hear but have not listened or heard.

The neglect of mystery and the hegemony of problem leads to a world wherein technique reigns with only sporadically disputed sway. There is an anonymity to technique that is antithetical to the singularity of existing. Technique involves a set of directives that can be used by all; the directives of a technique do not originate with the user but, if we desire success in the outcome, to these directives we must submit. Thus technique can breed a conformism, a certain standardization of the human being, an averaging. Uniqueness and recalcitrant singularity are levelled down.

This is a theme sounded loudly by Kierkegaard and Nietzsche. We have heard it so often that perhaps we are jaded. But weariness with a question does not mean it is solved. Technique shows the calculative mind in action. But there is no technique of human wholeness or integrity; there is no technique of ethical responsibility; there is no technique of honesty and truthfulness. Technicism is in flight from the unexpected and the uncontrollable. The idolatry of technique is really a metaphysical hostility to our vulnerability before the incalculable chance of being. The tyranny of technique drowns the deeper human in a conspiracy of efficiency and a frenzy of industry. It may erect a house but cannot make us a home.

Marcel's philosophizing takes shape at the opposite extreme to this technicism. It is appropriate to mention that this philosophizing owes much to his twin loves: music and drama. He repeatedly resorts to musical images, and was a composer and performer of no little talent. The image of improvisation is important. As applied to philosophy and life it means: the score is not settled before playing; the players are invited to create freely. This is not incidental to the pervasive post-Hegelian concern with the limits of systematic philosophy. Schopenhauer and Nietzsche are the major figures in the nineteenth century who believed that music was the metaphysical art. There are others in the twentieth century, Adorno most notably, who give some privilege to music. Philosophy, particularly in its logicist forms, can run roughshod over the subtleties, intimacies of being. Music may sing these, as it were, in a manner that forces philosophy to raise the question of the unsayable – the unsayable that yet is sung and so somehow said.

If music as metaphysically significant raises questions about the limits of philosophy, Marcel has no desire to yield to a dark romanticism. Nor does he thematically focus on the metaphysics of music, but uses musical images and metaphors again and again to illustrate some of his more elusive ideas. One has to conclude that there is an implicit community of meaning between his thought and music. Again consider the improvisatory style of some of his philosophizing: a theme is stated, developed, dropped; then resumed, restated; there come to be echoes back and forth; nor does Marcel offer any simple resolution, though there are moments of revelation. Does his thought then sing? Does his philosophy approach the condition of music? The analytical philosopher will squirm. But there is a rigour and discipline in this thinking that the analytical philosopher hardly suspects; there is a rigour and discipline in music too. Even Rudolp Carnap, one of the avatars of analytical philosophy, sensed a connection between metaphysics and music, though not surprisingly his judgment was topsy-turvy: metaphysics is just poor music.

The influence of drama is related to Marcel's preoccupation with the question of *the other*. Marcel was himself a successful playwright, with a lifelong interest in the theatre. Drama presents the concrete dilemmas of humans in their otherness and estrangements and solidarities.

It imaginatively enacts the resistance and reciprocity of the self and the other. It returns us to a point of emergent significance that is prior to abstract thought. Marcel said that he had interest not in the solitary 'I am' but in the concrete 'We are'. To exist is to be shaped in this solidarity of selves. Drama, of course, is enacted in and through language where again we face the other. Seemingly inconspicuous words may offer the revelation of the significant world of the other, its wounds, its conceit, its hospitality. Words are pregnant with more than can be rendered in the languages of function. Philosophy, like drama, should awaken vigilance for this 'more'.

One senses sometimes that his own plays were more important to Marcel than his philosophy. His preoccupations emerged in pristine form in his plays which were not meant as mere illustration of philosophical theories. What drama brings to birth, philosophy later may take hold of in reflection. It is as if the dramas were closer to the phenomenological matrix of being, wherein the basic perplexities appeared *in statu nascendi*, in a form more concrete than later conceptualizations could capture.

Some readers may find it tedious for Marcel to quote his own plays. I see it as a strategy of saying. In philosophy we always have a problem of writing about matters closest to the personal, to the intimacy of being. We refuse to be confessional. And yet we have to find strategies of confession, of saying the 'I' with a kind of elemental honesty. In quoting his plays, Marcel can confess without embarrassment. The citation offers not only a theme closer to the phenomenological matrix but also one with a space of possible distance. We do not have to collapse into the theme; it can become the basis for a secondary reflection. There is then a rhetorical complicity between his dramatic and philosophical writing.

In that sense Marcel might be called a plurivocal philosopher. He does not dramatize his philosophizing in the same way as Nietzsche does, who is poet and philosopher in one; or as Plato does in that great achievement of philosophical writing, the Platonic dialogue. Instead he creates a dialogue between his dramas and his philosophizing, in the philosophizing itself. There are times when he should have let the barrier between them break down, as do Plato and Nietzsche. Perhaps he did not, less for the sake of philosophy as out of respect for his dramatic art which one senses he wanted to preserve from the devitalizing encroachments of abstract philosophical categories.

To break down the barrier need not encourage this devitalization but rather promote a more radical vitalization of philosophical thinking. Admittedly the bureaucratic separation of philosophy and poetry is hard to get beyond. We should get beyond it, on Marcel's own terms, since the functionalizing mind, the bureaucratic mind, is an essentially technical mind. If Marcel too strongly insists on separating the function of drama and philosophy, he will show himself captive to the same narrow mind he denounces otherwise so rightly. He does not, to his credit. Beyond the functionalization of poetry and philosophy and religion, the one thing necessary is honesty nourished by spiritual seriousness. It does not matter whether we label it artistic, philosophic or religious. The dialogue of drama and philosophy points to modes of philosophizing outside system, entirely incomprehensible for an analytical philosopher in thrall to the plain prose of univocal writing.

The theme of the other is connected with Marcel's reflection on the body. His emphasis is on the incarnate person. The flesh is where we are in a primary contact with all otherness, both natural and human. The affirmation of being that arises there articulates a sense of the togetherness of the existing self and the rest of being in its otherness. It is as if the incarnate self is initially an inarticulate 'We are'. Marcel obviously sets himself against any form of Cartesianism and dualism here. There is some affinity with empiricism, stemming from his desire for phenomenological fidelity. The difference is in his interpretation of experience. Empiricist experience is an abstraction from the fullness of original fleshed incarnation. It is as alienated from concrete existence as is Cartesian dualism, from the side of the body in this case, rather than the reflective reason.

The subject is an incarnate self defined intersubjectively. The *inter*, the between of intersubjectivity, does not deny the flesh. The between is stressed by the concretization of spirit in the flesh of the human being. Again the intimacy of our involvement with the other matches the intimacy of our being our own bodies. Marcel is given to criticize the view that we have bodies; the connection of self with flesh is not thus external. Marcel wants to say: we are our body.

Here arises his concern with being and having. Like Marx and many other modern thinkers Marcel was concerned with the question of property, of possession, the nature of having. He denies that a person is what a person has. My property is something over which I have power; I can dispose of it as I please; we cannot so dispose of our own bodies, nor of our fellow human beings without a fundamental violation of our own nature and theirs. It is not that we ought not to take care of things. Marcel is quite aware that our care for things can draw them into the orbit of human attachment in a manner which transforms them, releases in them their promise. Our belongings too can have a more intimate relation to our selfhood. But this more authentic belonging is not simply a relation of dominating power. This applies even more radically to our belonging together in human community.

The theme of possession of the other has also been a major

concern in contemporary European philosophy, especially in the light of different interpretations of Hegel's dialectic of master and slave. Power and domination have been held to define the essence of human relations. This is currently a much debated issue, but Marcel has things to say that have not been surpassed. I mention here Marcel's fascination with Sartre's essentially degraded view of the other where the master/slave dialectic is concretized as a dialectic of sadist and masochist: either dominate or be dominated is the either/or that runs through all of Sartre. While fascinated with Sartre's view that hell is the other, Marcel is unrelentingly hostile to it. The Sartrean look is the look of the Gorgon that would reduce the other to stone. This look wants to have the other, wants to objectify the other and disarm by pre-emptive violence the suspected threat to the self's freedom.

Sartre's sense of the human body is tied to his understanding of our openness to the other. Sartre's body is the place of negativity, the nothingness that shapes our freedom in its power of refusal, like that of the child that asserts its own difference by repeating its 'No'. If the body incarnates a 'We are' and, in a manner that affirms a solidarity with what is other to self, then we are outside this Sartrean sense of the body, this sense of the other, and this apotheosis of negation as freedom. Against the Sartrean degradation, Marcel recommends the possibility of *disponabilité*. This availability to the other is not threatened by the other, nor concerned to threaten. It signals a reversal of the normal for-self of, say, the Spinozistic *conatus essendi*. It is the promise of an agape, rather than the drive of eros to possess the other.

In opposition to having, our relativity to the other is marked by the gift. The bestowal of a gift is never neutral, never just a transfer of a possession from one to the other. The gift given is the bearer of generosity towards the other and for the other. If human being were exhausted by will to power or *conatus* as self-insistence, giving would be a mere ruse to use the other for the self again. There would be no true giving as a movement of self towards the other but not for the sake of the self, but simply for the other as beloved. Without this giving over of the giver, a gift is not a genuine gift.

Similarly the receiving of the gift is not an indifferent addition to the receiver's inventory of possessions. The communication of self on one side, of course, can be met by refusal on the other. One might distrust the bestower's goodness and turn away, or take and suspect and wait for the appearance of the ulterior motive. The Sartrean self lives this suspicion of the goodness of the other. A thing given is received as a genuine gift in being hospitably welcomed. What touches one in the gift is not the thing or the possession. It is the generous freedom of the other that has made itself available without care for itself. The thanks that then may be voiced has nothing to do with abjectness before an other who has one in his or her debt. Thanks is simple, elemental appreciation of the transcendence of self-insistence by the goodness of the giver.

Marcel offers some important meditations on the family and on paternity in *Homo Viator*. He calls attention to a community of spirit beyond all objectification. There are ontological issues at stake in the shaping of a singular destiny by relation to the family. One might here compare Marcel's respect for paternity and the family to Sartre's contempt of the father in *The Words*, and his juvenile baiting of the bourgeois family. Of course, it is not only Sartre who displays this puerile disdain. Marcel distances himself from the pervasive attitude in post-romantic modernity that the father is always the tyrannical lord. Levinas's remarks on the family also escape the closed dialectic of master and slave.

Generosity is a condition of being beyond having which testifies to the human power of sacrifice. Sacrifice literally means to make sacred (*sacer facere*). Here Marcel's concern with generosity relative to the human other shades into his meditations on *the divine other*. For instance, Marcel draws attention to the difference of the martyr and the suicide. Suicides claim that their bodies are their own property and that they can do with them what they will. They claim the freedom to visit the ultimate violence on it. Martyrs look like suicides but are entirely different. They give up their bodies, their lives because neither belong to them. They belong to something higher than themselves and to this their death witnesses. Suicides attest to nothing but their own despair. Martyrs are centred beyond themselves; suicides find a centre in nothing, not even in themselves. The death of a true martyr is living testimony to a higher order of being and worth. Our existence is not our property but a gift of this order. The sacrifice makes sacred; even in this death the martyr gives himself or herself over to this order, gives thanks for its gift.

Marcel as philosopher was not primarily or directly interested in the traditional issues of natural theology. He was concerned with an existential phenomenology of significant occasions in human experience where the sense of the divine breaks through or is offered to us. While his conversion to Catholicism was profoundly influential, he tried to stay on the philosophical side of specifically theological reflections. He was reticent about making full-blown theological statements. He expressed some satisfaction when his reflections spoke to individuals outside Catholicism. His philosophical meditations were suggestive of theological possibilities, without determinately articulating anything even approaching a systematic idea of God.

Marcel's greatest fear, I suspect, and precisely out of religious reverence, was the reduction of God to our concepts. Yet clearly his religious faith provided a matrix that nurtured the characteristic ideas of his philosophical reflection. Reflections on the mystery of suffering and evil, and on the love that seeks to outlive death, take his thought again and again to the borders of religious faith.

He set himself against the traditional proofs of God as objectifying what ought never to be objectified. The very idea of proving God is a misconception, a misconception that might border on a kind of rationalistic sacrilege, if the living God is reduced to a mere toy in a parlour game of conceptual virtuosity. God is never an object, always a Thou that resists reification. Yet Marcel was profoundly disturbed at the godlessness of western modernity. There is in his writings a growing sense of the spiritual waste produced by godless modernity when coupled with the unbridled hubris of a Promethean technicism. He has much in common with Heidegger's later meditations on the absence of the holy in modernity.

Marcel does not fit a common view of existentialism as probing a world from which God has been barred. The atheistic existentialist, reduced to caricature by Sartre, sternly girds his or her loins before this Godforsaken world, and dismisses as a sentimental coward anyone seeking hope and ultimate sense. The stratagem began by being disturbing but ended in a different conformism. Its revolt against the old became its new dogma. To Marcel's credit he was not consoled by this comfort of negation. He willingly made love, fidelity, hope, transcendence his themes – against the grain of the times.

His suspicion of traditional philosophical concepts of God make him the heir of Pascal and his opting for the God of Abraham, Isaac and Jacob. Not that he accepted a fideistic rejection of reason, a fideism sometimes imputed to Pascal and Kierkegaard, both of whom are more sophisticated as thinkers than can be captured by a dualism of faith/reason. Faith and the spirit of truth are bound together, and reason too is bound by the spirit of truth.

Marcel's reflections on human fidelity take us to the border of religious faith. Thus his discussions of death and immortality have little to do with proving the immortality of the soul. They are meditations on a fidelity between the living and the dead others, a fidelity that transcends the divide between the living and the dead. Nor is the issue of death simply a question of my death; it is much more a matter of the death of the other arousing in the still living the promise of a fidelity beyond death. There is no objective certainty with respect to this fidelity. Nor is there with respect to faith in God. It is always on trial in its sojourn in the world. Fidelity is tied to hope, with the promise of being that cannot now be secured with complete certainty. Fidelity itself may flower into witnessing and testimony. Such existential realities – suffering, fidelity, hope, generosity, love, testimony – are the mysteries in which our sense of the sacred is shaped and on which the philosopher must reflect. The kinship with Kierkegaard is noticeable: the impossibility of objective certainty with respect to faith and fidelity. We are dealing with a trans-objective order, which for Marcel is not merely subjective.

Like Nietzsche he acknowledged the godless condition of modern man. But unlike Nietzsche, he did not see this condition as a gain for human freedom but as the sign of a catastrophic loss or refusal. Marcel admired Nietzsche's honest diagnosis about our godlessness but not his proposed solution in the Overman. Nietzsche offered a version of heroic sacrifice when he says: I love the man who creates beyond himself and thus perishes. But in the end there is no genuine beyond for Nietzsche, since all transcendence dissolves into human self-transcendence. Without transcendence beyond human self-transcendence, our sacrifice witnesses to nothing, except perhaps ourselves. The wasteland still grows.

Promethean humans may steal divine fire, but in absolutizing their own power they betray their community with the power of transcendence beyond them. The aspiration to transcendence is deformed. Its root is the divine ground; out of this ground, it grows; outside of it, the aspiration to transcendence withers. The howl of Nietzsche's Madman was heard by Marcel, but he also heard a different music. With neither Marcel nor Nietzsche had the horror of this howl been cheapened into the postmodern kitsch it has now become, with the chirpy nihilists who blithely claim to be at home in the wasteland.

❧ KARL JASPERS ❧

Karl Jaspers is often identified with German existentialism in that he speaks of one of the tasks of philosophy as the clarification of *Existenz*. He distinguished empirical being (*Dasein*) from *Existenz* which is peculiar to the human being. Some commentators have seen a desire to mark his own thought off from Heidegger's *Dasein*, used in the special Heideggerian sense to refer to human existence. The relationship between Jaspers and Heidegger would command a study in itself, yet both helped to mediate Kierkegaard's philosophy of existence in the twentieth century. Philosophy of existence emphasizes the singularity of the human being, and often in a manner that stresses the recalcitrance of that singularity to inclusion in any system of concepts. Jaspers shares this view but qualifies it with a different respect for the systematic impulse, and indeed a less closed sense of system than had been dominant since German idealism. The tension of *Existenz* and system, the necessity and the limits of system, the relation of *Existenz* and transcendence at the limit of all systems, constitute some of his major concerns.

Jaspers suffered from ill health since his youth, which he turned to good use by husbanding his strengths for thinking. His sense of philosophy was never that of an academic discipline but that of a noble calling. He was under threat during the Nazi regime, but he re-emerged into public prominence after the war with widespread respect for his ethical integrity. He willingly undertook the public task of raising the question of German guilt, and was always concerned with the spiritual condition of the time, the state of the university, the issues of politics, national and international, especially in a nuclear age, the questions of world religions in an age of mass communication.

Jaspers did not publicly commit himself to philosophy until around the age of 40. His background prior to that was in medicine and psychology. His first published work was *General Psychopathology* (1913), followed by *Psychology of Weltanschauungen* (1919). He was later to say that these were really philosophy all along, though not as overtly so as his subsequent work. His reverence for philosophy made him reluctant to claim its mantle, especially when professional philosophers frequently fell short of the nobility of its calling. His first major work, *Philosophie*, was published in 1931 and established him as a major voice. The point has been made that the publication of Heidegger's *Being and Time* in 1927 stole his existential thunder and dimmed somewhat the lustre of his achievement.

Existenz is Jaspers's counterpart to Heidegger's *Dasein*. For both, only the human being exists in this unique sense: only the human being is questionable to itself. *Existenz* is marked by this relatedness to self that is unique to human being; we are a being for self which is the possibility of free self-determination. Though Kierkegaard's influence marks both Heidegger and Jaspers, in Jaspers we find a strong respect for science grounded in his early training. This respect never wavered. Jaspers departs from the standard picture of existentialism as virulently anti-scientific. He never tires of insisting that science is one of the great works of the human mind. Moreover, any serious contemporary philosophizing worth the name must take due cognizance of its pervasive role in the modern world.

That said, the philosopher's task is not simply to be a methodologist of science. In reflecting on the meaning of science one inevitably inquires as to the precise status of scientific truth and science's role within the full economy of human life. One might even call Jaspers a philosopher of science in this generous sense that up to quite recently was almost unknown in Anglo-American analyses of science: science understood as a human achievement, and hence placed within a larger historical and cultural, indeed spiritual, milieu. To reflect on science is then not to abstract its methodological essence in a pseudo-ahistorical analysis; it is to meditate on the ideal of truth, and in Jaspers's case to open up a more fundamental sense of truth, which is constitutive of the milieu of scientific truth.

Jaspers's ideal of philosophy here is reminiscent of a certain reading and reconstruction of Kant's project. Many commentators have remarked on his debt to Kant, and Jaspers always acknowledged the depth of this debt. In Anglo-American philosophy Kant has been primarily read through the *Critique of Pure Reason*, interpreted as an anti-metaphysical tract, interspersed with some epistemological insights. Outside of Anglo-American analysis, Kant's more comprehensive ambitions are more willingly and widely recognized. Kant spoke of these ambitions in terms of the architectonic impulse. This means that reflection on science is certainly with a view to plotting the limits of valid cognition within a precisely delimited sphere. But – and this is where the more comprehensive sense of philosophy of science is relevant – to plot that limit is not necessarily to impute a merely negative judgment about other modes of meaning that may be other to science. One thinks the limits of science to know its strength but also its weakness in addressing no less pressing perplexities that transcend science. To assert that there are such perplexities that transcend science is not at all to depreciate science. It is to say that science is not the totality. The philosopher thinks what is other to science in thinking the greatness of science.

A careful reading of the Kantian enterprise will show that the heart of Kant's philosophy is not in the *First Critique* but in the *Second Critique*, and perhaps to an ambiguous extent (which has proved powerfully suggestive to Kant's German successors) in the *Third Critique*. German thinkers have this notable ability to hear voices in Kant's writing that to the outsider seem mere silences. In the scholastic twists and turns of the Kantian architectonic they sense that Kant was a tortured thinker. A tortured perplexity of thought is incessantly at work behind or beneath the scholastic encasing of concepts wherein Kant sheaths his explorations. Jaspers singles out many great thinkers for mention – Plato, Plotinus, Cusa, Spinoza, Hegel – but it is clear that his heart hears something in Kant that he hears nowhere else. Kant is often taken as a destroyer of Transcendence. Jaspers's reverence for Kant, I suspect, is as a thinker who tries to plot a winding way from finitude to Transcendence.

This sense of philosophy with a kind of Kantian architectonic is in tension with the singularity of human being as *Existenz*. Granting too the great power of science, there are questions that still exceed its proper competence. I underline the fact that the emphasis must first fall on *questioning*. We are here not talking about academic textbook puzzles. We are talking about the thinking human being as struck into questioning at the edge of all scientific rationalizing. There can be nothing anonymous or neutral about being struck into such questioning, and this is why the very unique selfhood of the philosopher is at stake in a way that is never quite the case in science. The stakes of perplexity are different in philosophy, for the mode of questioning that erupts is not one that can be completely objectified.

In scientific questioning the point is to detach oneself from oneself in the idiosyncrasy of selfhood, and to pose as univocal and determinate a question as possible. The singular I of *Existenz* becomes the anonymous one of univocal mind, consciousness in general. One represents univocal mind, anonymously the same for every rational consciousness, in search of a univocal answer to a univocal curiosity. This is related to Marcel's notion of the problem. But in philosophy a transformation of selfhood is called for which is energized in a new mode of perplexity which cannot be terminated by information about this object or that object. This perplexity is not a univocal curiosity about this thing or that thing. It is a kind of indeterminate wondering that may extend to the whole of what is, and indeed to the possibility of nothing. The 'objects' of philosophical perplexity are not univocal, determinate objectifiable themes. Nor can the 'results' of philosophical thinking be treated thus, be packaged thus. To do this would be to distort the true energy of living philosophical thinking. This indeterminate perplexity is the very self-transcending energy of human thinking. It was the ceaselessness of this that tortured Kant, even when he thought he had finally laid it to rest in the system and its categories.

I am putting the matter in terms Jaspers does not use but that do not betray his intent. Thus this perplexity is called forth when philosophy deals with what Jaspers calls 'boundary situations' (*Grenzsituationen*). Questions at the boundary are not just questions about the limits of science, though they are that too. They are questions on the limit, on the edge, *simpliciter*. The most obvious boundary situation is death. There is no answer to the meaning of death, because there is no determinate univocal concept that would put this event within an objective rational whole. Rather this event puts all objective rational wholes into question, and yet the genuine philosopher has to continue to think despite the severe strain put on the ideal of rational completeness. These are the boundary situations Jaspers considers in *Philosophie*: that I must die, that I cannot live without conflict and suffering, that I cannot escape guilt.

Boundary situations are not unrelated to Marcel's notion of the meta-problematic or mystery. They burst out of the system of scientific rationality. Yet philosophy does not end at this bursting. A more authentic philosophizing can then begin. Put in terms of Kant: Kant was obsessed with the desire to make metaphysics into a secure science, and to put behind him all the 'random gropings' of the past. Did Kant secure metaphysics as a science? The answer must be no. It will always be no. Metaphysics is not exhausted by the rationalistic scholasticism of the Wolffian school. Jaspers is critical of metaphysics in a vein reminiscent of Kant's attack on rationalistic science of being. But metaphysical thinking feeds on the indeterminate perplexity that takes us to the boundary and that is more radically energized in encounter with the boundary. There is a sense in which metaphysics really only begins at the limits of science. Despite his Kantian critique of 'metaphysics', I think Jaspers also hears this in Kant: the old rationalistic metaphysics may perhaps be put in its place; but at the limit, the old and ever fresh wonder is recalled into new life. A different kind of thinking has to take place at the boundary. This thinking Jaspers performs under the rubric of what he calls 'periechontology' as distinct from the old 'ontology'.

Consider here Jaspers's claim that truth cannot be reduced to correctness. Scientific truth does operate with some notion of correctness, Jaspers implies. Putting aside the complex disagreements in current philosophy of science, the ideal of correctness is based upon the presupposition that the ideal of determinate intelligibility is fundamental. A scientific proposition or theory or hypothesis is correct if it somehow 'corresponds' to the determinate state of affairs that it purports to report. The scientific proposition or theory or hypothesis must be stated with as much determinate precision as possible. The limit of this precision would be a mathematical univocity, a completely determinate formulation of a matter without any shade of equivocity or ambiguity or indefiniteness. Moreover, the reality thus propositionally determined is itself taken to be a more or less determinate manifestation of being. To be scientifically objective is thus to epitomize an objective mode of thinking relative to a reality that is objectified in just that sense of being appropriated as completely determinate. Scientific correctness objectively dispels the ambiguities of being. There is no objective *mathesis* of ambiguity, only a *mathesis* that dissolves ambiguity.

Within its sphere this is to the point, as Jaspers acknowledges. But philosophical thinking is already outside this sphere as reflecting upon this ideal of truth as correctness and the will to objective knowing inherent in it. Philosophy is thus already a non-objectifying thought. Jaspers pursues the question relative to truth as correctness by suggesting that determinate objects could not appear as determinable and hence as scientifically intelligible did they not appear out of or against a background that is not itself an object. This is the horizon of intelligibility that makes possible the appearance of determinate objects as determinate. The background horizon relative to which scientific truth determinately appears is not itself a determinate truth. There is no truth as correctness possible about this horizon. The horizon is truth in a sense that is not determinable or objectifiable.

Again one is hard put to forget Heidegger's analysis of the primordiality of *alētheia* relative to truth as *orthotes* or *adaequatio*. We might say that this indeterminable truth is the non-objective other to the indeterminate perplexity that drives the self-transcending thinking of philosophy. One wonders if in his own way Kant was aware of this finally indeterminable sense of truth. One of his most suggestive phrases in the *Third Critique* was 'purposiveness without purpose', (*Zweckmässigkeit ohne Zweck*). Kant does not extend the meaning of this phrase beyond the aesthetic, yet it has implications for the very self-transcending orientation of the human being towards truth as beyond every determinate truth. This is truth as the ultimate horizon of the truths of science and the determinate intelligibilities it discloses. There is, of course, a deep equivocity in Kant in tending to restrict truth to what is scientifically validated, and Jaspers shares in this equivocation, even while in practice extending the notion of truth well beyond scientific correctness. Jaspers's name for this horizon of truth is 'the Encompassing' (*Das Umgreifende*), one of the major ideas in his philosophy as a whole.

Das Umgreifende – the word carries the suggestion of being englobed by something that cannot be reduced to any definite object within the globe, the circle. Is this a variation of Parmenides' well-rounded truth? Yes. But any implication of a closed totality is something against which Jaspers will fight. The very language seems almost unavoidably to connote the closed circle. But if so, this is not something Jaspers intends. To close the circle would be to determine the indeterminable and so to objectify its non-objectifiable transcendence. Jaspers also claims that there is a plurality of modes of the Encompassing, and hence a Parmenidean monism will never do. This plurality of modes includes: Being in itself that surrounds us – this is further specified in terms of world and Transcendence; the Being that we are, further specified as empirical existence (*Dasein*), consciousness as such and spirit (*Geist*); finally the Encompassing as *Existenz* and reason (*Vernunft*).

Jaspers's philosophy is here a post-Kantian Kantianism of *finitude* in which the singularity of *Existenz* is thrust into the ambiguities of the Kantian architectonic. Jaspers's Kantianism appears again in that the ultimate indeterminability of the Encompassing makes it impossible to capture as a totality. Hegelian idealism makes what for Jaspers is the false claim to totality. To claim totality would be to imply a standpoint external to the Encompassing and this is impossible. Every determinate standpoint is relative to a determinate, objectified other, and hence is itself only possible on the basis of its englobement by the Encompassing.

We humans are not the encompassing of Encompassing. Still there is a sense in which for Jaspers we humans *are* the Encompassing; somehow our self-transcending thinking participates in the Encompassing; we are not determinate things but as *Existenz* participants in the truth in this more ultimate sense. We ourselves are a certain horizon of truth in a sense that cannot be reduced to objective correctness. The 'Kantianism' in this again brings us back to a certain finitude of thought, even in the indeterminate self-transcending of thought. The rejection of totality makes Jaspers join hands with Marcel in rejection of the speculative whole of Hegelian idealism. Marcel is very explicit in saying that the concept of totality is completely inappropriate to the idea of the spirit.

Jaspers, in my view, learned more from Hegel than he always explicitly acknowledged. His willingness to acknowledge the debt was spoken more clearly in his later life, but at the time of his earlier writing Hegel was not seen as an interlocutor that one could be respectably associated with, except to try to thrash. Nevertheless, Jaspers is very much a post-Hegelian philosopher in his refusal of totality, something he shares also with Heidegger. We will see in Levinas a divergence of totality and infinity, where the infinite ruptures every totality, beyond recuperation in any higher totality.

Our failure to determine the indeterminability of the Encompassing does not mean a surrender to the merely indefinite. The other thinking at the boundary of objective thought must be complemented by the project of *Existenz* clarification. Jaspers has some very important reflections on what he calls 'foundering' (*Scheitern*) and 'shipwreck' (*Schiffbruch*). Philosophy too founders, but in its foundering the possibility of breaking through to something other cannot be closed off. I cannot dwell on foundering here, but we can appropriately situate Jaspers relative to two exceptional predecessors he singles out for special mention: Nietzsche and Kierkegaard. These two could be said to live a sense of philosophical foundering that is deeply significant for all subsequent philosophizing.

Jaspers's writing shows a clear awareness that these two figures signal the end of a epoch, the end of modernity. Without exaggeration one can say that, to the extent that he appropriated their significance, Jaspers himself was a postmodern philosopher. I use the phrase with hesitation, since now postmodernism wastes itself with an academic anti-academic frivolity, the hermeneutics of suspicion gone chic, a scholastic scepticism without spiritual substance. A postmodern philosopher in any genuine sense is one who recognizes the spiritual sickness of modernity. Of course, a sick being is not a dead being, and a sick being continues to live, hence it must be in some other respects healthy. Modernity is sick in this ambiguous sense. Kierkegaard and Nietzsche not only diagnosed this sickness, they lived this sickness within themselves. Both were experimental thinkers, both experienced the illness they tried to cure in themselves, the illness of nihilism.

Kierkegaard's Christian cure, Nietzsche's Dionysian *pharmakon*, diverge. Jaspers thinks that philosophy can never be the same after them. They represent the radical rupture with idealistic totality. They stand before our future as exceptional thinkers who have lived through the spiritual sickness of modernity. Both founder for Jaspers. But this living through and foundering is informed by its own spiritual greatness. This greatness makes one reluctant to ally them completely with 'postmodernism', where the desire for spiritual seriousness or greatness seems feeble, if not terminal. Nietzsche and Kierkegaard would shudder at what passes for their current postmodern appropriations. Nietzsche would see the last men mouthing his songs, and sounding cacophonous. Kierkegaard would be dismayed at the aestheticization of his work, as if he did not call us to God – God, God and nothing but God. Let readers ask themselves if my reiteration of the word 'God' has not sent a shudder of uneasy embarrassment up their spines. Understand Nietzsche and Kierkegaard well. They are embarrassing thinkers; they shame us.

They call into question the traditional pretensions of reason. Jaspers is quite clear about this. Do they bring philosophy to an end? Perhaps philosophy of totality, but philosophy: no. Jaspers is himself a thinker of the end of philosophy, but he has a more nuanced historical sense than the fashionable proclaimers of the end of philosophy. There is an historical fairness. He does not totalize the tradition of philosophy in order to denounce it for totalizing thought – a blatant equivocation not avoided by anti-totalizing totalizers like Adorno, Derrida, Heidegger, Nietzsche himself. Though Jaspers is no Hegelian, there is much about him not entirely antipathetic to Hegel. He acknowledges that for a long time he got great sustenance for his own lectures from Hegel. Granting his greatness, eventually the totalizing Hegel became 'grotesque' for him. I mention his relation to Hegel again in that both have a much more generous attitude to the tradition of philosophy than almost all other post-Hegelian philosophers.

Hegel, Jaspers and Heidegger are perhaps the three greatest thinkers of the last 150 years who have tried to embrace, albeit very diversely, the heritage of millennia in their thinking. Jaspers's generosity to the tradition makes him finally distance himself from the exceptionality of Kierkegaard and Nietzsche. Their provocation of reason has to be balanced by the greatness of reason, as seen from a proper appropriation of the great thinkers of the past. Against the modern will to unprecedented originality – infecting Nietzsche and Heidegger – Jaspers wants to reaffirm the idea of *philosophia perennis*.

A major undertaking of Jaspers was to write a universal history of philosophy. This was never completed. Jaspers was interested not in a history of ideas but in a dialogue with the great thinkers by a genuine philosopher. The truth persists across time, though mediated through time. Nor is this truth identifiable with Heidegger's historicity of being, since Jaspers is not unwilling to invoke eternity, granting, of course, all the cautions and qualifications necessary in any such invocation. The tradition of philosophy is the privileged conversation of great thinkers. He includes himself in that conversation. Across the centuries a great thinker still calls to other thinkers. We later thinkers have to resurrect the greatness of the past thinker, not merely debunk them in the interests of spuriously elevating ourselves into a position of false originality. It is the spiritual truth of philosophical honesty that the great thinkers share. Each concretizes the self-surpassing transcendence of thinking, a personification of the extremity of honest perplexity before ultimacy.

Jaspers has not been as fashionable as Nietzsche and Heidegger precisely because of the generosity of his respect for tradition. In modernity we have been so infatuated with futurity that we have shortchanged the spiritual greatness of the past. In the future it will be great, it will be new, it will be unprecedented. A rhetoric of originality masks a lot of intellectual conceit. Nietzsche and Heidegger were not immune from thus puffing themselves up. As if a philosopher must strut and preen and crow: How different I am, how new! Cockcrow: and no, not dawn, as Nietzsche said; but flourish, flourish of the postmodern cock.

Jaspers addresses the theme of *the other*, especially in that philosophy for him is inseparable from communication. The dialogue with the tradition is one instance of communication. Communicative reason opens beyond monadic thinking at both ends: towards the past, towards the future. Nor did Jaspers deny the responsibility of the communicative reason of philosophy to shape the spiritual present. Again the other has to be accorded a different place in thought from that allowed for in idealistic totality. Reason in *Existenz* is always marked by a boundless will to communication. One sees some harbingers of Habermas. The communicative relation to the other is constitutive of the activity of reason. Indeed *Existenz* is not itself at all apart from the relation of the self to the other. The demand of communication with the other must be met for *Existenz* to be itself. Likewise we must be awakened to ourselves as *Existenz* if we are to do justice to the demand of communication.

Jaspers confessed to loneliness and incapacity to communicate in his youth. This was exacerbated by the isolating effects of his illness. Just as *Existenz* cannot be objectified, so our relatedness to the other can never be reduced to an objective relation such as might hold between things. Jaspers' primary emphasis is on the mutual reciprocity of communication between humans. He is a severe critic of the substitution in modernity of mass society for genuine community. The flattening of human beings into averageness, and hence the impoverishment of singularity, diminish, if not deform, what is essential to real community. In the singularity of *Existenz* there is always an opening to what is other than closed subjectivity.

As with Kierkegaard and Marcel, Jaspers offers a critique of the functionalization of man and the massification of societies. The sacrifice of singularity as *Existenz* is the defect of totalitarianism. But this defect also marks the competitive individualism of capitalism, for here singularity is merely atomized, and between atoms there is no deep bond of community. He does not display Nietzsche's elitist disdain for the many. He was deeply and ineradicably influenced by Weber. In many respects he also shares the sense of community at work in Kierkegaard's neglected social critique: each of us is an absolute singularity; this singularity is preserved in community, but genuine community is ultimately a community of spirit under God. The will of *Existenz* to communicate with the other stands under Transcendence as the absolute other.

Nor does Jaspers deny conflict in a mushy communitarianism. As already indicated, guilt and conflict are discussed as boundary situations in *Philosophie*. His suffering through Nazism was itself exposure to the violence of evil. He does underscore the possibility of a loving struggle. Love is not devoid of conflict, but the conflict is a creative war, *polemos*, as it were. Communication can be a contestation which is a mutual challenge to more authentic *Existenz*. His love for his wife, Gertrude, seem to have epitomized for him this creative contestation. This is close to Marcel's creative fidelity, and certainly beyond sadism and masochism, the degraded form of erotic struggle given so much attention by Sartre.

Communication is also central in Jaspers's ideas of reason and truth. Reason is an opening to the universal, but the true universal is not an anonymous generality in which singularity is submerged. So also for Jaspers truth is incomplete if it does not embody itself in a will to total communication. Truth is not closed on itself, timeless and unaffected by historicity. Jaspers even implies that truth actualizes itself in the movement of communication itself. Truth comes to completion in the process of communication.

One senses the shadow of Kant again. One is reminded of the Kantian *progressus*, the infinite task of the regulative ideal. When

Jaspers indicates a call on self-transformation in communication, to my mind he is talking about *truthfulness*, both singular and communal. Obviously this is constituted in the coming to truthfulness by the self and the community. This is a *becoming truthful* which would not be possible in the solitude of the self-communing thought, self-thinking thought. What about a sense of truth that is not constituted by what comes to be in a process of communication, but that makes possible that process of coming to be of social truthfulness? This sense of truth makes possible the constitution of truthfulness but is not itself constituted by truthfulness. This is truth that a process of communication unfolds or reveals, rather than creates or constitutes.

Residues of the constitutive language of Kantian idealism are here evident in Jaspers. The otherness of truth as for itself is compromised by this constitutive language. Jaspers does not want to deny this otherness but his submission to Kantian ways of thinking conditions a certain emphasis in his efforts to speak of Transcendence. This is applicable with respect to metaphysical transcendence, but also with respect to the possibility of divine revelation. The movement of our transcending, even in the communication of truthfulness, mingles with Transcendence as communicating with us out of its own integral otherness, such that we do not really know if there is this other otherness. What we do, our becoming truthful, seems hard to distinguish from what is done to us, our patience to truth. Does what is done to us collapse into what we do? How then are we to avoid a wrong appropriation of the other?

There is a principle of tolerance in Jaspers's sense of communicative reason. He knows that *vis-à-vis Existenz* we cannot just say there is one univocal truth. The truth is refracted singularly in the specific truthfulness of every singular *Existenz*. Reason must be honestly vigilant to the particularities of just that singular refraction. Communication is this vigilance, and this vigilance is respect for the other as other. I use the term 'refraction', which is not the language of constitutive idealism. And even though there is a quasi-constitutive language in Jaspers, his language of foundering must be seen to plot the limit of this, and indirectly to open a moment of radical receptivity in which we do not communicate but in which the other is communicating with us. Jaspers does not explicitly address the question of symmetrical and asymmetrical relativity in a manner that Levinas does.

Throughout I have referred to Transcendence. Here we approach the question of God. Transcendence for Jaspers is the ground of human *Existenz* and freedom. Jaspers treats of transcendence in volume III of *Philosophie* under the heading *Metaphysics*. The heading is not insignificant in the light of his critique of ontology from the standpoint of periechontology. The sense of metaphysical transcendence returns, proves unavoidable, even when all the Kantian strictures about metaphysics have been taken to heart. Transcendence is the absolute other. Again the Kantian modulation for Jaspers is that Transcendence is not to be known cognitively but to be reached existentially. There is no positive knowledge of Transcendence. Moreover, Transcendence grants itself gratuitously. Of course, if this is true the autonomy of reason is breached, and every trace of idealism, even Kantian idealism, will have to been reinspected.

Jaspers speaks of Transcendence as the absolute Encompassing, the Encompassing of all the encompassings. Transcendence is not the world, nor is it empty possibility, though Jaspers says that it shows itself only to *Existenz*. Transcendence is the absolute other in which *Existenz* is grounded. Wherever *Existenz* is authentically existing, it is not completely through itself. The human existent does not create itself. Relative to Transcendence I know that I have been given to myself. The more decisively *Existenz* is aware of its freedom the more it is aware of its relation to Transcendence.

I am tempted to think of both Augustine and Kierkegaard. Augustine speaks of being concerned with the soul and God and nothing more. This Augustinian theme is sounded in the correlation of *Existenz* and Transcendence. Moreover, Augustine speaks of God as *intimior intimo meo*: God is more intimate to me than I am to myself. The intimacy of this relation is beyond the world of objectivity; it happens in the deepest interiority of non-objectifiable *Existenz*, selfhood. Truth is subjectivity in Kierkegaard's sense: the truth of Transcendence will never be reduced to a set of general, public concepts. Perhaps this is why Jaspers insists, in Kantian manner, on our relation to Transcendence as non-cognitive. Why not speak of knowing in a different, non-objectifiable sense, a wisdom of idiocy, idiot wisdom of the intimacy of being? Why the obsessive insistence that validated cognition be confined to objective science?

Surely we can expand the notion of cognition without having to give ourselves over to full-blown Hegelian reason? For that matter, without this expansion does not Jaspers's way of talking fall foul of Hegel's critique of Kant's unknowable: If it is unknowable, you can say nothing; you cannot even know that it is unknowable; but you are saying something, then it must not be unknowable. I am enjoining the Hegelian question, not endorsing Hegel's answer to Kant in terms of a dialectical knowing of Transcendence. Hegel's answer sins in the opposite direction of cognitively subordinating Transcendence to immanence. We need a knowing other than Hegelian knowing and a non-knowing other than Kantian agnosticism.

Transcendence is, but is never adequately manifest in appearance. It eludes all thinking if we mean to think it as a determinate object. It seems easier to name it negatively than to say what it is positively. There is a sense in which we can find no final firm place in trying to say it, whether positively or negatively. Jaspers allows that there are many names for it. We can call it Being, Actuality, Divinity, God. Relative to thinking, he says we can call it Being; relative to life, it can be called Authentic Actuality; as demanding and governing, it can be called Divinity; relative to our encounter with it in our singular personhood, it can be called God.

Again we find a denial of cognitive content in favour of the naming of an existential experience. Self-transformation can occur in encounter with Transcendence; it can become a source out of which I live and towards which I die. *Amor Dei* can lead to a transformation of how we love and hate the world. Jaspers mentions the magnificent love of the world in Chinese life and the hatred of life in gnostic thought. This latter is finally a nihilism and despair: the godless creation of the world is brought forth by Lucifer. This diabolical creation is counter to God. When the world is God's creation the world is loved and God is loved in God's creation; the promise of human existence is affirmed.

We are always within the world and hence our relation to Transcendence is marked by finitude and foundering. We need the symbol and the cipher to articulate what in the end is beyond all articulation. In his later life Jaspers undertook a major dialogue with religious faith. He himself claimed the standpoint of what he called philosophical faith. Philosophy is often in tension with religion but their quests of ultimacy are akin. Like Hegel, Jaspers insists on the autonomy of philosophy, sometimes to the point of showing traces of a residual Enlightenment hostility to the claims of revealed religion. The same question can be put to both Hegel and Jaspers: To what extent are philosophical ideas rational transformations of religious themes, and hence not autonomous but heteronomous? Is philosophical faith religious faith rationalized?

For Hegel, of course, there is no philosophical faith; philosophy is knowing. Jaspers again stands closer to Kant. His philosophical faith attempts, among other things, to render articulate the 'faith' in favour of which Kant is willing to deny knowledge. This philosophical faith cannot be assimilated to poetry or science or religion. If philosophy is other to religion, it is with respect to critical self-consciousness, not with respect to any Hegelian speculative knowing wherein religion is dialectically *aufgehoben*. This critical self-awareness of limits nurtures a vigilance to the idolatry, whether fideistic or rationalistic, which mistakes the cipher of Transcendence for Transcendence itself. Religion and philosophy are different, not as opposites but as polar approaches to Transcendence. In this polarity they comprise a community of ultimates that are perennially a contestation and a challenge to each other.

❧ EMMANUEL LEVINAS ❧

Emmanuel Levinas was born in Lithuania into an orthodox Jewish family but has spent most of his life in France. His experience of the Second World War was to shape his thought deeply. He has written Talmudic studies, though he claims that his philosophy belongs in another category. Husserl's phenomenology and Heidegger's fundamental ontology influenced his first philosophical studies, influenced in the double sense of supporting his thinking and yet provoking him into struggle against that very support. His mature thought is expressed in *Totality and Infinity* (1961). Subsequently he has published collections of essays leading to *Otherwise than Being or Beyond Essence* (1973). He has also continued to write Talmudic studies of a more strictly religious character. Starting from phenomenology he has moved towards a recovery of metaphysical transcendence and an affirmation of what he calls 'ethics' as first philosophy.

Levinas became better known in English-speaking philosophy in the 1980s, partly mediated through the impact of deconstruction. English-speaking readers will find Levinas difficult without some sense of the context out of which he writes. Many consider *Totality and Infinity* to be his masterwork. It is a difficult book, for many philosophers as well as non-philosophers. Levinas's thinking is haunted by a whole host of philosophical ghosts. To get some sense of the peculiarities of his philosophizing, relative to his influences and claims, I name some of the ghosts.

There is the Cartesian heritage that seeks cognitive certainty in the foundation of the *cogito*, the 'I think'. Levinas evinces high respect for Descartes, surprising respect in that Descartes is often criticized as the originator of an understanding of mind that locks thought within itself, within its own immanence. Levinas wants to break out of that closed circle of immanence, without denying a certain inner integrity to the subject.

There is the phenomenological tradition, which can be interpreted as an ambiguous continuation of the Cartesian heritage. Levinas's first work was on the theory of intuition in Husserl, and his practice of phenomenology is not without debt to Husserl. He came to question the phenomenological doctrine of the intentionality of consciousness. He points to modes of consciousness where intentionality as a directedness on an object is not the final story. His discussion of enjoyment, for instance, reveals an engagement of consciousness, which cannot be reduced to the intention of an object. The structure of intentionality seems to point to a certain mastery of the object; but if there are modes of the subject beyond intentionality, then objectifying, hence dominating, consciousness does not have the last word.

The presence of Heidegger shadowed Levinas. Heidegger's stature is not denied. Yet the accusation against him is that his Being is an anonymous power that ultimately leads to an account of history as impersonal destiny. The person in its singularity is sacrificed to an ontology of anonymous powers. Heidegger's thought epitomizes ontology as a philosophy of power. Levinas opposes this with a metaphysics of the good wherein a nameless universal Being does not have final sway. Heidegger produces an ontology of the neuter; there is no basis for an ethics.

Levinas speaks against the neutering of being which he tends to identify with the horror and anonymity of what he calls the element. A different view of the elemental is possible, but for Levinas it is the faceless indefinite of the *prima materia* (sometimes wrongly identified with *to apeiron*). His account of the impersonality of the 'There is', as he calls it, reminds one of Sartre's account of being-in-itself, for instance in his phenomenology of the *viscous*: always threatening the integrity of the personal, the self as an integrity of innerness for itself. Levinas rejected the view of human being as derelict, as well as Sartre's alienated vision of man as nothingness. Heideggerian thrownness is counteracted by a phenomenology of enjoyment. Happiness, a prior agreement with being, is a more primordial condition of elemental being.

The question as to why Heidegger was an ardent Nazi is as important to Levinas as it was to Jaspers. Levinas spent time in a prisoner-of-war camp. Nazi philosophy was articulated in terms of a world-historical destiny as expressed in the German people. The others do not finally count; will to power subordinates all ethical concern to the victory of the mighty.

This relates to the influence in French philosophy of Kojève's reading of Hegel through the eyes of the master/slave dialectic in the *Phenomenology*. Hegelianism here becomes reduced to an all-devouring logic of domination and servitude. Sartre takes up a related interpretation in his infamous identification: hell is the other. Against the violence of the Sartrean look, Levinas sees the defencelessness of the other in the unguarded eyes, a powerlessness that nevertheless commands in the ethical injunction: Thou shalt not kill. Levinas rejects the identification of death as the master in Kojève's Heideggerian–Marxist Hegelianism. Contrary to the dialectic of master and slave and its violence, there is a pacific relation to the other that Levinas stresses as underlying the entire economy of labour and dwelling. This relates to the feminine. The grace of the feminine founds the home and the dwelling, out of which the labouring self is articulated, and with this the entire realm of economical, political and historical being. Things are conceived differently at the origins. These origins are not identical with the fullness of the ethical relation but they are consistent with it in a way that the dialectic of master and slave is not.

Kojève's Marxist Hegelianism also expresses a philosophy of history which culminates in the modern state as the earthly embodiment of the absolute. The world-historical universal sacrifices the intimate singularity of the self as person to the Moloch of the state. As world-historical universals, the state and history are ultimately idolatrous absolutes. Hegelian philosophy, like Heideggerian ontology, is seen by Levinas as an ontology of power which always is tempted to relate to the other by murder. The class struggle historically concretizes the master/slave dialectic. The course of history is war, the goal of history a homogeneous state in which otherness, the dissident other is suppressed in a universal sameness. Though this is abhorrent to Levinas, he is still concerned with labour, property, possession, reminding us of Marcel's concerns with being and having.

Levinas's repeated references to the philosophies of existence are guarded. He shares much with some existentialists, Kierkegaard for instance, in defending the singularity, the ipseity of the human self. Levinas's phenomenological background and its pretence that philosophy must be rigorous, indeed scientific, makes him uneasy with the so-called 'irrationalism' of the existentialists. He distances himself from a philosophy that is merely a protestation against the impersonal reason of the idealists and rationalists. He wants to defend a different sense of reason against individualistic irrationalism. This sense of reason will defend the ethical community of the same and the other. Though Levinas shuns the way of solitary genius, his sense of singularity aligns him with what is best in the philosophies of existence. This is an emphasis on what I called the intimacy of being with respect to Marcel. I find strong echoes of Marcel in some of the themes Levinas dwells on: the family, paternity, filiality, the home, enjoyment.

There is a groundswell of influence from Levinas's Jewishness. It is indicated very explicitly in his admiring reference to Rosenzweig's *The Star of Redemption*. Rosenzweig was initially a Hegelian who had written on Hegel's doctrine of the state. Then he had an astonishing quick conversion – reversion really – to Judaism, out of which *The Star of Redemption* sprung. This book is considered one of the landmarks of modern Jewish thought. Against the lure of Hegelian totality, a metaphysics of creation, as well as an affirmation of singularity as recalcitrant to inclusion in totality, is pursued. Though in *Totality and Infinity* Levinas says he is working in a purely philosophical vein, the distinctiveness of his philosophical voice owes much to the subterranean fermenting of the Jewish heritage.

In contrast to not a few poststructuralist thinkers, Levinas's philosophy has always exhibited a spiritual seriousness that refuses to playact with the matter itself. The return of sacred otherness in Levinas reminds us of Shestov's contrast of Athens and Jerusalem. Shestov is unjustly neglected today but he is a profound, radical thinker of the limits of philosophy in relation to religion as an other, and with a sense of the tradition of speculative metaphysics in some ways more profound than Levinas's.

With Heidegger and many post-structuralists, Levinas tends to totalize the tradition of philosophy. *All* philosophy is said to be only an imperialism of identity or the same. Levinas speaks of philosophy as allergic to otherness, an allergy that reaches its culmination in Hegel. This is surely not true of the philosophical tradition as a whole. This fact is revealed by Levinas's retraction: there is some philosophical acknowledgement of the other, as in Plato's doctrine of the Good beyond being.

The strategy is: totalize the tradition as imperialism of the same; suggest a different thinking of the other that is without precedent; then smuggle back ideas that in some form are found in the tradition; finally, acknowledge instances of such ideas in the tradition. Of course, most readers will have forgotten the first step by the time they reach the last. In fact, the total claim made in the first step is now effectively abolished. Why not acknowledge the last step *at the start*? But one cannot if one wants to claim to 'overcome the tradition'. That claim would be dissolved; suspicion would be cast on the hermeneutics of suspicion. To take the last step first would require a hermeneutics of generosity and perhaps also a different interpretation of the philosophical tradition.

Levinas is not to be confused with Derrida and Heidegger. He is very critical of Heidegger, and his writings evidence a spiritual seriousness that is lacking in Derrida. He mixes suspicion and generosity towards the philosophical tradition in his distinction between what he calls 'ontology' and 'metaphysics'. Ontology marks a philosophy of being that always ends up reducing the other to the same. Ontology is a philosophy of the neuter which cannot do justice to the other, and especially the other as ethical. It is built upon the logic of a movement from the same to the other which is always for the same, and always returning to the same. One is reminded of that strand of the tradition that privileges the movement of thought thinking itself.

By metaphysics Levinas implies a movement of thought that exceeds totality, most especially in the surplus to thought of the idea of infinity and the face-to-face relation of the ethical. Metaphysical thought goes from the same to the other, but not in order to return to the self. This metaphysical movement of mind has always been a philosophical possibility, evidenced in Levinas's own citation of Plato's

Good. Beyond thought thinking itself, thought thinks what is other to thought.

Levinas shows a tendency to identify the assumptions and analyses of Cartesian and transcendental idealism with the essential possibilities of philosophy. Relative to the Cartesian heritage, the *cogito* is privileged as the origin of all rigorously grounded philosophizing. Even Sartre's Cartesianism shows this: the availability of consciousness to itself seems to augur for a mode of philosophizing that is rigorously in possession of its own procedures and contents, for none of its thoughts escape its own immanence, and hence its own certainty and certification. Levinas differently underscores the Cartesian notion of infinitude to find a renewed pathway to the other beyond all mastering thought. Obviously phenomenology offers a more embracing sense of philosophizing than classical Cartesianism, but their basic presuppositions overlap significantly: immanence to consciousness is fundamental to phenomenology. This is just how the 'phenomenon' of phenomenology is defined: not as the *Sache* as given in itself, but as given to and for consciousness. Nevertheless, starting with many of phenomenology's presuppositions and methical strategies, Levinas ends up with conclusions that produce the subversion of phenomenological immanence, as well as classical versions of idealism.

Consider an important example: the discussion of representation in *Totality and Infinity*. Long passages are expository of an essentially Husserlian version of representation: representation is representability to consciousness; the immanence of the other is objectified as a representation for the same. This notion of representation has also been attacked by Heidegger, Derrida, Foucault and others. But to take this as *the* analysis of representation is questionable. We are offered analyses of representation and intelligibility which seem to cover the whole field, but do not at all. An account could be given which does not coincide with Husserl's view. Levinas himself goes on to do this, by claiming that there is an uprooted quality to the Husserlian analysis which privileges the theoretical consciousness. Turning to the phenomenon of enjoyment, Levinas finds a more primordial stratum in the genesis of representation that undercuts the analysis of the uprooted version. The 'intentionality' of enjoyment does not privilege self-constituting, or the primacy of the same over the other, as representation allegedly does.

One need not quarrel with this second aim. But Levinas sets up his account as undercutting the philosophical primacy of representation and intelligibility. In fact he is essentially criticizing representation and intelligibility as defined by Husserl's transcendental method. One could give an account of representation in which the privilege of the other over the self is primarily stressed. Instead of representation simply being a commandeering of the other to appear before the self as the self would dictate for itself, it might be an openness to the other in which the truth of the representation is a submission to heterogeneity, a humility before the other which the representation tries to approximate and respect.

Consider: if you ask me to represent you at a meeting, and if I truly want to represent you, I must subordinate my views to you and yours; I as representative must speak for you, the other; I cannot make you, the other, speak for me and yet honestly claim that I am representing you, the other. I am for you, as your representative. Representing is hence being-for-the-other in which the self subordinates the for-self of its own egoism to the truth of the other as it is for the other. This is exactly the opposite of the 'essence' to which Levinas reduces representation. Husserlian phenomenology is one philosophy; it is not philosophy, not the essence of philosophy. Nor is it the touchstone of all comparisons. Indeed its account is not true to the truth of representation as just indicated: a standing for the truth of the other as other.

I dwell on this example, for the standard moves of many post-structuralist thinkers, Derrida included, are already contained in Levinas's account of representation. But all philosophical discourse becomes skewed if Husserlian transcendentalism becomes *the* standard of philosophy against which other views are to be pitted. There is a certain historical, hermeneutical myopia here. When Marcel or Jaspers criticizes idealism, we do not find any tendency to hermeneutical special pleading. They do not totalize philosophy and its traditions. They are more judicious. Yet they too want to get beyond thought thinking itself to thought thinking what is other to thought.

It is impossible to separate Levinas's philosophy of the other from his sense of infinity and hence the idea of the divine other. Instead of conceiving the world as a fall or an emanation from the One, or a projection of constitutive subjectivity, Levinas's rethinking of the idea of infinity points towards a renewal of the metaphysics of creation. Metaphysics here again means a mode of thinking that is for the other as other, not simply for the same. Creation names the radically originative act by which the singular creature comes into being for itself, and is given its finite being for itself. The Creator absolves His creation from the Creator to let be the other as finite in its given freedom. In that sense, God is the ultimate other that is the giver of all otherness, including the radical otherness that is let be for itself, and in no way coerced into a return that would subordinate a part to an engulfing whole.

The strategic ambiguity here is that Levinas describes the for-self as atheist. On initial reading one might be inclined to think that Levinas espouses atheism. As I understand him, he is saying that the being of finitude as given in creation is atheist; it is a-theist in the most literal sense that it is not-God. God does not create Himself in creating the world, as Hegel and Spinoza might claim. God's creation is the giving of what is radically other to God, radically not-God; and this 'not' is the measure of an incommensurability between the Creator and the created being. This incommensurability is not a merely negative or lamentable disproportion; the 'not' of a-theism is the very space of transcendence in which the freedom of the creature can be enacted and called forth. The atheism of the self is the promise of its possible being-for-itself, and in its being-for-self its possible free relation across an irreducible difference to the divine source itself. Atheist being is then the product of divine generosity; atheism is the precondition of a different relativity between the human and divine which absolves the relata of complicity in relations of domination and violation.

Is there a little disingenuousness here? *Totality and Infinity* was written at a time when atheistic existentialism and Marxism were in their heyday. For well over a century and a half, the spiritual ethos of Europe has been dominated by a *de rigueur* atheism, as is nowhere more evident than in the popularizing of Sartrean existentialism. Levinas is a crafty writer in that he incorporates the truth of atheism within a project that aims to renew the metaphysical affirmation of God as transcendent. In the ambiguous creation, the human being as for-itself is atheist being; but atheist being can know its real otherness to ultimate transcendence and hence out of its atheist being turn towards the other, not as a part returns to its whole, not as an instance subordinates itself to its general, but as a free centre of ethical existence wills to enact the good of the Creator, the good of the creature and neighbour. This ethical affirmation stands sentinel against descent into the anonymous powers of demonic universality, the world-historical universal, whether idolized in Marxist or in Nazi form. In the latter we become agents, instruments of the anonymous universal, and all the more vile when we become judges and executioners of those who will not bow the knee before our murderously exacting idol. This is the malice of atheist being, which does not receive the expression or consideration in *Totality and Infinity* that it should.

Levinas's emphasis on infinity invokes a tale that spans the history of speculative metaphysics, from the pre-Socratics to our own time. Levinas exploits the Cartesian idea of infinity in a direction that I suspect would have astonished Descartes himself. Pascal was correct and saw right through Descartes when he said: 'I cannot forgive Descartes; in his whole philosophy he would like to do without God; but he could not help allowing him a flick of his fingers to set the world in motion; after that he had no more use for God.' Levinas, who often cites Pascal with approval, seems hardly to suspect the possible godlessness of Cartesianism.

There is also a strange approval of Cartesian doctrines of sensibility, praised because sensibility is held to be essentially other to thought and the concept. Kant is here praised on the same score for insisting on a heterogeneity between sensibility and understanding. One sees the point. The continuity of sensibility and thought, whether in Leibniz or in Hegel, is to be ruptured in defence of a heterogeneity not subsumable under the rational concept. But there is a sense in which such a thing as Cartesian sensibility hardly exists. There is a sensible body in Descartes but it is not the body of flesh; it is not the bodied self; it is the shape of the *res extensa* that in itself is lifeless. How can this lifeless *res extensa* enjoy life, since it is already a dead body? And from where could a Cartesian *res extensa* get a face? The *res extensa* has no face. The Cartesian body is like the featureless wax of Descartes' own example, entirely faceless, except for its automated mechanical movements. But human flesh has a face – just what Levinas wants to uphold.

In another place the Cartesian order is said to be prior to the Socratic order relative to teaching. But again what can the *res cogitans* teach to an other, or be taught itself? What is it taught by the idea of infinity? That God exists. But this is about all that is taught. Descartes is entirely lacking in the passion of religious inwardness that we find, for instance, in Augustine, Pascal and Kierkegaard. In fact, for Descartes the self and God are the two things most easily known, and once Descartes has placed them as foundational concepts to certify rational knowing methodologically, he gets down to the real business at hand: mathematicized science of nature. This Cartesian order of objective *mathesis* proves all but oblivious of the inward otherness of the self and the superior otherness of the divine transcendence. These become methodological means to an end, not enigmatic, mysterious realities that tax all thinking to the utmost, indeed defeat all its claims to the conceptual mastery, such as Descartes ardently pursued.

How superior here is the Socratic dialogue wherein the promise of openness to the other is inscribed from the outset. Levinas has nothing to say about dialogue as already articulating a concept of the soul that in its being is essentially relational; thought is never *kath' auto* in a manner that excludes relativity; for such a *kath' auto* would exclude the possibility of the face-to-face. Socratic dialogue is philosophical speech face-to-face. There is an implied Socratic sense of bodied speech – speech in the sight and in the hearing, and indeed within the touch of the other. Speech in a Socratic dialogue is as much a self saying as a something said.

Levinas's theme of the face-to-face must be noted here. This is his distinctive contribution to the discussion of 'intersubjectivity'. German idealism and phenomenology bequeathed the problem of the other: starting with subjectivity how do we genuinely constitute relatedness to the other as other? Is the other merely the means by which I recognize myself and return to myself? Is the other, seen from the primacy of the subject, just the mirror in which the self sees essentially itself, hence no radical otherness can ever be defended? As an heir of phenomenology and not German idealism, Levinas confronts phenomenology's same starting point in the subject. Levinas too starts with the self, in that earlier parts of *Totality and Infinity* are predominantly devoted to showing us a sufficiently strong sense of the *separation* of the self for itself. The self for itself is an irreducible ipseity that cannot be subsumed into an impersonal reason, or made the instance of an abstract universal. And yet this for-self in its radical separateness is not a transcendental ego. It is invested with the concreteness of the existing I in its primordial enjoyment of being.

How then is the problem of the *inter*, the 'between', tackled? The self expresses itself and enters into discourse and language. Expression for Levinas is such that the speaking subject always attends his or her expression. He or she does not abandon expression but attends it as willing to justify it, or indeed justify himself or herself, that is to say, apologize. To apologize does not here mean to ask pardon simply; it implies one standing there for oneself and owning up in expression to what one is or does. An apology, like Socrates', is a self-justification; the justice of the self in its personal particularity is at stake. But one apologizes always *before the other*. One attends one's expression in the sight of an other. Hence expression and the apologetic attending of expression by the self is an entry into social relatedness, is the social relation.

This entry of justification, justice, apology, attention of self before the sight of the other, comes to expression in the face-to-face. I encounter the face of the other and the other looks on me, not like Sartre's other that would petrify me and reduce the freedom of interiority to an objectified thing. The face of the other calls me to justification, to justice. The face presents itself with a nudity and destitution that is beyond all conceptualization. The face cannot be totalized, for the infinite comes to epiphany there. I cannot conceptually determine the face of the other; the eyes of the other look at me with an unguarded vulnerability, and call me to a response that is beyond power. This unguarded vulnerability of the eye of the other is radically opposite to Sartre's look. If looks could kill, Sartre's subject would be a mass murderer. In Levinas's case, the look offers itself as the other offering itself in unguarded frankness; in that look there appears the command 'Thou shalt not kill'.

The ethical is not an instrumental contract that the self of will to power, be it Nietzschean or Sartrean or Hobbesian, makes to defend itself against the other and to launch its self-aggrandizing onslaught on the freedom of the other. The unguarded face is beyond all instrumentality and beyond all finality in the sense that it does not constitute a determinate purpose or *telos* that could be conclusively comprehended and mastered or encompassed. Something overflows in the face of the other that is infinite, and this infinite is the command of goodness. The overflow of infinity into the between, the *inter*, calls the subject in its separateness to a relatedness with the other that does not compromise separateness, since the very between is an ethical respect of justice between the self and other.

Levinas finds the face absolutely irreducible, primordial. One cannot break it down into more basic constituents; it is elemental, though not in Levinas's sense. It cannot be contained within the economy of classical subjectivity, whether idealistic or transcendental/phenomenological. These latter finally give hegemony to the same over the other. While Levinas defends the separateness of the subject, the face-to-face and the overflowing of the other's infinitude reverse the hegemony of autonomy. There is a heteronomy more ultimate than autonomy. The self is for the other; and the other comes from a dimension of height, even when the other is the abject self, the poor, the widow, the orphan.

Levinas intends to transcend the master/slave dialectic, but there are occasions where the other is referred to as the master, and where the asymmetry between the same and the other seems to skirt dangerously another form of the master/slave relation. We find a peculiar mixture of elements: the radical separateness of the subject, who is not really separate, since he or she puts himself or herself in the between by his or her expression; the subject who in the between encounters the face of the other who commands against murder in the nakedness of the vulnerable eye; the separate self whose ineluctable destiny seems social. How then is the other radically other and the self still irreducibly separate? For it is their co-implication and infinite responsibility that seem the most important things. Is this no more than a verbal problem? Levinas defends the irreducibility of the self in its personal singularity, and yet against Enlightenment modernity he reinstates a heteronomous ethics, where the justice of the other, assumed in infinite responsibility, is absolutely central.

Eros is important for Levinas in breaking out of monadism and the 'egocentric predicament'. This is linked with his stress on fecundity. One is reminded of the speech of Socrates/Diotima concerning *eros* as generating on the good/beautiful. *Eros* generates beyond itself on the beautiful/good. This is a somewhat strange saying. I take it to mean that the highest point of *eros* is not, in fact, erotic in the sense of yielding just a completion of a lack in the self, and hence a culminating self-satisfaction in a final self-relatedness. *Eros* seems to start in lack and in final satisfaction makes the erotic being self-sufficient again by overcoming the lack. But this is not enough. Rather, the self generates beyond itself on the good. There is a transcendence of self that goes beyond the most embracing self-sufficiency and self-relativity.

Fecundity is the self generating beyond itself. I would prefer to call it the promise of *agape* rather than *eros*, in that it does not fill a lack of satisfaction but goes beyond self in an overflowing of being that is already full, overfull. As already full in itself the self agapeically goes towards the other as other; in this case goes towards the child as an other who is not yet known as a this, and who is the promise of the future, a continuation and a rupture, a relativity and a radical separateness at once.

It is noticeable here that Levinas emphasizes the father/son relation, rather than the relation of father/daughter, or mother/son. Paternity and filiality become the means of expressing the fecundity, the infinitude of time in its generative power. The feminine reduces to a certain equivocal form of being. There is ambiguity in the relation of the father and son: I the father am the son; I the father am not at all the son.

Levinas makes much of the infinity of time against what he seems to see as the jealous self-enclosure of eternity. It seems as if the fecundity of infinite time will pardon all. I think this will not do relative to the singularity and sociality Levinas wants to emphasize. Time, even infinite time, will not radically pardon radical evil. Later generations cannot provide justification for the radical evils visited upon present generations. Levinas does not want to instrumentalize present evil. But is infinite time enough to prevent time from being swept up into the instrumental justification of world history? It can only be from an entirely different dimension that the pardon for radical evil can come. This would be eternity in another sense to the one that Levinas plays with, namely, the catatonic absolute identity that knows no relativity to otherness. Levinas's reference to messianic time at the end of *Totality and Infinity* indicates that the work is a truncated book; its real import lies elsewhere.

For all the talk about the frankness of the face, and the person attending his expression, Levinas is perhaps a dissimulating writer. The entirety of *Totality and Infinity* points beyond itself to God, but God is foxily talked about throughout the entire book. One is reminded of the equivocation of discourse imputed to some Jewish thinkers, Spinoza for instance, or Derrida for that matter. In the present case, one speaks the language of atheism, while being a theist behind it all. Today the metaphysicians and theologians have to hide themselves from the inquisition of the atheist, while for the main part of recorded intellectual history it was the atheist who had to go in hiding in fear of the inquisition of the believer.

In Levinas's later work the sense of responsibility for the other is accentuated further. The claim that ethics is first philosophy is developed more fully. The central essay of *Otherwise than Being or Beyond Essence* is titled 'Substitution'. Here Levinas develops the idea of an anarchic subjectivity that is prior to all thematization. One is reminded of Sartre's non-positional consciousness, except that in Levinas's case the sense of being summoned by the other is to the fore; the self prior to the ego is marked by an obsession with the other. Levinas ties this with being a creature in which the trace of the absolute other is in passage.

'Substitution' is a bold and provocative meditation, brilliant and profound in many respects. I cannot do justice here either to its claims or to the questions it provokes. Levinas does claim that prior even to the absolute priority claimed for the transcendental ego, the call of the other in an infinite responsibility is at work. The concept of 'substitution' refers to the manner in which this anarchic self is a hostage for the other. It is in the place of the other; this power to be in the place of the other is the ground of all other acts of solidarity or sociality. The self is a subject in *being subject* to the other in infinite responsibility.

Levinas likes to quote Dostoevsky's Alyosha Karamazov: 'We are all responsible for everyone else – but I am more responsible than all the others.' This is a claim of hyperbolic responsibility, and some would criticize it as such. It may even ironically suggest an ethical hubris in which I place myself in the role of the absolute, substitute myself for God. Only God could be responsible thus, no mortal creature could. Yet Levinas wants to insist, and insist is the word, that human creatures are disturbed by this call of infinite responsibility. There are ambiguities here too complex to unravel in the space allotted. For substitution is a divine responsibility, substitution even to the point of death and sacrifice. Levinas is often presented as without precedents, and his singular style helps to foster this impression. But I cannot but remind the reader of the emphasis on testimony, witness and sacrifice in Marcel. Read in a certain way, Marcel's Catholicism and Levinas's Judaism generate some very deep affinities.

Levinas sets himself against transcendental phenomenology here and its regress to grounding in originary selfhood. He emphasizes the passivity, the patience to the other of the pre-synthetic self. Yet his mode of thinking, like transcendental philosophy generally, is regressive, a matter of what both call 'reduction'. Is there not after all a strange 'transcendentalism' in this? A transcendentalism of passivity rather than activity, or rather of patience to the other prior to both activity and passivity? This would be prior to the a priori of transcendental idealism. Substitution would be the condition of the possibility of all meaning, linguistic, cognitive, pragmatic as well as ethical. Ethics as first philosophy would then be a transcendental philosophy, though since it does not deal with the transcendental ego as the ultimate originary presence, it might be called an *atranscendental ethics* or a *negative transcendentalism*, on the analogy of negative theology.

Many of Levinas's ways of saying are strongly reminiscent of negative theology: It is not this, not that . . . ; it is as if it were, as though . . . it is neither this, nor that . . . . There is a sense in which we here have to make a *leap* beyond phenomenology. There are times when that leap could be made more intelligible for the reader if Levinas provided some phenomenological examples from human relations, for instance in the telling way Marcel appeals to the examples from his own dramatic works to suggest imaginatively the non-objectifiable.

There is generally a tendency to *dualistic* thinking in Levinas, for example, ontology versus metaphysics, being versus the good. This tendency can lead to significant equivocity. I will conclude with a relevant example and question. In 'Substitution' Levinas unrelentingly stresses the irreplaceability of the self that is summoned in ethical responsibility. But how can the irreplaceable be substituted? There cannot be a replacement for the non-substitutable, nor a substitute for the irreplaceable. The concept of hostage carried the idea of *equivalence*: one for the other, a tooth for a tooth. But the concept of equivalence is impossible without the idea of identity, and Levinas's whole discourse of the irreplaceable claims to be prior to the idea of identity and its cognate concepts like equivalence.

This is a logical problem with substitution, but it points to a tension that is not merely logical. If we privilege the irreplaceable, there must be a limit to human substitution; by contrast, if we privilege substitution, we compromise the absolute singularity of the irreplaceable. How then can we affirm substitution and the irreplaceable both together? Put this way: Job's second set of children seem to be replacements for the first dead children, they seem to be substitutes. But the whole thrust of Levinas's thought must be that there can be no replacement for the first irreplaceable children; there are no human substitutes.

Do we reach the limit of human substitution? And a limit of the fecundity of infinite time? Is there such a thing as divine substitution which would radically transfigure the notion of selfhood as irreplaceable? Do we need the idea of re-creation, the idea of a new creation to deal with the irreplaceability of the first creation, relative to the horrors we have heaped on it and its seemingly senseless death?

❧ SELECTED BIBLIOGRAPHY ❧

Marcel

Primary texts

5.1 'La Métaphysique de Josiah Royce', *Revue de métaphysique et de morale*, January–April 1919. Reprint: *La Métaphysique de Royce*, Paris: Aubier, 1945.

5.2 *Journal Métaphysique*, Paris: Gallimard, 1927. Reprint: 1935.

5.3 *Etre et avoir*, Paris: Aubier, 1935.

5.4 *Du refus à l'invocation*, Paris: Gallimard, 1940. Reprint: Paris: Aubier, 1945.

5.5 *Homo Viator: Prolégomènes à une métaphysique de l'espérance*, Paris: Aubier, Editions Montaigne, 1944.

5.6 *Les Hommes contre l'humain*, Paris: La Colombe, 1951. Reprint: Paris: Fayard, 1968.

5.7 *Le Mysterè de l'être*, vol. 1, *Réflexion et mystère*, Paris: Aubier, 1951. Contains the Gifford Lectures of 1949.

5.8 *Le Mysterè de l'être*, vol. 2, *Foi et réalité*, Paris: Aubier, 1951.

5.9 *Le Déclin de la sagesse*, Paris: Plon, 1954.

5.10 *Fragments philosophiques, 1909–1914*, Philosophes contemporains: Textes et études 11, Louvain: Nauwelaerts, 1962.

5.11 *La Dignité humaine et ses assises existentialles*, Collections Présence et pensée, Paris: Aubier, Editions Montaigne, 1964.

5.12 *Pour une sagesse tragique et son au-delà*, Paris: Plon, 1968.

5.13 *Coleridge et Schelling*, Paris: Aubier-Montaigne, 1971.

Translations

5.14 *Royce's Metaphysics*, trans. V. and G. Ringer, Chicago: Henry Regnery Co., 1956.

5.15 *Metaphysical Journal*, trans. B. Wall, Chicago: Henry Regnery Co., 1950. Reprints: 1952, 1967. London: Barrie & Rockliff, 1952.

5.16 *Being and Having*, trans. K. Farrer, Westminster: Dacre Press; Glasgow: University Press, 1949; Boston: Beacon Press, 1951. Reprinted under the expanded title *Being and Having: An Existentialist Diary*, London: Fontana Library and New York: Harper & Row, Harper Torchbooks, 1965.

5.17 *Creative Fidelity*. trans. R. Rosthal, New York: Farrar, Strauss, Cudahy, Noonday Press, 1964.

5.18 *Homo Viator: Introduction to a Metaphysic of Hope*, trans. E. Crauford, London: Victor Gollancz and Chicago: Henry Regnery Co., 1951. New York: Harper and Row, Harper Torchbooks, 1962.

5.19 *Men Against Humanity*, trans. G. S. Fraser, London: Harvill Press, 1952.

5.20 *Man Against Mass Society*, trans. G. S. Fraser, foreword by D. MacKinnon. Chicago: Henry Regnery Co., 1952. Reprint: Chicago: Henry Regnery Co., Gateway, 1962.

5.21 *The Mystery of Being*, vol. 1, *Reflection and Mystery*. trans. G. S. Fraser, London: Harvill Press and Chicago: Henry Regnery Co., 1950. Reprint: Chicago: Henry Regnery Co., Gateway, 1960.

5.22 *The Mystery of Being*, vol. 2, *Faith and Reality*. trans. R. Hague, London: Harvill Press and Chicago: Henry Regnery Co., 1951. Reprint: Chicago: Henry Regnery Co., Gateway, 1960.

5.23 *The Decline of Wisdom*, trans. M. Harari, London: Harvill Press and Toronto: Collins, 1954. New York: Philosophical Library, 1955.

5.24 *The Influence of Psychic Phenomena on My Philosophy*, London: London Society for Psychical Research, 1956. The Frederic W. H. Myers Memorial Lecture, December 1955.

5.25 *Philosophical Fragments, 1909–1914*, trans. L. A. Blain, published together with *The Philosopher and Peace*, trans. V. H. Drath, Notre Dame: University of Notre Dame Press, 1965.

5.26 *The Existential Background of Human Dignity*, Harvard University: The William James Lectures, 1961–2, Cambridge, Mass.: Harvard University Press, 1963.

5.27 *Philosophical Fragments 1909–1914*, trans. L. A. Blain. Notre Dame: University of Notre Dame Press, 1965.

5.28 *Tragic Wisdom and Beyond*, trans. S. Jolin and P. McCormick, Northwestern University Studies in Phenomenology and Existential Philosophy, Evanston: Northwestern University Press, 1973.

Criticism

5.29 Appelbaum, D. *Contact and Attention: The Anatomy of Gabriel Marcel's Metaphysical Method*, Lanham: University Press of America, 1986.

5.30 Davy, M. M. *Un Philosophe itinérant: Gabriel Marcel*, Paris: Flammarion, 1959.

5.31 Gallagher, K. T. *The Philosophy of Gabriel Marcel*, New York: Fordham University Press, 1962.

5.32 Hocking, W. E. 'Marcel and the Ground Issues of Metaphysics', *Philosophy and Phenomenological Research* 14: 4 (June 1954): 439–69.

5.33 O'Malley, J. B. *The Fellowship of Being*, The Hague: Nijhoff, 1966.

5.34 Peccorini, F. *Selfhood as Thinking in the Work of Gabriel Marcel*, Lewiston: Mellen Press, 1987.

5.35 Prini, P. *Gabriel Marcel et la méthodologie de l'invérifiable*, Paris: Desclée de Brouwer, 1953.

5.36 Ricoeur, P. *Gabriel Marcel et Karl Jaspers: Philosophie du mystère et philosophie du paradoxe*, Paris: Editions du temps présent, 1948.

5.37 Schilpp, P. and Hahn, L. (eds) *The Philosophy of Gabriel Marcel*, The Library of Living Philosophers, vol. XVII, La Salle: Open Court, 1983.

Jaspers

Primary texts

5.38 *Allgemeine Psychopathologie*, Berlin: Springer Verlag, 1913; 4th completely rev. edn, Berlin, Göttingen and Heidelberg: Springer Verlag, 1946; 8th edn, 1965.

5.39 *Psychologie der Weltanschauungen*, Berlin: Springer Verlag, 1919: 5th edn, Berlin, Göttingen, Heidelberg: Springer Verlag, 1960.

5.40 *Philosophie*, 3 vols, Berlin: Springer Verlag, 1932.

5.41 *Vernunft und Existenz: Fünf Vorlesungen*. Gröningen: J. B. Wolters, 1935; 4th edn, München: R. Piper, 1960.

5.42 *Die Schuldfrage*, Heidelberg: L. Schneider Verlag, and Zürich: Artemis Verlag, 1946.

5.43 *Von der Wahrheit: Philosophische Logik, Erster Band*. München: R. Piper, 1947; 3rd edn, 1980.

5.44 *Der philosophische Glaube: Gastvorlesungen*, Zürich: Artemis Verlag and München: R. Piper & Co., 1948; 7th edn, München: R. Piper, 1981.

5.45 *Vom Ursprung und Ziel der Geschichte*, Zürich: Artemis Verlag and München: R. Piper, 1949; 4th edn, München: 1963.

5.46 *Die grossen Philosophen: Erster Band*, München: R. Piper, 1957; 3rd edn, 1981.

5.47 *Die grossen Philosophen, Nachlass 1*, ed. H. Saner, München and Zürich: R. Piper, 1981.

5.48 *Die grossen Philosophen, Nachlass 2*, ed. H. Saner, München and Zürich: R. Piper, 1981.

5.49 *Der philosophische Glaube angesichts der Offenbarung*, München: R. Piper, 1962; 3rd edn, 1980.

5.50 *Weltgeschichte der Philosophie: Einleitung*, ed. H. Saner, München and Zürich: R. Piper, 1982.

Translations

5.51 *General Psychopathology*, trans. J. Hoening and M. W. Hamilton, Chicago: University of Chicago Press, 1963.

5.52 *Philosophy*, 3 vols, trans. E. B. Ashton, Chicago and London: University of Chicago Press, 1969–71.

5.53 *Reason and Existenz*, trans. W. Earle, London, Toronto and New York, 1955.

5.54 *The Question of German Guilt*, trans. E. B. Ashton, New York: Dial Press, 1947.

5.55 *Tragedy is not Enough*, (excerpt from *Von der Wahrheit*), trans. H. A. T. Reiche, H. T. Moore and K. W. Deutsch, Boston: Beacon Press, 1952 and London: V. Gollancz, 1953.

5.56 *Truth and Symbol* (excerpt from *Von der Wahrheit*), trans. J. T. Wilde, W. Kluback and W. Kimmel, New York: Twayne Publishers and London: Vision Press, 1959.

5.57 *The Perennial Scope of Philosophy*, trans. R. Manheim, New York: Philosophical Library, 1949 and London: Routledge & Kegan Paul, 1950.

5.58 *The Origin and Goal of History*, trans. M. Bullock, New Haven: Yale University Press and London: Routledge & Kegan Paul, 1953.

5.59 *Philosophical Faith and Revelation*, trans. E. B. Ashton, Chicago: University of Chicago Press, 1967.

5.60 *Anaximander, Heraclitus, Parmenides, Plotinus, Lao-tzu, Nagarjuna*, New York: Harcourt Brace Jovanovich, n.d. (excerpt from *The Great Philosophers: The Original Thinkers*).

5.61 *Anselm and Nicholas of Cusa*, New York: Harcourt Brace Jovanovich, n.d. (excerpt from *The Great Philosophers: The Original Thinkers*).

5.62 *The Great Philosophers: The Foundations, The Paradigmatic Individuals: Socrates, Buddha, Confucius, Jesus; The Seminal Founders of Philosophical Thought: Plato, Augustine, Kant*, ed. H. Arendt, trans. R. Manheim, New York: Harcourt, Brace & World, 1962.

5.63 *The Great Philosophers: The Original Thinkers: Anaximander, Heraclitus, Parmenides, Plotinus, Anselm, Nicholas of Cusa, Spinoza, Lao-Tzu, Nagarjuna*, ed. H. Arendt, trans. R. Manheim, New York: Harcourt, Brace & World, 1966.

5.64 *Kant*, New York: Harcourt, Brace & World, n.d. (excerpt from *The Great Philosophers: The Foundations*).

5.65 *Plato and Augustine*, New York: Harcourt, Brace & World, n.d. (excerpt from *The Great Philosophers: The Foundations*).

5.66 *Socrates, Buddha, Confucius, Jesus*, New York: Harcourt, Brace & World, n.d. (excerpt from *The Great Philosophers: The Foundations*).

5.67 *Spinoza*, New York: Harcourt Brace Jovanovich, n.d. (excerpt from *The Great Philosophers: The Original Thinkers*).

Criticism

5.68 Allen, E. L. *The Self and Its Hazards: A Guide to the Thought of Karl Jaspers*, New York: Philosophical Library, 1951.

5.69 Ehrlich, L. H. *Karl Jaspers: Philosophy as Faith*, Amherst: University of Massachusetts Press, 1975.

5.70 Kane, J. F. *Pluralism and Truth in Religion: Karl Jaspers on Existentialist Truth*, Chico: Scholars Press, 1981.

5.71 Lichtigfeld, A. *Jaspers' Metaphysics*, London: Colibri Press, 1954.

5.72 Olson, A. M. *Transcendence and Hermeneutics: An Interpretation of Karl Jaspers*, The Hague: Nijhoff, 1979.

5.73 Ricoeur, P. *Gabriel Marcel et Karl Jaspers*, Paris: Editions du Temps Présent, 1948.

5.74 Samay, S. *Reason Revisited*, Notre Dame: University of Notre Dame Press, 1971.

5.75 Schilpp, P. (ed.) *The Philosophy of Karl Jaspers*, 2nd edn, Lasalle: Open Court, 1981. Contains Jaspers's 'Philosophical Autobiography' (including chapter: 'Heidegger'), critical contributions by twenty-four authors, and Jaspers's 'Reply to His Critics'.

5.76 Schrag, O. O. *Existence, Existenz, and Transcendence*, Pittsburgh: Duquesne University Press, 1971.

5.77 Wallraff, C. F. *Karl Jaspers: An Introduction to His Philosophy*, Princeton: Princeton University Press, 1970.

5.78 Young-Bruehl, E. *Freedom and Karl Jaspers's Philosophy*, New Haven: Yale University Press, 1971.

Levinas

Primary texts

5.79 *La théorie de l'intuition dans la phénoménologie de Husserl*, Paris: Alcan, 1930 (Vrin, 1963).

5.80 *De l'existence à l'existant*, Paris: Fontaine, 1947 (Vrin, 1973).

5.81 *En découvrant l'existence avec Husserl et Heidegger*, Paris: Vrin, 1967.

5.82 *Totalité et infini: Essai sur l'extériorité*, The Hague: Martinus Nijhoff, 1961.

5.83 *Difficile liberté*, Paris: Albin Michel, 1963 (2nd edn, 1976).

5.84 *Quatre lectures talmudiques*, Paris: Editions de Minuit, 1968.

5.85 *Humanisme de l-autre homme*, Montpellier: Fata Morgana, 1972.

5.86 *Autrement qu'être, ou au-delà de l'essence*, The Hague: Martinus Nijhoff, 1974.

5.87 *Sur Maurice Blanchot*, Montpellier: Fata Morgana, 1975.

5.88 *Noms propres*, Montpellier: Fata Morgana, 1976.

5.89 *Du sacré au saint*, Paris: Editions de Minuit, 1977.

5.90 *Le Temps et l'autre*, Montpellier: Fata Morgana, 1947 (Paris: Presses Universitaires de France, 1983).

5.91 *L'Au-delà du verset*, Paris: Editions de Minuit, 1982.

5.92 *De Dieu qui vient a l'idée*, Paris: Vrin, 1982.

5.93 *De l'evasion*, Paris: Fata Morgana, 1982.

5.94 *Ethique et infini*, Paris: Fayard, 1982.

5.95 *Transcendance et intelligibilité*, Genève: Labor et Fides, 1984.

Translations

5.96 *The Theory of Intuition in Husserl's Phenomenology*, trans. A. Orianne, Evanston: Northwestern University Press, 1973.

5.97 *Existence and Existents*, trans. A. Lingis, The Hague: Martinus Nijhoff, 1978.

5.98 *Difficult Freedom*, trans. S. Hand, London: Athlone, forthcoming.

5.99 *Otherwise than Being or Beyond Essence*, trans. A. Lingis, The Hague, Martinus Nijhoff, 1981.

5.100 *Time and the Other*, trans. R. Cohen, Pittsburgh: Duquesne University Press, 1987.

5.101 *Ethics and Infinity*, trans. R. Cohen, Pittsburgh: Duquesne University Press, 1985.

5.102 *Collected Philosophical Papers*, trans. A. Lingis, Dordrecht: Martinus Nijhoff, 1987.

Criticism

5.103 Bernasconi, R., and Wood, D. (eds) *The Provocation of Levinas: Rethinking the Other*, London and New York: Routledge, 1988.
5.104 Burggraeve, R. *From Self-Development to Solidarity: An Ethical Reading of Human Desire in its Socio-Political Relevance according to Emmanuel Levinas*, trans. C. Vanhove-Romanik, Leuven: The Centre for Metaphysics and Philosophy of God, 1985.
5.105 Cohen, R. (ed.) *Face to Face with Levinas*, Albany: State University of New York Press, 1986.
5.106 Derrida, J. 'Violence and Metaphysics', in *Writing and Difference*, trans. A. Bass, London: Routledge & Kegan Paul and Chicago: Chicago University Press, 1978, pp. 79–153.
5.107 Libertson, J. *Proximity, Levinas, Blanchot, Bataille and Communication*, Phaenomenologica 87, The Hague: Martinus Nijhoff, 1982.
5.108 Lingis, A. *Libido: The French Existential Theories*, Bloomington: Indiana University Press, 1985.

CHAPTER 6

Philosophies of science
Mach, Duhem, Bachelard
Babette E. Babich

❦

❦ THE TRADITION OF CONTINENTAL ❦ PHILOSOPHY OF SCIENCE

If the philosophy of science is not typically represented as a 'continental' discipline it is nevertheless historically rooted in the tradition of continental thought. The different approaches to the philosophy of science apparent in the writings of Ernst Mach, Pierre Duhem and Gaston Bachelard suggest the range of these roots. But for a discussion of the tradition of continental philosophy of science – as the term 'continental' characterizes a contemporary style of philosophic thinking – it is important to emphasize that while Mach, Duhem and Bachelard may be said to be *historically* continental, a properly continental-style philosophy of science should not be ascribed to any one of them. Contemporary philosophy of science is pursued in what is largely an analytic or Anglo-American-style philosophic tradition. And Mach, Duhem and Bachelard made the formative contributions for which they are known in the philosophy of science within this same almost quintessentially analytic framework.[1]

Nevertheless, this very necessary historical precision is itself witness to a changing circumstance in mainline philosophy of science. Although continental philosophy has been marginalized in professional philosophy in general, and where this marginalization has perhaps been greatest within the philosophy of science, the very centre would seem to have shifted. In past years, traditional philosophers of science have begun to broaden their analytic conception of the philosophy of science to include approaches compatible with or even drawn from continental styles of philosophy. Such approaches reflect the philosophical reflections on science expressed from the tradition of important individual continental thinkers such as Edmund Husserl (Gethmann, Heelan, Orth, Rang, Seebohm, etc.) and Martin Heidegger (Gadamer, Heelan, Kisiel, Kockelmans), Habermas and Foucault (Radder, Rouse, Gutting), and even Friedrich Nietzsche (Babich, Maurer, Spiekermann). In this context, the philosophical reflections on science to be found in Mach, Duhem and Bachelard may be mined for what should prove to be a productive historical foundation between these two traditions addressed to a common focus. Exemplifying such a common focus, the philosophy of science is not inherently or essentially analytic if it is also not obviously continental.

The question of stylistic conjunction between continental and analytic philosophic perspectives is complicated and, before it can be addressed, one further preliminary clarification is necessary. Because of the possibility of geographic confusion, it must be emphasized that the rubric 'continental' in the context of the philosophy of science does not pertain to the geographic locus of the European continent except historically and circumstantially. Despite German and French scholars interested in specifically continental approaches to the philosophy of science in contemporary European philosophy, the character of the philosophy of science is decidedly analytic. It is telling and to the point in this last connection that Wolfgang Stegmüller, familiar as he was with traditional philosophy including phenomenological approaches, could find the appeal of analytic philosophy for a formalist and foundationalist interest in scientific theories so inspiring that he devoted his own life to its dissemination and through his influence analytic styles of philosophic thought consequently assumed their current leading role in German philosophy of science. In turn, this means that continental philosophy (and philosophy of science) remains as professionally marginal on the 'continent' as in English-speaking scholarly domains.

But if not defined as the dominant tradition in philosophy and if not a matter of geographic reference, continental philosophy (especially with respect to philosophic reflection on science) is also a multifarious tradition and not a single style or school. Just as Rom Harré could speak of 'philosophies' of science,[2] it is best to speak of 'continental philosophies' and hence of 'continental philosophies of science'. Not necessarily linked by 'family resemblances' – for example, Husserlian-influenced thinking bears almost no resemblance to Habermasian or Foucauldian social, critical theory – what is called 'continental philosophy' comprises several conceptual traditions and reflects a manifold of differing styles of philosophy with cross-disciplinary influences and applications. But one general characteristic might be said to be a strong historical sensibility. This sensibility distinguishes continental philosophic styles from analytic (progress-oriented and often expressly ahistoricist and sometimes expressly anti-historical) styles of philosophy.

A critically reflective historical sensibility in addition to an explicit reference to lived experience – the *life-world* of Husserlian and Diltheyan usage – indicates some of the major advantages to be brought by continental styles of philosophy to the broader and general philosophic project of reflection on science.

It is this historical dimension and reference to life (practice, experience, etc.) that makes continental styles of philosophy so important for the philosophy of science today. Since the radical critique of the received, analytic style of modern philosophy of science through the writings of N. R. Hanson and the work of Thomas Kuhn and Paul Feyerabend, contemporary philosophy of science has been increasingly transformed by an intensified and today decisive sensitivity to the importance of historical and sociological studies of actual scientific practice. The turn to history so characteristic of Mach's as of Duhem's philosophic writing on science, witnessed by their valuable contributions to the history of science, and implicit in Bachelard's reading of the culture of science, has come to be recognized as an irreducible component of the philosophy of science. In the same way, the resources of continental philosophy with a tradition of reflection on history seem increasingly essential to the practice of the philosophy of science beyond stylistic differences.

As *fons et origo*, the shared destiny and origin of continental philosophy and analytic philosophy is evident in a recent trend reviewing the connection between Husserl and Frege (Hill, Wiener, Cobb-Stevens, Dummett), suggesting that Husserlian-style philosophies of science may go furthest towards bridging the stylistic gap between analytic and continental philosophy. Likewise it is significant that the philosophy of technology, related to the philosophy of science because of its importance for reflection on experimental science, not only features continental practioners (Ellul, Ihde, Jonas, Schirmacher, Winner, Zimmerman) but is in its rigorously philosophic aspect a direct resultant of this same tradition (drawing as it does on the work of Heidegger but also Ricoeur and Gadamer).

Although Mach's (as indeed Duhem's) positivist successors were ultimately to disregard his concern with history in their focus on the formal analysis and logical reconstruction which characterizes the hypothetico-deductive account of theory formation and justification and which in its most developed form came to be known as the 'received view', recent reviews of Mach seek to examine his philosophy of science in terms germane to its own reflective scientific constellation and philosophical project (Feyerabend, Haller) rather than merely in terms of its influence on the logical empiricist tradition of the philosophy of science (beginning with Frank). Thus a reassessment of Mach's philosophy of science stresses his historical interests, while Feyerabend emphasizes aspects in his work which anticipate the insights of Hanson and Kuhn (as well as Michael Polanyi who is, according to Alasdair MacIntyre, significantly underacknowledged in this connection)[3] in Mach's sensitivity to the element of finesse (or in Polanyi's language: 'tacit knowledge'). Discussion of the role of tacit knowledge or finesse represents the researcher's 'art', an art which, if we follow Mach's words, is *unteachable* in the sense of being inherently unamenable to the programmatic Baconian project and which project, conversely for its part, was held by Bacon to have its singular advantage in being manageable by underlabourers – that is, by technicians literally, as Bacon has it: without 'wit'. For Mach, precisely such a programmatization (automatization, industrialization) is not desirable even if it were possible. We may note that the actuality of what Derek de Solla Price called 'big science' has long demonstrated that such 'programmatization' is possible and Hugh Redner details the same in his study of giant, industrial-sized science.[4] Against the artless routinization of science, Mach held that an unteachable 'art' must be indispensable for the practice of experimental science because, in Mach's conception of scientific inquiry, it is the *sine qua non* of invention and discovery.

A turn to history and the role of the experimenter's art is not the only parallel resonance between continental philosophies of science and traditional analytic approaches: there are others. Despite stylistic differences, analytic and continental styles of philosophy share a common future as complementary approaches to the philosophy of science where both disciplinary styles can enhance one another. But what is inevitably more important than the prospects of such stylistic reconciliation on a scholarly level, it now seems eminently clear that the philosophy of science cannot be conducted from an analytic perspective uninformed by the hermeneutic turn or, as analysts prefer to speak of it: the *interpretive* turn (Hiley *et al*). In concert with the phenomeno-logical turn (to the things themselves), the interpretive, hermeneutic turn represents the foundation of continental thought. And it goes without saying, or calling it hermeneutics, that the interpretive turn is a turn of thought in which, like the historical turn, the reflective advantage of continental philosophy comes to the fore.

In both existing and possible expressions, continental philosophy of science includes approaches drawn from the larger tradition of phenomenology (as found in the works expressed by Hegel, Husserl, Heidegger, Merleau-Ponty) as well as hermeneutics (beginning with some say Vico, but certainly with Schleiermacher and Dilthey, and also Heidegger, Gadamer, Betti, Gramsci, Ricoeur). Continental philosophy also reflects the influence of structuralism in linguistics, semiotics, and literary criticism and psychology, as well as the Heidegger-inspired *Daseinsanalyse* and existential psychoanalysis (Piaget, Binswanger,

Boss, Fromm, Merleau-Ponty, Sartre and Lacan). Related philosophic styles of deconstruction and recent postmodern conceptions of philosophy (Foucault, Derrida, Lyotard, Baudrillard) have had a decisive influence on late twentieth-century philosophic reflection on science in line with the hermeneutic perspective (Heelan, Kockelmans, Kisiel, Hacking, Böhme, Gadamer, Bubner). With specific reference to the philosophy of the social sciences, particularly representing the Frankfurt school, which often incorporates analytic-style distinctions in its focus on language and discourse (Habermas, Apel, Tugendhat), characteristically 'continental' influences are traced in a variety of lineages to Hegel or Schleiermacher, Marx or Feuerbach (Althusser, Bhaskar, LeCourt) and Kierkegaard or Dilthey, Heidegger, Weber, Simmel.

As representatives of nineteenth- and early twentieth-century empiricism and positivism, the particular names Ernst Mach (1838–1916), Pierre Duhem (1861–1916) and Gaston Bachelard (1884–1962) have of course and as already noted much more than a merely historical significance. In analytic philosophy of science, an ongoing tradition of reinterpretations of their work continues to influence the current linguistic or theoretical crisis in analytic philosophy and semiotics/semantics of scientific theory (Duhem not only as represented by W. V. O. Quine but also Stanley Jaki) as well as, on the other hand, the current emphasis on experiment representing the counter-absolutist turn to the history (and historiography) and practice of science in the philosophy of science (specifically Mach, as represented by Feyerabend and others, and Bachelard – and in routine conjunction with analyses of Michel Foucault – for Bruno Latour, Ian Hacking, Mary Tiles, Gary Gutting).

❧ MACH AND THE POSITIVIST CONNECTION: ❧ FROM ELEMENTS TO PHENOMENOLOGY

Ernst Mach was born in 1838 at Turas, formerly in Moravia – a region to be found in Bohemia, Silesia, and lower Austria which later was to become part of the modern republic of Czechoslovakia and is now part of the Czech republic. He studied in Vienna, teaching physics there in 1861, becoming professor at Graz in 1864, then at Prague in 1867, finally at Vienna in 1895. In 1901, upon his appointment to the upper house of the Austrian Parliament, Mach gave up his Vienna chair in the history and theory of inductive science. He spent the last three years of his life living with his son, Ludwig Mach and died in 1916 at Haar, near Munich.

At the risk of inviting distracting historical confusion, the above listing of the details of the historical name-changes concerning Mach's original nationality and the proper name or country of his birthplace – where names such as Moravia, Bohemia, Silesia, Lower Austria or, indeed, Czechoslovakia do not *currently* denominate legitimate nations within today's Europe – dramatizes the fortunes of the Austro-Hungarian empire and eastern Europe as well as the philosophy of science conceived within the broad European tradition of natural philosophy. Although this is also given as Galileo's achievement in historical accounts of science, it is usually claimed that the tradition of natural philosophy was transformed by Newton himself into modern physical science. But this is only to say that the practice of science (*natural* science) came to be regarded as identical to the practice of the more speculative and often explicitly metaphysical tradition known as natural philosophy, and, conversely, that the practice of natural science was identified with natural philosophy. By the turn of the century, the project of the philosophy of nature was identified with the project of natural science. In Mach's day and well before, then, philosophy (including the philosophy of science or natural philosophy) was not thought to be necessarily separate and distinct from (understood as a business of reflection, interpretive or speculative, either subsequent to or independent of) the physical or natural sciences in both theoretical and experimental manifestations as Duhem and more recently Jardine and Crombie have shown. As Kurt Hübner has it, 'theory of science coming into prominence at the turn of the century was still closely tied to the study of the history of science. Names like Mach, Poincaré, La Roy and especially Duhem clearly bear witness to this. However this development ceased to follow the path opened up for it by these men.'[5] Here we may add that the divisions between philosophy and science and between philosophy of science and other kinds of philosophy were not always the same. Thus the debate between Hobbes (a speculative philosopher not merely a theoretician) and Boyle (an experimentalist not merely a physical scientist) or Berkeley and Newton were not regarded by either the participants or their contemporaries as taking place across, let alone mixing, categories (of philosophical speculation or hypothesis and scientific experiment and theory). For Mach and Duhem, the importance of philosophic reflection was to be evaluated with respect to its contribution to the progress of science. Thus retaining a defining reference to and even identification with *natural* science (as) *natural* philosophy, *philosophia naturalis* acquired the methodological, historical and epistemological profile of what would later become modern philosophy of science. Around the turn of the century, as practised by Henri Poincaré and by Duhem, philosophy of science bore the name *critique des sciences* and this same science-critical emphasis (that is, philosophical critique expressed for the sake of scientific advance or progress) is echoed in Mach's empiriocriticism. Under the influence of Wittgenstein, Carnap and Schlick, Hempel's mature expression of the 'received view' of the philosophy of science or the hypothetico-deductive expression of professional analytic-style philosophy of science represents a decisive and increasingly bankrupt departure from this late nineteenth-century tradition of *critique des sciences* with its particular and explicit reference to science in practice.

Almost from its inception then, the analytic tradition of the philosophy of science lacked any reference to the historical 'fortunes' or 'scenes' of actual scientific inquiry (Jardine). If the 'new science' of the seventeenth century had involved a transformative turn (whether revolutionary and world-shattering as Koyré maintains or evolutionary and therefore less radical a transformation as Duhem and Crombie would argue) to experiment, analytic philosophy of science has so far found itself less able to complete the same turn. If the difference is between, as the Galileo experts have it, Platonic (formal) speculation and Aristotelian mathematical (functional) science, philosophers of science have tended towards Platonism. The turn away from history characteristic of logical positivism was only an expression of this idealizing, analytic tendency.

Although Mach in particular was especially devoted to experiment and its context in the history of science, many analytic authors nevertheless hold Mach to have been responsible for the divorce of traditional philosophical (metaphysical) concerns from the historical sensibility of the application of philosophic reflection to scientific practice. This is a misprision of a devastating kind but it was a constitutive one: seminal for the professional development of analytic-style philosophy of science.[6] The separation between philosophic expression and the lived world characteristic not only of logical positivism but of the division between continental and analytic styles of philosophy is no accident of location or tastes, as the talk of 'styles' may suggest. Rather, a necessary consequence, it might be argued, of the self-definition of modern science (as distinct from medieval and ancient science), the gap between theory and practice has shaped the analytic tradition of the philosophy of science, while at the same time leaving the philosophy of science as a theoretical discipline (*qua* philosophy) addressed to a particular theoretic practice (science) singularly unable to support the disjoint consequences of a separation between theory and historical practice.

Despite Mach's 'physicalism' or 'phenomenalism', the members of the Vienna circle, in the telling words of one commentator, 'wrote as though they believed science to be essentially a linguistic phenomenon'.[7] Hence this disposition to analyse 'language' – be it ordinary or logical language – together with a naive (non-historical, non-hermeneutic or ideal) view of *direct* observation (i.e., observation sentences) effectively limited the analytic concern of the philosophy of science to the analysis of theory, which last is the project of the received view or hypothetico-deductive nomological ideal of science (theory).

Such a focus on the elements of language – and not on the elements construed according to Mach's conception as *physical-physio-logical-psychological* – separates language and world. One obvious advantage of such a focus is the advantage of certainty. But this, its strength, to paraphrase Mach, and as is so often the case, is also its weakness. Philipp Frank, one of the founding members of the Vienna circle, who expressed the virtue of scientific analyticity, combining the essence of Mach's insights with Duhem's Kantian conventions, explains, 'the principles of pure science, of which the most important is the law of causality, are certain because they are only disguised definitions.'[8] If the essence of tautology or logical linguistic self-reference is not problematic when what is analysed is language use (the game or its rules), this same tautological expression becomes problematic when what is analysed must correspond to scientific facts or empirical matters. As Harré has observed, 'the philosophy of science must be related to what scientists actually do, and how they actually think'.[9] The imperative for such a correlative project between the philosophy of science and scientific practice, corresponding to the force of the socio-historical turn that comes after the linguistic turn, represents a much-needed philosophic mandate for the philosophy of science.

The revolutionary shifts, reversals and paradigmatic conflicts within the analytic tradition of the philosophy of science also correspond to the revolutionary shifts, reversals and paradigmatic conflicts in physical science. These witness to the need to develop a 'new' philosophy of science appropriate to the 'new science'. But the history of science tells us that novelty is itself relative, for the history of science is just such a record of 'new' sciences. One of the first 'new sciences', that of Galileo and Newton (and Hooke and Boyle), inaugurated a tradition that has since developed beyond its initial programme. That tradition was the tradition of modernity (as the cult of the new), and if one can speak of postmodern science today that is just because the programme of modernity can no longer be viewed unproblematically. The fortunes of the 'new' science and enlightenment thought mirror the problem of modernity and postmodernity, the problem of the conflict between the grand narratives of science and society and the distintegration of the promise of those same narratives throughout the modern era. This is not unconnected to the new historical and social turns in philosophic thinking about the sciences. These turns are not a sign of the times so much as they reflect a tension interior to post-Galilean science. As Mary Tiles explains the dynamics of this internal tension in post-Galilean (or 'new') science: 'The new science was to be abstract and mathematical, but also experimental; it was to yield both enlightenment and mastery of nature. It was to strive for an objective, purely intellectual, value-free view of the world in order to improve the lot of mankind by rendering technological innovations possible.'[10] There is an inherent conflict in this juxtaposition of material, practical progress and ideal or objective knowledge. Today's post-analytic or 'new' philosophy of science is manifestly directed to an expression of the consequences of this conflict.

Here, with reference to Mach's own particular historical context, it must be observed that Mach's declared opposition to philosophy – even where such an opposition may be rendered on Pascal's account as the best affective precondition for the best kind of philosophy – is, if taken literally as applying to philosophy today, anachronistic. Mach wished to avoid identification with the more metaphysical fashions often associated with or characteristic of philosophy. But his reflection on science was nothing other than a philosophy (albeit a philosophy of nature). This point highlights the value of a return to history for the sake of the broadening illumination of context. And where the return to history represents Mach's own phenomenalist version of Husserl's phenomenological call to return 'To the things themselves!', it cannot truly be Mach who is to be blamed for the logicization of the philosophy of science.

In all, the history of modern philosophy of science may be said to begin at the juncture epitomized by Mach's biography; but the rupture between theory and experiment that followed from the increasing logicization of empiriocriticism or critical positivism related to the rise of analytic-style philosophy of science has no precedent in Mach. This point is essential if one is to understand the growing attention paid to Mach's historical emphasis along with his very prescient sense of the importance of the art of the researcher, of the technical and social flair essential for the practice of the experimental life of the sciences.

Mach was greatly influenced by Berkeley and Fechner as well as by Kant and Hume. His thinking on the logical 'economy' of thought was shared by Richard Avenarius and his views on the nature of science engaged not only the scientists Helmholtz, Kirchhoff, Boltzmann, Einstein and Schroedinger but also the American pragmatist philosophers James and Pierce. It has been suggested that Mach's concern was to understand experience. But this concern with experience was not the same as the anglophone preoccupation with sensation. It has already been noted that many authors also tend to associate positivism's characteristic distance or alienation from the world with Mach's scepticism. Given Mach's sympathy with Berkeley and Hume, such an identification is not surprising. Mach's philosophy of science is commonly described as a 'sensationalism' or 'phenomenalism', expressed as an 'idealism', or by the catchwords positivist, empiricist, and anti-metaphysical. Endowed with the radical scepticism of a working scientist, as Mach was and because his sensationalism does not express an ontology as such, it is best to understand his perspective as fundamentally or even propaedeutically *heuristic*. Hence whatever metaphysical interests Mach may have had, they are not propositional but rather reflect his project of articulating what Paul Feyerabend describes as a non-foundational epistemology, and such an epistemology is not only essentially scientific but also represents the philosophic spirit of epistemology as such. In the same way, reference to a simplistic notion of parsimony, or *Denkökonomie*, linking that principle to an ontology, is misguided. And without emphasizing the extreme and today uncommon philosophical breadth of Mach's interests, the claim made in his *Analysis of Sensations* (1886) that 'the world consists only of our sensations' must be confusing. Again, Mach does not reduce the world to sensation so much as he finds the world *given in* and, as both Duhem and Bachelard would also stress, *knowable* only through sensation: 'Science does not create facts from facts, but simply *orders* known facts' (*Popular Scientific Lectures*). It is this connection that suggests a natural affinity between Mach's elemental phenomenalism and Husserlian phenomenology borne out by Mach's initial (and then specifically continental) reception (Brentano, Musil, Dingler) and which has more than once been reviewed in its connections not only with Husserl but even with Nietzsche (Sommer, Gebhard).

Mach deliberately sought to distance himself from the metaphysical pretensions of traditional philosophy as well as those assumed (sometimes by scientists) in the name of science. Like Duhem, Mach eschews the claims to certainty which have come to characterize traditional scientific expression and serve as an identifying feature of today's analytic heirs to the logical positivist tradition of the philosophy of science. For Mach, as for Duhem and Bachelard, *enquiry*, conceived via experiment, was the benchmark of the scientific enterprise and a classical but not necessarily pyrrhonian scepticism was the best guarantee of such an enquiring or open attitude. But this scepticism did not mean that Mach gave up any claim to offer an account of the scientific knowing enterprise, with respect to either practice or progress. Hence William James upon meeting Mach in 1882 could write not only that he had 'read everything' but that he 'knew everything'. James was not merely impressed with Mach, polymath extraordinaire, but by Mach's *pragmaticist* turn, which is one way to understand the very practical but not ontological imperative guiding Mach's endorsement of a logical economy. In this way, Mach's thinking illustrates the continental spirit of philosophy as questioning conceived in that *authentic* sense characterizing what Martin Heidegger calls thinking and which Nietzsche critically pronounces as the highest scientific virtue: intellectual probity or *Redlichkeit*. In Mach's *Popular Scientific Lectures* (1882), starting from the axiom that 'Physics is experience, arranged in economical order', such a questioning or open-ended reflection means that a philosophic consideration of the goals of science following the ordering value of economy as a thought principle is not proposed as or purported to yield a finished system: 'In the economical schematism of science lie both its strength and its weakness. Facts are always represented at a sacrifice of completeness and never with a greater precision than fits the needs of the moment.' This very Aristotelian practicality, which Gadamer has expressed in another context as the prudential core of hermeneutic judgment, works on Mach's account to exclude anything like 'absolute forecasts'.

Considered on its own terms, Mach's view is an *elemental* sensationalism, a factual, specifically non-factitious or empiri[ocriti]cism. Mach's thinking is radically sceptical. And it is a kind of conventionalism, like that of Duhem and Poincaré, which influenced the positivist protophysics of Dingler and the Erlangen school of Lorenzen's constructivism and its related development in evolutionary epistemology (Wuketis). But so far from the flat positivism of a reduction of the world to fact, Mach's 'mental mastery of facts' offers the only understanding to be had from or about those same 'facts', where the question of order or mastery in each case is hypothetical and ever subject to revision. This perspective in its historicist extension explains Mach's positivist appeal but an attention to the elemental mentality of this 'mastery of facts' shows its fruitfulness for current issues. This is evident in contemporary analytic philosophy of science after Kuhn and Feyerabend.

Thus Mach proposes that if the future of science may not be forecast as such (on pain of abandoning the open enterprise of science itself), its non-absoluteness may nevertheless be surmised and he suggests, in a fashion that is as Nietzschean as it is radically, elementally pluralistic, reflecting the spirit of what today has come to be called the 'new physics' – and what might likewise be named the 'new biology' and the 'new ecology' – that 'the rigid walls which now divide man from the world will gradually disappear; that human beings will not only confront each other, but also the entire organic and so-called lifeless world, with less selfishness and with livelier sympathy' (*Popular Scientific Lectures*).[11]

It has been noted that Mach sought to articulate the project of science in terms of its history and its practical or working functionality. But Mach's particular historicism was that of a philosopher – in spite of his protests against such an identification, where, as was also noted in a preliminary way, these protests themselves must be interpreted with reference to Mach's own, historical, circumstantial context. As a philosopher, Mach's historical focus shows him as a positivist, in the original, pristine Comtean sense of the word.[12] Ian Hacking, in a timely effort to broaden the current flattened and negative reading of 'positivism' with reference to August Comte's original use of the term, defines *positivity* as 'ways to have a positive truth value, to be up for grabs as true or false'.[13] Positivistic to this extent then, not only was Mach a philosopher, but he was a quasi-analytic – if also as we have seen a proto-phenomenological and even hermeneutic – kind of philosopher. Moreover, Mach remained as consistently committed to expressing the logical and philosophical foundations of science as any member of the Verein Ernst Mach (which was in fact and significantly the original name for the Vienna circle) or the modern heirs of the logical empiricist tradition in analytic philosophy of science.

Yet it must be emphasized that Mach was committed to the positivist ideal of science, that is, in Hacking's Comtean sense, to its 'positivity' but not its sheer logical expression. Thus, and, as we shall see, like Duhem, Mach's critical analytic turn far exceeds anything like an exclusive commitment to the expression or clarification of scientific method or theory as an end in itself where he criticizes the working functionality of the latter. More critical than Kant, Mach believes that there is no possibility of a priori knowledge *as such*: the basis of *all* knowledge is sense experience. Mach's *elementalism* – as his 'sensation-alism' is best described as outlined above and following the letter of Mach's own account – repudiates the 'arbitrary, one-sided theory' which is implied in talk of 'sensations' or 'phenomena'. This is important, for what Mach repudiates as 'arbitrary, one-sided theory' focusing upon 'sensations' or 'facts' represents the idea of the self or subject apart from or as substrate underlying or undergoing such 'sensations'. In this way, Mach's elementalism mirrors the critique of the subject familiar to continental scholars and others acquainted with the works of Nietzsche and Freud, as well as Heidegger, Lacan and Wittgenstein. As the central tenet of Mach's psychology, the self is a bundle of elements, an expression which must be understood not as Locke or Berkeley would understand it but rather as signifying a fundamental continuity between the unit of the perceiving self, or the physiological (elemental) subject, and the mental matter of psychological (elemental) knowing and the physical (elemental) world. Physical, physiological and psychological, Mach's convertible elements comprise his elemental-ism. This continuity suggests the *intentional* commonality requisite for developing a phenomenological reading of Mach's 'sensationalism' in the line of Husserl. This same connection also suggests the relevance of Mach's thought for interpretations of quantum physics. Mach's principle, so important on Einstein's own account for Einstein's theory of relativity, implies the interdependence of all things – that is: relativity (Mach's own views concerning relativity are no matter in this context). Hence there is no need for an absolute frame of reference (whether Newtonian space or time) but only for a relative frame of reference. The law of inertia stated by Newton can be understood either from the perspective of the body at rest or motion or from the related perspective of external impingent forces.

Scientific laws for Mach are abstract, general, and in all we might say: *abbreviated* descriptions of phenomena. The value of such laws, the 'meaning' of such laws for Mach, as for Nietzsche and Wittgenstein, lies in their use: their value for prediction. This too is not an ontological statement. Since Mach is not concerned with absolute truth as is the more metaphysically inclined philosopher of science, he is free to share the physical scientist's focus on working utility. It was this dedication which led to Mach's notorious repudiation of unobservables (unusable – untestable) as explanatory components in the atomic theory of physics and chemistry. Needless to say this prejudice, like his emphasis upon the researcher's 'unteachable' art (*Knowledge and Error*), has acquired the triumphant patina of prescience which is the fruit of a convergence with contemporary science, for today's atomic theorists have since discarded the nineteenth-century mechanistic vision of the atom.

❧ PIERRE DUHEM AND THE DAMNATION OF ❧ RELIGION: THE LIMITS OF ANALYTIC REHABILITATION

Pierre Maurice Marie Duhem was born in Paris in 1861, a son of a businessman of Flemish descent. Duhem's mother could trace her origins to the south of France and the village of Cabrespine, near Carcassonne, to the very house where Duhem himself was to die at the age of 54. In 1882, Duhem entered the Ecole Normale Supérieure at the head of the yearly competition. Proving his initial promise, Duhem completed a dissertation in thermodynamic physics in only three years. But through no evident fault of the work itself, Duhem's dissertation was none the less rejected by a jury headed by Gabriel Lippman. Two years after this first academic frustration, Duhem would successfully submit another thesis in thermodynamics, to earn his doctorate (in mathematics). Duhem's rejected first thesis was not only subsequently published but published to a broad and approbative scholarly reception. We shall have cause to note below that the complicated circumstances of this rejection are important for understanding Duhem's intellectual and academic career. In 1887, Duhem became *maître de conférences* at Lille, where he taught physical mechanics. Following a pedagogic dispute at Lille, Duhem moved to Rennes in 1893, but soon afterwards took a chair at Bordeaux in 1895, which he occupied until his death in 1916.

Duhem's philosophic interest in scientific theories is seen in his still-influential 1906 book, *La Théorie physique: son objet, sa structure* (*The Aim and Structure of Physical Theory*). Duhem, who shared Mach's belief in the vital importance of history for scientific progress, also made significant and substantial contributions to the history of science with his *Les Origines de la statique* (1905–6) and his voluminous study of medieval cosmology, *Le Système du monde* (1913–58), for the most part published posthumously and which has recently appeared in highly truncated form in English translation as the one-volume *Medieval Cosmology*.

If a discussion of place names can illuminate the changes necessary for an understanding of the transformation of natural philosophy into the kind of philosophy of science familiar today, the absent name of Paris is significant for understanding Duhem's intellectual position in that same tradition of the *critique des sciences*. For Duhem to all appearances had, with the submission of his first dissertation, opposed a then leading scholar, Marcellin Berthelot.[14] Duhem's biographers are largely agreed in reporting that the reasons for the jury's refusal of the thesis stem from the offence given to Berthelot in Duhem's theoretical repudiation of Berthelot's thermodynamical views on minimal work. And, indeed, more than a motive indicating a subjective and not an objective reason on Berthelot's part, we also have a tacit confession. In a 1936 biography written to secure support for the posthumous project of editing and publishing the remaining volumes (ultimately to number ten in all) of Duhem's *Système du Monde*, Duhem's daughter, Hélène, reported Berthelot's oft-cited professional edict which consigned (or better said, effectively damned) the Parisian-born Duhem to the provinces: 'This young man will never teach in Paris.'[15]

But to leave the question of the merits of Duhem's first dissertation to one side, and likewise to reserve the related question of the tactical wisdom of offending the leading scholar of one's day (for, as a recent biographer of Duhem's life and work, R. N. D. Martin, has observed, both are more properly questions to be directed to Duhem's teachers at the Ecole Normale than against Duhem himself), I would note that Berthelot's personal antagonism towards Duhem nevertheless retains resonant dimensions which exceed the indignant prejudice of the offended vanity of a leading Parisian scientist. For, betraying something more than a personal idiosyncrasy, Berthelot's views echo the general tenor of Duhem's philosophical reception, both then and now, where at least for our times it may be assumed that questions of professional conviction and ego are not similarly relevant. Nevertheless, questions of personality, understood in the broad, psychological and, in Duhem's particular case, confessional sense, play an essential role. Hence it is not insignificant that we are informed again and again that Duhem was a Catholic. Thus the newly published contribution to Duhem scholarship by Duhem's foremost English-language commentator, Stanley L. Jaki, bears the title *Scientist and Catholic*. Jaki, himself a priest, certainly does not mean to underline this conjunction unsympathetically. But Duhem's religious faith is common stock in reviews of his philosophical merit. And an evaluation of the objective significance of Duhem's faith with respect to Duhem's historical circumstance is not easy. And Martin's study of Duhem's intellectual biography, appropriately subtitled *Philosophy and History in the Work of a Believing Physicist*, begins by adverting to the significance of the specific fortunes of Duhem's intellectual reception. Martin notes that Duhem's work is from the start clouded by a number of persistent critical reservations. Thus it is essential to underline the fact that a French scholar of importance as, beyond all dispute, Duhem must be accounted, should none the less be denied, as Duhem was denied, a Paris chair. Whereas Bachelard, born in the provinces, and mentioned here for the sake of contrast, would not be similarly denied this same token of recognition. The difficulty here in the case of Duhem, arguably the superior philosopher, surely the superior scientist, is to trace the proximate cause.

In the conflict with Berthelot, reservations concerning Duhem's achievements preceded Duhem's scientific and academic career. Martin sums up the general scholarly judgment with respect to Duhem's historical stature with the resounding ambiguity of an understated reservation as, in a word, 'problematic'. For many, Martin writes, Duhem was 'a brilliant maverick who continually got things frustratingly wrong: producing brilliant arguments against atomic explanations in physics and chemistry, a muddled instrumentalism in the philosophy of science, and a voluminous collection of misreadings of mediaeval Scholastics' ([6.50], p. 194). In general, for Duhem's biographical commentators and interpreters, that is for Martin, for Jaki, Roberto Maiocchi, etc., Duhem's problem was fundamentally and in its essence a religious one, and, like most confessional affiliations, this was one that cut two ways. Not only was Duhem's Catholic faith an obstacle to the largely Protestant ideals of modern science but Catholics were uneasy with his totally modern (and in the Catholic view 'modernist') opposition to neo-scholasticism. Duhem for his part was an iconoclast, and his position in the provinces was not such as to inspire him to restraint (Duhem, let it be remembered, despite his lack of a Paris chair, was a native Parisian).[16] He was particularly impatient with the neo-Thomism of the day, evident in the works of Jacques Maritain with his quasi-

Aristotelian classification of the sciences. In the long run, what this meant was that Duhem could be dismissed as a Catholic apologist by non-Catholics while simultaneously being condemned as 'modernist' by the French Catholic intellectual elite.[17] And these reservations made on two sides were not the result of unthinking prejudice on one side or the other, but were in fact founded at least to some degree in both cases. For it is clear that the realist metaphysics and authoritarianism of the aims of the neo-scholastic movement in philosophy were undermined by the substance of Duhem's views. Conversely, Duhem's non-Catholic readers could regard Duhem's historical interest in medieval science as representing little more than another version of neo-scholasticism. The historical researches of Crombie and others suggest that the problem requires a clearer understanding of the differences between historical eras rather than matters of faith, but Martin's observation that 'Duhem seems to have fallen between every available stool' ([6.50], p. 211) would seem to be the least one could say not only of Duhem but of the judgments made concerning him. What the new concern with history illustrates is the value of Butterfield's insight that a 'Whig interpretation of history' (or 'presentism' as it is also called) – that is, an interpretation of other eras from the perspective of one's own era – illuminates only one's own prejudices (and that only from the point of view of a subsequent historiographer) without shedding light on the period in question. History without hermeneutics is blind.

Against Koyré's reading of the revolutionary transformation from the medieval to the modern world-view, which corroborates the non- or anti-Catholic reading of Duhem's reactionary scholasticism, Jaki maintains that Duhem's sympathetic account of the scholastic opposition to Aristotelian philosophy of natural place suggests that this medieval perspective fostered rather than hindered the modern scientific turn such as that associated with, for example, Galileo's speculations concerning the role of impetus. Other scholars, such as William Wallace, have offered corroborating readings of the 'Galileo affair', showing the importance of taking Galileo's terms not in a putatively modern context (following the conviction of Galileo's visionary genius) but in their more patent and for the modern reader all the more tacit historical and that is medieval context.[18] Wallace's discussion of Galileo's use of the Latin term *ex suppositione* illustrates this point.[19] The problem is not only that readers from the perspective of modern (analytic) philosophy of science tend to translate *ex suppositione* as *ex hypothesi*, but that the perspective of the Catholic Church is automatically identified with that of an anti-modern, progress-retarding influence. This, in the apposite context of the contest between religion and science, shows the tenacity of the Whig interpretation of history. For this reason, Butterfield writes, 'It matters very much how we start upon our labours –

whether for example we take the Protestants of the sixteenth century as men who were fighting to bring about our modern world, while the Catholics were struggling to keep the medieval or whether we take the whole present as the child of the whole past and see rather the modern world emerging from the clash of both Catholic and Protestant.'[20] For Butterfield the problem is the tendency to reduce the problem to one between Protestant and Catholic, between *enlightened* Whig and *dark-age* traditionalist. To understand Duhem, one must go beyond confessional prejudice.

In fact, as Martin takes pains to demonstrate, Duhem must be characterized as a reluctant convert to his ultimately continuous account of the transition from medieval science to modern science. Duhem moved towards this view *in spite* of his own original views as a scientist working at the peak of the modern self-understanding of the sciences, that is, despite his typically scientific (high modern or scientistic) formation at the turn of the last century. According to science's own self-understanding then, and which is in part still true for scientists today, the transition from the (in Koyré's words 'closed') medieval view of the world to the ('open') modern world-view was – like the birth of the fully armoured Athena from the forehead of her father Zeus – a sudden, completely discontinuous or punctual, radical leap from classical and hellenic to fully-fledged modern science. This view eclipsing the scientific value of the Middle Ages was as typical for the average scientist in Duhem's time as it can still be said to be true of scientists and of many philosophers today. Against the bias of this formation, it was less Duhem's religious faith, one could argue, than his rigorous education as a formal logician that brought him, indeed compelled him, to re-examine the historical record. In Jaki's view, a view now with considerable historiographical support, in addition to Duhem's axiomatician's rigour, the record suggests that the medieval cosmological viewpoint worked not to obstruct the path to modern science in effect, where even Galileo's term *impeto* may be traced to Jean Buridan in the fourteenth century, but rather to further its advance. Duhem's reading of medieval science as an essential bridge between classical science and Galileo's inauguration of Newton's project of modern scientific thinking reflects a revolution, but the revolution for Duhem takes place in his own thinking, against his modern scientist's ingrained thought-style but in accord with his trained axiomatician's loyalty to the importance of first principles and logical coherence.

Duhem's argument stressed both subtlety and complexity, but it is clear that for him the key question for any theory or hypothesis was its utility in 'saving' the phenomena. On such accounting, of course, not only was Galileo a child of his times, indebted to the scholasticism of Oresme and Buridan, but Galileo's account was less successful than the Ptolemaic alternative. From this point of view, Cardinal Bellar-mine's prudential caution may be read less as an illustration of jesuitry than as a representative of that kind of French common sense or Pascalian *bons sens* where the spirits of geometry *and* finesse intersect and for which, as both Martin and, years earlier, Dorothy Eastwood have argued, Duhem had a notable affinity. Yet beyond the still-unsettled questions of Duhem's personal reception, Duhem's signifi-cance for analytic philosophy of science is not in fact a subject of much debate owing to the prominence of the philosophers routinely listed as having responded to Duhem's influence, most notably Popper and Quine.

Duhem's argument against crucial experiments may also be seen to turn on his understanding of theories as axiomatic systems and his appreciation of the nature of such systems. For Duhem, physical experiments cannot refute isolated theories. Where alternative theoreti-cal views are to be tested, an experiment designed to enable the experi-menter to choose between them only confirms one hypothesis or another. But as an experiment confirms or refutes the theory and not the theoretical system, the results are inconclusive for not only may a subsequent experiment fail to confirm the theory, but a related experi-ment may refute a related theory; the experimenter is free to make ad hoc adjustments, and what has come to be called the 'theory-ladenness' of observations means that such adjustments may well be already or subsequently 'built into' the interpretation of the experimental results, without necessarily involving the awareness of the experimenter. Apart from such phenomenological hermeneutic questions as context-depen-dence and interpretation, the significance of the theory in any case is articulated only within the theoretical complex of which it is a part. Just as there are no isolated phenomena, there are no isolated theories but only theoretical systems. This interdependence points to the reason for Duhem's (as for Mach's own) conviction concerning the importance of history. Modification in the theory may preserve the system and vice versa, and an understanding of the system requires an understanding of the original meaning of its terms. For Duhem, experiment is crucial, but neither falsification nor demonstration provides certain or sure tests of eternal, unchanging truth. On this point, it is the history of science which justifies Duhem.

Apart from Duhem's views on history and related to his views on theoretical indecidability, Duhem held a form of instrumentalism that was shared not only by Mach and Poincaré, but also by Kirchoff, Hertz, Bridgman, Eddington and the Copenhagen school of quantum physics. For Duhem, two aspects of theory must be distinguished, the explanatory and the representational. As far as Duhem was concerned, although scientists and philosophers of science of a realist bent regarded theories as explanation, the value of theory is ultimately its instrumental or conventional value. Instrumentalism is a view of scientific theories founded, as Karl Popper says, by 'Osiander, Cardinal Bellarmine and Bishop Berkeley'.[21] Linking Osiander to Cardinal Bellarmine, as most theoreticians stage this drama, it is clear that the great antagonist to such instrumentalism for Popper and for others is Galileo. And, as Ian Hacking puts it, 'Galileo is everybody's favourite hero – not only Chomsky and Weinberg but also Husserl.'[22] To say as has already been suggested that Galileo was not as radical or as ahead of his times as had been thought is to oppose the general conception of Galileo as a canonic scientific hero (or saint). This is the associative point MacIntyre makes (arguing in a different direction) when he speaks of Feyerabend's 'anarchism' as Emersonian in spirit, advocating 'not "Every man his own Jesus" but "Every man his own Galileo" '.[23] If Duhem is an instrumentalist, he also stands opposed to Galileo. And he cannot do otherwise. Duhem, with his claim that 'a law of physics is properly speaking neither true nor false' (*The Aim and Structure of Physical Theory*), is consequently one of the principal antagonists not only of Popper's realist-falsificationist view of physical theories but of all realist views of science.

Duhem's instrumentalism continues to be important for the present profile of the philosophy of science in the English-speaking world. For Duhem, the same physical law has a potentially different extension at different times owing to the historical development of these laws and their embodiment in experimental *praxis*. The meaning of a physical law is to be determined in the final analysis by the context of scientific practice and the scheme of related laws involved in determining the meaning of that law. This principle provides the basis for the underdeterminist perspective on the relationship between experimental evidence and theory and the constellation of related theories. Through the work of Quine and Davidson, this notion of underdeterminism led to the current position on theoretical indecidability that has done so much to bring analytic philosophy to a (theoretical) cul de sac if also, albeit indirectly, generating the current emphasis on the importance of experiment in discussions within analytic philosophy of science.

It is a testimony to the seminal character of the influence of both Duhem and Mach that it is today thought necessary to return to their philosophic understanding of scientific practice (as theory and experiment/*praxis*). This is not to say that they were in individual agreement among themselves but rather that each had distinct insights which similarly failed to be transmitted in subsequent debates. And the current urgency of an historical turn in the philosophy of science, clear since the work of Hanson, Feyerabend and Kuhn, is accordingly necessary largely if not only because of a correspondent refusal of history in mainline or analytic philosophy of science.

❧ GASTON BACHELARD: SCIENTISM WITH A ❧ HUMAN FACE

Gaston Bachelard was born at Bar-sur-Aube in 1884. Bachelard's studies were conducted, as he himself was given to muse, under the sign of delay and he worked as a part-time mechanical technician for the French postal service until 1913 when he earned his *licence* in mathematics and science, becoming a teacher at the Collège of Bar-sur-Aube. Upon earning his doctorate in 1927, he assumed the chair of philosophy at Dijon and was then called to the chair of the history and philosophy of science at the Sorbonne in 1940, where he remained until his retirement in 1954. He died in Paris in 1962.

Bachelard's philosophy of science is expressed as a 'dialectical rationalism' or 'dialectical naturalism'. Just as Duhem's anti-idealist conventionalism was read as conducive to the aims of materialism, although instrumentalist and thus inherently anti-realist, so Marxist authors such as Louis Althusser and Roy Bhaskar have read Bachelard's naturalism as a kind of dialectical materialism to be employed against ideological appropriations of science. Although the current interest in Bachelard's epistemology and consequently in his philosophy of science doubtless owes a good deal to Althusser, and without denigrating the value of Althusser's reading for Marxist or materialist epistemology, the Marxist reception of Bachelard's work and the word 'dialectic', if drawn exclusively from Althusser's programme, can be misleading (LeCourt). Still it should be emphasized that those working from Marxist perspectives have been far more assiduous in examining Bachelard's philosophy for its epistemic component than other traditionally analytic philosophers of science (Bhaskar).

Bachelard's emphasis is on a dialogical exchange, that is to say, a dialogue between the knower and the known, a dialogue between poetic and scientific discourse. This is not to be construed as inherently (or essentially related to) a dialogue between *poetry* proper and *science* proper. Instead the capital dialogical exchange is that between the scientist and the dreaming scientist himself:[24] the scientist and himself poetizing, or projecting (and thus 'dreaming' or effectively constituting or technically constructing) the world of scientific nature. Thus Bachelard wrote on the psychoanalysis of the history of the discovery of fire as a dialogue between psychoanalysis and that history to find *its* psychoanalysis metaphorically in (and of) the history of sexual desire. The metonymic association between the origin of fire (and electricity) and the fire (and electricity) of sexual passion points to a dialogue between image (the discovery of fire) and the human reflection or projection of that same discovery. Similarly, the philosophy of no, by which expression Bachelard seeks to characterize the openness of the scientific attitude, is a dialogical philosophy – or better a dialogical account – of scientific practice. To say that the scientist constitutes the phenomena, the objects of science, is not to describe a unilateral construction; rather the constitution is a formative, informative, reciprocal creation, a making of the scientist himself as much as a making (a projection or constitution) of the scientist's world. This exchange with the world of scientific or technical experience articulates the scientist's characteristic capacity for an anticipatory openness to scientific phenomena, an attitude ever open to possible revision upon encountering a new phenomenon. Such a 'no' is then heuristic in function not destructive or eliminative: it describes what for Bachelard will be the enabling condition for the possibility of openness to (scientific) novelty. The scientist is thereby summoned to further innovative and creative efforts, reconstituting a new framework embracing the new experience.

Bachelard sought to go beyond phenomenology and regarded Husserl's own contributions as so many points of (dialectical) departure for Bachelard's own avowedly polemical reflections. Thus Bachelard could speak of the need for a 'phenomeno-technology' to reflect the engaged role of the human investigator and the world under investigation. Hermeneutically and phenomenologically sensitive authors have read this perspective as compatible with a hermeneutic phenomenology of (reading) scientific instrumentation.[25] But against such a tolerant syncretism of Bachelard's poetizing science and phenomenological hermeneutics of scientific culture, Bachelard's inherently antagonistic emphasis is more than clear in its original context. In the interest of and following upon the inspiration of science, Bachelard aims to *correct* phenomenology. Owing to the scientific phenomenology implicit in the doing of science, as Bachelard's philosophy of 'no', 'observation is always polemical; it either confirms or denies a prior thesis, a preexisting model, an observational protocol'. For Bachelard, philosophic reflection on science must be prepared to be instructed by science in practice. 'A truly scientific phenomenology is therefore essentially a phenomeno-technology' (*The New Scientific Spirit* [6.54]). The result of this perspective is not merely the banal pragmatism one might expect. Because Bachelard expects that the prime experience of science is to be a mathematical one, and that, as 'the mathematical tool affects the craftsman who uses it', it is not only safe to say that '*Homo mathematicus* is taking the place of *homo faber*', but that ultimately 'it is mathematics that opens new avenues to experience'. Close as this point of view is to Husserl, the gap remains and is widened by Husserl's sense of crisis, as a separation even more exacerbated by Heidegger's hermeneutic critique of technology along with the knowledge ideal of *mathesis*, or axiomatic certainty.

More negatively, resolutely committed as Bachelard was to the scientific and Enlightenment ideal disposition of a constitutional happiness or cheerfulness, Bachelard found the existentialist world-view particularly pernicious for it expressed what in his view was a false opposition between enquiring subject (poetizing poet or scientist – for they are or at least inherently can be considered the same) and world object (as created or as world to be known). Bachelard refused the distinction between the living subject and a dead or alien or meaningless world. The poetic world of human meaning was continuous with the scientific world, which for Bachelard bore the manifest imprint of the human projective imagination. Bachelard's positivism accordingly preserves the casual colloquial meaning of the word 'positive' as an optimistic outlook, or, in Bachelard's words, a 'happy' perspective. This affirmative and essentially scientistic humanism is expressed where Bachelard writes 'Science calls a world into being, not through some magic force, immanent in reality, but through a rational force immanent in the mind. . . . Scientific work makes rational entities real, in the full sense of the word' (*New Scientific Spirit* [6.54]).

Bachelard's work is extensively cited and has been the subject of numerous commentaries, less in the context of the philosophy of science than in principally literary and philosophical discussions of Bachelard's poetics. Beyond anglophone continental philosophic interests, Bachelard's eclectic style of reading between literature and science has found significant hearings in France and Germany in part through the efforts of a tradition of literary theorists (as Barthes recounts). In (particularly French) history and philosophy of science, this reception is due to the influence of Bachelard's student, Georges Canguilhem, the historian of physiological science, and R. Cavailles. In this company, Michel Foucault may also be regarded as within Bachelard's intellectual sphere. But if Foucault's value may be traced to – better and more significantly, if here it can be argued that Foucault's value for science can only be understood in terms of – Bachelard's influence (cf. Tiles who prefaces her own study [6.83] by saying that her representation of Bachelard 'is a rational construct',[26] or Gutting who reads Bachelard and Canguilhem as background to Foucault, or Bhaskar who also prefers not to treat of Bachelard on his own, or on his own terms, but sets and thus inevitably defines Bachelard in opposition to Feyerabend), the question of the nature of the enduring significance of Bachelard's philosophy for the philosophy of science is more elusive. This difficulty is not a matter of the conflict between

religion and modern scientific sensibility – as it was in Duhem's case
– but is doubtless due to Bachelard's style. This is a style that is less
esoteric than simply dated and rather specific to French literary culture,
at least according to Jonathan Culler's plausible and sympathetic
account. Culler implies that the lack of conceptual resonance among
philosophers of science or philosophers proper in response to Bachelard's works (a limitation which is also shared by non-francophone
literary theorists) is due to Bachelard's nineteenth-century style of
rhetorical and imaginative reference. The style in question is one of
diffuse allusion and allegory, like that of Jacques Lacan. In Culler's
view, Bachelard's style is simply out of synch with current modes of
expression and particularly unsuited for today's impatient styles of
reading.[27] To the late twentieth-century reader's impatience may be
added a fatal incapacity, that is an inability to appreciate the sense, to
infer and so to understand the full value of Bachelard's allusions. An
allusive, allegorical or metaphorical – in Bachelard's words *poetic* –
style presumes and is necessarily dependent upon the reader's aptness
for and familiarity with the conventions used.

The capacity to note such allusive resonances in Bachelard's work
is essential both for readers of Bachelard's philosophy of science and
for readers of his literary criticism. Accordingly, the literary theorist
Ralph Smith notes that it is Bachelard's 'philosophy of science [which]
must be understood in order to truly appreciate the full significance of
his essays on the imagination and to assess properly his contribution
to literary criticism'.[28] Where, for Bachelard, 'Science in fact creates
philosophy' (*The New Scientific Spirit* [6.54]), any clear distinction
between Bachelard's value for literary criticism and science must perforce be difficult to make. Still the lion's share of this attribution of
value is represented by studies in literary criticism. Apart from Gutting's background reference to Bachelard's work in line with the philosophy of science, and Tiles's related discussions, Bachelard is better
known for his literary contributions, in so far as Bachelard's emphasis
on the imaginary continues to appeal to a distinctively French fascination with fantasy and the domains of reverie and poetic invention.

Mary McAllester Jones's recent study [6.76] employs the term
'subversive' to emphasize Bachelard's predilection for the literary and
for the imagination not on the terms of humanism but rather as 'unhing-
ing' humanism.[29] This inverse, 'subverting' emphasis corresponds to
the fashionable celebration of the postmodern but also testifies to the
need to come to terms with scientism's recondite and irrecusable
humanism. Citing Bachelard's claim that 'Man's being is an unfixed
being. All expression unfixes him' (Bachelard in Jones [6.76], 193),
Jones reads this 'unfixing' in her account of Bachelard's focus on the
salutary *spiritual* value of challenge, dynamic flexibility and innovation.

Thus, in Jones's expression of such an *unhinged* humanism, the movement or fluidity of articulation is paramount: 'Man is unfixed by language, not decentered' (Jones [6.76], 193).

I think it helpful to add that this openness, as a very literal flexibility, is akin to Paul Valéry's anti-Platonic celebration of the divinity that is not given negative or oblique testament, that is, not at all missed or failing, but which *speaks* precisely in our muteness in the presence of beauty.[30] Such an awe or expression of silence in the face of the beautiful rather than revealing an incapacity (such silence betrayed in the human inability to hold to a steady glance in the face of beauty proves the body's counter-divinity as Plato maintains) is the caesura, the glancing gaping that affirms and confirms, sees, sings and consecrates what is seen. In Bachelard's words with reference to Valéry, 'the temporal structure found in ambiguity can help us to intellectualize rhythms produced by sound. . . . We have come to realize that it is the idea that sings its song, that the complex interplay of ideas has its own particular tonality, a tonality that can call forth deep within us all a faint, soft murmuring' (*La Dialectique de la durée*, cited in Jones [6.76], p. 73). Silence thus testifies to the moving power or *dynamis* so important for Bachelard, who was of course a reader of Valéry's poetry and theory as well as a high-school teacher of chemistry and university professor of epistemology. For Bachelard's enduring aim was to show that the work of the scientist was not only comparable to that of the poet, but was in its own and full sense a poetics as well. And if, as noted, 'science creates philosophy', for Bachelard it will also be science that, most properly said and equal to any poetic discipline, creates poetry.

In the creative processes of poet and scientist, the play of thought echoes or responds to what is in each case. This is what Bachelard means by writing, 'Science calls a world into being, not through some magic force, immanent in reality, but through a rational force immanent in the mind.' And it is in this creative, reflective way that Bachelard claims that 'Science in fact creates philosophy'. But that is to say that philosophy is science reflecting on itself. The scientist is creator (poet) and philosopher, a modern Prometheus calling 'a world into being'. Here, the different senses evoked by the idea of a 'modern Prometheus' in an English literary context (Mary Shelley's *Frankenstein*) and a continental context (romanticized Titanism) are significant and testify to the difficulties inherent in assimilating such an elusive and allusive author as Bachelard.

A contemporary physicist and philosopher of science, and one who may be counted within the continental tradition, Bernard d'Espagnat, takes Bachelard's important references to Valéry a step further. For d'Espagnat, Valéry's notion of spiritual value expresses a mysticism more veiled than obvious in Valéry's contrast between spiritual and material(ist) domains. D'Espagnat suggests that the nuance to be grasped here is that between a spiritual life without God (*a*theist) and spiritual life of a human (here, to be fair to d'Espagnat, perhaps not necessarily a *humanist*) kind. The difference is again not necessarily disjoint.

Yet the association with mysticism should perhaps only be emphasized in a limited way. Furthermore, for the sake of rigour, Bachelard's version of humanist scientism can be named a subversion of scientism only on the most fancifully esoteric level and that level is ambivalently problematic because of its insistent humanism. Bachelard's project must be conceived as a *subversive* humanism far more than a postmodern-style subversion of humanism as Jones maintains. Such a subversive humanism must, it would seem, be rethought if it may not in the end be said to yield the absence of the subject. Which is of course only to say that a subversive humanism remains a humanism. This subtle humanism is such as d'Espagnat, for example, finds in Valéry. It is elusive because it entails the conjunction of mysticism and what d'Espagnat calls Valéry's 'positivism of principle'.[31] As the proponent of a mysticism which is simultaneously, coextensively in the human, the ambiguity of Valéry's position is rightfully his as poet. Bachelard's poetics of science offers an illumination of why a contemporary scientist such as d'Espagnat could turn to Valéry, a poet, as guide for 'thinking' science. Bachelard's philosophy of science represents (a position on) science as the high point of human culture (as its most profitable-productive and progressive expression). But this science-approbative perspective offers a valorization of science echoing not only Bachelard's well-rounded conservative cultural views but in uncanny resonance with the spirit of the 'two cultures' debate (and their interplay) popularized for the anglophone and traditional reader in the philosophy of science by C. P. Snow's essay *The Two Cultures*.

In Bachelard's as well as Snow's approach to the human achievement of science, science remains an ideal to be valued (and, post-Foucault, we can observe that this value is also the power of science, a power Nietzsche and Lacan would tell us which contributes to the Enlightenment role or reign of terror). Where Snow glamorizes science, Bachelard renders science a kind of poetizing and its products, its 'phenomeno-technologies', a kind of poetry. In effect, science becomes myth. But this does not resolve the opposition between *logos* and *mythos*, an opposition which has been traditional since the beginnings of Socratic philosophy. Since a glamorization of science is a part of our contemporary high-industrialist culture, Bachelard's mythification of science, as a poetizing venture, far from being a revolutionary coding (much less a double or subversive coding) only underlines the ruling mystique of science. In this supplanting of *mythos* by *logos, mythos* is not eliminated but absorbed by or subsumed under *logos*. *Mythos* becomes (is and as so named always was) a function of *logos*. With a cultural presumption exceeding Mach or Duhem, Bachelard asserts the very poetic function of science. On Bachelard's enthusiastic account, science as scientistically – which is also to say (for such is the force of the mythic-logical conversion) science as *poetically* – conceived truly *is* poetry at its best.

Bachelard's express identification of the *project* of scientific practice and method, in theory and experiment, where the scientist is taken to *constitute* the manifest entities (and not merely the image) of science (what Bachelard calls poetizing) inspired the structure of the sociological turn so decisive for the development of the new philosophy of science beyond the received hypothetico-deductive or reconstructivist view (Latour, Bloor, Woolgar). Literally constructed, the poetic project of the world of science is a suitable object for a sociology of knowledge and scientific practice or, in Bachelard's esoteric coinage, a psycho-analysis of science.

❧ THE HISTORY OF CONTINENTAL PHILOSOPHY ❧ OF SCIENCE

From the perspective of Anglo-American analytic-style philosophy, continental philosophy may be identified as the tradition of philosophy committed to thinking within the philosophic tradition, that is, committed to explicitly reconstituting the enduring value of the history of philosophy. For its part, analytic philosophy is not concerned with the history of philosophy although to be sure it is rooted in it. Nor is analytic philosophy, as defined by Müller and Halder, concerned with the traditional objects of philosophic inquiry such as *things* or *relations* or *events*, but rather with 'expressions, concepts, axioms, principles'.[32] On the basis of such a distinction between the objects of continental and analytic philosophic concern, Husserl's otherwise putatively realist 'To the things themselves!' articulates an interest that is not merely stylistically but constitutively antithetical to analytic philosophy.

Patrick A. Heelan characterizes continental philosophy according to two interests: '(1) its preoccupation with the problem of the 'constitution' of knowledge, and (2) the effect of the historical and cultural world context of science on the 'social constitution' of scientific knowledge'.[33] Although the word 'constitution' occurs twice in this definition, rather than focusing on the phenomenological account of such constitution, recent efforts to articulate continental philosophies of scientific theory and practice emphasize the interpretive turn to hermeneutics

(Hiley, Bohman *et al.*). The hermeneutic turn is the interpretive turn taken by many analytic philosophers after Rorty, and in so far as this interpretive turn is necessarily an historical turn it is also, as mentioned above, one that is familiar to analytic philosophers of science after Kuhn. The interpretive and historic turn, which may be designated the hermeneutic turn, thus represents the most salient line of intersection between continental and analytic-style philosophy. But preliminary to any rigorous and significant expression of this intersection, as Rüdiger Bubner has demonstrated in a broader reflection on hermeneutics and critical theory, it is essential for the hermeneutic turn to be properly conceived in its technical and (that means) historical context.[34] This background critical context (and constellation of related interests) does not yet characterize the accepted path of received philosophy of science. Bubner's precision is of capital importance for the future of hermeneutic approaches to the philosophy of science. In recent historical studies of science (Hacking, Jardine, Crombie), a noteworthy attention is paid to the concept of the broadly hermeneutic rather than the specifically phenomenological philosophies of Husserl and Heidegger. Authors such as Gadamer and even Nietzsche may be invoked and references made to Ricoeur, but I think it important to consider the consequences entailed by Bubner's reservation that a genuine conversance with critical hermeneutics (in its theoretical and historical context) is often lacking.

What is more crucial than even this lack of interpretive and historical competency is the question of the advantage for the philosophy of science to be gained by taking the 'continental' turn, as it were, be that turn construed more narrowly as a historical turn or more radically as a hermeneutic turn. Would such a turn advance the fortunes of the currently becalmed (post-Kuhnian, post-sociology of science and knowledge) philosophy of science? Long ago, Immanuel Kant observed that philosophy itself seemed almost not to progress at all if compared to the natural, formalizable or mathematical sciences. For Kant, in the first *Critique* and the *Prolegomena*, to express the difference between philosophy and science, where science shows clear signs of cumulative and accelerating development, philosophy, in contrast, appears dissolutely aporetic: without issue or advance, and without consensus, lacking even a unified perspective or standard for what would count as such advance. To date, analytic-style philosophy seeks to be true to the scientific standard for philosophic progress as implied by Kant's criticism, and seeks the kind of absolutist or cumulative understanding, including formal precision and consensus, which constitutes or at least approximates the professional mien of a scientific endeavour.

If the ideal of science remains the ideal of our modern era, and where science, echoing Kant's reference, is offered as the standard for philosophy itself, it seems patently obvious that only a *scientific* (here, analytic) project of understanding the project of science could command our interest, and analytic philosophy, given its rightful or proper distinction, should also exclude other styles as irrelevant. Thus, as we have seen, Mach, a scientist who was hence already affiliated with the (as he thought) superior thought-style, eschewed the title of philosopher. If science shows *concrete* or factual progress where philosophy manifests only moribund confusion or intestine bickering, science by contrast would appear to have the most progressive part.

But the history of science shows that even in science the idea of progress is a conceptual chestnut. As Kuhn has it, one era's idea of progress is the 'paradigmatic' error to be overthrown by the 'revolutions' of another generation. Even with a cumulative, pre-Kuhnian scheme of simple progress, the philosophy of science, failing to approximate that ideal, is more 'philosophical' (indeed to the extent of following Kant's aporetic account) than Mach's ideal science. The philosophy of science, even analytically construed, even modelled as it is on science, is still not a science as such. Nor is it a metascience: if the philosophy of science is to be a science of science, complete with *concrete* progress and visible results, it has not been very successful. Offering an array (with no end in sight) of logical accounts, analytic philosophy of science may explain and offer an understanding of the workings of science as it conceives them. It is at this formal juncture that an analogy with the practice of science must end. For where science has to do with actual events, whether theoretically construed or experimentally constituted, where science is predictive, and thus amenable to verification or refutation, where related theories and experimental tests may be expected to proliferate, the *philosophy* of science, in its project of explaining science, does not similarly test or check its explanations against the substance or 'fact' of actual science. Thus the shock of the historical, interpretive or hermeneutic, and sociological turns in the philosophy of science. Far from a critique of science as a fact, the philosophy of science begins with science as it finds it: as a fact, a given, and a given to be accepted on the scientist's own terms. Neither Mach nor Duhem would champion this perspective, precisely because of their commitment to the project of science. And Bachelard was too much a scientist himself despite his celebration of science to petrify it by treating it as an accomplished fact. Thus if the least demanding definition of the business of science as an explanation of what the world is, of the world as it is (truly, or really, or practically-pragmatically), is to 'save the phenomena' on some level, either directly (observationally) or theoretically, the business of the philosophy of science (*qua* pretended science of science) will need to do the same for science. But that means that the philosophy of science cannot, despite its scientistic ambitions, become a science because such an account belongs within the perspective of philosophy.

CONTINENTAL CURRENTS IN ANALYTIC-STYLE PHILOSOPHY OF SCIENCE

The concern of analytic philosophy is, as its name betrays, a concern with the logical analysis of language. Indeed, for the sake of this distinction, it should be said that analytic philosophy is committed to the dissolution (that is, literally, the analysis) of philosophic problems through their clarification. Once the traditional questions concerning things in the world, cause and effect or freedom are analysed in terms of their meaning and significance one finds that one has to do with a logical account or tractatus concerning the world (i.e., statements, claims and assertions).

The analytic tradition of the philosophy of science is marked by its attention to questions relating to the structure of scientific explanation and theory-making. If science is characterized by reciprocal theoretical and experimental activity, the philosophy of science in its analytic mode has shed more light on theory than on experiment. Conversely its disposition *vis-à-vis* experimental procedure is such that the very mention of historical studies whether by historians of science (Kuhn, Crombie) or by sociologists of science (Barnes, Shapin, Bloor, Latour, Woolgar, Knorr-Cetina) has had a disruptive effect on the analytic programme. For the analyst, historical studies are often characterized by attempts at normative historical reconstruction. Feyerabend's work offers an example of such reconstruction, where efforts to restore the sense and significance of Mach's contribution to the foundations of the philosophy of science should be seen as a logical fulfilment of Mach's appreciation of science as historically and normatively progressive.

Note that this criticism of analytic-style philosophy of science is not a complaint raised against analytic style philosophy of science from the side of continental philosophy. These criticisms have been offered in tandem with the development of the philosophy of science itself from the start, beginning with Mach and Duhem and offered as well in various styles of historical reflection by philosophers and historians of science across cultural boundaries, from Bachelard and Canguilhem to Hanson, Kuhn and Feyerabend. None of these, not excepting Bachelard and Canguilhem (or French philosophy of science today which remains as addicted to analytic as to continental approaches), may be named a typical continental philosopher.

Mach, Duhem and Bachelard along with a number of other

scholars have argued that science itself is more critical, indeed more inherently 'hermeneutic', than philosophy. But this point too is problematic, and not only because of its counter-intuitive content – whereby science ends up with the virtue of being more hermeneutic than hermeneutics itself. It is overhasty to conclude as Mach for one would argue, with Duhem and Bachelard echoing him here, that scientists are the best judges of their own practice or that science provides its own best philosophy.

Feyerabend has argued eloquently against this view in *Against Method* and his recent books. But we should not need Feyerabend's warnings that if science is not inherently a socially *responsible* enterprise, science is nevertheless neither the Moloch nor the redeemer of culture and it *is* as a practical matter of funding in fact socially *responsive*.[35] We do need to add, that for Feyerabend's programme of taking responsibility for getting 'science' to respond to social interests and needs, that if one is not to sink into the platitudes of civic virtue, now more than Nietzsche could have imagined, we desperately need a critique of critique, a critique of reason, of truth, of morality.

If the analytic philosophic perspective represents the notion that (natural and objective) science is 'mankind's most successful truth enterprise', as Heelan puts it, the continental approach rejects the Whiggish implications of this ideal. However, this is a subtle point for it must again be emphasized that today there is no approach to the philosophy of science, analytic or otherwise, which would advocate an unreconstructedly Whiggish ideal. Yet if the perspective of a continental approach to the philosophy of science is inherently problematic owing to a perception of its views as 'anti-science', read off from its explicit rejection of scientific knowledge as a 'privileged kind', the pluralism of continental philosophy recommends a reconsideration. Such a review of continental prospects for the philosophy of science is under way.

This phenomenological tradition begins with Husserl's project of grounding mathematics and physics begun in his work on arithmetic and continued in his *Logical Investigations* and *Ideas*. Related to the Husserlian tradition in turn is Merleau-Ponty's *The Primacy of Perception*. Husserl's interests grew out of the same tradition as and to that extent matched analytic philosophy (Cobb-Stevens). Considering the common origins of analytic and continental philosophy as a response (variously expressed in Husserl and Frege) to the psychologism of Meinong and Brentano, one might propose, as Michael Dummett has done, that a basic standard for bridging the continental–analytic divide should be a scholarly conversance with *both* Husserl and Frege. In this way, Hugo Dingler, a positivist and in that measure an analytic philosophic thinker, may also be productively counted as one of Husserl's students, indeed as a student who memorialized the value of his teacher's influence (Gethmann, Dingler). Recent reviews of the history of the Vienna circle point to a revaluation of the historical relationship between phenomenology and logical positivism. In line with this analytic/continental connection, Ströker, Orth, Gethmann and Haller may be read as offering comprehensive discussions of the phenomenological tradition beginning with Husserl, while Gethmann in particular stresses the development of that tradition in Lorenzen and the Erlanger school and its further development and the continuation of constructivist themes in evolutionary epistemology (Wuketis, Löw, Maturana). According to Gethmann, beyond Husserl's transcendent phenomenology, Heidegger's specific brand of hermeneutic phenomenology may be counted as a indirect influence on the development of the Erlanger school. If Foucault is included, this line of association running from Husserl to Heidegger and beyond is more obviously seen to resonate with the Edinburgh school of strong sociology of science (Rouse, Latour).

Joseph Kockelmans defends as proto-analytic the realist perspective of hermeneutic continental approaches to the philosophy of science. For Kockelmans, a hermeneutic philosophy of science requires a 'new conception' of truth understood in Heideggerian terms as *alētheic* (truth as unconcealment), *horizonal* or, in Nietzsche's terms, *perspectival* truth (Kockelmans, Heidegger, Gadamer, Babich). But where Kockelmans's concern is meaning, his reading of truth and science is closer to a Fregean conception of *Sinn* (sense meaning) and to the traditional Diltheyan *Lebenswelt* (life-world), articulated in terms of a Gadamerian hermeneutics than to the later Heidegger's conception of truth and ambiguity.

Patrick Heelan's interest remains true to the formal constitutive (eidetic, transcendental, and genetic) phenomenology that is Husserl's project to found philosophy as a rigorous science and not just with respect to the so-called 'crisis' of his later work. Heelan's hermeneutic phenomenology expresses a realism which he calls a *horizonal realism*, articulating the basis for a phenomenology of experiment to be integrated with the theoretical expression of science. Heelan's phenomenology holds with Husserl's eidetic project the possibility of approximating the essence of a scientific object through successive profiles. The hermeneutic dimension reflects the necessity for considering the historical, social and disciplinary circumstance of the researcher. Theoretical descriptions denominate the experimental profiles that would be perceived under standard laboratory conditions and, with a hermeneutic of experimental work, become truly descriptive of what is eidetically perceived in the laboratory. Heelan's perspective accords with strong or robust realist readings of experimental science, but his is more promising than most for with a hermeneutic phenomenological expression the realist perspective becomes a matter of perception not faith.

In current English-language publications, the foremost representatives of so-called 'continental' approaches to the philosophy of science in addition to Heelan and Kockelmans include Theodore Kisiel and Thomas Seebohm. Older continental scholars seem rather more concerned with the special problems of phenomenology (intuition and formal logic, the meaning of transcendence, etc.) rather than with questions specific to the philosophy of science, while younger scholars read the value of Husserl's and Heidegger's thought with respect to science rather more historically and less theoretically. Recent studies (Gethmann, Orth, Harvey, Rouse, Crease) by contrast tend to argue for the historical influence upon rather than the current value of phenomenology and hermeneutic reconceptualizations of the expression of the philosophy of science.

In sum, this means that the work of Heelan, Kockelmans, Kisiel, Seebohm (all continental scholars, most originally of geographically continental nationality but working in the traditionally analytic academic world of United States philosophy of science), etc., must be seen as rather singular representatives of the philosophical development and application of the phenomenological and hermeneutic traditions towards an understanding of science including the natural sciences. And given the factually analytic profile of professional philosophy of science, by far the most influential contributions to the imperative value of a continental turn to historical and hermeneutic expressions of the philosophy of science must be said to have come from traditional analytic philosophers of science, complementing where not directly acknowledging the work of Heelan *et al*. This is not due to the greater perspicacity of scholars in the analytic tradition: it is only a function of its paradigmatic (and professional) dominance. Thus, for example, Hacking's recent work on statistics in *The Taming of Chance* and his recent articles is characterized by more than a historical turn but a turn that must be properly and fully named (although Hacking does not employ the term) hermeneutic. And this same reference to hermeneutics is implicit when not explicit in many recent historical studies of science (Jardine, Crombie). What is more, in the turn to the social (in old-fashioned terms, to the *life-world*) dimensions of science inspired by the sociology of science and knowledge (Hiley *et al*., Fuller, Latour, McMullin, Shapin/Scheffler), a new fusion of styles in the philosophy of science is emerging. If philosophy of science may not be said to be returning to its historical continental roots in all these revolutions, a review of these roots cannot but be salutary for the life of the broader discipline, for the range of styles, the plurality, of philosophies of science.

∾ NOTES ∾

1 The topic of the nature of a continental approach to the philosophy of science is almost necessarily esoteric rather than general. The intersection of continental thought and the philosophy of science is far from well defined in professional philosophy. Indeed, the focus on Mach, Duhem and Bachelard may even appear tendentious for these authors might well be represented as antecedent figures within traditional analytic philosophy of science. In fact they serve this antecedent function for both analytic and continental expressions of the philosophy of science. Hence the issues raised in this chapter correspond to the history of continental philosophy and the philosophy of science, their intersection, and the current state of research. As this last profile is constantly in flux, a more detailed bibliography has been included to indicate this ferment and to benefit further research.

2 R. Harré, *Philosophies of Science* (Oxford: Oxford University Press, 1976).

3 A. MacIntyre, 'Epistemological Crises, Dramatic Narrative, and the Philosophy of Science', in G. Gutting (ed.), *Paradigms and Revolutions: Appraisals and Applications of Thomas Kuhn's Philosophy of Science* (Notre Dame: University of Notre Dame Press, 1980), pp. 54–74.

4 H. Redner, *The Ends of Science* (Boulder: Westview Press, 1987).

5 K. Hübner, *Critique of Scientific Reason* (Chicago: University of Chicago Press, 1983), p. 35.

6 As a recent and comprehensive contribution to this perspective and the debate concerning it and the history of the Vienna circle as a whole in the North American context of what is by and large an American discipline, the philosophy of science, see G. Holton, 'Ernst Mach and the Fortunes of Positivism in America', *Isis*, 83: 1 (1992): 27–60.

7 C. Dilworth, 'Empiricism vs. Realism: High Points in the Debate during the Past 150 Years', *Studies in the History and Philosophy of Science*, 21 (3): 431–62 (447).

8 P. Frank, 'Kausalgesetz und Erfahrung', *Annalen der Naturphilosophie*, 6 (1906): 443–50.

9 Harré (note 1), p. 29.

10 M. Tiles [6.245], 227.

11 Blackmore cites Hans Kleinpeter's 1912 letter to Mach, reporting that 'Nietzsche read one of your essays in a scientific journal and spoke very favourably about it' ([6.8], 123). And according to Alwin Mittasch, Mach himself sent a copy of one of his articles to Nietzsche bearing the hand-written dedication 'Für Herrn Prof. Dr. Nietzsche hochachtungsvoll Ernst Mach' (Mittasch [6.151], 367). Mach's views correspond to Nietzsche's refusal to distinguish between the organic and the inorganic world as discontinuous (indeed, as opposed). For Nietzsche the living and the dead are representations of a non-discontinuous order.

12 It goes without saying that positivism has an almost uniformly negative connotation. This negative evaluation is not unique to our own times. F. Ringer notes that in the German universities between the 1890s and the 1930s, during the Weimar period, 'the label "positivist" was almost invariably used in a deroga-

tory sense' ('The Origins of Mannheim's Sociology of Knowledge', in McMullin [6.202], 55). This parallel with contemporary negative connotations of positivism extended to a critique that similarly accords with the corrective turns to the historical, the interpretive or hermeneutic and the social. For Ringer, the criticism of positivism entailed its own inherent ideology: 'positivism was seen as a kind of intellectual acid, a potentially disastrous dissolvent of wholistic concepts, traditional beliefs, and socially integrative certainties. To "overcome" the problems raised by specialization and positivism alike . . . there was an urgent need for a revitalization of philosophical idealism that would also reinstate *Wissenschaft* as a ground for an integral and partly normative *Weltanschauung*.'

13 I. Hacking, ' "Style" for Historians and Philosophers', *Studies in the History and Philosophy of Science*, 23: 1(1992): 1–20 (12).

14 Berthelot, Duhem scholars seem pleased to observe, is himself today very nearly forgotten and certainly more obscure than Duhem.

15 The issue is a socially and historically complicated one. For background information on this topic, see chapter 6 of M. J. Nye [6.51]. For a fuller discussion of the particular circumstances of Hélène Duhem's efforts on behalf of her father's unpublished work, see R. N. D. Martin [6.50].

16 Parisians – and New Yorkers – will understand the profound implications of such a circumstance. Although Duhem was characterized by his Bordeaux contemporaries as testy ('violence himself'), it is not hard to imagine this perception a result of a provincial point of view.

17 Today we might understand this perspective as a reaction against *scientism*, and it is still represented by thinkers such as Jacques Ellul and René Dubos. For a discussion of the French intellectual landscape with respect to the historical features of scientific dogma and religious belief including a discussion of Dubos' situation regarded within such a vista, see H. W. Paul [6.52].

18 W. A. Wallace, *Prelude to Galileo: Essays on Medieval and Sixteenth Century Sources of Galileo's Thought* (Dordrecht: Reidel, 1981).

19 See Wallace, *Prelude to Galileo*, 'Galileo and Reasoning *Ex Suppositione*', pp. 124–59. Among others, see M. Clavelin, *The Natural Philosophy of Galileo: Essay on the Origins and Formation of Classical Mechanics* (Cambridge, Mass.: MIT Press 1974) and R. E. Butts and J. Pitt (eds), *New Perspective on Galileo* (Dordrecht: Reidel, 1978).

20 Butterfield [6.212], 27.

21 K. A. Popper, *Conjectures and Refutations: The Growth of Scientific Knowledge* (New York: Harper & Row, 1963), p. 99.

22 Hacking (note 13), p. 7. Hacking feels compelled to add for reasons I dare not surmise, for Hacking does not comment on this addition, '. . . and also Spengler'.

23 A. MacIntyre, 'Epistemological Crises, Dramatic Narrative, and the Philosophy of Science', in Gutting (ed.) (note 3), p. 67.

24 It is hard to read Bachelard as conceiving of the scientist as a woman, hence I use masculine pronouns advisedly in what follows.

25 P. A. Heelan, 'Preface' to the English translation of Bachelard's *The New Scientific Spirit* [6.54], xiii.

26 Tiles [6.83], xv.

27 See J. Culler, *Framing the Sign: Criticism and Its Institutions* (Oxford:

Blackwell, 1988). See too J. Llewellyn, *Beyond Metaphysics: The Hermeneutic Circle in Contemporary Continental Philosophy* (Atlantic Highlands: Humanities Press, 1985). This dissonant reception may also account for the recurrent fascination with Bachelard.

28 R. Smith [6.82], preface.

29 Cf. J. Derrida's discussion of the 'hinge' (*brisure*) in *Of Grammatology*, trans. G. Spivak (Baltimore: Johns Hopkins University Press, 1974), pp. 65ff.

30 Paul Valéry (1871–1945), French poet, literary theorist and essayist.

31 B. d'Espagnat, *Penser la science ou les enjeux du savoir* (Paris: Bordas, 1990), p. 223.

32 M. Müller and A. Halder, '*Analytische Philosophie*', *Kleines Philosophisches Wörterbuch*, (Freiburg im Breisgau: Herder, 1971), p. 19.

33 P. A. Heelan, 'Hermeneutical Phenomenology and the Philosophy of Science', in H. Silverman, *Gadamer and Hermeneutics: Science, Culture, Literature* (New York: Routledge, 1991), p. 213.

34 See for example R. Bubner [6.131] and in particular Bubner [6.132].

35 See Feyerabend [6.218, 6.219, 6.220].

SELECT BIBLIOGRAPHY

Mach

Translations

6.1 'On the Definition of Mass', *History and Root of the Principle of the Conservation of Energy*, trans. P. E. B. Jourdain, Chicago: Open Court, 1872, 1911.

6.2 *The Science of Mechanics*, trans. T. J. McCormack, Chicago: Open Court, 1893, 1960.

6.3 *The Analysis of Sensations and the Relation of the Physical to the Psychical*, trans. C. M. Williams and S. Waterlow, Chicago: Open Court, 1914; New York: Dover, 1959.

6.4 *Popular Scientific Lectures*, trans. T. J. McCormack, with additional lectures from 1865 and 1897, La Salle: Open Court, 1894, 1943.

6.5 *Knowledge and Error: Sketches on the Psychology of Erring*, trans. T. J. McCormack (chaps xxi and xxii) and P. Foulkes, ed. B. McGuiness, Dordrecht and Boston: D. Reidel, 1976.

6.6 *Space and Geometry: In the Light of Physiological, Psychological, and Physical Inquiry*, trans. T. J. McCormack (three essays originally published in *The Monist*, 1901–3) La Salle: Open Court, 1906, 1960.

Criticism

6.7 Adler, F. *Ernst Machs Überwindung des mechanischen Materialismus*, Vienna, 1918.

6.8   Blackmore, J. T. *Ernst Mach: His Work, Life and Influence*, Berkeley: University of California Press, 1972.

6.9   Blackmore, J. T. *Ernst Mach – A Deeper Look: Documents and New Perspectives*, Dordrecht, Boston: Kluwer, 1992.

6.10   Bradley, J. *Mach's Philosophy of Science*, London: Athlone Press, 1971.

6.11   Brentano, F. *Über Ernst Machs 'Erkenntnis und Irrtum'*, Amsterdam: Rodopi, 1981.

6.12   Dingler, H. *Die Grundgedanken der Machschen Philosophie*, Leipzig: Barth, 1924.

6.13   Duhem, P. 'Analyse de l'ouvrage de Ernst Mach: La mécanique, étude historique et critique de son développement', *Bulletin des sciences mathématiques*, 1.26 (1903): 261–83.

6.14   Forman, P. 'Weimar Culture, Causality, and Quantum Theory, 1918–1927', *Historical Studies in the Physical Sciences*, 3 (1971): 1–11.

6.15   Frank, P. *Modern Science and its Philosophy*, Cambridge, Mass.: Harvard University Press, 1949, 1961, pp. 13–62 and 69–95.

6.16   Haller, R. and Stadler, F. (eds) *Ernst Mach: Werk und Wirkung*, Wien: Holder-Pichler-Tempsky, 1988.

6.17   Hentschel, K. 'Die Korrespondenz Duhem–Mach, zur "Modellbeladenheit" von Wissenschaftsgeschichte', *Annals of Science*, 14 (1988): 73–91.

6.18   Holton, G. 'Ernst Mach and the Fortunes of Positivism in America', *Isis*, 83: 1 (1992): 27–60.

6.19   Janik, A. and Toulmin, S. *Wittgenstein's Vienna*, New York: Simon & Schuster, 1973.

6.20   Jensen, K. M. *Beyond Marx and Mach: Aleksandr Bogdanov's Philosophy of Living Experience*, Dordrecht: Reidel, 1978.

6.21   Kaulbach, F. 'Das anthropologische Interesse in Ernst Mach's Positivismus', in J. Blühdorn and J. Ritter (eds) *Positivismus im 19 Jahrhundert*, Frankfurt: Klostermann, 1971.

6.22   Kraft, V. *The Vienna Circle*, New York: Greenwood Press, 1953.

6.23   Lenin, V. I. *Materialism and Empirio-Criticism*, trans. A. Fineberg, London, Peking, Moscow: Foreign Languages Publishers' House, 1952, 1972, (1930).

6.24   Losee, J. *A Historical Introduction to the Philosophy of Science*, Oxford: Oxford University Press, 1972, chapter 11.

6.25   Mises, R. von *Ernst Mach und die empirische Wissenschaftsauffassung*, The Hague: Nijhoff, 1938.

6.26   Mises, R. von *Positivism: A Study in Human Understanding*, trans. J. Bernstein and R. G. Newton, Cambridge, Mass.: Harvard University Press, 1951.

6.27   Musil, R. *On Mach's Theories*, Washington, DC: University of America Press and München: Philosophia Verlag, 1982.

6.28   Schlick, M. *Gesammelte Aufsätze*, Wien: Gerold, 1938; Hildesheim: G. Olms, 1969.

6.29   Smith, B. 'Austrian Origins of Logical Positivism', in B. Gower (ed.), *Logical Positivism in Perspective: Essays on Language, Truth, and Logic*, Totowa: Barnes & Noble, 1987, pp. 35–68.

6.30 Sommer, M. *Evidenz im Augenblick. Eine Phänomenologie der reinen Empfindung*, Frankfurt: Suhrkamp, 1987.

6.31 Stadler, F. *Vom Positivismus zur 'Wissenschaftlichen Weltfassung' am Beispiel der Wirkungsgeschichte von Ernst Mach in Österreich von 1895 bis 1934*, München (with bibliography), Wien: Locker, 1982.

6.32 Weinberg, C. B. *Mach's Empirio-Pragmatism in Physical Science*, New York: Albee Press, 1937.

Duhem

Translations

6.33 *The Aim and Structure of Physical Theory*, trans. P. Wiener, Princeton: Princeton University Press, 1954.

6.34 *Mediaeval Cosmology*, trans. and selection R. Ariew, Chicago: University of Chicago Press, 1985.

6.35 *To Save the Phenomena: An Essay on the Idea of Physical Theory from Plato to Galileo*, trans. E. Dolan and C. Maschier, Chicago: University of Chicago Press, 1969.

6.36 *The Origins of Statics: The Sources of Physical Theory*, trans. G. Leneaux, V. Vagliente and G. Wagener, Boston and Dordrecht: Kluwer, 1991.

Criticism

6.37 Brenner, A. *Duhem, science, realité et apparence, mathesis*, Paris: J. Vrin, 1990.

6.38 Eastwood, D. M. *The Revival of Pascal: A Study of his Relation to Modern French Thought*, Oxford: Clarendon Press, 1936.

6.39 Frank, P. *Modern Science and its Philosophy*, Cambridge, Mass.: Harvard University Press, 1949.

6.40 Harding, S. *Can Theories Be Refuted? Essays on the Duhem–Quine Thesis*, Dordrecht and Boston: Reidel, 1976.

6.41 Hentschel, K. 'Die Korrespondenz Duhem–Mach, zur "Modellbeladenheit" von Wissenschaftsgeschichte', *Annals of Science*, 14 (1988): 73–91.

6.42 Losee, J. *A Historical Introduction to the Philosophy of Science*, Oxford: Oxford University Press, 1972, chapter 11.

6.43 Lowinger, A. *The Methodology of Pierre Duhem*, New York: Columbia University Press, 1941.

6.44 Jaki, S. L. *Uneasy Genius: The Life and Work of Pierre Duhem*, The Hague: Kluwer, 1984.

6.45 Jaki, S. L. *Scientist and Catholic: An Essay on Pierre Duhem*, Front Royal: Christendom Press, 1991.

6.46 Maiocchi, R. *Chimica e filosofia, scienza, epistemologia, storia e religione nell' opera di Pierre Duhem*, Firenze: Le Lettre, 1985.

6.47 Martin, R. N. D. 'Darwin and Duhem', *History of Science*, 20 (1982): 64–74.

6.48   Martin, R. N. D. 'Saving Duhem and Galileo: Duhemian Methodology and the Saving of the Phenomena', *History of Science*, 25 (1987): 301–19.

6.49   Martin, R. N. D. 'The Trouble with Authority: The Galileo Affair and One of its Historians', *The Bulletin of Science, Technology, and Society* 9:5 (1989): 294–301.

6.50   Martin, R. N. D. *Pierre Duhem, Philosophy and History in the Work of a Believing Physicist*, La Salle: Open Court, 1991.

6.51   Nye, M. J. *Science in the Provinces: Scientific Communities and Provincial Leadership in France, 1860–1930*, Berkeley: University of California Press, 1986, chapter 6: 'Bordeaux: Catholicism, Conservativism, and the Influence of Pierre Duhem'.

6.52   Paul, H. W. *The Edge of Contingency: French Catholic Reaction to Scientific Change from Darwin to Duhem*, Gainesville: University of Florida Press, 1979.

6.53   Rey, A. 'La Philosophie scientifique de M. Duhem', *Revue de métaphysique et de morale*, 12 (1904): 699–744.

Bachelard

Translations

6.54   *The New Scientific Spirit*, trans. A. Goldhammer, Boston: Beacon Press, 1985.

6.55   *The Philosophy of No: A Philosophy of the New Scientific Mind*, trans. G. C. Waterston, New York: Orion Press, 1969.

6.56   *The Psychoanalysis of Fire*, trans. A. Ross, Boston: Beacon Press and London: Routledge & Kegan Paul, 1964.

6.57   *The Poetics of Space*, trans. M. Jolas, New York: Orion Press, 1964.

6.58   *The Poetics of Reverie*, trans. D. Russell, New York: Orion Press, 1969.

Criticism

6.59   *Présence de Gaston Bachelard: Epistémologie pour une anthropologie complète*, Aix-en-Provence: Librarie de l'Université, 1988.

6.60   *Gaston Bachelard: Profils epistémologiques*, Philosophica, 32, Ottawa: Presses de l'Université d'Ottowa, 1987.

6.61   *Hommage à Bachelard: Etudes de philosophie et d'histoire des sciences*, Paris: 1957.

6.62   Bhaskar, R. 'Feyerabend and Bachelard: Two Philosophers of Science', *New Left Review*, 94 (1975): 31–55.

6.63   Canguilhem, G. 'Sur une épistémologie concordataire', in [6.61].

6.64   Canguilhem, G. *Ideology and Rationality in the Hisory of the Life Sciences*, trans. A. Goldhammer, Cambridge, Mass.: MIT Press, 1988.

6.65   Caws, P. *Yorick's World: Science and the Knowing Subject*, Berkeley: University of California Press, 1993.

6.66 Dubrulle, G. *Philosophie zwischen Tag und Nacht: Ein Studie zur Epistemologie Gaston Bachelards*, Frankfurt: Peter Lang, 1983.

6.67 Gaukroger, S. W. 'Bachelard and the Problem of Epistemological Analysis', *Studies in the History and Philosophy of Science*, 7 (1976): 189–244.

6.68 Grieder, A. 'Gaston Bachelard: "Phénoménologue" of Modern Science', *Journal of the British Society for Phenomenology*, 17:2 (1986): 107–23.

6.69 Gutting, G. Chapter 1 in [6.167].

6.70 LaLonde, M. *La Théorie de la connaissance scientifique de Gaston Bachelard*, Montréal: Fidés 1966.

6.71 Lecourt, D. *Bachelard ou le jour et le nuit (un essai de matérialisme dialectique)*, Paris: Grasset, 1974.

6.72 Lecourt, D. *L'epistémologie historique de Gaston Bachelard*, Paris: Vrin, 1978.

6.73 Lecourt, D. *Marxism and Epistemology: Bachelard, Canguilhem, and Foucault*, trans. B. Brewster, London: NLB, 1979.

6.74 McAllester Jones M. (ed.) *The Philosophy and Poetics of Gaston Bachelard*, Washington, DC: University of America Press, 1989.

6.75 McAllester Jones, M. 'Unfixing the Subject: Gaston Bachelard and Reading', in [6.74], 149–61.

6.76 McAllester Jones, M. 'On Science, Poetry and the "honey of being": Bachelard's Shelley', in D. Wood (ed.) *Philosopher's Poets*, London: Routledge, 1990, pp. 153–76.

6.77 McAllester Jones, M. *Gaston Bachelard: Subversive Humanist*, Madison: University of Wisconsin Press, 1991.

6.78 Parker, N. 'Science and Poetry in the Ontology of Human Freedom: Bachelard's Account of the Poetic and the Scientific Imagination', in [6.74], 75–100.

6.79 Schaettel, M. *Bachelard critique ou l'achèmie du rêve: Un art de lire et de rêver*, Lyon: L'Hermes, 1977.

6.80 Schaettel, M. *Gaston Bachelard: le rêve et la raison*, Saint-Seine-L'Abbaye: Editions Saint-Seine-L'Abbaye, 1984.

6.81 Smith, C. 'Bachelard in the Context of a Century of Philosophy of Science', in [6.74], 13–26.

6.82 Smith, R. C. *Gaston Bachelard*, Boston: Twayne Publishers, 1982.

6.83 Tiles, M. *Bachelard: Science and Objectivity*, Cambridge: Cambridge University Press, 1984.

6.84 Vadée, M. *Bachelard ou le nouvel idéalisme épistémologique*, Paris: Editions Sociales, 1975.

Constructivism or evolutionary epistemology

6.85 Delbrück, M. *Wahrheit und Wirklichkeit: Über die Evolution des Erkennens*, Hamburg/Zürich: Rosch & Röhring, 1986.

6.86 Dürr, H. P. *Das Netz des Physikers*, München: Hanser, 1988.

6.87 Eisenhardt, P. *et al.* (eds) *Du steigst nie zweimal in denselben Fluss: Die Grenzen der wissenschaftlichen Erkenntnis*, Hamburg: Rohwolt, 1988.

6.88   Janich, P. 'Physics – Natural Science or Technology', in W. Krohn *et al.*,
       The Dynamics of Science and Technology, Dordrecht, Boston: D.
       Reidel, 1978.
6.89   Janich, P. *Grenzen der Naturwissenschaft*, München: Beck, 1992.
6.90   Maturana, U. and Varela, F. *Autopoiesis and Cognition: The Realization of
       the Living*, Dordrecht and Boston: Reidel, 1980.
6.91   Riedel, R. *Biology of Knowledge*, New York: Wiley, 1979.
6.92   Safranski, R. *Wieviele Wahrheit Braucht der Mensch: Über das Denkbare
       und das Lebbare*, München: Hanser, 1990.
6.93   Vollmer, G. *Was können wir wissen? Bd 1: Die Natur der Erkenntnis*,
       Stuttgart: Hizel, 1985.
6.94   Watzlawick, P. and Frieg P. (eds) *Das Auge des Betrachters: Beiträge zum
       Konstruktivismus*, München and Zürich: Piper, 1991.
6.95   Wolters, G. ' "The first man who almost wholly understands me." Carnap,
       Dingler and Conventionalism', in N. Rescher (ed.) *The Heritage of
       Logical Positivism*, Lanham: University Press of America, 1985.
6.96   Wolters, G. 'Evolutionäre Erkenntnistheorie – eine Polemik', *Vierteljahresch-
       rift der NaturforschendenGesellschaft in Zürich*, 133 (1988): 125–42.
6.97   Wuketis, F. M. (ed.) *Concepts and Approaches in Evolutionary Epistemology:
       Towards an Evolutionary Theory of Knowledge*, Dordrecht: Kluwer,
       1984.
6.98   Wuketis, F. M. (ed.) *Evolutionary Epistemology and Its Implications for
       Humankind*, Albany: State University of New York Press, 1990.

Phenomenologically oriented approaches to the philosophy of science: Husserl and Merleau-Ponty

6.99   Cho, K. K. (ed.) *Philosophy and Science in Phenomenological Perspective*,
       The Hague: Nijhoff/Kluwer, 1984.
6.100 Compton, J. 'Natural Science and the Philosophy of Nature', in J. Edie (ed.)
       Phenomenology in America, Athens: Ohio University Press, 1969.
6.101 Gutting, G. 'Phenomenology and Scientific Realism', *New Scholasticism*,
       48 (1976), 263–6.
6.102 Gutting, G. 'Husserl and Scientific Realism', *Philosophy and Phenomenologi-
       cal Research*, 39 (1979): 42–56.
6.103 Hardy, L. 'The Idea of Science in Husserl and the Tradition', in [6.104].
6.104 Hardy, L. and Embree, L. (eds) *Phenomenology of Natural Science*, Dord-
       recht: Kluwer, 1992. Includes Steven Chasan, 'Bibliography of
       Phenomenological Philosophy of Science'.
6.105 Harvey, C. W. *Husserl's Phenomenology and the Foundations of Natural
       Science*, Athens: Ohio University Press, 1989.
6.106 Harvey, C. W. and Shelton, J. D. 'Husserl's Phenomenology and the
       Ontology of the Natural Sciences', in Hardy/Embree, *Phenomenology
       of Natural Science*.
6.107 Heelan, P. A. *Quantum Mechanics and Objectivity*, The Hague: Nijhoff,
       1965.

6.108 Heelan, P. A. *Space-Perception and the Philosophy of Science*, Berkeley: California University Press, 1983.

6.109 Heelan, P. A. 'Husserl, Hilbert, and the Critique of Galilean Science', in R. Sokolowski (ed.) *Edmund Husserl and the Phenomenological Tradition*, Washington, DC: University Press of America, 1988, pp. 158–73.

6.110 Heelan, P. A. 'Husserl's Philosophy of Science', in J. Mohanty and W. McKenna (eds) *Husserl's Phenomenology: A Textbook*, Pittsburgh and Washington, DC: University Press of America, 1989, pp. 387–428.

6.111 Husserl, E. *Phenomenology and the Crisis of Philosophy: Philosophy as a Rigorous Science and Philosophy and the Crisis of Man*, trans. Q. Lauer, New York: Harper & Row, 1965.

6.112 Husserl, E. *The Crisis of European Sciences and Transcendental Phenomenology*, trans. D. Carr, Evanston: Northwestern University Press, 1970.

6.113 Kockelmans, J. *Phenomenology and Physical Science: An Introduction to the Philosophy of Physical Science*, Duquesne: Pittsburgh University Press, 1966.

6.114 Kockelmans, J. and Kisiel, T. (eds) *Phenomenology and the Natural Sciences*, Evanston: Northwestern University Press, 1970.

6.115 Langsdorf, L. 'Realism and Idealism in the Kuhnian Account of Science', in [6.104].

6.116 Lohmar, D. *Husserl's Phänomenologie als Philosophie der Mathematik*, Diss. Köln, 1987.

6.117 Lohmar, D. *Phänomenologie der Mathematik: Elemente der phänomenologische Aufklärung der mathematischen Erkenntnis*, Dordrecht and Boston: Kluwer, 1989.

6.118 McCarthy, M. *The Crisis of Philosophy*, Albany: State University of New York Press, 1990.

6.119 Merleau-Ponty, M. *Phenomenology of Perception*, trans. C. Smith, London: Routledge & Kegan Paul, 1962.

6.120 Orth, E. W. (ed.) *Die Phenomenologie und die Wissenschaften*, Freiburg im München: Alber, 1976.

6.121 Orth, E. W. 'Phänomenologie der Vernunft zwischen Szientismus, Lebenswelt und Intersubjektivität', *Phänomenologischen Forschungen*, 22 (1989): 63–87.

6.122 Rang, B. *Husserls Phänomenologie der materiellen Natur*, Frankfurt: Klostermann, 1990.

6.123 Seebohm, T. M., Føllesdal, D. and Mohanty, J. N. (eds) *Phenomenology and the Formal Sciences*, Dordrecht: Kluwer, 1992.

6.124 Sommer, M. *Husserl und die frühe Positivismus*, Frankfurt: Klostermann, 1985.

6.125 Strasser, S. *Phenomenology and the Human Sciences: A Contribution to a New Philosophic Ideal*, Atlantic Highlands: Humanities Press, 1974.

6.126 Ströker, E. 'Husserl's Principle of Evidence: The Significance and Limitations of a Methodological Norm of Philosophy as a Science', trans. R. Pettit, in *Contemporary German Philosophy*, University Park: Pennsylvania State University Press, 1982, pp. 111–38.

6.127 Ströker, E. *Husserls transzendentale Phänomenologie*, Frankfurt: Suhrkamp, 1987.

Hermeneuticist approaches to the philosophy of science: Nietzsche and Heidegger

6.128 Babich, B. E. *Nietzsche's Philosophy of Science: Reflecting Science on the Ground of Art and Life*, Albany: State University of New York Press, 1993.

6.129 Baier, H. 'Nietzsche als Wissenschaftskritiker', *Zeitschrift für philosophische Forschung*, 21 (1966): 130–43.

6.130 Bleicher, J. *The Hermeneutic Imagination: Outline of a Positive Critique of Scientism and Sociology*, London: Routledge & Kegan Paul, 1982.

6.131 Bubner, R. *Dialektik und Wissenschaft*, Frankfurt: Suhrkamp, 1973.

6.132 Bubner, R. 'On the Role of Hermeneutics in the Philosophy of Science', in *Essays in Hermeneutics and Critical Theory*, trans. E. Mathews, New York: Columbia University Press, 1988.

6.133 Connolly, J. and Keutner, T. *Hermeneutics versus Science: Three German Views*, Notre Dame: University of Notre Dame Press, 1988.

6.134 Connolly, J. and Keutner, T. 'Interpretation, Decidability, and Meaning', in [6.133].

6.135 Gadamer, H.-G. *Reason in Science*, trans. F. Lawrence, Cambridge, Mass.: MIT Press, 1981.

6.136 Gadamer, H.-G. 'On the Circle of Understanding', in [6.133], 68–78.

6.137 Gadamer, H.-G. and Böhme G. (eds) *Seminar: Die Hermeneutik und Die Wissenschaften*, Frankfurt: Suhrkamp, 1978.

6.138 Gebhard, W. *Nietzsches Totalismus: Philosophie der Natur zwischen Verklärung und Verhängnis*, Berlin and New York: Walter de Gruyter, 1983.

6.139 Heelan, P. A. 'Hermeneutics of Experimental Science in the Context of the Life-World', in D. Ihde and R. Zaner (eds) *Interdisciplinary Phenomenology*, The Hague: Nijhoff, 1975, pp. 7–50.

6.140 Heelan, P. A. 'Hermeneutical Phenomenology and the History of Science', in D. Dahlstrom (ed.) *Nature and Scientific Method: William A. Wallace Festschrift*, Washington, DC: University Press of America, 1991, pp. 23–36.

6.141 Hempel, H.-P. *Natur und Geschichte: Der Jahrhundertdialog zwischen Heidegger und Heisenberg*, Frankfurt: Anton Hain, 1990.

6.142 Hendley, S. *Reason and Relativism: A Sartrean Investigation*, Albany: State University of New York Press, 1991, chapters 1, 2, 5, 6.

6.143 Juranville, A. *Physique de Nietzsche*, Paris: Denoël/Gonthier, 1973.

6.144 Kirchhoff, J. 'Zum Problem der Erkenntnis bei Nietzsche', *Nietzsche-Studien*, 6 (1977): 16–44.

6.145 Kisiel, T. 'Hermeneutic Models for Natural Science', in [6.120], 180–91.

6.146 Kockelmans, J. J. *Heidegger and Science*, Washington, DC: University Press of America, 1985.

6.147 Kockelmans, J. J. 'Toward a Hermeneutic Theory of the History of the Natural Sciences', in [6.133].

6.148 Kolb, D. 'Heidegger on the Limits of Science', *Journal of the British Society for Phenomenology*, 14:1 (1983): 50–64.

6.149 Major-Poetal, P. *Michel Foucault's Archaeology of Western Culture: Toward a New Science of History*, Chapel Hill: University of North Carolina Press, 1983, chapters 1, 2, 3.

6.150 Mauer, R. 'The Origins of Modern Technology in Millenarianism', in P. T. Durbin and F. Rapp (eds) *Philosophy and Technology*, Dordrecht and Boston: Reidel, 1983: pp. 253–65.

6.151 Mittasch, A. *Friedrich Nietzsche als Naturphilosoph*, Stuttgart: A. Kroner, 1952.

6.152 Ormiston, G. and Sassower, R. *Narrative Experiments: The Discursive Authority of Science and Technology*, Minneapolis: University of Minnesota Press, 1989.

6.153 Richardson, W. J. 'Heidegger's Critique of Science', *The New Scholasticism*, 42 (1968): 511–36.

6.154 Ricoeur, P. *Hermeneutics and the Human Sciences*, trans. J. B. Thompson, Cambridge: Cambridge University Press, 1981.

6.155 Schirmacher, W. *Technik und Gelassenheit: Zeitkritik nach Heidegger*, Freiburg im München: Alber, 1985.

6.156 Schmidt, A. 'Zur Frage der Dialektik in Nietzsches Erkenntnistheorie', in M. Horkheimer (ed.) *Zeugnisse: Theodore W. Adorno zum sechszigsten Geburtstag*, Frankfurt: Suhrkamp, 1969, pp. 15–132.

6.157 Serrs, M. *Hermes: Literature, Science, Philosophy*, trans. J. V. Harari and D. F. Bell, Baltimore: Johns Hopkins University Press, 1982.

6.158 Stegmüller, W. 'Walther von der Vogelweide's Lyric of Dream-Love and Qasar 3C 273', in [6.133], pp. 102–52.

6.159 Vaihinger, H. *Nietzsche als Philosoph*, Berlin, 1902.

6.160 Vaihinger, H. *The Philosophy of As If. A System of the Theoretical, Practical and Religious Fictions of Mankind*, trans. C. K. Ogden, London: Routledge & Kegan Paul, 1935.

6.161 Wolff, J. *Hermeneutic Philosophy and the Sociology of Art*, London and Boston: Routledge & Kegan Paul, 1975, chapters 1–3.

Social, communicative and materialist (Marxist) continental approaches to the philosophy of science

6.162 Alford, C. *Science and the Revenge of Nature: Marcuse and Habermas*, Gainesville: University of Florida Press, 1985.

6.163 Aronowitz, S. *Science as Power: Discourse and Ideology in Modern Society*, Minneapolis: University of Minnesota Press, 1988.

6.164 Bhaskar, R. *Reclaiming Reality: A Critical Introduction*, London: Verso, 1989.

6.165 Bubner, R. 'Dialectical Elements of a Logic of Discovery' in [6.132].

6.166 Foucault, M. *The Order of Things: An Archaeology of the Human Sciences*, New York: Pantheon Books, 1973.
6.167 Gutting, G. *Michel Foucault's Archaeology of Scientific Reason*, Cambridge: Cambridge University Press, 1989.
6.168 Hacking, I. 'Michel Foucault's Immature Science', *Nous*, 13 (1979): 39–51.
6.169 Hiley, D. R., Bohman, J. and Schusterman R. (eds *The Interpretive Turn: Philosophy, Science, Culture*, Ithaca: Cornell University Press, 1991.
6.170 Lyotard, J.-F. *The Post-Modern Condition: A Report on Knowledge*, trans. G. Bennington and B. Massumi, Minneapolis: University of Minnesota Press, 1984.
6.171 Marcuse, H. *One Dimensional Man: Studies in the Ideology of Advanced Industrial Society*, Boston: Beacon Press, 1964.
6.172 Radder, H. *The Material Realization of Science: A Philosophical View on the Experimental Natural Sciences Developed in Discussion with Habermas*, Assen: Van Gorcum, 1988.
6.173 Rouse, J. *Knowledge and Power: Toward a Political Philosophy of Science*, Ithaca: Cornell University Press, 1987.
6.174 Whitebook, J. 'The Problem of Nature in Habermas', *Telos*, 40 (1979): 41–69.

Continental philosophy of technology

6.175 Beck, H. *Kulturphilosophie der Technik: Perspektiven zu technik-Menschheit-Zukunft*, Trier: Spee Verlag, 1979.
6.176 Guzzoni, U. 'Überlegungen zum Subjekt-Objekt-Modell Kritisches Denken und das Verhältnis von Technik und Natur', *Dialektik 14. Humanität, Venunft, und Moral in der Wissenschaft*, Köln: Pahl-Rugenstein, 1987: pp. 59–73.
6.177 Ihde, D. *Instrumental Reason: The Interface Between Philosophy of Science and Philosophy of Technology*, Indianapolis: Indiana University Press, 1991.
6.178 Loscerbo, J. *Being and Technology: A Study in the Philosophy of Martin Heidegger*, The Hague: Nijhoff, 1981.
6.179 Winner, L. *The Whale and the Reactor: A Search for Limits in an Age of High Technology*, Chicago: University of Chicago Press, 1986.

Related sociological studies of science and experimental epistemology

6.180 Anderson, G. 'Anglo-Saxon and Continental Schools of Meta-Science', *Continuum*, 8 (1980): 102–10. Also in [6.240].
6.181 Ashmore, M. *The Reflexive Thesis: Wrighting (sic) the Sociology of Scientific Knowledge*, Chicago: University of Chicago Press, 1989.
6.182 Barnes, B. *Interests and the Growth of Knowledge*, London: Routledge & Kegan Paul, 1977.
6.183 Barnes, B. *The Nature of Power*, Urbana: University of Illinois Press, 1988.

6.184 Bloor, D. *Knowledge and Social Imagery*, London: Routledge & Kegan Paul, 1976; 2nd edn, 1991.

6.185 Brannigan, A. *The Social Basis of Scientific Discoveries*, Cambridge: Cambridge University Press, 1981.

6.186 Brown, J. *The Rational and the Social*, New York: Routledge, 1989.

6.187 Collins, H. *Changing Order: Replication and Induction in Scientific Practice*, London: Routledge & Kegan Paul, 1985.

6.188 Collins, H. and Pinch, T. *Frames of Meaning: The Social Construction of Extraordinary Science*, London and Boston: Routledge & Kegan Paul, 1987.

6.189 Crane, D. 'The Gatekeepers of Science: Some Factors Affecting the Selection of Articles for Scientific Journals', *American Sociologist*, 2 (1967): 195–201.

6.190 Crane, D. *Invisible Colleges: The Diffusion of Knowledge in Scientific Communities*, Chicago: University of Chicago Press, 1972.

6.191 Gallison, P. *How Experiments End*, Chicago: University of Chicago Press, 1987.

6.192 Haraway, D. J. *Simians, Cyborgs, and Women: The Reinvention of Nature*, New York: Routledge, 1991.

6.193 Heelan, P. A. 'The Quantum Theory and the Phenomenology of Social-Historical Phenomena', in P. Blosser, L. Embree and S. Kojima (eds), *Japanese and American Phenomenology*, Washington, DC: University Press of America.

6.194 Krige, J. *Science, Revolution and Discontinuity*, Atlantic Highlands: Humanities Press and Brighton: Harvester, 1980.

6.195 Knorr-Cetina, K. *The Manufacture of Knowledge*, Oxford: Oxford University Press, 1980.

6.196 Knorr-Cetina, K. and Mulkey, M. (eds) *Science Observed: Perspectives on the Social Study of Science*, London and Beverly Hills: Sage, 1983.

6.197 Kutschmann, W. *Der Naturwissenschaftler und sein Körper: Die Rolle der 'inneren Natur' in der Experimentellen Naturwissenschaft der frühen Neuzeit*, Frankfurt: Suhrkamp, 1986.

6.198 Latour, B. *Science in Action*, Cambridge, Mass.: Harvard University Press, 1987.

6.199 Latour, B. *The Pasteurization of France/Irreductions: A Politico-scientific Essay*, Cambridge: Mass.: Harvard University Press, 1988.

6.200 Latour, B. and Woolgar, L. *Laboratory Life*, London: Sage, 1979.

6.201 Laudan, L. *Progress and its Problems*, Berkeley: University of California Press, 1977.

6.202 McMullin, E. (ed.) *The Social Dimensions of Science*, Notre Dame: University of Notre Dame Press, 1991.

6.203 Myers, G. *Writing Biology, Texts in the Social Construction of Scientific Knowledge*, Madison: University of Wisconsin Press, 1990.

6.204 Prelli, L. *A Rhetoric of Science*, Columbia, South Carolina: University of South Carolina Press, 1989.

6.205 Redner, H. *The Ends of Science*, Boulder: Westview Press, 1987.

6.206 Ringer, F. 'The Origins of Mannheim's Sociology of Knowledge', in [6.202].

6.207 Sapp, J. *Where the Truth Lies: Franz Moewus and the Origins of Molecular Biology*, Cambridge: Cambridge University Press, 1990.

6.208 Shapin, S. and Schaffer, S. *Leviathan and the Air Pump: Hobbes, Boyle, and the Experimental Life*, Princeton: Princeton University Press, 1985.

6.209 Winch, P. *The Idea of a Social Science and its Relation to Philosophy*, London: Routledge & Kegan Paul, 1958.

Related studies in the philosophy and history of science

6.210 Agassi, J. *Towards an Historiography of Science: History and Theory*, vol. 2, The Hague, 1963.

6.211 Butterfield, H. *The Origins of Modern Science*, New York: Macmillan, 1951, 1957, 1965.

6.212 Butterfield, H. *The Whig Interpretation of History*, New York: Norton, 1965 (1931).

6.213 Cartwright, N. *How the Laws of Physics Lie*, Oxford: Oxford University Press, 1983.

6.214 Churchland, P. M. and Hooker, C. A. (eds) *Images of Science: Essays on Realism and Empiricism*, Chicago and London: 1985.

6.215 Crombie, A. C. *Augustine to Galileo*, Cambridge, Mass.: Harvard University Press, 1961.

6.216 Cushing, J. T., Delaney, C. F. and Gutting, G. M. (eds) *Science and Reality: Recent Work in the Philosophy of Science*, Notre Dame: University of Notre Dame Press, 1981.

6.217 Dijksterhuis, E. J. *The Mechanization of the World Picture*, trans. C. Dikshoorn, London: Clarendon, 1961.

6.218 Feyerabend, P. *Against Method: Outline of an Anarchistic Theory of Knowledge*, London: Verso, 1975.

6.219 Feyerabend, P. *Farewell to Reason*, London: Verso: 1987.

6.220 Feyerabend, P. *Three Dialogues on Knowledge*, London: Verso, 1990.

6.221 Gower, B. 'Speculation in Physics: The History and Practice of *Naturphilosphie*', *Studies in History and Philosophy of Science*, 3 (1973): 301–56.

6.222 Hacking, I. *The Emergence of Probability: A Philosophical Study of Early Ideas about Probability, Induction and Statistical Inference*, London and New York: Cambridge University Press, 1975.

6.223 Hacking, I. *Representing and Intervening: Introductory Topics in the Philosophy of Natural Science*, Cambridge: Cambridge University Press, 1983.

6.224 Hacking, I. *The Taming of Chance*, Cambridge: Cambridge University Press, 1990.

6.225 Hanson, N. R. *Patterns of Discovery: An Inquiry Into the Conceptual Foundations of Science*, Berkeley: University of California Press, 1958.

6.226 Harman, P. M. *Energy, Force, and Matter: The Conceptual Development of Nineteenth-Century Physics*, Cambridge: Cambridge University Press, 1982.

6.227 Hesse, M. *Revolutions and Reconstructions*, Bloomington: University of Indiana Press, 1980.

6.228 Jardine, N. *Fortunes of Inquiry*, Cambridge: Cambridge University Press, 1986.

6.229 Jardine, N. *Scenes of Inquiry*, Oxford: Oxford University Press, 1991.

6.230 Kockelmans, J. *Philosophy of Science: The Historical Background*, New York: Free Press, 1968.

6.231 Kuhn, T. *The Structure of Scientific Revolutions* (2nd edn), Chicago: University of Chicago Press, 1962, 1970.

6.232 Kuhn, T. *The Essential Tension*, Chicago: University of Chicago Press, 1977.

6.233 Ladrière, J. *The Challenge to Culture Presented by Science and Technology*, Paris: Unesco, 1977.

6.234 Lakatos, I. *The Problem of Inductive Logic*, Amsterdam: North Holland Publishing Co., 1968.

6.235 Lakatos, I. 'Falsification and the Methodology of Scientific Research Programmes', in Lakatos and A. Musgrave (eds) *Criticism and the Growth of Knowledge*, Cambridge: Cambridge University Press, 1970, pp. 91–196.

6.236 Priyogine, I. and Stengers, I. *La Nouvelle Alliance: Metamorphose de la science*, Paris: Editions Gallimard, 1979.

6.237 Polanyi, M. *Personal Knowledge: Towards a Post-Critical Philosophy*, Chicago: University of Chicago Press, 1974.

6.238 Price, D. J. de Solla *Little Science, Big Science*, New York: Columbia University Press, 1963.

6.239 Price, D. J. de Solla *Science Since Babylon*, New Haven: Yale University Press, 1975.

6.240 Radnitzky, G. and Andersson, G. (eds) *Progress and Rationality in Science*, Dordrecht: Reidel, 1978.

6.241 Stegmüller, W. *Metaphysik, Skepsis, Wissenschaft*, Berlin: Springer, 1969.

6.242 Stegmüller, W. *The Structuralist View of Theories: A Possible Analogue of the Bourbaki-Programme to Physical Science*, Berlin: Springer, 1979.

6.243 Suppe, F. (ed.) *The Structure of Scientific Theories*, Urbana: University of Illinois Press, 1974.

6.244 Suppe, F. *The Semantic Conception of Scientific Theories and Scientific Realism*, Urbana: University of Illinois Press, 1989.

6.245 Tiles, M. 'Science and the World,' in G. H. R. Parkinson *et al.*, *The Handbook of Western Philosophy*, New York: Macmillan, 1988, pp. 225–48.

6.246 Toulmin, S. 'The Construal of Inquiry: Criticism in Modern and Post-Modern Science', *Critical Inquiry*, 9 (1982): 93–111.

CHAPTER 7

Philosophies of Marxism
Lenin, Lukács, Gramsci, Althusser
Michael Kelly

⟫⟪

⟫ INTRODUCTION ⟪

Marxist philosophy can be seen as a struggle with Hegel or a struggle with capitalism, that is, as an intellectual or a political movement. Neither of these views can be very readily reduced to the other, but nor can they be entirely separated. It is difficult to deal with Marxism in terms of a particular discipline when so much of it sprawls awkwardly across the lines which delineate disciplinary boundaries within the English-speaking institutions of knowledge. The attempt here to approach it within a philosophical context can scarcely avoid transgressing that context and introducing material which, in a narrow definition of philosophy, may be thought out of place. To consider Marxism at all, philosophy may need to consider itself a more commodious enterprise.

A history of Marxist philosophy cannot be innocent. The Marxist tradition includes histories of philosophy and philosophies of history. It also includes notoriously conflicting accounts of the nature and status of both history and philosophy. Nor is there any better agreement among non-Marxist thinkers on the nature and status of Marxist philosophy. A study of its history must enter a fiercely contested field of combat, where, more than in any other philosophical tradition, the struggle is waged not only in the intellectual realm but also in the social and geopolitical arenas. The context in which this study is written, in the turbulent and uncertain aftermath of the collapse of communist regimes throughout Europe, carries its quantum of intellectual risk, and confers a certain untimeliness on what is to be said.

Far from being a *philosophia perennis*, Marxist philosophy is in constant mutation, spurred not only by the shifting contours of its environment but also by the changing problems and purposes of its practitioners. With the passage of time, there has grown up an increasing multiplicity of re-interpretations of canonical texts and commentaries, several divergent accounts of who the founder (or founders) were, which of their writings may be relied on and which subsequent commentators should be consulted. In many cases, such issues have been the occasion of bitter controversy, and several schools of Marxist thought have vigorously claimed to possess the only authentic version. Some have, for a time at least, been willing and able to support that claim with judicial or even military coercion. An initial question is therefore that of identity: in what sense can a substantive Marxist philosophy be coherently defined across the diversity of its forms? Eschewing orthodoxies, the present study will be content with a looser understanding of the Marxist tradition as a family of movements, connected in complex and often conflictual relationships. In such a brief span as this chapter, it will not be possible to examine more than a few moments in the tradition, and the main lines of their interrelation. Such a broad approach to Marxism carries a price. In particular, it cannot do more than gesture at the coherence and breadth of view which some versions of Marxism have achieved, and which some, but not all, Marxists have regarded as a major strength and achievement.

A closely related issue is what status to accord to philosophy within Marxism. Invariably, this refers back to the relationship between Marx and Hegel. Marx's much repeated distinction between Hegel's system (castigated as the idealist shell) and his method (lauded as the rational kernel) has given rise to deeply conflicting interpretations. Whereas some have argued that Marxism continues the Hegelian project of providing a general philosophical framework which unifies the entire field of human knowledge, others have contended that Marx's signal achievement was to abandon philosophy, having exposed its ambitions as illusory. There are many other positions between these two poles. Without invoking an easy dialectical supersession of these terms, the present study grasps the nettle at least to the extent of accepting that there is a field of discourse within Marxism which must be recognized as philosophical, even when (perhaps especially when) it purports to announce the end of philosophy.

At the heart of the problem is the relation between theory and practice. The starting point lies in the major insight of Marxist thought that in addition to understanding or interpreting the world it should seek to change it. Implied in this notion is the view that in the first instance thought is a product of human social activity and that in the second instance it contributes to producing or shaping the future course of that activity. Applied to philosophy specifically, it suggests that philosophers who refrain from seeking change are by default helping to maintain the existing social order. It may then be inferred that philosophers who declare themselves as Marxist (or vice versa) are engaged, through their philosophy, in a project of social change. The consequences of such an inference for Marxist philosophers personally have at different times and places ranged from exile, torture and execution to celebrity, fame and fortune: more often the former than the latter. The shadow of the philosopher-king also looms in the important historical figures who inhabit the pantheon of Marxist philosophy, including Lenin, Stalin and Mao Tse-tung in their day. Their example compounds the tension between theory and practice in urging Marxist political figures to exercise leadership in philosophy and philosophers to don the mantle of statecraft: a wider gulf to bridge within some cultures than within others.

Karl Marx's own discomfort on the interface between his theoretical and political responsibilities was summed up in his reaction to French 'Marxists', whose work prompted his much-quoted comment that 'I am not a Marxist'. While it may be rash to place too much weight on this *boutade*, it usefully illustrates the problematic relationship between Marxist philosophy and an individual author. Perhaps more than elsewhere, there are visible limits on the extent to which an author can, or would wish to, claim ownership of the texts or ideas ascribed to him or her. If Marx was led to disown his self-appointed disciples during his lifetime, it would be prudent not to assume too close a correspondence between his or other thinkers' writings and the positions with which they are usually associated. Such prudence would be encouraged by the common phenomenon in Marxism of texts coming to exercise influence only long after they were written and in quite different circumstances from those in which they were produced. This is eminently true of major works of Marx, Lenin, Gramsci and Lukács. A thinker is often brandished as a banner, designating a particular view which may or may not be found explicitly in his or her work. Frequently, by a process of displacement, a thinker or even a philosophical concept will also come to function as a coded reference to a political position or programme, which cannot be directly addressed. An author or idea is in this respect primarily a signifier, whose meaning is closely dependent on the context of its utterance. They can in this way be emptied of meaning, though it is also common for them to become supersaturated with meaning, when accumulated layers of commentary effectively come to bar access to a heavily glossed text.

Marxist philosophy is largely inextricable from the groups and movements for which it has been formulated or which have adopted it as a theoretical approach likely to promote the achievement of their political purposes and programmes. Among them have been the labour

and trade union movements, the political parties of the left, the movements for national self-determination and the states and regimes which
under one guise or another have espoused Marxism. Institutionalization
of this kind has several effects which often differentiate Marxist philosophy from other philosophies. One which is rarely remarked upon is
that the channels of its communication are frequently those of a spon-
soring organization, whether a political paper or journal, a political
training programme or a publishing house with a recognizable political
or social complexion. Not infrequently, work of Marxist inspiration has
been excluded from the channels available to professional philosophy.
Marxist texts are always characterized by high levels of intertextuality,
such that their importance is often only grasped by a reader who is
familiar with other canonical or contemporary texts from which they
are specifically distinguished. Another distinguishing feature is the frequent effort to express Marxist ideas in a way which is sufficiently
simple and systematic to be widely understood and applied, particularly
by a non-specialist readership. Allied to this is the degree of constraint
under which work is produced, ranging from standard formats and
house styles to varying degrees of editorial intervention and collective
authorship. No doubt this is inseparable from the effect institutions
have of vesting philosophy with authority beyond the intrinsic merit
of rational discussion.

There remains one final question for the present historical study:
what is the object of study? Is it a history of philosophers, however
defined, or of ideas, or of intellectual movements? And what criterion
of selection and ordering is to be applied in the face of a daunting
abundance of material? The close dependence of Marxist philosophy
on the material conditions of its production and its reception suggests
that it should be approached as a history of ideas, though the confines
of space dictate that it will here be examined most often in terms of
an individual philosopher. But while ideas and philosophers do have
individual and collective histories, their history is not wholly their own.
Concepts, propositions or arguments appear, change and disappear at
times and in places that can be charted, but their development cannot
be adequately understood in isolation from other historical processes,
which provide both the conditions of intelligibility and the main motive
force for change. Ideas, in other words, draw their life and strength
more from social than from logical relations, though in the present
study the social context can be only lightly sketched.

If ideas do not entirely have their own history, then they may
best be approached through entities which do have their own history.
From this perspective, it is clear that countries, or regions, offer the
most manageable historical framework. Countries certainly do have
their own history, and it may even be argued that having a history is

what makes a country a country. The identity of a modern nation is closely bound up with the construction, by itself and others, of a historical narrative in which it figures as the subject. Philosophy is one of the cultural forms through which a nation represents itself, articulating a general statement of its own identity and its history, especially in relation to the acquisition of state power. Marxist philosophy has for most of the twentieth century been a major participant in defining and representing this process, and the remainder of this chapter will therefore be structured in terms of national and regional Marxist philosophical movements.

⚭ SOVIET MARXISM ⚭

The Soviet Union was the first country to adopt Marxism as an official philosophy. Supported by resources of the state and the prestige of the October Revolution, Soviet Marxism was for most of the twentieth century the dominant version of Marxist philosophy in the world. Its domination was never complete, of course, and much of the debate among Marxist philosophers has been directed towards attacking or defending all or part of the Soviet synthesis.

Towards the end of the nineteenth century, Russian socialists discovered Marxist ideas, and, largely under the direction of George Valentinov Plekhanov (1856–1918), elaborated them into a schematic and all-embracing philosophy. Plekhanov's major work, *The Development of the Monist View of History* (1895) became both an authoritative statement and a model for later Soviet approaches to Marxism. He critically analysed several currents of previous European philosophy, drawing out the strengths and limitations of their thought as a preparation for the resolution of their problems in the Marxist materialist conception of history. The materialism of the eighteenth-century French Enlightenment, the conception of history of nineteenth-century French historians, the French utopian socialists' concept of society and the dialectical philosophy of the German idealists were each examined and found to be useful but flawed. He then expounded Marx's solutions, based on Engels's short accounts of his own and Marx's philosophy, which Plekhanov characterized as a 'modern dialectical materialism', thus coining the term which later became the generic title for official Soviet Marxism. He laid a particularly strong emphasis on the determining role played by the economic base of society, as against the political, legal and ideological superstructures, which he saw as merely a function of the base, facilitating or impeding economic developments.

Without dwelling on the detail of his interpretation, it may be noted that Plekhanov firmly established the practice of approaching

Marxism through the exegesis of passages from Marx and Engels, confirming a scriptural tradition in which texts are the authoritative source of truth. He also approached Marxism through the intellectual history of its antecedents, with several important consequences. In the first instance, it situated Marxism in the mainstream of European thought, with all the intellectual prestige attaching to it, particularly among the Francophile Russian intelligentsia. Second, it suggested that, within this tradition, Marxism appears as a modern and therefore better solution to long-running problems, the very example of human progress. Third, it confirmed the contestatory and polemical character of Marxism, which is almost defined by its conflict with other schools of thought. These characteristics were amplified over the years, as Plekhanov became the catechist of Russian Marxism. Even though he became a leader of the Mensheviks from 1903, his philosophical writings were warmly endorsed by Lenin, and his influence continued for several years after the Revolution and his own death in 1918.

Lenin's main philosophical work is *Materialism and Empiriocriticism* (1908). In it he attacked what he considered to be idealist deviations in the theory of knowledge, canvassed by leading intellectuals within the Marxist movement, among them Plekhanov, who saw convergences with religious thought. Lenin contested the view that discoveries in modern physics, challenging Newtonian mechanics, lent support to these 'revisionist' tendencies. Apart from the reiteration of classical statements of principle drawn from Engels, the major impact of the work was to reinforce the polemical mode in which Russian Marxist philosophy was increasingly couched, with the invective and stigmatizing labels which were more common in political discourse. Lenin also published a number of short popularizing accounts of Marxism, including an essay, *The Three Sources and Three Component Parts of Marxism* (1913), which identified the founding triad of Marxism as German philosophy, English economics and French politics, each superseded by Marx's theoretical advances.

The importance of these works is primarily that they were written by the leader of the revolutionary movement which took power in 1917, and founder of the Soviet state. In this capacity, they underwent the same canonization as Lenin himself, after his death in 1924. Used to support several sides in the philosophical debates of the 1920s, they achieved the status of scripture when, in the early 1930s, Joseph Stalin declared Lenin to have made such a significant advance in Marxism that it was henceforth to be known as Marxism–Leninism. The sanctification was selective, however. In particular, Lenin's notes on his enthusiastic reading of Hegel, published in 1929, did not attract Stalin's approval.

The process by which Marxism–Leninism became the state philosophy of the Soviet Union was marked by bitter controversies, particularly among the professional philosophers who vied with one another to secure the support of Stalin. The groundwork of Marxism–Leninism was laid in the codification of historical materialism by Nikolai Ivanovitch Bukharin (1888–1938), in his manual *The Theory of Historical Materialism* (1921). It sparked an intense debate, much of it conducted in the pages, and editorial premises, of the leading philosophical journal *Pod znamenem marksizma* ('Under the banner of Marxism' – 1922–44). On one side, the 'mechanists' (Skvortsov-Stepanov, Timiryazev and others) held, with Bukharin, that Marxism now had no need of philosophy since it had advanced to the stage of scientific knowledge. Consequently there was no place for philosophers and ideologists to intervene in matters of natural science.

On the other side, the 'dialecticians' (Deborin, Tymyansky, Sten and others) argued, in the tradition of Plekhanov, that Marxist philosophy was increasingly needed to generalize, unify and direct enquiry in all areas of knowledge, as a 'science of sciences'. The debate was concluded in 1929 when Bukharin's fall into political disfavour took the mechanists with him. The dialecticians' victory was, however, short-lived. Their general position passed into orthodoxy, but they themselves were criticized by a new generation of 'bolshevizing' philosophers who accused them of overestimating Plekhanov at the expense of Lenin, and of unspecified links with Trotsky (who had in fact generally been reluctant to pronounce on philosophical matters).

At the centre of these debates was the question of authority, which fell into two parts. First, what authority did philosophy have to direct activity in other areas of society, especially the strategic areas of science and technology? The answer to this was that it had complete authority to legislate and pronounce: Marxist philosophy was fundamental to the successful construction of socialism, both in one country and worldwide. Second, what authority is philosophy itself subject to? The answer to this is that it was subject not to some internal philosophical principle or tradition but to the interests of the working class, represented by the Communist Party, embodied in its General Secretary, Stalin, whose authority was derived from Lenin. The specific contribution of Lenin to Marxism was in turn declared to be his championing of partisanship in philosophy, interpreted ultimately as the obligation of submission to the Party. This was the point at which Marxism–Leninism assumed the position of official state philosophy.

The 1930s were a period during which Stalin extended his power over the whole of Soviet life, and over the expanding communist movement throughout the world. Codification and 'bolshevization' went hand in hand under the banner of Marxism–Leninism, and reached their apogee in the era of the great purges with the publication in 1938 of the definitive Stalinist manual, *History of the Communist Party of the Soviet Union (Bolsheviks), A Short Course*. One chapter of the *Short Course*, credited to Stalin himself, laid out in simple schematic form the basic dogma of dialectical and historical materialism. The four principle features of dialectics, as opposed to metaphysics, are listed as interconnection, change, qualitative leaps and contradiction, while the three features of materialism, as opposed to idealism, stipulate that the world is material, exists independently of mind, and is knowable. This dialectical materialism is the guiding star of the party of the proletariat and when applied to the study of history it yields historical materialism. This recognizes that spiritual life (including ideas and institutions) is a reflection of economic production, and that the determining force in historical development is the mode of production, composed of forces of production and relations of production. Five types of productive (i.e. property) relations have existed: primitive communal, slave, feudal, capitalist and socialist, and the transitions between them have always occurred through revolutions triggered by the faster progress of productive forces (instruments, people, skill) than their associated relations.

The authority of the *Short Course*, assisted by its blunt clarity, channelled Marxist philosophy into a narrow and dogmatic orthodoxy, which held absolute sway in the Soviet Union and in world communism until after Stalin's death. Since that time it has been the implicit reference point of much of Marxist debate, even (perhaps especially) when Stalinism is most vehemently denounced. Soviet dogmatism was given a further twist in the early days of the Cold War when, under the direction of Andrei Zhdanov, culture, including philosophy, was relentlessly confined to the defence and illustration of Soviet Marxist preeminence in all things. This included strong discouragement of interest in non-Marxist philosophy, even where, as with Hegel, it had strong connections with Marxism, and even extending to Marx's own noncanonical writings, particularly the Paris Manuscripts of 1844.

After the death of Stalin in 1953, and his denunciation by Krushchev at the 20th Congress of the Soviet Communist Party in 1956, the rigidly dogmatic approach began to ease. But an indelible pattern was set, which no amount of destalinization could remove. The authority of the state, the primacy of the party, the obligatory teaching of Marxism-Leninism at all stages of the Soviet education system and a strongly hierarchical academic establishment, all served to maintain the social and intellectual structure of Soviet Marxism largely unchanged. The Stalinist 'Vulgate' developed into an elaborate scholastic system, in which controversies might rage over the interpretation of a particular passage of the canon, or over the status of a particular doctrine. A good example was the successful campaign to rehabilitate the negation of the negation, omitted by Stalin from the *Short Course*, as one of the universal dialectical laws of development.

Paradoxically, the very close identification of Marxism–Leninism with the state and party also largely insulated it from developments which took place elsewhere in Marxist philosophy. The logic was simple: if a foreign thinker was not a member of a communist party, he or she was not an authentic Marxist, and could be recognized only as some form of renegade or deviant from Marxism; conversely, if he or she was a party member, his or her work could not be publicly discussed without infringing the principle of non-interference in the affairs of a fraternal party. The result was inevitably a thriving underground preoccupation with foreign Marxist philosophers, and with major non-Marxist philosophers. The resulting gulf between the public and private face of Soviet Marxism rendered it extremely friable under pressure of events. Marxism–Leninism in the USSR's eastern European satellites, and in pro-Soviet communist movements elsewhere, was clearly marked as a coded acceptance of Russian domination, political or ideological. In those parties which espoused the Eurocommunist line in the 1970s, it was symbolically rejected, while in many others it was discreetly abandoned. In any event, it had no independent strength on which to draw, and when the state and party which sponsored it collapsed at the beginning of the 1990s, Soviet Marxism effectively came to an end. Since it has been the focus and archetype of Marxism for most of the twentieth century, it remains to be seen whether its demise will also prove to be the end of Marxism as such.

The Chinese variant of Stalinist Marxism has also been influential. Chinese communism developed two main currents of philosophy, one being the orthodox Marxism–Leninism of the *Short Course*, introduced by Moscow-trained intellectuals and promoted by the Comintern, the Third or Communist International (1919–43) founded by Lenin to direct the policy and activities of Communist parties worldwide. The other current was an adaptation of the first by intellectuals based in the revolutionary headquarters at Yenan during the late 1930s, of whom the most successful was Mao Tse-tung (1893–1976). Apart from a much greater emphasis on the role of the peasantry, Mao developed a classification of contradictions in terms of whether they were antagonistic or non-antagonistic in nature, primary or secondary in the specific context, and what their primary and secondary aspects were. He argued that contradictions and their aspects could in certain circumstances pass from one type to another, particularly when they were handled correctly in the practice of the revolutionary party.

With the success of the Chinese revolution in 1948, and particularly after the death of Stalin, Mao was increasingly presented as a second Lenin, and Peking as an alternative to Moscow in the leadership of the world communist movement. During the 1960s, most countries witnessed the rise of Maoist communist movements, which in western Europe were small, but particularly successful in student circles. They were particularly influenced by the events of the Cultural Revolution, during which the 'little red book' of *Quotations from Chairman Mao Tse-tung* elevated his neo-Stalinism to cult status, condensing the official philosophy, renamed Marxism–Leninism–Mao-Tse-tung Thought, into all-purpose gobbets and slogans. From this apotheosis, Chinese communism returned from an internationalist to a nationalist Marxism–Leninism, and for a time during the 1980s began to allow the expression of humanist forms of Marxism associated with Lukács and Gramsci. Whether and how soon Chinese communism will incur a fate comparable to its Soviet counterpart can only be a matter of speculation, but it is clear that its influence on Marxist philosophy elsewhere largely ceased in the mid-1970s.

CENTRAL EUROPEAN MARXISM

In the early years after the First World War, before root and branch bolshevization had set them all marching to the rhythm of Moscow, there was still a flourishing culture of philosophical debate among central European Marxists. To a large extent this was conducted in the German-speaking circles which had been the intellectual centre of gravity of pre-Bolshevik Marxism. Pervaded by the humanism of the Second International, the organization which brought together the social-democratic and labour parties of Europe (1889–1914), and oriented toward a respect for intellectual and cultural values, it was blotted out by triumphant Marxism–Leninism and lay largely ignored until the post-Stalinist era of the 1960s. At that stage it was rediscovered in the writings of Korsch, Lukács, Benjamin, Bloch and others, and given widespread currency, largely by movements opposed to the dominant communist orthodoxy.

Several attempts have been made to construct an alternative tradition by aggregating these writers with the Frankfurt school, with Italian Marxists, and with French writers as diverse as Althusser and Sartre, to create a 'western Marxism'. Such has been the project of the British *New Left Review*, which has done a great deal to create an appropriate canon of texts in English, and has rendered accessible a broad range of non-Soviet Marxist theorists. None the less, the notion of 'western Marxism', coined in the mid-1950s by Maurice Merleau-Ponty, loses historical coherence as soon as it is extended beyond the germanophone debates of the interwar period. For this reason, it is more helpful to consider the diverse central European writers without having to wrestle them into an artificial unanimity with each other and with writers from other intellectual and political traditions.

Undoubtedly, the giant among these philosophers is Georg (György) Lukács (1885–1971). Born in Budapest to a wealthy and cultured family, and educated in the universities of Germany and the Austro-Hungarian Empire, he wrote with equal facility in German and Hungarian, and played a significant role in the political history of Hungary and of the international communist movement, as well as being the central figure in major literary and philosophical debates. Brought up in the German philosophical tradition of Kant, Dilthey and Simmel, he came to espouse Marxism via Max Weber and then Hegel, whose thought exercised an enduring fascination for him. A leading figure of the leftist faction in the Hungarian Communist Party during the turbulent events of 1919–20, Lukács developed an interpretation of Marxism sharply at odds with the dialectical materialism which gained ascendancy in Moscow. Through most of his career he was the target of repeated attacks on his 'revisionist' positions, despite his efforts at different times to assert his own orthodoxy. There has been considerable discussion as to whether Lukács's philosophical positions can be directly correlated with his political shift towards a conciliatory attitude to the non-communist left. But since his political sympathies were in many respects close to Bukharin, whose philosophy he opposed, it would be rash to draw any reductive conclusions.

Undoubtedly Lukács's major work is his collection of essays *History and Class Consciousness*, published in 1923. It was the focus for controversy in the years following its publication, and again at the beginning of the Cold War. It was widely circulated in French translation in the 1960s, before Lukács approved its reappearance in German and English in 1967. The basic thrust of the book was to relocate Marx firmly in the tradition of Hegel, and to draw out the Hegelian concepts which Marx had sought to refashion. In the first essay ('What is orthodox Marxism?') Lukács argues that Marx had adopted the progressive part of the Hegelian method, namely the dialectic, setting it against the mythologizing remnants of 'eternal values' which Hegel himself had been struggling against. In this sense, Marx was directing against Hegel the very criticism that Hegel had levelled against Kant and Fichte, that they immortalized particular moments of abstract reflection at the expense of an awareness of process, concrete totality, dialectics and history. Hegel, he argued, had been unable to progress from the level of abstractions to a perception of the real driving forces of history, and it had been Marx's originality to discover these forces.

Perhaps the most influential essay in the book, entitled 'Reification and the consciousness of the proletariat', launched the interpretation of Marxism as a theory of alienation, remarkably anticipating the argument of Marx's Paris Manuscripts of 1844, which had not yet been brought to light. Lukács highlighted the exchangeable commodity as the basic unit of capitalist economies, and the fetishism of commodities as an inevitable consequence, leading people to neglect the human content of activity in favour of its quantifiable exchange value. He argued that it was a logical necessity for the development of capitalism that all relations must eventually be reduced to the structure of commodity-exchange. This process of reification led, he thought, to all aspects of life being calculated and quantified, alienating the individuality of both people and things. Carried to its conclusion, it also stamped its imprint on human consciousness and reified the most intimate areas of human relations and the most rigorous of scientific investigations. Within bourgeois society there was clearly no prospect of a radical escape from the ravages of reification. The only hope of a solution was to transform philosophy into *praxis*, a practical orientation of thought and consciousness towards reality. Reality in this sense was understood as a process of becoming, a totality. Only the practical class consciousness of the proletariat, grasping itself as the subject of the social totality, could be expected to transform a theory of *praxis* into a practical theory which overturns the real world, revolutionizes the totality and overcomes the process of reification. Even then it would succeed only as long as it retained its practical orientation and avoided the Hegelian pitfalls of schematization, repetitive mechanical patterns (such as the famous triad: thesis, antithesis, synthesis), and the undialectical project of extending its attention beyond human society to a philosophy of nature.

Lukács's reaffirmation of Hegel's relevance was in one sense a reclamation of Marx for the European philosophical tradition, and a challenge to the increasing tendency to sanctify Lenin, visible in the last months of the latter's life and stridently pursued by Stalin in the campaign of bolshevization. His strictures against Hegel's shortcomings were in another sense an implicit reproach to the codification of Marxism into a set of rigid abstractions, culminating in the *Short Course*. He reaffirmed the dialectical relationship between subject and object, between theory and practice, as a fundamental tenet of Marxism which guaranteed its progressive and transformative potential. The alternative, he argued, would be a relapse into utopian dualism, characteristic of revisionism, and generating an ossified theory which would serve as a catch-all justification of any kind of practice. This would most likely lead to a conservative right–Hegelian worship of the state from which Marx had rescued the posterity of Hegel. It is not difficult to see the Marxist–Leninist equivalent looming over the argument.

But Lukács did not only set a challenge to Soviet Marxism, he also set an intellectual agenda for an alternative, Hegelianizing Marxism.

Cultured and humanistic in its ethos, it drew strength from romantic idealism and traditions of religious fervour. The philosophy of alienation offered a subtle dialectic with a strong appeal to intellectuals, while the philosophy of *praxis* offered a basis for activism and engagement in the political struggles of the working class, cast as the secular source of salvation. Over the longer term, the richness of Lukács's conceptualization, and the many philosophical links it made with the European intellectual mainstream, made *History and Class Consciousness* a bridge between the western New Left of the 1960s and the non-Stalinist roots for which it was so ardently searching. Lukács himself, though long-lived, played a singularly distant role in his own rediscovery, obliged as he was to play intellectual hide and seek with the political authorities in Moscow and Budapest. For most of his career, he was much more widely recognized as a literary theorist and critic of European literature, deeply involved in the cultural controversies, and more than a little reticent about his earlier philosophy.

Though he was much read, Lukács had few disciples in central Europe. Perhaps the most noteworthy is the Romanian scholar, Lucien Goldmann (1913–70), who met and admired Lukács in Vienna but spent most of his adult life in Paris, where he distinguished himself primarily through his analysis of French literature using approaches drawn from Lukács and from the structuralism of Jean Piaget.

Closer in spirit and preoccupations was Lukács's contemporary and friend Karl Korsch (1886–1961). A leading figure in the powerful German Communist Party of the 1920s, Korsch took a leftist stance vehemently opposed to the bolshevization of the Communist International. His most influential work, *Marxism and Philosophy* (1923), aroused sharp hostility and, with other oppositional leaders he was eventually ousted from the Party. In 1936 he emigrated permanently to the United States.

Korsch noted that nineteenth-century Marxism had largely ignored philosophy, and he traced the fact to Marx's and Engels's view that their materialist conception of history and society was destined to supersede classical German philosophy, from which it sprang, and ultimately destined to replace philosophy. He castigated the undialectical approach of those who had assumed that philosophy was therefore abolished, and of those who wished to reinstate it, pointing out that its abolition was necessary but dependent on the revolutionary transformation of the historical circumstances which produced it. Since this transformation had not taken place, the rejection of philosophy was premature, while its reinstatement was retrograde. The result of abolition was that Marxist economic or political theory were being proposed as value-free sciences which could equally be used by opponents of socialism, and that in practice socialists were combining Marxism with various substitute philosophies which did provide systems of values. Conversely, the result of reinstatement was to reinforce philosophy as an obstacle to the process of its own historical suppression.

Since Korsch was attacking both the theorists of the Second International, who had abandoned philosophy, and those of the Comintern, who were reinstating it, he attracted fierce criticism from both sides. There were strong affinities between his position and that of Lukács, but both were increasingly isolated voices in the political aftermath of the failure to achieve socialism internationally. The revolutionary fervour and the messianic tone of their thought did not chime with the increasingly inhospitable social and political climate in central Europe.

More consonant with the disillusioned and embattled left of the interwar period is the work of Walter Benjamin (1892–1940), a Berliner who largely avoided political activism but expressed a revolutionary Marxist approach in his critical essays. Benjamin was a critic and historian of culture, rather than a philosopher, sharing the perception of the Frankfurt school (which is treated elsewhere in this volume) that culture had in some respects overtaken politics as the main field of struggle. His work on Brecht (with whom he enjoyed a close friendship) and Baudelaire, and his more philosophical essays collected as *Illuminations*, began to attract renewed attention in western Europe during the 1970s. Benjamin was a deliberately non-systematic thinker, considering images, aphorisms and allegories as a more potent means of gaining purchase on the course of history. Progressive change was likely, he thought, to arise either from a long-term strategy of attrition or from an extremely focused unleashing of explosive social forces. In either event, his approach was expressed in the contemporary maxim of 'pessimism of the intellect, optimism of the will', and he summed up his conception of history by reference to a drawing by Paul Klee showing the angel of history facing backwards to look with pity on the debris of its victims, but propelled into the future by a storm blowing from paradise, which constitutes progress. Benjamin himself fell victim to the upheavals of history, taking his own life to avoid falling into the hands of the Gestapo as he attempted to flee from occupied France into Spain.

Central European intellectuals, caught between the hammer of fascism and the anvil of Marxism–Leninism, plunged into an understandable slough of despond with the approach of war. The basis for any optimism was slender, but, such as it was, it was articulated in the philosophy of possibility of Ernst Bloch (1885–1977). Born and educated in Berlin, Bloch developed a syncretic philosophy in which Marxist elements jostled with religious mysticism, vitalism and classical German philosophy. During his wartime exile in the United States, he wrote most of his major work, *The Principle of Hope*, which was published in East Germany, where he had returned, during the 1950s. He later fled to West Germany following disagreements with the communist authorities which he had generally supported, without becoming a party member.

Bloch's thought, expressed almost as aphoristically as Benjamin's, follows a humanist inspiration to argue that the basic nature of a human being is characterized by living and working towards a future goal which is in the process made real, actualizing one out of the many potential forms of existence. The task of creating a utopia is central to human existence, and falls not only to the intellect but also to the imagination and emotions, which can awaken latent possibilities within the present. Ever since earliest times, human societies have woven images and stories of utopias, which they have variously attempted to bring into being, without ever completely succeeding. The constantly renewed drive to do this is a principle of hope which energizes human activity and finds its highest expression in the Marxist project of a concrete utopia, which can be compared with the kingdom of heaven.

Bloch's very unspecific characterization of what kind of utopia may be hoped for is in sharp contrast with his euphoric endorsements of East German social achievements, and he has been criticized for both. But, assisted by his own longevity, Bloch's work is another important contribution from the generation of central European Marxist philosophers who were formed and continued to write outside the orthodox Marxist–Leninist framework. Though Bloch, Benjamin, Korsch and Lukács are in many respects different both politically and philosophically, they do share common roots in the classical German philosophical tradition which culminated in Hegel, and a deep regard for the value and efficacity of European cultural traditions. It is this shared culture which gives them their potential for resisting the reduction of philosophy to an instrument to be used, modified or discarded as it suits a particular political purpose.

ITALIAN MARXISM

From the end of the First World War to the end of the Second, Italian Marxism led an underground life, most of which was only brought to wider attention long afterwards. It was not born in the underground, however. Before the Great War, Marxists were well-established figures in the Italian mainstream, active participants in debates which were shaped by the neo-Hegelian revival.

Most prominent of the early Italian Marxists was Antonio Labriola (1843–1904), whose *Essays on the Materialist Conception of History* (1895–1900) were read throughout Europe at the turn of the century.

His undogmatic and humanist approach was alert to the sinuosities of history but lyrical about the mission of the proletariat to give meaning to it. His thought left its mark on philosophers like Benedetto Croce (1866–1952) and Giovanni Gentile (1875–1944), who both grappled with Labriola's Marxism before taking an avowedly Hegelian path away from it towards liberal and, in Gentile's case, fascist conclusions. The triumph of Mussolini in the early 1920s created extraordinary difficulties for communists and Marxists in Italy, with activists driven into exile, or hiding, or prison. In exile, a leader like Palmiro Togliatti (1893–1964) was able to shape the political direction of the Comintern, though not the development of Marxist philosophy.

Paradoxically, it was the imprisonment of the Italian Communist Party leader, Antonio Gramsci (1891–1937) that produced the most influential theoretical and philosophical development. Born of a poor family in Sardinia, Gramsci studied history and philosophy at the university of Turin before throwing himself into revolutionary politics early in the First World War. He became an editor of the influential socialist review *Ordine nuovo* ('New order') in 1919 and played a key role in the foundation of the Italian Communist Party, becoming its leader in 1923, when his policy of broad alliances eventually prevailed. His political activity in Italy and abroad ended when he was arrested in Rome and imprisoned in 1926. Spending the rest of his life in appalling conditions in prison and hospital, Gramsci wrote prolifically, reflecting deeply on Marxist principles in virtual isolation from current events. His influence stems mainly from his *Prison Notebooks*, which were published in Italy soon after the Second World War but only became widely known during the late 1960s, when they were identified as offering an attractive alternative to Soviet Marxism.

Philosophically, Gramsci's affinities were with the Hegelian tradition which he had encountered through Croce. He considered that Marx's achievement had been to create a synthesis from the two opposing schools into which Hegelianism had divided. He also thought that Marx's own posterity had divided into two schools, mechanistic materialism and dialectical idealism, which now needed to be welded into a new synthesis. His proposal was a philosophy of *praxis*, a name he chose partly as a code-word for Marxism to placate the prison censors but partly also because it encapsulated his distinctive conception of history as an aggregation of human practical activity.

At the core of Gramsci's philosophy was the humanist question: what is man? A later generation, attempting to meet feminist critiques, has rephrased the question: What is human existence? Gramsci's answer was that humanity is reflected in every individual person, and consists of the individual, other people and nature. The individual enters into relationships with other people and with nature, primarily through work, generating a network of relationships. These relationships form organic social entities, which become conscious of themselves and become capable of purposeful and effective action. Thus the individual is an integral part of the process of change which is history, its conscious motive force, and the whole complex of changing relationships is part of each individual. Human existence is synonymous with the socio-historical process and the question 'what is human existence?' must therefore be reformulated as 'what can human existence become?'

Within Gramsci's humanist vision, philosophy appears as the consciousness of the historical process, not only a dimension of the totality of human *praxis*, and therefore inherently political, but also part of the consciousness of each individual within it. It was in a sense a collective subjectivity, and its value lay in its appropriateness to the task of the collectivity rather than in its relation to any objective reality. In any case, he questioned whether it was meaningful to speak of a reality existing independently from human *praxis*. He thought it necessary for the unity and advancement of humanity that philosophy should overcome the distance, frequently observed, between the doctrine of the intellectuals and that of ordinary people. There was in particular, he argued, a need for Marxism to foster intellectuals who were an organic part of the working people and capable of raising the level of consciousness of the masses, without bringing elitist ideas from outside. In this way, it would, he suggested, be possible to build a unity of ideas and political action which could challenge the hegemony of bourgeois philosophy and politics.

The concept of hegemony is Gramsci's most influential and contentious innovation, since it emphasizes that the exercise of power in a society is secured not only by the repressive use of state power but also more crucially by the maintenance of a moral, intellectual and cultural consensus. For the working class and its allies to win power, it is not sufficient to engineer a *coup d'état*, it is also necessary to build an alternative cultural consensus capable of securing hegemony. This is a much broader and more long-term task, requiring a different kind of organization from the highly centralized and disciplined parties built by the Comintern. Learning lessons from the ideological power exercised by the Catholic Church, Gramsci was responding to the fact that Mussolini's fascism had been successful in gaining popular support, and recognizing that a long 'war of position' would be needed to win over the masses for socialism. The alternative, which he rejected, was to fall back on faith in the likelihood of the blind workings of history producing a suitable revolutionary opportunity. For socialists reading Gramsci thirty years later, however, hegemony appeared to emphasize the strategic importance of ideological and cultural struggle as an alternative to traditional politics, which seemed to offer no prospect of radical change.

Because of their fragmentary, allusive and often obscure nature, Gramsci's prison writings allow of a range of interpretations. At one end of the range, they can be seen as a restatement of fairly orthodox Marxism–Leninism, somewhat veiled by the circumstances in which they were produced. That is largely how they were presented when they were first published. At the other end of the range, they can be interpreted as a penetrating rebuttal of Soviet Marxism which offers an entirely different basis on which to develop Marxist philosophy. That is largely how they have been received since their rediscovery in the 1960s. The philosophy of *praxis* served to challenge the distinction between theory and practice, obviating the need for a body of theory and thus for the scholastic apparatus of hitherto existing Marxism. The concept of hegemony served to challenge the distinction between base and superstructure, reducing the importance of economics, at a time of relative prosperity, and increasing that of cultural theory, at a time of rapid expansion in audiovisual communication. In this way Gramsci's posthumous reputation grew both from his conceptual innovations and from the new political directions his ideas opened up.

In postwar Italy, Gramsci's humanist and historicist positions dominated Marxist debate for many years, assisted by the success of the Communist Party in giving intellectuals an organic role to play within political activity. His influence was not unchallenged, however. In particular, Galvano della Volpe (1895–1968) maintained a persistent critique of historicism, which he regarded as a product of the contamination of Marxism by Italian idealist philosophy. An academic rather than an activist, della Volpe drew on the egalitarian and democratic thought of Rousseau, counterposed to the Hegelian theory of the state, and argued that Marxism should concern itself with specific scientific knowledge of the world, rather than with indeterminate abstractions.

With the political effervescence of the 1960s came a flourishing Marxist culture which permeated most areas of intellectual inquiry, prompting intense philosophical debates between the diverse movements and schools of thought which sprang up inside and outside the Communist Party. Two philosophers of the far left may be mentioned as having been influential in the English-speaking world. Lucio Colletti, brought up in the tradition of della Volpe, sought to demystify the historicism of Gramsci and to refute the view that Marxism could draw on an underlying materialism in the dialectic of Hegel, whom he regarded as essentially a Christian philosopher. Ultimately, however, he concluded that dialectical mystification was present even in Marx, and he began to distance himself from Marxism. His hostility to idealism was shared by Sebastiano Timpanaro, who attacked the French attempts to reconcile Marxism with existentialist (Sartre) and structuralist (Althusser) theories. A strong proponent of materialism, which he saw as lacking in Gramsci, Timpanaro asserted the objectivity of scientific knowledge and sought recognition for the autonomous existence of the natural world, necessary as a theoretical basis for science and for ecological awareness.

These philosophers are not proposed as representative of debates over the past thirty years, and the present study cannot offer an extensive survey of the variety of Italian Marxists. They include a utopian Marxism strongly imbued with Christian spiritualism, and several suggested combinations of Marxism with other contemporary schools of thought (psychoanalytical, ecological, feminist among others). Moreover, as the example of Colletti suggests, Marxist philosophy shades into other philosophical movements. With the transformation of the Italian Communist Party into a social democratic party, it may be that Italy has largely lost the institutional framework which made it important, or even possible, to distinguish Italian Marxism from other philosophies which are not specifically Marxist.

❧ FRENCH MARXISM ❧

Marxist philosophy came late to France, despite the close contacts which Marx and Engels had with French socialists. This was partly because Proudhon's syndicalist socialism continued to have a deep and abiding influence, and partly because of the periods of repression following the failed revolutions of 1848 and 1871. In the 1890s, Marx's daughters, Laura and Jenny, and his two French sons-in-law, Paul Lafargue and Charles Longuet, did a great deal to make his ideas known in France. Lafargue (1842–1911), the most active of them, propagated a highly simplified economic determinism which Marx himself was wont to criticize. His main opponent, Jean Jaurès (1859–1914), countered this with a neo-Kantian ethical socialism in which he hoped to synthesize Marx's ideas with various other progressive doctrines. Their debate was largely curtailed by the intellectual truce which followed the unification of the main socialist groupings in 1905.

The most sophisticated French contributor to pre-war Marxism, Georges Sorel (1847–1922), was a maverick whose unorthodox Marxism included an unusually vigorous attack on rationalism, and a corresponding advocacy of revolutionary myth. At odds with most of his contemporaries, Sorel's ideas were more influential outside France, especially in Italy, where Mussolini claimed them as an inspiration for his fascist movement.

After the First World War, a new generation of young intellectuals gradually introduced a thriving Marxist culture, within or on the margins of the Communist Party. Most prominent of them was Henri Lefebvre (1901–91), a prolific and long-lived thinker who set his mark on sociology as well as on Marxist philosophy. Emerging from the surrealist movement of the 1920s, he used his energy and erudition to popularize the early writings of Marx, some of which he translated into French, and to publish several volumes by or about Hegel, who was just beginning to arouse interest in France. Enjoying the more intellectually relaxed climate of the Popular Front period, Lefebvre wrote what eventually became the most successful short exposition of Marxism in France, *Dialectical Materialism* (1939). Despite its orthodox-sounding title, it set out a humanist Marxism fundamentally opposed to that of the *Short Course*, which appeared at about the same time.

Lefebvre affirmed the superiority of Hegel's dialectic over formal logic, based on the dialectic's attempt to achieve a synthesis of the concept and its content, and thence a synthesis of thought and being. What distinguished the Marxist dialectic was that, whereas Hegel had sought to derive the content from the concept, Marx saw the need to enable the content to direct the development of the concept. The resulting dialectical materialism, he thought, transcended both idealism and materialism, and oriented the dialectic towards a resolution of contradictions in practical activity, or *praxis*. The unfolding of dialectical *praxis* in history would, he believed, lead to the practical realization of the full potential of human existence in what he called 'Total Man'.

Recognizing the obstacles to the fulfilment of the dialectic of *praxis*, Lefebvre systematized the analysis of alienation, which he argued was a fundamental structure of human activity, and could be summarized in terms of a three-stage evolution. In the first (spontaneous) stage, activity generates some form of order in response to needs; in the second (conscious) stage, the spontaneous order is shaped into rational structures so as to work more effectively; and in the third (illusory) stage, the rational structures become fixed and fetishized, beginning to hinder further development, and being misappropriated and used as an instrument of oppression by one group over another. The revolutionary overthrow of alienated structures thus appears as a requirement of human self-realization. It is clear that, by its generality, Lefebvre's analysis can be applied to the oppressive role of the state under communism as much as under capitalism, and to the sclerosis of thought in the Communist Party as much as in the Sorbonne.

In the first years after the Second World War, Lefebvre was lionized by the French Communist Party (PCF) as one of its most distinguished intellectuals but, unlike its Italian counterpart, the PCF tended to regard major intellectuals as figures of symbolic rather than practical importance. With the tightening of the Cold War, he was reproached for his lack of orthodoxy, and withdrew from philosophy into sociology, which provided the focus for his subsequent work. In the late 1950s he became an influential figure on the non-communist left, where his dialectical humanism was widely welcomed as an open and non-dogmatic basis for social critique. His conception of philosophy also shifted to a suspicion that any general philosophical assertions would be likely to fall into mystification. Ontological or cosmological statements should, he thought, be left to poets and musicians, and Marxist philosophy should concentrate on honing the concepts of dialectics as a critical method, to be part of what he termed metaphilosophy. This meant that *praxis*, which was action-oriented, should be supplemented by other dimensions, including a creative function, which he termed *poesis*, to form a concept of 'everyday life'. More productive in sociology than in philosophy, Lefebvre's humanist and Hegelian Marxism offered plausible explanations for the uprising of students and workers in France in May 1968 and proved an attractive conceptual framework for some members of the radical movements involved.

The chief spokesman for Marxist–Leninist philosophy in the post-war period was Roger Garaudy (b. 1913), who articulated a Stalinism of strict obedience up to the 20th Congress of the CPSU in 1956. In its aftermath, he had the task not only of leading the philosophical denunciation of Stalin but also, implicitly at least, of finding a suitable replacement philosophy for the French Communist Party. His first step was to propose a Marxist humanism directed towards the discovery of Total Man, little different in substance from that of Lefebvre, though political difficulties made it impossible to acknowledge the debt. His second step was more original, however, in that he sought an explicit dialogue with other forms of humanism, particularly in the Catholic and existentialist intellectual movements. The vitalist philosophy of Teilhard de Chardin, exercising widespread posthumous influence, seemed to offer significant common ground, though Garaudy stopped short of accepting that evolution would culminate as Teilhard suggested, in the creation of God. Garaudy turned to Hegel, who was also attracting the interest of theologians, as a possible basis for a common humanist philosophy. The alarm his 'God-building' caused in communist circles was a material factor in leading the Party to abandon the notion of an official philosophy in 1966. Disavowed by the Party for disagreements over the events of 1968, Garaudy underwent a religious conversion, first to Catholicism and then to Islam.

The most trenchant opponent of the path followed by Garaudy was Louis Althusser (1918–90), who developed a critique of humanist Marxism, producing in the process an innovative and influential philosophical reworking of Marx, expressed in two studies published in 1965, *For Marx* and *Reading Capital*. A professional philosopher rather than an activist, he was initially inspired by Mao Tse-tung's writings on practice and on contradiction, and was widely followed in French Maoist circles of the 1960s and early 1970s. Althusser began from a re-examination of the history of Marxist philosophy, in which he argued that there was a radical discontinuity between Marx and his predecessors, Hegel and Feuerbach. He suggested that Marx had first rejected the idealist system of Hegel, and then the materialist humanism of Feuerbach, in order to emerge with a distinctive and scientific theory. He dismissed the view that the theory was a supersession of Hegel and Feuerbach, which would imply that it conserved important parts of their philosophy, and argued that Marx had made an epistemological break, establishing his theory as a science of history, entirely distinct from the ideological conceptions from which it has emerged. He noted that ideas and concepts tended to emerge in response to a historical situation and to aggregate into more or less coherent combinations, each of which formed a problematic. Retaining a particular concept generally implied accepting the entire problematic to which it belonged, and thus mature Marxism had to exclude ideas drawn from pre-Marxist problematics. Marx's own early writings with their notions of alienation, human self-realization and Hegelian dialectics came before the epistemological break and should therefore be considered as belonging to pre-Marxist and unscientific problematics. Althusser conceded that Marx's later writings sometimes contained ideological residues, but generalized his argument to assert that the concept of the epistemological break could be applied to distinguish what was scientific (or theoretical, as he preferred to say) from what was ideological in Marx's work, or in the work of anyone else. In this way theoretical practice could be clearly separated from ideological practices.

Althusser next identified the problem that while the mature Marxist theoretical practice was well developed, Marx had never gone back to reformulate the philosophical principles which it implied. There was, in other words, no theory of theoretical practice. In its absence, various ideological approximations were made to serve, most of them Hegelian in origin. He suggested that these had now become an obstacle to the further development of Marxism, and set himself the task of undertaking a philosophical reading of Marx, Engels and Lenin, especially Marx's major work *Capital*, attempting to elucidate a theory of theoretical practice. Since such a theory was not articulated explicitly, the texts would need to be read 'symptomatically', to detect symptoms which might point to the theory at work in a practical way. If the theory had not been supplied by Marx, it could certainly not be taken from Hegel or Feuerbach. Althusser consequently drew from Spinoza's rationalism, Freudian psychoanalysis and Saussurean structural linguistics to provide usable concepts.

Althusser began with the concept of contradiction. The Hegelian notion of a struggle of opposites was replaced by the notion of a process of production, in which a raw material of some kind was transformed into a product by some process of transformation involving human work, or practice, and an appropriate means of production. In societies, or social formations, there are four main processes of production, each with many subsidiary processes: they are the economic, political, ideological and theoretical practices. These practices are highly interlocking in that each is conditioned by all the others, a situation which he designated 'overdetermination', borrowing from Freud's analysis of dream images. Contradictions, or transformations, in one level of practice might transfer to or condense in another, and if contradictions in several or all practices came to fuse together, then a general transformation or revolution would be likely to ensue.

The concept of overdetermination was presented as a more complex, and more rigorous, basis for the analysis of history than the Hegelian dialectic it replaced, and contained a different conception of causality. The linear cause-and-effect principle of classical physics, and the expressive causality of the Hegelian dialectic, were replaced by a structural causality in which a particular event is not determined by an earlier event or a more fundamental event, but is overdetermined by a structure of practices to which it belongs. There is no centre to the structure, and since practices develop unevenly, one of them is dominant in the structure at a given time, though none is permanently so. Even economic practice has no permanent domination, though it has the special power of determining which practice does dominate. This is Althusser's version of the base-and-superstructure model of society, reformulated to give greater relative autonomy to the superstructures, which no longer merely reflect the economic base. Thus, although economic developments are determinant in the last instance, there is no moment at which they abruptly take over, and so 'the lonely hour of the last instance never comes'.

Althusser's model was crowned in effect by philosophy (designated as Theory, or the theory of theoretical practice) which had the role of ensuring the coherence and rigour of other theories (and their corresponding practices), and therefore appeared as a science of sciences. Criticized for his theoreticism, he devoted most of his writings after 1968 to self-criticism in which a series of retreats from 'high' Althusserian positions was accompanied by further conceptual innovations. Three of these may be mentioned as particularly influential. First, he advanced an alternative conception of philosophy as class struggle in theory, and as a weapon in the revolution. This suggested that its role was to ensure the theoretical correctness of political practice and the political correctness of theory. Second, he redefined the dialectic of history as a process without a subject or a goal, as opposed to the Hegelian dialectic which was both humanist, in seeing human existence as the subject of history, and teleological, in seeing history as advancing purposefully towards some final end. And third, he offered an account of ideology as the necessary illusion of a lived relationship between individuals and their circumstances. In this, he argued that most of the apparatuses of a modern state are primarily ideological, rather than repressive, in that their main function is to elicit the consent of the governed. People are incorporated into these ideological state apparatuses by the effect, which all ideology has, of calling on individuals to recognize themselves as subjects, in the sense both of being persons responsible for themselves and of being subordinated to an authority. His analysis of ideology has been widely adopted in critical theory and political philosophy internationally.

Of the philosophers who have continued Althusser's work, three are particularly worthy of note. Etienne Balibar developed a critique of the abandonment, in France and elsewhere, of the concept of the dictatorship of the proletariat, and has applied Althusserian analysis to issues of nation, race and class. Pierre Macherey developed a theory of how literature is produced, rather than created, and reveals the contradictions which ideology serves to conceal. He also advocated an appropriation of Spinozist conceptions by Marxism in preference to Hegelian ideas. Georges Labica re-examined Marx's early writings, criticizing the simplistic schema of his adoption of English political economy, French socialism and German philosophy, and arguing that he finally succeeded in escaping from philosophical mystifications only by substantially abandoning philosophy in favour of a science of history. Labica is also the major French instigator of academic research into the history of Marxist thought.

Althusser's ideas remained oppositional on the French left, partly because of his political disagreements with the French Communist Party, of which he was a member, and partly because non-communist critics tended to view his enterprise as an attempt to rescue Stalinist conceptions. His name was largely erased from public discussion after 1980 when he killed his wife, in a bout of his recurrent psychiatric disorder. None the less, many of his ideas became common currency in Marxist philosophy, and have had widespread influence particularly in literary and cultural criticism. Paradoxically, his onslaught against Hegel also had the effect of stimulating renewed interest in Hegelian studies in France.

Several Marxist philosophers responded to the challenge by carefully re-examining the concepts which had come through Hegel.

Jacques D'Hondt sought to rehabilitate the progressive content of Hegel's own life and thought. Solange Mercier-Josa argued that it was productive to look at the original Hegelian versions of Marx's main concepts so as to grasp the originality of his reworking of them, and also perhaps to retrieve some useful Hegelian concepts which Marx neglected to rework. Perhaps the most comprehensive of the attempts to find a synthesis in the Hegelian style is the work of Lucien Sève. In a series of studies, culminating in a compendious work, *An Introduction to Marxist Philosophy* (1980), Sève sought to systematize the concept of contradiction, suggesting that the distinction between antagonistic and non-antagonistic forms should not exclude their mutual interpenetration. He maintained the Hegelian distinction between objective and subjective dialectics and consequently between real historical development and the logical ordering of concepts with which to grasp it, while at the same time affirming the dialectical relationship between them. Sève also argued that Marxist materialism, understood as a scientific approach to knowledge rather than as a political ideology, was not specifically atheistic and should be open to learning from what religious thought expressed in intuitive or imaginative terms.

The breadth and erudition of Marxist philosophy in the 1960s and 1970s made it one of the dominant currents in French and European intellectual life, with a strong place in the schools and universities, as well as in political discourse. Towards the end of the seventies it began to run out of steam, under a combination of pressures which included the alternative attraction of other schools of thought (feminism, poststructuralist, psychoanalysis, ecology, spiritualism and postmodernism), as well as shifts in national politics and the accelerating decline of communism internationally. A variety of strategies was proposed to rejuvenate Marxism, including the incorporation of Italian Gramscian and Anglo-Saxon analytical versions of Marxism, but more often including eclectical borrowings from non-Marxist currents. Perhaps most significant was the impact of questioning from various quarters as to the need for, or legitimacy of, such a comprehensive intellectual enterprise (or master-narrative) as Marxism had historically undertaken. It was a question which struck an undeniable chord with intellectuals who were increasingly working without reference to a real or imagined Marxist collectivity (state, party or professional grouping) which could give a communal identity or an institutional basis to their thought. As a result, Marxist philosophy was in serious disarray even before the historical events of 1989 plunged it into catastrophe.

❧ CONCLUSION ❧

Since the present study is undertaken in the perspective of 'continental philosophy', it would not be appropriate to conclude without evoking the implied standpoint of the observer, that is, the philosophy of the English-speaking world, and in particular of the British Isles. The supposition that continental philosophy is something which happens elsewhere, on a real or imagined continent of Europe, indicates the extent to which the dominant currents of English-speaking philosophy have sought to isolate their intellectual traditions from foreign influences. In practice, English-speaking academic philosophy has been deeply engaged with continental European philosophers, even though they have often, like Popper or Wittgenstein, been regarded as honorary English philosophers. The strategy of exclusion implied by the term 'continental' serves to keep out undesirables, of which the least desirable has generally been the Marxist tradition. Until recent times, the exclusion of Marxism from at least academic philosophy has been largely complete, with the result that it has fallen to other disciplines, particularly literary and cultural studies, sociology, politics, history, geography and archaeology, to introduce continental Marxist philosophers to English-speaking intellectuals.

Marxism–Leninism was given some currency through the agency of communist parties, whose small size tended to exacerbate their dependence on Moscow. But for most of the period from the 1920s to the 1960s its influence was confined to the trade union movement. During the 1930s a small number of intellectuals were attracted to communism, and one of them, Christopher Caudwell, might have founded an indigenous Marxism in Britain had he not been killed fighting for the Republic in Spain. Later, Maurice Cornforth (1909–80) was an effective exponent of Marxist–Leninist philosophy, applying it in polemics against Popperian positivism and linguistic philosophy during the 1960s, and began to formulate a more critical view of Marxism shortly before his death. During the 1970s, English-speaking communist parties, in rapid decline, divided between Marxist–Leninists and Eurocommunists, who took Gramsci as their main philosophical inspiration.

During the 1960s a strong interest in Marxism emerged in the New Left groupings which were founded by dissident communists and Trotskyists. They drew on the non-Marxist–Leninist writings which were being published in France and Italy. The American journal *Telos* and the English journal *New Left Review*, and its publishing house, played a major role in the cultural, political and historical fields, in translating and introducing the work of Marxists who have been discussed above. From the early 1970s, the journal *Radical Philosophy* played a similar role with particular emphasis on philosophical discussion, by no means all Marxist. The growth of a flourishing English-speaking Marxist culture was visible from the 1960s with the emergence of literary and cultural critics like Raymond Williams, Stuart Hall, Terry Eagleton and Fredric Jameson, and historians such as E. P. Thompson, Christopher Hill, Eric Hobsbawm and Perry Anderson, among others. Philosophy proved more resistant to Marxist influence, though it is visible in the philosophy of science, particularly in the work of Roy Bhaskar, whose theory of scientific realism was linked to a project of general human emancipation. More ambitious and influential has been the work of Jon Elster and G. A. Cohen, who have attempted to reformulate the main principles of Marxism in terms of analytical philosophy. The confrontation of Marx with Popper, Keynes and Austin produces insights which are refreshing within the analytical tradition and challenging to Hegelian dialectics. The reconciliation is inevitably incomplete, however, and involves rejecting much of Marx's socialism and historical materialism.

English-speaking Marxist theory has developed in relative dissociation from powerful Marxist political movements. It has keenly observed such movements abroad, but their domestic counterparts have been either far left groups with marginal influence or mainstream parties with little commitment to particular doctrines. Its academic detachment has to some extent insulated it from the debacle of communism in 1989. That year did not bring Marxist philosophy to an end, but it does provide a convenient point at which to end the narrative of its history. Though it is always rash to extend history so far towards the present that it cannot be seen at any historical distance, 1989 is mainly significant in that the collapse of communism, symbolized by the breaching of the Berlin Wall, was a turning point in international history heavy with consequences for Marxist philosophy. While some English-speaking writers have continued to feel at ease in a broadly Marxist moral and philosophical framework, the political fall-out of 1989 has impelled others to take a more sympathetic view of other alternatives. This latter tendency is also encouraged by the increasingly chill winds blowing from the continent on unreconstructed Marxism.

Marxist philosophy has generally been distinguished by its close relationship to its social context, and in particular to the institutional forms through which its practical and political orientation is mediated. In its most institutional form, Marxism–Leninism, it became inextricably tied to the Soviet state and to the network of communist parties and client states which pledged their allegiance to it, including *mutatis mutandis* the Chinese variant. To a large extent, it has collapsed with the states and parties which sustained it, and, in Europe at least, writings in this tradition are now unreadable, except as historical documents, or as liturgy for the fragmented groups of old believers who continue to keep the faith. The question which remains posed is how far this erasure will affect other Marxist traditions which have been outlined in the present chapter.

The answer can as yet be only speculative, but it is probable that the future of Marxism as an identifiable philosophy will depend on the persistence or emergence of states, groupings or movements which can provide a plausible institutional basis for the imperative to change the world as well as interpreting it. It is unlikely for the foreseeable future that any individual state will provide such a basis, and the calamities which have overtaken those which did so in the past will more probably serve as a counter-example. Similarly the health and influence of those political parties which still claim the name communist or Marxist suggests that they are scarcely better placed. If the link between theory and practice is taken seriously, then the failure of practice must call into question the validity of the theory. It is only a partial defence to argue that the previous practical implementation of the theory was deficient, since that accepts a substantive severance of the link.

If the chief originality of Marxism is that it claimed to have the means to put its theory into practice, then it has largely lost that originality. An attenuated commitment to change would effectively place Marxism in the same position as any of a number of philosophies which express moral or social imperatives with general hortatory effect. Viewed in this light, it becomes less important to set precise limits on what may be called Marxism. For most of its history, Marxist philosophy has had an active and influential place as a strand in many currents of thought. Some, like the Frankfurt school, took it as a starting point; some, like the French existentialists, attempted to marry it with another tradition; and some, like the structuralists, accepted it as one element feeding into their theory. There is no reason to suppose that the process of intellectual cross-fertilization is likely to come abruptly to an end.

The loss of a distinct and coherent tradition of Marxist philosophy would in some respects liberate its proponents from their obligations to a collectivity, and perhaps also from the authority of a canon. In other respects, however, it would remove a point of reference and an identity, which has had the unusual role of forming common links between the different cultural and intellectual environments of Europe whether western, central or eastern, and of opening them out to a wider world outside. The resistance to overarching world-views or master narratives is no doubt in part a response to the constricting effects of international Marxism especially in its dogmatic forms. In a world where postmodernism is setting the intellectual and cultural agenda, there may be a role for a humanist post-Marxism which retained its varieties and its international dimensions without proclaiming the necessity or authority to synthesize them. But if Benjamin's angel of history is still being driven by the storm from paradise, it is unlikely to linger over the debris that it leaves behind, and it remains to be seen how much of Marxist philosophy will survive from the wreckage.

❧ BIBLIOGRAPHY ❧

The following is a list of some of the relevant texts published in English. It is divided into primary texts and critical texts, though in the nature of the subject, the distinction between the two is in some respects arbitrary.

Primary texts

7.1 Althusser, L. *Essays in Ideology*, London: Verso, 1984.

7.2 Althusser, L. *Essays in Self-criticism*, London: New Left Books, 1976.

7.3 Althusser, L. *For Marx*, London: Verso, 1990.

7.4 Althusser, L. *Reading Capital*, London: New Left Books, 1970.

7.5 Balibar, E. and Wallerstein, I. *Race, Nation, Class: Ambiguous Identities*, London: Verso, 1991.

7.6 Benjamin, W. *Charles Baudelaire, a Lyric Poet in the Era of High Capitalism*, London: New Left Books, 1972.

7.7 Benjamin, W. *Illuminations*, London: Jonathan Cape, 1970.

7.8 Bhaskar, R. *Dialectic*, London: Verso, 1992.

7.9 Bhaskar, R. *Scientific Realism and Human Emancipation*, London: Verso, 1986.

7.10 Bloch, E. *The Principle of Hope*, 3 vols, Oxford: Blackwell, 1986.

7.11 Colletti, L. *From Rousseau to Lenin*, London: New Left Books, 1972.

7.12 Colletti, L. *Marxism and Hegel*, London: New Left Books, 1973.

7.13 Cornforth, M. *Communism and Philosophy*, London: Lawrence & Wishart, 1980.

7.14 Cornforth, M. *The Open Philosophy and the Open Society*, London: Lawrence & Wishart, 1968.

7.15 Della Volpe, G. *Critique of Taste*, London: New Left Books, 1978.

7.16 Della Volpe, G. *Rousseau and Marx and Other Writings*, London: Lawrence & Wishart, 1978.

7.17 Engels, F. *Anti-Dühring*, London: Lawrence & Wishart, 1975.

7.18 Engels, F. *Dialectics of Nature*, Moscow: Progress Publishers, 1972.

7.19 Garaudy, R. *Marxism in the Twentieth Century*, London, 1970.

7.20 Garaudy, R. *The Turning Point of Socialism*, London, 1970.

7.21 Goldmann, L. *The Hidden God*, London: Routledge & Kegan Paul, 1964.

7.22 Goldmann, L. *The Human Sciences and Philosophy*, London: Jonathan Cape, 1969.

7.23   Gramsci, A. *Letters from Prison*, ed. L. Lawner, New York: Harper & Row, 1973.

7.24   Gramsci, A. *Selections from his Cultural Writings*, ed. D. Forgacs and G. Nowell-Smith, London: Lawrence & Wishart, 1985.

7.25   Gramsci, A. *Selections from the Prison Notebooks*, ed. Quintin Hoare and G. Nowell-Smith, London: Lawrence & Wishart, 1971.

7.26   Ilyenkov, E. V. *Dialectical Logic: Essays in its History and Theory*, Moscow: Progress Publishers, 1977.

7.27   Konstantinov, F. V. (ed.) *The Fundamentals of Marxist-Leninist Philosophy*, Moscow: Progress Publishers, 1974.

7.28   Korsch, K. *Marxism and Philosophy*, London: New Left Books, 1970.

7.29   Labriola, A. *Essays on the Materialist Conception of History*, Chicago: Charles H. Kerr, 1908.

7.30   Lenin, V. I. *Collected Works*, London: Lawrence & Wishart; Moscow, Progress Publishers, 1972. Volume 18 contains *Materialism and Empiriocriticism*, and volume 38 contains his *Philosophical Notebooks*.

7.31   Lefebvre, H. *Critique of Everyday Life*, London: Verso, 1991.

7.32   Lefebvre, J. *Dialectical Materialism*, London: Jonathan Cape, 1968.

7.33   Lukács, G. *The Destruction of Reason*, London: Merlin, 1980.

7.34   Lukács, G. *History and Class Consciousness*, London: Merlin, 1971.

7.35   Lukács, G. *The Ontology of Social Being*, 3 vols, London: Merlin, 1978–80.

7.36   Macherey, P. *A Theory of Literary Production*, London: Routledge & Kegan Paul, 1978.

7.37   Mao Tse-tung, *Four Essays on Philosophy*, Peking: Foreign Languages Press, 1966.

7.38   Mao Tse-tung, *Selected Works*, vols 1–4, Peking: Foreign Languages Press, 1967–9.

7.39   Marx, K. *Selected Writings*, ed. D. McLellan, Oxford: Oxford University Press, 1977.

7.40   Marx, K. and Engels, F. *Basic Writings on Politics and Philosophy*, ed. by L. S. Feuer, London: Fontana, 1969.

7.41   Marx, K., and Engels, F. *Collected Works*, London: Lawrence & Wishart, 1975– . About two-thirds of the planned fifty volumes have now appeared.

7.42   Oizerman, T. I. *The Making of the Marxist Philosophy*, Moscow: Progress Publishers, 1981.

7.43   Plekhanov, G. V. *Selected Philosophical Works*, 5 vols, London: Lawrence & Wishart; Moscow, Progress Publishers, 1974. Volume 1 contains *The Development of the Monist View of History*.

7.44   Roemer, J. (ed.) *Analytical Marxism*, Cambridge: Cambridge University Press, 1986.

7.45   Timpanaro, S. *On Materialism*, London: New Left Books, 1975.

Critical texts

7.46 Acton, H. B. *The Illusion of the Epoch*, London: Cohen & West, 1955.

7.47 Anderson, P. *Considerations on Western Marxism*, London: New Left Books, 1976.

7.48 Anderson, P. *Arguments within English Marxism*, London: Verso, 1980.

7.49 Avinieri, S. *Varieties of Marxism*, The Hague: Martinus Nijhoff, 1977.

7.50 Benton, T. *The Rise and Fall of Structural Marxism*, London: Macmillan, 1984.

7.51 Berki, R. N. *The Genesis of Marxism*, London: Dent, 1988.

7.52 Berlin, I. *Karl Marx*, Oxford: Oxford University Press, 1978.

7.53 Boggs, C. *Gramsci's Marxism*, London: Pluto Press, 1976.

7.54 Borkenau, F. *European Communism*, London: Faber, 1953.

7.55 Borkenau, F. *World Communism*, University of Michigan Press, 1962.

7.56 Bottomore, T. (ed.) *A Dictionary of Marxist Thought*, London: Blackwell, 1983.

7.57 Callinicos, A. *Althusser's Marxism*, London: Pluto Press, 1976.

7.58 Callinicos, A. *Marxism and Philosophy*, Oxford: Clarendon Press, 1983.

7.59 Carver, T. *Marx and Engels*, London: Wheatsheaf Books, 1983.

7.60 Caute, D. *Communism and the French Intellectuals*, London: Macmillan, 1964.

7.61 Caute, D. *The Fellow-travellers*, London: Weidenfeld & Nicolson, 1973.

7.62 De George, R. T. *Patterns of Soviet Thought*, Ann Arbor, 1966.

7.63 De George, R. T. *The New Marxism*, New York, 1968.

7.64 Derfler, L. *Paul Lafargue and the Founding of French Marxism*, Cambridge, Mass.: Harvard University Press, 1991.

7.65 Deutscher, I. *Stalin: A Political Biography*, Harmondsworth: Penguin Books, 1966.

7.66 Deutscher, I. *Marxism in Our Time*, London: Jonathan Cape, 1972.

7.67 Eagleton, T. *Walter Benjamin, or Towards a Revolutionary Criticism*, London: Verso, 1981.

7.68 Elliott, G. *Althusser, the Detour of Theory*, London: Verso, 1987.

7.69 Evans, M. *Lucien Goldmann*, Brighton: Harvester Press, 1981.

7.70 Fiori, G. *Antonio Gramsci: Life of a Revolutionary*, London: New Left Books, 1970.

7.71 Gorman, R. A. (ed.) *A Biographical Dictionary of Neo-Marxism*, Westport: Greenwood Press, 1985.

7.72 Hirsh, A. *The French New Left*, Boston: South End Press, 1981.

7.73 Holub, R. *Antonio Gramsci: Beyond Marxism and Postmodernism*, London: Routledge, 1992.

7.74 Hudson, W. *The Marxist Philosophy of Ernst Bloch*, London: Macmillan, 1982.

7.75 Hunt, I. *Analytical and Dialectical Marxism*, London: Avebury, 1993.

7.76 Hyppolite, J. *Studies on Marx and Hegel*, New York, 1969.

7.77 Jacoby, R. *Dialectic of Defeat: The Contours of Western Marxism*, Cambridge: Cambridge University Press, 1981.

7.78 Jameson, F. *Marxism and Form*, Princeton: Princeton University Press, 1971.

7.79 Judt, T. *Marxism and the French Left*, Oxford: Clarendon Press, 1986.

7.80 Kelly, M. *Modern French Marxism*, Oxford: Blackwell, 1982.

7.81 Kolakowski, L. *Main Currents of Marxism*, 3 vols, Oxford: Oxford University Press, 1978.

7.82 Labedz, L. *Revisionism: Essays on the History of Marxist Ideas*, London and New York, 1961.

7.83 Leonhard, W. *The Three Faces of Marxism*, New York: Holt, Rinehart & Winston, 1974.

7.84 Lichtheim, G. *Marxism in Modern France*, London and New York: Columbia University Press, 1966.

7.85 Lichtheim, G. *Marxism*, London: Routledge & Kegan Paul, 3rd impression, 1967.

7.86 Lichtheim, G. *Lukács*, London: Fontana, 1970.

7.87 Lukes, S. *Marxism and Morality*, Oxford: Clarendon Press, 1985.

7.88 MacIntyre, S. *A Proletarian Science: Marxism in Britain 1917–1933*, London: Lawrence & Wishart, 1986.

7.89 Matthews, B. (ed.) *Marx 100 Years on*, London: Lawrence & Wishart, 1983.

7.90 Merquior, J. G. *Western Marxism*, London: Paladin, 1986.

7.91 Mészáros, I. *Lukács' Concept of Dialectic*, London: Merlin, 1972.

7.92 Mouffe, C. (ed.) *Gramsci and Marxist Theory*, London: Routledge & Kegan Paul, 1979.

7.93 Poster, M. *Existential Marxism in Postwar France*, Princeton: Princeton University Press, 1975.

7.94 Rossi-Landi. F. *Marxism and Ideology*, Oxford: Clarendon Press, 1990.

7.95 Scanlan, J. P. *Marxism in the USSR*, Ithaca: Cornell University Press, 1985.

7.96 Schram, S. R. *Mao Tse-tung*, Harmondsworth: Penguin Books, 1966.

7.97 Schram, S. R. *The Political Thought of Mao Tse-tung*, Harmondsworth: Penguin Books, 1969.

7.98 Sowell, T. *Marxism, Philosophy and Economics*, London, George Allen & Unwin, 1985.

7.99 Tismaneaunu, V. *The Crisis of Marxist Ideology in Eastern Europe*, London: Croom Helm, 1988.

7.100 Wetter, G. *Dialectical Materialism*, London: Routledge & Kegan Paul, 1958.

CHAPTER 8

Critical theory
Horkheimer, Adorno, Habermas
David Rasmussen

❧⦂❧

Critical theory[1] is a metaphor for a certain kind of theoretical orientation which owes its origin to Hegel and Marx, its systematization to Horkheimer and his associates at the Institute for Social Research in Frankfurt, and its development to successors, particularly to the group led by Jürgen Habermas, who have sustained it under various redefinitions to the present day. As a term, critical theory is both general and specific. In general it refers to that critical element in German philosophy which began with Hegel's critique of Kant. More specifically it is associated with a certain orientation towards philosophy which found its twentieth-century expression in Frankfurt.

What is critical theory? The term bears the stamp of the nascent optimism of the nineteenth century; a critical theory can change society. Critical theory is a tool of reason which, when properly located in a historical group, can transform the world. 'Philosophers have always interpreted the world, the point is to change it.' So states Marx's famous eleventh thesis on Feuerbach. Marx got this idea from Hegel who, in his *Phenomenology of Spirit*,[2] developed the concept of the moving subject which, through the process of self-reflection, comes to know itself at ever higher levels of consciousness. Hegel was able to combine a philosophy of action with a philosophy of reflection in such a manner that activity or action was a necessary moment in the process of reflection. This gave rise to one of the most significant discourses in German philosophy, that of the proper relationship between theory and practice. Human practical activity, *praxis* in the sense that classical Greek philosophy had defined it, could transform theory. There are two famous instances where Hegel attempted to demonstrate the interrelationship of thought and action in his *Phenomenology of Spirit*, namely, the master/slave dialectic and the struggle between virtue and the way of the world. In the former example, which attempts to demonstrate the proposition, 'Self-Consciousness exists in and for itself when, and by the fact that, it so exists for another: that is, it exists only in being acknowledged,'[3] the slave transforms his or her identity by moulding and shaping the world and thus becomes something other than a slave. In the latter example, the modern way of the world (essentially Adam Smith's concept of the political economy of civil society) triumphs over the ancient classical concept of virtue as a higher form of human self-knowledge oriented toward freedom. Historical development, as the institutionalization of human action, became an element in human rationality. Critical theory derives its basic insight from the idea that thought can transform itself through a process of self-reflection in history.

Marx, early on in his development in a text that has come down to us under the title *On the Jewish Question*,[4] argued from Hegel's critical insight into the context of modern society. Having already done an analysis a few months before of Hegel's *Philosophy of Right*, he turned his attention to the development of the modern state by reflecting on Bruno Bauer's essay by the same name. Here, he would come to the conclusion that the course of human freedom culminating in the modern state (which Hegel had so brilliantly documented as leading from slavery to emancipation – the so-called course of human reason) was no emancipation at all. Indeed, the promised liberation of modern society from the shackles of the Middle Ages had not occurred. Hence, the task of social emancipation which could be carried on by critical reflection would lead the very agents of that reflection to a further task, namely, the transformation of society through revolution. Consequently, the promise of critical theory would be radical social transformation. The ancient assumption that the purpose of reflection was for knowledge itself, allied with the further assumption that pure contemplation was the proper end of the human subject, was replaced by another end of reflection also to be derived from classical thought, but with its own peculiarly modern twist; theory when allied with *praxis* has a proper political end, namely, social transformation.

However, for Marx this was not enough. Two factors remained. First, whence was such knowledge to be derived? Second, what would be the nature of such knowledge? Between the autumn of 1843 and the summer of 1844, Marx would provide answers to both questions. The answers came in the form of a class theory in which the newly emerging 'proletariat' were to play the central role. For Marx, they became the concrete subject of history with the result that hopes for emancipation would be anchored in a critical theory, which would in turn be associated with the activity of a particular class. Again, Hegel had provided the groundwork for this understanding by associating the basic interest in civil society in his philosophy of law with the interest of a particular *Stände*. Of the three orders of society – agricultural, business and civil service – it was only the latter which could represent the universal interests of humankind. With Marx, that latter task was transferred from the civil servants, who could no longer be trusted, to the proletariat, who he somewhat confidently asserted would bring about the social revolution necessary to overcome the contradictions with modern political society.

With regard to the second question, it was again Hegel, the philosopher of modernity *par excellence*, who taught Marx to look not to intuition *per se* but to the manifestation of reason in practical institutional form for an appropriate understanding of the world. Hegel had been the first philosopher both to understand and to use the work of the political economists in his work. Marx, first in a review of James Mill's *Elements of Political Economy* and later in a much more elaborate fashion, would work out a thesis about the dynamics of history leading him to assert that economic activity had a certain priority in the development of history.

This thesis would lead Marx to assert shortly thereafter, in *The German Ideology*,[5] that for the first time real history could begin. The very assumption behind a book which had the audacity to put the term 'ideology' into the title was that thought alone was ideological. There was a higher truth which Marx, through his methodology, would be able to attain, namely the 'productive' activity of humankind. Human history would then be simultaneous with human production. The term for this new approach to the world of reflection and action would be 'historical materialism' and it would attack other more 'idealistic' modes of thinking as 'ideological'. Hence, a critical theory would be able to unearth the false presumptions that had heretofore held humanity in their sway. Later, in *Capital*, Marx would label the kind of thinking which he had characterized as 'ideology' in *The German Ideology* as 'fetishism'. He did so in the famous last section of the first chaper of volume 1, entitled 'The fetishism of commodities and the secret thereof'. Marx's choice and use of metaphor is interesting, if not compelling. He uses 'ideology', 'fetishism' and 'secret' as if there was some ominous conspiracy against humankind which a certain kind of critical and theoretical orientation could unmask. The term 'fetishism' had a religious origin designating a fundamental confusion regarding perceptual orientations to the world. The very assumption that a certain theoretical orientation could unleash the 'secret' behind ideology as a kind of 'fetishism' represented a kind of confidence that would not only shape the historical development of critical theory in the future, but also unearth its problematic nature.

At the risk of oversimplification, one might state that there are two basic strains in the history of German philosophy. One strain argues that thought or reason is constitutive, the other that it is transformative. The former orientation can be traced to the debate initiated by Kant over the limits of human reason, while the latter can be traced to Hegel's philosophy of history, which attempted to locate philosophical reflection in a discourse about the history of human freedom.

Critical theory could be said to ally itself with this latter theme, even though the constitutive element would play an ever more significant role. In its classical, Hegelian–Marxist, context, critical theory rests on the nascent Enlightenment assumption that reflection is emancipatory. But what is the epistemological ground for this claim? In other words, how is thought constitutive for action? Which form of action is proper, appropriate or correct? In the early writings, Marx attempted to ground the epistemological claims of transformative action in the concept of *Gattungswesen*, i.e., species being. This concept, taken directly from Ludwig Feuerbach, who in turn had constructed it from both Hegel and Aristotle, affirms that in contrast to the radical individuation of the subject in modern thought, the aim or purpose of a human being is to be determined through intersubjective social action. In Hegelian terms, one constitutes valid self-knowledge through social interaction defined as human labour. According to Marx, the problem with the modern productive process is that it fails to allow the worker to constitute him- or herself as a species being, i.e., as a person who can function *for* another human being. Hence, the labour process reduces him or her to an animal, as opposed to a human, level making him or her autonomous, competitive and inhuman – co-operating with the productive process and not with other human beings. The point of revolution would be to bring the human being to his or her full and proper capacities as a being for whom the species would be the end, object and aim.

There were problems with this view. To be sure, Marx represents the culmination of a certain kind of political theory that began with Hobbes, and which was in turn critical of original anthropological assumptions that saw the human being as an autonomous agent emerging from a state of nature. However, in a certain sense, the concept of species-being was as metaphysical as the Hobbesian notion of the human being in a state of nature, a view which was so aptly and appropriately criticized by Rousseau. It is my view that Marx was aware of the essentially epistemological problem that lay at the foundation of his own thought. Does one ground a theory of emancipation on certain anthropological assumptions regarding the nature of the species, assumptions which were as metaphysical as those the theory was attempting to criticize? Marx attempted to overcome this dilemma by providing historical evidence. In this context, his later work, the volumes of *Capital*, represent a massive attempt to give an account of human agency which was both historical and scientific. Hence, the quest for a valid constitutive ground for critical theory began with Marx himself. Marx as a political economist would bring massive historical research to bear on the claim that capitalism is merely a phase in human development and not the be-all and end-all of history. Hence, as a true Hegelian, he would assert that like any economic system it bore the seeds of its own destruction. As a consequence, the metaphysical claims present in the notion of species-being would re-emerge as a claim about the implicit but incomplete socialization present in capitalism, which, when rationalized, would transform the latter into socialism. As is well known, Marx even went beyond that to attempt to develop, on the basis of his historical investigations, a scientific, predictive formula announcing the end of capitalism on the basis of the 'falling rate of profit'. The formula assumed that as capital advanced it would be able to generate less and less profit and so would lose its own incentive. Hence, the force of capitalism, unleashed, would lead to its own imminent self-destruction. The victor, of course, would be socialism, which would emerge from the fray, new-born and pure, the ultimate rationalization of the irrationalism implicit in capitalism. As the family would inevitably give way to the force of civil society in Hegel's philosophy of law, so capitalism would break down and re-emerge as socialism.

In 1844 the young Marx had accused his one acknowledged theoretical mentor, Hegel, of harbouring a certain 'latent positivism'.[6] There are those who would accuse the older Marx of having done the same. If capitalism is to fall of its own weight, what is the link between thought and revolutionary action that so inspired the younger Marx? Indeed, what role would the proletariat, the heretofore messianic class of underlings, play in the transformation of society? And what of critical theory? It too would be transformed into just one more scientific, predictive positivistic model. In Marx's favour, this desire to secure the claims of a critical theory on the firm foundation of positivistic science was always in tension with the more critical claims of exhaustive historical analysis. But it was Marx himself who bequeathed to the late nineteenth century, and subsequently by implication to the twentieth century, the ambiguities of a critical theory. One could imagine the great social thinkers of the nineteenth and twentieth centuries coming together to pose a single question: upon what can we ground a critical theory? Would it be the proletariat now transformed into the working class? economic scientific analysis? the critical reflection of a specific historically chosen agent (the vanguard)? informed individual *praxis?* Perhaps critical theory would produce a 'dialectic of enlightenment' so cunning that its very inauguration would produce its own destruction as certain later heirs would predict. Certainly, the late nineteenth and the early twentieth centuries saw the concretization of a particular form of Marxism in a political society, not merely in the former USSR but also in the various workers' movements in Europe and elsewhere, as well as in the founding of the International, which would raise these questions. A kind of critical theory found its apologists from Engels to Lenin, from Bernstein to Luxemburg, from Kautsky to Plekhanov. Yet the systematization of critical theory as a model of reflection owes its life in the twentieth century to a group of academics who, originally inspired by the German workers' movement, attempted to give to critical theory a life in the German university.

∾ FROM GRÜNBURG TO HORKHEIMER: THE ∾ FOUNDATION OF CRITICAL THEORY

Although the term 'critical theory' in the twentieth century owes its definition primarily to an essay written in 1937 by Max Horkheimer,[7] the institute which became associated with this term was founded almost two decades earlier. Certainly one of the more interesting experiments in the history of German institutional thought began when Felix Weil, the son of a German exporter of grains from Argentina, convinced his father, Hermann, to provide an endowment which would enable a yearly income of DM 120,000 to establish, in the year 1922, an Institute for Social Research in affiliation with the University of Frankfurt. Weil, inspired by the workers' movement, and having written a thesis on socialism, wanted an institute which could deal directly with the problems of Marxism on a par equal to other established disciplines in the University. The first candidate for director, Kurt Albert Gerlach, who planned a series of inaugural lectures on socialism, anarchism and Marxism, died of diabetes before he could begin. His replacement, Karl Grünberg, a professor of law and political science from the University of Vienna, an avowed Marxist, who had begun in the year of 1909 an Archive for the History of Socialism and the Worker's Movement, was present at the official creation of the Institute on 3 February 1922. In his opening address, he indicated that Marxism would be the guiding principle of the Institute. And so it was for a decade. To be sure, it was the kind of Marxism that was still inspired by the nineteenth century, by the idea of the proletariat, by the workers' movement, by the example of the Soviet Union and the Marx–Engels Institute in Moscow, by the conception of Marxism as a kind of science which could penetrate heretofore unknown truths which had been obscured by so-called 'bourgeois' thought. Indeed, mocking Frankfurt students celebrated its orthodoxy by referring to it as 'Café Marx'.

Certainly, Marxism need not be vulgar to be orthodox. Academic problems which were standard fare for a now more or less established theoretical tradition were commonplace. Principal among them was the study of the workers' movement. Indeed, if Marxian class theory was correct, the proletariat were to bear the distinctive role of being those who were able to interpret history and bring about the transformation that such insight would sustain. *Praxis* would then be associated solely with their activity. From an epistemological point of view, the problem of the relation of theory to *praxis* would be revealed. As Lukács would later think, there would be a certain transparent identity between Marxian social theory and the activity of the working class. Hence, academic study of the working class would be the most appropriate, indeed, the most proper, subject of study for an institute which conceived itself in Marxist terms.

For the Institute for Social Research at that time, Marxism was conceived by analogy to science. Hence, the original works of the Institute were associated with capitalist accumulation and economic planning, studies of the economy in China, agricultural relations in France, imperialism and, along with this, through close collaboration with the Soviet Union, the establishment of a collection of the unpublished works of Marx and Engels. However, it wasn't until the leadership passed from Grünberg to the more able hands of one of the young assistants at the institute, Max Horkheimer, in 1931, that the Institute was to make its mark through both productivity and scholarship. Although Horkheimer was never the believing Marxist Grünberg had been, certain events in Germany and the world would shape the Institute, distancing it from Marxian orthodoxy. The rise of fascism and the splintering of the workers' movement as well as the Stalinization of Russia would force the Institute to stray from the conventional Marxist wisdom about both theory and science as well as shake its confidence in the workers' movement.

During the 1930s, the roster of the institute would include Theodor Adorno, Leo Lowenthal, Erich Fromm, Fredrich Pollach, Herbert Marcuse, Walter Benjamin (indirectly though, since he never became a fully-fledged member) and others. Although each figure would eventually be known for independent work, and although certain members would break with the general orientation of the Institute, in retrospect what is somewhat amazing about this illustrious group of scholars was its concern for sharing a common theoretical programme under a distinctive directorship. Indeed, the two most powerful theoretical minds, Adorno (1903–69) and Horkheimer (1895–1973), continued to collaborate for their entire lifetimes. Also, it was during this period that the distinctive perspective with which this group came to be identi-fied began to be developed. Modern critical theory can be dated from this period.

The problematic which sparked a critical theory of the modern form was the demise of the working class as an organ of appropriate revolutionary knowledge and action coupled with the rise of fascism and the emergence of Stalinization. Taken together, these events would de-couple the link between theory and revolutionary practice centred in the proletariat which had become commonplace in Marxian theory. What became apparent to Horkheimer and others at the Institute was that once this link was broken, essentially the link with a certain form of ideology, it would be necessary to forge a unique theoretical perspective in the context of modern thought in general and German thought in particular. It would not be enough either comfortably to study the workers' movement or to define Marxist science. The road upon which the Institute embarked would have to bear its own distinc-tive stamp and character. In brief, not only would this de-coupling give critical theory its peculiar dynamic for the 1930s but, as the torch was passed in the 1960s to a younger generation, this same thrust would give it definition. Hence, while Grünberg's Archive for the History of Socialism and the Workers' Movement would define the Institute in more traditional Marxian terms, the chief organ of the Institute under Horkheimer, *The Journal for Social Research*, would record a different purpose, namely the movement away from Marxian materialism. Writing in 1968 Jürgen Habermas would put it this way:

> Since the years after World War II the idea of the growing wretch-edness of the workers, out of which Marx saw rebellion and revolution emerging as a transitional step to the reign of freedom, had for long periods become abstract and illusory, and at least as out of date as the ideologies despised by the young. The living conditions of laborers and employees at the time of *The Com-munist Manifesto* were the outcome of open oppression. Today they are instead motives for trade union organization and for discussion between dominant economic and political groups. The revolutionary thrust of the proletariat has long since become realistic action within the framework of society. In the minds of men at least, the proletariat has been integrated into society.
>
> (*Critical Theory* [8.104], vi)

Horkheimer's 1937 essay, 'Traditional and Critical Theory', which attempted to systematically define critical theory, does not begin by underlining an association with the Marxist heritage which still distin-guished the Institute and journal with which it was associated. Rather the essay begins by trying to answer the more general question regarding theory *per se*, 'What is theory?' (*ibid.*, p. 188). In the traditional sense, theory is a kind of generalization based upon experience. From Descartes to Husserl theory has been so defined, argues Horkheimer. As such, however, theory traditionally defined has a peculiar kind of prejudice which favours the natural sciences. Horkheimer, reflecting the great Diltheyian distinction between *Geisteswissenschaften* (social sciences) and *Naturwissenschaften* (natural sciences) makes the appropriate criticism. Social science imitates natural science in its self-definition as theory. Put simply, the study of society must conform to the facts. But Horkheimer would argue that it is not quite so simple. Experience is said to conform to generalizations. The generalizations tend to conform to certain ideas present in the minds of the researchers. The danger is apparent: so defined, theory conforms to the ideas in the mind of the researcher and not to experience itself. The word for this phenomenon, derived from the development of the Marxist theoretical tradition following Lukács's famous characterization in 1934, is 'reification'. Horkheimer doesn't hesitate to use it. Regarding the development of theory he states, 'But the conception of theory was absolutized, as though it were grounded in the inner nature of knowledge as such, or justified in some other ahistorical way, and thus it became a reified ideological category' (*ibid.*, p. 194). Although various theoretical approaches would come close to breaking out of the ideological constraints which restricted them, theoretical approaches such as positivism, pragmatism, neo-Kantianism and phenomenology, Horkheimer would argue that they failed. Hence, all would be subject to the logico-mathematical prejudice which separates theoretical activity from actual life. The appropriate response to this dilemma is the development of a critical theory. 'In fact, however, the self-knowledge of present-day man is not a mathematical knowledge of nature which claims to be the eternal logos, but a critical theory of society as it is, a theory dominated at every turn by a concern for reasonable conditions of life' (*ibid.*, p. 199). Of course, the construction of a critical theory won't be easy. Interestingly enough, Horkheimer defines the problem epistemologically. 'What is needed is a radical reconsideration not of the scientist alone, but of the knowing individual as such' (*ibid.*).

Horkheimer's decision to take critical theory in the direction of epistemology was not without significance. Critical theory, which had heretofore depended upon the Marxist tradition for its legitimation, would have to define itself by ever distancing itself from that tradition. Indeed, one of the peculiar ironies resulting from this particular turn is that the very tradition out of which critical theory comes, namely Marxism, would itself fall under the distinction between traditional and critical theory. Ultimately, in many ways the Marxist tradition was as traditional as all the other traditions. But, of course, the 1937 essay fails to recognize this. Indeed, this dilemma of recognition would play itself out in the post–1937 period. This is the very irony of the systematization of critical theory. Equally, this epistemological turn would change permanently the distinction and approach of critical theory. As I suggested earlier, critical theory found its foundation in the transformative tradition in German thought as inspired by Hegel and Marx. Now, having embarked upon an epistemological route, it would find it necessary to draw upon the constitutive dimension of German thought. If one could not ground critical theory in Marxian orthodoxy, certainly the assumption behind the 1937 essay, it would be necessary to find the constitutive point of departure for critical theory in an analysis of knowledge as such. Unfortunately, Horkheimer was unprepared to follow his own unique insight. Instead, the constitutive elements of knowledge to which he refers are taken in a more or less unexamined form from the Marxian heritage. The distinction between individual and society, the concept of society as bourgeois, the idea that knowledge centres in production, the critique of the so-called liberal individual as autonomous, the primacy of the concept of history over logos – these so-called elements which are constitutive of a critical theory were part of the Marxist heritage.

Taken as a whole, 'Tradition and Critical Theory' is strongly influenced by the Hegelian–Marxist idea that the individual is alienated from society, that liberal thought obscures this alienation, and that the task of critical theory must be to overcome this alienation. Horkheimer put it this way,

> The separation between the individual and society in virtue of which the individual accepts as natural the limits prescribed for his activity is relativized in Critical Theory. The latter considers the overall framework which is conditioned by the blind interaction of individual activities (that is, the existent division of labour and class distinctions) to be a function which originates in human action and therefore is a possible object of painful decision and rational determination of goals.
>
> (*ibid.*, p. 207)

Horkheimer is vehement in his critique of the kind of thought that characterizes so-called 'bourgeois' individualism. For him, 'bourgeois thought' harbours a belief in an individual who is 'autonomous' believing that it, the autonomous ego, is the ground of reality. Horkheimer counters this view with another, reminiscent of the early Marx. 'Critical thinking is the function neither of the isolated individual nor a sum total of individuals. Its subject is rather a definite individual in his real relation to other individuals and groups, in his conflict with a particular class, and, finally, in the resultant web of relationships with the social totality and with nature' (*ibid.*, pp. 201–11).

Of course, this view is dangerously close to traditional Marxian class theory and Horkheimer knows it. After all, who is this 'definite individual' whose 'real relation' is to other individuals? Traditional Marxist theory answered, the proletariat. Horkheimer is suspicious. 'But it must be added that even the situation of the proleteriat is, in this society, no guarantee of correct knowledge' (*ibid.*, p. 213). Horkheimer is hard pressed to find the appropriate replacement of the proletariat without falling back into what he called 'bourgeois individualism'. He is doubtful of the proletariat's ability somehow to 'rise above ... differentiation of social structure ... imposed from above'. But if he wants to eliminate the proletariat as a source of truth or correct knowledge, he doesn't quite do it. Indeed, the intellectual or critic can proclaim his or her identity with the proletariat. Horkheimer is not entirely without optimism. 'The intellectual is satisfied to proclaim with relevant admiration the creative strength of the proletariat and finds satisfaction in adapting himself to it and canonizing it' (*ibid.*, p. 214). Indeed, Horkheimer is optimistic about this identification. If, however, the theoretician and his specific object are seen as forming a dynamic unity with the oppressed class, so that his presentation of societal contradictions is not merely the expression of the concrete historical situation but also a force within it to stimulate change, then his real function emerges' (*ibid.*, p. 215).

Horkheimer's reliance on Marxian doctrine as the epistemological foundation for critical theory becomes more apparent as the essay develops. Hence, a critical theory of society will show 'how an exchange economy, given the condition of men (which, of course, changes under the very influence of such an economy), must necessarily lead to a heightening of those social tensions which in the present historical era lead in turn to wars and revolution' (*ibid.*, p. 266). As such, critical theory has a peculiar insight into the potential history of modern society. As Marx used political economy and the theory of the primacy of production, Horkheimer will use this model of economic determinism to predict the development of social contradictions in the modern world. Indeed, he goes as far as to state that critical theory rests upon a 'single existential judgment', namely, 'the basic form of the historically given commodity economy, on which modern history rests, contains in itself the internal and external tensions of the modern era' (*ibid.*, p. 227).

Equally, critical theory will be able to overcome the 'Cartesian dualism' that characterized contemporary traditional theory by linking critical with practical activity, theory and *praxis*. Indeed, it was this belief that critical theory was somehow related to practical activity that would distinguish this kind of theoretical endeavour. 'The thinker must relate all the theories which are proposed to the practical attitudes and social strata which they reflect' (*ibid.*, p. 232).

In retrospect, one may view this 1937 declaration as something of a *tour de force* attempting to break away from at least some of the most fundamental tenets of traditional Marxist theory, while at the same time in a curious way being caught in the very web of the system from which it was trying to escape. Hence, while dissociating itself from the assumption that truth and proper knowledge were to be rendered through the proletariat, the fundamental tenet of Marxian class theory, this treatise on critical theory celebrated concepts such as economic determinism, reification, critique of autonomy and social contradiction – assumptions derived from traditional Marxian social theory – as valid notions. Simultaneously, this position could not seek to justify itself independently of the events of the time. As the French Revolution determined Hegel's concept of the political end of philosophy as human freedom, and as the burgeoning Industrial Revolution determined Marx's thought, critical theory attempted to respond to the events of the time, the decline of the workers' movement and the rise of fascism. Hence, the indelible mark of the Institute, and of the essay on critical theory in the decade of the 1930s, was the conviction that thought was linked to social justice. The thesis, as old as the German Enlightenment itself, was that thought could somehow be emancipatory. The predominance of this view gave the Institute its particular character, especially when contrasted to the other German philosophical movements of the time, phenomenology, existentialism and, to some extent, positivism. Although influenced by the same set of events as the other German philosophical movements it was critical theory that was to distinguish itself by addressing the political oppression of the day.

❧ HORKHEIMER, ADORNO, AND THE DIALECTICAL ❧ TRANSFORMATION OF CRITICAL THEORY

Critical theory in the post-1937 period would be characterized by two essentially related perspectives, one which broadened its critique of modes of rationality under the heading 'critique of instrumental reason' and the other which attempted a grand analysis of culture and civilization under the heading 'dialectic of enlightenment'. With the onslaught of the Second World War, Horkheimer and Adorno shared not only a deep pessimism about the future course of rationality but also a loss of hope in the potentialities of a philosophy of history for purposes of social transformation. The confidence in the great potentialities of thought as unleashed by the German Enlightenment went underground, replaced by the pessimism of the two major thinkers of critical theory who gave up not only on being thinkers in solidarity with the proletariat but also on the redemptive powers of rationality itself. In this sense, not only do they represent a critique of what is now quite fashionably called 'modernity', but they may be the harbingers of postmodernity as well.

In the course of the development of critical theory under the ever more pessimistic vision of its principal representatives, the focus would change from Hegel and Marx to Weber. Although they were never to give up entirely on Hegel and Marx, it was Weber who would articulate the pessimistic underside of the Enlightenment which Horkheimer and Adorno would come to admire. Hegel, through his notion of reflection which made a distinction between true and false forms of externalization, between *Entaüsserung* and *Entfremdung*, always sustained the possiblity of reason being able to overcome its falsifications. Marx, although less attentive to this distinction, retained the possibility of overcoming falsification or alienation through social action. Hence, whether it was through the reconciliatory power of reason in the case of Hegel, or the transformative force of social action in the case of Marx, a certain emancipatory project was held intact. Horkheimer, and eventually Adorno, initially endorsed that project. However, when Horkheimer wrote his *Critique of Instrumental Reason* [8.105] it was under the influence of Weber's brilliant, sobering vision regarding reason and action forged through a comprehensive analysis of the genesis and development of western society. Weber had speculated that in the course of western history, reason, as it secularizes, frees itself from its more mythic and religious sources and becomes ever more purposive, more oriented to means to the exclusion of ends. In order to characterize this development, Weber coined the term *Zweckrationalität*, purposive-rational action. Reason, devoid of its redemptive and reconciliatory possibilities, could only be purposive, useful and calculating. Weber had used the metaphor 'iron cage' as an appropriate way of designating the end, the dead-end of modern reason. Horkheimer would take the analysis one step further. His characterization of this course was designated by the term, 'instrumental reason'. Implied in this usage is the overwhelming force of reason for purposes of social control. The combined forces of media, bureaucracy, economy and cultural life would bear down on the modern individual with an accumulated force which could be described only as instrumental. Instrumental reason would represent the ever-expanding ability of those who were in positions of power in the modern world to dominate and control society for their own calculating purposes. So conceived, the kind of analysis which began with the great optimism inaugurated by the German Enlightenment (which sustained the belief that reason could come to comprehend the developing principle of history and therefore society) would end with the pessimistic realization that reason functions for social control, not in the name of enlightenment or emancipation. And what then of a critical theory?

No doubt that question occurred to Horkheimer and Adorno, who, as exiles, now southern Californians, collaborated on what in retrospect must be said to be one of the most fascinating books of modern times, *Dialectic of Enlightenment*. Is enlightenment, the avowed aim of a critical theory, 'self-destructive'? That is the question posed by the book, the thesis of which is contained in its title. Enlightenment, which harbours the very promise of human emancipation, becomes the principle of domination, domination of nature and thus, in certain hands, the basis for the domination of other human beings. In the modern world, knowledge is power. The book begins with an analysis of Bacon's so-called 'scientific attitude'. The relation of 'mind' and 'nature' is 'patriarchal' (*ibid.*, p. 4); 'the human mind, which overcomes superstition, is to hold sway over a disenchanted nature' (*ibid.*). 'What men want to learn from nature is how to use it in order wholly to dominate it and other men. That is the only aim' (*ibid.*). Hence, 'power and knowledge' are the same. But the thesis is more complex. The term 'dialectic' is used here in a form which transcends Hegel's quasi-logical usage. Here dialectic circles back upon itself in such a manner that its subject, enlightenment, both illuminates and destroys. Myth is transformed into enlightenment, but at the price of transforming 'nature into mere objectivity' (*ibid.*, p. 9). The increment of power gained with enlightenment has as its equivalent a simultaneous alienation from nature. The circle is vicious: the greater enlightenment, the greater alienation. Magic, with its desire to control, is replaced by science in the modern world, which has not only the same end but more effective means. According to this thesis, the very inner core of myth is enlightenment. 'The principle of immanence, the explanation of every event as repetition, that the enlightenment upholds against mythic imagination, is the principle of myth itself' (*ibid.*, p. 12). Indeed, they observe, in the modern obsession with the mathematization of nature (the phenomenon so accurately observed by Edmund Husserl in his famous *The Crisis of European Science and Transcendental Phenomenology*) they find representatives of a kind of 'return of the mythic' in the sense that enlightenment always 'intends to secure itself against the return of the mythic'. But it does so by degenerating into the 'mythic cult of positivism'. In this 'mathematical formalism', they claim, 'enlightenment returns to mythology, which it never knew how to elude' (*ibid.*, p. 27). Such is the peculiar character of the dialectic of enlightenment, which turns upon itself in such a way that it is sub-sumed by the very phenomenon it wishes to overcome.

Critical theory distinguishes itself in this period by ever distancing itself from the Marxian heritage with which it originally associated. Some would see this as a departure from the very sources of reason from which it was so effectively nourished. Hence, a form of rationality gone wild. Others might see it from a different perspective. Perhaps the *Dialectic of Enlightenment* represents the coming of age of critical theory as critical theory finally making the turn into the twentieth century. As such, the philosophy of history on which it so comfortably rested, with its secure assumptions about the place of enlightenment in the course of western history (to say nothing of the evolution of class and economy), was undercut by the authors' curious insight into the nature of enlightenment itself. Enlightenment is not necessarily a tem-poral phenomenon given its claims for a particular time and place in modern historical development. Rather, for Horkheimer and Adorno, enlightenment is itself dialectical, a curious phenomenon associated with rationality itself. In this view, the dialectic of enlightenment could be traced to the dawn of human civilization. Here we encounter a form of critical theory influenced not only by Kant, Hegel, Marx and Weber but also by Nietzsche and perhaps Kierkegaard. It would follow that texts that witnessed the evolution of human history would be placed side by side with those which gave testimony to its origin. Enlighten-ment can then be traced not to the so-called German Enlightenment, or to the western European Enlightenment, but to the original written texts of western civilization, which, as any former Gymnasium student knows, were those of Homer. Nietzsche is credited with the insight. 'Nietzsche was one of the few after Hegel who recognized the dialectic of enlightenment' (*ibid.*, p. 44). They credit him with the double insight that while enlightenment unmasks the acts of those who govern, it is also a tool they use under the name of progress to dupe the masses. 'The revelation of these two aspects of the Enlightenment as an historic principle made it possible to trace the notion of enlightenment as progressive thought, back to the beginning of traditional history' (*ibid.*).

Horkheimer and Adorno do not concentrate much on the illusory character of the enlightenment in Homer, 'the basic text of European civilization' as they call it. That element has been over-emphasized by the so-called fascist interpreters of both Homer and Nietzsche. Rather, it is the use or interpretation of myth as an instrument of domination as evidenced in this classic text that they perceive as fundamental. Here, Weber and Nietzsche complement one another. The other side of the dialectic of enlightenment is the thesis on instrumental reason. Hence, the 'individuation' of self which is witnessed in the Homeric text is carried out through what seems to be the opposition of enlightenment and myth. 'The opposition of enlightenment to myth is expressed in the opposition of the surviving individual ego to multifarious fate' (*ibid*., p. 46). The Homeric narrative secularizes the mythic past in the name of the hero's steadfast orientation to his own 'self-preservation'. It secularizes it by learning to dominate it. Learning to dominate has to do with the 'organization' of the self. But the very instrumentality associated with domination has its curious reverse side; something like that which Marcuse would later call 'the return of the repressed'. As they put it regarding Homer, 'Like the heroes of all the true novels later on, Odysseus loses himself in order to find himself; the estrangement from nature that he brings about is realized in the process of the abandonment to nature he contends in each adventure; and, ironically, when he, inexorably, returns home, the inexorable force he commands itself triumphs as the judge and avenger of the legacy of the powers from which he has escaped' (*ibid*., p. 48).

There is no place where this curious double thesis is more effectively borne out than in the phenomenon of sacrifice. Influenced by Ludwig Klage's contention regarding the universality of sacrifice, they observe that individuation undercuts the originary relation of the lunar being to nature which sacrifice implies. 'The establishment of the self cuts through that fluctuating relation with nature that the sacrifice of the self claims to establish' (*ibid*., p. 51). Sacrifice, irrational though it may be, is a kind of enabling device which allows one to tolerate life. 'The venerable belief in sacrifice, however is probably already an impressed pattern according to which the subjected repeat upon themselves the injustice that was done them, enacting it again and again in order to endure it' (*ibid*.). Sacrifice, when universalized and said to apply to the experience of all of humanity, is civilization. Its elimination would occur at enormous expense. The emergence of rationality is based on denial, the denial of the relationship between humanity and nature. 'The very denial, the nucleus of all civilizing rationality, is the germ cell of a proliferating mythic irrationality: with the denial of nature in man not merely the *telos* of the outward control of nature but the *telos* of man's own life is distorted and befogged' (*ibid*., p. 54). The great loss is of course that the human being is no longer able to perceive its relationship to nature in its compulsive preoccupation with self-preservation. The dialectic of enlightenment continues to play itself out. To escape from sacrifice is to sacrifice oneself. Hence the sub-thesis of *Dialectic of Enlightenment*: 'the history of civilization is the history of the introversion of sacrifice. In other words, the history of renunciation' (*ibid*., p. 55). It is this sub-thesis that they associate with the 'prehistory of subjectivity' (*ibid*., p. 54).

The text to which Horkheimer and Adorno have turned their attention is written by Homer, but the story is about the prehistory of western civilization. Odysseus is the prophetic seer who in his deeds would inform the course of action to be followed by future individuals. Odysseus is the 'self who always restrains himself', he sacrifices for the 'abnegation of sacrifice' and through him we witness the 'transformation of sacrifice into subjectivity'. Above all, Odysseus 'survives', but ironically at the 'concession of one's own defeat', an acknowledgement of death. Indeed, the rationality represented by Odysseus is that of 'cunning': a necessity required by having to choose the only route between Scylla and Charybdis in which each god has the 'right' to do its particular task. Together the gods represent 'Olympian Justice' characterized by an 'equivalence between the course, the crime which expiates it, and the guilt arising from that, which in turn reproduces the curse' (*ibid.*, p. 58). This is the pattern of 'all justice in history' which Odysseus opposes. But he does so by succumbing to the power of this justice. He does not find a way to escape the route charted past the Sirens. Instead, he finds a way to outwit the curse by having himself chained to the mast. As one moves from myth to enlightenment, it is cunning with its associated renunciation which characterizes reason. The great promise held by enlightenment is now seen when perceived in retrospect from the perspective of the earlier Horkheimer and Adorno to be domination, repression and cunning.

The thesis contained in *Dialectic of Enlightenment* can be extended beyond the origin of western civilization. As its authors attempt to show, it can be brought back to critique effectively the eighteenth-century Enlightenment as well as attempts to overcome it. As self-preservation was barely seen in Homer as the object of reason, the so-called historical Enlightenment made a fetish of it. 'The system the Enlightenment has in mind is the form of knowledge which copes most proficiently with the facts and supports the individual most effectively in the mastery of nature. Its principles are the principles of self-preservation.' 'Burgher', 'slave owner', 'free entrepreneur' and 'administrator' are its logical subjects. At its best, as represented in Kant, reason was suspended between 'true universality' in which 'universal subjects' can 'overcome the conflict between pure and empirical reason in the conscious solidarity of the whole' (*ibid.*, p. 83), and calculating rationality 'which adjusts the world for the ends of self-preservation'. In this view, Kant's attempts to ground morality in the law of reason came to naught. In fact, Horkheimer and Adorno find more base reasons for Kant's attempt to ground morality in the concept of 'respect'. 'The root of Kantian optimism' is based in this view on the fear of a retreat of 'barbarism'. In any case, in this view the concept of respect was linked to the bourgeois which in latter times no longer existed in the same way. Totalitarianism as represented in fascism no longer needed such concepts nor did it respect the class that harboured them. It would be happy with science as calculation under the banner of self-preservation alone. The link between Kant and Nietzsche is said to be the Marquis de Sade. In Sade's writings, it is argued, we find the triumph of calculating reason, totally individualized, freed from the observation of 'another person'. Here, we encounter a kind of modern reason deprived of any 'substantial goal', 'wholly functionalized', a 'purposeless purposiveness' totally unconcerned about effects which are dismissed as 'purely natural'. Hence, any social arrangement is as good as any other and the 'social necessities' including 'all solidarity with society duty and family' can be dissolved.

If anything, then, enlightenment means 'mass deception' through its fundamental medium of the 'culture industry' where the rationality of 'technology' reigns. 'A technological rationale is the rationale of domination itself' (*ibid.*, p. 121). In film, in music, in art, in leisure this new technology has come to dominate in such a way that the totality of life and experience have been overcome. In the end, in accord with this view, the so-called enlightenment of modern civilization is ironic, total, bitter and universal. Enlightenment as self-deception manifests itself when art and advertising become fused in an idiom of a 'style' that fashions the modern experience as an ideology from which there is no escape. In the blur of modern images, all phenomena are exchangeable. Any object can be exchanged for any other in this 'superstitious fusion of word and thing' (*ibid.*, p. 164). In such a world, fascism becomes entertainment, easily reconciled with all the other words and images and ideologies in the vast arena of modern assimilation.

In the end, *Dialectic of Enlightenment* can be viewed as a kind of crossroads for modern philosophy and social theory. On the one hand, reason can function critically, but on the other, it cannot ground itself in any one perspective. Reason under the image of self-preservation can only function for the purpose of domination. This is critical theory twice removed; removed from its foundations in the Marxism of the nineteenth century from which it attempted to establish its own independence, and removed once again from any foundation to function as a raging power of critique without foundation. In this sense, this book, more than any other to come from the so-called Frankfurt school, hailed the end of philosophy, and did so in part to usher in the era now designated as postmodernity. Thus, it was not only to the successive reconstruction of phenomenology from Husserl through Heidegger that the harbingers of postmodernity could point as legitimate forebears of their own movement, but to the voices which rang out in the *Dialectic of Enlightenment* whose prophetic rage led the way. It was left to Foucault to probe the multiple meanings of the discipline of the self and the institutional repression of the subject unleashed by the

Enlightenment, and to Derrida to articulate the groundlessness of a position which seeks the role of critic but cannot find the way to a privileged perspective which would make possible the proper interpretation.

❧❧ ADORNO AND THE AESTHETIC ❧❧ REHABILITATION OF CRITICAL THEORY

But if critical theory was willing in the late 1940s to give up partially on the Enlightenment and the possibility of a modality of thought that harboured within it a potential for emancipation, it was not totally ready to do so. Hence, critical theory in its curious route from the early 1920s to the present would make one more turn, a turn toward aesthetics. The wager on aesthetics would keep alive, if in muted fashion, the emancipatory hypothesis with which critical theory began. Adorno, inspired in part by Benjamin, would lead the way out from the ashes left in the wake of an instrumental rationality whose end, as the end of philosophy, was almost apparent. If the general claims of the *Dialectic of Enlightenment* were to be sustained, the theoretical consequences for critical theory would be devastating. Hence the question regarding the manner in which a critical theory could be rehabilitated, but this time under the suspicion of a full-blown theory of rationality. In a sense, through Horkheimer's and Adorno's rather devastating analysis of rationality as fundamentally instrumental, and of enlightenment as fundamentally circular, it would have seemed that the very possibility for critique itself would be undermined. The aesthetic redemption of the claims of critical theory would have to be understood from the perspective of the framework of suspicion regarding the claims of cognition. Since cognition would result inevitably in instrumentality, it would be necessary to find a way in which critique could be legitimated without reference to cognition *per se*. Aesthetics, with which Adorno had been fascinated from the time of his earliest published work, would provide a way out. If *Dialectic of Enlightenment* could be read as a critique of cognition, art represents for Adorno a way of overcoming the dilemma established by cognition. Adorno sees the capacity of a non-representational theory in the potentiality of art as manifestation. The explosive power of art remains in its representing that which cannot be represented. In this sense it is the non-identical in art that can represent society, but only as its other. Art functions then for Adorno in the context of the programme of critical theory as a kind of stand-in for a cognitive theory, which cannot be attained under the force of instrumentality.

Adorno, however, was not quite ready to give up on a philosophy of history which had informed his earlier work. Hence, under the influence of Benjamin and in direct contrast to Nietzsche and Heidegger, he was able to incorporate his understanding of art within a theory of progress. At the end of his famous essay 'The Work of Art in the Age of Mechanical Reproduction',[8] originally published in the *Zeitschrift für Sozialforschung* in 1936,[9] Benjamin has postulated the thesis that with photography, 'for the first time in world history, mechanical reproduction emancipates the work of art from its parasitical dependence on ritual'. As a consequence, art no longer needed to sustain a claim on authenticity. After photography, the work of art is 'designed for reproducibility'. From this observation, Benjamin drew a rather astonishing conclusion: 'But the instant the criterion of authenticity ceases to be applicable to artistic production, the total function of art is reversed. Instead of being based on ritual, it begins to be based on another practice – politics' (*ibid.*, p. 244). However, it should not be assumed that the politics with which modern art was to be associated was immediately emancipatory. The thesis was as positive as it was negative. 'The logical result of Fascism is the introduction of aesthetics into political life' (*ibid.*, p. 241). But for Benjamin this was a form of the relationship between aesthetics and politics which would attempt to rekindle the old association between art and ritual. 'The violation of the masses, whom Fascism, with it the Führer cult, forces to their knees, has its counterpart in the violation of an apparatus which is pressed into the production of ritual values' (*ibid.*). However, the tables can be turned; while fascism 'equals the aestheticism of politics', Benjamin claimed, Marxist as he was, that 'communism responds to politicizing art' (*ibid.*, p. 242).

Adorno would use this insight into the nature of art and historical development freed of Benjamin's somewhat materialist orientation. While he affirmed that 'modern art is different from all previous art in that its mode of negation is different' because modernism 'negates tradition itself', Adorno addressed the issue of the relation of art not to fascism but to capitalist society. Beyond that, Adorno's task was to show how art could overcome the dilemma of rationality as defined through the critique of instrumentality, while at the same time sustaining the claim that art had a kind of intelligibility. How could art be something other than a simple representation of that society? Adorno would return to the classical aesthetic idea of mimesis in order to make his point. Art has the capacity to represent, but in its very representation it can transcend that which it is representing. Art survives not by denying but by reconstructing. 'The modernity of art lies in its mimetic relation to a petrified and alienated reality. This, and not the denial of that mute reality, is what makes art speak' (*Aesthetic Theory* [8.23], 31). Art, in other words, represents the non-identical. 'Modern art is constantly practicing the impossible trick of trying to identify the non-identical' (*ibid.*).

Art then can be used to make a kind of claim about rationality. 'Art's disavowal of magical practices – art's own antecedents – signifies that art shares in rationality. Its ability to hold its own *qua* mimesis in the midst of rationality, even while using the means of that rationality, is a response to the evils and irrationality of the bureaucratic world.' Art then is a kind of rationality that contains a certain 'non-rational' element that eludes the instrumental form. This would suggest that it is within the power of art to go beyond instrumental rationality. This is what art can do which cannot be done in capitalist society *per se*. 'Capitalist society hides and disavows precisely this irrationality, whereas art does not.' Art then can be related to truth. Art 'represents truth in the twofold sense of preserving the image of an end smothered completely by rationality and of exposing the irrationality and absurdity of the status quo' (*ibid.*, p. 79).

It is Adorno's claim then that although art may be part and parcel of what Weber described as rationalization, that process of rationalization in which art partakes is not one which leads to domination. Thus, if art is part of what Weber called the 'disenchantment of the world', it leads us in a direction different from that of instrumental reason. Hence, the claim that 'Art mobilizes technology in a different direction than domination does' (*ibid.*, p. 80). And it is for this reason, thinks Adorno, that we must pay attention to the 'dialectics of mimesis and rationality that is intrinsic to art' (*ibid.*).

Whereas the *Dialectic of Enlightenment* could be conceived as a critique of cognition, Adorno uses art to rehabilitate a cognitive claim. 'The continued existence of mimesis, understood as the non-conceptual affinity of a subjective creation with its objective and unposited other, defines art as a form of cognition and to that extent as "rational"' (*ibid.*). Hence, in a time when reason has, in Adorno's view, degenerated to the level of instrumentality, one can turn to art as the expression of the rehabilitation of a form of rationality which can overcome the limitation of reason by expressing its non-identity with itself. In this sense, the claims of critical theory would not be lost but be transformed. Indeed, the earlier emancipatory claims of critical theory would be reappropriated at another level. Here again, Adorno's view seems to be shaped by that of his friend Walter Benjamin. Art can reconcile us to the suffering which can never be expressed in ordinary rational terms. While 'reason can subsume suffering under concepts' and while it can 'furnish means to alleviate suffering', it can never 'express suffering in the medium of experience'. Hence, art has a unique role to play under a transformed understanding, i.e., the role of critical theory. 'What recommends itself, then, is the idea that art may be the only remaining medium of truth in an age of incomprehensible terror and suffering' (*ibid.*, p. 27). In other words, art can anticipate emancipation, but only on the basis of a solidarity with the current state of human existence. 'By cathecting the repressed, art internalizes the repressing principle, i.e. the unredeemed condition of the world, instead of merely airing futile protests against it. Art identifies and expresses that condition, thus anticipating its overcoming' (*ibid.*, p. 26). For Benjamin it was this view of and solidarity with suffering experienced by others in the past which has not been redeemed. For him then, happiness is not simply an empty Enlightenment term. It has a slightly messianic, theological twist. His fundamental thesis was 'Our image of happiness is indissolubly bound up with the image of redemption' (*ibid.*, p. 254).

Finally, if it is possible to look at Adorno's later work on aesthetics from the perspective of the position worked out with Horkheimer in *Dialectic of Enlightenment*, it appears that a case can be made for the retrieval of the earlier emancipatory claims of critical theory on the basis of the non-identical character of the work of art. To be sure, Adorno, along with Horkheimer, had left little room to retrieve a critical theory in the wake of their devastating critique of the claims of reason. Indeed, the claims for art would have to be measured against this very critique. Yet, in a peculiar way, Adorno was consistent with the prior analysis. If reason would always lead to domination, then art would have to base its claim on its ability to express the non-identical. However, the task remained to articulate those claims precisely. In order to do so Adorno would often find himself falling back on a philosophy of history which, by the standards articulated in his earlier critique, he had already invalidated.

❧❧ HABERMAS AND THE RATIONAL ❧❧ RECONSTRUCTION OF CRITICAL THEORY

With Jürgen Habermas, Adorno's one-time student, the discourse over the rehabilitation of critical theory was taken to a higher level. Habermas's initial strategy was to rehabilitate the notion of critique in critical theory. Clearly, Habermas has long-held doubts about the way in which his philosophical mentors in Frankfurt failed to ground a critical theory in a theory of rationality which would harbour an adequate notion of critique. On this he has written eloquently in both *The Theory of Communicative Action* (1981, [8.85]) and *The Philosophical Discourse of Modernity* (1985, [8.88]). What I have found interesting in studying the works of Habermas is the manner in which the argument for a critical theory of rationality began to take shape as an alternative argument to the one which Horkheimer and Adorno put forth. In this context, Habermas would avail himself of certain resources within the tradition of contemporary German philosophy which his mentors overlooked. I suggested earlier that German philosophy since Kant has been shaped by the interaction between the themes of constitution and transformation. If modern critical theory began with a relatively firm belief that the grounds for the emancipatory assumptions regarding critique were clear and given in a certain orientation toward theory, in retrospect that foundation became ever less secure. Eventually, critique, as in *Dialectic of Enlightenment*, became caught in a never-ending circle of internal repression and external domination. Hence, the promise of critical theory had been undermined. It was the great merit of Habermas's early work to have seen the dilemma and to have addressed it in terms of turning not to the transformative but to the constitutive element in the German philosophical tradition. Critical theory was for Habermas, at least originally, the problem of 'valid knowledge', i.e., an epistemological problem.

It should come as no surprise then that when Habermas first juxtaposes traditional and critical theory, following in the footsteps of Horkheimer's 1937 article, he engages Edmund Husserl not only on the status of theory but also on the nature of science. By so doing, he appropriates two of the themes that were germane and of a piece in late transcendental phenomenology, namely, the association of the concept of theory with a more or less political notion of liberation or emancipation and the preoccupation of phenomenology with the status of science.

As early as the writing of *Knowledge and Human Interests* (1969, [8.82]), Habermas sustained the thesis that critical theory could be legitimated on the basis of making apparent the undisclosed association between knowledge and interest. This association, however, could be specified only on the basis of the clarification of theory in its more classical form. According to Habermas *theoria* was a kind of mimesis in the sense that in the contemplation of the cosmos one reproduces internally what one perceives externally. Theory then, even in its traditional form, is conceived to be related to the 'conduct of one's life'. In fact, in this interpretation of the traditional view, the appropriation of a theoretical attitude creates a certain ethos among its practitioners. Husserl is said to have sustained this 'traditional' notion of theory. Hence, when Husserl approached the question of science he approached it on the basis of his prior commitment to the classical understanding of theory.

In Habermas's view, it is this commitment to theory in the classical sense which determines Husserl's critique of science. Husserl's attack on the objectivism of the sciences led to the claim that knowledge of the objective world has a 'transcendental' basis in the pre-scientific world, that sciences, because of their prior commitment to mundane knowledge of the world, are unable to free themselves from interest, and that phenomenology, through its method of transcendental self-reflection, can free this association of knowledge and mundane interest through a commitment to a theoretical attitude which has been defined traditionally. In this view, the classical conception of theory, which phenomenology borrows, frees one from interest in the ordinary world with the result that a certain 'therapeutic power', as well as a 'practical efficacy', is claimed for phenomenology.

Habermas endorses Husserl's procedure, while at the same time pointing out its error. Husserl is said to be correct in his critique of science, which, because of its 'objectivist illusion', embedded in a belief in a 'reality-in-itself', leaves the matter of the constitution of these facts undisclosed with the result that it is unaware of the connection between knowledge and interest. In Husserl's view, phenomenology, which makes this clear, can rightfully claim for itself, against the pretensions of the sciences, the designation 'pure theory'. Precisely here Husserl would bring the practical efficacy of phenomenology to bear. Phenomenology would be said to free one from the ordinary scientific attitude. But phenomenology is in error because of its blind acceptance of the implicit ontology present in the classical definition of theory. Theory in its classical form was thought to find in the structure of the 'ideal world' a prototype for the order of the human world. Habermas says in a rather insightful manner, 'Only as cosmology was *theoria* also capable of orienting human action' ([8.82], 306). If that is the case, then the phenomenological method which relied on the classical concept of theory was to have a certain 'practical efficacy', which was interpreted to mean that a certain 'pseudonormative power' could be derived from the 'concealment of its actual interest'.

In the end, phenomenology, which sought to justify itself on the basis of its freedom from interest, has instead an undisclosed interest which it derived from a classical ontology. Habermas believes classical ontology in turn can be characterized historically. In fact, the concept of theory is said to be derived from a particular stage in human emancipation where *catharsis*, which had been engendered heretofore by the 'mystery cults', was now taken into the realm of human action by means of 'theory'. This in turn would mark a new stage, but certainly not the last stage, in the development of human 'identity'. At this stage, individual identity could be achieved only through the indentification with the 'abstract laws of cosmic order'. Hence, theory represents the achievements of a consciousness that is emancipated, but not totally. It is emancipated from certain 'archaic powers', but it still requires a certain relationship to the cosmos in order to achieve its identity. Equally, although pure theory could be characterized as an 'illusion', it was conceived as a 'protection' from 'regression to an earlier stage'. And here we encounter the major point of Habermas's critique, namely, the association of the contemplative attitude, which portends to dissociate itself from any interest, and the contradictory assumption that the quest for pure knowledge is conducted in the name of a certain practical interest, namely, the emancipation from an earlier stage of human development.

The conclusion is that both Husserl and the sciences he critiques are wrong. Husserl is wrong because he believes that the move to pure theory is a step which frees knowledge from interest. In fact, as we have seen, the redeeming aspect of Husserl's phenomenology is that it does in fact have a practical intent. The sciences are wrong because although they assume the purely contemplative attitude, they use that aspect of the classical concept of theory for their own purposes. In other words, the sciences use the classical concept of pure theory to sustain an insular form of positivism while they cast off the 'practical content' of that pure theory. As a consequence, they assume that their interest remains undisclosed.

Significantly, when Habermas turns to his critique of science, he sides with Husserl. This means that Husserl has rightly critiqued the false scientific assumption that 'theoretical propositions' are to be correlated with 'matters of fact', an 'attitude' which assumes the 'self-existence' of 'empirical variables' as they are represented in 'theoretical propositions'. But not only has Husserl made the proper distinction between the theoretical and the empirical, he has appropriately shown that the scientific attitude 'suppresses the transcendental framework that is the precondition of the meaning of the validity of such propositions' (*ibid.*, p. 307). It would follow, then, that if the proper distinction were made between the empirical and the theoretical and if the transcendental framework were made manifest, which would expose the meaning of such propositions, then the 'objectivist illusion' would 'dissolve' and 'knowledge constitutive' interests would be made 'visible'. It would follow that there is nothing wrong with the theoretical attitude as long as it is united with its practical intent and there is nothing wrong with the introduction of a transcendental framework, as long as it makes apparent the heretofore undisclosed unity of knowledge and interest.

What is interesting about this analysis is that the framework for the notion of critique is not to be derived from dialectical reason as Horkheimer originally thought but from transcendental phenomenology. One must be careful here. I do not wish to claim that Habermas identifies his position with Husserl. Rather, it can be demonstrated that he derives his position on critique from a critique of transcendental phenomenology. As such, he borrows both the transcendental framework for critique and the emphasis on theory as distinguished from empirical fact that was established by Husserl. Therefore, at that point he argues for a 'critical social science' which relies on a 'concept of self-reflection' which can 'determine the meaning of the validity of critical propositions'. Such a conception of critical theory borrows from the critique of traditional theory the idea of an 'emancipatory cognitive interest' which, when properly demythologized, is based not on an emancipation from a mystical notion of universal powers of control but rather from a more modern interest in 'autonomy and responsibility'. This latter interest will appear later in his thought as the basis for moral theory.

On the basis of this analysis, one might make some observations. Clearly, from the point of view of the development of critical theory, Habermas rightfully saw the necessity of rescuing the concept of critique. Implicit in that attempt is not only the rejection of *Dialectic of Enlightenment* but also Adorno's attempt to rehabilitate critical theory on the basis of aesthetics. However – and there is considerable evidence to support this assumption – the concept of critical theory which had informed Horkheimer's early essay on that topic had fallen on hard times. As the members of the Institute for Social Research gradually withdrew from the Marxism that had originally informed their concept of critique, so the foundations upon which critical theory was built began to crumble. Habermas's reconceptualization of the notion of critique was obviously both innovative and original. It was also controversial. Critique would not be derived from a philosophy of history based on struggle but from a moment of self-reflection based on a theory of rationality. As Habermas's position developed it is that self-reflective moment which would prove to be interesting.

❧ HABERMAS: CRITIQUE AND VALIDITY ❧

Critique, which was rendered through the unmasking of an emancipatory interest *vis-à-vis* the introduction of a transcendentalized moment of self-reflection, re-emerges in the later, as opposed to the earlier, works of Habermas at the level of validity. The link between validity and critique can be established through the transcendentalized moment of self-reflection which was associated with making apparent an interest in autonomy and responsibility. Later, that moment was transformed through a theory of communicative rationality to be directed to issues of consensus. Validity refers to a certain background consensus which can be attained through a process of idealization. As critique was originally intended to dissociate truth from ideology, validity distinguished between that which can be justified and that which cannot.

Hence, it readdresses the claims for autonomy and responsibility at the level of communication. It could be said that the quest for validity is superimposed upon the quest for emancipation. There are those who would argue that moral theory which finds its basis in communicative action has replaced the older critical theory with which Habermas was preoccupied in *Knowledge and Human Interests*. I would argue somewhat differently that Habermas's more recent discourse theory of ethics and law is based on the reconstructed claims of a certain version of critical theory.

However, before justifying this claim, I will turn to the basic paradigm shift in Habermas's work from the philosophy of the subject to the philosophy of language involving construction of a theory of communicative action on the one hand and the justification of a philosophical postion anchored in modernity on the other. Both moves can be referenced to the debate between earlier and later critical theory.

If Horkheimer's, and later Adorno's, concept of 'instrumental rationality' is but a reconstruction of Max Weber's concept of purposive-rational action, it would follow that a comprehensive critique of that view could be directed to Weber's theory of rationalization. In Habermas's book, *The Theory of Communicative Action*, it is this theory that is under investigation as seen through the paradigm of the philosophy of consciousness. Weber's thesis can be stated quite simply: if western rationality has been reduced to its instrumental core, then it has no further prospects for regenerating itself. Habermas wants to argue that the failure of Weber's analysis, and by implication the failure of those like Horkheimer and Adorno who accepted Weber's thesis, was to conceive of processes of rationalization in terms of subject–object relations. In other words, Weber's analysis cannot be dissociated from Weber's theory of rationality. According to this analysis, his theory of rationality caused him to conceive of things in terms of subject–object relations. Habermas's thesis, against Weber, Horkheimer and Adorno, is that a theory of rationality which conceives of things in terms of subject–object relations cannot conceive of those phenomena in other than instrumental terms. In other words, all subject–object formulations are instrumental. Hence, if one were to construct a theory of rationalization in non-instrumental terms, it would be necessary to construct an alternative theory of rationality. The construction of a theory of communicative action based on a philosophy of language rests on this assumption.

In Habermas's view, the way out of the dilemma of instrumentality into which earlier critical theory led us is through a philosophy of language which, through a reconstructed understanding of speech-act theory, can make a distinction between strategic and communicative action. Communicative action can be understood to be non-instrumental in this sense: 'A communicatively achieved agreement has a rational basis; it cannot be imposed by either party, whether instrumentally through intervention in the situation directly or strategically through influencing decisions of the opponents' ([8.85], p. 287). It is important to note that the question of validity, which I argued a moment ago was the place where the emancipatory interest would be sustained, emerges. A communicative action has within it a claim to validity which is in principle criticizable, meaning that the person to whom such a claim is addressed can respond with either a yes or a no based, in turn, on reasons. Beyond that, if Habermas is to sustain his claim to overcoming the dilemma of instrumental reason he must agree that communicative actions are foundational. They cannot be reducible to instrumental or strategic actions. If communicative actions were reducible to instrumental or strategic actions, one would be back in the philosophy of consciousness where it was claimed by Habermas, and a certain form of earlier critical theory as well, that all action was reducible to strategic or instrumental action.[10]

It is Habermas's conviction that one can preserve the emancipatory thrust of modernity by appropriating the discursive structure of language at the level of communication. Hence, the failure of *Dialectic of Enlightenment* was to misread modernity in an oversimplified way influenced by those who had given up on it. Here is represented a debate between a position anchored in a philosophy of history which can no longer sustain an emancipatory hypothesis on the basis of historical interpretation, and a position which finds emancipatory claims redeemable, but on a transcendental level. Ultimately, the rehabilitation of critical theory concerns the nature and definition of philosophy. If the claims of critical theory can be rehabilitated on a transcendental level as the claims of a philosophy of language, then it would appear that philosophy as such can be defined *vis-à-vis* a theory of communicative action. Habermas's claim that the originary mode of language is communicative presupposes a contrafactual communicative community which is by nature predisposed to refrain from instrumental forms of domination. Hence, the assertion of communicative over strategic forms of discursive interaction assumes a political form of association which is written into the nature of language as such as the guarantor of a form of progressive emancipation. In other words, if one can claim that the original form of discourse is emancipatory, then the dilemma posed by instrumental reason has been overcome and one is secure from the seductive temptation of the dialectic of enlightenment.

❧❧ NOTES ❧❧

1 There are three excellent works on the origin and development of critical theory. The most comprehensive is the monumental work by R. Wiggershaus [8.140]. M. Jay's historical work [8.131] introduced a whole generation of Americans to critical theory. Helmut Dubiel [8.128] presents the development of critical theory against the backdrop of German and international politics.

2 Hegel, *Phenomenology of Spirit*, Oxford: Oxford University Press, 1977.

3 *Ibid.*, p. 111.

4 K. Marx, 'On the Jewish Question', in *The Marx–Engels Reader*, ed. R. Tucker, New York: Norton, 1972.

5 *Ibid.*, pp. 110–65.

6 *Ibid.*, pp. 83–103.

7 M. Horkheimer, 'Traditional and Critical Theory', in *Critical Theory*, New York: Herder & Herder, 1972.

8 W. Benjamin, 'The Work of Art in the Age of Mechanical Reproduction', *Illuminations* [8.36].

9 *Zeitschrift für Sozialforschung*, 5:1 (1936).

10 For a more comprehensive analysis of the issues involved in this distinction, see my discussion in [8.96].

❧❧ SELECT BIBLIOGRAPHY ❧❧

Journals of the Institute of Social Research

8.1 *Archiv für die Geschichte des Sozialismus und der Arbeiterbewegung*, I-XV, 1910–30.

8.2 *Zeitschrift für Sozialforschung*, vols 1–8, 2, Leipzig, Paris, New York, 1932–9.

8.3 *Studies in Philosophy and Social Science*, New York, 1940–1.

8.4 *Frankfurter Beiträge zur Soziologie*, Frankfurt, 1955–74.

Adorno

Primary texts

For Adorno's collected works, see *Gesammelte Schriften* [GS] (23 volumes), ed. R. Tiedemann, Frankfurt: Suhrkamp, 1970– . See also *Akte: Theodor Adorno 1924–1968*, in the archives of the former philosophy faculty at the University of Frankfurt.

For a bibliography of Adorno's work, see René Görtzen's 'Theodor W. Adorno: Vorläufige Bibliographie seiner Schriften und der Sekundärliteratur', in *Adorno Konferenze 1983*, ed. L. Friedeburg and J. Habermas, Frankfurt: Suhrkamp, 1983.

8.5 *Kierkegaard: Konstruktion des ästhetischen*, Tübingen, 1933.

8.6　*Philosophie der neuen Musik*, Tübingen: Mohr, 1949.
8.7　*The Authoritarian Personality*, co-authored with E. Frenkel-Brunswick, D. Levinson, and R. Sanford, New York: Harper, 1950 (2nd edn, New York: Norton, 1969).
8.8　*Minima Moralia: Reflexionen aus dem beschädigten Leben*, Berlin and Frankfurt: Suhrkamp, 1980.
8.9　*Prismen: Kulturkritik und Gesellschaft*, Frankfurt: Suhrkamp, 1955.
8.10　*Noten zur Literatur I*, Frankfurt: Suhrkamp, 1974.
8.11　*Jargon der Eigentlichkeit*, Frankfurt: Suhrkamp, 1964.
8.12　*Negativ Dialektik*, Frankfurt: Suhrkamp, 1966.
8.13　*The Positivist Dispute in German Sociology*, introduction and two essays by Adorno, London: Heinemann, 1969.
8.14　*Ästhetische Theorie*, in *GS*, vol. 7, 1970.
8.15　*Noten zur Literatur*, ed. R. Tiedemann, in *GS*, vol. 11, 1974.
8.16　*Hegel: Three Studies*, Cambridge, Mass.: MIT Press, 1993.

Translations

8.17　*Philosophy of Modern Music*, London: Sheed & Ward, 1973.
8.18　*Minima Moralia: Reflections from Damaged Life*, London: New Left Books, 1974.
8.19　*Prisms*, London: Neville Spearman, 1967.
8.20　*Jargon of Authenticity*, London: Routledge & Kegan Paul, 1973.
8.21　*Negative Dialectics*, New York: Seabury Press, 1973.
8.22　*Against Epistemology: A Metacritique*, Cambridge, Mass.: MIT Press, 1982.
8.23　*Aesthetic Theory*, London: Routledge & Kegan Paul, 1984.
8.24　*Notes to Literature*, 2 vols, New York: Columbia University Press, 1992.

Criticisms

8.25　Brunkhorst, H. *Theodor W. Adorno, Dialektik der Moderne*, München: Piper, 1990.
8.26　Früchtl, J. and Calloni, M., *Geist gegen den Zeitgeist: Erinnern an Adorno*, Frankfurt: Suhrkamp, 1991.
8.27　Jay, M. *Adorno*, Cambridge, Mass.: Harvard University Press, 1984.
8.28　Lindner, B. and Ludke, M. (eds) *Materialien zur ästhetischen Theorie Theodor W. Adorno's: Konstruktion der Moderne*, Frankfurt: Suhrkamp, 1980.
8.29　Wellmer, A. *Zur Dialektik von Moderne und Postmoderne: Vernunftkritik nach Adorno*, Frankfurt: Suhrkamp, 1985.

Adorno and Horkheimer

8.30　*Dialektik der Aufklärung*, Amsterdam: Querido, 1947.
8.31　*Sociologia*, Frankfurt: Europäische Verlagsanstalt, 1962.

Benjamin

Primary texts

For Benjamin's collected works, see *Gesammelte Schriften* (7 vols), ed. R. Tiedemann and H. Schweppenhäuser, Frankfurt: Suhrkamp, 1972–89. See also *Briefe* (2 vols), ed. G. Scholem and T. Adorno, Frankfurt: Suhrkamp, 1966; *Schriften* (2 vols), ed. T. Adorno and G. Scholem, Frankfurt 1955. See also *Habilitationakte Walter Benjamins* in the archive of the former philosophy faculty at the University of Frankfurt. For a bibliography see R. Tiedemann, 'Bibliographie der Erstdrucke von Benjamins Schriften', in *Zur Aktualität Walter Benjamins*, Frankfurt: Suhrkamp, 1972, pp. 227–97.

8.32 *Deutsche Menschen: Eine Folge von Briefen*, written under pseudonym Detlef Holz, Frankfurt: Suhrkamp, 1977.
8.33 *Zur Kritik der Gewalt und andere Aufsätze*, Frankfurt: Suhrkamp, 1965.
8.34 *Berliner Chronik*, ed. G. Scholem, Frankfurt: Suhrkamp, 1970.
8.35 *Moskauer Tagebuch*, ed. G. Smith, Frankfurt: Suhrkamp, 1980.

Translations

8.36 *Illuminations, Essays and Reflections*, ed. and introduced by H. Arendt, New York: Schocken, 1968.
8.37 *Charles Baudelaire; A Lyric Poet in the Era of High Capitalism*, London: New Left Books, 1973.
8.38 *Understanding Brecht*, London: New Left Books, 1973.
8.39 *Communication and the Evolution of Society*, Boston: Beacon Press, 1979.

Criticism

8.40 Buck-Morss, S. *The Dialectics of Seeing: Walter Benjamin and the Arcades Project*, Cambridge, Mass.: MIT Press, 1989.
8.41 Roberts, J. *Walter Benjamin*, London: Macmillan Press, 1982.
8.42 Scheurmann, I. and Scheurmann, K. *Für Walter Benjamin: Dokumente, Essays und ein Entwurf*, Frankfurt: Suhrkamp, 1992.
8.43 Scholem, G. *The Correspondence of Walter Benjamin and Gerschom Scholem*: Mass.: Harvard University Press, 1992. Frankfurt, 1975.
8.44 Tiedemann, R. *Studien zur Walter Benjamins*, Frankfurt: Suhrkamp, 1973.

Fromm

For his collected works, see *Gesamtausgabe* (10 vols), ed. R. Funk, Stuttgart: Deutsche Verlags-Anstalt, 1980–1. A bibliography is found in vol. 10.

8.45 'Die Entwicklung des Christusdogmas: Eine psychoanalytische Studie zur sozialpsychologischen Funktion der Religion', *Imago*, 3:4 (1930).
8.46 *Escape From Freedom*, New York: Farrar & Rinehart, 1941.

8.47 *Man for Himself: An Inquiry into the Psychology of Ethics*, New York: Rinehart, 1947.

8.48 *The Sane Society*, New York: Rinehart, 1955.

8.49 *The Art of Loving*, New York: Rinehart, 1956.

8.50 *Beyond the Chains of Illusion: My Encounter with Marx and Freud*, New York: Simon & Schuster, 1962.

8.51 *The Heart of Man*, New York: Harper & Row, 1964.

8.52 *The Anatomy of Human Destructiveness*, New York: Holt, Rinehart, Winston, 1973.

8.53 *To Have or To Be?* New York: Harper & Row, 1976.

Grünberg

8.54 'Festrede gehalten zur Einweihung des Instituts für Sozialforschung an der Universität Frankfurt a.M. am 22 Juni 1924', *Frankfurter Universitätsreden*, 20 (1924).

Habermas

Primary texts

8.55 *Das Absolute und die Geschichte: von der Zweispaltigkeit in Schellings Denken*, dissertation, Universität Bonn, 1954.

8.56 *Strukturwandel der Öffenlichkeit*, Berlin: Luchterland, 1962.

8.57 *Technik und Wissenschaft als Ideologie*, Frankfurt: Suhrkamp, 1968.

8.58 *Erkenntnis und Interesse*, Frankfurt: Suhrkamp, 1969.

8.59 *Theorie und Praxis*, (2nd edn) Frankfurt: Suhrkamp, 1971.

8.60 *Kultur und Kritik: Verstreute Aufsätze*, Frankfurt: Suhrkamp, 1973.

8.61 *Legitimationsprobleme im Spätkapitalismus*, Frankfurt: Suhrkamp, 1973.

8.62 *Zur Rekonstruktion des Historischen Materialismus*, Frankfurt: Suhrkamp, 1976.

8.63 *Communication and the Evolution of Society*, Boston: Beacon Press, 1979.

8.64 *Theorie des kommunikativen Handelns*, 2 vols, Frankfurt: Suhrkamp, 1981.

8.65 *Zur Logik der Sozialwissenschaften*, 5th edn, Frankfurt: Suhrkamp, 1982.

8.66 *Moralbewußtsein und kommunikatives Handeln*, Frankfurt: Suhrkamp, 1983.

8.67 *Vorstudien und Ergänzungen zur Theorie des kommunikativen Handelns*, Frankfurt: Suhrkamp, 1984.

8.68 *Philosophische Diskurs der Moderne*, Frankfurt: Suhrkamp, 1985.

8.69 *Eine Art Schadensabwicklung*, Frankfurt, Suhrkamp, 1987.

8.70 *Nachmetaphysisches Denken*, Frankfurt: Suhrkamp, 1988.

8.71 *Texte und Kontexte*, Frankfurt: Suhrkamp, 1990.

8.72 *Erläuterungen zur Diskursethik*, Frankfurt: Suhrkamp, 1991.

8.73 *Vergangenheit als Zukunft*, Zürich: Pendo Interview, 1991.

8.74 *Faktizität und Geltung: Beiträge zur Diskurstheorie des Rechts und des demokratischen Rechtsstaats*, Frankfurt: Suhrkamp, 1992.

Translations

8.75 *Structural Change of the Public Sphere*, Cambridge, Mass.: MIT Press, 1989.
8.76 *Toward a Rational Society*, London: Heinemann, 1971.
8.77 *Knowledge and Human Interests*, Boston: Beacon Press, 1971.
8.78 *Theory and Practice*, London: Heinemann, 1974.
8.79 *Legitimation Crisis*, Boston: Beacon Press, 1975.
8.80 *The Theory of Communicative Action*, 2 vols, Boston: Beacon Press, 1984, 1987.
8.81 *On the Logic of the Social Sciences*, Cambridge, Mass., MIT Press, 1988.
8.82 *Moral Consciousness and Communicative Action*, Cambridge, Mass.: MIT Press, 1989.
8.83 *The Philosophical Discourse of Modernity*, Cambridge, Mass.: MIT Press, 1987.
8.84 *The New Conservatism: Cultural Criticism and the Historians' Debate*, Cambridge, Mass.: MIT Press, 1989.
8.85 *Post-Metaphysical Thinking*, Cambridge, Mass.: MIT Press, 1992.

Criticism

8.86 Arato, A. and Cohen J. (eds) *Civil Society and Political Theory*, Cambridge, Mass.: MIT Press, 1992.
8.87 Bernstein, R. (ed.) *Habermas and Modernity*, Cambridge, Mass.: MIT Press, 1985.
8.88 Calhoun, C. (ed.) *Habermas and the Public Sphere*, Cambridge, Mass.: MIT Press, 1992.
8.89 Dallmayr, W. (ed.) *Materialen zu Habermas 'Erkenntnis und Interesse'*, Frankfurt: Suhrkamp, 1974.
8.90 Flynn, B. *Political Philosophy at the Closure of Metaphysics*, London: Humanities Press, 1992.
8.91 Held, D. and Thompson, J. (eds) *Habermas: Critical Debates*, Cambridge, Mass.: MIT Press, 1982.
8.92 Honneth, A. *Kritik der Macht*, Frankfurt: Suhrkamp, 1985.
8.93 Honneth, A. and Joas, H. (eds) *Communicative Action: Essays on Jürgen Habermas' Theory of Communicative Action*, Cambridge, Mass.: MIT Press, 1991.
8.94 Honneth, A. *et al.* (eds) *Zwischenbetrachtungen im Prozess der Aufklärung*, Frankfurt: Suhrkamp, 1989.
8.95 McCarthy, T. *The Critical Theory of Jürgen Habermas*, Cambridge, Mass.: MIT Press, 1978.
8.96 Rasmussen, D. *Reading Habermas*, Oxford: Basil Blackwell, 1990.
Rasmussen, D. (ed.) *Universalism and Communitarianism*, Cambridge, Mass.: MIT Press, 1988.
8.97 Schnädelbach, H. *Reflexion und Diskurs*, Frankfurt: Suhrkamp, 1977.

8.98   Thompson, J. *Critical Hermeneutics: A Study in the Thought of Paul Ricoeur and Jürgen Habermas*, New York: Cambridge University Press, 1981.

Horkheimer

For Horkheimer's collected works, see *Gesammelte Schriften* (18 vols), ed. G. Noerr and A. Schmidt, Frankfurt: Fischer, 1987– . Most of Horkheimer's essays in the *Zeitschrift für Sozialforschung* are found in *Kritische Theorie: Eine Dokumentation* (2 vols), ed. A. Schmidt, Frankfurt: Fischer, 1968. See also *Akte Max Horkheimer, 1922–65* in the archives of the former philosophy faculty at the University of Frankfurt. For a bibliography, see *Horkheimer Heute*, ed. A. Schmidt and N. Altwicker, Frankfurt: Fischer, 1986, pp. 372–99.

8.99   'Die Gegenwärtige Lage der Sozialphilosophie und die Aufgaben eines Instituts für Sozialforschung', *Frankfurter Universitätsreden*, 37 (1931).
8.100 *Dämmerung*, written under the pseudonym Heinrich Regius, Zürich: Oprecht and Helbling, 1934.
8.101 *Eclipse of Reason*, New York: Oxford University Press, 1974.
8.102 'Zum Begriff der Vernunft', *Frankfurter Universitätsreden*, 7 (1953).
8.103 *Kritische Theorie: Eine Dokumentation*, 2 vols, ed. A. Schmidt, Frankfurt: Fischer, 1968.
8.104 *Critical Theory*, New York: Herder & Herder, 1972.
8.105 *Critique of Instrumental Reason*, New York: Seabury Press, 1974.

Criticism

8.106 Gumnior, H. and Ringguth, R. *Horkheimer*, Reinbeck bei Hamburg: Rowohlt, 1973.
8.107 Tar, Z. *The Frankfurt School: The Critical Theories of Max Horkheimer and Theodor Adorno*, New York: Wiley, 1977.

Lowenthal

For his collected works, see *Schriften* (4 vols), ed. H. Dubiel, Frankfurt, 1980.

8.108 *Prophets of Deceit: A Study of the Techniques of the American Agitator*, Palo Alto: Pacific Books, 1970.
8.109 *Literature and the Image of Man*, Boston: Beacon Press, 1957.
8.110 *Literature, Popular Culture, and Society*, Palo Alto: Pacific Books, 1968.
8.111 *Critical Theory and Frankfurt Theorists: Lectures, Correspondence, Conversations*, New Brunswick: Transaction Books, 1989.

Marcuse

For Marcuse's collected works, see *Gesammelte Schriften* (9 vols), Frankfurt: Suhrkamp, 1978–87. For a complete bibliography of Marcuse's works, see *The Critical Spirit: Essays in Honor of Herbert Marcuse*, ed. K. Wolff and B. Moore, Boston: Beacon Press, 1967.

8.112 *Reason and Revolution: Hegel and the Rise of Social Theory*, New York: Oxford University Press, 1941.
8.113 *Eros and Civilization: A Philosophical Inquiry Into Freud*, Boston: Beacon Press, 1955.
8.114 *Reason and Revolution: Hegel and the Rise of Social Theory*, 2nd edn, Boston: Beacon Press, 1960.
8.115 *Eros and Civilization*, 2nd edn, with preface, 'Political Preface, 1966', Boston: Beacon Press, 1966.
8.116 *Negations: Essays in Critical Theory*, Boston: Beacon Press, 1968.
8.117 *Counterrevolution and Revolt*, Boston: Beacon Press, 1972.
8.118 *The Aesthetic Dimension: Towards a Critique of Marxist Aesthetics*, Boston: Beacon Press, 1978.

Criticism

8.119 Görlich, B. *Die Wette mit Freud: Drei Studien zu Herbert Marcuse*, Frankfurt: Nexus, 1991.
8.120 Institut für Sozialforschung (eds) *Kritik und Utopie im Werk von Herbert Marcuse*, Frankfurt: Suhrkamp, 1992.
8.121 Pippin, R. (ed.) *Marcuse: A Critical Theory and the Promise of Utopia*, South Hadley: Bergin & Garvey, 1988.

Pollock

8.122 *The Economic and Social Consequences of Automation*, Oxford: Basil Blackwell, 1957.

General criticism

8.123 Benhabib, S. *Critique, Norm, and Utopia: A Study of the Foundations of Critical Theory*, New York: Columbia University Press, 1986.
8.124 Benhabib, S. and Dallmayr, F. (eds) *The Communicative Ethics Controversy*, Cambridge, Mass.: MIT Press, 1990.
8.125 Bubner, R. *Essays in Hermeneutics and Critical Theory*, New York: Columbia University Press, 1988.
8.126 Dallmayr. F. *Between Freiberg and Frankfurt: Toward a Critical Ontology*, Amherst: University of Massachusetts Press, 1991.
8.127 Dubiel, H. *Kritische Theorie der Gesellschaft*, München: Juventa, 1988.

8.128 Dubiel, H. *Theory and Politics*, Cambridge, Mass.: MIT Press, 1985.

8.129 Guess, R. *The Idea of Critical Theory*, Cambridge: Cambridge University Press, 1981.

8.130 Held, D. *An Introduction to Critical Theory*, London: Hutchinson, 1980.

8.131 Jay, M. *The Dialectical Imagination: A History of the Frankfurt School and the Institute of Social Research, 1923–1950*, Boston: Little Brown, 1973.

8.132 Kearney, R. *Modern Movements in European Philosophy*, Manchester: Manchester University Press, 1987.

8.133 Kellner, D. *Critical Theory, Marxism and Modernity*, Baltimore: Johns Hopkins University Press, 1989.

8.134 McCarthy, T. *Ideal and Illusions: On Reconstruction and Deconstruction in Contemporary Critical Theory*, Cambridge, Mass.: MIT Press, 1991.

8.135 Marcus, J. and Tar, Z. (eds) *Foundations of the Frankfurt School of Social Research*, London: Transaction Books, 1984.

8.136 Norris, C. *What's Wrong with Postmodernism: Critical Theory and the Ends of Philosophy*, Baltimore: Johns Hopkins University Press, 1990.

8.137 O'Neill, J. (ed.) *On Critical Theory*, New York: Seabury Press, 1976.

8.138 Schmidt, A. *Zur Idee der Kritischen Theorie*, München: Hanser, 1974.

8.139 Wellmer, A. *Critical Theory of Society*, New York: Seabury Press, 1974.

8.140 Wiggershaus, R. *Die Frankfurter Schule*, Munchen: Hanser, 1986.

I wish to thank James Swindal for his assistance in the preparation of the bibliography.

CHAPTER 9

Hermeneutics
Gadamer and Ricoeur
G. B. Madison

❧•❀•☙

❧❧ THE HISTORICAL BACKGROUND: ❧❧
ROMANTIC HERMENEUTICS

Although the term 'hermeneutics' (*hermeneutica*) is, in its current usage, of early modern origin,[1] the practice it refers to is as old as western civilization itself. Under the traditional appellation of *ars interpretandi*, hermeneutics designates the art of textual interpretation, as instanced in biblical exegesis and classical philology. In modern times, hermeneutics progressively redefined itself as a general, overall discipline dealing with the principles regulating all forms of interpretation. It was put forward as a discipline that is called into play whenever we encounter texts (or text-analogues) whose meaning is not readily apparent and which accordingly require an active effort on the part of the interpreter in order to be made intelligible. In addition to this exegetical function, hermeneutics also viewed its task as that of drawing out the practical consequences of the interpreted meaning ('application'). This dual role of understanding (or explanation) (*subtilitas intelligendi, subtilitas explicandi*) and application (*subtilitas applicandi*) is perhaps especially evident in the case of juridical hermeneutics where the task is not only to ascertain the 'meaning' or 'intent' of the law but also to discern how best to *apply* it in the circumstances at hand.

In the early nineteenth century, at the hands of Friedrich Schleiermacher (1768–1834), the scope of hermeneutics was expanded considerably. Indeed, Schleiermacher claimed for hermeneutics the status of an overall theory (*allgemeine Hermeneutik*) specifying the procedures and rules for the understanding not only of textual meaning but of cultural meaning in general (*Kunstlehre*). Rooted in the romantic tradition, Schleiermacher, often referred to as the 'father of hermeneutics', empha-

290

sized the 'psychological' or 'divinatory' function of hermeneutics – the purpose of interpretation being that of 'divining' the intentions of an author, or, in other words, reconstructing psychologically an author's mental life ('to understand the discourse just as well as and even better than its creator').[2] The purpose of hermeneutics is thus that of unearthing the original meaning of a text, this being equated by Schleiermacher with the meaning originally intended by the author.[3] This view of hermeneutics as a form of cultural understanding (understanding another culture or historical epoch, for instance) and the concomitant, 'psychological' view of understanding (as a grasping of the subjective intentions of authors or actors) was developed more fully towards the end of the century by Wilhelm Dilthey (1833–1911).

One of the most salient features of the nineteenth century was the rapid expansion of the human sciences (*Geisteswissenschaften*), historiography in particular. The task that Dilthey set himself was that of furnishing a methodological foundation for these new sciences, similar to the way in which, a century earlier, Kant had sought to 'ground' the natural sciences philosophically. Conceding, like Kant, an exclusivity in the explanation of natural being to the natural sciences (*Naturwissenschaften*), Dilthey sought to go beyond Kant by arguing (as the historian J. G. Droysen had before him) that the human sciences have their own specific subject matter and, accordingly, their own, equally specific, method. A spokesperson for the *Lebensphilosophie* current at the time, Dilthey maintained that the proper object of the human sciences is something specifically *human*, namely the inner, psychic life (*Erlebnis*, lived experience) of historical and social agents. Whereas the natural sciences seek to explain phenomena in a causal and, so to speak, external fashion (*Erklären*), the method proper to the human sciences is that of emphathetic understanding (*Verstehen*). The task of the human scientist is, or should be, that of transporting himself or herself into an alien or distant life experience, as this experience manifests or 'objectifies' itself in documents, texts ('written monuments') and other traces or expressions (*Ausdrucken*) of inner life experiences and world-views (*Weltanschauungen*). The *Lebensphilosophie* assumption operative here is that, because the human scientist is a living being, a part of life, he or she is, as a matter of principle, capable of reconstructively understanding other objectifications of life. Understanding (the method proper to the human sciences) is thus a matter of *interpretation*, and interpretation (*Deutung*) is the means whereby, through its outward, objective 'expressions', we can come to know in its own innerness what is humanly other, can, in effect, imaginatively coincide with it; *relive* it. Dilthey thus viewed the goal or purpose of interpretation as that of achieving a *reproduction* (*Nachbildung*) of alien life experiences.

Dilthey's purpose in conceptualizing the hermeneutical enterprise in this way was, as I indicated, to secure for the human sciences their own methodological autonomy and their own scientific objectivity *vis-à-vis* the natural sciences. The human sciences can lay claim to their own rightful epistemological status, can, indeed, lay claim to *validity*, if, as was Dilthey's aim, it can be shown that there is a 'method' which is specific to them, and which is different from the one characteristic of the natural sciences. This, Dilthey argued, was the method of *Verstehen*, as opposed to that of *Erklärung*; the task of the human sciences is not to 'explain' human phenomena, but to 'understand' them.

As a matter of historical interest, it may be noted that Dilthey's 'solution' to what could be called the 'problem of the human (or social) sciences' was revived several decades later in the mid twentieth century by Peter Winch, at roughly the same time that Gadamer and Ricoeur were developing their own quite different version of hermeneutics. In opposition to the then dominant positivist approach to the human sciences, which (as in the case of Carl Hempel and his 'covering law' model)[4] maintained that these disciplines could be made 'scientific' if they could manage, somehow, to incorporate the explanatory methods of the natural sciences, Winch argued that the 'explanatory' approach is totally inappropriate in the human sciences. With Wittgenstein's notion of 'forms of life' in mind, Winch maintained that 'the concepts used by primitive peoples can only be interpreted in the context of the way of life of those peoples'. The task of the anthropologist, for instance, can be no more than that of empathetically projecting himself or herself into an alien 'form of life'. When one has empathetically described in this way a particular 'language game', there is nothing more to be done. Like Dilthey, Winch drew a radical distinction between empathetic understanding and causal explanation and suggested that the human sciences should limit themselves to the former, arguing that human or social relations are an 'unsuitable subject for generalizations and theories of the scientific sort to be formulated about them'. 'The concepts used by primitive peoples', he insisted, 'can only be interpreted in the context of the way of life of those peoples.'[5] Winch's position is accurately characterized by Richard J. Bernstein in the following terms:

> Winch's arguments about the logical gap between the social and the natural can be understood as a linguistic version of the dichotomy between the *Naturwissenschaften* and the *Geisteswissenschaften*. Even the arguments that he uses to justify his claims sometimes read like a translation, in the new linguistic idiom, of those advanced by Dilthey.[6]

The important thing to note in this regard is how this Diltheyan-style attempt to make of life a special and irreducible category and to set it up as the foundational justification for a special and irreducible sort of science is, by that very fact, to oppose it to another distinct category, that of nature, which generates another, opposed kind of science. Explanation and understanding are viewed as two different, and even antagonistic, modes of inquiry. As we shall see later in this chapter, one of the prime objectives of Ricoeur's hermeneutics has been to overcome the understanding/explanation dichotomy inherited from Dilthey which has bedevilled so much of the debate in the twentieth century as to the epistemological status of the human sciences. Indeed, it could be said that one of the principal tasks of contemporary phenomenological hermeneutics[7] continues to consist, on the one hand, in 'depsychologizing' or 'desubjectivizing' the notion of meaning (rejecting thereby an empathetic notion of understanding) and, on the other hand, and correlatively, in attempting to specify the particular sense in which (or the degree to which) it can properly be said that the human sciences are indeed 'explanatory'.

In order to position ourselves for understanding what is distinctive about the hermeneutics of Gadamer and Ricoeur, it should also be noted that the Schleiermacher–Dilthey tradition in hermeneutics (customarily referred to as 'romantic hermeneutics') has been carried on in this century in the work of Emilio Betti and E. D. Hirsch, Jr, both of whom have strenuously objected to the version of hermeneutics put forward by Gadamer and Ricoeur. In an attempt to revive traditional hermeneutics (which they view phenomenological hermeneutics as having unfortunately displaced), Betti and Hirsch have sought to argue anew for hermeneutics as a general body of methodological principles and rules for achieving validity in interpretation.

Betti, the founder in 1955 of an institute for hermeneutics in Rome, has sought to resuscitate Dilthey's concern for achieving objective validity in our interpretations of the various 'objectifications' of human experience. He has attacked Gadamer for, as he sees it, undermining the scientific concern for objectivity and, because of the emphasis that Gadamer places on the notion of 'application' (to be discussed below), of opening the door to arbitrariness (or 'subjectivism') in interpretation and, indeed, to relativism. At the outset of his major work of 1962, *Die Hermeneutik als allgemeine Methodik der Geiteswissenschaften*,[8] Betti indirectly accused Gadamer of abandoning the 'venerable older form of hermeneutics' by having turned his back on its overriding concern for correctness or objectivity in interpretation.

Betti's critique was taken up by Hirsch with the publication in 1967 of the latter's *Validity in Interpretation*,[9] the first original and systematic treatise on hermeneutics written in English. As the title of his book so clearly indicates, Hirsch, like Betti and the other romantic hermeneuticists before him, was concerned to make of hermeneutics a *science* capable of furnishing 'correct' interpretations of 'verbal meanings' presumed to exist independently of the interpretive process itself. Hirsch's critical arguments are much the same as those of Betti, but he does add a new, methodological twist to his overall position. Hirsch's strategy for transforming interpretation into a genuine science is, quite simply, to transfer – lock, stock and barrel – the method of hypothetico-deductionism and Popperian falsificationism from the philosophy of the natural sciences to the humanities and, in particular, to the interpretation of literary texts. Like Popper's 'logic of scientific discovery', Hirsch's 'logic of validation' maintains that there can be no *method* for 'guessing' ('understanding') an author's meaning but that once such 'conjectures' or 'hypotheses' happen to be arrived at, they can subsequently be subjected to rigorous testing in such a way as to draw 'probability judgments' supported by 'evidence'. 'The act of understanding', Hirsch writes, 'is at first a genial (or a mistaken) guess, and there are no methods for making guesses, or rules for generating insights. The methodological activity of interpretation commences when we begin to test and criticize our guesses' (*Validity*, p. 207). And the activity of testing 'interpretive hypotheses', he says, 'is not in principle different from devising experiments that can sponsor decisions between hypotheses in the natural sciences' (p. 206).

The curious result of Hirsch's attempt to make of hermeneutics a science is to have narrowed considerably the scope that, traditionally, was claimed for it by the romantics. Hermeneutics is no longer concerned with understanding, interpretation and application but with interpretation alone, and this conceived of merely as 'validation'. In Hirsch's hands hermeneutics becomes essentially no more than an interpretive technique (*technē hermeneutikē*) for arbitrating between possible meanings, conflicting interpretations, with the aim of deciding which of them is the *one and only* true meaning of the text, i.e., the one intended by the author. Moreover, in conceiving of 'validation' in a Popperian and positivistic fashion, Hirsch effectively collapses the distinction between the natural and the human sciences,[10] sacrificing in the process the concern of Dilthey and others to safeguard the integrity and autonomy of the latter. Hirsch resolves the long-standing explanation/understanding debate – but at the total expense of 'understanding'. He uncritically endorses the scientistic claim that the natural sciences represent a model for all legitimate knowledge and are canonical for all other forms of knowledge.

In the wake of Betti and Hirsch, critics of Gadamer and Ricoeur continue to iterate the (by now well-worn) objection that their version of hermeneutics is incapable of generating a method by means of which 'correct' interpretations of textual meaning can be conclusively arrived at and that, because of this, it inevitably results in subjectivism and relativism.[11] We can begin to understand what is specific to phenomenological hermeneutics when we can understand its own reasons for rejecting the modernist obsession with 'method' and when, moreover, we can see why phenomenological hermeneutics should in its turn accuse traditional hermeneutics of falling prey to a naive form of *objectivism*.

❧ MOVING BEYOND THE TRADITION: ❧ PHENOMENOLOGICAL HERMENEUTICS

It would seem to be something of a general rule that any specifically human phenomenon is understood best when understood in terms of that from which it differs. It is certainly the case in any event that what goes to make up the specificity of the hermeneutics defended by Hans-Georg Gadamer (1900–   ) and Paul Ricoeur (1915–   ) is the way in which it differs from, and stands opposed to, traditional hermeneutics, as portrayed in the preceding remarks. For his part Ricoeur has explicitly characterized his hermeneutics in terms of its oppositional role when he declared: 'I am fighting on two fronts.' The two fronts he is referring to are, on the one hand, the 'romantic illusion' of empathetic understanding and, on the other hand, the 'positivist illusion' of a textual objectivity closed in upon itself and wholly independent of the subjectivity of both author and reader' (*OI*, 194–5).[12] In the latter case Ricoeur had the structuralist approach to texts in mind, but his remark would apply equally well to Hirsch's brand of hermeneutics to the degree that the latter seeks to maintain the pristine objectivity of a text closed in upon itself and wholly independent of the subjectivity of the reader (of its 'application'). Gadamer has sought in a similar way to clarify his position by differentiating it from that of Betti.

In the Foreword to the second edition (1965) of his *magnum opus, Truth and Method*, Gadamer attempted to defend himself against Betti's criticisms. His response was basically two-sided. On the one hand, he sought to justify his lack of concern for 'method' and, on the other, to defend himself against the charge of 'subjectivism'. In regard to the question of method he stated:

> My revival of the expression 'hermeneutics', with its long tradition, has apparently led to some misunderstandings.[13] I did not intend to produce an art or technique of understanding, in the manner of the earlier hermeneutics. I did not wish to elaborate a system of rules to describe, let alone direct, the methical procedure of the human sciences.... My real concern was and is

philosophic: not what we do or what we ought to do, but what happens to us over and above our wanting and doing.[14]

In other words, the goal that Gadamer set himself was that of envisaging hermeneutics in a way thoroughly different from the way in which it traditionally had been envisaged. In stark contrast to the positivist-inspired view of hermeneutics that Hirsch was subsequently to defend, Gadamer's goal was not *prescriptive* (laying down 'rules' for (correct) interpretation) but, in the phenomenological sense of the term, *descriptive* (seeking to ascertain what actually occurs whenever we seek to understand something). The difference between Gadamer's hermeneutics and traditional hermeneutics could be aptly compared to the difference between traditional philosophy of science, of either a positivist or Popperian sort, and the radically new approach to the philosophy of science instituted by Thomas Kuhn in *The Structure of Scientific Revolutions* (first published in 1962, two years after the original German edition of Gadamer's *Truth and Method*), a work which was to revolutionize the philosophy of science. Analogously to Gadamer, Kuhn sought not (like, for instance, Popper) to lay down methodological criteria that scientists must meet if what they do is to merit the appellation 'science', but sought instead simply to describe that particular activity which we refer to when we speak of someone 'doing science' (the actual characteristics of which are more often than not significantly different from what scientists are liable to say they are doing when pressed to make philosophical statements about their actual practice). With Gadamer explicitly in mind, Kuhn was later to describe his own work as 'hermeneutical'.

As the text cited above clearly indicates, Gadamer's purpose was not 'methodological' but, as he says, 'philosophic'. That is, Gadamer's goal was to elaborate a general *philosophy* of human understanding, in all of its various modes. It is precisely for this reason that his thought is often referred to as 'philosophical hermeneutics'.[15] A couple of pages further on in the Foreword Gadamer, again with reference to Betti, states his 'philosophic concern' in the following way:

> The purpose of my investigation is not to offer a general theory of interpretation and a differential account of its methods (which E. Betti has done so well) but to discover what is common to all modes of understanding and to show that understanding is never subjective behaviour toward a given 'object', but towards its effective history – the history of its influence; in other words, understanding belongs to the being of that which is understood.
>
> ([9.7], xix)

What in the present context is to be noted is how, in this last remark, Gadamer is attempting to respond to Betti's accusation of 'subjectivism'. Understanding, Gadamer is effectively saying, is not so much a 'subjective' as it is an *ontological* process. Understanding is not something that the human subject or we 'do' as it is something that, by reason of our 'belonging' to history (*Zugehörigkeit*), *happens* to us. Understanding is not a subjective accomplishment but an 'event' (*Geschehen*), i.e., 'something of which a prior condition is its being situated within a process of tradition' ([9.7], 276).

If, as we shall see, phenomenological hermeneutics is adamantly opposed to all forms of objectivism, it is equally opposed to all forms of modern subjectivism. As Ricoeur would say, it is continually constrained to do battle on two fronts. The central thrust of phenomenological hermeneutics is to move beyond *both* objectivism *and* subjectivism, which is to say, also, beyond relativism. One of the core features of Ricoeur's hermeneutics has been his ongoing attempt to articulate a notion of 'the subject' which would be free from all forms of modern subjectivism.[16] Unlike other forms of postmodern thought, hermeneutics has strenuously resisted the current, and very fashionable, antihumanist calls for the abolition of 'the subject' (the 'end of "man" '). The notion of the subject, hermeneutics insists, is not to be abandoned – but it must indeed be stripped of all its modernist, metaphysical accretions. This continued allegiance on the part of hermeneutics to the notion of the subject testifies to its rootedness in the phenomenological tradition inaugurated by Edmund Husserl.

❧ THE PHILOSOPHICAL BACKGROUND OF ❧ PHENOMENOLOGICAL HERMENEUTICS: HUSSERL AND HEIDEGGER

All of Husserl's philosophizing, from roughly 1900 onwards, was a sustained attempt to overcome the debilitating legacy of modern philosophy and, in particular, the subject/object dichotomy instituted by Descartes.[17] A pivotal moment in the unfolding of Husserl's phenomenology occurred in 1907 with a series of five lectures delivered in Göttingen (published subsequently in 1950 by Walter Biemel under the title *Die Idee der Phänomenologie*). In these lectures Husserl introduced his celebrated 'phenomenological reduction', the express purpose of which was to achieve a decisive overcoming of what the French translator of this work, Alexandre Lowit, has called 'la situation phénoménale du clivage', in other words, the subject/object split which presides over the origin and subsequent unfolding of modern philosophy from Descartes onwards. To speak in contemporary terms, what Husserl was seeking to accomplish by means of the 'reduction' was a thoroughgoing 'deconstruction' of the central problematic of modern philosophy itself, namely, the 'epistemological' problem of how an isolated subjectivity, closed in upon itself, can none the less manage to 'transcend' itself in such a way as to achieve a 'knowledge' of the 'external world'.[18] This, it may be noted, is, in one of its many variants, the problem which continues to inform the work of Betti and Hirsch (how to 'validate objectively' our own 'subjective ideas').

Thanks to the 'reduction' however, Husserl effectively displaced or deconstructed the epistemological problematic itself. He did so by discrediting (revealing the 'philosophical absurdity' of) its two constitutive notions: the notion of an 'objective', 'in-itself' world and the correlative notion that 'knowledge' consists in forming inner 'representations' on the part of an isolated 'cognizing subject' of this supposedly objective or 'external' world. The subsequent history of the phenomenological movement in the twentieth century – from Heidegger and Merleau-Ponty to Gadamer and Ricoeur – could be viewed as nothing other than an attempt 'to extract the most extreme possibilities'[19] from Husserl's own deconstruction of the epistemological problematic. Building on Husserl's own point of departure, phenomenological hermeneutics has systematically defined itself in terms of its opposition to both objectivism and subjectivism.

If the key methodological notion in Husserl's phenomenology is that of the reduction, the key substantive notion is the one that Husserl uncovered late in his life, that of the life-world (*Lebenswelt*). This too was to play a decisive role in the evolution of hermeneutics.[20] As was later pointed out by Merleau-Ponty (who in his own revision of Husserlian phenomenology anticipated a great many of the themes developed later on in greater detail by hermeneutics), what Husserl's phenomenological reduction serves ultimately to reveal is the life-world itself and this, Merleau-Ponty observed, is exactly what Heidegger referred to as 'being-in-the-world'.[21] The basic paradigm of modern epistemologism, dominated as it is by the subject/object dichotomy, is that of an isolated subjectivity (the 'mind') which is supposed to be related to the 'external' or 'objective' world by means of ideas or sense impressions (subsisting *within* the 'mind' itself) which are said to be 'true' (a 'true likeness') to the degree that they adequately 'represent' or 'refer to' facts or states of affairs in 'reality'. This modernist view of things (which could appropriately be labelled 'referentialist-representationalism') is one that continues to prevail with theorists such as Betti and Hirsch. It was in opposition to modern epistemologism, however, that Martin Heidegger argued in *Being and Time* (1927) that a relation (a *commercium*) between the subject and the world does not first get established on the level of 'cognition' or 'knowledge'.[22] Before any explicit awareness on its part, the human subject (*Dasein*) finds itself already in a world, 'thrown' into it, as it were. This surrounding world, the life-world, is thus one which is 'always already' there. What this pregivenness (as Husserl would say) of the life-world means is that, by virtue of our very existence, i.e. our 'being-in-the-world', we possess what Heidegger called a 'pre-ontological understanding' of the world (of 'being'). All explicit understandings or theorizings do no more than build on this always presupposed – and thus never fully thematizable – 'ground'. For Heidegger, therefore, understanding is not so much a mode of 'knowing' as it is one of 'being'. As Gadamer would subsequently put it, consciousness is more *Sein* than *Bewusstsein*.

Heidegger refers to this situation as 'facticity': if there is an always presupposed element in all our explicit understandings, this means that, in our various interpretations of things, we can never hope to achieve total transparency. The lesson that phenomenological hermeneutics was to draw from this Heideggerian position is that human understanding is essentially 'finite'. As Ricoeur has said: 'The gesture of hermeneutics is a humble one of acknowledging the historical conditions to which all human understanding is subsumed in the reign of finitude.'[23] What this means is that there can be no 'science', in the traditional philosophical sense of the term (*episteme, scientia intuitiva*), of existence (or of 'being'). The hermeneutics of Gadamer and Ricoeur could most fittingly be characterized as nothing other than a systematic attempt to draw all the philosophical conclusions that follow from a recognition of the inescapable finitude of human understanding (this is why they will argue, against objectivists such as Betti and Hirsch, that it is impossible ever to arrive at *the* (one and only) correct interpretation of a text or any other human product). Their hermeneutics will be 'a hermeneutics of finitude' ([9.15], 96).

Heidegger's 'existential analytic' – his phenomenological-interpretive description of human existence and its basic structures (what he referred to as *Existentialen*), his attempt to elaborate a 'hermeneutics of facticity', of everyday life, the life-world – provided the crucial impetus for subsequent hermeneutics. What is peculiar to Heidegger's hermeneutics is that it is an *ontological* hermeneutics. It is ontological (rather than 'methodological') in that, unlike what traditionally had gone under the heading 'hermeneutics', it was not concerned to specify criteria for 'correct' interpretations but instead had for its object something much more fundamental (Heidegger referred to his project as 'fundamental ontology'), namely a properly philosophical elucidation or interpretation of the basic (ontological) structures of human understanding which is to say, human existence) itself. The move that Heidegger made in this connection was to prove decisive for the subsequent development of hermeneutics. Understanding, Heidegger insisted, is not merely one attribute of our being, something that we may 'have' or not (in the sense in which we are said to 'have knowledge'); understanding is rather that which, as existing beings, we most fundamentally *are*.

As existing beings, we exist only in the mode of becoming (as Kierkegaard – from whom Heidegger drew much of his inspiration – would have said), and thus *what* we most fundamentally are is not anything fixed and given but rather what we can *become*, i.e., *possibility*. This in turn means that the understanding which we are is itself nothing other than an understanding of the possible ways in which we could be ('Understanding is the Being of such potentiality-for Being', *BT*, 183). As existing, understanding beings, we are continually 'projecting' possible ways of being (our being is defined in terms of these 'projects'). What Heidegger calls 'interpretation' (*Auslegung*) is itself nothing other than a possibility belonging to understanding. That is, when our pre-thematic, pre-predicative or tacit understanding is developed, it becomes interpretation.[24] Interpretation (explication, laying-out, *Auslegen*) is the working-out (*Ausarbeitung*) of the possible modes of being that have been projected by the understanding. The point that Heidegger is insisting on is that interpretation is always derivative; interpretation discloses only what has *already* been understood (albeit only tacitly).

In other words, interpretation is never without presuppositions (Heidegger referred to these as 'fore-structures'). It is never the mere mirroring of an 'objectivity' which simply stands there naked before us (the 'bare facts'); in interpretation there is always something that is 'taken for granted'. With the example of textual interpretation in mind, Heidegger pointedly remarks that if in one's interpretations one appeals to 'what "stands there"', then one finds that what "stands there" in the first instance is nothing other than the obvious undiscussed assumption [*Vormeinung*] of the person who does the interpreting' (*BT*, 192). There is, then, an essential *circularity* between understanding and interpretation.

In this way Heidegger effectively ontologizes what traditional hermeneutics had called the 'hermeneutical circle', which, as a methodological rule, simply meant that when interpreting a text one ought continually to interpret the parts in terms of the whole, and the whole in terms of the parts. For Heidegger, however, the 'circle' of understanding goes much deeper; it is in fact rooted in the existential constitution of human being itself. Human understanding itself has a circular structure. This amounts to saying that all interpretive understandings are presuppositional or 'anticipatory' by nature (interpretation must . . . already operate in that which is understood' (*BT*, 194).

Since the 'circle' is constitutive of our very being – since, in other words, it constitutes the very condition of possibility of our understanding anything at all – it would be altogether misleading to view it, as a logician might, as a 'vicious circle'. Even to view the circularity involved in all understanding – its 'presuppositional' nature – as an inevitable or unfortunate imperfection of human understanding that, in an ideal situation, could or ought to be overcome would mean, Heidegger says, that one has misunderstood the act of understanding 'from the ground up' (*BT*, 194). Indeed, all attempts to deny the 'circle' or to escape from it testify to a false consciousness. What Heidegger is here calling into question is the Cartesian ideal that has dominated all of modern philosophy, namely, the notion that truly 'objective' knowledge must be presuppositionless or 'foundational', grounded upon some rock-solid, 'objective' foundation (even the logical positivists continued to demand such a foundation and believed that they had found it in a combination of the laws of logic and raw 'sense data'). Thus, he maintains that the objectivistic ideal of 'a historiology which would be as independent of the standpoint of the observer as our knowledge of Nature is supposed to be' is a false ideal, an idol, in fact, of the understanding. Both scientistic objectivism and common sense (the 'natural attitude', as Husserl would have said) misunderstand understanding (see *BT*, 363). The important thing, Heidegger says, the lesson to be drawn from the phenomenological analysis of human being-in-the-world, is that we ought not even to try to get out of the circle but should attempt rather 'to come into it in the right way' (*BT*, 195). We must, in other words, learn in our theorizing to do without 'foundations' (such as, in textual interpretation, the supposedly original intention of the author). It would not be too much of an exaggeration to say that the whole meaning and significance of post-Heideggerian hermeneutics consists in its strenuous attempt to take this lesson to heart and, accordingly, to elaborate a theory of understanding and interpretation that could most properly be termed 'non-foundational'.

PHENOMENOLOGICAL HERMENEUTICS: THE BASIC THEMES

The putative purpose of Heidegger's lengthy analysis in *Being and Time* of the basic structures of human being was to set the stage for raising anew the age-old question of the meaning of Being, a question which Heidegger believed had increasingly been lost sight of since the time of the ancient Greeks. In subsequent writings Heidegger attempted to find a more direct approach to the Being-question (*die Seinsfrage*), abandoning in the process the existential orientation of his earlier work which, he believed, had distracted him from this overriding issue. The key actor in Heidegger's later writings is no longer the human being

(*Dasein*) but Being itself, Being-as-such. Neither Gadamer nor Ricoeur chose to follow Heidegger in this all-out pursuit of 'Being'. The following remark of Gadamer reflects well the agenda that hermeneutics has set itself – and which is not that of Heidegger's ontological eschatology: 'What man needs is not only a persistent asking of ultimate questions, but the sense of what is feasible, what is possible, what is correct, here and now' ([9.7], xxv).

Throughout his career Ricoeur has, for his part, held fast to a fundamentally existential motivation, conceiving of hermeneutics as an attempt on the part of the reflecting subject to come to grips with 'the desire to be and the effort to exist which constitute us'[25] (his 'existentialism' is at the root of his opposition to scientistic objectivism), and over the last several decades Gadamer has greatly expanded the scope of Heidegger's earlier, existential hermeneutics (the 'hermeneutics of facticity'), elaborating in the process an all-inclusive philosophical discipline. As he once remarked: 'I bypass Heidegger's philosophic intent, the revival of the "problem of Being".'[26] Unlike Heidegger, Gadamer has focused his interest not on the question of 'Being' but on the *Geisteswissenschaften*, on the nature and scope of the human sciences. 'We make', he said, 'a decided relation between the human sciences and philosophy. . . . The human sciences are not only a problem *for* philosophy, on the contrary, they represent a problem *of* philosophy' (*PHC*, 112). As the subject matter of his writings testifies, Ricoeur has also devoted a great deal of his philosophical attention to human science issues. If there is a difference between the two hermeneuticists in this regard, it is that Ricoeur feels that Gadamer has slighted important methodological issues having to do with the human sciences in his concern to accord them a special ontological status *vis-à-vis* the natural sciences ('an entirely different notion of knowledge and truth' [*PHC*, 113]). We shall, accordingly, return to the relation between hermeneutics and the human sciences after having explored some of the basic tenets of hermeneutics *qua* philosophy.

In responding to Betti's charge that his shift away from the concern of traditional hermeneutics for verificatory method encourages subjectivism and arbitrariness in interpretation, Gadamer, it will be recalled, asserted: 'understanding is never subjective behaviour toward a given "object", but towards its effective history – the history of its influence.' One of the most outstanding features of Gadamer's hermeneutics is the emphasis he places on the 'historicality' or tradition-laden nature of human understanding. 'It is not really ourselves who understand', he in fact says, 'it is always a past that allows us to say, "I have understood"' ([9.5] 58). Gadamer defends himself against the charge of subjectivism by maintaining that interpretation is never – indeed, can never be – the act of an isolated, monadic subject, for the subject's own self-understanding is inevitably a function of the historical tradition to which he or she belongs. In fact, Gadamer attempts to turn the tables on the objectivists by arguing that the 'presuppositionless' or 'objective' view of understanding that their theory of interpretation calls for is an existential impossibility, that, as Heidegger would say, it involves a thoroughgoing misunderstanding of human understanding.

It is in this context that Gadamer's famous 'rehabilitation' of *prejudice* must be understood. When Gadamer provocatively asserts that prejudices are integral to all understanding, he is not condoning wilful bias or bigotry. He is simply generalizing on Heidegger's observations on the 'anticipatory' nature of understanding, the fact that all understanding operates within the context of certain pre-given 'fore-structures'. 'Prejudice' must be understood in the literal sense of a 'pre-judgment' (or a pre-reflective judgment), a presupposition, not in the pejorative sense of the term which has prevailed since the Enlightenment. The polemical thrust of Gadamer's speaking of 'prejudice' is in fact directed against what he calls the Enlightenment 'prejudice against prejudice' ([9.7], 240). There can be, he wants to argue, 'legitimate prejudices'. Here is yet another, and most basic, instance of how phenomenological hermeneutics essentially defines itself in opposition to modernist objectivism. The aim of Gadamer's rehabilitation of prejudice is to call into question the very notions of reason and knowledge that we have inherited from Cartesianism and the rationalism of the Enlightenment.

In this rationalist view of things *reason* stands opposed to *authority*; the 'prejudice against prejudice' is indeed, on a deeper level, a prejudice against 'authority' itself and as such. The peculiarly rationalist prejudice is that true knowledge can be had only by freeing ourselves from all inherited beliefs and opinions (the 'authority of the tradition') so as to create a *tabula rasa* on which genuinely 'objective' knowledge can be erected. What Gadamer objects to here is the quite arbitrary way in which Enlightenment rationalism equates authority with blind obedience and domination; as there can be 'legitimate prejudices', so likewise the recognition of authority can itself be fully rational. Gadamer asserts:

> It is true that it is primarily persons that have authority; but the authority of persons is based ultimately, not on the subjection and abdication of reason, but on recognition and knowledge – knowledge, namely, that the other is superior to oneself in judgment and insight and that for this reason his judgment takes precedence, i.e., it has priority over one's own. This is connected with the fact that authority cannot actually be bestowed, but is

acquired and must be acquired, if someone is to lay claim to it. It rests on recognition and hence on an act of reason itself which, aware of its own limitations, accepts that others have better understanding. Authority in this sense, properly understood, has nothing to do with blind obedience to a command. Indeed, authority has nothing to do with obedience, but rather with knowledge.

([9.7], 248)

As Gadamer goes on to say, if we accord recognition to anything, it is because 'what authority states is not irrational and arbitrary, but can be accepted in principle' ([9.7], 249). There is, therefore, something like rightful authority, the recognition whereof is itself fully rational.

Gadamer contends that the Enlightenment ideal of Reason, as a 'faculty' enabling the individual to make contact with 'reality' unmediated by authority and tradition, is in fact an idol of modernity. He is especially opposed to the modernist assumption that reason so conceived (in an objectivistic-instrumentalist fashion) should serve as the basis for the complete reorganization ('rationalization') of society. As Richard Bernstein points out: 'We can read his philosophic hermeneutic as a meditation on the meaning of human finitude, as a constant warning against the excesses of what he calls "planning reason", a caution that philosophy must give up the idea of an "infinite intellect".'[27]

Curiously enough (though not surprisingly), the modernist quest for 'objective knowledge' is itself supremely subjectivistic. It presupposes that the thinking subject has direct access only to the contents of its own 'mind' (which is assumed to be fully transparent to itself) but that, with suitable methodological procedures, this isolated individual can, by means of Reason, achieve genuine knowledge on his or her own. An appropriate label for this view would be 'methodological solipsism'. For Gadamer, however, 'Understanding is not to be thought of so much as an action of one's subjectivity, but as the placing of oneself within a process of tradition, in which past and present are constantly fused' ([9.7], 258).

It can thus be seen that Gadamer's defence of 'prejudice' goes hand in hand with the emphasis he places on *tradition*; indeed, for Gadamer the ultimate locus of authority is tradition itself. It is interesting to note in this regard that post-positivist philosophy of science has, in the case of Thomas Kuhn, Paul Feyerabend and others, sought to highlight the role that tradition plays in that rational enterprise called 'science'. Scientists, it is now recognized, do not simply 'observe and describe' bare facts; what they look for, and what they accordingly find, is a function not of an abstract method ('the experimental method') but of the 'paradigms' or research traditions in which they happen to be working (and into which they have been enculturated in their training as scientists). This parallel between the new philosophy of science and Gadamerian hermeneutics is perhaps especially interesting and noteworthy in that in his work Gadamer has focused exclusively on the human sciences and has not sought to indicate what a hermeneutical approach to the natural sciences might look like. But the point that the new philosophers of science are making is a properly Gadamerian one: there are no answers 'in themselves'; the only answers that scientists get is to the questions they have asked, and these are ones which they owe to the tradition within which they are working.

In his reflections on the human sciences Gadamer has devoted particular attention to the importance of the *question*. The logic of the human sciences, he says, is 'a logic of the question' ([9.7], 333, see also 325ff.). All knowledge comes only in the form of an answer to a question. And much as Feyerabend was later to do in his *Against Method*, Gadamer insists that 'There is no such thing as a method of learning to ask questions, of learning to see what needs to be questioned' ([9.7], 329). This of course does not mean, as a neopositivist like Hirsch would maintain, that there is no 'art of questioning'. There is indeed such an art, and this is precisely one we learn from the tradition to which, as thinking beings, we belong.

From what has been said, it can be readily appreciated why, in his attempt to elaborate an overall philosophy of human understanding, Gadamer should devote so much of his attention to the notion of tradition. If there is no understanding without presuppositions or 'prejudices', then it is incumbent on a philosophical hermeneutics to thematize the role that tradition plays in our understanding, since our enabling presuppositions are historical by nature, something handed down to us by the tradition(s) to which we belong – a prime instance of 'the historicality that is part of all understanding' ([9.7], 333). In highlighting tradition in this way, Gadamer is led to articulate one of the core notions in his work, that of *wirkungsgeschichtliche Bewusstsein*.

Like so many other German terms, this one defies easy translation. The 'hermeneutical consciousness' it designates is 'the consciousness of effective history' or, alternatively, 'the consciousness in which history is effectively at work'. What effective-history 'means' is that 'both what seems to us worth enquiring about and what will appear as an object of investigation' are determined in advance ([9.7], 267–8). The term connotes a consciousness which is at once affected by history and aware of itself as so affected, an awareness which precludes our regarding history as an object since it is itself already implicated in history.[28] As Ricoeur characterizes it, effective-history is 'the massive and global fact whereby consciousness, even before its awakening as such, belongs to and depends on that which affects it' ([9.15], 74). 'Effective-history' is Gadamer's response to 'historical objectivism'. Gadamer not only argues that there can be no purely 'objective' knowledge of history – since history is already effectively at work in all historiological attempts at understanding it – he argues also that the rootedness of understanding in its own history (a history which it therefore continually 'presupposes') must not be viewed as an impediment to genuine understanding, to 'truth'. Or as Ricoeur sums it up: 'The action of tradition [effective-history] and historical investigation are fused by a bond which no critical consciousness could desolve without rendering the research itself nonsensical' ([9.15], 76).

That indeed is Gadamer's main point. Effective-history does not signal a limitation on our ability to understand (unless, of course, one wishes to contrast human understanding with divine understanding, in which case human understanding will always come out the loser) as much as it designates the positive and productive possibility of any understanding that lays claim to truth. To speak in traditional philosophical terms, effective-history is the very condition of possibility of understanding. Effective-history provides us with our 'enabling' presuppositions.

There is a phenomenological parallel between the world in which we exist as thinking beings and the world in which we exist as perceiving beings: both have *horizons*.[29] Effective-history provides us with the intelligible horizon within which, as thinking beings, we 'live, move, and have our being'. Now, what occurs in the case of historical or intercultural understanding is what Gadamer calls a 'fusion of horizons' (*Horizontsverschmelzung*). The term 'fusion' is perhaps misleading, however. When we attain to a 'hermeneutical consciousness' of another historical or cultural horizon, we do not coincide with the other (cf. Dilthey's notion of *nachleben*, re-living), but our horizon and that of the other partially overlap, as it were. The best illustration of such a 'fusion' is that of a meaningful conversation. As Gadamer writes:

> Just as in a conversation, when we have discovered the standpoint and horizon of the other person, his ideas become intelligible, without our necessarily having to agree with him, the person who thinks historically comes to understand the meaning of what has been handed down, without necessarily agreeing with it, or seeing himself in it.[30]

([9.7], 270)

Were one inclined to draw out the applicational significance of Gadamer's notion of a fusion of horizons, it would be most instructive to interpret it in the light of recent debates about 'incommensurability'.[31] What this would serve to reveal is how the notion of a fusion of horizons, like so many other hermeneutical notions, is an intrinsically oppositional or dialectical notion. In regard, for instance, to the question as to whether different cultural world-views are in any way 'commensurable', the fusion-of-horizons notion would oblige one to defend a position which would be *neither* absolutist *nor* relativist. On the one hand, the hermeneuticist would want to argue – as Richard Rorty, for instance, has done – against the idea of 'universal commensuration', the idea, that is, that the values operative in different cultures can be measured or ranked according to some univocal, hierarchical standard of comparison, by means of some kind of epistemological algorithm. On the other hand, however, the hermeneuticist would want to argue just as strenuously against an unrestrained 'particularism', i.e., against the outright rejection of universalism altogether (cf. Rorty's defence of 'ethnocentrism'). The hermeneutical notion of a fusion of horizons means (in practical or pragmatic terms) that a meaningful dialogue with the 'other' (a genuine contact with the other, as other) is always possible, given the necessary effort and good will – even though a Hegelian-like *Aufhebung* of differences in a univocally uniform understanding is neither possible nor even, for that matter, desirable.[32] Expressing much the same point, though in a somewhat different way, Ricoeur observes:

> This [the fusion of horizons] is a dialectical concept which results from the rejection of two alternatives: objectivism, whereby the objectification of the other is premissed on the forgetting of oneself; and absolute knowledge, according to which universal history can be articulated within a single horizon. We exist neither in closed horizons, nor within an horizon that is unique. No horizon is closed, since it is possible to place oneself in another point of view and in another culture. . . . But no horizon is unique, since the tension between the other and oneself is unsurpassable.
>
> ([9.15], 75)

To sum up: what Gadamer has called 'tradition' is nothing other than the way in which our own horizons are constantly shifting through 'fusion' with other horizons. 'In a tradition,' he says, 'this process of fusion is continually going on, for there old and new continually grow together to make something of living value, without either being explicitly distinguished from the other' ([9.7], 273). The all-inclusive name for the phenomenon in question is 'understanding'.

To highlight in this way the 'horizonal' nature of understanding is, once again, to underscore the essential finitude of all understanding. 'Philosophical thinking', Gadamer insists, 'is not science at all. . . . There is no claim of definitive knowledge, with the exception of one: the acknowledgement of the finitude of human being in itself.'[33] The important thing to note in this regard, however, is that while an emphasis on finitude rules out the possibility of our ever attaining to 'definitive knowledge', it does not exclude the possibility of *truth*. It does not, that is, if and when truth is no longer conceived of in a metaphysical fashion, as a state of rest in which one has achieved a final coincidence with the object in question (e.g., the meaning of a text), but is reconceptualized to mean a mode of existence in which we keep ourselves open to new experiences, to further expansions in our horizons. Truth, for Gadamer, is not a static but a dynamic concept. It is not an epistemological but an existential concept, designating a *possible mode of being-in-the-world*. When, in the very last line of *Truth and Method*, Gadamer speaks of 'a discipline of questioning and research, a discipline that guarantees truth', what he means by 'truth' tends to coincide with the notion of *openness*. This is why he writes: 'The truth of experience always contains an orientation towards new experience. . . . The dialectic of experience has its own fulfilment not in definitive knowledge, but in that openness to experience that is encouraged by experience itself' ([9.7], 319).[34]

If human understanding is effectively historical, this means that it is also *linguistic* through and through, since it is through language that the tradition is effectively mediated and 'fused' with the present (which means also that in the language we speak and by means of which we achieve understanding the past continues to be effectively present). 'The linguistic quality of understanding', Gadamer remarks, 'is the concretion of effective-historical understanding'; 'it is the nature of tradition to exist in the medium of language' ([9.7], 351). Ricoeur has summed up the chief consequence of the 'new ontology of understanding' in the following way: 'there is no self-understanding which is not *mediated* by signs, symbols and texts . . . that is to say that it is *language* that is the primary condition of all human experience' (*OI*, 191). For both Gadamer and Ricoeur the ultimate goal of all understanding is self-understanding, and, to the degree that this occurs, it occurs by means of language. As was mentioned earlier, hermeneutics for Ricoeur is nothing other than an attempt on the part of the reflecting subject to come to grips with 'the desire to be' ('le désire d'être'), and there is, he says, a basic 'proximity between desire and speech'. In fact, the path to self-understanding, he says, 'lies in the speech of the other which leads me across the open space of signs'. Like Gadamer, Ricoeur believes that the condition for understanding and self-understanding is the linguistically mediated tradition to which we belong, 'the whole treasury of symbols transmitted by the cultures within which we have come, at one and the same time, into both existence and speech' (*OI*, 192–3).

At one point in his career,[35] Ricoeur equated hermeneutics with the interpretation of symbols, i.e., various double-meaning expressions such as stain, fall, wandering, captivity, and so on, the purpose of hermeneutics being that of explicating the non-literal meaning of these expressions, thereby recollecting and restoring the fullness of their symbolic meaning. In work undertaken subsequent to what he calls his 'linguistic turn', Ricoeur's view of the scope of hermeneutics expanded to include the entire range of human linguisticality, the issue of textuality in particular. Gadamer for his part devoted fully one-third of *Truth and Method* to a discussion of language. If 'all understanding is interpretation', it is equally the case, Gadamer insists, that 'all interpretation takes place in the medium of language'. Language, he says, 'is the universal medium in which understanding itself is realized' ([9.7], 350).

This is Gadamer's thesis concerning the 'linguisticality' (*Sprachlichkeit*) of experience, regarded by some as 'his most original contribution to the history of hermeneutics'.[36] As he formulates it, the thesis is a strong one:

> Linguistic interpretation is the form of all interpretation, even when what is to be interpreted is not linguistic in nature, i.e., is not a text, but is a statue or a musical composition. We must not let ourselves be confused by these forms of interpretation which are not linguistic, but in fact presuppose language.
>
> ([9.7], 360)

A natural reaction on the part of many readers is to object that, surely, we have experiences which are not linguistic in nature. As if in realization of the somewhat counter-intuitive nature of his thesis, Gadamer goes on to say:

> We must understand properly the nature of the fundamental priority of language asserted here. Indeed, language often seems ill-suited to express what we feel. In the face of the overwhelming presence of works of art the task of expressing in words what they say to us seems like an infinite and hopeless undertaking. It seems like a critique of language that our desire and capacity to understand always go beyond any statement that we can make. But this does not affect the fundamental priority of language.
>
> ([9.7], 362)

It is indeed necessary, as Gadamer says, to understand properly the nature of the priority being asserted here. Gadamer is not advocating a kind of *Sprachidealismus*, a linguistic idealism. He is not defending a metaphysical thesis to the effect that there is nothing outside of language or that everything can be reduced to language – as Derrida was subsequently perceived to be saying ('Il n'y a pas de hors-texte'). The linguisticality-thesis does not *deny* the meaningfulness of non-linguistic modes of experience; rather it *affirms* that meaningfulness by maintaining that it can always, in principle, be brought to expression (can be interpreted) in language. If the pre-linguistic could not be so interpreted, it would indeed be meaningless to speak of it as having any meaning at all. Thus, as Gadamer says:

> language always forestalls any objection to its jurisdiction. Its universality keeps pace with the universality of reason. Hermeneutical consciousness is only participating in something that constitutes the general relation between language and reason. If all understanding stands in a necessary relation of equivalence to its possible interpretation and if there are basically no bounds set to understanding, then the linguistic form which the interpretation of this understanding finds must contain within it an infinite dimension that transcends all bounds. Language is the language of reason itself.
>
> ([9.7], 363)

Ricoeur too insists on this 'general relation between language and reason'. The operant presupposition or 'central intuition'[37] underlying his hermeneutical endeavours is that existence is indeed meaningful, that, notwithstanding the very real existence of unmeaning, necessity (unfreedom) and evil, there is in existence 'a super-abundance of meaning to the abundance of non-sense'.[38] The core of what could be called Ricoeur's philosophical faith is his belief in the *dicibilité*, the 'sayability', of experience. He formulates this 'wager for meaning' or this 'presupposition of meaning' in the following way: 'It must be supposed that experience in all its fullness . . . has an expressibility [*dicibilité*] in principle. Experience can be said, it demands to be said. To bring it to language is not to change it into something else, but, in articulating and developing it, to make it become itself' ([9.15], 115).

Perhaps no more forceful statement could be adduced to highlight the fundamental difference between hermeneutics and other forms of postmodern philosophy which also emphasize the centrality of language but which proceed to draw from such a recognition conclusions of a philosophically agnostic sort (cf. Derrida's notions of *différance* and 'undecidability'). For hermeneutics the fact that our understanding of things is always *mediated* by language does not mean that language is a *barrier* preventing us from having genuine access to 'reality'. Precisely because of the linguisticality of understanding, hermeneutics insists that there is – 'in principle', as Ricoeur would say – nothing that we might wish to understand which cannot, in one way or another, be brought to language. As Gadamer states: 'everything that is intelligible must be accessible to understanding and to interpretation. The same thing is as true of understanding as of language' ([9.7], 365). 'Every language', he maintains, '. . . is able to say everything it wants' ([9.7], 363). This of course is not to say that one could ever succeed in saying everything that there is to be said about anything; experience of the world is not only expressible, it is infinitely expressible and is, therefore, inexhaustible in its meaning.[39]

It should be noted that the hermeneutical 'postulate of meaningfulness', of expressibility, is not merely an article of (philosophical) faith but is based on an ontological thesis as to the relationship between human understanding (what traditional philosophy would have called the 'mind') and reality. The thesis is one to which Gadamer gave the following succinct formulation: 'Being that can be understood is language' ([9.7], 432). Let us attempt to unpack this very provocative assertion.

What exactly the thesis as to the 'linguisticality of the world' means can perhaps best be grasped when it is reinserted in the phenomenological context from which it derives; for hermeneutics the relation between language and the world parellels the relation between consciousness and the world as described by Husserl. As was mentioned earlier, the 'phenomenological reduction' was the means by which Husserl sought to overcome the subject/object split of philosophical modernity. What the reduction served to reveal is the 'intentionality' of consciousness: 'all consciousness is consciousness *of* its object, *of* the world.' In other words, in being conscious, one is not first of all conscious of one's own consciousness and then, only subsequently, of an object; on the contrary, self-consciousness is derivative – 'parasitical', even – upon an immediate consciousness of the object.[40] Consciousness is therefore not something we have to break out of in order to encounter the world. As Merleau-Ponty remarked, 'there is no inner man';[41] consciousness is 'always already' in a world and thus is itself a mode of being-in-the-world.

Transposed from the register of consciousness to that of language, the intentionality-thesis means that between language and the world there exists, as Gadamer puts it, a mutual belonging, an 'affiliation'. What language 'expresses' is nothing other than the world itself, and thus, as Gadamer says, 'language has no independent life apart from the world that comes to language within it' ([9.7], 401). Echoing, as it were, Heidegger's characterization of language as 'das Haus des Seins', the home of being, Gadamer insists on 'the intimate unity of word and object'. Objecting to 'the instrumentalist devaluation of language that we find in modern times' ([9.7], 365), Gadamer maintains that language is not simply a tool, 'a mere means of communication' ([9.7], 404). 'Language', he says, 'is not just one of man's possessions in the world, but on it depends the fact that man has a world at all.' By strict phenomenological logic, the conclusion follows: 'this world is linguistic in nature' ([9.7], 401). Thus, to speak of 'the nature of things' or of 'the language of things' is, Gadamer remarks, to use two expressions 'that for all intents and purposes mean the same thing' ([9.5], 69).

Like the notion of a fusion of horizons, the hermeneutical view of language is a dialectical concept resulting from a rejection of two alternative views of language. On the one hand, just as phenomenology rejects the modernist view of consciousness as a mere 'representation' of the 'external' world, so likewise hermeneutics rejects the modernist view of language as nothing more 'than a mere sign system to denote the totality of objects' ([9.7], 377). The words of a natural language, Gadamer insists, are not merely 'signs' that 'refer' to an alinguistic, pre-given reality. Words are not mere labels that we stick on things that are fully defined in themselves; they are the very means by which the things themselves exist for us. To say that language is the universal medium of our experience of the world means, practically or pragmatically speaking, that it is quite devoid of meaning to speak of a totally extra-linguistic reality. The age-old goal of transcending language in such a way as to coincide with reality as it is 'in itself', with a transcendental signified (as Derrida would say), is thereby shown to be a vain and meaningless pursuit. Hermeneutics spells the 'end of metaphysics' when it insists that being itself is (to borrow a phrase from Jacques Lacan) 'structuré comme un langage', structured like a language.

On the other hand, hermeneutics also rejects not only modernism but also those *post*modern views of language which, in addition to viewing language as a mere system of signs, maintain as well that the system is closed in upon itself and that it 'refers' to nothing other than itself – which is to say, to nothing 'real' at all. That indeed would be a form of linguistic idealism.

For hermeneutics, language is neither a mere tool nor an autonomous object in its own right; it is the medium of understanding itself, and all understanding is in the last analysis a form of self-understanding. Faithful to its origins in existential phenomenology, hermeneutics views language as the means whereby a speaking subject arrives at understanding in dialogue with other speaking subjects. For his basic model of linguistically-mediated understanding, Gadamer invariably takes as his privileged example what is itself an instance of language as *praxis: conversation (Gespräch)*.[42] He seeks, as he says, 'to approach the mystery of language from the conversation that we ourselves are' ([9.7], 340). Language, he says, 'has its true being only in conversation, in the exercise of understanding between people' ([9.7], 404). By 'conversation' Gadamer understands

> a process of two people understanding each other ['fusion of horizons']. Thus it is characteristic of every true conversation that

each opens himself to the other person, truly accepts his point of view as worthy of consideration and gets inside the other to such an extent that he understands not a particular individual, but what he says. The thing that has to be grasped is the objective rightness or otherwise of his opinion, so that they can agree with each other on the subject.

([9.7], 347)

We should note that, as Gadamer defines it, conversation is an instance of *dialogue*. What makes the conversation a dialogue is that it is not simply the intersection of two monologues; in a conversation there exists a genuine *commonality*. What makes for this commonality is not the individual 'subjectivities' of the interlocutors but rather what the conversation is 'about', 'what is being said', i.e., the 'topic' or 'subject' of the conversation or what Gadamer calls *die Sache*, that which is at issue (at play, *en jeu*) in the conversation.[43] As in a game situation, what guides and rules over the conversation is not the subjective intentions of the participants but 'the object to which the partners in the conversation are directed' ([9.7], 330). It should also be noted how the above definition of conversation also contains an implicit reference to the concept of truth, as hermeneutics conceives of it: truth (according to one reading of Gadamer's somewhat ambiguous remarks on the subject) is essentially the *agreement* that the interlocutors arrive at in the course of a conversation on the issue at stake.

Gadamer's portrayal of language under the aegis of conversation is typically 'ontological': it is part and parcel of his overall attempt to elaborate a philosophy (an ontology) of human understanding. However, privileging as it does the point of view of the speaking subject (or subjects), it bypasses the approach to language taken by the science of linguistics and the methodological implications thereof. One of Ricoeur's chief preoccupations has been to remedy this situation by engaging in a debate with the objective science of language. Resisting Gadamer's separation of 'truth' from 'method', Ricoeur defines his own approach *vis-à-vis* that of Heidegger and Gadamer as wanting to contribute 'to this ontological vehemence an analytical precision which it would otherwise lack' (*OI*, 196).

Like Gadamer, Ricoeur holds to 'the conviction that discourse never exists *for its own sake*, for its own glory, but that in all of its uses it seeks to bring into language an experience, a way of living in and of Being-in-the-world which precedes it and which demands to be said' (*OI*, 196). However, he believes that it is not sufficient simply to assert this conviction but that it must be justified given what could be called the 'semiological' challenge. What exactly is this challenge?

For structural or Saussurian linguistics (from which philosophical poststructuralism was to draw much of its inspiration and, in particular, its rejection of the notion of 'the subject'), language is an autonomous system of differences, one of internal dependencies which are self-referential and self-defining. In this respect the system has no outside, only an inside, and, as a mere code, it is anonymous. This means that, from a 'semiological' point of view, language has neither subject nor meaning nor reference, nor, a fortiori, is it to be viewed as a means of communication. It would seem, therefore, that in their views on language hermeneutics and 'semiology' are irreconcilably opposed.[44]

Typically of his general approach to issues, Ricoeur has sought to arbitrate this dispute and to elaborate 'a new phenomenology of language which would take seriously the challenge of semiology, of structural linguistics, of all the "structuralisms" '.[45] He has done so by arguing that while on the micro level of phonological and lexical units the structuralist approach to language is, *qua* science, fully justified, it none the less fails to account for what is uniquely characteristic of language when one considers larger linguistic units, such as the sentence and, above all, the text. When language is considered no longer merely as an atemporal *system* of *signs* but as an *event* of *discourse*, as an 'actualisation of our linguistic competence in performance', it becomes apparent, Ricoeur argues, that language does indeed communicate something meaningful about the world to a subject attuned to it (see [9.15], 132ff.). As we shall see in the next section when considering the hermeneutical principles of text-interpretation, what a text communicates is indeed a *world*, i.e., a possible mode of being-in-the-world.

Ricoeur's debate or *Auseinandersetzung* with structural linguistics illustrates very well one of the persistent elements in his philosophizing. From his early work in philosophical anthropology (where he sought to overcome the idealist limitations of Husserl's philosophy of consciousness) to his current concern with textuality, semantic innovation and the narrative function, Ricoeur has throughout waged a philosophical battle on two fronts. While seeking to overcome all forms of modern subjectivism and, in particular, all psychologistic theories of meaning (e.g., those which equate meaning with authorial intention), he has consistently opposed various structuralist and poststructuralist attempts to get rid of the notion of subjectivity altogether. What Ricoeur has worked to articulate is a renewed, transformed and, above all, decentred notion of the subject, i.e., one which views subjectivity not as a metaphysical 'origin' of meaning but as the result ('effect') of its transformative encounter with the 'other'. If, as Habermas has done in a recent work, we were to take as one of the more noteworthy traits of contemporary philosophy its critique of 'a self-sufficient subjectivity that is posited absolutely'[46] ('the philosophy of the subject', the 'philosophy of consciousness'), the hermeneutics of Gadamer and Ricoeur would

stand out as exemplary in this regard. In its basic philosophical orientation – key elements of which we have surveyed in this section –
hermeneutics is a prime instance of the general movement in twentieth-
century philosophy which has been a movement away from the paradigm of (monological) consciousness to that of (dialogical) intersubjectivity. To insist, as hermeneutics does, on the effective-historical and
linguistic nature of consciousness is, *eo ipso*, to insist on its intersubjective nature. To maintain that 'the goal of all communication and understanding is agreement concerning the object' ([9.7, 260) is to aim at a
conception of meaning and truth which is neither objectivistic nor
subjectivistic. Truth is not to be thought of objectivistically as 'correspondence' to some in-itself reality, nor is meaning to be thought of
subjectivistically as something residing 'within' subjectivity itself. The
attempt on the part of phenomenological hermeneutics to move decisively beyond both objectivism and relativism is especially evident in
regard to its theories on text-interpretation, an issue to which we now
turn.

THE HERMENEUTICAL THEORY OF TEXT INTERPRETATION

'The best definition for hermeneutics', Gadamer writes, 'is: to let what
is alienated by the character of the written word or by the character
of being distantiated by cultural or historical distances speak again.
This is hermeneutics: to let what seems to be far and alienated speak
again.'[47] As we have seen, however, Gadamer distances himself from the
tradition of romantic hermeneutics by insisting that his 'philosophical'
hermeneutics is not intended as a skilled procedure, a body of knowledge that 'can be brought under the discipline of consciously employed
rules and thus be deemed a technical doctrine'. Rather, it is, as he says
(borrowing a phrase from Habermas), a 'critical reflective knowledge',
i.e., an attempt to articulate what is ontologically presupposed in all acts
of text-interpretation which seek to bridge over cultural or historical
distances.[48] As a *critical* reflection, it seeks to uncover 'the naive objectivism within which historical sciences, taking their bearings from the
self-understanding of the natural sciences, are trapped'.

In regard to text-interpretation, the 'naive objectivism' to be
uncovered and overcome is the belief that (as with respect to 'reality'
naturalistically or scientistically conceived) texts contain within themselves (as Hirsch would say) a perfectly well-defined, determinate, self-
same, and unchanging meaning that it is the business of interpretation
merely to lay bare. It goes without saying that this objectivistic view
of 'knowledge' is thoroughly at odds with the philosophical theory of

human understanding outlined above. How then, we may ask, does philosophical hermeneutics conceive of textual meaning and the business of interpretation?

The basic point can be stated fairly tersely: what interpretation seeks to understand is not the *intention* of the *author*, but the *meaning* of the *text*. To put the matter yet another way: textual meaning is not reducible to authorial intention. A 'good' text is precisely one which has something to say to us, its readers, over and above what its author may (or may not) have intended and willed.[49] As Gadamer pointedly asks: 'Does an author really know so exactly and in every sentence what he means' ([9.7], 489)? 'The sense of a text', Gadamer says, 'in general reaches far beyond what its author originally intended.' And thus 'the task of understanding is concerned in the first place with the meaning of the text itself' ([9.7], 335).[50] The task of interpretation is to develop or explicate these textual meanings – by means, as we shall see, of 'application'. The distinctive tenet of philosophical hermeneutics is that, as Gadamer says, *interpretation* is never simply *reproduction* ([9.7], 345).

Gadamer's rejection of authorial intention as the supreme criterion of textual meaning follows from his views on conversation. As we have seen, a genuine conversation is one wherein we are not preoccupied with 'reading the other person's mind' but are concerned, instead, with coming to a mutual understanding ('agreement') with him or her on the topic under discussion. For Gadamer, the same is, or ought to be, the case in our encounter with texts. Reading involves 'not a mysterious communion of souls, but a sharing of a common meaning'. The goal of interpretive understanding is not 'to recapture the author's attitude of mind but . . . the perspective within which he has formed his views' ([9.7], 259–60) – in other words, to join with him or her in a conversation on the issue at stake in the text. Such is the 'hermeneutic situation' with regard to texts.

To speak of 'conversation' is necessarily also to speak of a 'fusion of horizons'. What occurs in the act of reading or interpretation is a 'fusion' of the 'horizon' of the text (what Ricoeur calls the 'world of the text') with that of the reader. The meaning of the text is the result of this 'fusion'. Textual meaning is therefore nothing substantial in itself but exists rather in the form of an *event*, and this event is the act of reading.[51] If, as we have seen, there are no answers but to questions we ourselves pose, then it is the presupposition of 'fore-meanings' we bring to bear on a text which are decisive in what the text 'tells' us. 'The only "objectivity" here', Gadamer insists, 'is the confirmation of a fore-meaning in its being worked out' ([9.7], 237).

This of course is not to say that we are free to project our own presuppositions on to the text arbitrarily – this would precisely *not* be a conversation in the Gadamerian sense. Indeed, to the degree that in reading a 'fusion' actually does occur, to that very degree our own presuppositions are put at risk. The mark of arbitrary prejudices, Gadamer says, is that 'they come to nothing in the working-out' ([9.7], 237). This not infrequently happens. Our fore-meanings are often not confirmed but challenged, and it is precisely in this way that our own horizons are transformed, such that we gain in understanding. Not only is understanding, in the final analysis, a form of self-understanding, but all self-understanding is ultimately a matter of *self-transformation*. When we encounter a text or object whose newness is a challenge to our acquired presuppositions, what that object says to us is: 'You must change yourself.' Thus, in the act of reading, by means of the fusion of horizons effected thereby, we achieve an understanding of what is other by relating its horizon to our own; however, in order to do so, we are at the same time challenged to expand our own horizons, such that, through and by means of reading, our own selves are renewed. The postmodern paradigm of intersubjectivity under which philosophical hermeneutics operates is perhaps no more in evidence than here, in its theory of text-interpretation. 'Only through others', Gadamer says, 'do we gain true knowledge of ourselves' (*PHC*, 107).

Another way of expressing this whole matter would be to say that all interpretation necessarily involves *application* (*Anwendung, applicatio*). We can be said to have understood a text, grasped its meaning, only when we are able to relate ('apply') what it says to our own situation, our own historical horizon. Indeed, if there would be *no* way in which we could relate what a text says (what it means, 'wants to say', *veut dire*) to our own situation, if, in other words, there were no way we could *translate* the language of the text into our own historically conditioned language – then it would be meaningless to speak of our having to do with a *text* in the first place, i.e., something presumed to have *meaning*. We would have no more grounds for viewing the thing in question as a text than we would to view markings on the floor of the Peruvian desert as traces of alien subjectivities from outer space, rather than as mere curiosities of nature.

For Gadamer, the three moments of the 'hermeneutical situation' – understanding, interpretation and application – are inseparable. Just as understanding always involves interpretation, so also interpretation always includes the element of application. In asserting this interconnection ('the truly distinctive feature of philosophic hermeneutics', in the words of one commentator[52]), Gadamer is once again distancing himself from the tradition of romantic hermeneutics and, indeed, from the basic paradigms of modern epistemology in general. In linking together understanding, interpretation and application, he is rejecting outright the modernist view of 'knowledge' as correct 'representation' of an in-itself state of affairs. He is insisting, in a decidedly postmodern fashion, that all genuine knowledge is in fact *transformation*. Understanding, he maintains, is never merely 'a reproductive, but always a productive attitude as well. . . . It is enough to say that we understand in a different way, if we understand at all' ([9.7], 264). What that means in regard to text-interpretation is that, since understanding a text involves its application to the situation of the interpreter, it is necessarily the case that in changing circumstances a text is understood appropriately 'only if it is understood in a different way every time' ([9.7] 275–6). This is yet another inevitable consequence of linking up meaning with the event of understanding. If, indeed, understanding (truth) is itself in the nature of an event then, as Gadamer remarks – provocatively, but with perfectly good reason none the less: 'the same tradition must always be understood in a different way' ([9.7], 278). An understanding of things which failed constantly to renew itself in this way – through 'application' – would be nothing more than (to borrow a phrase from Hegel) 'the repetition of the same majestic ruin'.[53]

It may be noted in passing that Gadamer's notions of the fusion of horizons and, consequent upon this, the transformative nature of understanding is enough to deflect one of the main criticisms often directed at his work, namely that it amounts to a form of cultural or intellectual conservatism. From what we have seen, it should be obvious that Gadamer's defence of tradition is in no way a paean to an incessant repetition of the same. If the 'same' – the tradition – is not always understood differently, it ceases to what Gadamer understands by 'tradition'. What are commonly referred to as 'traditional' societies – ones which seek to deny change and transformative becoming and to perpetuate inviolate a particular societal order – are precisely ones which are devoid of tradition in the Gadamerian sense, i.e., a *living* tradition animated by a 'historical consciousness'. The fact that language and its effective-history preforms our experience of the world does not, Gadamer insists, 'remove the possibilities of critique'. 'Conversation' always holds open 'the possibility of going beyond our conventions' and ensures 'the possibility of our taking a critical stance with regard to every convention'. In short, tradition does not present 'an obstacle to reason' ([9.7], 495–6). Gadamer's response to charges of conservatism could not be more categorical:

> It is a grave misunderstanding to assume that emphasis on the essential factor of tradition which enters into all understanding implies an uncritical acceptance of tradition and socio-political conservatism. . . . In truth the confrontation of our historic tradition is always a critical challenge of the tradition.
>
> (*PHC*, 108)

Gadamer's position in this matter could be summed up in the following way: given the presuppositional nature of human understanding, the idea of a *total* critique of what has been handed down to us by tradition is utopic and is an existential impossibility, for the only way in which we can critically scrutinize certain presuppositions is by tacitly appealing to others. However, the fact that we stand always within tradition and cannot, for that reason, criticize everything *at once*, does not mean that there are things that cannot be criticized, as a cultural conservative might maintain. The fact of the matter is that, for Gadamer, there is nothing that cannot, at some time or other, be subjected to criticism in the light of reason. For Gadamer reason and tradition do not stand in an antithetical relation. 'Reason', he in fact says, 'always consists in not blindly insisting upon what is held to be true but in critically occupying oneself with it.'[54]

Thus, in contrast to intellectual conservatives such as Alasdair MacIntyre and Leo Strauss, Gadamer's trenchant critique of philosophical modernity is not intended to justify a return to an idealized, pre-modern, metaphysical past. When, as he often does, Gadamer makes use of notions drawn from the philosophical tradition, it is with the aim of articulating a decidedly post-metaphysical and post-foundationalist – which is to say, postmodern – theory of human being and understanding (albeit one which differs in important ways from other forms of postmodern thought in that it seeks to avoid their relativistic and nihilistic tendencies).

Gadamer's way of summing up his notion of application by saying that the 'same' tradition must always be understood 'in a different way' may strike one as being, to say the least, paradoxical. It would be meaningless indeed were Gadamer presenting his theory of interpretation as a *science* in the traditional sense of the term; from a scientific point of view the same conclusions should invariably follow from the same premises. Unlike Betti and Hirsch, however, Gadamer is not attempting to make of hermeneutics a science; indeed, he is resolutely turning his back on the age-old Platonic notion of science (*episteme*). What he is arguing for is 'a knowledge that is not a science'.[55] In order to indicate what such a knowledge could be, Gadamer effectuates, in the course of his discussion of application, a creative retrieval of Aristotle's notion of *phronesis*.

Phronesis is the key concept in Aristotle's practical philosophy (ethics, politics) and is concerned with the crucial issue of how something *universal* is to be applied in *particular* circumstances. *Phronesis* designates a form of historically informed, prudential judgment which seeks to determine not what is eternally true or valid (as in mathematics) but, as Gadamer would say, 'what is feasible, what is possible, what is correct, here and now' ([9.7], xxv). In opposition to Plato,

Aristotle argued that in matters of practical reasoning (whose object is human action) there can be no hard and fixed rules which, as in logic, can mechanically generate particular decisions. In practical reasoning there is, as it were, a dialectical relation between the universal and the particular; the relation between the two is one not of logical subsumption but of codetermination. The universal in question (an ethical maxim, a law, a principle of political philosophy, and so on) is oriented entirely towards its application and has no real meaning apart from it – in that, precisely, its *raison d'être*, as a theoretical principle, is itself entirely practical, in that it is meant to serve as a guide to action – and yet the universal is not reducible to its particular applications, either, since no single application of the universal is unequivocally dictated by it and, consequently, can claim to exhaust it (to express its 'univocal' meaning). It is just this sort of reciprocal or codetermining relation, Gadamer holds, that obtains between a text (which, as something that is in a sense 'self-same', functions as a universal) and various interpretations ('applications') of it. He writes:

> The interpreter dealing with a traditional text seeks to apply it to himself. But this does not mean that the text is given for him as something universal, that he understands it as such and only afterwards uses it for particular applications. Rather, the interpreter seeks no more than to understand this universal thing, the text; i.e., to understand what this piece of tradition says, what constitutes the meaning and importance of the text. In order to understand that, he must not seek to disregard himself and his particular hermeneutical situation. He must relate the text to this situation, if he wants to understand at all.
>
> ([9.7], 289)

Gadamer's preferred model for text-interpretation is the interpretive activity of the jurist. 'Legal hermeneutics', he maintains, 'is able to point out what the real procedure of the human sciences is.' As he goes on to say:

> Here we have the model for the relationship between past and present that we are seeking. The judge who adapts the transmitted law to the needs of the present is undoubtedly seeking to perform a practical task, but his interpretation of the law is by no means on that account an arbitrary re-interpretation. Here again, to understand and to interpret means to discover and recognise a valid meaning. He seeks to discover the 'legal idea' of a law by linking it with the present.

From this Gadamer generalizes as follows:

Is this not true of every text, i.e., that it must be understood in terms of what it says? Does this not mean that it always needs to be restated? And does not this restatement always take place through its being related to the present? . . . Legal hermeneutics is, then, in reality no special case but is, on the contrary, fitted to restore the full scope of the hermeneutical problem and so to retrieve the former unity of hermeneutics, in which jurist and theologican meet the student of humanities.

([9.7], 292–3)

It follows as a general conclusion that in text-interpretation it is altogether inappropriate – indeed, quixotic – to seek to determine the single correct interpretation of a text. However, it also follows, and with equal force, that in text-interpretation, as in practical reasoning in general, it is never the case that 'anything goes'. If hermeneutics is an instance of practical reasoning, as indeed Gadamer insists that it is – 'The great tradition of practical philosophy lives on in a hermeneutics that becomes aware of its philosophic implications'[56] – this means that while it is never possible to *demonstrate* the validity of one's interpretations, it is nevertheless always possible to *argue* for them in cogent, non-arbitrary, indeed, prudent ways. As an instance of practical philosophy, hermeneutics is as remote from dogmatic scientism as it is from interpretive anarchism. It is precisely because hermeneutics is a practical philosophy in the Aristotelian sense of the term that it can legitimately claim to have transcended both objectivism and relativism.

Godamer's interest in practical philosophy has led him to explore the relationship between hermeneutics and rhetoric. The relationship between the two is both extensive and deep.[57] If it is the case that hermeneutical reasoning is not a form of scientific *demonstration* but of *persuasive argumentation* and that its object is not what is *certain* but what is *probable* or *likely*, then it is obvious that it is to traditional rhetoric – the theory of argumentation (in the words of Chaim Perelman[58]) – that hermeneutics is obliged to look for its theoretical and methodological grounding. The scope of rhetoric, Gadamer says, is truly unlimited, and thus to the universality of hermeneutics corresponds the ubiquity of rhetoric. As he further remarks:

Where, indeed, but to rhetoric should the theoretical examination of interpretation turn? Rhetoric from oldest tradition has been the only advocate of a claim to truth that defends the probable, the *eikos* (verisimile), and that which is convincing to the ordinary reason, against the claim of science to accept as true only what can be demonstrated and tested! Convincing and persuading, without being able to prove – these are obviously as much the aim

321

and measure of understanding and interpretation as they are the aim and measure of oration and persuasion.

([9.5], 24)

Ricoeur shares with Gadamer the same basic approach to text-interpretation, the most common element in which is perhaps the attempt to work out a 'non-subjective' theory of meaning. However, there are some noticeable differences between these two leading representatives of phenomenological hermeneutics, differences not so much in substance, perhaps, as in what they choose to accentuate. Three such differences may be noted.

In the first instance, Ricoeur has always been uncomfortable with Gadamer's apparent dichotomizing of 'truth' and 'method'. Throughout his career Ricoeur has maintained a strong interest in the relationship between philosophy and the human sciences; accordingly, and in contrast to Gadamer, the focus of much of his attention has been on specific methodological issues. While he fully subscribes to the basic ontological concerns of both Heidegger and Gadamer, he feels none the less that this particular preoccupation on their part has tended to prevent philosophical hermeneutics from entering into a serious dialogue with the more empirically oriented sciences. Reacting no doubt to Gadamer's somewhat underdefined notion of 'truth',[59] Ricoeur insists that questions of 'validation' cannot simply be bypassed. Gadamer's 'ontological' hermeneutics, he maintains, ignores the quite legitimate question of validation which so preoccupied romantic hermeneutics. In Ricoeur's eyes Gadamer develops not only the anti-psychologistic tendencies of Heidegger's philosophy but also, unfortunately, its anti-methodological tendencies as well. As a result, he says, a crisis is opened in the hermeneutical movement: 'in correcting the "psychologizing" tendency of Schleiermacher and Dilthey, ontological hermeneutics sacrifices the concern for validation which, with the founders, provided a balance for the divinatory aspect.'[60] Ricoeur distinguishes his own 'methodological' hermeneutics from Gadamer's 'ontological' hermeneutics by saying that it attempts to place 'interpretation theory in dialogue and debate with the human sciences'. It is not surprising, therefore, that – in his continuing attempt to mediate the 'conflict of interpretations' – Ricoeur should make an explicit attempt to incorporate Hirsch's concerns for validation into his own interpretation theory (though in a way which is hardly likely to have won Hirsch's allegiance to the cause of phenomenological hermeneutics).[61]

Another aspect of Gadamer's interpretation theory about which Ricoeur has expressed reservations is the conversation model on which Gadamer relies so extensively. In the light of his concern over the nature of textuality as such, Ricoeur argues that the relationship between reader and text is significantly different from that between two conversational partners. The latter should not be taken as a model for all instances of understanding, and it is definitely not appropriate for conceptualizing our relationship with texts: 'the dialogical model does not provide us with the paradigm of reading' ([9.15], 210).[62]

Far from viewing the act of reading as a kind of dialogue, we should, Ricoeur provocatively remarks, consider even living authors as already dead and their books as posthumous – for only then does the readers' relationship to the book become 'complete and, as it were, intact' ([9.15], 147). The reason for Ricoeur's saying this is the profound transformation that he believes writing has on language. Ricoeur defines a text as 'any discourse fixed by writing' ([9.15], 145), but with this 'fixation' something important happens: the text achieves, as it were, an 'emancipation with respect to the author' ([9.15], 139). More specifically, in writing, the *intention* of the author and the *meaning* of the text cease to coincide (in spoken discourse, Ricoeur holds, the intention of the speaker and the meaning of what he says overlap) (see [9.15], 200). In other words, when language is transformed into a text, it assumes a life of its own, independent of that of its author. As Ricoeur expresses the matter: 'the text's career escapes the finite horizon lived by its author. What the text says now matters more than what the author meant to say, and every exegesis unfolds its procedures within the circumference of a meaning that has broken its moorings to the psychology of the author' ([9.15], 201).

This leads directly into the third difference between Ricoeur and Gadamer to be noted in the present context, having to do with the notion of 'distantiation'. It will be recalled how at the outset of the present section I quoted Gadamer as saying: 'The best definition for hermeneutics is: to let what is alienated by the character of the written word or by the character of being distantiated by cultural or historical distances speak again.' This remark might seem to imply that distantiation is a negative factor which it is the task of interpretation to overcome as much as possible. Ricoeur for his part appears to read Gadamer in this way; he perceives as 'the mainspring of Gadamer's work . . . the opposition between alienating distantiation and belonging' – an opposition reflected in the very title of Gadamer's *Truth and Method* ([9.15], 131). He sees Gadamer as wanting to renounce the concern of the human sciences for objectivity so as to reaffirm our 'belongingness' to the tradition. In opposition to this, Ricoeur states: 'My own reflection stems from a rejection of this alternative and an attempt to overcome it.'

The point that Ricoeur wishes to emphasize is that the phenomenon of textuality overcomes 'the alternative between alienating distantiation and participatory belonging' in such a way as to introduce 'a positive and, if I may say so, productive notion of distantiation.' Why is distantiation a 'productive function'? Distantiation is productive in that, in 'alienating' a text from its original context, it confers on the text a kind of 'autonomy', thereby freeing it for what is in fact its true vocation, namely, that of being 'reactualized' in ever new contexts (becoming in this way a genuinely 'living' text).[63] This reactualization (or recontextualization) is what Ricoeur calls 'appropriation' (*Aneignung*). He prefers this term to 'application' (*Anwendung*), since it underscores the central role that the reader plays in regard to the text. To 'appropriate' means ' "to make one's own" what was initially "alien" ' ([9.15], 185). It is the reader's function to actualize ('make actual, real') the meaning of the text. A text is, by its very nature, addressed to someone, to 'an audience which extends in principle to anyone who can read' ([9.15], 139). In a very real sense, the text's audience is one 'that it itself creates' ([9.15], 202). In any event, without an audience (an addressee) to reactualize it, the meaning of a text would remain for ever 'undecidable', as Derrida has quite rightly remarked. Thus, for Ricoeur, 'reading is the concrete act in which the destiny of the text is fulfilled' ([9.15], 164)

Ricoeur's position in this matter is a strict consequence of his rejection of the psychologistic theory of meaning. The meaning of a text is its 'reference', but this is neither the psychological intention of the author nor an empirical state of affairs in the so-called 'objective' world ('ostensive reference'). The true referent of a text is what it is 'about', what Gadamer calls *die Sache*, the 'matter of the text'. Ricoeur calls this the 'world of the text'. He defines it as 'the ensemble of [non-situational] references opened up by the text' – as when we speak of the 'world of the Greeks', meaning thereby not an empirical reality but a particular *understanding* of the world ([9.15], 202). The 'intended meaning of the text' is the 'world' that it discloses; the projecting of a world is 'the process which is at work in the text' ([9.15], 164).

For Ricoeur there is no text that does not express a 'world', that 'does not connect up with reality', no matter how fictional the text may be ([9.15], 141). In opposition to Roland Barthes, Ricoeur strenuously maintains that the language of texts does not merely 'celebrate itself'. Poetry and novels may not refer to any merely empirical reality, but they most definitely do have a 'second-order reference'.[64] The central task of interpretation is that of explicating this higher-level reference; herein lies, according to Ricoeur, 'the center of gravity of the hermeneutical question' ([9.15], 132), 'the most fundamental hermeneutical problem' ([9.15], 141):

If we can no longer define hermeneutics in terms of the search for the psychological intentions of another person which are concealed *behind* the text, and if we do not want to reduce interpretation to the dismantling of structures [as in the structuralist, purely explanatory approach], then what remains to be interpreted? I shall say: to interpret is to explicate the type of being-in-the-world unfolded *in front of* the text.

This last remark provides a more precise indication of what Ricoeur means by the 'world of the work'. This 'world' is none other than Husserl's life-world or Heidegger's being-in-the-world. That is to say, the 'possible world' ([9.15], 218) unfolded in a text is nothing other than a *possible mode of being*. In other words, *it is a world which I, the reader, could (possibly) inhabit*. By opening up a world for us, a text provides us with 'new dimensions of our being-in-the-world' ([9.15], 202); it suggests to us new and different ways in which we ourselves could be. 'To understand a text', Ricoeur says, 'is at the same time to light up our own situation' ([9.15], 202). It is at this point that Ricoeur's theory of text-interpretation links up with his overriding concern to articulate a non-metaphysical concept of subjectivity, 'a new theory of subjectivity' ([9.15], 182).

The key point here is that in appropriating the meaning (the 'world') of a text, the reader – the self – reappropriates *it*self, acquires in effect a new self. 'What would we know of love and hate,' Ricoeur asks, 'of moral feelings and, in general, of all that we call the *self*, if these had not been brought to language and articulated by literature' ([9.15], 143)? The relation between text and reader is thus, as it were, a two-way street: the text depends on its readers for its actualization, but in the process of reading – giving the text a meaning – readers are themselves actualized ('metamorphosed') – given a self – by the text. In exposing ourselves to the text, we undergo 'imaginative variations' of our egos (see [9.15], 189) and receive in this way from the text 'an enlarged self, which would be the proposed existence corresponding in the most suitable way to the world proposed' ([9.15], 143). Thus, as Ricoeur remarks:

> In general we may say that appropriation is no longer to be understood in the tradition of philosophies of the subject, as a constitution of which the subject would possess the key. To understand is not to project oneself into the text; it is to receive an enlarged self from the apprehension of proposed worlds which are the genuine object of interpretation.
>
> ([9.15], 182–3)

It can thus be seen that while Ricoeur's interpretation theory situates the reader at the heart of the interpretive process, it does not legitimate any form of interpretational subjectivism; what it calls for is 'instead a moment of dispossession of the narcissistic *ego*' ([9.15], 192).[65] However, by linking up the understanding of meaning with self-understanding, it does illustrate in a striking way Ricoeur's basic philosophical motives which derive from the tradition of reflective (or reflexive) philosophy and, more particularly, the concern for the 'self' that he inherits from existentialism.[66] In all text-interpretation what is ultimately at stake is a self in search of self-understanding, in search of 'the meaning of his own life' ([9.15], 158). Thus Ricoeur writes: 'By "appropriation", I understand this: that the interpretation of a text culminates in the self-interpretation of a subject who thenceforth understands himself better, understands himself differently, or simply begins to understand himself' ([9.15], 158). It is accordingly not surprising that when in the course of a famous debate Lévi-Strauss asserted that for him meaning is always phenomenal and that underneath meaning (conceived of as nothing more than the combination of elements meaningless in themselves) there is only non-meaning, Ricoeur should have insisted most strongly: 'If meaning is not a segment in self-understanding, I don't know what it is.'[67] The position that Ricoeur adopts in his consideration of the human sciences and, in particular, the explanation/ understanding debate is, as we shall see in what follows, dictated by this fundamental conviction.

❧ HERMENEUTICS AND THE HUMAN SCIENCES: ❧ FROM TEXT TO ACTION

If Gadamer's major contribution to philosophical hermeneutics is to have provided it with a general theory of human understanding, Ricoeur's vital contribution to the discipline could perhaps be said to consist in his having drawn from this ontology of understanding *methodological* conclusions of direct relevance to the practice of the human sciences. In doing so, he has also addressed the key problem in the philosophy of the human sciences that Gadamer's hermeneutics tends to leave unresolved, namely, the problem of the relation between *explanation* and *understanding*.

What is it about hermeneutics, one might ask, that makes it especially relevant to the human sciences? Or, again, what is it about the human sciences that allows one to maintain that they themselves are most properly understood when viewed as a form of 'applied' hermeneutics? The proper objects of these disciplines might seem, on the face of it, to have very little in common: the traditional concern of hermeneutics is *texts*, whereas the proper object of the human sciences is human *action*. The human sciences are concerned with what people do, the meaning of what they do, why and how they do it, and the consequences of their doing what they do. Hermeneutics is concerned, at its core, with the right reading of texts. But perhaps, to be understood properly, human action needs also to be *read* in the right way. Perhaps the common element here is the notion of *meaning*.

What indeed constitutes the specificity of the human sciences *vis-à-vis* the natural sciences? The difference lies first and foremost in the respective objects of these sciences. What is unique about the objects of the human sciences is that these objects are also *subjects*. As three human scientists remark: 'the objects studied are subjects, embedded in cultural practices, who think, construe, understand, misunderstand, and interpret, as well as reflect on the meanings they produce.'[68] This difference in the objects (or subject matter) of the two kinds of science dictates a difference in *method* (it does, that is, if one adheres to Aristotle's injunction to the effect that a science should always adapt its method to the nature of the object under consideration). From a methodological point of view, human *action* falls under a different category altogether than does mere physical *motion*. Motion can be 'explained' in purely mechanistic terms, in terms of physical cause and effect relations, but action cannot properly be 'understood' except in terms of *meaning*. As the object of a science, human agents are not only interpreted objects (as in the case of the natural sciences), they are also self-interpreting subjects. Phenomenologically speaking, what is unique about that entity called 'man' is that he is a *self*-interpreting animal (this is, of course, simply another way of saying that 'man' is the 'speaking animal'). What this all means is that (in the words of the hermeneutical anthropologist Clifford Geertz) 'man is an animal suspended in webs of significance he himself has spun' and that, accordingly, the analysis of human culture (understood as precisely those 'webs') is not 'an experimental science in search of [nomological-deductive] law but an interpretive one in search of meaning'.[69]

Human action is essentially meaningful (significative) in that action is, by definition and in contrast to purely physical systems, intentional, teleological or purposeful. Humans *act* in order to bring into being states of affairs that would not, or would not likely, prevail without their acting. If, for instance, humans engage in economic activities (the only species to do so), it is, as economist Ludwig von Mises has remarked, *in order to* improve their material position, to make their lives more liveable, more meaningful.[70] That human action is essentially meaningful can therefore be taken as an ontological (or phenomenological) fact. The crucial question, as concerns the human sciences, is a methodological one: if the human sciences cannot look to the natural sciences for their method (since the concept of meaning or purpose is itself meaningless in a purely physicalistic or mechanistic context), where are they to look? This is where hermeneutics comes in.

In a famous article, 'The Model of the Text: Meaningful Action Considered as a Text', Ricoeur addressed the above mentioned question. Meaningful action, he said, can be the object of a science only if the meaning of action is 'objectified' in a way equivalent to that in which the meaning of discourse is 'fixated' by writing (see [9.15], 203) – only if, in other words, action can properly be viewed as a text-analogue (a 'quasi text'). Ricoeur maintains that this is indeed the case. He writes:

> In the same way that a text is detached from its author, an action is detached from its agent and develops consequences of its own. This autonomisation of human action constitutes the *social* dimension of action. An action is a social phenomenon . . . because our deeds escape us and have effects which we did not intend. One of the meanings of the notion of 'inscription' ['fixation'] appears here. The kind of distance which we found between the intention of the speaker and the verbal meaning of a text occurs also between the agent and its action.
>
> ([9.15], 206)

This is an important text, in that it specifies clearly that aspect of meaningful human action which makes of it the proper object of a *social* science: as in the case of texts, the meaning of action is not reducible to the psychological intentions of the agents themselves. The meaning of what people do displays an autonomy similar to that of texts in regard to their authors' intentions. Thus here too the notion of meaning must be 'depsychologized' or 'desubjectivized'. The proper objects of the social sciences are various social *orders* (the equivalent of texts) which are the *result* of human action – the result, it must be added, of human action but not necessarily of human design.[71] As Ricoeur remarks: 'our deeds escape us and have effects which we did not intend.' Our deeds escape us in the same way that the text's career escapes the finite horizon of its author. Strictly speaking, therefore, the meaningful action or, better expressed, the meaningful *patterns of action* that the social sciences seek to understand are *neither* subjective *nor* objective (in the purely physicalistic sense of the term). As the Canadian hermeneuticist Charles Taylor has emphasized, we are dealing here with meanings which are not subjective (residing in the heads of the actors) but rather *intersubjective*. 'The meanings and norms implicit in these practices', Taylor observes, 'are not just in the minds of the actors but are out there in the practices themselves, practices which cannot be conceived as a set of individual actions, but which are essentially modes of social relation, of mutual action.'[72] Although, as Ricoeur reminds us, it is only individuals who do things, it is nevertheless also the case that human action is meaningful – and thus understandable – only in terms of a shared public world.[73] As one psychotherapist observes:

> The meaning of action can be read from the directedness of the action seen within the pattern of practices that constitute the individual's social milieu. It is these practices, and not any representations in the individual's head, that determine the meanings attributable to the individual. The background of social practices and cultural institutions give specific objects and actions – and even mental representations when they do occur – their meanings.[74]

Another way of expressing the matter would be to say that just as what constitutes a text is that it has a certain 'logic' which it is precisely the task of text-interpretation to lay bare (Ricoeur speaks in this regard of 'the internal dynamic which governs the structuring of the work' (*OI*, 193)), so also there is a certain objective logic to human events or practices which it is precisely the task of social science to explicate. The social orders or 'wholes' that social scientists (anthropologists, economists, historians, etc.) seek to render intelligible possess their own unique ontological status in that their mode of being is *neither* psychological *nor* physical; it is, as Merleau-Ponty would say, an 'ambiguous' mode of being, neither that of the for-itself nor that of the in-itself. These wholes are indeed *objective* (or incarnate) *logics*, which exist as the sedimented results (in the form, ultimately, of sociocultural *institutions*) of the activities of a myriad of individual human agents, each of whom was pursuing meaning in his or her own life. If this is indeed the case, the crucial methodological question becomes: what method is most appropriate to the task of explicating these logics?

From what has been said, it should be evident that a purely *descriptive* approach (in terms of mental states) is no more appropriate than would be a purely 'explanatory', cause-and-effect approach; in both cases the object to be understood – meaning embedded in intersubjective practices – would be lost sight of. Human agents are self-interpreting beings, but it is not the task of a social science simply to 'describe' these interpretations. It is not their task, if it is indeed the case that the meaning of action surpasses the intentions of the actors themselves. The function of interpretation cannot simply be that of *Verstehen* in the classical sense of the term, i.e., that of articulating the self-understanding of human actors, in such a way as to achieve an empathetic understanding of them. The unavoidable fact of the matter is that the human sciences are *doubly interpretive*; they are interpretations of the interpretations that people themselves offer for their actions. As Clifford Geertz has observed: 'what we call our data are really our own constructions of other people's constructions of what they and their compatriots are up to.'[75] The fact that the proper object of social science is the logic of *practices* and not merely the psychological intentions of actors means that social scientists often have to discount the self-interpretations of the actors themselves.[76] Ricoeur has long insisted that the consciousness that we have of ourselves is often a false consciousness, which means that the hermeneutical enterprise must include as one of its moments, a 'hermeneutics of suspicion'.

This amounts to saying that the role of an interpretive social science is necessarily *critical*. The fact that there is inevitably a certain non-coincidence between the interpretations worked out by the social scientist and the self-interpretations proffered by the actors themselves means that there exists, in the words of John B. Thompson, a 'methodological space for . . . *the critical potential of interpretation*'.[77] Because there is always, to one degree or another, a certain *décalage* or discrepancy between what people do and what they say they do, critique is in fact integral to interpretive understanding, and this is why philosophical hermeneutics can, with Habermas in mind, insist on the *emancipatory* function of interpretive theory.

In conceptualizing the interpretive function in a way such as this, Ricoeur is able, he believes, to resolve the long-standing conflict between 'explanation' and 'understanding' (Gadamer had already portrayed Dilthey's dichotomizing distinction as a relic of the Cartesian dualism which has infected all of modern thought).[78] From what has been said, it is obvious that interpretation cannot be reduced to 'understanding', in the narrow (empathetic) sense of the term. Indeed, precisely because the meaning of human action is not 'subjective', there is, Ricoeur maintains, a legitimate, albeit strictly limited, place for explanatory techniques of a purely objective nature in the overall interpretive process. If (as in psychotherapy, for instance) meaning-intentions are not open to, or cannot be exhaustively grasped by, direct inspection, and thus cannot simply be described 'from within', but must be deciphered and interpreted, as it were, 'from without', it follows that there is, by principle and of necessity, a rightful place for 'explanation' (in the traditional sense of the term) in the human sciences.

Just as, in the case of text-interpretation, it may be useful at the outset to approach a text in a purely objective way, in terms of an analysis of its formal structure or computer analysis of word distribution, for instance, so also, in an attempt to understand human action, an objective approach, e.g., in terms of statistical analysis, may alert social scientists to the existence of patterns they might otherwise overlook. What Ricoeur wishes nevertheless to emphasize is that the intelligibility provided by purely explanatory techniques is essentially partial and one-sided. The phenomena themselves cannot properly be understood, in the last analysis, until the results of the explanatory approach are integrated into a wider, interpretive understanding. For Ricoeur, 'explanation' amounts to a *methodological distantiation* from what is 'said' in the text (the 'world of the text'), but, unlike Gadamer (in Ricoeur's view), he holds that this is a proper, and even necessary, moment in the overall process of understanding, conceived of, in the last analysis, as 'appropriation'. With Ricoeur there is, therefore, as one commentator says, a 'dialectic of an understanding which takes the detour of methodic distantiation so as to return to understanding'.[79]

Ricoeur's strategy in this regard consists in locating 'explanation and understanding at two different stages of a unique *hermeneutical arc*' ([9.15] 218), integrating thereby the opposed attitudes of explanation and understanding within an overall conception of interpretation as the recovery of meaning. In accordance with his hermeneutical conviction that all understanding is ultimately a form of self-understanding, Ricoeur maintains that, as he says, 'the final brace of the bridge [is] anchorage of the arch in the ground of lived experience' ([9.15], 164). In accordance as well with his underlying existential motivations, Ricoeur also insists that social structures are 'attempts to cope with existential perplexities, human predicaments and deep-rooted conflicts' ([9.15], 220). Thus, the ultimate goal of the social sciences is no different from that of text-interpretation, namely 'appropriation', a heightened understanding of the meaning of our being-in-the-world. 'We are not allowed', Ricoeur insists, 'to exclude the final act of personal commitment from the whole of objective and explanatory procedures which mediate it' ([9.15], 221). In applying Ricoeur's notion of the 'fixation' or 'inscription' of meaning to the study of cultures, Clifford Geertz for his part insists that the ultimate concern of the anthropologist is 'the existential dilemmas of life' and that the 'essential vocation' of interpretive anthropology is that of making 'available to us answers that others, guarding other sheep in other valleys, have given, and thus to include them in the consultable record of what man has said'.[80]

Ricoeur has long maintained that human phenomena – texts, action – cannot properly be understood until the results of the explanatory approach have been integrated into a wider, interpretive understanding. In his latest work culminating in his three-volume study *Time and Narrative* (1983–8), he has argued that the attempt to understand the specifically human must, in the final analysis, assume the form of a *narrative*. To the teleological nature of action, discussed above, corresponds the plot structure of narrative.[81] 'Objective data' (that is, the data that are produced as a result of the application of objective measuring techniques) achieve their maximum intelligibility not when, as is the goal of the natural sciences, they have been subsumed under (supposedly) binding and timeless 'covering laws' (whose putative purpose is that of 'explanation' and 'prediction') but when, as in history or psychotherapy, they have been interrelated and integrated into a narrative account, one which, precisely, confers meaning on them through narrative emplotment. For Ricoeur, the most primordial of all forms of understanding is thus that of story-telling. He writes:

> to follow a story is to understand the successive actions, thoughts and feelings as displaying a particular *directedness*. By this I mean that we are pushed along by the development and that we respond to this thrust with expectations concerning the outcome and culmination of the process. In this sense, the 'conclusion' of the story is the pole of attraction of the whole process. But a narrative conclusion can be neither deduced nor predicted. There is no story unless our attention is held in suspense by a thousand contingencies. Hence we must follow the story to its conclusion. So rather than being *predictable*, a conclusion must be *acceptable*. Looking back from the conclusion towards the episodes which led up to it, we must be able to say that this end required those events and that chain of action. But this retrospective glance is made possible by the teleologically guided movement of our expectations when we follow the story. Such is the paradox of the contingency, 'acceptable after all', which characterises the understanding of any story.
>
> ([9.15], 277)

As Kierkegaard pointed out, understanding comes always only after the event, and, as Ricoeur has sought to show, the full measure of whatever understanding is available to us is made possible not by formalistic modes of explanation but by retrospective, narrative emplotment. Ricoeur has developed his theory of the narrative function primarily with respect to historiography,[82] but it can be, and has been, extended to other human sciences.[83] If Gadamer has argued for the universality of hermeneutics on the grounds that hermeneutics is concerned with the entire range of human *linguisticality* – which, in turn, is coextensive with 'being that can be understood' – Ricoeur advances this claim even further when, in his later writings, he maintains that the object of hermeneutics is *textuality*, and that this notion is coextensive with human existence itself. As one commentator remarks: 'Hermeneutics is concerned with the interpretation of any expression of existence which can be preserved in a structure analogous to the structure of the text. . . . Taking it to the limit, the entirety of human existence becomes a text to be interpreted.'[84]

As Ricoeur's work on narrative clearly demonstrates, good history shares many of the same traits as good fiction. In showing how understanding is ultimately a form of story-telling – and in undermining in this way the modernist opposition between the 'real' and the 'imaginary' – Ricoeur has also shown how hermeneutical truth is itself a result of the *productive imagination*.[85] For Ricoeur the poetic imagination (the means whereby that 'higher order referent' he calls the 'world of the text' is brought into being) is necessarily a 'subversive force' in regard to what is customarily (or traditionally) taken to be 'real'. If Ricoeur stresses the role of the imagination in the overall understanding process, it is because he perceives this to be a strategic means of defending hermeneutics against Habermas's charge that it is inherently 'conservative'. The hermeneutics of the text conceived of as a 'hermeneutics of the power-to-be' (and thus as a critique of the illusions and false consciousness of the subject) would itself, he argues, provide the necessary underpinnings for a critique of ideology [9.15], 94). Of particular interest to Ricoeur is the theme of the 'social-imaginary' ('l'institution imaginaire de la société', in the words of Cornelius Castoriadis), an interest which testifies to his overriding concern with social and political, i.e., practical, philosophy – a concern shared by Gademer, as we shall see in what follows.[86]

❧ HERMENEUTICS AND PRACTICAL PHILOSOPHY: ❧ ETHICAL AND POLITICAL IMPLICATIONS

The ultimate task of hermeneutical reflection consists in explicating the values that inform and guide hermeneutical practice itself. These are values that are inherent in the 'hermeneutical experience' (as Gadamer calls it), i.e., in that most natural and universal of all human activities: the persistent attempt on the part of humans to achieve understanding, self-understanding, and, above all, mutual understanding. In articulating these values, hermeneutics seeks to do no more than to spell out the (practical) 'conditions of possibility' of the interpretive-communicative process itself. It may be noted that the values arrived at in this way are the core values of traditional liberal theory: tolerance, reasonableness, the attempt to work out mutual agreements by means of discourse ('conversation') rather than by means of force.[87] The values in question are ones that Gadamer would call 'principles of reason' – in that they are integral to communicative understanding or rationality.

Hermeneutical values are those having to do with respect for the freedom and dignity of one's conversational partners, one's fellow dialogical beings. A fundamental value in this regard is that of *equality*. Since for an agreement to count as 'true' – from the viewpoint of communicative rationality – it must be reached by non-coercive means, the right of dialogical partners to equal and fair consideration cannot rationally be denied. The hermeneutical notion of 'good will'[88] points to a core precept of democratic pluralism: the other may possibly be right over against oneself and thus must be accorded a freedom equal to one's own. Of all the principles of reason, the highest is of course *freedom* itself. In the course of a discussion of Hegel, Gadamer asserts:

> There is no higher principle of reason than that of freedom. Thus the opinion of Hegel and thus our own opinion as well. No higher principle is thinkable than that of the freedom of all, and we understand actual history from the perspective of this principle: as the ever-to-be-renewed and the never-ending struggle for this freedom.
>
> ([9.6], 9)

Freedom is the highest 'principle of reason' in that (as the theory of argumentation – the 'new rhetoric' – has shown) no one can claim to be 'reasonable' if he or she denies freedom of opinion and expression to others. No one, that is, can deny this freedom without undermining his or her own demand for due consideration (recognition) that is implicit in the expressing of any opinion whatsoever, and without thereby ostracizing himself or herself from collective or intersubjective deliberations as to what is true and right. For Gadamer *freedom* and *reason* are inseparable concepts; freedom is precisely the freedom (the right) to possess a meaningful voice in the common dialogue, in that 'conversation' which is constitutive of our humanity.

In advocating the 'freedom of all' as the highest principle of reason, Gadamer, it will be noted, is defending the *universality* of certain basic human values. Here again is an illustration of how hermeneutics differs in a most important way from other forms of anti-foundational postmodernism; unlike them, hermeneutics does not believe that a rejection of objectivism need entail an anti-humanist relativism. To the universality of human linguisticality corresponds the universality of certain basic human rights. 'It is no longer possible', Gadamer insists, 'for anyone still to affirm the unfreedom of humanity' ([9.6], 37). Unlike Heidegger and recent poststructuralists, both Gadamer and Ricoeur defend the tradition of philosophical and political humanism.[89]

It may be noted as well that hermeneutics' defence of normative universalism is what allows for the possibility of a *philosophical or rational critique* of existing practices. 'The task of bringing people to a self-understanding of themselves', Gadamer says, 'may help us to gain our freedom in relation to everything that has taken us in unquestion-ingly' ([9.6], 149–50). To the degree that this or that form of human community fails to embody the universal values of communicative rationality, it is a legitimate object of critique. To fail to expose various forms of 'social irrationality' ([9.6], 74) for fear of being accused of 'ethnocentrism' and, more specifically, of 'Eurocentrism' would, her-meneutics believes, amount to nothing less than a betrayal of reason.[90]

This is yet another reason why Gadamer's own version of hermen-eutics is improperly understood when, as is often the case, it is thought to entail 'an uncritical acceptance of tradition and sociopolitical con-servatism' (*PHC*, 108). Richard Bernstein is one commentator who has clearly perceived the 'radical' element in Gadamer's hermeneutics that follows from its stress on practical philosophy. Bernstein notes how, in attempting to draw out the practical consequences of philosophical hermeneutics, Gadamer appropriates from Hegel the principle of free-dom ('a freedom that is realized only when there is authentic mutual "recognition" among individuals'), and he remarks: 'This radical strain is indicated in his emphasis – which has become more and more domi-nant in recent years – on freedom and solidarity that embrace all of humanity.'[91]

Although he meant it as a criticism, Stanley Rosen was quite right when he said: 'Every hermeneutical program is at the same time a political manifesto or the corollary of a political manifesto.'[92] Gadamer openly acknowledges this when he characterizes hermeneutics as *scientia practica sive politica*.[93] Hermeneutical philosophy is inevitably politi-cal – to the degree, that is, that it is a form of practical philosophy, which is to say, to the degree that it privileges practical reason, *phron-esis*, dialogue. In addition, hermeneutical politics inevitably assumes the form of what Ricoeur calls 'political liberalism'. 'This apologia of dialogue', he says, 'implies, in the context of politics, an unremitting censure of tyranny and authoritarian régimes, and a plea for discussion as also for the free expression and unrestricted interplay of all shades of opinion.'[94] In many of his shorter writings after *Truth and Method* Gadamer returns again and again to socio-political issues, defending the values of communicative rationality and denouncing the subtle forms of oppression that tend to subvert these values in an age domi-nated by science and technology and a purely instrumentalist concep-tion of reason. 'It is the function of hermeneutical reflection, in this connection [the conservation of freedom],' Gadamer says, 'to preserve us from naïve surrender to the experts of social technology' ([9.5], 40).[95]

The term used by Gadamer to refer to the normative ideal defended by hermeneutics is *solidarity*. What 'practice' means, Gadamer says, 'is conducting oneself and acting in solidarity. Solidarity . . . is the decisive condition and basis of all social reason' ([9.6], 87). The task incumbent upon hermeneutics is a universalist one; it is, as Gadamer might say, that of 'reawakening consciousness of solidarity of a humanity that slowly begins to know itself as humanity' ([9.6], 86). The solidarity advocated by Gadamer is not, it should clearly be noted, one based solely on ethnic or cultural commonalities (*Gemeinschaft*, 'culture'). What he means by solidarity is, rather, 'rational identification with a universal interest', with 'the universals of law and justice'.[96] Unlike present-day communitarians of either the left or the right, Gadamer is not extolling the virtues of any particular ethos or way of life ('community'), purely as such; he is arguing for the need for a genuine, philosophical (and thus universalist) *ethics*. The relation here between ethics (*Moralität*) and ethos (*Sittlichkeit*) parallels the more general relation between 'understanding' (the universal) and 'application' (the particular) discussed above; the former requires the latter, but is not reducible to it.[97] Practical reason is indeed a form of *reason*, which means that it makes a claim to *universality*.[98] In the final analysis, the solidarity Gadamer defends is the solidarity of *reason* seeking 'general agreement';[99] it is the solidarity of mutual recognition (*Anerkennung*) binding together the citizens of a liberal society (*Gesellschaft*), i.e., a polity, or what Kant called 'a universal civic society',[100] founded upon the rational idea of human rights and universal freedom.[101]

In opposition to anarchism in both its leftist and rightist versions (the latter sometimes referred to as 'anarcho-capitalism'), hermeneutics insists that for freedom and solidarity to prevail in practice liberal *institutions* are required (or what Gadamer refers to as 'moral and human arrangements built on common norms').[102] As Merleau-Ponty had already pointed out, invoking the name of Hegel: 'freedom requires something substantial; it requires a State, which bears it and which it gives life to.' The essential thing is the existence of 'institutions which implant this practice of freedom in our customs [*moeurs*]'.[103] Ricoeur reiterates this point. In the Hegelian view that Ricoeur adopts, an 'institution' is the 'whole of the rules relating to the acts of social life that allow the freedom of each to be realized without harm to the freedom of others'.[104] Ricoeur refers to this institutional set-up as 'un Etat de droit', i.e., the liberal-democratic state or the rule of law. Such a state is democratic in that it 'does not propose to eliminate conflicts but to invent procedures permitting them to be expressed and to remain negotiable. The State of Law, in this sense,' Ricoeur goes on to say, 'is the State of organized free discussion.' Ricoeur refers in this connection to Hegel's definition of the most rational state as 'the State in which each would be recognized by all'.[105] In arguing for 'a synthesis of freedom and institution' Ricoeur is expressly arguing against those contemporaries of his – referred to by some as the 'philosophers of

'68'[106] – who exalt a kind of 'liberté sauvage' outside of any institutional framework and who denounce institutions as being essentially coercive and repressive. And he insists that 'it is only in the form of the liberal State that this synthesis [of freedom and institutions] can be seen at work in the depths of history'.[107] The liberal-democratic state defended by hermeneutics is, one could say, nothing other than the institutional-ization of (dialogical) reason. In this connection Richard Bernstein describes the practical task of hermeneutics as that of fostering 'the type of dialogical communities in which *phronesis* becomes a living reality and where citizens can actually assume what Gadamer tells us is their "noblest task" – "decision-making according to one's own responsibility – instead of conceding that task to the expert" '.[108] What democratic theory has long referred to as the 'common good' is in fact nothing other than an order of social institutions binding people together, one whose *raison d'être* is to facilitate and encourage in them the exercise of practical-dialogical reason ('solidarity').

In conclusion, it is apparent that philosophical or phenomenological hermeneutics not only provides a general theory of human under-standing in its various modes, it also prescribes very specific tasks in the realm of socio-political *praxis*. With the recent demise of anti-liberal socialism and the triumph of democratic values throughout much of the world, 'the end of history' is said by some to have occurred. Although Gadamer too does not see any alternative to liberalism, he is under no illusions as to the ultimate triumph of freedom and reason in history. He agrees with Hegel that it is no longer possible for anyone (rationally) to deny the supreme value of the freedom of all. 'The principle that all are free never again can be shaken.' It cannot be shaken to the degree that the principle is, precisely, a principle of reason. However, he adds:

> But does this mean that on account of this, history has come to an end? Are all human beings actually free? Has not history since then [Hegel's time] been a matter of just this, that the historical conduct of man has to translate the principle of freedom into reality? Obviously this points to the unending march of world history into the openness of its future tasks and gives no becalm-ing assurance that everything is already in order.
>
> ([9.6], 37)

The task of realizing freedom in history is like the task of under-standing and self-understanding itself – it is an endless task. 'To exist historically', Gadamer says in reply to Hegel, 'means that knowledge of oneself can never be complete' ([9.7], 269). Like humanism or the belief in the 'subject' – the human subject in search of meaning in his or her own life and, as such, the bearer of basic human rights –

hermeneutics or the belief in meaning in history must recognize, as Ricoeur says, that it is without metaphysical foundations, that it is a wager, a cry.[109]

 NOTES

1 The term was apparently first used by J. C. Dannhauer in his *Hermeneutica sacra sive methodus exponendarum sacrarum litterarum* (1654).

2 F. Schleiermacher, *Hermeneutics: The Handwritten Manuscripts*, ed. H. Kimmerle, trans. J. Duke and J. Forstman (Missoula: Scholars Press, 1977), p. 93.

3 Both Gadamer and Ricoeur concur in ascribing to Schleiermacher a 'psychologistic' view of understanding of the sort described here. This interpretation has been challenged, however, by Manfred Frank; see his *What is Neostructuralism?*, trans. S. Wilke and R. Gray (Minneapolis: University of Minnesota Press, 1989), pp. 8–9.

4 See C. G. Hempel, 'The Function of General Laws in History' (1942), reprinted in *Theories of History*, ed. P. Gardiner (New York: Free Press of Glencoe, 1959), pp. 344–56.

5 See P. Winch, *The Idea of a Social Science and Its Relation to Philosophy* (London: Routledge & Kegan Paul, 1958), as well as his articles 'The Idea of a Social Science' and 'Understanding of a Primitive Society', both in *Rationality*, ed. B. R. Wilson (New York: Harper Torchbooks, 1971).

6 R. J. Bernstein [9.29], 30.

7 'Phenomenological hermeneutics' aptly designates the hermeneutics of Gadamer and Ricoeur since, as I shall indicate in more detail below, their thought is rooted in the phenomenology of Edmund Husserl and Martin Heidegger. Ricoeur has said of his own position: 'it strives to be a *hermeneutical* variation of this [Husserl's] phenomenology' ('On Interpretation' in A. Montefiore (ed.), *Philosophy in France Today* (Cambridge: Cambridge University Press, 1983), p. 187; hereafter cited in the text as *OI*). On another occasion Ricoeur stated: 'I do not believe that hermeneutics replaces phenomenology. It is only opposed to the idealist interpretation of phenomenology' ('Response to My Friends and Critics' in C. E. Reagan [9.25], no page no.).

8 Tübingen: J. C. B. Mohr; see also his earlier encyclopaedic work, *Theoria generale della interpretazione*, 2 vols (Milan: Dott. A. Giuffrè, 1955).

9 E. D. Hirsch, Jr, *Validity in Interpretation* (New Haven: Yale University Press, 1967).

10 See *Validity*, p. 264: 'The much-advertised cleavage between thinking in the sciences and the humanities does not exist. The hypothetico-deductive process is fundamental in both of them, as it is in all thinking that aspires to knowledge.'

11 A particularly mean-spirited attack against Gadamer along these lines was published by J. Barnes: 'A Kind of Integrity', *London Review of Books*, 6 Nov. 1986, pp. 12–13.

12 As Ricoeur recently pointed out in response to the Canadian hermeneuticist Jean Grondin, hermeneutic's polemical opposition to objectivism is an integral

part of hermeneutics as it is of the Husserlian phenomenology from which it derives. 'L'herméneutique ... est polémique', Ricoeur says, 'parce que la *compréhension* dont elle s'autorise doit sans cesse se reconquérir sur diverses figures de la *méconnaissance*' (Ricoeur, 'Réponses' in C. Bouchindhomme and R. Rochlitz (eds), *'Temps et récit' de Paul Ricoeur: en débat* (Paris: Editions du Cerf, 1990), pp. 201–2).

13 Gadamer here refers in a note to Betti's work.

14 Hans-Georg Gadamer, *Truth and Method* [9.7], xvi.

15 This was in fact the title given to an edited collection of essays by Gadamer published in 1976: *Philosophical Hermeneutics* ([9.5]).

16 For a detailed treatment of this issue see 'Ricoeur and the Hermeneutics of the Subject' in Madison [9.34]; forthcoming also in *The Philosophy of Paul Ricoeur* (Library of Living Philosophers), ed. I. E. Hahn. For a good overview of the basic themes in Ricoeur's philosophizing, centred on the notion of the subject, see John W. Van Den Hengel [9.27]. Van Den Hengel includes in his study a remarkably extensive bibliography (483 titles) of Ricoeur's writings from 1935 to 1981.

17 Husserl provides a historical reconstruction of the modernist tradition to which he is opposed in *The Crisis of European Sciences and Transcendental Phenomenology: An Introduction to Phenomenological Philosophy*, trans. D. Carr (Evanston: Northwestern University Press, 1970).

18 See E. Husserl, *The Idea of Phenomenology*, trans. W. P. Alston and G. Nakhnikian (The Hague: Martinus Nijhoff, 1964), lecture I.

19 The phrase is that of Ludwig Landgrebe, one of Husserl's late assistants. See his 'Husserl's Departure from Cartesianism', in R. O. Elveton (ed.), *The Phenomenology of Husserl* (Chicago: Quadrangle Books, 1970), p. 261.

20 Cf. Ricoeur, 'On Interpretation' (see note 7), p. 190: 'The theme of the *Lebenswelt*, a theme which phenomenology came up against in spite of itself, one might say, is adopted by post-Heideggerian hermeneutics no longer as something left over, but as a prior condition.'

21 See M. Merleau-Ponty, *Phenomenology of Perception*, trans. C. Smith (London: Routledge & Kegan Paul, 1962), p. xiv: 'Far from being, as has been thought, a procedure of idealistic philosophy, phenomenological reduction belongs to existential philosophy: Heidegger's "being-in-the-world" appears only against the background of the phenomenological reduction.'

22 M. Heidegger, *Being and Time*, trans. J. Macquarrie and E. Robinson (New York: Harper & Row, 1962), p. 90: hereafter cited in the text as *BT*.

23 Ricoeur, *Hermeneutics and the Human Sciences* [9.15], 87.

24 'In it [interpretation] the understanding appropriates understandingly that which is understood by it' (*BT*, 188).

25 Ricoeur, 'The Question of the Subject', in D. Ihde (ed.), *The Conflict of Interpretations:Essays in Hermeneutics* (Evanston: Northwestern University Press, 1974), p. 266 (translation corrected).

26 Gadamer, 'The Problem of Historical Consciousness', in P. Rabinow and W. M. Sullivan (eds), *Interpretive Social Science: A Reader* (Berkeley: University of California Press, 1979), p. 106; hereafter cited in the text as *PHC*. Ricoeur also bypasses Heidegger's concern for Being. Grounded as his thinking is in the French tradition of reflexive philosophy, Ricoeur's guiding question is

not so much 'What is the meaning of being?' as 'Who am I?' He writes: 'L'herméneutique devenait pour moi le long détour d'une philosophie de la réflexion, la médiation interminable de l'auto-compréhension . . . [M]a philosophie s'est développée – grossièrement parlant – comme une anthropologie philosophique, où la question de l'être se réduit à celle du mode d'être de cet être capable de se désigner comme sujet parlant, comme agent et patient de l'action, comme sujet moral et politique, porteur de responsabilité et de citoyenneté' ('Réponses' in *'Temps et récit' de Paul Ricoeur* (note 12), p. 211).

27 Bernstein [9.29], 159.

28 I owe this particular observation to Paul Fairfield.

29 The parallel between the two was one of the principal objects of concern of Merleau-Ponty's hermeneutical phenomenology.

30 What Gadamer says here of historical understanding could be applied, *mutatis mutandis*, to intercultural or ethnological understanding and could be usefully contrasted with the position defended by Peter Winch.

31 For a good overview and discussion of the issues involved in this debate, see Bernstein [9.29].

32 It would not be desirable, in that it is incompatible with the philosophical-political values to which hermeneutics subscribes – a topic to be considered later in this chapter.

33 Gadamer, 'The Science of the Life-World', *Analecta Husserliana*, 2 (1977): 185. It should be noted that this text differs from the version published subsequently under the same title in *Philosophical Hermeneutics*.

34 Ricoeur makes a similar remark: 'The truth is . . . the lighted place in which it is possible to continue to live and to think. And to think *with* our very opponents themselves, without allowing the totality which constrains us ever to become a knowledge about which we can overestimate ourselves and become arrogant' ('Reply to My Friends and Critics' [9.25], no page no.). It could thus be said that for hermeneutics 'truth' is primarily not 'cognitive' but a 'moral' concept; it refers not so much to bits and pieces of 'information' we may *possess* as it does to a general mode of *living* (being-in-the-world). In this connection Ricoeur remarks, in a very Jamesian sort of way: 'We wager on a certain set of values and then try to be consistent with them; verification is therefore a question of our whole life. No one can escape this. . . . I do not see how we can say that our values are better than all others except that by risking our whole life on them we expect to achieve a better life, to see and to understand things better than others' (*Lectures on Ideology and Utopia* [9.16], 312).

35 In *La symbolique du mal* (*Philosophie de la volonté: Finitude et culpabilité*, vol. II) (Paris: Aubier, 1960). English translation: *The Symbolism of Evil* [9.20].

36 D. C. Hoy [9.33], 61.

37 See T. M. Van Leeuwen [9.28] 1.

38 Ricoeur, *The Conflict of Interpretations* [9.13], 411.

39 In what is said, there is always, Gadamer insists, 'an infinity of what is not said' ([9.7], 426).

40 This point is developed by Sartre in *La transcendance de l'ego: Esquisse d'une description phénoménologique* (Paris: J. Vrin, 1966).

41 Merleau-Ponty, *Phenomenology of Perception* (note 21): there is no inner man, man is in the world, and only in the world does he know himself' (p. xi).

42 It should perhaps be noted that, from a Gadamerian point of view, conversation is not so much an *instance* of language as it is what language essentially *is*.

43 As Gadamer goes on to point out: 'Where a person is concerned with the other as individuality, e.g. in a therapeutical conversation or the examination of a man accused of a crime, this is not really a situation in which two people are trying to understand one another.' (In a footnote Gadamer remarks that in such a situation the questions which arise are 'marked by insincerity'.) As we shall see later, this view of conversation has important consequences for the theory of text-interpretation.

44 For a discussion of these issues see Ricoeur, 'Structure, Word, Event' in *The Conflict of Interpretations* [9.13].

45 Ricoeur, 'New Developments in Phenomenology in France: The Phenomenology of Language', trans. P. Goodman, *Social Research*, 34: 1 (spring 1967): 14.

46 See J. Habermas, *The Philosophical Discourse of Modernity*, trans. F. Lawrence (Cambridge, Mass.: MIT Press, 1987), pp. 41–2.

47 Gadamer, 'Practical Philosophy as a Model of the Human Sciences', *Research in Phenomenology*, 9 (1980): 83.

48 See Gadamer, 'Reply to My Critics' in G. L. Ormiston and A. D. Schrift, *The Hermeneutic Tradition: From Ast to Ricoeur* (Albany: State University of New York Press, 1990), pp. 275–6.

49 For Hirsch, in contrast, meaning is always *willed* meaning (see *Validity* (note 9), p. 51).

50 See also pp. xix, 321, 336, 338, 353, 356.

51 This point is developed in aesthetic response theory and reader reception theory by Wolfgang Iser and Hans Robert Jauss, respectively (see Iser, *The Act of Reading: A Theory of Aesthetic Response* (Baltimore: Johns Hopkins University Press, 1978) and Jauss, *Towards an Aesthetic of Reception*, trans. T. Bahti (Minneapolis: University of Minnesota Press, 1982). Ricoeur discusses the views of Iser and Jauss in *Time and Narrative* [9.21], vol. 3, pp. 166ff.

52 Bernstein [9.29], 145.

53 G. W. F. Hegel, *The Philosophy of History* (New York: Dover Publications, 1978), p. 106.

54 Gadamer, 'The Power of Reason', *Man and World*, 3: 1 (1970): 15. In response to Habermas's charge that 'tradition', as hermeneutics understands it, is not subject to a critique guided by an 'emancipatory interest', Gadamer makes the following counter-charge: 'unconsciously the ultimate guiding image of emancipatory reflection in the social sciences [i.e., Habermas's position] must be an anarchistic utopia. Such an image, however, seems to me to reflect a hermeneutically false consciousness, the antidote for which can only be a more universal hermeneutical reflection' ([9.5], 42).

Gadamer's emphasis on tradition is not meant to deny either (1) the universality of certain *values* or (2) the critical function of *reason*. What it does deny is the existence of an *ahistorical* reason (the kind of 'transcendental' reason appealed to by Habermas that can escape tradition altogether). In *Truth and*

Method Gadamer states his position in the following way: 'Does the fact that one is set within various traditions mean really and primarily that one is subject to prejudices and limited in one's freedom? Is not, rather, all human experience, even the freest, limited and qualified in various ways? If this is true, then the idea of an absolute reason is impossible for historical humanity. Reason exists for us only in concrete, historical terms, i.e., it is not its own master, but remains constantly dependent on the given circumstances in which it operates' ([9.7], 245).

We shall return to the question of values and rational critique in the concluding section of this chapter.

55 Gadamer, 'Reply to My Critics' (note 48), p. 273.

56 Gadamer, 'Hermeneutics as Practical Philosophy', in *Reason in the Age of Science* [9.6], 111.

57 For a detailed treatment of this issue see my 'The New Philosophy of Rhetoric', *Texte: Revue de critique et de théorie littéraire*, 8/9 (1989): 247–77.

58 See C. Perelman and L. Olbrechts-Tyteca, *Traité de l'argumentation: la nouvelle rhétorique* (Bruxelles: Editions de l'Institut de Sociologie, Université Libre de Bruxelles, 2nd edn, 1970).

59 R. Bernstein remarks in this regard: 'Although the concept of truth is basic to Gadamer's entire project of philosophic hermeneutics, it turns out to be one of the most elusive concepts in his work' ([9.29], 151).

60 Ricoeur, 'Langage (Philosophie)' *Encyclopaedia Universalis*, vol. 9 (1971), p. 780.

61 See Ricoeur, 'The Model of the Text' in *Hermeneutics and the Human Sciences* [9.15], 212–13.

62 See also pp. 146–7, 203. Ricoeur also says that whereas Gadamer, with his reliance on the model of conversation, places a great deal of confidence in *Einverständnis* – profound agreement – he himself is 'beaucoup plus sensible au caractère conflictuel du champ d'interprétation' ('De la volonté à l'acte' in *'Temps et récit' de Paul Ricoeur* (note 12), p. 19.

63 'Distantiation is not the product of methodology and hence something superfluous and parasitical; rather it is constitutive of the phenomenon of the text as writing' ([9.15] 139). Critics of Ricoeur might argue that his own critique of Gadamer is not entirely fair, in that Gadamer himself argues for a 'positive' notion of distantiation. See, *inter alia*, the following remarks that Gadamer made in his lectures at the University of Louvain in 1957: 'Contrary to what we often imagine, time is not a chasm which we could bridge over in order to recover the past: in reality, it is the ground which supports the arrival of the past and where the present takes its roots. "Temporal distance" is not a distance in the sense of a distance to be overcome. . . . Actually, it is rather a matter of considering "temporal distance" as a fundament of positive and productive possibilities for understanding' (*PHC*, 155–6).

If it is the case that Ricoeur has misread Gadamer on this score, then it is also the case that he concedes too much to Habermas in the latter's criticism of Gadamer (for Ricoeur's attempt to mediate the dispute between Habermas and Gadamer, see 'Hermeneutics and the Critique of Ideology' in *Hermeneutics and the Human Sciences*) [9.15]. If Ricoeur argues for a positive notion of distantiation, it is because he wants to maintain (against Habermas) that hermeneutics has to do not only with the transmission of the past (as Habermas portrays Gadamer as saying) but that it can also incorporate a *critical* moment in the appropriation process. However, if Gadamer's notion of distantiation is itself of a positive sort, then there is *already* a critical element in Gadamer's hermeneutics (which therefore does not need to be supplemented with borrowings from Habermas's critical theory). As I have already indicated, Gadamer does indeed make this claim.

64 The 'second order referentiality' of metaphorical discourse was one of the main things that Ricoeur sought to demonstrate in *La métaphore vive* (Paris: Seuil, 1975); English trans.: *The Rule of Metaphor* [9.19].

65 This highlights an important difference between Ricoeur's theory of text-interpretation and other postmodern theories which indeed do legitimate 'projecting oneself into the text' in whatever way, i.e., engaging in 'strong misreadings' of the text. An outstanding example of just how 'strong' misreadings of a deconstructionist sort may be is provided by the American literary critic J. Hillis Miller. In a review of Ricoeur's *Time and Narrative*, Miller asserts that 'hermeneutic theories', such as Ricoeur's, assume 'the existence of stable monological texts of determinable meanings, meanings controlled in each case by the intentions of the author and by the text's reference to a pre-linguistic "real world out there"'. One's astonishment over such a manifestly absurd remark (do deconstructionists even bother any more to read the texts they pretend to 'interpret'?) is compounded when a few paragraphs further on one reads: 'his view of language remains a more or less unambiguous copy theory. Language, for him, mirrors, represents or "expresses" the lived world' ('But Are Things as We Say They Are?', *Times Literary Supplement*, 9–15 October 1987: 1104).

66 See in this regard 'On Interpretation' (see note 7), pp. 185ff. The subject of the 'self' was the topic of Ricoeur's 1986 Gifford Lectures, 'On Selfhood, The Question of Personal Identity', published in book form under the title *Soi-même comme un autre* (Paris: Seuil, 1990), trans.: *Oneself as Another* [9.17].

67 'Si le sens n'est pas un segment de la compréhension de soi, je ne sais pas ce que c'est' (*Esprit*, November 1983: 636).

68 S. B. Messer, L. A. Sass, R. L. Woolfolk (eds), *Hermeneutics and Psychological Theory: Interpretive Perspectives on Personality, Psychotherapy, and Psychopathology* (New Brunswick: Rutgers University Press, 1988), p. xiii.

69 C. Geertz, *The Interpretation of Cultures* (New York: Basic Books, 1973), p. 5.

70 By way of underscoring the purposive nature of human action, Mises writes: 'There is no human being to whom the intent is foreign to substitute by appropriate conduct one state of affairs for another state of affairs that would prevail if he did not interfere' (*The Ultimate Foundation of Economic Science: An Essay on Method* (Kansas City: Sheed Andres & McMeel, 1978), p. 71).

71 That various social orders are the result of human action but not necessarily of human design has been one of the major themes in the work of F. A. Hayek whose work anticipates, in many ways, that of Gadamer and Ricoeur. See in this regard my 'Hayek and the Interpretive Turn', *Critical Review*, 3: 2 (spring 1989).

72 C. Taylor, 'Interpretation and the Sciences of Man', in P. Rabinow and W. M. Sullivan (eds), *Interpretive Social Science: A Reader* (note 26), p. 48.

73 See Ricoeur, 'History as Narrative and Practice', interview with P. Kemp, *Philosophy Today* (fall 1985): 216.

74 J. Wakefield, 'Hermeneutics and Empiricism: Commentary on Donald Meichenbaum' in Messer *et al.* (eds), *Hermeneutics and Psychological Theory* (note 68), p. 143.

75 Geertz, *The Interpretation of Cultures* (note 69), p. 9.

76 The interpretive economist D. Lavoie remarks in this regard: 'The fact that the objects of our study *already have* an interpretation of what is going on does not release the social scientist from the responsibility to develop and defend her own explication of what is going on. The interpreter should not try to rid herself of her own perspective in order to 'adopt' that of the interpreted, but must try to find new ways to use her presuppositions to attain a better understanding of the human activities under study.... Thus interpretation always means *adding* to what is said through a mediation of the 'horizons' of the interpreter and the interpreted' ('The Account of Interpretations and the Interpretation of Accounts: The Communicative Function of "The Language of Business" ', *Accounting, Organizations and Society*, 12: 6 (1987): 594).

77 J. B. Thompson, *Ideology and Modern Culture: Critical Social Theory in the Era of Mass Communication* (Stanford: Stanford University Press, 1990), p. 323. In his analysis of ideology Thompson draws extensively on suggestions put forward by Ricoeur. For a comparative study of Ricoeur's hermeneutics and the critical theory of Jürgen Habermas, see his earlier work [9.26].

78 See Gadamer's discussion of Dilthey in 'The Problem of Historical Consciousness' (note 26).

79 Jean Grondin, 'L'herméneutique positive de Paul Ricoeur' in *'Temps et récit' de Paul Ricoeur* (note 12), p. 125.

80 Geertz, *The Interpretation of Cultures* (note 69), p. 30.

81 In *Time and Narrative* [9.21], vol. I, Ricoeur refers to 'explanation' and 'understanding' as 'a now obsolete vocabulary'; he prefers to speak instead of 'nomological explanation and explanation by emplotment' (p. 181).

82 Of Ricoeur's work in this area historian H. White has said: 'Ricoeur's is surely the strongest claim for the adequacy of narrative to the realization of the aims of historical studies made by any recent theorist of historiography' ('The Question of Narrative in Contemporary Historical Theory', *History and Theory*, 1 (1984): 30).

For a discussion of Ricoeur's treatment of the imagination over the course of his writings see Richard Kearney, 'Paul Ricoeur and the Hermeneutic Imagination', in T. P. Kemp and D. Rasmussen (eds) [9.24] (reprinted in Kearney, *Poetics of Imaging: From Husserl to Lyotard* (London: Harper Collins Academic, 1991)). The thesis defended by Kearney is that 'a poetic hermeneutic of imagination' represents 'the ultimate, if discreet, agenda of his philosophical project' (p. 2). The following remark of Ricoeur lends support to this thesis: 'Despite appearances the one problem that has interested me from the beginning of my work as a philosopher is that of creativity. I worked from the angle of individual psychology in my early work on the will, then on the cultural level with my studies on symbolisms. My present work on narrative puts me right at the heart of this social, cultural, creativity' ('History as Narrative and Practice', *Philosophy Today* (fall 1985): 222).

83 Thus, for example, economist D. Lavoie writes, with reference to Ricoeur: 'History is in this view not an attempt to find quantitative covering laws that fully determine a sequence of events, but an attempt to supply a qualitative interpretation of some part of mankind's "story". The whole purpose of the theoretical social sciences (including economics and accounting research) is to equip people with the capacity to better distinguish acceptable from unacceptable historical narratives. . . . What we find ourselves doing in the social sciences is not so much the testing of *ex ante* predictions but is more of the nature of what the Austrian economist F. A. Hayek calls an *ex post* explanation of principles. The only "test" any theory can receive is in the form of a qualitative judgment of the plausibility of the sequence of events that has been strung together by narrative' ('The Account of Interpretations and the Interpretation of Accounts' (note 76), pp. 595–6).

84 D. Pellauer, 'The Significance of the Text in Paul Ricoeur's Hermeneutical Theory' in [9.25], 112, 109.

85 Ricoeur's interest in history and narrative can be seen to be the logical outgrowth of his abiding concern over the issue of human action, since, in being 'fixated', action is transformed into institutionalized social patterns, which is to say that it generates historical processes.

86 Ricoeur deals at length with the issue of the 'social imagination' (of which ideology and utopia are two basic modes) in *Lectures on Ideology and Utopia* [9.16].

87 See Ricoeur's remarks on violence and discourse in *Main Trends in Philosophy* (New York: Holmes & Meier, 1979), pp. 224–7. On p. 227 Ricoeur writes: 'It is because we, as men, have chosen discourse – that is, discussion, seeking agreement by means of verbal confrontation – that the defence of violence for violence's sake is forever forbidden us.'

88 'Reaching an understanding in conversation presupposes that both partners are ready for it and are trying to recognize the full value of what is alien and opposed to them' ([9.7], 348).

89 Speaking of the humanistic ideal of the German historical school, Gadamer says that it 'does not contain any particular content, but is based on the formal ideal of the greatest variety. This kind of ideal is truly universal, for it cannot be shaken by any historical evidence, any disturbing evidence of the transience of human things. History has a meaning in itself' ([9.7], 178).

The political motivation for Ricoeur's defence of philosophical humanism is evident in the following remark: 'If anti-humanism is true, there is also no theoretical basis on which the legal subject can oppose the abuse of political authority' (*Main Trends in Philosophy*, p. 369).

90 The real 'ethnocentrist', hermeneutics maintains, is the person who denies the universal validity ('applicability') of the principles of freedom and reason and who asserts that any criticism of non-western societies for failing to recognize these principles is an instance of 'Eurocentrism'. As a leading spokesperson for democratic values ('such basic ideas as representative government, human rights, and the rule of law') in the 'third world', Aung San Suu Kyi, recipient

in 1991 of the Nobel Peace Prize, has stated: 'The proposition that the Burmese are not fit to enjoy as many rights and privileges as the citizens of democratic countries is insulting' ('In Quest of Democracy', *Journal of Democracy*, 2: 1 (January 1992): 6 and 11). Anti-universalist ethnocentrism ('reverse Eurocentrism') is indeed an affront to basic human dignity.

91 Bernstein [9.29], p. 163.

92 S. Rosen, *Hermeneutics as Politics* (New York: Oxford University Press, 1987), p. 141.

93 Gadamer, 'The Power of Reason', *Man and World*, 3: 1 (1970): 8.

94 Ricoeur, *Main Trends in Philosophy* (note 87), p. 315.

95 In 'Hermeneutics and Social Science', *Cultural Hermeneutics*, 55 (1970), Gadamer writes: 'the chief task of philosophy is . . . to defend practical and political reason against the domination of technology based on science. That is the point of philosophical hermeneutic' (p. 316).

96 'The Power of Reason' (note 93), p. 13.

97 See in this regard Gadamer's remarks on natural law in *Truth and Method* [9.7].

98 Cf. Gadamer, 'The Power of Reason' (note 93): 'Clearly reason has an immediate connection with the universal' (p. 6); 'identification with the Universal – what is Reason if not that?' (p. 12). Reason is 'the self-realizing identification with the universal' (p. 14). On p. 13 of this text Gadamer identifies 'loss of freedom' with 'lack of possibility of identifying with the universal'.

99 See Gadamer. 'Reply to My Critics' (note 48), p. 289.

100 I. Kant, 'Ideas for a Universal History from a Cosmopolitan Point of View', in *On History*, L. W. Beck (ed.) (Indianapolis: Bobbs-Merrill, 1963), p. 16. Kant goes on to characterize such a society as 'the society with the greatest freedom. Such a society is one in which there is a mutual opposition among the members, together with the most exact definition of freedom and fixing of its limits so that it may be consistent with the freedom of others'.

101 The notion of human rights, as hermeneutics conceives of it, is not a metaphysical notion and does not appeal to essentialist or foundationalist modes of thinking. Human rights are not 'natural rights' (as Gadamer's critic, L. Strauss, would maintain); they are *rational rights*, *rights of reason*. That is to say, they are injunctions as to how people *ought* to be treated, given what they in fact *are*, namely rational beings. That means: beings who have the *logos* (as Isocrates said), i.e., are capable of engaging in dialogical or communicative rationality. Basic rights such as freedom of speech, of conscience, of association, and so on, are simply enumerations of the legal–institutional guarantees that are required for the unimpeded exercise of this form of rationality. Since, as Gadamer recognizes, the 'power of reason' is not a 'natural faculty' but a social attribute ('This is not simply a capacity that man has, but something of the sort that must be developed' ('The Power of Reason' (note 93), p. 7), people can be fully rational (and thus fully human) only when they have the good fortune of living within the kind of institutional set-up that these rights make possible. Human rights are what those rational beings who are reflectively aware of what they are will claim for themselves, in order to be recognized for what they are and in order to become what they are (cf. Tiananmen Square, 1989).

102 'The Power of Reason' (note 93), p. 8.

103 M. Merleau-Ponty, *Signs*, trans. R. C. McCleary (Evanston: Northwestern University Press, 1964), p. 349.

104 Ricoeur, 'Le Philosophe et la politique devant la question de la liberté', in *La liberté et l'ordre social* (Neuchâtel: La Baconnière, 1969), p. 53.

105 Ricoeur, *Du texte à l'action* (Paris: Seuil, 1986), p. 404.

106 See L. Ferry and A. Renaut, *French Philosophy of the Sixties: An Essay on Antihumanism* (Amherst: University of Massachusetts Press, 1990).

107 Ricoeur, 'La raison pratique' in T. Gearets (ed.), *La Rationalité aujourd'hui/ Rationality Today* (Ottawa: Editions de l'Université d'Ottawa, 1979), p. 238.

108 Bernstein [9.29], p. 159.

109 See Ricoeur, *Main Trends in Philosophy* (note 87), p. 372. On another occasion, Ricoeur says that 'the lament of modern philosophy [is] that we have to raise Hegelian problems without the Hegelian solutions.' While rejecting the notion of absolute knowledge and all-encompassing theories of history, he neverthe-less concedes: 'Maybe we cannot have passionate history without a certain expectation of what *could be* the global meaning of history, but that must remain at the level, I think, of hypothesis; that must remain a kind of working hypothesis' ('The Conflict of Interpretations' in R. Bruzina and B. Wilshire (eds), *Phenomenology: Dialogues and Bridges* (Albany: State University of New York Press, 1982), pp. 319–20).

❧ SELECT BIBLIOGRAPHY ❧

For an exhaustive bibliography of both the primary and the secondary literature in various languages, see Jean Grondin, *Einführung in die Philosophische Hermeneutik* (Darmstadt: Wissenschaftliche Buchgesellschaft, 1991).

Gadamer

Translations

9.1 *Dialogue and Dialectic: Eight Hermeneutical Studies on Plato*, trans. P. C. Smith, New Haven: Yale University Press, 1980.

9.2 *Hegel's Dialectic: Five Hermeneutical Studies*, trans. P. C. Smith, New Haven: Yale University Press, 1976.

9.3 *The Idea of the Good in Platonic–Aristotelian Philosophy*, trans. P. C. Smith, New Haven: Yale University Press, 1985.

9.4 *Philosophical Apprenticeships*, trans. R. Sullivan, Cambridge, Mass.: MIT Press, 1985.

9.5 *Philosophical Hermeneutics*, trans. D. E. Linge, Berkeley: University of California Press, 1976.

9.6 *Reason in the Age of Science*, trans. F. Lawrence, Cambridge, Mass.: MIT Press, 1981.

9.7 *Truth and Method*, New York: Seabury Press, 1975, 2nd rev. edn, New York: Crossroad, 1990.

Criticism

9.8 Foster, M. *Gadamer and Practical Philosophy: The Hermeneutics of Moral Confidence*, Atlanta: Scholar's Press, 1991.

9.9 Michelfelder D., and Palmer, R. (eds) *Dialogue and Deconstruction: The Gadamer–Derrida Encounter*, Albany: State University of New York Press, 1989.

9.10 Sullivan, R. *Political Hermeneutics: The Early Thinking of Hans-Georg Gadamer*, University Park: Pennsylvania State University Press, 1989.

9.11 Warnke, G. *Gadamer: Hermeneutics, Tradition and Reason*, Stanford: Stanford University Press, 1987.

9.12 Weinsheimer, J. *Gadamer's Hermeneutics: A Reading of Truth and Method*, New Haven: Yale University Press, 1985.

Ricoeur

Translations

9.13 *The Conflict of Interpretations: Essays in Hermeneutics*, ed. D. Ihde, Evanston: Northwestern University Press, 1974.

9.14 *Freud and Philosophy: An Essay on Interpretation*, trans. D. Savage, New Haven: Yale University Press, 1970.

9.15 *Hermeneutics and the Human Sciences*, trans. J. B. Thompson, Cambridge: Cambridge University Press, 1981.

9.16 *Lectures on Ideology and Utopia*, ed. G. H. Taylor, New York: Columbia University Press, 1986.

9.17 *Oneself as Another*, trans. K. Blamey, Chicago: University of Chicago Press, 1992.

9.18 *Political and Social Essays*, ed. D. Steward and J. Bien, Athens: Ohio University Press, 1974.

9.19 *The Rule of Metaphor*, trans. R. Czeny, K. McLaughlin and J. Costello, Toronto: University of Toronto Press, 1977.

9.20 *The Symbolism of Evil*, trans. E. Buchanan, New York: Harper & Row, 1967.

9.21 *Time and Narrative*, trans. K. McLaughlin and D. Pellauer, 3 vols, Chicago: University of Chicago Press, 1984, 1985, 1988.

Criticism

9.22 Clark, S. H. *Paul Ricoeur*, London: Routledge, 1990.

9.23 Ihde, D. *Hermeneutic Phenomenology: The Philosophy of Paul Ricoeur*, Evanston: Northwestern University Press, 1971.

9.24 Kemp, P. and Rasmussen, D. (eds) *The Narrative Path: The Later Works of Paul Ricoeur*, Cambridge, Mass.: MIT Press, 1989.

9.25 Reagan, C. E. (ed.) *Studies in the Philosophy of Paul Ricoeur*, Athens: Ohio University Press, 1979.

9.26 Thompson, J. B. *Critical Hermeneutics: A Study in the Thought of Paul Ricoeur and Jürgen Habermas*, Cambridge: Cambridge University Press, 1981.

9.27 Van Den Hengel, J. W. *The Home of Meaning: The Hermeneutics of the Subject of Paul Ricoeur*, Washington: University Press of America, 1982.

9.28 Van Leeuwen, T. M. *The Surplus of Meaning: Ontology and Eschatology in the Philosophy of Paul Ricoeur*, Amsterdam: Rodopi, 1981.

General commentaries and analysis

9.29 Bernstein, R. J. *Beyond Objectivism and Relativism: Science, Hermeneutics, and Praxis*, Philadelphia: University of Pennsylvania Press, 1983.

9.30 Bleicher, J. *Contemporary Hermeneutics: Hermeneutics as Method, Philosophy, and Critique*, London: Routledge, 1980.

9.31 Heckman, S. J. *Hermeneutics and the Sociology of Knowledge*, Notre Dame: Notre Dame University Press, 1986.

9.32 Hollinger, R. (ed.) *Hermeneutics and Praxis*, Notre Dame: University of Notre Dame Press, 1985.

9.33 Hoy, D. *The Critical Circle: Literature and History in Contemporary Hermeneutics*, Berkeley: University of California Press, 1978.

9.34 Madison, G. B. *The Hermeneutics of Postmodernity: Figures and Themes*, Bloomington: Indiana University Press, 1988.

9.35 Palmer, R. E. *Hermeneutics: Interpretation Theory in Schleiermacher, Dilthey, Heidegger, and Gadamer*, Evanston: Northwestern University Press, 1969.

9.36 Weinsheimer, J. *Philosophical Hermeneutics and Literary Theory*, New Haven: Yale University Press, 1991.

CHAPTER 10

Italian idealism and after
Gentile, Croce and others
Giacomo Rinaldi

❧ ❧ ❧

❧ INTRODUCTION ❧

The history of twentieth-century Italian philosophy is strongly influenced both by the peculiar character of its evolution in the preceding century and by widespread tendencies of contemporary continental (especially German) thought. In nineteenth-century Italian philosophy we can distinguish four main trends: (1) St Augustine's and Aquinas's traditional *dualistic metaphysics*, which was renewed with some originality by the priest Antonio Rosmini Serbati (1797–1855), and was regarded by the Roman Catholic church as its 'official' philosophical doctrine; (2) *methodological empiricism*, which was developed since the Renaissance especially by the founder of modern mathematical physics, Galileo Galilei, and which found its most prominent exponent in the *positivist* thinker Roberto Ardigò (1828–1920); (3) the speculative German tradition of *Kantian–Hegelian idealism*, according to its interpretation as a *metafisica della mente*, i.e. as a philosophy of pure self-consciousness, outlined by the greatest nineteenth-century Italian thinker, Bertrando Spaventa (1817–83); and finally (4) Marx's and Engels's *historical materialism*, which was spread and fostered especially by Antonio Labriola (1843–1904), who worked out a 'humanistic' (anti-naturalistic) interpretation of it.

The influence of 'classical German philosophy' from Kant to Marx on twentieth-century Italian thought thus turns out to be strictly determined and 'mediated' by the peculiar character of its interpretation and appropriation in the preceding century. But other trends of German thought too are studied, interpreted and further developed by contemporary Italian philosophers, thus exerting a direct, 'immediate' influence on them: e.g., the German tradition of 'speculative mysticism' (one might recall the philosophies of the later Fichte and the later Schelling, as well as Gadamer's 'hermeneutics'), the 'philosophy of immanence' (Schuppe and Schubert-Soldern), the 'empiriocriticism' of Mach and Avenarius; Husserl's 'phenomenology' and Heidegger's 'existentialism', etc.

The peculiar political-cultural context in which the above-mentioned trends of contemporary Italian thought arise and spread can be sketched as follows. The philosophy of German idealism, and especially its Hegelian version, owing both to its origin in Protestant theology and religiosity and to its insistence on the state's 'ethical' essence as the supreme moral law of the individual's practical activity, met the spiritual exigencies of those 'liberal-national' movements of the Italian *Risorgimento* which aimed at the foundation of a unitary state, and which saw their major adversary in the Catholic church's temporal power.[1] Augustine's and Aquinas's dualistic metaphysics, on the contrary, prevailed in the most conservative classes and political trends in Italian society, and can be safely regarded, as it were, as the Roman Catholic church's secular arm in its intellectual and moral life. At the extreme opposite of the social-political array, Marx's historical materialism seemed able to offer an 'objective', 'scientific' foundation to the political aspirations of those who dreamt of radically transforming Italian society's traditional order, be it the more archaic one sanctioned by the Roman Catholic church or the more recent one of the national unitary state. Finally, positivistic empiricism became, as it were, the 'official' ideology of the rising Italian industrial bourgeoisie, concentrated especially in the country's northern regions.

One can easily distinguish three fundamental evolutionary phases in twentieth-century Italian philosophy. In the first (*c.* 1900–45) we witness an indisputable prevalence of the idealistic trends, among them especially Giovanni Gentile's thought. This is despite the often exaggerated cultural influence of his 'actual idealism', which from its first 'official' statement (1911) was strongly opposed by other no less famous representatives of Italian idealism such as Pietro Martinetti, Benedetto Croce and Pantaleo Carabellese. In the second phase (*c.* 1945–80), a widespread violent reaction against idealistic philosophy in general, and 'actual idealism' in particular, occurred. Antonio Banfi, Nicola Abbagnano, etc. set against it not only the materialistic conception of history, but also later tendencies of German thought such as, e.g., Husserl's phenomenology and Heidegger's existentialism. The distinction between the first and the second phase, however, must be understood not simply as a rigid separation, but as indicating a *prevalence* of the idealistic orientation in the first half of the twentieth century and of the anti-idealistic one in the second. In effect, the influence of nineteenth-century positivism does not disappear in the age dominated by Croce's and Gentile's thought (it suffices to think, in this regard, of the writings of sociologists such as Vilfredo Pareto (1868–1923), of economists such as Luigi Einaudi (1874–1961), and of methodologists of science such as Antonio Aliotta (1881–1964). Furthermore, many of the most prominent exponents of the reaction against idealism in the second half of the century (e.g., Antonio Gramsci, Abbagnano and Banfi) had already worked out their fundamental conceptions before 1945. On the other hand, although in weakened and often speculatively unfruitful forms, the philosophical traditions of Gentile's 'actual idealism' and of Croce's 'absolute historicism' have survived up to today.[2] In the 1980s, the final phase, something like a widespread 'decline of ideology' ('tramonto dell'ideologia') has, as Lucio Colletti says, taken place. The most remarkable consequence of it is likely to be the perhaps definitive dissolution of the cultural influence of the materialistic conception of history, which in the second half of the century has often represented one of the most powerful and unrelenting adversaries of any idealistic speculation. Although, then, the current situation of the 'spirit' of Italian culture is undoubtedly pervaded with a general feeling of bewilderment and creative impotence, yet it might also disclose new horizons and real possibilities for a critical resumption and further original development of the most glorious and speculatively fruitful trend in Italian thought – i.e., the Kantian–Hegelian tradition.

❧ 'ACTUAL IDEALISM': GIOVANNI GENTILE ❧

Giovanni Gentile (1875–1944), who was rightly defined by Michele Federico Sciacca as 'the greatest Italian philosopher in our century',[3] was the author of numerous philosophical and historiographical works which are to be counted among the masterpieces of Italian thought in any age and have left an indelible trace also on the development of contemporary European philosophy. Here I can confine myself to mentioning the most relevant ones: *La riforma della dialettica hegeliana* (*The Reform of Hegelian Dialectic*) (1913 [10.32]), *Sommario di pedagogia come scienza filosofica* (*An Outline of Pedagogy as a Philosophical Science*), two volumes (1913–14 [10.33]), *Teoria generale dello spirito come atto puro* (*General Theory of Mind as Pure Act*) (1916 [10.35]), *I fondamenti della filosofia del diritto* (*The Foundations of the Philosophy of Law*) (1916 [10.34]), *Sistema di logica come teoria del conoscere* (*A System of Logic as a Theory of Knowledge*), two volumes (1917–22 [10.36]), *Le origini della filosofia contemporanea in Italia* (*The Origins of Contemporary Philosophy in Italy*), three volumes (1917–23 [10.37]), *Discorsi di religione* (*Speeches on Religion*) (1920 [10.38]), *La filosofia dell'arte* (*The Philosophy of Art*) (1931 [10.42]), *Introduzione alla filo-*

sofia (*An Introduction to Philosophy*) (1933 [10.43]), and finally his posthumously published book *Genesi e struttura della società* (*Genesis and Structure of Society*) (1946 [10.44]). Gentile's works organically merge a vigorous theoretical development of his own original philosophical doctrine, 'actual idealism' (or 'actualism') with an immense, philologically very accurate, historiographical erudition, focusing especially upon the history of Italian philosophy and culture.

The doctrine of 'actual idealism' can be safely regarded as an attempt to press to its extreme consequences Spaventa's interpretation of Hegelian philosophy as a metaphysics of pure self-consciousness. Philosophy is the search for truth – not for this or that particular 'abstract' truth, but for the unique 'absolute' truth (and reality). And such a truth cannot possibly 'transcend' thought's self-conscious act which aspires to its possession. For in such a case not only could the latter never be 'certain' of any truth whatsoever, but as essentially 'other' than (absolute) truth it could not but turn into a mere contingent phenomenon. This, however, is clearly disproved by the fact that, as Descartes had already pointed out, one can deny the 'evidence' of self-conscious thought only by virtue of a further, more original act of thinking. Gentile can therefore assert: 'cogito ergo sum; sum substantia cogitans; quatenus substantia in me sum et per me concipior; hoc est mei conceptus non indiget conceptum alterius rei, a quo formari debeat' ('I think, therefore I am. I am a thinking substance. As a substance I am in myself and can be thought of only through myself – i.e., the concept of myself need not any concept of another thing in order to be thought of').[4] Yet according to Gentile, unlike Descartes, not only is consciousness actual but the whole of reality turns into consciousness. For any possible objectivity, in the final analysis, turns out to be *absolutely* enclosed in it, as its own immanent content, or rather 'opposite'. Since the act of consciousness is *one* and 'unmultiplicable' (*immoltiplicabile*),[5] the object's essence, then, will be radically *manifold*. On the other hand, as the object is but a *negative* content of knowing, that of which consciousness can be *actually* aware is only *itself*. As Hegel had already maintained, the 'truth' of consciousness is therefore *self-consciousness*. 'The Ego's act is consciousness as self-consciousness; the Ego's object is the Ego itself. Any conscious process is an act of self-consciousness.'[6] In such an act, then, subject and object *coincide*. But their identity is never 'immediate'. For self-consciousness is every truth *only* as the *necessary* consciousness of the *error* that essentially inheres to any 'immediate' (i.e. sensuous, manifold, natural, etc.) being as such. As a consequence, its 'being' can become actual only as the negation of a 'not-being' originally immanent to it – and thus is a *dialectical unity of opposites*. Now, as Hegel himself had shown by 'deducing' Becoming from the opposite 'abstractness' of Being and

Nothing, such a unity can be consistently conceived only as 'movement' or 'process': 'The subject that resolves the object into itself, at least when this object is a spiritual reality, is neither a being nor a state of being: it is nothing immediate, as we said, but a constructing process – a process constructing the object as a process constructing the very subject.'[7]

One of the deepest and most fascinating aspects of 'actual idealism' is certainly Gentile's insightful distinction between his 'transcendental' concept of the self-conscious Ego and the 'empirical Ego' (the sensuous-finite individual), and consequently between the former's peculiar processuality and the form of 'time'. In fact, both the empirical Egos and time (which to Gentile, unlike Kant, is, like 'space', the essential form of *nature*, *not* of consciousness) imply a *plurality* of 'facts', or 'points', which exclude each other, either in the simultaneity of spatial existence or in the succession of temporal becoming. The transcendental Ego, on the contrary, as *necessarily* existing (*cogito ergo sum*), is of necessity *universal*, and thus *unique*. The mutual transcendence (exclusion) of the empirical Egos as well as of the moments of sensuous time (past, present and future), therefore, is in the final analysis negated (in the Hegelian sense of 'negation', i.e. as *Aufhebung*) in the *timeless*, 'eternal' process of the transcendental Ego – of the *pensiero pensante*. 'Thought as actual, or as the universal Ego, contains, and therefore overcomes not only the spatiality of pure *nature*, but also the temporality of pure natural becoming. Thought is beyond time, is eternal.'[8] 'And therefore the moment [*istante*], the ἐξαίφνης of thought, is not a moment among the moments, is not in time; it has no 'before', and no 'after'; it is eternal.'[9]

Gentile deduces with admirable logical cogency the overall articulation of spirit's whole life from his concept of human self-consciousness as 'mediate', dynamic unity of subject and object. If their unity cannot in principle be 'immediate', this means that they are immediately different, and even opposite. Pure ('abstract') subject, pure ('abstract') object, and their ('concrete') mediation (identity of subject and object) – these are the three fundamental 'phases' of self-conscious thought's process, the three 'absolute forms of spirit'.[10] The form of spirit's abstract subjectivity coincides, according to Gentile, with 'pure feeling' (*sentimento puro*), which constitutes the specific element of *art*.[11] It is not to be mistaken for the *psychological* sensations of pleasure and pain, although these latter do constitute the opposite 'poles' of its immanent dialectic, for it is not conditioned by any alleged extramental reality,[12] and thus is 'infinite'. Although acknowledging that feeling, art, beauty, etc. *are* the origin, and even the 'root' (*radice*), of spirit's whole development, Gentile emphatically denies that they constitute something more than a merely 'abstract', 'inactual' moment of it. For in the act of thinking in which they are thought of as such, they necessarily negate themselves as 'pure' feeling, 'pure' beauty, etc., and rather identify themselves with the very (concrete) objectivity of pure thought. In fact, Gentile says, '[k]nowing is identifying, overcoming otherness as such'.[13] The very moment, then, the self-conscious subject becomes fully aware of the 'intimacy' (*intimità*) of its feelings, it cannot but objectify them, and thus transform them into a thought-content. Not unlike Hegel, Gentile therefore denies any possible *autonomous* development of art.[14]

The pure, 'abstract' object, we have seen, is the immanent negation of the act of thinking. Gentile can therefore proceed to set spirit's unity, universality, necessity, activity, freedom, eternity, etc. over against the radical multiplicity, particularity, contingency, passivity, temporality, etc. of *nature*, which is just the object of thought as 'immediately' other than it. He consequently holds to a rigidly *deterministic* and *mechanical* conception of nature. For him this *is* immanent to spirit, but the latter is not immanent at all to it *as such*. To the extent that nature's reality is (abstractly, and therefore 'erroneously') posited, the actuality of the spiritual subject must be negated. This is also the case with the positive (both 'natural' and 'historico-social') sciences, since they describe or explain an essentially manifold object (the 'phenomenal' plurality of natural 'facts' or of historical 'events'), and, moreover, abstract from its essential relation to the self-conscious act of thinking as its ultimate origin and condition of possibility. Yet no less abstractly objective, and therefore in the final analysis negative and 'erroneous', than sensible nature and the positive sciences is the *intelligible* multiplicity of the concepts, principles, and logical laws that constitute the subject matter of traditional formal logic. Although the first volume of his *Sistema di logica come teoria del conoscere* (*A System of Logic as a Theory of Knowing*) is devoted to a close examination of its fundamental structures,[15] such a logic, whose peculiar object he defines in terms of *logo astratto* (abstract thought) or of *pensiero pensato* (thought thought of), is radically unable adequately to express the logical essence of thought's *self-conscious* process (or *autoconcetto*). Just as was the case with nature and the positive sciences, Gentile does recognize the necessity of the *logo astratto* but for no other reason than that in his *dialectical* conception of spirit's becoming the negative, the 'abstract' is no less essential than the positive, the 'concrete', to its 'self-positing' (*autoctisi*).

As an 'abstractly' objective form of spirit Gentile does not hesitate to consider religion itself, both as confessional religiosity[16] and as subjective mystical experience. This is because religion generally sets against pure self-consciousness, as the creating principle of its being, an absolutely transcendent personal God, who, as such, is obviously an 'other' with respect to its 'pure immanence', and thus an 'inactual' abstraction. On the other hand, in mystical experience the subject does try to identify itself with the objectivity of the 'divine', but at the cost of *annihilating* itself as consciousness, and, a fortiori, as *self-consciousness*.[17] Not unlike spirit's artistic form, then, to Gentile religion too remains incurably 'abstract'. The 'concrete' unity of subject and object, therefore, can be attained only by a higher spiritual form, in which the object is conceived as essentially immanent to the subject, and this latter not as merely 'subjective' feeling but as the 'substantial', 'objective' subjectivity of *actual thought*. And this, of course, can be explicated only by *philosophy*, which for Gentile coincides without residue with spirit's *ethico-political* activity. For it is possible to distinguish them only by somehow opposing thought to action, theory to praxis, or, within the latter, the 'morality' of the individual to the 'ethicality' of society (or of the state). Yet for him the very intrinsic absoluteness, creativity and actuality of the *autoconcetto* excludes in principle the possibility that it may be conceived as *mere* theory, as a *passive* 'reflection' of a 'given' it does not itself 'posit'. As a consequence, it does not lack that creative energy which traditional philosophy (before and after him) is rather inclined to ascribe to the will alone. On the other hand, to Gentile the only concrete effective moral life the human individual can realize is that which unfolds in the organic, 'spiritual' unity of *social* institutions, from the family up to the state.[18] The very moment, then, speculative philosophy theoretically 'constructs' absolute truth in the 'pure act' of self-consciousness, it also actualizes itself in those ethico-political institutions which are the 'kernel', as it were, of humanity's spiritual history.

Despite the extremely summary character of this outline of Gentile's idealism I believe that the reader can easily grasp its fundamental difference from Hegel's, whose paternity, on the other hand (through the mediation of Spaventa's interpretation), he openly recognizes. Whereas to Hegel there exists a dialectical movement of the logical categories and of natural reality which is *not yet*, as such, (explicitly) *self-conscious*, to Gentile the only possible dialectical process, and then concrete actuality, is that of self-conscious spirit. Whereas to Hegel an organic, teleological development of the *Denken*, of speculative reason, is immanent in nature (despite its being nothing more than the Absolute Idea's self-alienation), to Gentile (not unlike, at least in this regard, Kant and the positivists old and new) it is nothing more than a dead mechanism determined by merely quantitative and causal connections. Whereas to Hegel the identity of knowing and the will in the Absolute Idea does not exclude a no less substantial 'logical' difference between them, which, in the Philosophy of Spirit, renders possible the further distinction between the 'finite' sphere of ethico-political life ('objective'

Spirit) and the higher one of the artistic, religious and philosophical contemplation of the Absolute (Absolute Spirit), to Gentile there is no other 'Absolute' than spirit's ethico-political history, nor any other 'spirit' than the 'infinite' unity of the 'Ego=Ego' (i.e., Absolute Spirit).

To these fundamental differences two others can be added, which seem to me no less relevant, although strictly logico-methodological in character. First of all, Hegelian dialectic unfolds in a succession of categories (*Denkbestimmungen* and *Begriffsbestimmungen*) in which the preceding are (relatively) more 'abstract' than the subsequent ones, while the latter are (relatively) more 'concrete', and constitute the 'truth' of the former, which are both 'negated' and 'preserved' (*aufgehoben*) in them. To Gentile, on the contrary, the 'concrete', the 'Ego=Ego' is the beginning of the dialectical process not only in the *ontological* order of reality and truth, but also in the *methodological* one of its dialectical explication. Second, while to Hegel the speculative synthesis of opposites constitutes itself as a *Stufenfolge*, a hierarchical succession of categories, or 'spiritual forms', more and more adequate to the Absolute's concreteness, Gentile openly denies that spirit's development unfolds 'in a series of typical degrees'.[19] For its self-identity is *equally immanent* in all 'concrete' moments in which its evolutionary process is being articulated. In fact, if one should admit, with Hegel, a hierarchy of spiritual forms, the Absolute and the higher ones would turn out to be (at least relatively) *transcendent* to the most elementary and inadequate ones. And this would undermine the fundamental methodological assumption of 'actual idealism': i.e. the 'absolute immanence' of truth to self-conscious thought.

This is not the place to try to strike a balance (however summary) of Gentile's philosophy,[20] still less of his 'reform of Hegelian dialectic'. As compared with the speculative doctrine from which it stems, it might certainly be regarded as little more than a mere 'simplification'[21] of it that risks mutilating, if not even irreparably distorting, the rich, systematic complexity of Hegel's thought. Yet in such a case one would too easily forget that that concept of 'spirit' as 'pure act', on which all of Gentile's theoretical reflections and constructions hinge, does constitute the most living, profound and up-to-date aspect of the whole Hegelian system. Moreover, while Hegel distinguishes religion from philosophy only owing to their 'form', and emphatically asserts the identity of their 'content', thus seeming to forget that according to his own logic[22] they on the contrary determine each other, Gentile's distinction between religion as the 'abstractly objective' form of spirit and philosophy as the fully 'concrete' and 'actual' one does bring to light a difference concerning their very content, and thus saves – against Hegel – the validity of his very principle of the mutual determination of the form and the content of thought.

Finally, an undeniably original, creative development of Gentile's thought with respect to Hegel's is certainly to be found in his pedagogical theory. The dialectical opposites that are constitutive of the educational act, which he conceives as an essentially 'spiritual' activity, are the subjectivity of the 'pupil' and the objectivity of 'science', which is embodied in the person of the 'teacher'. As long as these two terms of the educational relation remain in the 'immediate' form of their mutual exclusion – which constitutes, as such, the original 'antinomy of education'[23] – no real spiritual progress in the pupil's self-consciousness can take place. For it to occur, indeed, it is necessary that the latter should turn the teacher's objectivity into his or her own self-consciousness, thus becoming, in a sense, the 'teacher of himself or herself'. In the fullness of the educational act, Gentile profoundly observes, the pupil 'does learn, and throbs and lives in the teacher's word, as if he heard a voice sound in it that bursts out from the inwardness of his own being'.[24] Any true knowing, therefore, is never mere passive learning of dead and fragmentary notions, but rather free spiritual creation of knowledge by the pupil's inner personality. The spirit which 'actually' thinks, Gentile concludes, is always, in one way or another, an 'autodidact'. From his deep-rooted conception of education as a 'spiritual' process Gentile does not fail explicitly to draw a consequence that seems to me to be still today of the utmost cultural relevance and up-to-dateness. True culture and education is only that in which the human mind knows and 'creates' itself. Hence it is an essentially *humanistic* (philosophical) culture and education. Any technological cognition or ability (which as such constitutes the object of what he calls 'realistic instruction'),[25] therefore, can be legitimately ascribed some sort of meaning and value only to the extent that it constitutes a useful (although of necessity always subordinate) *means* for the pupil's *spiritual formation*, this being in one both philosophical and ethico-political.[26]

❧ 'ABSOLUTE HISTORICISM': BENEDETTO CROCE ❧

Both to Hegel and to Gentile 'the Absolute is Subject', and as such it necessarily manifests itself in humanity's *historical* development. Yet this does not mean at all that for them historical reality, as a multiplicity of spiritual 'facts' or events, and historiography, as the subjective representation of such a reality, constitute, respectively, the unique true actuality, and the only possible 'objective' knowledge of which the human mind could dispose. Any historico-factual manifestation of the Absolute, as such, is incurably 'finite', and thus inadequate to its pure ideal self-identity, whose full concreteness is actualized only in the process of 'absolute knowing' (Hegel) or of the *autoconcetto* (Gentile), as absolute identity of knowing and the will. The 'absolute historicism' of Benedetto Croce (1866–1952), on the contrary, aims at resolving without residue any possible reality into historical facticity. The fundamental error of any metaphysical speculation consist in the *filosofismo*,[27] i.e., in the illegitimate claim that the concept's immanent development would of itself be able to offer us an adequate knowledge of objective reality. Croce appeals to Kant's famous dictum that 'concepts without intuitions are empty, and intuitions without concepts are blind', in order to vindicate the element of the intuitive, individual, 'historical' representation as an essential condition for any possible knowing. Actual knowledge, then, is neither the pure concept (as metaphysics, and especially Hegel's 'panlogism', maintains),[28] nor the singular sensuous representation (as empiricism generally holds), but rather the logical activity of the 'individual judgment',[29] in which the human mind predicates of an historico-individual 'fact' four fundamental 'categories' (the Beautiful, the True, the Useful, the Good), to which Croce ascribes universal, necessary and thus a priori validity.

But is not nature's reality itself constituted by a multiplicity of individual 'facts', and do not the natural 'laws' which the positive sciences discover in such facts imply some sort of a priori cognitive 'forms' (e.g., space and time) or 'categories' (causality, substance, etc.) either? Why, then, restrict the area of application of the 'individual judgments' to historical reality alone? Croce resorts to the idealistic principle of the identity of being and consciousness in order to deny in principle the actuality of any alleged natural, and then extra-mental, facts. On the other hand, he borrows from one of the most fashionable *Wissenschaftstheorien* (theories of science) of the early 1900s, Mach's and Avenarius's 'empiriocriticism', the idea that the concepts and laws of the positive sciences are devoid of intrinsic universality and necessity, and are rather 'abbreviations' of a contingent plurality of sensuous, particular representations, which are worked out only in view of their practical *utility*, this consisting in the 'economy' of mental 'effort' which their employment would allow to the scientists.[30]

Having denied the reality of the Absolute and of nature, and consequently the truth of metaphysics and the positive sciences, Croce can easily identify the whole theoretical activity of the human mind with *historiography*. Philosophical knowledge differs from it only as the reflective explication of the conditions for the possibility of those 'logical a priori syntheses' (the 'individual judgments') which the actual historiographical praxis mostly carries out in an unconscious way. Contrary to what all great metaphysicians had concordantly maintained, then, philosophy can no longer be regarded as an 'autonomous' science but as the mere 'methodological moment of historiography'.[31]

Its specific subject matter would consist, in substance, in a clarification of the contents and mutual relations of those a priori categories which constitute, as we have seen, an essential moment of the 'individual judgments'. The category of the Beautiful coincides with spirit's *artistic* activity, or sense-perception, and its essential products are just those individual intuitive representations which become the subject of the judgments laid down by spirit's *logical* activity.[32] This latter, then, does not exhaust as such the essence of the category of the True, whose concrete content, rather, turns into the multiplicity of the individual judgments historical knowledge consists of. As to the category of the Useful, according to Croce it defines a form of spirit's activity no less concrete and 'autonomous' than art, knowledge or morality. In this regard, the influence of Marx's thought on Croce, through the mediation of its 'humanistic' interpretation worked out by Labriola at the end of the nineteenth century (see p. 350), *is* undeniable.[33] Unlike Hegel and Gentile, who emphasize the fact that the economic activity of the human mind is but the 'phenomenal', 'negative', 'abstract' side of the only true practical activity, i.e., moral activity as social morality (*Sittlichkeit, eticità*) or ethico-political praxis, to Croce the world of economic processes and relations instead constitutes a fully actual and autonomous factor in human history. Of course, since Croce identifies being in general with history, and defines this latter in terms of 'spirit', he can acknowledge the actual reality of economy only by interpreting the latter as a human activity no less 'spiritual' than, e.g., aesthetic contemplation or historical knowledge. As to the category of the Good, finally, Croce decidedly rejects Hegel and Gentile's contention that it can be concretely embodied only in social institutions. As was already the case with Kant, he confines moral activity to the private sphere of individual conscience, or, at best, to those social relations which an individual can freely join.

These are the main lines of the 'philosophy of spirit' set forth by Croce in his four 'systematic' works: *Estetica come scienza dell'espressione e linguistica generale* (*Aesthetics as the Science of Expression and General Linguistics*) (1902 [10.15]), *Logica come scienza del concetto puro* (*Logic as the Science of the Pure Concept*) (1905 [10.16]), *Filosofia della pratica* (*The Philosophy of Practice*) (1908 [10.18]), and *Teoria e storia della storiografia* (*A Theory and History of Historiography*) (1917 [10.19]). In the later years of his long literary, philosophical and political career, he seemed deeply to modify such a conception, at least with respect to two fundamental issues. On the one hand, in his *Storia d'Europa nel secolo decimonono* (*A History of Europe in the Nineteenth Century*) (1932 [10.20]),[34] he sees at the root of the progressive historical realization of the ethico-political ideal of 'liberalism' the spiritual energy of a new 'religion', although non-confessional in character: the so-called 'religion of freedom'. In the systematic exposition of his 'philosophy of spirit', on the contrary, religion is not regarded as a peculiar form of spirit's activity. On the other hand, in his *La storia come pensiero e come azione* (*History as Thought and as Action*) (1938 [10.22]),[35] he denies that the category of the Good constitutes, as such, a 'distinct' and autonomous form of spirit's life. Now morality seems to him to turn without residue into each of the three previous categories: the True, the Beautiful, and the Useful. Furthermore, in an essay collected in his last book, *Indagini sullo Hegel e schiarimenti filosofici* (*Inquiries into Hegel and Philosophical Explanations*) (1952 [10.23]),[36] he stresses the spiritual form of 'vitality' (*vitalità*) – which coincides, at least *prima facie*, with the category of the Useful – as the unique, common origin and 'root' of all the 'distinct' forms of spirit, whose 'autonomy', on the contrary, he had once so emphatically vindicated.

Despite the wide influence exerted by Croce's 'historicism' on twentieth-century Italian and European culture, I do not believe that he was actually able to offer a speculatively relevant contribution to the development of philosophical thought in our age. Elsewhere I have pointed out those which seem to me to be the fundamental short-comings both of his general conception of history and, in particular, of his logic.[37] Here I can confine myself to remarking that Croce's negation of the possibility of metaphysics is based upon the uncritical ontological presupposition of the actual reality of the 'finite' (as 'historical fact'). As soon as its intrinsic negativity becomes evident to self-conscious reflection, the radical inconsistency of such a presupposition can easily be unmasked. Second, the empiriocriticistic and Crocean denial of the universality of the concepts and laws of the positive sciences turns out to be possible only by surreptitiously presupposing the immediate evidence of sense-perception, which in truth is no less negative and contradictory than the 'finite' as such. Third, Croce declares that the four 'categories' in which he articulates the essence of spirit's development are a priori, i.e., 'universal' or absolute (and this is just the reason why, as against historical relativism, he defines his own philosophy as '*absolute* historicism'). A merely historico-inductive justification of their peculiar content and relations, then, is clearly out of place. The only possible foundation of their objective validity would obviously be their 'deduction' (however this may be conceived). Now, in no passage of his extensive writings does Croce appear to be able to provide us with the least 'deduction' of the specific categorial content of his 'theory of the distincts', and still less with any coherent conception of their mutual 'dialectical' relations. On the other hand, the groundlessness of his claim that they are a priori is proved *ad oculos* by his subsequent reduction of their number through the suppression of the category of the Good as an autonomous form of spirit's life as well as by his conclusive resolution of the whole categorial order into the sensuous immediacy of the *vitalità*. Fourth, how is it possible meaningfully to speak of an alleged 'religion of freedom' while at the same time openly *denying* (unlike Gentile and Hegel!) that religion as such is a specific form of spirit's dialectical development? Finally, Croce's vindication of the a priori character of the category of the Useful and, correlatively, of the 'spiritual' value and meaning of man's economic activity *as such* clearly implies the absurd transmogrification of a merely *external* and *finite* categorial relation such as that of 'utility'[38] into a self-contained, 'infinite' concept, since *any* authentic 'spiritual' category must necessarily be such. The final outcome of Croce's critical destruction of metaphysics in general, and especially of his sometimes very virulent polemic against Hegel's and Gentile's thought, then, appears to be, on the one hand, the sanctification of the most immediate, arbitrary and egoistic *utilitarian interests* of the 'private' individuals, and, on the other, the replacement of the living profundity of speculative thought with the dead superficiality of the most trivial and fragmentary historical *erudition*.

❧ HISTORICAL RELATIVISM AND SCEPTICISM ❧

Despite his polemic against Hegel and Gentile, Croce's historicism nevertheless holds to two fundamental assumptions of any *idealistic* philosophy: i.e., the identification of being with *consciousness* and the distinction, within the latter, between a system of *universal* (absolute) categories (or 'values') and the multiplicity of the particular, contingent representations which they somehow determine and qualify. A widespread theoretical and historiographical trend in twentieth-century Italian philosophy, represented especially by former fellows of Croce and Gentile, although holding fast to the first assumption, decidedly rejects the second. It *is* a 'dogmatic' prejudice, they acknowledge, to assert the actuality of a reality different from, and transcendent to, human consciousness – broadly speaking, of an 'external world' (however this may be conceived). Yet this would not imply at all that there exists something like a Universal Consciousness or an Absolute Subject, or a mere plurality of a priori concepts, unifying the multiplicity of individual consciousnesses and of their historical, temporal and subjective contents in a universally valid objective experience. The very idea of 'truth' as an *absolute* norm and principle of human knowledge is regarded as nothing more than a 'metaphysical prejudice'. Not only do they deny the existence of a unique, universal truth, of which the manifold determinate truths would be but internal, organic manifestations, but human knowing could not even come to any intrinsic, 'apodeictic' *certainty* of the specific content of a mere plurality of finite, particular truths. Any judgments that can be actually stated, indeed, are always merely 'problematic'. According to the *problematicismo* of Ugo Spirito (1896–1979), such a relativistic, and in the final analysis *sceptical*, conception of knowing would be the unavoidable outcome of Gentile's dialectical logic itself. This, as we have seen, identifies the essence of spirit with its becoming. Yet as a 'theory of spirit as pure act' it cannot but negate itself *as* becoming to the very extent that it claims a priori, and thus immutable and eternal, validity for its own theoretical tenets. As a consequence, one can do justice to reality's intimate processuality only by denying, in principle, the possibility of anything like a 'general theory of spirit' – more generally, of *metaphysics* as such.[39] Reality would thus turn into a 'historical' flux of states of consciousness, in which any alleged universal or absolute truth and reality dissolves, as a follower of Spirito puts it, into 'an unrestrainable rhapsody of sensations'.[40] Any human knowledge would consist of nothing other than mere '[p]robabilistic assertions, hypotheses and conjectures', and these 'are propositions which reality itself, in its daily or even hourly becoming, undertakes to compromise in their objectivity and to defeat in their claim to universality'.[41] According to Raffaello Franchini (1920–90), metaphysics and (historical) becoming 'cannot get along with each other',[42] and the former's claim to an 'absolute unification' and to 'conclusiveness' must give place to the 'infinity of particular researches'.[43] 'The survival . . . of the metaphysical conception of philosophy is very harmful to philosophy itself.'[44] Although not hesitating to see in Croce's historicism the epilogue and culmination of the whole history of western dialectic,[45] Franchini declares that not even Croce 'can avoid paying a tribute to the archaic philosophy of Being, despite his effective polemic against it'.[46] Such a tribute would obviously consist in his 'systematic' conception of spirit's forms as 'distinct' a priori categories, whereas they too would be nothing else than the product of 'a distinguishing *activity*, which in the final analysis is the judgement which Croce himself did not by chance call "historical" ',[47] i.e. merely contingent and relative.

It is out of place to go deeply here into a more detailed exposition and critique of the 'problematistic' and 'relativistic' outcomes of Italian idealism. In this context it will suffice to point out that, first of all, there is no actual contradiction between spirit's essential becoming and its reflective self-comprehension in a (metaphysical) 'theory' provided that the former is conceived (as with Gentile no less than with Hegel) not as mere temporal change but as 'eternal process': not as a simple negation of the eternal's self-identity, but as a self-identity which *eternally* 'returns-into-itself' from its 'self-alienation'.[48] Second, 'problematicism' and 'historical relativism', like any more or less radically *sceptical* sort of relativistic subjectivism, is plainly a *self-refuting* philosophical conception. For on the one hand it denies the metaphysical ideal of an absolute, 'definitive' truth; on the other, it undeniably ascribes absolute, 'definitive' value to its unjustified and unjustifiable, and therefore 'dogmatic',[49] denial of truth.

🙠 'CRITICAL ONTOLOGY': 🙠 PANTALEO CARABELLESE

Not unlike Croce's 'historicism' or Spirito's 'problematicism', the philosophy of Pantaleo Carabellese (1877–1948) can itself be safely regarded as a critical reaction to 'actual idealism'. Yet what he sets against Gentile's metaphysics of the 'pure act' is not a subjectivistic and relativistic conception of historical becoming so much as an 'ontology' of the 'pure Object', of absolute Being. In any case, such an ontology is still based upon an *idealistic* conception of reality (unlike all the other trends of twentieth-century 'metaphysics of Being', which I shall examine below) in that Carabellese shares with Gentile and Croce the fundamental epistemological assumption that 'being is in consciousness'.[50] Hence he explicitly disallows any attempt to 'overcome'[51] consciousness and to make the latter dependent, in the manner either of naturalistic empiricism or of traditional dualistic metaphysics, on a reality radically alien to it. Any possible actuality is either an act, or an object (a content), of consciousness. The peculiar problematic of metaphysics thus comes to coincide, for Carabellese, with a 'critical' analysis of the immanent formal-general structures of consciousness as the only 'concrete' reality. He distinguishes in it two 'transcendental conditions' mutually connected: the 'subject' and the 'object'; and three 'determinate forms' of its activity, which also imply one another: 'feeling', 'knowledge' and the 'will'. In each of the latter it is possible to bring out a peculiar configuration of the subject–object relation. Carabellese's whole polemic against Gentile is rooted in a different, and even alternative, conception of such a relation. Setting out from Kant's famous contention that the 'objectivity' of a perception coincides with its intersubjective validity, i.e. with its 'universality', he identifies the very essence of the object as such with the most 'universal' concept, i.e. the indeterminate 'idea of Being'. Yet this latter, as Rosmini (see p. 350) had already pointed out against Kant,[52] is not to be regarded as the product of an act of the knowing subject. Rather, it is passively 'given' to it. But what about the 'singular' objects, e.g. 'this' pen 'here'? Carabellese appeals in this regard to Berkeley's immaterialism, and emphatically denies that consciousness can actually refer to an extended, material, bodily, etc. object.[53] The only objective actuality it can become aware of is a 'spiritual reality', and this coincides with the *universal* idea of Being. The subject of the act of consciousness, on the contrary, must necessarily be merely 'singular': 'one among many', a 'monad'[54] bearing a relation of 'mutual otherness'[55] to infinite other possible singular subjects. As a consequence, contrary to what Kant, Hegel and Gentile held, the *unity* of conscious experience cannot be the result of a spontaneous 'synthesis' by the subject (for this is 'in itself' merely passive and manifold). It will therefore be rendered possible by the object alone, which, as universal, is also of necessity *unique*.[56]

The universal uniqueness of the object, then, *unifies* the singular plurality of the subjects; these latter, conversely, *individuate* the indeterminate universality of ideal Being. As we have already said, this takes place in three 'determinate forms of consciousness', to which three distinct ideal objectivities correspond: to feeling the idea of the Beautiful, to knowing the idea of the True, to willing the idea of the Good. In polemic with Gentile, who held 'pure feeling' to be 'inactual', and identified knowing with the will in the concrete actuality of the transcendental Ego (see p. 356), Carabellese vindicates, no less emphatically than Croce, the mutual *autonomy* of such concepts (and, of course, of the corresponding forms of consciousness). Hence it turns out to be impossible to raise any of them to the unconditioned principle of the others. Yet, unlike Croce, he not only excludes economic activity (and the corresponding category of the Useful) from his 'table' of the 'determinate forms of consciousness', but also tries to offer something like a 'deduction' of their specific content, which should bestow on them that *necessity* of which Croce's 'theory of the distincts', as we have seen, is devoid. In this regard, Carabellese appeals to consciousness's *temporal* form. While Kant regarded time as the mere form of 'inner sense', according to Carabellese it expresses rather the inmost essence of the whole life of consciousness.[57] Hence he thinks it possible to 'deduce' from the three 'moments' involved in the essence of time – past, present and future – the concepts of the True, of the Beautiful, and of the Good in the following way:

> In the certainty of having already been, the subjects are said intellect, the object is said true, and the concrete act is said *knowledge*; therefore *knowledge is consciousness of the being that was, is consciousness of the past*. In the certainty of being now, instead, the subjects are said feeling; the object is said beautiful, and the concrete act is said *intuition*; this therefore is consciousness of the being that is, is *consciousness of the present*. Finally, in the certainty of having to be [*dover essere*], the subject is said the will, the object is said good, and the concrete act is said *action*. This therefore is consciousness of the being that will be, *consciousness of the future*.[58]

Unlike Gentile (and Hegel), Carabellese refuses to deduce from the idealistic principle of the identity of being and consciousness the further consequence that the truth of immediate consciousness is the pure act of *self-consciousness*. For in such an act the Ego should be the object of itself; but to Carabellese, as we know, the object is essentially distinct from the subject (although being immanent in, and inseparable from, it). I therefore can be conscious of an object different from me (i.e., the idea of Being), but cannot possibly become aware of my own conscious act. The resolution of the objectifying act of consciousness into pure self-consciousness thus appears to Carabellese to be nothing less than 'the fundamental falsehood' of 'post-Kantian idealism'.[59]

A summary critical examination of Carabellese's ontology suffices to show that it is certainly not preferable to Croce's 'historicism' as a plausible alternative to 'actual idealism'.[60] First of all, his attempt to deduce the 'determinate forms of consciousness' from the essence of temporality is quite unsuccessful. His raising of temporality from a mere form of 'inner sense' to the constitutive structure of consciousness as such appears to be wholly arbitrary and unjustified. He does not seem to realize the intrinsic *negativity* (contradictoriness) of temporality, of whose 'moments' the past and the future, as such, *are not*, and the (sensuous) present is but an *abstract*, unreal limit between them. Moreover, if the origin of the concept of the True (and of knowing) lay in the temporal moment of the past, not only would the knowledge of the present and the future be obviously impossible, but also any logical and metaphysical knowing whatsoever (for this as such transcends the whole sphere of temporality). No less inconsistent is Carabellese's identification of the subject's essence with the 'plural singularity', and of that of the object with the unique universality of the idea of Being. As Kant himself, to whose authority Carabellese so often resorts, had already shown, I can become aware of a multiplicity (be it objective or subjective, and, in the latter case, be it the 'manifold' of the states of consciousness within the single subject or an 'intersubjective' plurality of individual subjects) only if I keep *self-identical* during the whole process of knowing in which I become aware of such a multiplicity. It is, then, the absolute identity of the self-conscious Ego, and not that of the object, which renders possible, in the final analysis, the 'synthetic unity' of concrete experience. Moreover, on what grounds can I assert that the object is 'in itself' *unique*? In effect, apart from the fact that sense-perception manifests an indefinite *plurality* of singular objects ('this' pen 'here', etc.), *all* objective *concepts* too, as determined, are essentially manifold. Only the *indeterminate* idea of Being is likely to be actually 'unique'. Yet, just as indeterminate, it is, in truth, but a mere 'abstraction', an empty *nothing*. How, then, can it render possible the objective unity of the 'concrete' as consciousness? Finally, Carabellese does not realize that his denial of the possibility of self-consciousness undermines nothing less than the most original conditions for the possibility of his own idea of philosophy as a 'critique of the concrete'. For we already know that to Carabellese the 'concrete' coincides with consciousness, and that his 'critique of the concrete' consequently turns into a reflective explication of consciousness's formal-general structures. Such an explication is obviously an act of consciousness. But its object, unlike that of 'immediate' consciousness, is by no means the indeterminate idea of Being, but *the very concrete actuality of knowledge*, so that it clearly takes the shape of a determinate form of *pure self-consciousness*, whose real possibility, then, it as such proves, as it were, *ad oculos*.

❧ 'MYSTICAL IDEALISM': PIETRO MARTINETTI ❧

When outlining the historical genesis of 'actual idealism' I have remarked that it stems from Hegel's idealism through the mediation of its interpretation by Spaventa in the nineteenth century. And the conceptions of thinkers such as Croce, Carabellese, Spirito, etc., can to a great extent be regarded as a mere reaction to Gentile's philosophy. The thought of Pietro Martinetti (1872–1943), on the contrary, derives both its concrete problematic and its fundamental speculative inspiration from a direct, and very detailed, acquaintance with the German idealistic tradition from Kant[61] to the neo-Kantianism of Riehl, Wundt and others. Not unlike the other exponents of Italian idealism, however, for him too the term 'idealism' fundamentally means an epistemological conception of the subject–object relationship according to which the latter is nothing more (nor less) than a pure immanent content of consciousness. The entire world-becoming thus turns without residue into that of consciousness. '[T]he reality which is given us in perception is conscious reality itself, and nothing other than it.'[62] If consciousness is considered from the standpoint of its immanent multiplicity, it constitutes the object. If, conversely, it is considered from the viewpoint of its active, unifying function, it constitutes the subject or the 'Ego' *stricto sensu*. The peculiar orientation of Martinetti's philosophical idealism with respect to that of Croce, Gentile or Carabellese is revealed, in my opinion, by two fundamental aspects of his thought. On the one hand, he seems to hold that a clear understanding of consciousness's process can be offered us rather by a *psychological* analysis of our inner experience than by a purely logical deduction of its a priori forms (Fichte, Hegel). Indeed, he does not hesitate to define his own position in terms of 'psychological idealism',[63] and to lay down a very favourable judgment about the 'idealistic empiricism flourishing in contemporary philosophy'[64] – for example Schopenhauer's theory of 'representation' or Schuppe's and Schubert-Soldern's 'philosophy of immanence'. But, on the other hand, no less crucial than the influence of that 'psychologism' which held sway over German thought at the end of the nineteenth century is that of *pantheistic mysticism* – from the Indian philosophy of the 'system' Sankhya (to which he devoted his doctoral dissertation) to the metaphysics of Plotinus, Spinoza[65] and the later Fichte. In substance, according to Martinetti, the analysis of psychological experience *is* a necessary moment of the process of knowing, but only as the groundwork for the construction of an 'idealistic metaphysics'[66] of the Absolute as an immanent Whole.

The fundamental philosophical principle bestowing unity and coherence on Martinetti's thought, in fact, has little or nothing to do, in my opinion, with psychological experience, but seems rather to coincide with the chief speculative assumption of Plotinus's metaphysics.[67] The most universal categories on the basis of which it is possible to interpret to totality of experience are Unity and Multiplicity. Contrary to what Hegel (and, before him, Plato himself at least in the *Parmenides*) maintained, they are, as such, *mutually exclusive*. This means that in an entity, experience or concrete spiritual activity, the more the moment of unity prevails, the less relevant the role played by multiplicity becomes, and conversely. The implications of such an assumption are not only ontological but also axiological and ethical in character. Unity is the principle of the intelligibility and 'perfection' of an entity; multiplicity, on the contrary, that of its irrationality and 'imperfection'. As a consequence, the differences revealed by our experience of the world and the Ego are ordered in a hierarchical succession, at the lower levels of which the moment of multiplicity predominates, while unity is the peculiar feature of the higher ones. Absolute Reality, therefore, is to be identified with an absolutely 'formal', 'indeterminate' Unity, devoid of any content, properties, relations, etc., since these are all clearly unthinkable apart from the manifold. Any other form of unity, even the 'concrete unity' of the system of Plato's 'ideas' or of Hegel's 'categories', is but mere *appearance*. Since intelligent activity too involves a manifold content (the plurality of the concepts which it distinguishes and/or unifies), the Absolute Unity necessarily *transcends* intelligence itself. 'But also this intelligible world is nothing else than a relative expression of a unity which in itself transcends intelligence.'[68] This latter, Martinetti rightly points out, is but a 'development' (*potenziamento*) of 'consciousness'. As a consequence, the Absolute Unity will transcend the totality of conscious experience as well: 'the highest constructions of logical thought are imperfect expressions of a Reality whose absolute unity transcends any consciousness'.[69] Although, then, all of our world-experience turns without residue into a dynamic, hierarchical succession of forms and states of consciousness, the ultimate aim (which to Martinetti, just as to Hegel, is at the same time the 'absolute foundation' of the whole cosmic becoming) of its evolution is not a possible act or content of consciousness.

It should be noted, however, that Martinetti's insistence on the absolute *epistemological* transcendence of Unity to consciousness does not exclude an unambiguous vindication of its substantial *ontological immanence* to the multiplicity of phenomenal experience. Perhaps the most intriguing aspect of Martinetti's metaphysics seems to me to be precisely his unrelenting polemic against the traditional theistic conception of God as an absolutely transcendent, 'otherworldly' entity. For him, on the contrary, the absolute, 'divine' unity is immanent even in the most negligible details of world-becoming.

> And therefore, as Leibniz already saw, every single phenomenon always expresses in the unity it realizes the unity of the world to which it belongs; every most simple unity reflects, owing to the infinite multiplicity of its factors, the universal order of existences; every most trifling being encloses in the mystery of its laws the secret of the world.[70]

The vulgar conception of the (first) cause as external to its effects (*causa transiens*) is to be rejected *in toto*. For the a priori necessity of their connection can be accounted for only by presupposing the intrinsic identity of them as their common foundation. But the cause, in truth, is not only identical with its effects: rather, it 'potentiates', 'reveals' itself in them.[71] In polemic with Aquinas and, more generally, with the whole scholastic ontology, Martinetti therefore declares: 'The whole system of the forms *in re* and *post rem* dissolves in such a case as an unhelpful complication. The world is but the very system of the divine thoughts, of the forms *ante rem*, that, before the obscure power of sense, as it were breaks and is refracted in the indefinite multiplicity of sensuous appearances.'[72]

Martinetti's reference to the 'obscure power of sense' in this passage is critical for the interpretation and evaluation of his whole philosophy. For his doctrine of sensible knowledge is perhaps that which gives rise to the greatest difficulties in his theoretical perspective. I have said that to Martinetti the manifold is a principle of unreality and imperfection, and that the more the process of consciousness approximates the Absolute Unity, the less relevant the former's actuality becomes. 'Sensible intuition' is obviously the most rudimentary phase in consciousness's development, since its content coincides with the heterogeneous, unreal multiplicity of material things and of sensuous qualities. A loose unification of the manifold is rendered possible, within the sphere of sense, by the (relatively) a priori functions[73] of 'space' and 'time'. The whole sphere of spatio-temporal reality, then, becomes the content of further, higher-order *logical* unifications by virtue of the fundamental categories of 'causality'[74] and 'logical identity'.[75] Now, not unlike Hegel, Martinetti explicitly declares that in the evolution of a lower form of spirit into a higher one the latter represents the 'truth', the 'actual reality' of the former, which with respect to it turns out to be 'virtually negated': 'the logical unity is not a reality coexisting with pure sensuous multiplicity, is not a reality of the same degree, but is a qualitatively higher reality, which *virtually denies sensuous reality*.'[76] Yet, on the other hand, he tries to differentiate his own position in this regard from Hegel's 'panlogism' by asserting that the logical unification of the sensuous 'given' does not undermine its autonomous, independent *reality*: 'An abyss subsists between the logical world of panlogism and sensuous reality.' 'The sensible and the logical order are two absolutely distinct orders, and their forced overlapping only succeeds in bringing out – here better than elsewhere – the absolute impossibility of making them coincide.'[77] The sharp contradiction in which Martinetti's thought here gets entangled is self-evident. In effect, in the final passage of his major work he himself somehow tries to solve it by declaring that 'if from the logical viewpoint the distinction between logical and sensuous reality turns into the distinction between being and not-being . . . from the absolute viewpoint both are but two subsequent forms of one reality, which in its absolute form is neither the one nor the other'.[78] Yet we know that for Martinetti the 'absolute viewpoint' is that of the absolutely 'formal' Unity, which as such radically transcends any consciousness and intelligence. How, then, can *we* take up such an alleged 'absolute viewpoint'? The 'logical' viewpoint therefore remains the only one we can legitimately resort to (and, strictly speaking, not only 'we', but also a possible infinite 'divine' *intelligence*). Hence his vindication of the original autonomy of sensuous reality is clearly self-refuting, and consequently his attempt to differentiate his own position from Hegel's 'panlogism' turns out to be, at least in this regard, quite unsuccessful.

The other fundamental objections that Martinetti's idealistic monism raises against Hegel's philosophy concern the dialectical method; his doctrine of the immanent becoming of the logical Idea; his identification of the latter with the very Absolute Reality; and finally his 'realistic' admission of the possibility of a philosophy of 'nature' as the process of the Idea in a still 'unconscious form'. Given the validity of the idealistic principle of the identity of being and consciousness, how can one still deem it possible to construct a priori a succession of natural categories that is not, at the same time, the content of a series of subjective 'syntheses' of consciousness?

Martinetti's reproach to Hegel's thought, in this regard, is clearly that it is not yet sufficiently 'idealistic'. It seems to me to be historically enlightening to point out that the gist of this Martinetti objection coincides *in toto* with one of the fundamental results of Gentile's 'reform of Hegelian dialectic': i.e., the denial of the possibility of any dialectical process which is not the pure becoming of the *pensiero pensante*, i.e. of the self-conscious Ego (p. 356).

As for the relation between the Hegelian Idea and Absolute Reality, it is undeniable that, if the latter really is, as Martinetti maintains, a Unity which transcends any multiplicity, and therefore the very element of consciousness and intelligence, it cannot possibly coincide with Hegel's Absolute Idea, which is indeed the pure self-consciousness of a systematic totality of thought-determinations. Moreover, any becoming (be it temporal or logical) is clearly possible and thinkable only as a synthesis of unity (continuity) and multiplicity (discretion, as the *plurality* of the successive 'phases' discernible in it). If, then, Absolute Reality is actually devoid of any multiplicity whatsoever, becoming must certainly be nothing more than a mere 'phenomenon'. The Absolute Unity, therefore, is *eo ipso* absolutely motionless and static. Finally, according to Martinetti (who strangely seems to share, in this regard, some of the most popular tenets of contemporary logical empiricism), there are only two scientifically valid 'logical' methods: 'analysis', which is merely formal and reconstructive in character; and 'synthesis', or 'induction', which consequently is the only method actually able originally to constitute, and then to extend, our knowledge. The latter's 'genetic order', he says, 'is invariably inductive, and springs forth from a unique source which is experience'.[79] As a consequence, induction is the proper method not only of the *positive sciences* but also of philosophy itself. As a consequence, the only real difference between them is that, while the positive sciences limit themselves to a more or less 'relative' unification of the multiplicity of the immediate 'given', philosophy on the contrary essentially aspires to a 'total', 'absolute' unification. The undeniable non-inductive character of Hegel's dialectical method, then, would ineluctably undermine the 'scientificity' of his 'panlogistic' conception of the Absolute. In Martinetti's critique of Hegelianism, then, (psychological) empiricism and (immanentistic) mysticism work hand in hand in a somewhat surprising way. While, indeed, his rejection of the dialectical method (like his theory of sensible intuition I have outlined above) relies on arguments of clear empiricist origin, his polemic against Hegel's Absolute Reason has no other ground, nor any other aim (so at least I believe), than the vindication of the ontological and ethical primacy of *mystical–religious experience* over rational–philosophical thought. In fact, on one occasion he does not hesitate openly to define in terms of 'mysticism' the deepest possible form of unity between the Absolute and the human mind: 'our knowing . . . is an act of mystical union with the eternal Logos which is the absolute ground of our nature.'[80]

The plausibility of Martinetti's anti-Hegelian polemic thus appears to depend *in toto* upon two decisive speculative assumptions: (1) the epistemological validity of induction; and (2) the ontological reality of an absolute Unity absolutely devoid of any moment of difference or multiplicity. But, in truth, Aristotle and Kant had insightfully pointed out already in the antinomy of 'complete induction' the irremediable shortcoming of the inductive method; and Plato, in his *Parmenides*, had already brilliantly shown that the statement 'The One is' actually means the very opposite of what it purports to mean, i.e. the *unreality* of the One as One. For the existential predicate 'is' constitutes of itself an element *different* from it, and thus immediately posits an *original manifold* in the alleged pure 'unity' of the One itself.

❧ METAPHYSICS OF BEING ❧

The peremptory rejection of the 'idealistic' identification of being and consciousness and the unrelenting polemic against all the logical, metaphysical and ethical consequences drawn from it by both Croce and Gentile constitute the fundamental and historically most relevant features of a widespread tendency in twentieth-century Italian philosophy which one could generally define in terms of 'metaphysics of Being'.[81] The divergences among the spiritual traditions of (1) Thomism, (2) Augustine's and Rosmini's 'spiritualism', and (3) Kierkegaard's mystical irrationalism – to which thinkers such as (1) Armando Carlini (1878–1959), Augusto Guzzo (1894–1986), Gustavo Bontadini (1903–90), and Michele Federico Sciacca (1908–79), (2) Francesco Olgiati (1886–1968) and (3) Luigi Pareyson (1918–91) respectively go back – turn out to be negligible as compared with the substantial affinity of both the theoretical content and the historico-cultural finalities of their philosophical activity. Being, Truth, the Absolute, God, they maintain, radically *transcend* the whole sphere of self-consciousness, and especially the activity of rational thought. Even those who are most willing to acknowledge the actuality and value of speculative reason, i.e. the neo-Thomists, hold nevertheless that this is a function of spirit which is in the final analysis *subordinate* (or rather: 'subaltern') to an alleged more original immediate *intuition* of the 'idea of Being' – and, a fortiori, to religious revelation such as is sanctioned by the authority of the Roman Catholic church, and to mystical experience. 'The absolute objective truth', Sciacca declares, 'is before its being known, and it would remain such even though no thinking subject ever knew, or sought for, it.'[82] '[T]he *ratio* is a cognitive power inferior to the *intellectus*, on which it depends.'[83] 'What counts,' Pareyson echoes him, 'is not reason, but truth.'[84] The vindication of the absolute epistemological transcendence of truth to human self-consciousness finds a close counterpart, at the ontological level, in their common intent to 'restore', as Bontadini openly says, in contemporary philosophy and culture a decidedly 'dualistic' conception[85] of the relations between God and man, process and eternity, spirit and nature, the One and the Many, etc. '[T]ranscendence means *duality*, immanence means *monism*', Sciacca asserts. 'The condition of culture turns out to us still to be the dualistic conception of the reality of "this" world and of that of the "other" world, of the world of man and of the world of God.'[86] 'Hegel's *Gott-in-Werden* [God-in-becoming] is a nonsense, in that one uses the term "God", but one ascribes to him a predicate that denies him, that is contrary to his nature.'[87] From this dualistic ontological perspective the reality of nature, of life, of the 'cosmos' cannot obviously but be regarded as something quite alien to spirit, and as such even unworthy of philosophical consideration. 'Analogy', Guzzo maintains, 'can be held to be the only means truly fit to dispel any temptation of identifying nature and man, either in the naturalistic sense of a reabsorption of man into nature or in the sense of an idealistic epistemology which aims at drawing back and dissolving "nature" into "spirit" '.[88] In his polemic against the metaphysical reality of nature, Carlini goes as far as to accuse of *cosmologismo*, i.e. of naturalism, the very 'Christian Neoplatonism with its *Ens Realissimum*'![89]

According to Olgiati, 'if there were no realities there would be no relations, for it is not the relations which create reality, but it is reality which gives rise to the relations'.[90] In Bradley's terminology one could say that the fundamental ontological point this neo-Thomist intends to make is that the only actual relations are the 'external' ones occurring among an original plurality of logically indifferent entities that are irreducible to any higher, more concrete Unity or organic Totality. No surprise, then, that in the light of such an ontological conception of reality as mere plurality the *only* concept of man's personality that appears to be tenable to the upholders of the metaphysics of Being is still that of the traditional 'soul-substance', i.e. of a self-contained, finite and contingent entity. '[T]he concept of person', a follower of Sciacca observes, 'cannot avoid that individualistic-intimistic closure which seems to be wholly peculiar to the level of singularity.'[91] Its only possibility of, and hope for, 'immortality', consequently, far from consisting in its absolute identity with the Totality of the cosmos and human history, will rather coincide with its alleged indefinite duration 'after death' in the temporal dimension of the *future*: i.e., as Sciacca openly declares, with its 'ultramundane [*ultraterreno*] destiny'.[92]

If it is an indisputable merit of the upholders of the metaphysics of Being to have revived interest in the metaphysical problem in contemporary philosophy, one must also acknowledge that its statement and solution in the ambit of their philosophical perspective does appear to be wholly unsatisfying. The fundamental concept of 'Being' they concordantly resort to as the first and most original truth of the human 'intellect', indeed, is but a dead, unfruitful, *unthinkable* abstraction – both because it is devoid of any determinate content whatsoever and because it presupposes the actual *abstraction* from the concrete becoming of the 'act of thinking', of which, in truth, such a concept is a mere product, and which is thus necessarily presupposed by any alleged categorial negation of it. In other words, the self-conscious ('subjective') process of thinking cannot possibly be transcended, and consequently the object is originally and substantially *identical* with the subject. The dualistic conception of reality, which is on the contrary based on the original *opposition* of subject and object, is therefore inconsistent and untenable, and any attempt to 'restore' it in the spiritual life of contemporary humanity appears to be ineluctably destined to failure.[93]

❧ MARXISM AND PHENOMENOLOGY ❧

While for the upholders of the metaphysics of Being the fundamental shortcoming of Croce's and Gentile's idealism consists in its rigorously 'immanentistic' and/or 'historicistic' orientation, most theorists of twentieth-century Italian Marxism, on the contrary, regard it as the most 'living' and up-to-date legacy of the idealistic-Hegelian tradition (if not even of the whole history of 'bourgeois' philosophy). One can distinguish three main trends in Italian Marxism just on the basis of their different relation to that tradition. According to Antonio Gramsci (1890–1937), 'in a sense . . . the philosophy of praxis [i.e., Marxism] is a reform and development of Hegelianism'.[94] Croce's and Gentile's Hegelian idealism is therefore the only twentieth-century 'bourgeois' philosophy which he holds to be able to furnish a helpful conceptual contribution to the theoretical elaboration of historical materialism. Not unlike Croce's 'absolute historicism', indeed, 'the philosophy of praxis has been the translation of Hegelianism into a *historicistic* language'.[95] And not unlike 'actualism', it is itself a philosophy of the 'act' – even though not of the 'pure', but of the ' "impure" (*impuro*), real act, in the most profane and mundane sense of this word'.[96] The possibility and necessity of an 'integration' of historical materialism with any other contemporary philosophical-cultural tendency whatsoever is emphatically rejected by Gramsci. 'Marxist orthodoxy', he says, consists 'in the fundamental concept that the philosophy of praxis is "self-sufficient", i.e. contains in itself all the fundamental concepts needed to build up a total, integral conception of the world'.[97]

Quite opposed to the 'subjective'[98] conception of historical materialism worked out by Gramsci is the interpretation of Marx's thought as a 'logic of existence', or of 'contingent reality', put forward by Galvano Della Volpe (1895–1968).[99] In his opinion, Marx's methodology would bear a close resemblance to the 'kind of critical instances from which *modern experimental science* originates'.[100] In open polemic against Hegelianism, and, more generally, against any 'metaphysics' or 'mysticism', the school of Della Volpe (Mario Rossi,[101] Lucio Colletti,[102] etc.) stresses the radical difference between thought and being, vindicates the 'positive reality', the objectivity of the 'instance of *matter*, or the manifold, or the discrete',[103] and reduces Hegel's concept of 'reason' as a unity of opposites (an 'identità tauto-eterologica', as Della Volpe also says) to a merely logical ideal devoid of concrete actuality.

The interpretation of Marxism put forward by the 'Milan phenomenological school' founded by Antonio Banfi (1896–1957), whose most prominent exponent was probably Enzo Paci (1911–76), shares with Gramsci's the insistence on the 'subjective', 'humanistic' character of historical materialism, and on its consequent substantial divergence from any kind of traditional naturalistic and deterministic materialism. But the most radical, and up-to-date, understanding of human subjectivity would certainly not be the excessively 'speculative' and 'metaphysical' one worked out by Hegel's philosophy, so much as the 'descriptive' and 'intuitive' explication of its 'formal-general structures' rendered possible by Husserl's 'phenomenological' method. Whereas, then, for Gramsci Marxism is a 'self-sufficient' world-view, for Paci it needs to be 'integrated', and in some respects even 'rectified', by the most original theoretical achievements of 'transcendental phenomenology'.

The fundamental shortcomings of traditional idealistic philosophy, according to Gramsci, consist, on the one hand, in its being an 'abstractly' *theoretical*, or 'speculative', conception of the world which unduly ignores the essential *practical*, or rather 'political', origin and finality of any alleged 'autonomous' spiritual or rational activity; and, on the other, in its more or less explicit 'solipsism'. 'The history of philosophy', he asserts, is nothing more than 'the history of the attempts . . . to modify practical activity as a whole'.[104] 'One can believe in solipsism, and indeed *any form of idealism* necessarily falls into solipsism.'[105] Gramsci therefore goes on to set against the idealistic (rationalistic) principle of 'coherence' as truth criterion the more trivially *quantitative* one of the wideness of the consent which a philosophy (or rather, as he says, an 'ideology') enjoys in the 'masses'. The truth of a philosophy, he declares, 'is witnessed by the fact that it is appropriated, and permanently appropriated, by the majority [*gran numero*], so as to become a culture'.[106] 'One can say that a philosophy's historical value can be "calculated" by the "practical" effectiveness it has won.'[107] Also Gramsci's polemic against 'vulgar' materialism and positivism, which reduce in one way or another humanity's spiritual reality to the passive and ineffective 'superstructure' or 'epiphenomenon' of its material life, is based, in the last analysis, on grounds that are strictly practical-political in character. Idealistic philosophy is right to insist on the 'reality' of 'ideologies' – but not because they would express an 'eternal' or 'autonomous' being or truth so much as because the 'cultural factor' would constitute an essential 'instrument of practical action'[108] in view of the establishment of the 'political domination', of the 'hegemony' (*egemonia*),[109] of one social class over another. 'According to the philosophy of praxis, ideologies are not arbitrary at all; they are *real historical facts*.'[110]

Far more akin to traditional materialism and positivism is Della Volpe's interpretation of historical materialism. In his opinion, Marx's Hegel critique would have rendered possible the foundation of philosophy 'as a scientific ontology, this being a *material ontology* and no longer a *formal ontology* or *metaphysics* as the traditional one from Plato and Aristotle up to Hegel'.[111] It would thus allow us to replace Hegel's 'metaphysics of the state' with a far more realistic 'sociology of the state', whose peculiar inspiration would be 'experimental' or 'Galileian'.[112] Its fundamental epistemological assumptions consist, according to Della Volpe, in the vindication of the original reality of the sensuous-contingent 'facts' (of the 'manifold') as well as of the objective validity of the principle of non-contradiction, of the 'finite understanding', of experiment, and of formal or 'classificatory' logic. Della Volpe decidedly denies the authentically 'scientific' character of Engels's 'laws of dialectic',[113] and against any activistic or pragmatistic interpretation of historical materialism insists on the fact that it is Marxism as a 'science' that grounds practical activity, and not conversely.[114]

In open polemic against 'naturalistic' materialism, and the very logico-experimental method of the positive sciences which would be but a peculiar form of the 'alienation' typical of 'bourgeois' society, Paci emphasizes no less than Gramsci the 'subjective', 'historical' character of Marx's concept of 'matter'. Yet, unlike Gramsci, he holds that it at least virtually finds a close counterpart in Husserl's conception of 'transcendental consciousness' as 'virtual intentional life' (*vita intenzionale fungente*), or as a 'world-of-life' (*mondo-della-vita*). 'Inert matter is in some way *subjective*. Materialism is not a metaphysics of a substance [*sostanzialismo*] alien to the subject: I am the world, I am the whole world.'[115] The plausibility of an 'idealistic' interpretation of such a fundamental phenomenological conception is ineluctably undermined, according to Paci, by the fact that to Husserl consciousness is always originally and radically *sensuous, passive,* and *temporal,* even when it is regarded as a 'pure' transcendental 'function'. 'The error fraught with the worst consequences in the interpretation of Husserl's phenomenology is that of those who see in [Husserl's] Ego the consciousness or self-consciousness in the creative [*creativistico*] sense of idealism.'[116] The phenomenological analysis of the 'world-of-life' would thus render it possible to 'correct' the erroneous 'naturalistic' tendencies or interpretations of historical materialism without falling once again into the alleged 'categorial' abstractness of the 'idealistic' metaphysical tradition. The phenomenological point of view, Paci maintains, 'allows us . . . to stress the necessity and the conditioning of the material structure or of the structure of the needs on human-historical praxis, but forbids us, at the same time, to apply to history a scientific dialectic in the sense in which physics is scientific'.[117]

Except for the school of Della Volpe, then, Italian Marxism generally tends to emphasize the decisive role played by *human subjectivity* in the self-constructing process of history – and even of universal reality itself. Yet its uncritical allegiance to the assumption of the original reality and truth of sensible perception and praxis, of time and finitude, as fundamental constitutive structures of 'history', or even of the 'transcendental consciousness', does not allow either Gramsci or Banfi and Paci to realize the 'abstractness' (in the sense of 'mutilated' one-sidedness) and thus contradictoriness of a 'subjectivity' that is not at the same time 'objective' (infinite), since the 'eternal' reality of the Absolute is not held to be immanent in it.[118] Furthermore, they do not seem to be sufficiently aware that their denial of the *unconditional* autonomy of logico-speculative reason (of the philosophical 'categories') in the final analysis undermines the 'coherence', and then objective validity, of any conception or interpretation (be it philosophical or scientific) of the very evolutionary process of human social history.

❧ EXISTENTIALISM AND EMPIRICISM ❧

The reaction against the speculative tradition of Italian idealism does reach a climax in the philosophical perspective of Nicola Abbagnano (1901–90) and his followers, which he defines in terms of both 'positive existentialism' and 'methodological empiricism' or 'neo-illuminism'. His interpretation of Heidegger's existential ontology, indeed, emphatically disallows any possible 'metaphysical stiffening'[119] of it, and reduces the method of 'existential analysis' to a mere empirical and contingent description 'of those human situations which can be regarded as "fundamental" or "essential" or "decisive" or as "limit-situations" [*situazioni-limite*], etc.'.[120] On the other hand, as the American pragmatists had already pointed out, that 'experimental method' which any empiricist philosophy is used to appealing to cannot and must not be conceived in a strictly 'theoretical' or 'objective' sense,[121] but as 'the structure of action *par excellence*, in that it is destined to modify such [human] situations'.[122] This is because to Abbagnano, just as to all existentialists, the 'being-in-the-world' of man is a 'relation to being' which is originally 'emotional' and 'practical' in character (something like a series of 'decisions'), and as such is absolutely alien and impenetrable to rational, theoretical consciousness. 'Existence cannot be enlightened by knowledge or by reason, but can throw light on them.'[123]

The originally 'irrational' nature of 'existence', according to Abbagnano, excludes the possibility that it might be adequately qualified by those ontological categories which most typically express the essence of pure rationality, such as universality, necessity, infinity, 'progress'. The only 'really existing man', he declares, is neither the Absolute Subject of the idealistic systems, nor the ideal of 'humanity', nor world-history, but nothing else than the 'singular individuality'.[124] This would be determined by a particular factual 'situation' which radically distinguishes it from any other human individual, and which one-sidedly conditions any possible 'activity' – or 'project' – of its own. Human existence, then, is by its nature 'contingent', 'uncertain', 'risky', and the most general ontological category needed to understand its fundamental structures is therefore that of 'possibility'. Indeed, the essence of 'freedom' itself would turn into the mere possibility of 'choosing' among a range of 'given' alternatives (or 'choices'), and therefore is not, nor can it in principle ever be, infinite or absolute. 'Existentialism asserts that man is a finite reality, that he exists and operates at his own risk and danger.'[125]

According to Abbagnano, then, the only object of which philosophy and the sciences can meaningfully speak is 'finite' (temporal, contingent, relative, etc.) reality. The fundamental *idealistic*, or 'romantic', assumption that the finite as such is not actually real, but is rather the mere manifestation of a 'superior Reality'[126] (the Totality of the Universe, Spirit, Absolute Reason, etc.), is purely 'mythological' in character. But not only is a unique, infinite Reality or Totality quite inexistent, but it does not even make sense to speak of 'absolute' *moral*, or 'spiritual', values. Also the faith in the objectivity of such values would be but a mere 'romantic' prejudice, and it is just the task of 'existential analysis' to show its inconsistency.

Romanticism always has a certain spiritualistic bent. It tends to extol the importance of inwardness, of spirituality, as well as of the values that are called 'spiritual', at the cost of what is earthly, material, mundane, etc. Existentialism shamelessly recognizes the importance and value for man of externality, of materiality, and of 'mundanity' in general, and thus of the conditions of human reality that are included under these terms: the needs, the use and production of things, sex, etc.[127]

[F]rom the empirical standpoint, the moral problem cannot obviously be coped with by resorting to an apology for morals, or by claiming to be able to establish hierarchies of 'absolute' values, which ought to provide us with necessary criteria for evaluation.[128]

The fundamental philosophical error that undermines the 'positive existentialism' of Abbagnano and his followers throughout is the absurd claim that the human subject may become 'immediately' aware of its own 'existence' as a 'structure' originally 'other' than rational self-conscious thought. In truth, any reliance on the 'evidence' of 'immediate', sensible, 'pre-logical' perception, intuition, praxis, etc. is purely illusory, since it does not account for the intrinsically 'mediate' character of any subject–object relation, and, furthermore, for the fact that any 'mediation', connection or 'relation', in the last analysis, is nothing more (as Kant had already stressed) than a product of the 'synthetic' activity of the pure self-conscious Ego. And even the most elementary act by which this 'posits itself' necessarily involves (as the 'dialectical' development of its pure immanent content could easily show) the objective validity of those very categories of 'necessity', 'universality', 'infinity', etc., which Abbagnano's 'positive existentialism' dogmatically denies, or rather is simply unable to account for. In face of the luminous 'self-evidence' of the thinking concept's immanent self-explication, then, all the too often banal, trivial, and worn-out arguments of his polemic against 'romanticism' and 'idealism' cannot but 'dissolve as fog in the sun'.

❧ CONCLUSION ❧

If now, having come to the conclusion of this brief outline of twentieth-century Italian philosophy, we take a fleeting retrospective glance at its most significant vicissitudes and achievements, we can first of all remark that the debate between the upholders and the adversaries of idealist-speculative thought does constitute the crux of its whole development. It is undeniable that in the second half of the twentieth century the anti-idealistic trends – empiricism, existentialism, phenomenology, Marxism, dualistic metaphysics, etc. – have somehow prevailed. Yet this does not mean at all that their contributions to the progress of Italian philosophical culture have *eo ipso* turned out to be more convincing, valuable, or lasting. On the contrary, our summary analysis of their fundamental assumptions outlined above seems to have clearly brought out their indisputable theoretical inferiority with respect to both the content and the method of the idealistic perspective.

As far as the latter is concerned, then, we have witnessed the polemic between the rigorously dialectical, monistic, and 'speculative' development of the philosophical principle of idealism carried out by Gentile's 'actualism' and other antidialectical, pluralistic or historicistic forms of idealism such as Martinetti's mystical monism, Carabellese's 'critical ontology', and Croce's 'absolute historicism'. Despite the sharp critiques to Gentile's thought put forward by the latter, none of their speculative constructions can bear comparison – as to coherence, lucidity and intimate force of persuasion – with the theoretical perspective of 'actual idealism'. Hence this is and remains up to the present the essential reference point for any further development and progress of philosophical research in Italy.

This, however, is not tantamount at all to saying that a fair evaluation of the actual speculative achievements of Gentile's thought cannot and must not bring to light in it more than one fundamental limit.[129] In this context I can confine myself to remarking that the actual result of his 'reform of Hegelian dialectic' appears to consist, in more than one respect, rather in a one-sided formalistic 'simplification' of the very complex totality of Hegel's Absolute Idea than in the positive explication of a speculative truth which in the Hegelian system would still be merely implicit. After all, Bosanquet's famous objection to Gentile's philosophy – that it would be a sort of 'narrow humanism' which, unlike the Hegelian one, does no justice to the intrinsic 'dialectical' nature both of the logical categories and of the processes of natural reality – is likely to be sound and tenable. The *speculative task* which the critical reflection on the theoretical limits of 'actual idealism' proposes to contemporary philosophy thus seems to be the integration of the brightest and most fruitful idea of Gentile's thought – i.e., that Absolute Reality is the totality-in-becoming of self-conscious, active 'spirit' – with a 'holistic' and 'systematic' interpretation of the fundamental achievements of scientific and methodological research in our century such as is being developed, for example, by the latest and most significant trends of the philosophical tradition of Anglo-Saxon Hegelianism.[130]

 NOTES

1 Cf. H. Marcuse, *Reason and Revolution: Hegel and the Rise of Social Theory*, 2nd edn, New York: The Humanities Press, 1954, pp. 402–9.

2 For a detailed, although somewhat uncritical, reconstruction of the 'external' events of the development of twentieth-century Italian philosophical culture, see E. Garin [10.31] A summary overview of the fundamental trends of Italian thought from 1945 up to 1980 is offered by the collection of essays, ed. E. Garin [10.53].

3 M. F. Sciacca [10.86], vol. 3, p. 214.

4 G. Gentile, 'L'atto del pensare come atto puro', 1911; in Gentile, *La riforma della dialettica hegeliana* [10.32], 193.

5 G. Gentile, *Teoria generale dello spirito come atto puro* [10.35]; in Gentile [10.45], p. 491.

6 'L'atto del pensare come atto puro' [10.32], 194.

7 *Teoria generale dello spirito come atto puro* [10.35], 475.

8 'L'atto del pensare come atto puro' [10.32], 190.

9 *Ibid.*, p. 191.

10 G. Gentile, *Il modernismo e i rapporti tra religione e filosofia*, 1909, ch. 10: 'Le forme assolute dello spirito', in Gentile, *La religione*, [10.38], pp. 259–65.

11 Cf. G. Gentile, *La filosofia dell'arte* [10.42], 144–70. See also Gentile, *Introduzione alla filosofia* [10.43], 34–60.

12 Cf. *La filosofia dell'arte* [10.42], 150–2.

13 Cf. *Teoria generale dello spirito come atto puro* [10.35], 470.

14 Cf. *La filosofia dell'arte* [10.42], 117ff.

15 Cf. G. Gentile, *Sistema di logica come teoria del conoscere* [10.36], vol. 1.

16 The most developed and accomplished form of which remains, in his opinion, Catholicism: cf. G. Gentile, 'La mia religione' [10.40], 405–26.

17 Cf., e.g., G. Gentile, *Discorsi di religione* [10.38], 382: 'The most deeply religious (= mystical) element of religion is not the affirmation of the abstract object so much as the *negation of the subject*' (my italics).

18 In Gentile's terminology: in the '*societas in interiore homine*'. Cf. Gentile, *I fondamenti della filosofia del diritto* [10.34], 75–6; and *Genesi e struttura della società* [10.44], ch. 4, pp. 33–43.

19 Cf. G. Gentile, *Sommario di pedagogia come scienza filosofica* [10.33], vol. 1, p. 25.

20 For a more detailed critical examination of his fundamental logical and epistemological doctrines, see my paper [10.83] and my book [10.82], part 3, ch. 2, no. 51.

21 H. S. Harris [10.52], 274. A careful outline of Gentile's philosophy is offered by the same author in his essay [10.51]. Nothing more than a somewhat grotesque distortion of Gentile's thought in a relativistic-materialistic sense is the 'interpretation' put forward by A. Negri in his book [10.64] and by V. A. Bellezza in his papers [10.7] and [10.8].

22 Cf., e.g., Hegel, *Enzyklopädie der philosophischen Wissenschaften*, Frankfurt: Suhrkamp, 1970, vol. I, no. 133, *Zusatz*.

23 G. Gentile, *La riforma dell'educazione* [10.41], 32–47.

24 *Sommario di pedagogia* [10.33], 127.

25 *Ibid.*, p. 253.

26 *La riforma dell'educazione* [10.41], 176.

27 Cf. B. Croce, *Logica come scienza del concetto puro* [10.16], 249–54.

28 Cf. B. Croce, *Saggio sullo Hegel seguito da altri scritti di storia della filosofia,* [10.17], 126ff.

29 Cf. *Logica* [10.16], 91ff.

30 Cf. *ibid.*, pp. 323–5.

31 Cf. *Teoria e storia della storiografia* [10.19], 140.

32 In an essay of 1936, however, Croce, explicitly contradicting a fundamental assumption of the aesthetic theory outlined by him in 1902, asserts that one of the essential features of 'poetry' is the '*cosmicità*', i.e. its 'universality' (cf. B. Croce, *La poesia* [10.21], 11–14).

33 Croce's critical discussion and (partial) appropriation of the theory of Marx's historical materialism is documented especially by his book *Materialismo storico ed economia marxistica* [10.14].

34 Cf. B. Croce, *Storia d'Europa nel secolo decimonono* [10.20], 7–21.

35 Cf. B. Croce, *La storia come pensiero e come azione* [10.22], 44.

36 B. Croce, *Indagini sullo Hegel e schiarimenti filosofici* [10.23], 29–55.

37 Cf. my paper [10.81], and my book [10.82], part 3, ch. 2, no. 52.

38 Cf. *ibid.*, part 2, ch. 4, note 19, p. 280.

39 Cf. U. Spirito [10.89]. For an outline of the development of Spirito's thought see A. Negri [10.64], vol. 2, pp. 65–73.

40 A. Negri [10.65], 58.

41 *Ibid.*, p. 57.

42 R. Franchini [10.30], 167.

43 *Ibid.*, p. 57.

44 *Ibid.*, p. 172.

45 R. Franchini [10.29], 347.

46 R. Franchini [10.30], 167.

47 *Ibid.*

48 'Relativistic historicism' is also the final outcome of the spiritual itinerary of one of the major Italian historians of philosophy, Guido de Ruggiero (1888–1948). See especially [10.25]. For a critique of his misguided polemic against Hegel's absolute idealism, which he accuses of 'theologism' and even of 'fetishism', cf. G. Rinaldi [10.82], part 3, ch. 2, note 87. The denial of the constitutive immanence of the logical universal in individual consciousness led Julius Evola (1898–1974) to identify the essence of the human subject with Nietzsche's 'will to power': cf. J. Evola, *Teoria dell'Individuo Assoluto* [10.27].

49 In fact, Franchini (not unlike, in this regard, the contemporary empiricists) denies the epistemological value of any possible logical 'foundation' or 'demonstration', as merely 'tautological' (cf. [10.30], 171). His very denial of the possibility of metaphysics, then, is to be held to be *ungrounded* – more the expression of individual subjective impotence than the ascertainment of human reason's objective, insuperable 'limits'.

50 P. Carabellese, *Critica del concreto* [10.11], 23. The second edition of this work considerably differs from the first, and can be legitimately regarded as the definitive version of Carabellese's 'critical ontology'.

51 *Ibid.*, pp. 101, 184.

52 And, after him, Bernardino Varisco (1850–1933), a spiritualistic and theistic Italian thinker who has remarkably influenced the development of Carabellese's thought.

53 In Carabellese's ontological perspective the very concept of 'nature' turns out to be simply nonsensical. As a consequence, he cannot but deny *in toto* the theoretical value of the positive sciences. Cf., e.g., *Critica del concreto* [10.11], 189.

54 *Ibid.*, p. 109.

55 *Ibid.*, p. 199.

56 In more than one context Carabellese does not even hesitate to identify the objective unity of the idea of Being with God himself (cf., e.g. *ibid.*, p. 7, note). In any case, since such an idea, as we know, is but an abstract 'transcendental condition' of knowing, radically *different* from the subject which is its other essential condition, he is bound to conclude, somewhat absurdly, that God as such *does not exist actually*, nor is he 'subject', 'person', 'self-consciousness', 'spirit' (cf. *ibid.*, pp. 151–2, 171, 194).

57 Cf. *ibid.*, pp. 113–15 and 181. Note the analogy of this Carabellese doctrine with Husserl's and Heidegger's more known 'phenomenological' conceptions of 'temporality'.

58 *Ibid.*, p. 24.

59 Cf. *ibid.*, pp. 126–39.

60 Garin rightly stresses the 'obscurity' and 'haziness of expression' of Carabellese's thought (cf. [10.31], vol. 2, pp. 357, note 16, and 455). And R. Donnici suitably observes that 'as compared with Gentile and Croce's idealism, his most immediate polemical targets, Carabellese's critical ontology appears to be very frail' (R. Donnici [10.26], 7). In my opinion, this holds good more for his critique of Gentile than for that of Croce.

61 His book *Kant* [10.61] is devoted to a decidedly 'spiritualistic' interpretation of Kant's whole 'critical philosophy'.

62 P. Martinetti, *Introduzione alla metafisica* [10.55], 45.

63 *Ibid.*, p. 40.

64 *Ibid.*, p. 259.

65 To Spinoza's thought, which Martinetti interprets and criticizes from a substantially *neo-Platonic* point of view, he devoted numerous insightful essays. Cf. P. Martinetti, 'La dottrina della conoscenza e del metodo nella filosofia di Spinoza' [10.56], 289–324; 'La dottrina della libertà in Benedetto Spinoza' [10.57], (reprinted in his book *La libertà* [10.59]); 'Modi primitivi e derivati, infiniti e finiti' [10.58]; 'Problemi religiosi nella filosofia di B. Spinoza' [10.60]. For a general critical evaluation of Martinetti's Spinoza interpretation see my 'Introduction' to my Italian translation of E. E. Harris's book *Salvezza dalla disperazione. Rivalutazione della filosofia di Spinoza*, Milano: Guerini, 1991, pp. 29–31.

66 *Introduzione alla metafisica* [10.55], 261.

67 Cf., e.g., Plotinus, *Enneads* VI, 9.

68 *Introduzione alla metafisica* [10.55], 471.

69 *Ibid.*, p. 476.

70 *Ibid.*, p. 478.

71 Cf. *ibid.*, pp. 435–43.

72 *Ibid.*, p. 273.

73 I say 'relatively', because for Martinetti their ultimate psychological origin is itself merely empirical. They are a priori only with respect to experience's sensible qualities, which they unify in a 'unique', 'absolute' order. Cf. *ibid.*, pp. 423ff.

74 Cf. *ibid.*, pp. 434–43.

75 Cf. *ibid.*, pp. 443–55.

76 *Ibid.*, p. 468.

77 *Ibid.*, p. 403. Such a vindication of the autonomy of sensible intuition seems to find a close counterpart in Martinetti's critique of Kant's doctrine that the 'manifold' of sensuous impressions is merely subjective, and the objective unity is introduced in it only by the understanding's 'synthetic' activity. In his opinion, on the contrary, sense-perception is an inseparable unity of subject and object before, and independently of, its subsequent unification in the logical forms of thought (cf. *ibid.*, pp. 241–2).

78 *Ibid.*, p. 472.

79 *Ibid.*, p. 18.

80 *Ibid.*, p. 433.

81 Among the numerous, although often speculatively mediocre, writings of today's upholders of the metaphysics of Being, I confine myself to mentioning: F. Olgiati [10.66]; A. Carlini [10.12]; A. Guzzo [10.49]; V. La Via [10.54]; C. Mazzantini [10.63]; F. Olgiati [10.67]; V. A. Padovani [10.73]; M. F. Sciacca [10.87]; L. Stefanini [10.90]; F. Olgiati [10.68]; V. Mathieu [10.62]; M. F. Sciacca [10.88]; P. Prini [10.77]; G. Bontadini [10.10]; C. Arata [10.4]; C. Arata [10.5]; M. Gentile [10.46]; D. Pesce [10.76]; C. Fabro [10.28]; A. Guzzo [10.50]; L. Pareyson [10.74]. Guzzo's broad essay [10.48] is devoted to an excellent exposition of Spinoza's thought and to a lucid critique of it from a still 'actualistic' (and by no means 'spiritualistic' or 'neo-Thomistic') point of view. The reductive 'irrationalistic' interpretation of Fichte's thought put forward by L. Pareyson [10.75] is, on the contrary, wholly questionable.

82 M. F. Sciacca [10.88], 36.

83 *Ibid.*, p. 163.

84 L. Pareyson [10.74], 147.

85 Cf. G. Bontadini [10.10], 4.

86 M. F. Sciacca [10.88], 241.

87 *Ibid.*, p. 206.

88 A. Guzzo [10.50], 77.

89 A. Carlini [10.12], 192.

90 F. Olgiati [10.68], 27.

91 C. Arata [10.5], 18.

92 M. F. Sciacca [10.88], 66–7.

93 A lucid, thoroughgoing critique of Thomism from the standpoint of Gentile's 'actual idealism' is carried out by Giuseppe Saitta (1881–1965) in his admirable essay [10.85].

94 A. Gramsci [10.47], 115.

95 *Ibid.*, p. 244 (my italics).

96 *Ibid.*, p. 54.

97 *Ibid.*, p. 195.
98 *Ibid.*, p 238.
99 G. Della Volpe [10.24], 36.
100 *Ibid.*, p. 123.
101 Cf. especially M. Rossi [10.84].
102 Cf. especially L. Colletti [10.13].
103 G. Della Volpe [10.24], 103.
104 A. Gramsci [10.47], 26.
105 *Ibid.*, p. 27.
106 *Ibid.*
107 *Ibid.*, p. 28.
108 *Ibid.*, p. 52.
109 *Ibid.*, p. 219.
110 *Ibid.*, p. 292. For a critique of Gramsci's Hegel interpretation see my book [10.79], vol. 1, pp. 14f., 24f., 136f., 201f.
111 G. Della Volpe [10.24], 169.
112 *Ibid.*, p. 121.
113 *Ibid.*, p. 201.
114 *Ibid.*, p. 184.
115 E. Paci [10.71], 222.
116 E. Paci [10.69], 3. For his critique of Gentile's idealism see especially Paci [10.72]), 62–6. Husserl's theory of consciousness's 'original temporality' is developed by Paci especially in his essay [10.70].
117 [10.71], 226.
118 Banfi's open denial of the original truth and reality of the Absolute is unambiguously witnessed, for example, by the following passage: 'in general one must say that according to phenomenological thought an absolute reality is as absurd as a round quadrilateral, for there is nothing absolute but the ideal moment of pure immanence' (A. Banfi [10.6], 94–5). For a more detailed exposition and critique at Banfi's and Paci's 'phenomenological Marxism' see my book [10.78], Appendices, pp. 214–31.
119 N. Abbagnano [10.2], 157.
120 *Ibid.*, p. 156.
121 Cf. Abbagnano [10.3], 45–9.
122 [10.2], 156.
123 [10.3], 48.
124 *Ibid.*, p. 47.
125 [10.2], 26f.
126 *Ibid.* p. 26.
127 *Ibid.*, p. 27. The stiff opposition between the philosophical-cultural perspectives of 'Illuminism' (or 'existentialism') and of 'Romanticism' (or 'idealism') constitutes the fundamental historiographical criterion by which Abbagnano interprets and judges the whole development of contemporary philosophy. Cf., e.g., Abbagnano [10.1], vol. 3, parts VI and VII.
128 [10.2], 157.
129 Cf. above, note 20.
130 Errol Harris's epistemological researches appear especially interesting in this

regard. For a summary exposition and interpretation of his philosophy see my
books [10.80] and [10.82], part 3, ch. 3 no. 61.

❧ SELECT BIBLIOGRAPHY ❧

Primary texts and criticism

10.1 Abbagnano, N. *Storia della filosofia*, 3 vols, 1946; 3rd edn, Torino: UTET, 1974.

10.2 Abbagnano, N. *Possibilità e libertà*, Torino: Taylor, 1956.

10.3 Abbagnano, N. *Introduzione all'esistenzialismo*, 1965; 4th edn, Milano: Il Saggiatore, 1972.

10.4 Arata, C. *Lineamenti di un ontologismo personalistico*, Milano: Marzorati 1955.

10.5 Arata, C. *Principi di un'interpretazione trascendentalistica e personalistica della metafisica classica*, Milano, 1955.

10.6 Banfi, A. *Filosofi contemporanei*, ed. R. Cantoni, Milano: Parenti, 1961.

10.7 Bellezza, V. A. 'La riforma spaventiano-gentiliana della dialettica hegeliana', in *Incidenza di Hegel*, ed. F. Tessitore, Napoli: Morano, 1970, pp. 5–74.

10.8 Bellezza, V. A. 'La razionalità del reale: Hegel, Marx, Gentile', in *Enciclopedia '76–'77: Il pensiero di Giovanni Gentile*, Roma, 1977, pp. 59–75.

10.9 Bellezza, V.A. *La problematica gentiliana della storia*, Roma: Bulzoni, 1983.

10.10 Bontadini, G. 'L'attualità della metafisica classica', *Rivista di filosofia neoscolastica*, 45: 1 (1953): 1–18.

10.11 Carabellese, P. *Critica del concreto*, 1921; 2nd edn, Roma: A. Signorelli, 1940.

10.12 Carlini, A. 'Lineamenti di una concezione realistica dello spirito umano', in *Filosofi italiani contemporanei*, ed. M. F. Sciacca, Como: Marzorati, 1944, pp. 189–97.

10.13 Colletti, L. *Il marxismo e Hegel*, 2 vols, Bari: Laterza, 1976.

10.14 Croce, B. *Materialismo storico ed economia marxistica*, 1900; 3rd edn, Bari: Laterza, 1978.

10.15 Croce, B. *Estetica come scienza dell'espressione e linguistica generale*, 1902; 11th edn, Bari: Laterza, 1965.

10.16 Croce, B. *Logica come scienza del concetto puro*, 1905; 2nd edn, Bari: Laterza, 1971.

10.17 Croce, B. *Saggio sullo Hegel seguito da altri scritti di storia della filosofia*, 1906; 5th edn, Bari: Laterza, 1967.

10.18 Croce, B. *Filosofia della pratica*, 1908; 9th edn, Bari: Laterza, 1973.

10.19 Croce, B. *Teoria e storia della storiografia*, 1917; 11th edn, Bari: Laterza, 1976.

10.20 Croce, B. *Storia d'Europa nel secolo decimonono*, 1932; 3rd edn, Bari: Laterza, 1972.

10.21 Croce, B. *La poesia*, 1936; 3rd edn, Bari: Laterza, 1971.

10.22 Croce, B. *La storia come pensiero e come azione*, 1938; 3rd edn, Bari: Laterza, 1973.

10.23 Croce, B. *Indagini sullo Hegel e schiarimenti filosofici*, 1952; 2nd edn, Bari: Laterza, 1967.

10.24 Della Volpe, G. *Logica come scienza positiva*, 1950; 2nd edn, Messina-Firenze: D'Anna, 1965.

10.25 De Ruggiero, G. *Storia della filosofia*, 12 vols, Bari: Laterza, 1918–47.

10.26 Donnici, R. *Comunità e valori in Pantaleo Carabellese*, Venezia: Marsilio, 1982.

10.27 Evola, J. *Teoria dell'Individuo Assoluto*, 1927; 2nd edn, Roma: Edizioni Mediterranee, 1973.

10.28 Fabro, C. *Dall'essere all'esistente*, Brescia: Morcelliana, 1957.

10.29 Franchini, R. *Le origini della dialettica*, Napoli: Giannini, 1961.

10.30 Franchini, R. 'Che cos'è la metafisica', *Criterio*, 7 (1990): 165–73.

10.31 Garin, E. *Cronache di filosofia italiana 1900/1943. Quindici anni dopo. 1945/1960*, 2 vols, Bari: Laterza, 1966.

10.32 Gentile, G. *La riforma della dialettica hegeliana*, 1913; 4th edn, Firenze: Sansoni, 1975.

10.33 Gentile, G. *Sommario di pedagogia come scienza filosofica*, 2 vols, 1913–14; 4th edn, Firenze: Sansoni, 1959.

10.34 Gentile, G. *I fondamenti della filosofia del diritto*, Pisa: Mariotti, 1916.

10.35 Gentile, G. *Teoria generale dello spirito come atto puro*, 1916; 6th edn, Firenze: Sansoni, 1959.

10.36 Gentile, G. *Sistema di logica come teoria del conoscere*, 2 vols, 1917–1922; Bari: Laterza, 1922.

10.37 Gentile, G. *Le origini della filosofia contemporanea in Italia*, 3 vols, Messina: Principato, 1917–23.

10.38 Gentile, G. *Discorsi di religione*, 1920; in Gentile, *La religione*, Firenze: Sansoni, 1965, pp. 281–389.

10.39 Gentile, G. *Il modernismo e i rapporti tra religione e filosofia*, in Gentile, *La religione* [10.38], 1–275.

10.40 Gentile, G. 'La mia religione', in Gentile, *La religione* [10.38], 405–26.

10.41 Gentile, G. *La riforma dell'educazione*, 1920; 6th edn, Firenze: Sansoni, 1975.

10.42 Gentile, G. *La filosofia dell'arte*, 1931; 3rd edn, Firenze: Sansoni, 1975.

10.43 Gentile, G. *Introduzione alla filosofia*, 1933; 2nd edn, Firenze: Sansoni, 1981.

10.44 Gentile, G. *Genesi e struttura della società*, 1946; 2nd edn, Firenze: Sansoni, 1975.

10.45 Gentile, G. *Opere filosofiche*, ed. E. Garin, Milano: Garzanti, 1991.

10.46 Gentile, M. *Come si pone il problema metafisico*, Padova, 1955.

10.47 Gramsci, A. *Il materialismo storico e la filosofia di Benedetto Croce*, 1929–35, Roma: Editori Riuniti, 1977.

10.48 Guzzo, A. *Il pensiero di Spinoza*, Firenze: Vallecchi, 1924.

10.49 Guzzo, A. 'L'Uomo', in *Filosofi italiani contemporanei* [10.12], 243–53.

10.50 Guzzo, A. 'Idealismo 1963', *Filosofia*, 14 (1963): 25–84.

10.51 Harris, H. S. *The Social Philosophy of Giovanni Gentile*, Urbana & London: University of Illinois Press, 1966.

10.52 Harris, H. S. 'Gentile's Reform of Hegel's Dialectic', in *Enciclopedia 76–77: Il pensiero di Giovanni Gentile*, Roma, 1977.

10.53 *La filosofia italiana dal dopoguerra ad oggi*, ed. E. Garin, Bari: Laterza, 1985.

10.54 La Via, V. 'La restituzione del realismo', in *Filosofi italiani contemporanei* [10.12], 255–72.

10.55 Martinetti, P. *Introduzione alla metafisica*, 1st edn, Torino, 1904; 2nd edn, Milano: Libreria Editrice Lombarda, 1929; 3rd edn, Milano, 1987.

10.56 Martinetti, P. 'La dottrina della conoscenza e del metodo nella filosofia di Spinoza', *Rivista di filosofia* 8: 3 (1916): 289–324.

10.57 Martinetti, P. 'La dottrina della libertà in Benedetto Spinoza', *Chronicon Spinozanum*, 4 (1926): 58–67.

10.58 Martinetti, P. 'Modi primitivi e derivati, infiniti e finiti', *Rivista di filosofia*, 18: 3 (1927): 248–61.

10.59 Martinetti, P. *La libertà*, Milano: Libreria Editrice Lombarda, 1928.

10.60 Martinetti, P. 'Problemi religiosi nella filosofia di B. Spinoza', *Rivista di filosofia*, 30: 4 (1939): 289–311.

10.61 Martinetti, P. *Kant*, posthumously published in 1946; 2nd edn, Milano: Feltrinelli, 1974.

10.62 Mathieu, V. *Limitazione qualitativa della conoscenza umana*, Torino, 1949.

10.63 Mazzantini, C. 'Linee di metafisica spiritualistica come filosofia della virtualità ontologica', in *Filosofi italiani contemporanei* [10.12].

10.64 Negri, A. *Giovanni Gentile*, 2 vols, Firenze: La Nuova Italia, 1975.

10.65 Negri, A. 'Modernity as Crisis and Permanent Criticism', *Idealistic Studies*, 21: 1 (1991): 48–65.

10.66 Olgiati, F. 'Come si pone oggi il problema della metafisica', *Rivista di filosofia neoscolastica*, 14 (1922): 14–28.

10.67 Olgiati, F. 'La filosofia cristiana e i suoi indirizzi storiografici', in *Filosofi italiani contemporanei* [10.12], 183–197.

10.68 Olgiati, F. *Il concetto di metafisica*, Milano, 1945.

10.69 Paci, E. 'Coscienza fenomenologica e coscienza idealistica' *Il Verri*, 4 (1960): 3–15.

10.70 Paci, E. *Tempo e verità nella fenomenologia di Husserl*, Bari: Laterza, 1961.

10.71 Paci, E. *Funzione delle scienze e significato dell'uomo*, 1963; 4th edn, Milano: Il Saggiatore, 1970.

10.72 Paci, E. *La filosofia contemporanea*, Milano: Garzanti, 1974.

10.73 Padovani, V. A. 'Filosofia e religione', in *Filosofi italiani contemporanei* [10.12], 319–31.

10.74 Pareyson, L. *Verità e interpretazione*, 1971; 3rd edn, Milano: Mursia, 1982.

10.75 Pareyson, L. *Fichte: Il sistema della libertà*, Milano: Mursia, 1976.

10.76 Pesce, D. *Saggio sulla metafisica*, Firenze, 1957.

10.77 Prini, P. *Itinerari del platonismo perenne*, Torino, 1950.

10.78 Rinaldi, G. *Critica della gnoseologia fenomenologica*, Napoli: Giannini, 1979.

10.79 Rinaldi, G. *Dalla dialettica della materia alla dialettica dell'Idea. Critica del materialismo storico*, vol. 1, Napoli: SEN, 1981.

10.80 Rinaldi, G. *Saggio sulla metafisica di Harris*, Bologna: Li Causi, 1984.

10.81 Rinaldi, G. 'A Few Critical Remarks on Croce's Historicism', *Idealistic Studies*, 17: 1 (1987): 52–69.

10.82 Rinaldi, G. *A History and Interpretation of the Logic of Hegel*, Lewiston: The Edwin Mellen Press, 1992.

10.83 Rinaldi, G. 'Attualità di Hegel: Autocoscienza, concretezza, e processo in Gentile e in Christensen', *Studi filosofici*, 12–13 (1989–90): 63–104.

10.84 Rossi, M. *Marx e la dialettica hegeliana*, 4 vols, Roma: Editori Riuniti, 1960–3.

10.85 Saitta, G. *Il carattere della filosofia tomistica*, Firenze: Sansoni, 1934.

10.86 Sciacca, M. F. *La filosofia nel suo sviluppo storico*, 3 vols, 1940; 12th edn, Roma: Cremonese, 1976.

10.87 Sciacca, M. F. 'Spiritualismo cristiano', in *Filosofi italiani contemporanei* [10.12], 365–74.

10.88 Sciacca, M. F. *Filosofia e metafisica*, Brescia: Morcelliana, 1950.

10.89 Spirito, U. 'Finito e infinito', in *Filosofi italiani contemporanei* [10.12], 375–83.

10.90 Stefanini, L. 'Spiritualismo cristiano', in *Filosofi italiani contemporanei* [10.12], 385–93.

Translations

See also 10.51 above.

10.91 Croce, B. *What is Living and What is Dead in the Philosophy of Hegel*, trans. D. Ainslie, London, 1915.

10.92 Croce, B. *My Philosophy and Other Essays on the Moral and Political Problem of our Time*, selected by R. Klibansky, trans. E. F. Carritt, London: Allen & Unwin, 1951.

10.93 Croce, B. *History – As the Story of Liberty*, trans. S. Sprigge, London: Allen & Unwin, 1951.

10.94 Gentile, G. *The Theory of Mind as Pure Act*, trans. from the third edition with an introduction by H. W. Carr, London: Macmillan, 1922.

10.95 Gentile, G. *The Reform of Education*, trans. D. Bigongiari, with an introduction by B. Croce, New York: Harcourt, Brace, 1922.

10.96 Gentile, G. *Fragments From La filosofia dell'arte*, trans. E. F. Carritt, Oxford, 1931.

10.97 Gentile, G. *Genesis and Structure of Society*, trans. H. S. Harris, Urbana: University of Illinois Press, 1960.

10.98 Gentile, G. *The Philosophy of Art*, trans. and with an introduction by G. Gullace, Ithaca and London: Cornell University Press, 1972.

CHAPTER 11

French structuralism and after
De Saussure, Lévi-Strauss, Barthes, Lacan, Foucault
Hugh J. Silverman

❦

❧ FERDINAND DE SAUSSURE ❧

The history of structuralism cannot be thought without Ferdinand de Saussure (1857–1913). The Swiss linguist lecturing in Geneva in the early twentieth century set the scene for what in the two and a half decades following the Second World War came to be known as structuralism. The figures who dominated the development of the movement in the 1940s and 1950s were Claude Lévi-Strauss (b. 1908), Jacques Lacan (1901–82), and Roland Barthes (1915–80). By the 1960s Michel Foucault's (1926–84) reformulations and even rejections of structuralism indicated the new directions for what became poststructuralism.

Curiously, the parallel development of existential phenomenology in France ran a different course. With the possible exception of Maurice Merleau-Ponty's (1908–61) interests in the structuralist alternative, structuralism had little or no effect upon the development of phenomenology as a philosophical movement. With poststructuralism, however, the confluence of these two different philosophical methods marked the appearance of an entirely new mode of thinking – one which is exemplified in Foucault's archaeology of knowledge on the one hand and Jacques Derrida's (b. 1930) deconstruction on the other. For the purposes of the present chapter however, I shall take Foucault as exemplary of this new development.[1]

Structuralism – and especially French structuralism – cannot be understood apart from de Saussure's semiology. According to de Saussure – as articulated clearly in the posthumously published *Course in General Linguistics* (1916), a compilation of several years of the Swiss linguist's Geneva lectures [11.1] – semiology is 'the general science of signs'. De Saussure proposed a new understanding of the notion of 'sign'. He argued that the sign is not just a word but rather that a sign is both a word and concept. He named these two components of the sign the 'signifier' [*signifiant*] and the 'signified' [*signifié*]. The signifier is the word, that which does the signifying. The signified is the concept, that which is signified. Together these two components constitute a binary pair called the sign. The standard example which de Saussure offers for this binary relation is the word *tree* and the concept 'tree'.

A sign, however, is not yet a sign until it is distinguished from other signs in the same system, or language [*langue*]. A sign cannot be on its own – apart from all other elements of the language. Indeed, de Saussure defines a sign as determined by its difference from all other signs in the sign system. Hence the sign *tree* is the sign *tree* by its difference from other signs such as *house*, *bird* and *sky*. Now the sign *tree* is also different from the sign *arbre* or the sign *Baum*, *arbor* or *arbol*. Each of these other signs is part of a different sign system: *arbre*, the French language, *Baum*, the German language, *arbol*, the Spanish language. Because they are not part of the same sign system, they are signs only in their respective sign systems.

De Saussure also remarks that the relation between a signifier and a signified is entirely 'arbitrary'. That the concept or signified 'tree' is designated by the word *tree* in English is simply arbitrary. It could have been called *arbre*, *Baum* or *arbol* – and indeed in different languages it does acquire such signifiers. Only in the limited instances of onomatopoeia in which a signifier corresponds in a motivated way to a particular signified is the arbitrary nature compromised. Hence *bow-wow* for a dog's bark, or *smooth*, for something soft and gentle, or *Being-in-the-world* for the extensiveness of our existence are connected in a more related way than most words with their corresponding concepts.

A sign – a signifier [*un signifiant*] and a signified [*un signifié*] – is one among many signs in a language [*langue*]. A *langue* can be English, French, German, Japanese, Russian, etc. In the account of a *langue* nothing need be spoken as such. Hence, de Saussure offers a correlative concept called the speaking of the language or *parole*. While *langue* is constituted by elements that make up a particular language, *parole* is the speaking of that language in a determinate context and at a determinate time. Hence when I say: 'Tall evergreen trees inspire a sense of grandeur', I am saying [*parole*] these words (with their corresponding concepts) in English. Were I to say: 'Ces grands arbres verts sont magnifiques', I am saying something else in French but I am enacting the French language in a particular context and at a specific time – the saying is *parole*.

Another binary pair (or binary opposition), as Saussure sometimes calls them, is the relation between 'syntagm' and 'system' (or 'paradigm'). The sentence 'Tall evergreen trees inspire a sense of grandeur' is a sequence of signs; one follows the other. As a sequence, the signs follow a syntagmatic line. Each sign is contiguous with the next, and there is a meaning produced by the sequence. By contrast, were one to substitute alternate signs such as 'short', 'broad', or 'imposing' for 'tall', for instance, the sentence would read: 'Short (or broad, or imposing) evergreen trees inspire a sense of grandeur.' The new sentence with the substituted term still makes sense, but the sense is of course different – and even in the first two instances a bit curious. What does not quite fit with 'tall', 'short', and 'broad' is 'imposing'. The first three are all signs of size. 'Imposing' is of another order, yet it is also substitutable for 'tall'. All of these substitutable terms are part of the same system (or paradigm) if broadly interpreted. If more narrowly interpreted, the system could be restricted to signs of size and not just signs that are substitutable. Each of the elements of the sentence could be examined in terms of substitutable signs, and each would be part of a different system.

A fourth binary opposition is that between diachrony and synchrony. A diachronic study of the Greek sign of excellence *aretē* would follow it through its Latin version in *virtus*, its Italian reformulation as *virtú*, its French usage as *vertu*, a term which is also repeated in English (virtue). To study the same work over time, chronologically, allows for the consideration of a development over time, historically, as it were. However, such a study isolates what is studied from its context and framework. It takes the element and reviews the whole development independently of related concerns. A synchronic study, by contrast, is ultimately concerned with the set of relations among a whole complex of signs and elements that arise at the same time and in the same context. The sign *aretē* is studied in relation to other signs at the time: *paideia* (education and the ideals of the culture), *sophrosyne* (moderation or temperance), and so forth. In this respect a given notion is understood in a broad context – in this case, a cultural context. Once the synchronic study has been accomplished for a given time-slice, it will be possible to compare that time-slice with other periods of time – in order to show similarities and/or differences across a number of different time-slices.

As a linguist, de Saussure was ultimately concerned with language. Indeed, the whole project of structuralism is framed according to a linguistic model. This model presumes that what is outside language is not relevant to the linguist's task. Hence the earliest forms of structuralism were restricted to the formulations of a semiology based on language study. Roland Barthes, by contrast, in his *Elements of Semiology*

(1964 [11.7]), remarks that while de Saussure believed that linguistics is a part of semiology – that there are domains of semiology that are not relevant for the linguist – in his view, semiology is a part of linguistics. Barthes's formulation presumes that all sign systems are already language systems of one sort or another – I shall return to Barthes later.

∾ CLAUDE LÉVI-STRAUSS ∾

What is significant here is that when Lévi-Strauss in the late 1940s began to apply structuralist principles to anthropological concerns, he was already extending the linguistic model far beyond language study. This meant that although Lévi-Strauss as an anthropologist was concerned with structures of thought, he had already made the shift that Barthes articulates: ethnology is already a language which can be studied by the structuralist.

Although de Saussure was lecturing on structural linguistics in the first decades of the century, it took until the 1930s for his work to become noticed and accessible to a broader context. This was the fate of his *Course in General Linguistics*. When Lévi-Strauss travelled to the United States during the Second World War, it was out of political and personal necessity as he narrates in considerable detail in *Tristes tropiques* [11.3]. When he arrived in New York, he began teaching at the University in Exile (which has subsequently come to be called The New School for Social Research). During that time, he met and conferred often with Roman Jakobson (1896–1982) (whose own itinerary had taken him from Russia to Prague to Paris to New York). Jacobson was a linguist whose development of Russian formalism was an important contribution to the concept of structure. Indeed both Lévi-Strauss and Jakobson worked together on a groundbreaking reading of a Baudelaire poem, 'Les Chats'. The idea was to offer a structural study of the poem. Their reading was careful and meticulous. They were interested in how the poem exhibits structural, stylistic and syntactic features in order to constitute the work as a whole. Jakobson's further interest in metaphor and metonymy was worked out in his *Fundamentals of Language* [11.50] in terms of two types of aphasia: metaphor as replacement by substitution, metonymy as replacement by contiguity.[2]

After the war, Lévi-Strauss served as cultural adviser to the French ambassador to the United States (1946–7). Then he returned to France where he took up his position at the Ecole Pratique des Hautes Etudes en Sciences Sociales (the 'Pratique' has subsequently been dropped) and resumed his research in structural anthropology. In 1949, he produced his major contribution, *The Elementary Structures of Kinship* [11.2].

Here the concept of kinship was developed in connection with Lévi-Strauss's understanding of structuralism and his collation of many different ethnographic accounts of kinship throughout the world. His view was that despite many significant differences in kinship practice in different cultures, common structures are repeated underneath these multiple instances of kinship practices. These structures have a basic form according to a determinate set of relations. The actual character of the relation might change from one context to another, but what does not change is the relation itself. Each relation is part of a whole structure of relations, where no element is strictly independent of any of the others. Thus a one-to-one correspondence of one part of a structure with one part of another cannot be made. The whole structure must be compared with another whole structure in order to provide an appropriate analysis. For instance, Lévi-Strauss is particularly interested in the 'avunculate' or uncle-relation. He finds from his extensive research of many different cultures, societies and social groups that the role of the uncle is critical. Hence there is the mother–father relation, the mother–father and son relations, the son–maternal uncle relation, and the mother–brother relation.

Understood independently, each of these relations has a particular content: positive and socially supported in one case, negative and outcast in another. Lévi-Strauss determined that by assigning a positive or negative value to each of these relations in a particular context, he could determine the nature of the whole structure. For three hypothetical societies, it might look like Fig. 11.1.

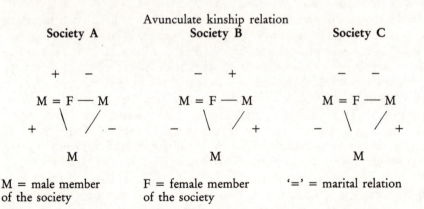

Figure 11.1

In each of these societies, the mother and father, the mother's brother and the brother's sister's son constitute the key kinship relations. While the structure recurs, the nature of the relations change from one society to the next. The repetition of the same structure is matched with the differences in the nature of the relations among the social roles in each society.

This concept of structure indicates a latent set of relations that underlie the actual, particular and real relations of specific individuals in a determinate context. Lévi-Strauss broadens his reading of kinship relations to the account of totems and taboos in different societies as well as to the detailed study of myths. These further explorations of the application of structural method resurface in a variety of essays written between 1944 and 1957 and are collected together in the first volume of *Structural Anthropology* (1958 [11.4]). The appearance of *Structural Anthropology* marked a significant phase in the development of structuralism. *Elementary Structures* (1949, [11.2]) was highly detailed and technical. The new book solidified the role of structuralism in France. It indicated that there was now an alternative research programme that would ultimately match that of existentialism and the existential phenomenology that had reigned unopposed since the early 1940s. While it would take another decade for structuralism to establish its foothold firmly, Lévi-Strauss's new book was an important link between the growing interest in de Saussure's semiology and the full-fledged structural studies that Barthes, Lacan and Foucault would carry on into the 1960s. This is not to say that Lévi-Strauss has not been a continuing and dominant force in the development of structuralism even today. At the beginning of the 1970s, when I attended his lectures at the Collège de France where he occupies the Chair of Social Anthropology, he was still defending his position against the comments and criticisms of the British anthropologist Rodney Needham. And many books have followed the appearance of *Structural Anthropology*. His four-volume study of world mythologies, his second volume of *Structural Anthropology*, his autobiographical *Tristes tropiques*, his many essays on masks and race all add up to a major contribution to late twentieth-century French thought.

Louis Marin (1931–92) used to comment that when he was a young man in the early 1950s, he and his wife Françoise were invited to the apartment of M. and Mme Maurice Merleau-Ponty for what was then described as a 'dîner intime'. When he and his wife arrived, he discovered that it was indeed a small diner party: M. and Mme Merleau-Ponty, M. and Mme Lévi-Strauss, and M. and Mme Lacan. That these three were all friends indicates a certain collaboration and dialogue that was highly charged in the early period in which structuralism was gaining hold. Although Merleau-Ponty is known for his ground-breaking work as a phenomenologist of perception (1945), only a year later he was lecturing on de Saussure at the Ecole Normale Supérieure in Paris. Merleau-Ponty's turn to semiology as a topic of interest began to blend with his commitment to the achievements of Gestalt psychology, but even more with those of phenomenology which he saw as superior even to the Gestalt theories of Köhler and Koffka, Gelb and Goldstein. Yet with his growing interest in language, Merleau-Ponty found real value in the Saussurian theory of the sign.[3] His courses on 'Language and Communication' (1946–7) stressed his new commitment to language – a topic which he had only broached in *Phenomenology of Perception* (1945), notably in the chapter on 'The Body as Speech and Expression'. Hence concurrently with Lévi-Strauss's return to France and his intense work on kinship relations, his friend Merleau-Ponty, who was by then Professor of Child Psychology and Pedagogy at the Institut de Psychologie in Paris, was also developing a serious interest in the implications of Saussure's structural linguistics.

When Merleau-Ponty set himself the task of writing a kind of literary theory which was to have seen the light of day in the early 1950s, he was setting the stage for an important debate that would take shape throughout the 1950s and 1960s – even long after his death in 1961. What became *The Prose of the World* (published posthumously in 1969) [11.64]) , was to have been completed in 1952. However, Merleau-Ponty was elected to the Collège de France that year and his research took him in other directions, most notably in his critique of 'dialectic' and towards his theory of visibility in *The Visible and the Invisible* (1964). There were two companion pieces that have been included in *Signs* (1960 [11.62]) which addressed the question of language: 'The Phenomenology of Language' and 'Indirect Language and the Voices of Silence'. These two essays, written in 1951–2, indicate the convergence between phenomenology and structuralism as it was under development in the French context. While Sartre continued to reject structuralism vigorously,[4] Merleau-Ponty continued to be intrigued. While Sartre published his own theory of literature in *Qu'est-ce que la littérature?* in 1947, he oriented this theory toward the act of communicating the freedom of a writer to the freedom of a reader. Writing, for Sartre, was both an act of commitment and an expression of freedom. Merleau-Ponty's response came in 1952 with *The Prose of the World*: there are many aspects of language and expression that are simply not direct, that do not give an algorithmic reading of experience – literature and painting are prime examples. Here there is language but indirectly expressed – even silence for Merleau-Ponty speaks.

⌘ ROLAND BARTHES ⌘

Like Merleau-Ponty, the second major figure of French structuralism, Roland Barthes, was also preparing in 1952 a response to Sartre's literary theory: *Writing Degree Zero* [11.5] was of mould-breaking merit. It offered an entirely different way of understanding the role and status of writing. Writing was no longer an act of communication, but rather an articulation that links up both style and language. The writer's style (whether romantic, or surrealist or existentialist) is matched with the writer's *langue* or language. This language is not simply idiosyncratic. For Barthes, language partakes of a social context and experience. Language and style at the intersection of the two marks the locus of writing (*écriture*). Hence revolutionary writing or bourgeois writing or romantic writing occur in terms of a particular language and a determinate style. And such revolutionary writing can be found equally in the times of Thomas Jefferson, Robespierre and Brecht. Though the times are radically different, even the language and style are different, the writing can be called 'the same'. Although Barthes found that different texts could be characterized in terms of these repeatable forms of writing, he was also fascinated with the new writing of Alain Robbe-Grillet. Barthes is credited with having 'discovered' Robbe-Grillet, whose style of writing is officially a radical break with the nineteenth-century novel, but whose writing itself marks the beginning of an impassionate language where the subject is decentred and the discursive proliferations are structurally identifiable. *Le Voyeur* and *La Jalousie* are excellent examples of a language stripped of emotion – or at least emotion as described by the typical nineteenth-century omniscient author. There is still emotion, but it is described through the surfaces and the ways in which surfaces are affected.

With the 1964 publication of *Elements of Semiology* [11.7], Barthes at last linked up his critical practice with the theoretical writings of de Saussure. In this short piece, which was originally published in *Communications*, the official journal of the Ecole Pratique des Hautes Etudes en Sciences Sociales, Barthes outlines the theory of the sign: the signifier/signified relation, the *langue/parole* link, the connection between diachrony and synchrony, and the opposition between denotation and connotation. But the critical year was 1966, which saw the publication of his own *Criticism and Truth* [11.8], Lacan's *Ecrits*, [11.15] and Foucault's *The Order of Things* [11.17]. Hence over a decade after Barthes produced *Writing Degree Zero*, structuralism finally came of age. *Elements of Semiology* set the stage for that crowning moment. In his seminar at the Ecole Pratique des Hautes Etudes which I attended for the whole year in 1971–2, Barthes focused on what he called 'The Last Decade of Semiology'. He considered 1966 as the watershed year. In the following year, Jean-Luc Godard produced his revolutionary film *La Chinoise* (which prefigured the student-worker revolts of 1968) and Derrida published *Speech and Phenomena* [11.30], *Of Grammatology* [11.29], and *Writing and Difference* [11.31]. Hence by 1967, a whole new phase had begun – for lack of a more precise term it was called poststructuralism. Of course, there were still many who were committed to structuralism for another decade and many of the so-called poststructuralist theories continued to build upon the languages and lessons of structuralism.

Once the scene was set and the terminology clarified in *The Elements of Semiology* [11.7], Barthes himself began to develop his own position further. He rejected those critical theories that gave special place to the author and authorial presence. And in his famous essay 'From Work to Text' (1971 [11.10]), he outlined very clearly the distinction between the traditional notion of the 'work' and his notion of the 'text'. The 'work' (*oeuvre*, *opera*, *Werk*) results from an act of filiation: an author produces or creates a work which is then a 'fragment of substance, occupying a part of the space of books (in a library for example)'.[5] The author requires authority over the meaning of the work. And the critic seeks to understand the author's meaning. This hermeneutic concern pervades work-centred studies. And it was also a dominant feature of the Sartrian theory as well. Barthes proposes to place the emphasis on the text, which he describes as a 'methodological field'. He elaborates: 'The Text can be approached, experienced, in reaction to the sign. The work closes on a signified' (p. 158). This means that the text can be read in terms of the sign system which participates in it, while the work focuses on what is meant by it. The plurality of the text permits a full and elaborate network of intertextuality which is closed off by the work. 'The Text', he says, 'is bound to *jouissance*, that is to a pleasure without separation' (p. 164).

Two years later, Barthes published *The Pleasure of the Text* (1973, [11.11]). For Barthes, the Text is not an object of desire or even a result of a creative act. Rather the Text is a site – a locus for a reading, a place in which *jouissance* occurs. Something happens in the critical reading of a Text. The Text's network of signifying dynamic is brought out. In the Introduction to *S/Z* (1970), Barthes had already shown how the distinction between the 'readerly' (*lisible*) and 'writerly' (*scriptible*) text marks the difference between a text which is simply read through for the pleasure of it and the text which is read as a methodological field – one in which the codes and sign systems are elaborated in detail and available for careful decoding. The 'writerly text is not a thing,' Barthes writes, 'we would have a hard time finding it in a bookstore.'[6] The 'writerly is the novelistic without the novel, poetry without the poem, the essay without the dissertation, writing without style, production without product, structuration without structure' (p. 5). The writerly occupies only a methodological and theoretical space, it is not a product like the readerly text.

In this frame, Barthes outlined five different codes which constitute what he calls 'the plural text', and the plural text is the writerly text critically disclosed. The five codes include: the semic code (the elaboration of the signifier), the hermeneutic code (disclosure of the enigma), the symbolic code (one element stands for another), the actantial code (the action code), and the reference code (the cultural indicators marked in the text). These codes are only possible codes for the reading of a text. Although Barthes does not dwell upon the alternatives, it is only plausible that alternative sets of codes function as well as those Barthes invokes.

Barthes was at his most daring when he took up an age-old topic, namely autobiography, but in a radically new way. *Roland Barthes* (1975, [11.12]) by Roland Barthes is certainly a break with the traditional diachronic mode of writing one's own life. He organizes his life not according to the succession of years, but according to the alphabetical arrangement of topics, themes and oppositions that played an important role in his life. And as to the typical chronology, that can be found in two pages at the back of the essay. Barthes should not have died so early. He was run over by a milk truck outside the Collège de France where he had been elected to the Chair of Semiology in 1977. He was only sixty-five when he died in 1980.

❧ JACQUES LACAN ❧

Jacques Lacan, by contrast, born in 1901 only one year after Hans-Georg Gadamer, lived to a ripe old age of eighty-one. There is a wonderful cartoon which Barthes includes in his *Roland Barthes* of Lévi-Strauss, Lacan, Barthes, Foucault and Michel Leiris all sitting together in Tahitian skirts. Although reflecting different ages, they all came together around the structuralist enterprise. Lacan provided the basis for a structural psychoanalysis. His early 1936 study of the mirror stage was first presented in Marienbad (later made famous by Robbe-Grillet in the film *Last Year at Marienbad*). Lacan's theory is rather simple: the child at first does not detect any difference between it and its mother. The sensory world around it is all integrated. It begins to notice a difference between it and the mother. This becomes clear when it looks into the mirror and sees no longer just motion or another person, but recognizes an identity between what it sees and itself. It waves an arm and the image waves its arm, etc. It notices then that the mirror image is itself. But then the father intercedes: the *nom du père/*

non du père/non-dupe erre are all forms of interdiction. The father with his name and his prohibition – after all, he is somewhat jealous of the close relationship that his child has with his wife – attempts to break the harmony, introduces a negation, his paternal law, his 'No'. The father is no fool. He knows what he wants and he knows what he does not want. By interceding between the child and the mother, he imposes his authority, his will, his name. Now the child cannot but recognize difference. The *Verneinung* is effective. The father imposes his will and the child learns to affirm its own identity. Thus the mirror stage is the critical moment at which the child takes on an identity of its own.

The inclusion of the revised version of the 'Mirror Stage' in *Ecrits* (1966 [11.15]) correlates with a number of other essays of major importance. In 1966 there was a conference held at Johns Hopkins University subsequently entitled *The Structuralist Controversy*. While Richard Macksey and Eugenio Donato edited the volume, the leadership of René Girard was crucial. At Stanford, for instance, in the late 1960s one heard of the Johns Hopkins experiment and those professors of literature committed to an earlier model of literary study were deeply opposed to the Johns Hopkins scene. Curiously, René Girard is now Professor of Humanities at that very same Stanford University after trying out the State University of New York at Buffalo for a brief period.

Lacan was one of the speakers at the 1966 Hopkins conference. Also presenting papers were Jean Hyppolite and Jacques Derrida. It was an important moment. And Lacan's essay was no less important. His paper was entitled 'The Insistence of the Letter in the Unconscious', an essay which also appears in *Ecrits*. The question is, how does the chain of signifiers mark off and bar the range of the signified? The signified especially in the metonymic line is barred from access by the signifier. This exclusion of the signified leads to a veering off of the signifier from one sign to the next. The signified however remains unaccessible. The line between the signifier and the signified is strong and resistant. In such cases in which the signifier has no access to the signified, it must act in terms of that repression.

In the case of metaphor, there is an overdetermination of signifieds for a particular signifier. In such a case, the bar is weak and a multiplicity of meanings intrude. Throughout Lacan's account, 'the unconscious is structured like a language'. Where there is resistance in language, there would be resistance in the unconscious. But for Lacan whatever there is of an unconscious is read in terms of the play of signifiers. Repression results when the letter is unable to insist in the signified. Meaning is kept at bay. A stream of words and utterances follows but the relation to the signified is repressed. With Lacan, as later with Derrida, the self is decentred, the subject is dispersed throughout language. The language of the self is the language of the chain of signifiers. The subject *per se* remains absent.

❧ MICHEL FOUCAULT ❧

The theme of the absent subject is especially notable in the philosophy of Michel Foucault, who met an untimely AIDS-related death at the early age of fifty-eight. In his *magnum opus*, *The Order of Things* (*Les Mots et les choses*) [11.17] also published in 1966 – the theme of the absent subject pervades not only his reading of Velázquez but also his account of the contemporary human sciences. For contemporary (poststructuralist, or what would now be called 'postmodern') thought, there is no centred origin, no unique place of focus, no present subject as there once was for the modern age.

Foucault's reading of origins is marked off by his reading of discursive practices. As he demonstrates in *The Order of Things*, history does not begin at a certain moment and then continue – in linear fashion – from then on. Rather, moments of dominance of certain discursive practices prevail for a time and are then succeeded by a new set of discursive practices. Where a discursive practice ends, a new one is about to begin. Origin then will occur where a new discursive practice starts to take place. But where and when do such new practices begin to take place? They clearly do not occur at a determined moment in time such as a date or year. Certain discursive practices pertinent to a particular epistemological space, as Foucault calls it, continue into a new epistemological space, while others die out.

But what is a discursive practice? For Foucault, a discursive practice is a whole set of documents produced within a broadly general period of time in which common themes or ideas occur across that period in a wide variety of disciplines and areas of human knowledge production. For instance, in the nineteenth century the relations between biology, economics and philology would seem to be entirely unrelated. However Foucault has shown that they all consolidate in terms of a relatively singular conceptual unity, or what Foucault calls an *episteme*. For the broad space of the nineteenth century, Foucault identifies the theme in question with what he calls an 'anthropology', that is, the theory of 'man' as defined by the 'empirico-transcendental doublet',[7] the particular Kantian idea that empirical (objective) considerations must always be understood in connection with a transcendental (subjective) set of conditions that permeates the discursive practices of the nineteenth century. The theme of subjectivity in relation to objectivity pervades the nineteenth-century understanding of life, labour and language. Thus the discursive practices of the nineteenth century repeat themselves in a variety of contexts – all explicitly unrelated to each other. These differences then form an *epistemé*.

The *epistemé* of the nineteenth century succeeds the *epistemé* of the 'classical age'. This prior epistemological space is marked by another set of discursive practices. These include the classification of species, the analysis of wealth and natural grammar. What one would take to be entirely unrelated concerns are here brought into relation to one another in that they each exhibit features of the 'classical age' *epistemé*, namely 'representation'. As Foucault reads the general period of the seventeenth century and first half of the eighteenth century, the idea of 'representation' – the projection or postulate of ideas before the mind – formed the frame for a distinctly 'classical' way of thinking. The relation between this classical *epistemé* and the nineteenth-century *epistemé* is much less significant than the relation between the various practices at each of these respective time-slices.

The origin of the *epistemé* is not the beginning of the *epistemé*. A particular *epistemé* is marked by a certain dominance. The place where the *epistemé* dominates is the place of its origin. The place of dominance for the empirico-transcendental doublet is the place of origin within that epistemological framework. Similarly the place of dominance of *representation* in the classical age is the place of origin within that epistemological framework. However, where is this place of origin in each case? Dispersed throughout the epistemological space, the place of origin occurs wherever there is a discursive practice that exhibits it. Hence the origin is in many places: reappearing in many locations throughout the epistemological space itself. In the nineteenth century, one can find the empirico-transcendental doublet not only in Hegel and Hölderlin but also in biologists such as Cuvier (whose 'fixism' is set off against the backdrop of human historicity), economists such as Ricardo (for whom history is a vast compensating mechanism) and philologists such as Schlegel (with his 1808 essay on the language and philosophy of the Indians), and philologists such as Grimm (most notably in the 1818 *Deutsche Grammatik*) and Bopp (whose 1816 study of the Sanskrit conjugation system became an object of study).

Each of these places constitutes itself as an origin, as a locus in which the concept of 'man' as a subject–object is brought into discourse production itself. No longer does language, for instance, operate between words and things resulting in an operation of representation. And in the nineteenth century, words are objects themselves, objects for scrutiny and study by a scientific practice that hopes to judge them and their interrelationships. Origin, then, for Foucault is not a source from which all historical events follow. Origin is not the beginning from which history begins to unfold. Origin is not the inception from which development ensues. Origin does not establish the moment before which nothing else will have occurred. Rather origin springs up in many places within a broad, general, historical time-frame. Origins occur in various discourses, scarring them with marks of a common practice that is unaware of its own commonality.

Foucault's enterprise disperses origin throughout a kind of methodological field (as Barthes would have called it). And his appeal to the English reader to ignore those 'tiny little minds that persist in calling him a structuralist', indicates that he is already beyond the mere repetition of structuralist methods. Although his own archaeology of knowledge could be characterized as largely synchronic, it also relies upon the assessment of periods or time-slices in order to compare one time-slice with another. What Foucault rejects is the necessity of a concept of continuity in favour of discontinuity. Structuralists were already concerned with a discourse of the past. Nietzsche and Mallarmé are invoked as threshold figures marking the break with the older empirico-transcendental doublet of the modern age. They mark the beginning of a new mode of thought in which dissemination, dispersal, metonymy and decentring of the subject are the dominant frames of knowledge production.

Where Sartre had announced in his 1936 *Transcendence of the Ego* that the self or ego could not be located in consciousness but is at best an object of consciousness, Foucault in 1966 places that claim in a historical context. He situates the end of the age of modernism with the end of the centred subject, the dominant self, the focal 'I'. Like Nietzsche's madman who ran through the streets proclaiming the 'death of god', Sartre had already proclaimed 'the end of man', but in a sense that would not be fully understood for another thirty years. The linguistic turn in continental philosophy took on a different shape from that in the analytic tradition. It did not fully take place until the Saussurian epistemology became the principle according to which language, culture and knowledge production would be understood. The structural analysis of kinship, totems and myths in Lévi-Strauss, the speaking subject's chain of signifiers in Lacan, the semiological analysis of text and culture in Barthes were themselves placed in context by Foucault. In this respect, Foucault is indeed already after structuralism, for he is able to situate it as a movement in a period of time. The subsequent development of Foucault's own genealogy, Derrida's deconstruction, Deleuze's nomadologies, Kristeva's semanalysis and Lyotard's postmodernist sublimities are all themes for another story in the history of continental thought. Suffice it to say that structuralism played a critical role in offering an alternative to existential phenomenology and at the same time a complement to it. What comes after structuralism (and after the age of the modern subject) is identified by those such as Foucault who were themselves marked by both phenomenology and structuralism and who were in a position to succeed them as well.

❧ NOTES ❧

1 Derrida's deconstruction is left aside here for the simple reason that it is taken up in another contribution to this same volume. A portion of the discussion of Foucault is taken from H. J. Silverman, *Textualities: Between Hermeneutics and Deconstruction* (New York and London: Routledge, 1993).

2 The role of metaphor and metonymy have been subsequently linked with what Freud calls 'condensation' and 'displacement' in dream interpretation. Hence metaphor as substitution and condensation implies the replacement of a father by a big bear (for instance) in a young boy's dream, while metonymy as contiguity and displacement results in a dream about a neighbour's garden hose (for instance) instead of her passion for him. In structural political theory, developed most notably by Louis Althusser – in an essay called 'Freud and Lacan' from *Lenin and Philosophy* [11.23] metaphor is associated with overdetermination in a reading of a political text or context, while metonymy is represented as underdetermination. In making this point, Althusser is building on the account of metaphor and metonymy offered by Lacan in his famous essay 'The Insistence of the Letter in the Unconscious' (included in *Ecrits* [11.15]) and H. J. Silverman [11.72], especially the chapter on 'Merleau-Ponty on Language and Communication (1946–47)'.

3 See Maurice Merleau-Ponty, *Consciousness and the Acquisition of Language* [11.65].

4 See H. J. Silverman [11.72], esp. chapters on 'Sartre and the Structuralists' and 'Sartre versus Structuralism'.

5 R. Barthes, 'From Work to Text' [11.10], 155–64.

6 R. Barthes, *S/Z* [11.9], 5.

7 See Silverman [11.72], esp. chapter 18 on 'Foucault and the Anthropological Sleep'.

❧ BIBLIOGRAPHY ❧

de Saussure

11.1 *Course in General Linguistics* (1916), trans. W. Baskin, New York: McGraw-Hill, 1959.

Lévi-Strauss

11.2 *The Elementary Structures of Kinship* (1949), trans. from the revised edition by J. H. Bell and J. von Sturmer, and ed. R. Needham, Boston: Beacon, 1969.

11.3 *Tristes tropiques* (1955), trans. J. and D. Weightman. New York: Atheneum, 1974.

11.4 *Structural Anthropology* (1958), trans. C. Jacobson and B. G. Schoepf, New York: Basic Books, 1963.

Barthes

11.5 *Writing Degree Zero* (1953), trans. A. Lavers and C. Smith, New York: Hill & Wang, 1968.

11.6 *Michelet*, Paris: Seuil, 1954.

11.7 *Elements of Semiology* (1964), trans. A Lavers and C. Smith, New York: Hill & Wang, 1968.

11.8 *Criticism and Truth* (1966), trans. K. P. Kenneman, Minneapolis: University of Minnesota Press, 1987.

11.9 *S/Z* (1970), trans. R. Miller, New York: Hill & Wang, 1974.

11.10 'From Work to Text', in [11.13], 155–64.

11.11 *The Pleasure of the Text* (1973), trans. R. Miller, New York: Hill & Wang, 1975.

11.12 *Roland Barthes* (1975), trans. R. Howard, New York: Hill & Wang, 1977.

11.13 *Image–Music–Text*, trans. S. Heath, New York: Hill & Wang, 1977.

11.14 *Recherche de Proust*, Paris: Seuil, 1980.

Lacan

11.15 *Ecrits* (1966), trans. A. Sheridan, New York: Norton, 1977.

11.16 'Seminar on "The Purloined Letter"', trans. J. Mehlman, *French Freud: Structural Studies in Psychoanalysis*, *Yale French Studies* 48 (1972): 38–72.

Foucault

11.17 *The Order of Things: An Archeology of the Human Sciences* (1966), trans. anon., New York: Vintage, 1970.

11.18 *The Archeology of Knowledge* (1969), trans. A. Smith, New York: Pantheon, 1972.

11.19 'Nietzsche, Genealogy, History', in *Language, Counter-Memory, Practice (1971)*, trans. D. Bouchard and S. Simon, Ithaca: Cornell University Press, 1977, pp. 139–64.

11.20 *Discipline and Punish* (1975), trans. A. Sheridan, New York: Vintage, 1979.

Other works and criticism

11.21 Allison, D. B. (ed.) *The New Nietzsche*, Cambridge, Mass.: MIT Press, 1977, 1985.

11.22 Allison, D. B. 'Destruction/Deconstruction in the Text of Nietzsche', *Boundary 2*, 8: 1 (fall 1979): 197–222.

11.23 Althusser, L. *Lenin and Philosophy and Other Essays*, trans. B. Brewster, New York: Monthly Review Press, 1971.

11.24 Blanchot, M. 'Discours Philosophique' in *L'Arc: Merleau-Ponty*, 46 (1971): 1–4.

11.25 Blanchot, M. *Death Sentence*, trans. L. Davis, New York: Station Hill, 1978.

11.26 Culler, J. *Structuralist Poetics*, Ithaca: Cornell University Press, 1975.

11.27 Culler, J. *On Deconstruction: Theory and Criticism After Structuralism*, Ithaca: Cornell University Press, 1982.

11.28 Derrida, J. *Edmund Husserl's Origin of Geometry: An Introduction* (1962), trans. J. Leavey, Lincoln: University of Nebraska Press, 1989.

11.29 Derrida, J. *Of Grammatology* (1967), trans. G. C. Spivak, Baltimore: Johns Hopkins University Press, 1975.

11.30 Derrida, J. *Speech and Phenomena, and Other Essays on Husserl's Theory of Signs* (1967), trans. D. B. Allison, Evanston: Northwestern University Press, 1973.

11.31 Derrida, J. *Writing and Difference* (1967), trans. A. Bass, Chicago: University of Chicago Press and London: Routledge & Kegan Paul, 1978.

11.32 Derrida, J. *Dissemination* (1972), trans. B. Johnson, Chicago: University of Chicago Press and London: Athlone Press, 1981.

11.33 Derrida, J. *Margins of Philosophy* (1972), trans. A. Bass, Chicago: University of Chicago Press and Hassocks: Harvester Press, 1982.

11.34 Derrida, J. *Positions* (1972), trans. A. Bass, Chicago: University of Chicago Press and London: Athlone, 1982.

11.35 Derrida, J. 'The Deaths of Roland Barthes' (1981), trans. P. A. Brault and M. B. Naas, in H. J. Silverman (ed.) *Philosophy and Non-Philosophy since Merleau-Ponty (Continental Philosophy-I)*, London and New York: Routledge, 1988, pp. 259–96.

11.36 Derrida, J. 'The Time of a Thesis: Punctuations', in Alan Montefiore (ed.) *Philosophy in France Today*, Cambridge: Cambridge University Press, 1982.

11.37 Derrida, J. *Signéponge/Signsponge*, trans. R. Rand, New York: Columbia University Press, 1984. (Parallel French and English translation.)

11.38 Descombes, V. *Modern French Philosophy*, trans. L. Scott-Fox and J. M. Harding, Cambridge: Cambridge University Press, 1980.

11.39 Donato, E. and Macksey, R. (eds) *The Structuralist Controversy*, Baltimore: Johns Hopkins University Press, 1972.

11.40 Eco, U. *A Theory of Semiotics*, Bloomington: Indiana University Press, 1976.

11.41 Fekete, J. (ed.) *The Structural Allegory: Reconstructive Encounters with the*

New French Thought, Minneapolis: University of Minnesota Press, 1984.

11.42 Felman, S. (ed.) *Literature and Psychoanalysis: The Question of Reading – Otherwise*, Baltimore: Johns Hopkins University Press, 1982.

11.43 Gasché, R. 'Deconstruction as Criticism', *Glyph* 7 (1979): 177–216.

11.44 Gasché, R. *The Tain of the Mirror: Deconstruction and the Philosophy of Reflection*, Cambridge, Mass.: Harvard University Press, 1986.

11.45 Hartman, G. *Beyond Formalism*, New Haven: Yale University Press, 1970.

11.46 Hartman, G. *The Fate of Reading*, Chicago: University of Chicago Press, 1975.

11.47 Hartman, G. *Criticism in the Wilderness*, New Haven: Yale University Press, 1980.

11.48 Hartman, G. *Saving the Text: Philosophy/Derrida/Literature*, Baltimore: Johns Hopkins University Press, 1981.

11.49 Hawkes, T. *Structuralism and Semiotics*, Berkeley and Los Angeles: University of California Press, 1977.

11.50 Jakobson, R. 'Two Aspects of Language and Two Types of Aphasia', in *Fundamentals of Language*, The Hague: Mouton, 1971.

11.51 Kearney, R. *Dialogues with Contemporary Continental Thinkers: The Phenomenological Heritage*, Manchester: Manchester University Press, 1984.

11.52 Kearney, R. *Modern Movements in European Philosophy*, Manchester: Manchester University Press, 1986.

11.53 Kristeva, J. *Desire in Language*, trans. T. Gora, A. Jardine and L. Roudiez, New York: Columbia University Press, 1980.

11.54 Kristeva, J. *Revolution in Poetic Language*, trans. M. Waller with an introduction by L. S. Roudiez, New York: Columbia University Press, 1984.

11.55 Kristeva, J. *The Kristeva Reader*, ed. Toril Moi, New York: Columbia University Press, 1986.

11.56 Kristeva, J. *Black Sun*, New York: Columbia University Press, 1989.

11.57 Lacoue-Labarthe, P. 'Fable (Literature and Philosophy)', trans. H. J. Silverman, *Research in phenomenology*, 15 (1985): 43–60.

11.58 Lyotard, J.-F. *The Postmodern Condition*, trans. G. Bennington, Minneapolis: University of Minnesota Press, 1984.

11.59 Marin, L. *Utopics: The Semiological Play of Textual Spaces*, trans. R. Vollrath, Atlantic Highlands: Humanities Press, 1990.

11.60 Merleau-Ponty, M. *Sense and Non-Sense* (1947), trans. H. L. Dreyfus and P. A. Dreyfus, Evanston: Northwestern University Press, 1964.

11.61 Merleau-Ponty, M. *L'Oeil et l'esprit* (1960), Paris: Gallimard, 1964.

11.62 Merleau-Ponty, M. *Signs* (1960), trans. R. C. McCleary, Evanston: Northwestern University Press, 1964.

11.63 Merleau-Ponty, M. *The Primacy of Perception*, ed. J. M. Edie, Evanston: Northwestern University Press, 1964.

11.64 Merleau-Ponty, M. *Prose of the World* (1969), trans. J. O'Neill, Evanston: Northwestern University Press, 1973.

11.65 Merleau-Ponty, M. *Consciousness and the Acquisition of Language*, trans. H. J. Silverman, Evanston: Northwestern University Press, 1973.

11.66 Merleau-Ponty, M. *Texts and Dialogues*, ed. H. J. Silverman and J. Barry, Jr., Atlantic Highlands: Humanities Press, 1992.

11.67 Montefiori, A. (ed.) *Philosophy in France Today*, Cambridge: Cambridge University Press, 1982.

11.68 Peirce, C. S. *Philosophical Writings of Peirce*, ed. J. Buchler, New York: Dover, 1940/1955.

11.69 Said, E. *The World, the Text, and the Critic*, London: Faber & Faber, 1984.

11.70 Silverman, H. J. 'Phenomenology', *Social Research*, 47: 4 (winter 1980): 704–20.

11.71 Silverman, H. J. 'Phenomenology: From Hermeneutics to Deconstruction', *Research in phenomenology*, 14 (1984): 19–34. Reprinted, with 'Afterthoughts', in A. Giorgi (ed.) *Phenomenology: Descriptive or Hermeneutic?*, Pittsburgh: Duquesne University Phenomenology Centre, 1987, pp. 19–34 and 85–92.

11.72 Silverman, H. J. *Inscriptions: Between Phenomenology and Structuralism*, London and New York: Routledge, 1987.

11.73 Silverman, H. J. (ed.) *Philosophy and Non-Philosophy since Merleau-Ponty* (*Continental Philosophy – I*), London and New York: Routledge 1988.

11.74 Silverman, H. J. (ed.) *Derrida and Deconstruction* (*Continental Philosophy – II*), London and New York: Routledge, 1989.

11.75 Silverman, H. J. (ed.) *Postmodernism – Philosophy and the Arts* (*Continental Philosophy – III*), New York and London: Routledge, 1990.

11.76 Silverman, H. J. (ed.) *Gadamer and Hermeneutics* (*Continental Philosophy – IV*), New York and London: Routledge, 1991.

11.77 Silverman, H. J. (ed.) *Writing the Politics of Difference*, Albany: SUNY Press, 1991.

11.78 Silverman, H. J. and Aylesworth, G. E. (eds) *The Textual Sublime: Deconstruction and its Differences*, Albany: SUNY Press, 1989.

11.79 Sini, C. *Semiotica e filosofia: Segno e linguaggio in Peirce, Heidegger e Foucault*, Bologna: Il Mulino, 1978.

11.80 Sini, C. *Images of Truth*, trans. M. Verdicchio, Atlantic Highlands: Humanities Press, 1993.

11.81 Sturrock, J. (ed.) *Structuralism and Since: From Lévi-Strauss to Derrida*, London: Oxford University Press, 1979.

11.82 Wurzer, W. S. 'Heidegger and Lacan: On the Occlusion of the Subject', in H. J. Silverman *et al.* (eds) *The Horizons of Continental Philosophy*, Dordrecht: Nijhoff-Kluwer, 1988, pp. 168–89.

CHAPTER 12

French feminist philosophy
De Beauvoir, Kristeva, Irigaray, Le Doeuff, Cixous
Alison Ainley

❧❧✣❧❧

❧❧ INTRODUCTION ❧❧

Although women have been active philosophers for many centuries,[1] the development of a specifically feminist viewpoint in the context of philosophy has gained credence only comparatively recently; partly as a result of more widespread debates about sexual politics in recent years, and partly as a result of social changes in the status of women. While recognizing that feminism did not spring fully formed and fully armed from the last twenty years like Athena from the brow of Zeus,[2] for reasons of brevity I will discuss in this chapter only a few of the better-known contemporary contributors to feminist philosophy, and focus particularly on those feminists whose work overlaps with or draws upon continental philosophy.

At the outset, it should be stressed that the strands of feminist thinking in relation to philosophy have been and continue to be diverse and do not necessarily present a unified point of view. Feminist thinking in relation to philosophy can take place at a number of levels and from different perspectives, and indeed this has been one of the strengths of its position(s). In general terms, it can take the form of a critique of philosophers' images of women (for example, criticisms of Schopenhauer's description of women as 'defective, trivial, silly and shortsighted',[3] or Kant's account of women as more sentimental and more 'delicate in judgment' than men).[4] It can be historical research into past women philosophers whose work may have been unjustly disregarded.[5] It can be a political critique of the organization of the discipline of philosophy, or a critique of the whole of philosophy as 'male' or 'masculine'.⁶ Or it can be positive contributions to philosophy from a feminist perspective.⁷ Feminist philosophy may take all or some of these approaches to be important. However, as a general guide, feminist philosophy will assume the question of sexual difference to be a philosophical issue at some level and, depending on the point of departure, produce very different ways of theorizing this question. Having said this, not all women philosophers are necessarily feminist philosophers (although there may be feminist implications in their work); for example Hannah Arendt and Simone Weil are twentieth-century thinkers whose work I will not discuss here;⁸ and not all feminists accept the relevance of philosophy to their work.

Despite these qualifications, a notable amount of feminist thinking has been greatly influenced and aided by developments in recent continental philosophy, borrowing from thinkers such as Jacques Derrida, Michel Foucault, Jean-Paul Sartre and Jacques Lacan, and earlier figures such as Hegel, Freud and Heidegger.⁹ Such borrowings have furnished many different aspects of feminist approaches to questions of sexual difference, subjectivity and selfhood, ethics and epistemology. Because the above thinkers have been concerned to raise questions about the discipline of philosophy itself – for example, what they see as philosophy's tendency to organize its enquiries in particular ways around notions of truth or knowledge, the use of binary oppositions or dualisms of mind/body, spirit/matter, order/chaos and hierarchical structures, and the issues of power and politics – they have been helpful in the search for ways of theorizing sexual difference for feminists.

However, feminist theorists have also been highly critical of the above thinkers, sometimes finding their work reduplicating some of the problems they had already identified with the discipline of philosophy in general, i.e. the exclusion of women as philosophers, the use of such symbolic values as 'the feminine' to indicate chaos and plurality without considering how such values relate to women, or the tendency to speak 'on behalf of' women.¹⁰ In other words, feminists have been concerned about the apparent loss or lack of political agency which seems to accompany critiques of identity in recent postmodernist theory. Postmodernists such as Jean Baudrillard respond that 'there is a strange, fierce complicity between the feminist movement and the order of truth'¹¹ and women would do better to recognize that 'woman is but appearance. And it is the feminine as appearance that thwarts masculine depth. Instead of rising up against such insulting counsel, women would do well to let themselves be seduced by its truth, for here lies the secret of their strength.'¹²

The critiques of identity which thinkers such as Derrida, Baudrillard and Gilles Deleuze advance mean that women, characteristically stereotyped as lacking agency in the past, are ironically now 'already' in an enviable position.[13] But feminists have been alarmed or suspicious of the passivity implied in such characterizations of the feminine.

Such disagreements have often been placed in the context of the modernism/postmodernism debate, where feminist theorists are seen to be holding on to notions of emancipatory Enlightenment projects and 'essentialist' notions of identity in the face of, and in opposition to, unassimilatable heterogeneity and the feminine as 'mere' surface. However, the feminist thinkers I discuss below have, I believe, a subtle and complex approach to political questions and are not easily placed into this either/or debate. In addition to raising questions of sexual difference in the context of philosophy, they also raise questions about the connection (or lack of it) between theory and practice/lived experience – women *are* the ones (amongst others) over whose heads this discussion often seems to take place, and deserve to be able to make their own contribution.

❧ SIMONE DE BEAUVOIR ❧

Simone de Beauvoir is perhaps the best-known feminist philosopher of the twentieth century. Her lifelong association with Jean-Paul Sartre seems to have been on the whole one of mutual intellectual inspiration and companionship.[14] De Beauvoir's work on the moral implications and the social context of existentialism, for example in her 1947 work *Pour une morale de l'ambiguité* (translated as *The Ethics of Ambiguity*)[15] was influential upon Sartre, an influence discernible in his shift of focus from the individual consciousness in *Being and Nothingness*[16] to the more collective or situated concerns of his later work. The publication in 1949 of de Beauvoir's best-known work, *The Second Sex*,[17] continued her interest in these themes, a work which provoked reviewers to express outrage at a book which was seen to herald the breakdown of social relations. However, given that de Gaulle had granted French women the vote only five years earlier, the radical impact of this book should not be underestimated.

The Second Sex is a rich and complex work which draws upon literature, myth and religion, theories of biology, accounts of social and economic development (Marxism and psychoanalysis), but also existentialist philosophy. De Beauvoir's aim is to address the question 'What is a woman?'[18] It is because her painstaking analysis uncovers and addresses the nature of the oppression and exclusion of women that it has been significant in the history of feminist thought. But de Beauvoir is also responsible for the promotion of questions of sexual difference on to the philosophical agenda, and for probing questions about the social context of the existentially free individual. Sartre,

Merleau-Ponty and other existentialist thinkers agreed that sexuality was an issue that had been largely disregarded in philosophy, but de Beauvoir's work most insistently asks questions of the relevance of sexual difference to philosophical notions of identity, an insistence Michèle Le Doeuff has called 'a characteristic genius for the inappropriate'.[19] De Beauvoir points out that sexuality is not just 'added on' to human beings but plays a fundamental role in the meaning of an individual's existence: that we are 'embodied'.

However, she rejects the accounts of sexual difference which subscribe to an 'essential' notion of identity, whether this is found in the biological differentiation of the sexes (male/female) or in the 'eternal feminine', an ideal 'essence' of feminine qualities.[20] She rejects these accounts first because she sees individuals as dynamic, engaged in struggles towards freedom, and second because she fears that to suggest an 'essential' nature of woman will allow women to be imprisoned back in the problematic identity of the oppressed. This identity is unacceptable for ideals of existential freedom, and for feminist claims that women should have equal opportunities to engage freely in projects in the world. Her overwhelming historical evidence points to the fact that, in general, men possess such freedom and women do not.

De Beauvoir takes up the concerns of existentialist thinking with the freedom of the individual, the capacity of the individual to make choices and the conflicts which arise between individuals in the context of social relations. She claims that *The Second Sex* is 'an existentialist ethics',[21] and hence agrees with Sartre about the need for individuals 'to engage in freely chosen projects'.[22] The Sartrean individual, striving to maximize freedom, becomes aware that he or she exists as an object in the consciousness of others, a compromising objectification for an individual striving towards freedom. Individuals may become locked into opposing the determinations that others, with their own projects and their capacity to objectify an individual, present. This means that social relations are inherently conflictual, basically relations of dominance and submission. For de Beauvoir, it is important that freedom be maintained as an open horizon, since this is what gives meaning to an individual's existence. However, she immediately questions the apparent neutrality of the individual and the equal starting point of human freedom and autonomy that existentialist individuals are supposed to possess. She points out that, rather than beginning from a neutral and autonomous point, women are already in the position of the determined and objectified, as the Other. 'She is defined and differentiated with reference to man and he not with reference to her; she is the incidental, the inessential as opposed to the essential. He is the Subject, he is the Absolute – she is the Other.'[23]

The freedom of the existential individual is immediately compromised by the socially constructed roles for men and women; rather than various neutral possibilities presented to equal individuals, women are unable to exercise their freedom, because they inherit a pre-given set of assumptions shaping the range of possibilities available to them.

This seems to suggest that women are doomed to be inauthentic because of their sex, if inauthenticity is the failure to maximize one's freedom. Women are in the position of being the second sex. Their existence is constantly conflated with their gender in a way that men's is not, and they seem to be more confined to being bodies or objects.

De Beauvoir accepts that biology plays an important part in one's identity (we live our bodies), but argues that it cannot be used to determine one's destiny. Women's role in reproduction has caused her to be exclusively identified with this role, but with adequate social changes such as childcare and medical advances, there is no reason why reproduction should limit a woman's capacity for freedom. The problem with a biological account of sexual difference, she argues, is that it may attribute essences to men and women, splitting human beings into two types or essential identities.[24] There may be perceptible differences (in physical strength for example), but there is no intrinsic reason why strength should be given a superior value. Such values depend on social context, and are therefore open to revision.

De Beauvoir may wish to dissociate herself from the 'biology is destiny' position, but she often seems to come close to rejecting biology altogether. If women are restrictively defined as 'mere' bodies or as mothers then such restrictions must be overcome, to ensure that women are able to realize their choices consciously. But de Beauvoir does not always consider the extent to which she may be echoing a misogynistic distaste for the female body in trying to overturn such determinations. 'It has been well said that women have "infirmity in the abdomen", and it is true that they have within them a hostile element – it is the species gnawing at their vitals.'[25]

These aspects of her argument are an attempt to escape from essentialism or biologism and to affirm the demand for self-determination. But de Beauvoir has also argued that women's own experience is important and should be validated, even if such experience is of a less independent nature than men's. After sex, she suggests, men are free to take up their individuality once again, whereas women feel themselves to be more 'connected' to biology and more embodied, with responsibility for reproduction within themselves – an experience of their own 'immanence'.[26] De Beauvoir's commitment to projects of transcendence and freedom on the one hand, and her argument that women are more immanently 'in' their bodies on the other, seems to suggest that women are placed in the impossible position of having to transcend their own bodies. It suggests that if women do not seek transcendence they are 'inauthentic' or guilty of bad faith, but if they do seek transcendence it will be a project of self-defeat, an attempt to escape from the immanent realm which is 'feminine'.[27] This contradiction has led some feminists to interpret de Beauvoir either as essentialist or as suggesting that sexual identity is culturally constructed. In fact she seems to be in both positions, and the tension here can be interpreted as part of the contradictions in her existentialist framework.

In keeping with her initial socialist perspective on oppression, de Beauvoir does seem to locate inequalities between the sexes in a social or cultural context. Such declarations as 'One is not born a woman, one becomes one'[28] or 'the body is not a thing, it is a situation'[29] would tend to support this interpretation. Her concern is to ensure that inequalities can be diagnosed, and so combated, at this level. She refuses to accept that any biological or essentialist reason could be given to prevent women overcoming their 'secondary' position. Sheer effort of will, the widespread recognition of women's freedom and choices (which must also be recognized by men) and the fuller availability of choices will bring about greater equality of the sexes. This uncompromising stance often leads her to be stern about the efforts women must make to transcend determination for themselves, in effect to 'stop colluding' in becoming the other for men. Her objective is to galvanize women into asserting their autonomy and formulating projects which will allow them to develop their own identity. She has been criticized for apparently suggesting that it is only if women become more like men that equality will be attained, partly because the kinds of projects she values as important are derived from a framework which itself could still be described as masculine – emphasizing fewer domestic ties, the need for recognized (and paid) labour, perhaps specifically the work of individual creative artists. However, she does suggest that even complete equality in this sphere would not cancel out all differences between the sexes, and women would still maintain a specific understanding of their own sexuality.[30]

AFTER DE BEAUVOIR

The increasingly complex account of otherness that feminist theory in France has developed owes a clear debt to de Beauvoir's analysis of Woman as Other. Feminists have sought to combine the forceful political critique provided by drawing attention to sexual difference, with an analysis of identity drawn from developments in poststructuralist and psychoanalytic theory. Such an analysis draws attention to the self's vulnerability to the displacing effects of desire, as well as to the socially and culturally constructed nature of identity, implicating systems of language and meaning in such a critique.[31]

Rather than situating projects for change and emancipation within existing political and cultural practices, many feminists have subjected such practices to a sustained critique, asking questions about the very constitution of meaning and the concepts of power and politics as such. Whereas de Beauvoir stressed the strong will and self-control required in struggling for equality and autonomy, subsequent theories have raised questions about the very nature of equality and the extent to which such self-control can be practised. In this respect, feminist critiques of identity as rational or masculine coincide with psychoanalytic theory regarding the displacement of consciousness by forces which call into question the epistemological privilege of the subject. Such forces are seen as all-pervasive and unsettling, manifest in systems of representation and language and are understood as corresponding linguistically to the processes of desire. This theory, shaped in part by Lacan's work in structuralism and psychoanalysis, looks at difference as a relation operating not only intersubjectively between self and other, but also as sets of relations of differences within the very systems of signification which order and create meaning. This expanded version of difference means that apparently unified or singular terms are seen to operate by processes of exclusion or suppression, occluding their relation to, or reliance upon, other terms. Discrete or autonomous identities are shown to be disrupted or undermined by 'otherness' and concepts such as 'truth' or 'knowledge' are put into question.

Hence the maintenance of identity as rational and autonomous and the notion of truth as objective and independent are viewed as a defence of territory by the exclusion of that which is other. Anything which lies outside the 'normal' circuits of knowledge or identity gets classified as madness, chaos, darkness or ignorance, and the borders between the two realms are characterized as the site of constant power struggles. Many thinkers also draw attention to a symbolic equation between the excluded otherness and the feminine. Whether this connection is made explicitly or implicitly, the feminine as otherness is seen as multiple, dissembling and excluded, yet capable of disrupting limits and disturbing the status quo.

Thus a connection is established between sexual difference (male/female or masculine/feminine) and polarized oppositions such as self/other, knowledge/ignorance, spirit/body. De Beauvoir makes it possible to draw these parallels from a feminist viewpoint, and to politicize the hierarchical arrangement of such oppositions. Apparent neutrality is thus opened up for analysis as an imbalance of power. But de Beauvoir retains her existentialist/humanist framework when discussing a possible feminist practice, whereas other feminist thinkers take up the critique of the humanist subject as besieged and intersected by unruly forces of desire and structures of power. Thinkers such as Julia Kristeva, Hélène Cixous or Luce Irigaray are influenced by understandings of otherness inherited from Hegel, Sartre and Heidegger, as well as by Derrida's account of western thinking as phallo-logo-centric, unduly centred on a particular account of truth which is infused with masculine values, and Foucault's analyses of the connections between power and knowledge. They are also influenced by Lacanian theory concerning sexuality, language and identity.[32]

Psychoanalytic theory has proved useful to feminist theory, in that it can show the extent to which identity and sexuality are constructed by conflicting and quasi-deterministic forces, as well as indicating the penetration of such forces to psychic structures.[33] At the same time there is an acknowledgement of the implicitly sexual nature of structures and economies which are ostensibly neutral. Hence on one level it provides a generalizable account of identity construction, cross-culturally and trans-historically. Despite the danger of universalizing identity which such an analysis courts, it does give a certain force to the analysis of sexual difference: the dominant structures which divide sexuality into two essential types may need to be challenged and addressed at precisely this level. However, the determinism implied by such internalized constructions is offset somewhat by the notion of the unconscious. The unconscious can act as a constant reminder of the overall failure of the internalization process: 'a resistance to identity at the very heart of psychic life',[34] as Jacqueline Rose puts it. The splits, forcings and divisions of psychic life place pressure against the notion of coherent identity, a widespread replay of an incomplete adjustment to the norm. This moment of failure, negativity, fluidity or formlessness is symbolically bound up with the feminine. As Rose suggests, feminists may recognize certain similarities with their own projects – a 'symbolic failure to adjust to normality'[35] and the resistance this implies.

Lacan suggests that the whole social and cultural context of meaning, the Symbolic Order, is premised on a suppression or repression of the symbolically feminine/maternal. Symbolically otherness stands as excessive, ex-centric and ecstatic, beyond or outside the dominant order of meanings, which allows Lacan to state 'the woman does not exist'.[36] Whether this is the pre-Oedipal mother or the quintessentially feminine, the Ideal woman or the dark absence of negativity, it is the process by which such a realm is designated as Other or otherness which allows the dominant meanings to retain their hold on truth, singularity and power, although paradoxically such otherness is the hidden ground or unacknowledged axis of such an economy.

In its very construction the Lacanian framework is emphatically unfeminist. Nevertheless, Lacan accords women, or the feminine, a kind of power, the possibility of disrupting signifying systems, albeit without the agency to do anything other than constantly disrupt, efface, move on. 'I believe in the jouissance of the woman in so far as it is something more, on condition that you screen off that *something more* until I have properly explained it.'[37] The force of feminist theory influenced by Lacan may be understood as a kind of 'return of the repressed'.[38] The unnameable and unrepresentable feminine jouissance Lacan has proscribed is taken up as the power of disruption and destabilization, and works to unsettle fixation, particularly in the realm of sexual stereotypes.

❧❧ JULIA KRISTEVA ❧❧

The interdisciplinary nature of Julia Kristeva's work, drawing from linguistic theory, Marxism, philosophy and psychoanalysis, makes her a versatile and wide-ranging thinker. She sees herself as a cultural critic and analyst rather than particularly as a feminist thinker, although many feminists see potentials in her work for developing critiques of western thinking and for understanding problems of identity, and she certainly deals with questions about 'the feminine', cultural representations of figures such as 'the mother', or topics such as Chinese women. Coming to Paris from Bulgaria in the mid-1960s, she brought with her a mixture of left-wing politics and an approach to literary criticism influenced by Russian formalism: in brief, a materialist approach to signification and social structures, tempered by her commitment to aesthetic and cultural practices and her desire to change oppressive conditions.[39] The common themes running through her work are an interest in language, politics and sexual identity, themes initially broached in her doctoral thesis *Revolution in Poetic Language* (1974),[40] where she attempts to develop a theory of identity formation in the context of Lacanian psychoanalysis and structuralism. Her main concern in this book is to understand the structuring effects of language without relinquishing the creative, poetic and marginal aspects. She then links her theory to a political account of marginalized but revolutionary forces, exemplified in the figure of the avant-garde poet.

Through a complex intersection of theoretical perspectives, Kristeva develops her account of the material/linguistic forces which constantly disrupt identity, but are still located within the corporeal body. She suggests that identity is forged in a precarious and dynamic relation between various positionalities which can be taken up according to the social and cultural meanings in the Symbolic, and a force of negativity which is persistently engaged in undermining such positions. Her analysis has proved intriguing for many feminist theorists for a number of reasons. First, she emphasizes the critique of identity as a fixed or essential notion. Second, she identifies the constructed nature of meaning and sexuality, and the determining or restrictive effect which existing definitions, stereotypes and cultural roles can have in shaping identity. Third, she identifies a transgressive force which, if activated, can have a disruptive or revolutionizing effect on the social/cultural context in question. Her account of 'the subject-in-process'[41] analyses the cost involved in subject formation, but it also hints at ways of subverting the dominant forms of understanding sexual difference. For feminist theorists, she seems to negotiate essentialism on the one hand by suggesting that subject 'positions' are being created and destroyed in the ongoing dialectic of signification, and yet she refuses to diffuse subjectivity into merely an effect of language.

For Kristeva, Lacan's 'return to Freud' (his reworking of Freud)[42] is important in that it shifts the focus from biology to a linguistic shaping of sexuality and identity. This shift, she thinks, will allow for a different way of understanding identity. If sexual difference is implicated in the conceptual framework itself, Kristeva's characterization of language as a shifting process of the production and decay of meaning allows her a potential for mobility on the question of identity formation. The Freudian focus on a visible/biological structure seems very limiting in the light of the fluid freeing of sexual difference into the Symbolic arena (many potential positionalities or social roles to be fulfilled). But in some ways all that has happened is a shifting of the terms of formation. Lacan's point that a framework of cultural reference is the only place from which any account of sexual difference can be produced, is meant to negate any simplistic biological starting point. Now that difference is seen as being produced by systems of meaning, there is no direct access to a pure biological understanding of physical bodies, since it would be impossible to recognize such bodies outside of the system of meaning. This is the basis of the development of the imaginary, the realm which severs full cognisance of the body and renders its relation metaphorical or 'morphological'. If identity is seen as *structuration* rather than as psycho-physical development through time, the issue shifts from questions of anatomical difference (at what point in development do differences appear?) to questions as to what such differences *mean* within the symbolic, and the extent to which they are open to subversion. But because Lacan denies any access to an 'other' realm, for him there can only be the conceptions of sexual difference which already exist, but which are inherently 'masculine' (because created in the Symbolic).[43]

For Lacan, the primary relation with the mother's body, which he had characterized as fluid and plural, the realm of unmediated jouissance, was what had to be overcome so that identity could be established. Successfully relinquishing this realm of non-separation allows for successful entry into the Symbolic and identification with the masculine or patriarchal values of social/cultural meaning. The price to be paid for attaining linguistic competence and a place in the Symbolic is the loss of the blissful, unselfconscious pleasure before the entry into language. However, Kristeva argues that the overcoming of this 'other' realm can never be wholly successful, and it will continue to break through or irrupt into the Symbolic Order, where its effects will be felt bodily as pleasurable disturbances. Symbolically, such disruptions will connote the pre-Oedipal and the feminine.

The focus of Kristeva's work on femininity is governed by this understanding. If the structuration of identity is at the level of language, but this process is constantly invaded by the 'language' of the other realm, then its stability is called into question. Perhaps by insisting upon the disruptive rather than the constitutive elements of language, a sufficiently transgressive notion of the subject can be produced to allow it to reformulate itself, 'more or less' masculine or feminine?

Kristeva is critical of theorists who focus on language as a homogeneous, logical system with internal coherence. It would seem she has in mind the prioritizing of communication, consensus and competence she finds in the work of Saussure and Chomsky and in Lacan's symbolic. In contrast, Kristeva focuses on the 'edges' of language, the points at which language appears to break down: the 'pathologies' of madness and schizophrenia, the hermetic and difficult poetries of the avant-garde, and the 'hysteria' of women. She theorizes these aspects in a different way from other linguists, who had seen these forms of language as continuous with conventional signification, but less successful. If the formal practice of language uses is emphasized, these deviant practices are judged according to their conformity or deliberate flouting of the rules. Structuralist linguists minimized reference to 'subjective' elements. Kristeva seeks to identify a connection, but, as she makes clear, it is a productive and dynamic relation she is interested in, not a relation of stasis or a revival of a humanist subject.

Focusing on rhythm, repetition, elision and displacement reinforces a notion of the subject-in-process, rather than an ideal enunciator, since it concerns the apparent failures rather than the successes of the struggle to maintain a coherent identity. It is also indicating the points at which the 'other' realm is discernible through its effects.

Kristeva's notions of 'the semiotic' and the *'chora'* present an attempt to theorize this untheorizable, pre-discursive realm which is described in terms of 'space' or a locus to avoid pinning it to a stage of development. She writes of the semiotic as a kind of primordial writing or signifying of the body, although this is not strictly an accurate description, since it is concerned with 'the body of a subject who is not yet constituted as such'.[44] Still, this pre-signifying signification is a textuality of the body which is more experiential than meaningful. 'We understand the term semiotic in its Greek sense; σημεῖον = distinctive mark, trace, index, precursory sign, proof engraved or written sign, imprint, trace, figuration.'[45] It is an ordering of energies which initiates the inscription and conditions for representation. Hypothesized as both the material rhythms and forces underlying the possibility of textuality, and the imprinting of psychical energies to connect sensation to movement, it acts as a preparation for entry into language. This space is as yet undifferentiated but it cannot be described as homogeneous, shot through with 'psychical marks' and in a state of motility. Kristeva names it as 'the *chora* . . . an essentially mobile and extremely provisional articulation constituted by movements and their ephemeral stases'.[46]

That this notion is positioned 'prior' to signification should not be taken to indicate a necessary chronology in time, since this realm is symbolically 'other' to temporal order as well as topographical space. Therefore although it is given an apparently archaic and originary status, it does not constitute a reified origin divided from the subject in the symbolic. This would replicate a duality which Kristeva is concerned to resist; the terms are not equal and the notion of origin is reconstructed only in retrospect from positions already in language. In fact, Kristeva is explicitly critical of Lacan for making the repression of the mother the condition of subjectivity. As she draws attention to the symbolic connection of the *chora* with feminine or maternal notions, she is taking up pre-figured connections which identify the notion of an origin with a primordial mother: 'This place which has no thesis and no position, the process by which significance is constituted. Plato himself leads us to such a process when he call this receptacle or chora nourishing or maternal.'[47] However, the semiotic is in one important sense opposed to the Symbolic: it is a site of resistance and disruption against which the organization of the Symbolic is to be compared. Kristeva takes up the equation of otherness with the feminine or maternal, in order to demonstrate the sacrificial process involved in identity construction, and to suggest how the inherent violence might be made less painful or channelled in more creative ways.

Despite the alignment of otherness and the feminine, for Kristeva it does not constitute an alternative identity for women, nor does it allow a specifically female or feminine language. However, there are ways of maximizing its disruptive effects in order to combat the restrictive impact of the Symbolic. The figures of the avant-garde poet and the political dissident are focal points in Kristeva's earlier work, while later on she considers women as potential disruptive figures.

What the father doesn't say about the unconscious, what sign and time repress in their impulses, appears as their *truth* (if there is no absolute, what is truth, if not the unspoken of the spoken?) and this truth can be imagined only as a woman. A curious truth: outside time, with neither past nor future, neither true nor false; buried underground, it neither postulates nor judges. It refuses, displaces, breaks the symbolic order before it can re-establish itself.[48]

Kristeva suggests three ways in which this curious truth may be understood: 'Jouissance, pregnancy, and marginal speech: the means by which this "truth", cloaked and hidden by the symbolic order and its companion, time, functions through women'.[49] Here Kristeva is linking 'a vigilance, call it ethical',[50] with the figuration of the feminine and the maternal as 'other'. It is a critical and disruptive kind of ethicality, linked to a capacity to resist the fixation of subjectivity and to remain critical, but also seeking a means to express such 'otherness'.

To refuse all roles, in order, on the contrary, to summon this timeless 'truth' – formless, neither true nor false, echo of our jouissance, of our madness, of our pregnancies – into the order of speech and social symbolism. But how? By listening; by recognising the unspoken in speech; by calling attention at all times to whatever remains unsatisfied, repressed, new, eccentric, incomprehensible, disturbing the status quo.[51]

Here she seems to be suggesting that the location of ethicality is no longer adequately situated in the reformulation and attempted perfection of codes of behaviour, rules and laws. Unless the disruptive traces of the subject, constantly being rewritten in its processes, can also be accounted for, these projects are destined to keep retreading the same ground. The constant transgression and renewal of positioning in relation to the process of signification leads to the possibility of new practices, forged at the very boundaries of thinking.

Kristeva finds in maternity the metaphoric expression of the above boundary location of ethicality, which is given the force of subversion but still embodied. Maternity connotes a possible irruption and interruption of the Symbolic, centrally placed, yet disruptive, a disturbance between stasis and dynamism, cyclical/monumental time and discursive/grammatical time. In her essay 'Stabat Mater',[52] the poetic, left-hand (sinister?) 'other' side of the text irrupts into the historical and chronological mapping of motherhood. Textually this corresponds to a writing of the metaphoric mother, positioned as a body in signification and yet already split, separated, pleasuring; 'the heterogeneity not subsumed under any law'. A space is opened for different subjective possibilities, yet retaining the specificity of women. This 'heretical ethics' (her-ethics) is based not upon avoiding the law, but upon enriching it. 'Now, if a contemporary ethics is no longer seen as being the same as morality; if ethics amounts to not avoiding the embarrassing and inevitable problematics of the law but giving it flesh, language, jouissance – in that case its reformulation demands the contribution of women.'[53] A similar position is taken in Kristeva's analysis of the role of the Virgin Mary. In 'Stabat Mater' she draws heavily upon Marina Warner's book *Alone of All Her Sex; the Myth and Cult of the Virgin Mary*[54] to indicate how the Virgin Mary becomes a symbolic axis of the conjunction between hebraic and hellenic; and as a conjunction between virginity and maternity. As a moment of undecidability, the figure presents a potential site of ambivalence, for the two traditions as well as for understandings of women. There is a potential disruption of the Greek logos and Jewish monotheism in the presence of a divine feminine figure, central to religion but neither one thing nor another. But this dangerous ambivalence is conscripted for control and synthesis, in that the virginal aspect becomes a pure and holy asceticism, and maternity becomes the continuity of the community via reproduction. The freezing of undecidability sets up an ideal, fusing with the existing ideal of virginity in courtly love and the ideal of devoted maternal love. The impossible totality of the virgin mother is not only disseminated within patriarchal cultures but becomes the prototype for western love relations. In Kristeva's terms, the dangerous moment of rupture is contained by erasing jouissance, in virginity, and channelling it, in maternal reproduction, to sustain the deathless ideal of the masculine, whether this is the law, the community or the subject.

This maternal figure, the epitome of romantic sentimentality and utterly serene icon, ideal and untroubled, functions as a sublimating vessel for various cultures. And yet Kristeva indicates that its 'cleverly balanced architecture today appears to be crumbling', the 'psychotic sore of modernity' is 'the incapacity of contemporary codes to tame the maternal'.[55] Thus it reveals that which it cannot contain even in trying to cover over this slippage.

Despite Kristeva's characterization of the subject as 'an open system', I don't think she is committed to the denial of sexual difference or the 'erasure' of the subject. However, she does argue that the positionality which may lead to a metaphysical hypostatization of identity is to be found in feminist discourse too. This is perhaps what leads her to be unnecessarily harsh on the variety of feminist positions which do not coincide with her own; a fear of the reintroduction of the essentialist subject which has led women to 'sacrifice or violence'. If this is a challenge to feminist theory, is it the kind of critique which feminist theory needs? Many feminist writers on Kristeva find her

attacks on feminism uncomfortable, especially when they seem to emanate from an apparently powerful position as the 'queen of theory'.
But on occasion her work is compatible with feminist approaches to
the body, offering a potential rethinking of corporeality in keeping
with a radical perspective on difference. As Rosi Braidotti puts it:

> the body thus defined cannot be reduced to the biological, nor can
> it be confined to social conditioning. In a new form of 'corporeal
> materialism', the body is seen as an inter-face, a threshold, a field
> of intersection of material and symbolic forces; it is a surface
> where multiple codes of power and knowledge are inscribed; it is
> a construction that transforms and capitalises on energies of a
> heteronomous and discontinuous nature. The body is not an
> essence, and therefore not an anatomical destiny.[56]

❧ LUCE IRIGARAY ❧

Like Kristeva, Irigaray has a background in linguistics, psychoanalysis,
philosophy and feminist theory, and is currently practising therapy or
analysis. However, she takes a set of premises very different from
Kristeva's from these areas, and produces markedly different conclusions.

Born in 1930 in Belgium, Luce Irigaray began her work with
research into psycholinguistics, specifically the language of patients
diagnosed schizophrenic or suffering from senile dementia (see some
of the essays in *Speaking/Language is Never Neutral/Neuter* first published in 1986).[57] Her conclusions concerning the loss or lack of identity
of such patients who seem 'overwhelmed' by language led her to draw
comparisons with the position of women in relation to language. In
the process of the analytic session, understood as a dialogue between
two speakers, Irigaray noted a number of factors which continue to
be important throughout her work. First, the emergence of identity
formulated as possible positions in such locutionary exchanges. Second,
the differences (specifically sexual difference) dramatized or enacted in
speech. Third, the points at which grammatical formulations of language begin to break down, and the experience of speakers caught in
this position. Her focus is the vulnerability of subjectivity and the
attempts to secure a place for it against the destructive technologization
of communication in the present age. However, her concern is not the
resurrection of a humanist subject but a critique of the language and
thinking which presents itself as neutral or neuter.

Irigaray combines this research with her understanding of Lacanian psychoanalysis and structuralism concerning the construction of

identity, to throw light on what she sees as a sacrificial culture and the position of women in such a culture. One of her concerns, which has been extensively misinterpreted, is her attempt to develop an alternative strategy to allow 'feminine identity' to take (a) place. Although she has often been understood to be positing a language of the female body, the level of her intervention is markedly that of cultural and social formations. She does suggest that the dominant form of discourse has been 'isomorphic' with masculine sexuality, and it is this relation which has been difficult to understand or translate. It is not simply a representational model but a relation itself to be understood as metaphoric or metonymic. If this relation has dominated in the past, perhaps there could be a form of discourse which has morphological suggestions of images of the female body? It is this 'hypothetical' style she deploys in the essay *This Sex Which is Not One'* (first published in 1977),[58] and which has led to the assumption that she is 'writing the body'. Rather, it appears that this stylistic deployment is a strategic intervention in what she feels has been a monologic or 'phallo-logo-centric' approach to questions of sexuality and language. In her later work it appears that she is concerned more with existing social formations and linguistic practices than with developing a completely alternative female language, and her recent empirical studies into language use and sexual difference would seem, with hindsight, to support this analysis of her early writings. However, this does not lessen her attempts to restore, or rather to create, a less damaged and damaging understanding of sexual difference.

At the beginning of her book *The Ethics of Sexual Difference*, (first published in 1984),[59] she states her belief that sexual difference is the burning issue of our age, the issue of difference which potentially could be 'our salvation on an intellectual level . . . the production of a new age of thought, art, poetry and language; the creation of a new *poetics'*. However, she suggests that the development of this event is hampered and constrained by the systematic repetition of sameness being compulsively reiterated in the spheres of philosophy, politics, religion and science. This repetition, or reworking of the same ground, is evident in many contexts, which Irigaray lists as 'the consumer society, the circular nature of discourse, the more or less cancerous diseases of our age, the unreliable nature of words, the end of philosophy, religious despair or the regressive return to religion, scientistic imperialism or a technique that does not take the human subject into account, and so on'.[60] According to Irigaray, this repetition works to conceal or efface a possible way of articulating otherness. This articulation, she thinks, can best take place in the context of questions of sexual difference. Apart from the explicit feminist perspective, her reasons for privileging sexual difference lie in her specific appropriation of psychoanalytic discourse, particularly the work of Lacan. Despite her use of a psychoanalytic framework, her work is also a strategic departure from it, or an attempt to subvert it from within. She suggests that psychoanalysis has enabled a theoretical treatment of sexuality and identity to take place via the (generalizable) analysis of forms of patriarchal identity as constructions. Her focus on the *constructed* nature of such notions as identity, philosophical discourse and its concepts has a number of implications. She is able to diagnose a bias running through the history of such notions and to point to the permeation of such forces to psychic levels. She is also able to conduct a sustained critique of the damaging nature of such constructions as exclusion or suppression. She thus sees her work as 'jamming the machinery'[61] of western theory, a process of analysing and uncovering the fantasies, projections and repressions which are taken to be normal or necessary. The nature of this work is extensive and radical.

> For the work of sexual difference to take place, a revolution in thought and ethics is needed. We must re-interpret the whole relationship between the subject and discourse, the subject and the world, the subject and the cosmic, the microcosmic and the macrocosmic. . . . In order to think and live through this difference, we must reconsider the whole question of space and time.[62]

If such apparently foundational notions are shown to be constructions, then there is a possibility that they may be modified or changed in the future. For Irigaray, the usefulness of psychoanalytic theory rests in some part on its capacity to analyse the symbolism of masculine and feminine as a pair of terms which pervade wide and various sets of relations, such that the symbolization becomes tangled up in the very process of conceptualization. The common oppositions of the Pythagorean table of opposites become aligned with a symbolic interpretation of anatomical difference, and, significantly, the unified, non-contradictory and homogenous terms come to dominate. Across a range of systems and at different levels, exclusion and censorship operate to prioritize the masculine term at the expense of the feminine, such that the very operation itself is obscured from view. The status quo is maintained at the price of a peculiar violence – the exclusion of the feminine, or its characterization as object, matter, inferior term. As regards subjectivity, masculine/feminine forces or values may become aligned with male and female sexes, but, she suggests, the very notion of subjectivity itself has 'already been appropriated to the masculine', despite the way that such a notion is presented as neutral. It is because such structures are built upon repression and denial that inevitably the tension of maintaining such a territory begins to show and the cracks, failures and breakdowns indicate the spaces through which the potentiality of the feminine may begin to be built. It is through her understanding and seizure of a certain *lack* of synchronization, therefore, that Irigaray situates her project.

Irigaray's engagement with philosophy has been extensive. If she sees philosophical discourse as 'the master discourse . . . the discourse on discourses'[63] – adding, 'the philosophical order is indeed the one that has to be questioned, and disturbed, inasmuch as it covers over sexual difference[64] – she has also identified philosophy's resources as crucial in reinterpreting questions of sexual difference. She sees her focus as philosophical, but her work is a dramatic testimony to the ambivalence she feels as a woman in philosophy, and as such displays an equivocation between her critique of philosophy and her more positive reconstructions of female subjectivity.

In the context of philosophy, she announces her desire to 'have a fling with the philosophers',[65] paradoxically to indicate the seriousness of her engagement with philosophical questions. This means 'going back through the male imaginary', and gives rise to 'the necessity of "reopening" the figures of philosophical discourse – idea, substance, subject, transcendental subjectivity, absolute knowledge – in order to pry out of them what they have borrowed that is feminine, from the feminine, to make them "render up" and give back what they owe the feminine.'[66]

She means to be as intimate and familiar with philosophical history as possible, but also to challenge it from the position of a woman; that is, one who is symbolically positioned outside or other to philosophy, one who can only 'flirt' with ideas, or conversely, deflate them by being too playful, refusing to take them seriously. This positioning allows Irigaray to follow through some of the main canonical texts of western philosophy; in *Speculum of the Other Woman* (first published in 1974), she takes on Plato, Aristotle, Meister Eckhart, Descartes, Hegel, Spinoza, Plotinus, Kant, Marx, Freud, and in *The Ethics of Sexual Difference* she adds Hegel, Merleau-Ponty and Levinas, while other texts deal with Nietzsche and Heidegger, for example,[67] reconstructing their logic carefully in order to show how it interrupts itself. What she calls 'the blind spot in an old dream of symmetry',[68] the hidden assumption so necessary to the symmetry and so necessarily hidden, will entail analysing philosophy's unconscious.

For Irigaray, what is repressed is 'the feminine', that which allows philosophy to get off the ground, but must remain essentially unspoken, as the ground. The negativity of symbolically occupying this groundless ground constantly places women in an impossible position. As primal matter or 'mother-matter', the feminine or maternal acts an archaic past, the 'nature' placed in opposition to culture. 'The mother-woman remains the place separated from its "own place", a place deprived of a place of its own. She is, or ceaselessly becomes, the place of the other who cannot separate himself from it.'[69] One of Irigaray's concerns is to explore the suppressed or superseded nature of this element or 'the elemental' space, partly to remind philosophy of its debt to this unexplored 'pre-rational' world-view and partly to try to develop a vocabulary which could articulate this otherness. Irigaray writes: 'I wanted to go back to this natural material which makes up our bodies, in which our lives and our environment are grounded; the flesh of our passions.'[70] Her 'elemental' texts deal with air, earth, water and fire, her 're-invention' of the material origins of philosophical thinking and its elision with maternal or feminine symbolism (for example in *Marine Lover of Friedrich Nietzsche* (first published in 1980) she shows a certain aversion in Nietzsche's writing to water, which is symbolically feminine). In trying to imagine this 'other region' she employs a strategic syntactical style, an interplay of weaving in the writing of the body as she had expressed it – multiplicity and plurality, with frequent changes of tense, and questions disrupting her work and interrupting whichever position she was speaking from. Speaking (as) woman is a tactical means of restoring specificity to a non-specific discourse, and also corresponds to her aim to put the philosophical subject back into a material context – the body and the materiality of its surroundings.

Irigaray's strategy in reading these canonical texts is to imitate their movements, a mimicry which is, in its very exaggerated miming, in excess of the limits and definitions which had been set.

> There is in an initial phase, perhaps only one 'path', the one historically assigned to the feminine: that of mimicry. One must assume the feminine role deliberately. Which means already to convert a form of subordination into an affirmation and thus to begin to thwart it. . . . To play with mimesis is thus, for a woman, to try to recover the place of her exploitation by discourse, without allowing herself to be simply reduced to it.[71]

Her strategy of mimicry is directly related to the notion of 'mirroring' which runs throughout her texts. This notion is part of a complex set of interwoven strands which explore the preoccupation of western thinking with accurate 'reflection', illumination, and clarity. Not only do metaphors of the 'ocular' and 'specular' seem to dominate, but, she suggests, they are essential for the establishing of the self-reflexive subject, and the apparent autonomy of the philosopher. The narcissism of the subject that results is, for Irigaray, part of the logic of 'the same'. However, she also suggests that the speculations which privilege this version of the epistemological subject are based upon a (hidden) reliance upon women or the feminine to act as a mirror for such a subject, at the expense of their own identity. Women are either frozen into static representations dictated by the logic of the same, or they are positioned wholly outside the system as a conceptual 'black hole'; the elsewhere and otherwise without a status of its own. In *Speculum* Irigaray suggests equivalencies with Freud's dark continent or Plato's cave, the exploration of which is deemed essential and yet produces, according to Irigaray, theory still caught within its own expectations, more of the same. In order to broach the question of sexual difference, Irigaray produces a critique of the 'flat mirror' of 'the processes of specula(riza)tion that subtend our social and cultural organisations'[72] and suggests, through such a critique, another mode of approach which will allow for feminine subjectivity: '*a curved mirror*, but also one that is *folded back on itself*, with its impossible appropriation "on the inside" of the mind, of thought, of subjectivity. Whence the *intervention of the speculum and the concave mirror*, which disturb the staging of representation.'[73] If mimesis is no longer direct and accurate 'reflection', then the distorting mirror in which women have been confined can throw back 'disturbed' and disturbing reflections, thereby beginning the process of allowing the feminine to take (a) place. This is a mimicry which not only twists and parodies, but effects a change in the process.

Irigaray proposes a particular conception of psychic health to counteract the crisis and fragmentation of the present age, which would involve the adequate conceptualization of both masculine and feminine elements in a non-hierarchical exchange and process. However, we are far from this stage. The feminine is still inadequately conceptualized. It is only by intervening on the destructive circuit that another age of difference might be broached, an intervention which Irigaray describes as ethical. The revaluation of 'passion' and 'wonder' (*admiration*)[74] could lead to relations which, while retaining the radical otherness of the other, allow for an ethical encounter to take place.

Irigaray's more explicitly political proposals include interventions in the legal, civil and representional status of women[75] and her own work with various women's groups in Italy for example. But she has also explored more 'mystical' approaches; lyrical poetic expressions of love between women, between mothers and daughters and lovers, and her work on 'the divine', which is an attempt to explore the forms of sacred meaning which have also acted to exclude women, and to revalue divisions between sacred/profane, carnal/celestial, matter/spirit.[76]

Irigaray's equivocations may strike her critics as contradictory or difficult to place. How are we to understand what seem to be utopic projections of 'amatory exchanges' and a new fertile dialogue of sexual difference in the light of her sustained critique of subjectivity and philosophy, the 'sacrificial culture'? Is she writing for all women? From where? However, at present she is perceived to be a thinker who manages to negotiate the minefields and sustain the tensions with acuity, a position which itself invites further responses and engagements with her writings.[77]

❧ MICHÈLE LE DOEUFF ❧

Michèle Le Doeuff was born in 1948, taught philosophy at the Ecole Normale Supérieure and is currently doing research at the CRNS. Her focus on the apparently innocuous illustrative devices used in philosophy (and she shows that 'the feminine' is a constantly recurring item) uncovers a tension at the heart of such texts which has repercussions for women's relation to philosophy. Although metaphors and images may appear to be harmless, especially when they are explicitly given a secondary status, one of Le Doeuff's concerns is to expose such an assumption. Her reading of the history of philosophy shows how philosophy draws upon a very specific set of such devices which function in quite particular ways in the texts, even as 'philosophical discourse . . . labels itself as philosophical by means of a deviation from the mythic, the poetic and all that is image making'.[78] For Le Doeuff, these images point to tensions or stress lines in the organization of the philosophical enterprise, the 'sensitive nerve endings' which say more about philosophical discourse than it would prefer to speak. For not only do they provide continuity markers in the history of philosophy, but they also indicate the 'obsessions, neuroses and dangers', or the more uncontrollable elements intrinsically bound up in the progress of reason. In her book *The Philosophical Imaginary* (first published in 1986) she analyses such images and figures in Kant, Rousseau, Plato, Moore, Bacon and Descartes. She argues that philosophy sets up the feminine as an internal enemy: 'a hostile principle, all the more hostile because there is no question of dispensing with it . . . the feminine, a support and signifier of something that, having been engendered by philosophy whilst being rejected by it, operates within as an indispensable deadweight'.[79]

Despite the psychoanalytic tones of this analysis, Le Doeuff rejects any notion of the unconscious at work. For her, the metaphors of 'the feminine' are expressed as part of the philosophical imaginary (which at times seems to resemble a bestiary), but she uses this term more in the sense of 'a collection of images' than in the sense which Lacan, or Irigaray, employ it. She argues that greater awareness of this process will have certain implications for changes in the practice of philosophy, but she rejects overarching frameworks such as Marxism or psychoanalysis, partly because of her concern that women in philosophy will exchange one set of orthodoxies for another, sitting at the feet of 'new masters' (Lacan and Derrida, amongst others), a process which sets up new forms of political correctness.

This is why she is careful to examine the specific relation of student and teacher in her more recent book *Hipparchia's Choice* (first published in 1989).[80] She conducts an analysis of the way an apprenticeship is served in philosophy, considering what techniques of assessment, training and control are used. Seeing this relation in terms of influence and power or lack of it, she locates it within a wider set of relations, the relation of the academic institution to the particular social setting and historical inheritance, with connections between knowledge and power being made in a manner reminiscent of Foucault. Her 'case study' for this analysis is the relationship between Sartre and Simone de Beauvoir, a complex site of tensions between male/female, teacher/disciple (de Beauvoir's own description), philosophy/feminism.

Rather than concentrate upon the exclusion of women from philosophy, Le Doeuff emphasizes their incorporation into the very centre. Far from them appearing as victims of rigid expulsion, she points out, women have been philosophers all along, learning, corresponding, discussing and writing. However, the terms of their admission into philosophy have been, she suggests, quite strictly controlled, presenting a more complex and subtle picture of philosophy's process of self-legitimation.

Despite the cheerful optimism which Le Doeuff seems to display about the possibility of 'retraining' philosophy to be more open and tolerant, she doesn't underestimate the difficulties which such a demand presents. Rather, I would see her strategy as 'entrism', borrowing scholarly techniques in order to gain a legitimate foothold in philosophy, and from there developing the feminist challenges and provoking the changes which she believes the discipline must address. She wishes to redeem, restore and rehabilitate philosophy, arguing for a pluralistic 'contest of faculties', or 'constrained disagreement' in academia, which could allow for uncertainty and resisting closure, and prevent domination of any one viewpoint at the expense of other, more hesitant viewpoints. This approach, which Rosi Braidotti calls 'a reasoned critique of reason',[81] comparing it with the work of Lorraine Code or Genevieve Lloyd,[82] means that her work does not indict the whole of western philosophy for 'masculinism'. Her work is not really compatible with that of, for example, Irigaray's, because Le Doeuff does not subscribe to the discourse of radicality or revolution. Her 'common-sense' approach contrasts with the 'poetic-hysteric' style of other French feminists, but some critics find her occasionally too cautious.

❧ HÉLÈNE CIXOUS ❧

Hélène Cixous was born in Algeria in 1937, and has been professor of English literature at the University of Paris VIII at Vincennes, located in Saint-Denis, since 1968. It is with Cixous that the notion of *écriture féminine* (feminine, or female, writing) is most readily associated. Through her explorations of the relationship between sexuality and writing, mostly in her texts of the 1970s (which deliberately defy classification as poetry or theory), she tries to encourage the scripting of Lacan's forbidden feminine jouissance. While she seems to pay even less heed to the theoretical demands of philosophical rigour and clarity than Kristeva and Irigaray, she elaborates on the construction and uncovering of feminine sexual pleasure as it might be given shape in a subversive practice of writing, but the implicit background is Derrida's analysis of *différance* and the poststructuralist problematizing of logos, power and knowledge. Cixous takes up the notion of the feminine as symbolically other, plural and multivocal, positioned as such by the classical oppositions which classify and divide values. Her texts may be said to work at the knots which tie such an economy in place, loosening the rigidity of dualisms to free the expression of heterogeneity. Through the exploration of this more open and fluid form of difference, from the strategic standpoint of a woman 'lost' in her corporeal sexuality, her dreams of her marginalized, inessential nature, Cixous believes that the fixity of our present conceptual schema will be shaken. Her work initiates and celebrates the experiential dimensions of feminine desire. She raids classical literature to uncover 'lost voices' through reinvesting in powerful figures – mothers, mythical heroines, goddesses and the ecstatic and excessive aspects of a sexual 'dark continent'. It is also an attempt to enrich a particular vocabulary coextensive with 'the feminine'; poetic and allusive, metaphorical and 'incandescent'. Rather than merely replicating the static, fragmented or silenced position she has diagnosed women as occupying, her texts attempt to transgress these positions by 'overloading' them, and lyrically exploding them. The notions of 'spending' and 'the gift' are significant in her piece 'Sorties':[83] showing up an economy of exchange to be one of exploitation by miming its carefully monitored limits to the point of parody is for Cixous a political and transgressive activity.

There are many problematic aspects of Cixous' work – she may seem to lapse into the versions of women's bodies she was critical of, or into a fascination with her own fabulous textual labyrinths at the expense of more explicit political engagement. She does extricate herself from any collective feminism which she believes to be a quest for recognition and legitimation in an inadequately interrogated patriarchal economy and so a 'reactionary ideology'. It is also unclear whether

Cixous is celebrating and uncovering the quintessential 'feminine' in her work, or if she is demonstrating a strategy which all women are invited to explore for themselves. The use of 'we' for women in her texts is an ambivalent point in this regard. However, the celebratory tone of her texts is inspirational and creative: 'a laughter that breaks out, overflows, a humour no one would expect to find in a woman . . . she who laughs last. And her first laugh is at herself.'[84]

CONCLUSION

The philosophical paradox of scepticism bears, I think, many similarities to feminist work in philosophy. 'Scepticism may be understood as an expression of an extreme form of dissatisfaction with the logos in its philosophical form. Scepticism tries to evade philosophy; but is there any logos-free space where it could settle to enjoy a human life?'[85] If thinking is continually involved in movements of imprisonment, encompassing and repulsing, 'Which experiences, adventures of the mind, or events of history do not permit the gathering of logos to enclose them within its horizons?'[86] How are we to find a strategy of critique which is not merely repetition of the same, but manages to avoid the infinite regress of a scepticism forced to be sceptical of its own position? This is the problematic which faces those thinkers who seek to reproach philosophy for what it has repressed or left out, and to reproach it in the name of a legitimate cause, and yet this reproach contaminates the basis of an appeal to legitimation in reproaching philosophy. How to dodge philosophical containment while at the same time utilizing its resources to articulate otherness? Engaging in this 'impossible' enterprise is to offer an ethical reproach to philosophy, the conditions of this reproach being a determination to avoid quietism.

The questioning of identity belongs to an immense volume of work which aims to uncover the conflation of singularity, ontology and presence, and the connection to the power structures which not only create such formations but maintain them as the most successful means of sustaining the status quo. The totalitarian thinking which occludes difference in the name of a more coherent theorization of unity is not confined to those political regimes more immediately identifiable as repressive, but also to the liberal framework which argues for equality at the expense of celebrating difference. If feminist theory has been concerned to question identity in the context of postmodernist thinking, it is in order to analyse the alignment of presence and power. But the recent 'return to the subject' in philosophical theory, which is heralded as the chance to reconsider questions of ethics and political responsibility now that subjectivity has been unsettled from its complacent fixity, is not really new to feminist theory, in that feminism is in general seeking an effective version of agency to be able to conduct a struggle, whether reformist or revolutionary.

 NOTES

1 See M. E. Waite (ed.) [12.87].
2 In [12.85], 169, G. Spivak suggests that the professional woman philosopher may be comparable to Athena: 'Women armed with deconstruction must be aware of becoming Athenas, uncontaminated by the womb, sprung in armour from the father's forehead'.
3 A. Schopenhauer, 'On Women', in [12.84], 102–13.
4 I. Kant [12.69].
5 See some of the contributors to [12.87].
6 Many feminists have drawn attention to masculine traits in philosophy (see [12.73, 12.80] for examples) although this does not often extend so far as to see philosophy as all and irredeemably 'male'.
7 I have tried to include a representative sample of feminist philosophers in the Bibliography.
8 See E. Young-Bruehl [12.93], and C. Herman, 'Women in Space and Time', in E. Marks and I. de Courtivron (eds), *New French Feminisms, an Anthology* (Brighton: Harvester, 1980), pp. 168–74, for just two examples of feminist readings of Arendt and Weil.
9 See A. Jardine [12.68], R. Braidotti [12.50] or E. Grosz [12.65] for a mapping of the influence of such thinkers on contemporary feminist theory.
10 The works cited in note 9 also give examples of critiques of these thinkers. See also A. Nye [12.79].
11 J. Baudrillard [12.46], 8.
12 *Ibid.*, p. 9.
13 See J. Derrida [12.57], J.-F. Lyotard, 'One of the Things at Stake in Women's Struggles', in A. Benjamin (ed.), *The Lyotard Reader* (Oxford: Blackwell, 1989), pp. 111–21, or G. Deleuze [12.57] for examples of the fragmentation and dispersal of identity being linked to the feminine.
14 Texts dealing with Sartre's and de Beauvoir's relationship are extensive: see for example M. Le Doeuff's discussion in *Hipparchia's Choice* [12.43]. Many of the themes discussed above are given shape in de Beauvoir's novels, for example in *The Woman Destroyed*, or in her short stories, *When the Things of the Spirit Come First*. Portraits of women struggling with social contradictions and moral dilemmas and attempting, succeeding or failing to assert their freedom, complement her more theoretical work on this topic. Such themes are also given poignant expression in her autobiography, from 'dutiful daughter' to 'old age'.
15 S. de Beauvoir [12.27].
16 J.-P. Sartre, *Being and Nothingness*, trans. H. Barnes (London: Methuen, 1968).
17 S. de Beauvoir *The Second Sex* [12.28].
18 *Ibid.*, p. 13.
19 M. Le Doeuff, *Hipparchia's Choice* [12.43], 58.

20 De Beauvoir, *The Second Sex* [12.28], 15.

21 *Ibid.*, p. 28.

22 *Ibid.*, p. 29.

23 *Ibid.*, p. 16.

24 *Ibid.*, pp. 35–69.

25 *Ibid.*, p. 62.

26 *Ibid.*, p. 57.

27 See G. Lloyd [12.73], 102, for a discussion of this paradox in relation to de Beauvoir.

28 De Beauvoir, *The Second Sex* [12.28], 249.

29 *Ibid.*, p. 66. De Beauvoir also considers a Marxist analysis of sexual difference, which attributes inequalities to economic conditions and the historical development and transmission of such conditions. The division of labour which leads to the unequal distribution of property and wealth still does not explain why women should be seen as secondary, confined to the home and themselves valued as part of property. Sexual difference cuts across all class distinctions, yet in each class women are seen as subordinate. Although she agrees that at some indeterminate moment in history women became the other for men, and, once occupying a secondary role, continued to perpetuate such conditions through the centuries, she rejects the idea that the abolition of the family will resolve women's subordination, since without a fuller account of interpersonal relations (how dominant and subordinate roles between individuals come about), she argues, the inequalities may continue to exist.

30 See J. Pilardi, 'Female Eroticism in the Works of Simone de Beauvoir', in J. Allen and I. M. Young (eds) [12.44], 18–34. Another aspect of sexuality which de Beauvoir explores is the psycho-physical development of an individual in the context of the family. She agrees with Freud that women's positioning as subordinate is a consequence of her own emotional and sexual development, as a woman she identifies with or reacts against certain models of sexuality and incorporates such attitudes into her own self-understanding. But she also questions the universality of the Freudian scheme, being suspicious of the apparent inevitability with which men and women achieve their sexual identity in Freud's view, motivated by drives and prohibitions into particular socially determined roles, mainly because it represents an encroachment on her valorization of freedom.

31 See C. Duchen [12.61] for a clear historical perspective on the shifts in thinking.

32 See E. Grosz [12.66].

33 See J. Mitchell and J. Rose (eds) [12.76], or J. Gallop [12.63], for discussions of this influence. Feminist theory influenced by ego-psychology and object relations psychoanalysis, such as the work of Jessica Benjamin or Nancy Chodorow ([12.48], [12.54]) differs, in that it tends to analyse patterns of identification and difference or relations of dominance and submission between individuals, rather than the fragmented individual of Lacanian theory.

34 J. Rose, cited in G. C. Spivak, 'Feminism and Deconstruction, Again: Negotiating Unacknowledged Maculinism', in T. Brennan (ed.) [12.51], 206–24.

35 *Ibid.*

36 J. Mitchell and J. Rose (eds) [12.76], 166.

37 *Ibid.*, p. 147.

38 Although this is Freud's phrase, it is often used to describe feminist theory influenced by psychoanalysis.

39 See J. Lechte [12.72] for an account of Kristeva's work and influences upon her.

40 J. Kristeva, *Revolution in Poetic Language* [12.35]. Only the first part is translated. The poets she discusses in the later section are Lautréamont and Mallarmé.

41 *Ibid.*, p. 22.

42 See Lechte [12.72], 32, where he writes: 'On 7 November 1955, Jacques Lacan – doctor of medicine, psychoanalyst, friend of surrealism – "officially" announced his famous "return to Freud" in a paper given at a neuro-psychiatric clinic in Vienna.' See J. Lacan, 'The Freudian Thing, or the Meaning of the Return to Freud in Psychoanalysis' in [12.71], 114–45.

43 Lacan writes: 'It is the name-of-the-father that we must recognize as the support of the symbolic function, which from the dawn of history has identified his person with the figure of the law' [12.71], 67.

44 Kristeva, *Revolution in Poetic Language* [12.35], 25.

45 *Ibid.*

46 *Ibid.*

47 *Ibid.*, p. 26.

48 Kristeva, *About Chinese Women* [12.36], 35.

49 *Ibid.*, p. 36.

50 *Ibid.*, p. 16.

51 *Ibid.*, p. 35.

52 Kristeva 'Stabat Mater' in *Tales of Love* [12.40], and in *The Kristeva Reader* [12.41]. Quotations from *The Kristeva Reader*.

53 *Ibid.*, p. 185.

54 M. Warner [12.88].

55 Kristeva 'Stabat Mater', in [12.40], 162.

56 R. Braidotti [12.50], 219. In contrast to the so-called 'feminists of difference' stand those thinkers who see all identity as social construction, and as a consequence see the notion of sexual difference as constructed. Such thinkers as Monique Plaza and Christine Delphy return to the ground of materialist/ humanist thinking because they see the adoption of sexual difference and 'the language of the female body' as too hasty or naive, in the face of the material and social oppression which women face. While it may be timely to remind philosophy of such concerns, overall the rejection of difference may lead once again to the marginalization or postponement of issues about sexual difference, or to very specific or localized areas of concern. Monique Wittig is perhaps an example of this approach. She rejects all binarisms of male/female or masculine/ feminine, and opts for a 'third' category, the lesbian, which, in her terms, involves advancing a strategic utopia and utilizing guerrilla-type tactics of subversion. Opting out or refusing any given terms may ultimately render this tactic less than effective.

57 L. Irigaray, *Parler n'est jamais neutre* [12.12].

58 L. Irigaray 'This Sex Which is Not One', in *This Sex Which is Not One* [12.34], 23–33. Reprinted from Marks and de Courtivron (eds) (note 8), pp. 99–106.

59 L. Irigaray, *Ethique de la différence sexuelle* [12.11]. First part translated in T. Moi (ed) [12.78] as 'Sexual difference', pp. 118–32. Quotes from translation.

60 *Ibid.*, p. 118.
61 Irigaray, *This Sex* [12.34], 78.
62 Irigaray, 'Sexual difference' (note 59), p. 119.
63 Irigaray, *This Sex* [12.34], 149.
64 *Ibid.*, p. 159.
65 *Ibid.*, p. 150.
66 *Ibid.*, p. 74.
67 L. Irigaray, *Speculum of the Other Woman* [12.33]. See also *Marine Lover of Friedrich Nietzsche* [12.31] and *L'oubli de l'air chez Martin Heidegger* [12.10].
68 The title of the first section of *Speculum of the Other Woman*.
69 Irigaray, 'Sexual difference' (note 59), p. 122.
70 L. Irigaray, 'Divine Women', Sydney: Local Consumption Occasional Papers 8, trans. S. Muecke, from *Sexes et parentés* [12.13].
71 Irigaray, *This Sex* [12.34], 76.
72 *Ibid.*, p. 154.
73 *Ibid.*, p. 155.
74 Irigaray takes this notion from Descartes, *The Passions of the Soul*, article 53 in *The Philosophical Writings of Descartes*, vol I, trans. J. Cottingham *et al.*, Cambridge: Cambridge University Press, 1985, p. 350.
75 See L. Irigaray, *Sexes et parentés* [12.13], *Je, Tu, Nous, pour une culture de la différence* [12.15] and *Le Temps de la différence: pour une révolution pacifique* [12.14] for examples of Irigaray's recent concerns. See *The Irigaray Reader* [12.32] for representative translations, particularly pp. 157–218.
76 See *Ethique de la difference sexuelle* [12.11] or *Elemental Passions* [12.29] for examples.
77 See M. Whitford's excellent and comprehensive study [12.90] and her introduction to *The Irigaray Reader* [12.32] where she writes: 'Holding the tension here, walking this particular tightrope, is what makes her work so challenging and so insistent' (p. 13). See also R. Braidotti [12.50], 262–3.
78 M. Le Doeuff, 'Women and Philosophy' in T. Moi (ed.) [12.78], 195, revised from version printed in *Radical Philosophy*, 17 (summer 1977): 2–11. Originally from *The Philosophical Imaginary* [12.42].
79 *Ibid.*, p. 196.
80 M. Le Doeuff, *Hipparchia's Choice* [12.43].
81 R. Braidotti [12.50], 197.
82 See G. Lloyd [12.73] and L. Code, 'Experience, Knowledge and Responsibility', in M. Griffiths and M. Whitford (eds) [12.64], 187–204.
83 H. Cixous, 'Sorties' in Marks and de Courtivron (eds) (note 8), pp. 90–8.
84 H. Cixous, 'Castration or Decapitation?' [12.24], 55.
85 A. Peperzak, 'Presentation', in R. Bernasconi and S. Critchley (eds) [12.49], 51–66 (p. 54).
86 *Ibid.*, p. 53.

❧❧ SELECT BIBLIOGRAPHY ❧❧

Primary texts by de Beauvoir, Kristeva, Irigaray, Le Doeuff, Cixous

12.1 Cixous, H. 'Le Rire de la Méduse', *L'Arc (Simone de Beauvoir)*, 61 (1975): 39–54.

12.2 Cixous, H. 'Le Sexe ou la tête?' *Cahiers du GRIF*, 13 (1976): 5–15.

12.3 Cixous, H. *La Jeune Née* (en collaboration avec C. Clément), Paris: Union Générale d'Editions, 10/18, 1975.

12.4 de Beauvoir, S. *Pour une morale de l'ambiguité*, Paris: Gallimard, 1948.

12.5 de Beauvoir, S. *Le Deuxième sexe*, Paris: Gallimard, 1949.

12.6 Irigaray, L. *Speculum de l'autre femme*, Paris, Editions de Minuit, 1974.

12.7 Irigaray, L. *Ce Sexe qui n'en est pas un*, Paris, Editions de Minuit, 1977.

12.8 Irigaray, L. *Amante marine, de Friedrich Nietzsche*, Paris: Editions de Minuit, 1980.

12.9 Irigaray, L. *Passions élémentaires*, Paris: Editions de minuit, 1982.

12.10 Irigaray, L. *L'oubli de l'air chez Martin Heidegger*, Paris: Editions de Minuit, 1983.

12.11 Irigaray, L. *Ethique de la différence sexuelle*, Paris: Editions de Minuit, 1984.

12.12 Irigaray, L. *Parler n'est jamais neutre*, Paris: Editions de Minuit, 1986.

12.13 Irigaray, L. *Sexes et parentés*, Paris: Editions de Minuit, 1987.

12.14 Irigaray, L. *Le Temps de la différence: pour une révolution pacifique*, Paris: Librairie Générale Française/Livre de Poche, 1989.

12.15 Irigaray, L. *Je, Tu, Nous, pour une culture de la différence*, Paris: Grasset, 1990.

12.16 Kristeva, J. *La révolution du langage poétique; l'avant-garde à la fin du XIXe siècle, Lautréamont et Mallarmé*, Paris: Editions du Seuil, 1974.

12.17 Kristeva, J. *Des chinoises*, Paris: Editions des Femmes, 1974.

12.18 Kristeva, J. *Polylogue*, Paris: Editions du Seuil, 1977.

12.19 Kristeva, J. 'Le Temps des femmes', *33/44, Cahiers de recherche des sciences textes et documents*, 5 (winter 1979): 5–19.

12.20 Kristeva, J. *Histoires d'amour*, Paris: Denoel, 1983 and Gallimard, 1985.

12.21 Le Doeuff, M. *L'Imaginaire philosophique*, Paris: Payot, 1980.

12.22 Le Doeuff, M. *L'Etude et le rouet*, Paris: Editions du Seuil, 1989.

Translations

12.23 Cixous, H. 'The Laugh of the Medusa', trans. K. and P. Cohn, in E. Marks and I. de Courtivron (eds) *New French Feminisms*, Brighton: Harvester, 1980, pp. 254–64. Reprinted from *Signs*, 1 (summer 1976): 875–99.

12.24 Cixous, H. 'Castration or Decapitation?', trans. A. Kuhn, *Signs*, 7 (1981): 36–55.

12.25 Cixous, H. (with C. Clément) *The Newly Born Woman*, trans. B. Wing, Theory and History of Literature Series 24, Manchester: Manchester University Press, 1986.

12.26 Extract from 'Sorties' in E. Marks and I. de Courtivron (eds) *New French Feminisms*, Brighton: Harvester, 1980, pp. 90–8.

12.27 de Beauvoir, S. *Ethics of Ambiguity*, trans. B. Frechtman, Secancus: Citadel Press 1980.

12.28 de Beauvoir, S. *The Second Sex*, trans. H. M. Parshley, Harmondsworth: Penguin, 1978.

12.29 Irigaray L. *Elemental Passions*, trans. J. Collie and J. Still, London: Athlone Press, 1992.

12.30 Irigaray, L. *The Ethics of Sexual Difference*, trans. C. Burke, Ithaca: Cornell University Press, forthcoming.

12.31 Irigaray, L. *Marine Lover of Friedrich Nietzsche*, trans. G. C. Gill, New York: Columbia University Press, 1991.

12.32 Irigaray, L. *The Irigaray Reader*, ed. M. Whitford, trans. D. Macey *et al.*, Oxford: Blackwell, 1992.

12.33 Irigaray, L. *Speculum of the Other Woman*, trans. G. C. Gill, Ithaca: Cornell University Press, 1985.

12.34 Irigaray, L. *This Sex Which is Not One*, trans. C. Porter and C. Burke, Ithaca: Cornell University Press, 1985.

12.35 Kristeva, J. *Revolution in Poetic Language*, trans. M. Waller, New York: Columbia University Press, 1984 (first part translated only).

12.36 Kristeva, J. *About Chinese Women*, trans. A. Barrows, New York and London: Marion Boyars, 1977.

12.37 Kristeva, J. *Desire in Language: a Semiotic Approach to Literature and Art*, trans. S. Gora, A. Jardine, and L. Roudiez, Oxford: Blackwell, 1984 (8 essays of 20 translated).

12.38 Kristeva, J. 'Women's Time', *Signs* 7: 1 (autumn 1981): 13–55. Reprinted in N. O. Keohane, M. Z. Rosaldo, and B. G. Gelpi (eds), *Feminist Theory: A Critique of Ideology*, Chicago: University of Chicago Press, 1982 and in [12.41], pp. 187–214.

12.39 Kristeva, J. 'Julia Kristeva in Conversation with Rosalind Coward', in *ICA Document: Desire*, London: ICA, 1984, pp. 22–7.

12.40 Kristeva, J. *Tales of Love*, trans. L. S. Roudiez, New York: Columbia University Press, 1987.

12.41 Kristeva, J. *The Kristeva Reader*, ed. with an introduction by T. Moi, Oxford: Blackwell, 1986.

12.42 Le Doeuff, M. *The Philosophical Imaginary*, trans. C. Gordon, London: Athlone, 1986.

12.43 Le Doeuff, M. *Hipparchia's Choice: An Essay Concerning Women, Philosophy etc.*, trans. T. Selous, Oxford: Blackwell, 1991.

Other works and criticisms

12.44 Allen, J. and Young, I. M. (eds) *The Thinking Muse: Feminism and Modern French Philosophy*, Bloomington: Indiana University Press, 1989.

12.45 Atack, M. 'The Other; Feminist', *Paragraph*, 8 (Oct. 1986): 25–39.

12.46 Baudrillard, J. *Seduction*, trans. B. Singer, London: Macmillan, 1990 (*De la seduction*, Paris: Galilée, 1979).

12.47 Benhabib, S. and Cornell, D. (eds) *Feminism as Critique*, Oxford: Blackwell, 1987.

12.48 Benjamin, J. *The Bonds of Love: Psychoanalysis, Feminism and the Problem of Domination*, London: Virago, 1990.

12.49 Bernasconi, R. and Critchley, S. (eds) *Re-reading Levinas*, Bloomington: Indiana University Press, 1991.

12.50 Braidotti, R. *Patterns of Dissonance: A Study of Women in Contemporary Philosophy*, London: Polity Press, 1991.

12.51 Brennan, T. (ed.) *Between Feminism and Psychoanalysis*, London: Routledge, 1989.

12.52 Burke, C. 'Romancing the Philosophers: Luce Irigaray', in D. Hunter (ed.) *Seduction and Theory; Feminist Readings on Representation and Rhetoric*, Chicago: University of Illinois Press, 1981, pp. 226–40.

12.53 Butler, J. *Gender Trouble: Feminism and the Subversion of Identity*, London: Routledge, 1990.

12.54 Chodorow, N. *The Reproduction of Mothering: Psychoanalysis and the Sociology of Gender*, Berkeley: University of California Press, 1978.

12.55 Conley, V. A. *Hélène Cixous: Writing the Feminine*, Lincoln: University of Nebraska Press, 1984.

12.56 Deleuze, G. *Différence et répétition*, Paris: PUF, 1969.

12.57 Derrida, J. *Eperons/Spurs, the styles of Nietzsche*, trans. B. Harlow, Chicago: University of Chicago Press, 1978.

12.58 Derrida, J. 'Women in the Beehive: An Interview with Jacques Derrida', *Subjects/Objects*, 2 (1984). Reprinted in A. Jardine and P. Smith (eds) *Men in Feminism*, London: Methuen, 1987.

12.59 Derrida, J. and Conley, V. A. 'Voice ii', *Boundary 2*, 12: 2 (1984): 180–6.

12.60 Derrida, J. and McDonald, C. V. 'Choreographies', *Diacritics*, 12 (summer, 1982): 66–76.

12.61 Duchen, C. *Feminism in France from May '68 to Mitterand*, London: Routledge & Kegan Paul, 1986.

12.62 Eisenstein, H. and Jardine, A. (eds) *The Future of Difference* Boston: G. K. Hall, 1980.

12.63 Gallop, J. *Feminism and Psychoanalysis: The Daughter's Seduction*, London: Macmillan, 1982.

12.64 Griffiths, M., and Whitford, M. (eds) *Feminist Perspectives in Philosophy*, London: Macmillan, 1988.

12.65 Grosz, E. *Sexual Subversions*, Sydney: Allen & Unwin, 1989.

12.66 Grosz, E. *Jacques Lacan: A Feminist Introduction*, London: Routledge, 1990.

12.67 Harding, S. and Hintikka, M. *Discovering Reality: Feminist Perspectives on Epistemology, Metaphysics, Methodology and the Philosophy of Science*, Dordrecht: Reidel, 1983.

12.68 Jardine, A. *Gynesis. Configurations of Women and Modernity*, Ithaca: Cornell University Press, 1985.

12.69 Kant, I. 'Of the Distinction of the Beautiful and the Sublime in the Interrelations of the Sexes', in *Observations on the Feeling of the Beautiful and the Sublime*, trans. J. T. Goldthwaite (1763) Berkeley: University of California Press, 1960.

12.70 Kofman, S. *The Enigma of Woman: Women in Freud's Writing*, Ithaca: Cornell University Press, 1985.

12.71 Lacan, J. *Ecrits: A Selection*, trans. A. Sheridan, London: Tavistock, 1977.

12.72 Lechte, J. *Julia Kristeva*, London: Routledge, 1991.

12.73 Lloyd, G. *The Man of Reason. 'Male' and 'Female' in Western Philosophy*, London: Macmillan, 1984.

12.74 Miller, N. K. (ed.) *The Poetics of Gender*, New York, Columbia University Press, 1986.

12.75 Mitchell, J. *Psychoanalysis and Feminism*, Harmondsworth: Pelican, 1974.

12.76 Mitchell, J. and Rose, J. (eds) *Feminine Sexuality: Jacques Lacan and the Ecole Freudienne*, trans. J. Rose, London: Macmillan, 1985.

12.77 Moi, T. *Sexual/Textual Politics: Feminist Literary Theory*, London: Methuen, 1985.

12.78 Moi, T. (ed.) *French Feminist Thought: A Reader*, Oxford: Basil Blackwell, 1988.

12.79 Nye, A. *Feminist Theory and the Philosophies of Man*, London: Routledge, 1988.

12.80 Okin, S. M. *Women in Western Political Thought*, Princeton: Princeton University Press, 1979.

12.81 Pateman, C. *The Sexual Contract*, Cambridge: Polity Press, 1988.

12.82 Pateman, C. *The Disorder of Women: Democracy, Feminism and Political Theory*, Cambridge: Polity Press, 1990.

12.83 Schiach, M. *Hélène Cixous: A Politics of Writing*, London: Routledge, 1991.

12.84 Schopenhauer, A. *The Essential Schopenhauer*, London: Unwin Books, 1962.

12.85 Spivak, G. C. 'Displacement and the Discourse of Woman', in M. Krupnick (ed.) *Displacement: Derrida and After*, Bloomington: Indiana University Press, 1983, pp. 169–91.

12.86 Vetterling-Braggin, M., Elliston, F., and English, J. (eds) *Feminism and Philosophy*, Totowa: Littlefield, Adams & Co., 1977.

12.87 Waite, M. E. (ed.) *A History of Women Philosophers*, 4 volumes, The Hague: Martinus Nijhoff, 1987.

12.88 Warner, M. *Alone of All Her Sex*, London: Picador, 1981.

12.89 White, A. 'L'Eclatement du sujet: The Theoretical Work of Julia Kristeva', Birmingham Centre for Contemporary Cultural Studies, Stencilled Occasional Paper 49, 1977.

12.90 Whitford, M. *Luce Irigaray: Philosophy in the Feminine*, London: Routledge, 1991.

12.91 Wilcox, H., McWatters, K., Thompson, A. and Williams, R. (eds) *The Body and the Text: Hélène Cixous, Reading and Teaching*, London: Harvester, 1990.

12.92 Wittig, M. *The Lesbian Body*, trans. Peter Owen, New York: Avon, 1986 [*Le Corps lesbien*, Paris: Editions de Minuit, 1973].

12.93 Young-Bruehl, E. *Mind and the Body Politic*, London: Routledge, 1988.

CHAPTER 13
Deconstruction and Derrida

Simon Critchley and Timothy Mooney

❦❖❦

❦ DERRIDIAN DECONSTRUCTION[1] ❦

In the last twenty-five years or so, particularly in the English-speaking world, no philosopher has attracted more notoriety, controversy and misunderstanding than Jacques Derrida. Caricatural summaries of deconstruction and 'deconstructionism' abound in introductory text-books, newspaper articles, radio and television programmes. The word 'deconstruction' has found a home in everyday language, and positions pro and contra Derrida are taken up and held with a vehemence that is difficult for the uninitiated to grasp. 'Derrida' and 'deconstruction' have become integral terms in the debate on the meaning of western culture in the late twentieth century. However, in this chapter I would like to take a step back from the sound and fury of the cultural debate around Derrida and sketch, as clearly and simply as possible, what appears to take place in deconstruction, that is to say, what is the method of reading employed by Derrida and what, in brief, are the consequences of the latter for the philosophical tradition.

What is deconstruction? Or, as it is perhaps initially easier to give a negative response to this question, what is *not* deconstruction? Employing a short text of Derrida written in 1983 and published in 1985, 'Letter to a Japanese Friend', which was specifically written in order to aid the possible translation of the word *déconstruction* into Japanese, one can quickly sketch some important caveats. First, Derrida insists that deconstruction is not negative; it is not a process of demolition (which does not automatically entail that deconstruction is positive – [13.17], 390). Furthermore, deconstruction needs to be sharply distinguished from analysis, which presupposes a reduction of entities to their simple or essential elements, elements which themselves would

441

stand in need of deconstruction. Crucially, deconstruction is not critique, either in the general or Kantian sense; Derrida writes, 'The instance of the *krinein* or of *krisis* (decision, choice, judgement, discernment) is itself, as is moreover the entire apparatus of transcendental critique, one of the essential "themes" or "objects" of deconstruction' ([13.17], 390). Similarly, deconstruction is not a method or way that can be followed in the activity of interpretation. This is also to say that deconstruction cannot be reduced to being a methodology (amongst competing methodologies) in the human or natural sciences, or becoming a technical procedure assimilable by academics and taught in educational institutions ([13.17], 390–1). In addition, deconstruction is not an *act* produced and commanded by a subject, nor is it an *operation* that sets to work on a text or an institution. Derrida concludes the 'Letter' characteristically by writing, 'What deconstruction is not? But everything! What is deconstruction? But nothing!' ([13.17], 392). All ontological statements of the form 'deconstruction is x' miss the point a priori, for it is precisely the ontological presuppositions of the copula that provide one of the enduring 'themes' of deconstruction. Rather, carefully avoiding the verb 'to be', Derrida claims that deconstruction takes place ('a lieu'), and that it does so wherever there 'is' something ('où il y a quelque chose'). Such is the *enigma* (Derrida's word – [13.17], 391) of deconstruction: it cannot be defined and therefore resists translation; it is not an entity or a thing, it is not univocal or unitary. Derrida writes, paying careful attention to reflexivity of the statement, 'Ça se déconstruit' ('It deconstructs itself', the *Ça* being both a translation of *Es* – the id, the unconscious – and a homophone for *Sa* – 'Savoir Absolu', Absolute Knowing – [13.17], 391). It deconstructs itself wherever something takes place.

However, such a formulation, although subtle and faithful, risks being unhelpful because of its generality. Having taken on board the negative caveats in the problem of defining deconstruction, I should now like to assemble a more 'constructivist' account of deconstruction by asking the question: *how* does deconstruction take place? Derrida addressed this question concisely and lucidly in *Of Grammatology* (1967) [13.4, 13.29], in a chapter entitled, 'The Exorbitant. Question of Method'. The first essential point to make, however, trivial it may seem, is that deconstruction is always the deconstruction of a *text*. Derrida's thinking is always thinking *about* a text, from which flows the obvious corollary that deconstruction is always engaged in a *reading* of a text. The way of deconstruction is always opened through reading, what Derrida calls 'a first task, the most elementary of tasks' ([13.21], 35; [13.43], 41). Any thinking that is primarily concerned with reading will clearly be dependent upon the text that is being read. Thus, Derrida's readings are parasitic because they are close readings of texts that draw their sustenance from within the flesh of the host. What takes place in deconstruction is reading, and, I shall argue, what distinguishes deconstruction as a textual practice is *double reading*. That is to say, a reading that interlaces at least two motifs or layers of reading, most often by first repeating what Derrida calls 'the dominant interpretation' ([13.22], 265; [13.44], 143) of a text in the guise of a commentary, and second, within and through this repetition, by leaving the order of commentary and opening a text up to the blind spots or ellipses within the dominant interpretation.

Now, when Derrida reads Rousseau, he organizes his reading around the word *supplément*. It is claimed that this word is the 'blind spot' (*tâche aveugle* [13.4], 234; [13.29], 163) in Rousseau's text, a word which he employs but whose logic is veiled to him.[2] Derrida's reading of Rousseau traces the logic of this supplement, a logic which allows Rousseau's text to slip from the grip of its intentions and achieve a textual position that is other than the logocentric conceptuality that Rousseau intended to affirm. Thus, Derrida's reading of Rousseau occupies the space between the writer's intentions and the text, or between what a writer commands and fails to command in a language. It is into this space between intentions and text that Derrida inserts what he calls the 'signifying structure' ([13.4], 227; [13.29], 158) of the reading that constitutes part two of *Of Grammatology*.

How does one perform a deconstructive reading? In 'The Exorbitant. Question of Method', Derrida pauses in his reading of Rousseau in order to justify his own methodological principles. The signifying structure of a deconstructive reading cannot, he claims, simply be produced through the 'respectful doubling of commentary' ([13.4], 227; [13.29], 158). Although Derrida is acutely aware of the exigencies of the traditional instruments of commentary as an 'indispensable guardrail' in critical production, he claims that commentary 'has always only *protected*, it has never *opened*, a reading' (*ibid.*).

Here I would like to pause for a moment to consider what Derrida could possibly mean by the word 'commentary' in this context: is he claiming, oblivious to the achievements of Heideggerian and especially Gadamerian hermeneutics, that there can be a pure commentary or literal repetition of a text that is not already an interpretation? Derrida corrects and clarifies the above remarks from *Of Grammatology* in one of his responses to Gerald Graff in the 'Afterword' to *Limited Inc*. Derrida writes that 'the moment of what I called, perhaps clumsily, "doubling commentary" does not suppose the self-identity of "meaning", but a relative stability of the dominant interpretation (including the auto-interpretation) of the text being commented upon'. He continues, 'perhaps I should not have called it commentary' ([13.22], 265;

[13.44], 143). Thus, for Derrida, the moment of commentary refers to the reproducibility and stability of the dominant interpretation of a text, for example the traditional logocentric reading (or misreading) of Rousseau. Commentary is always already interpretation and Derrida does not believe in the possibility of a pure and simple repetition of a text. However, and this is a crucial caveat, there is an unavoidable need for a competence in reading and writing such that the dominant interpretation of a text can be reconstructed as a necessary and indispensable layer or moment of reading. 'Otherwise', Derrida writes, echoing a sentence from *Of Grammatology* effectively ignored by many of its opponents and proponents alike, 'one could indeed say just anything at all and I have never accepted saying, or being encouraged to say, just anything at all' ([13.22], 267; [13.44], 144–5; cf. [13.4], 227; [13.29], 158).

Derrida goes on to argue that the moment of 'commentary' or of the dominant interpretation reflects a minimal *consensus* concerning the intelligibility of texts, establishing what a given text means for a community of readers. Although such a search for consensus is 'actively interpretive', Derrida adds, 'I believe that no research is possible in a community (for example, academic) without the prior search for this minimal consensus' ([13.22], 269; [13.44], 146). Thus, although 'commentary' alone does not open a genuine reading, the latter is not possible without the moment of commentary, without a scholarly competence in reading, understanding and writing, without a knowledge of texts in their original languages (for example, Rousseau's or Derrida's French), without knowing the corpus of an author as a whole, without knowing the multiple contexts – political, literary, philosophical, historical and so forth – which determine a given text or are determined by that text. This is what one might call the deconstructive duty of scholarship. I would go further and claim that there is a hermeneutic principle of fidelity – one might even say 'an "ethico-political duty" ' ('un "devoir éthico-politique" ') ([13.22], 249; [13.44], 135) – and a minimal working notion of truth as *adaequatio* underlying deconstructive reading, as its primary layer of reading. If deconstructive reading is to possess any demonstrative necessity, it is initially in virtue of how faithfully it reconstructs the dominant interpretation of a text in a layer of 'commentary'.

To choose an extreme example, in *Limited Inc.* every word of Searle's 'Reiterating the Differences: A Reply to Derrida' is repeated or re-reiterated. Derrida clearly views this as a way of responding responsibly to the brutality of Searle's essay, which decides to 'insult' ([13.22], 257; [13.44], 139) Derrida's work – for example Searle writes of 'Derrida's distressing penchant for saying things that are obviously false'[3] – rather than engaging in the necessary critical demonstration.

Thus, bearing the above qualifications in mind, one might say a reading is *true* in the first instance to the extent that it faithfully repeats or corresponds to what is said in the text that is being commented upon. This is perhaps the reason why Derrida quotes at such length and with such regularity in his writings, and it is also the basis for his accusation of falsity against Habermas's critique of his work in 'Excursus on Leveling the Genre Distinction between Philosophy and Literature', where Derrida is not cited a single time ([13.22], 244; [13.44], 156).[4]

Returning to *Of Grammatology*, it is clear that although the respectful repetition of the text which 'commentary' produces fails to open a reading, this in no way entails that one should then transgress the text by reductively relating it to some referent or signified outside of textuality (i.e. historical material or the psychobiography of the author). To determine textual signifiers by referring them to a governing signified – for example, to read *A la recherche* in terms of Proust's asthma – would be to give what Derrida calls a transcendent reading. The axial proposition of *Of Grammatology* is 'il n'y a pas de hors-texte' ('there is no outside text' [13.4], 227; [13.29], 158), or again, 'il n'y a rien hors du texte' ('there is nothing outside of the text' [13.4], 233; [13.29], 163). One should be attentive to the nuanced difference between these two sentences: the first claims that there is no 'outside-text', no text outside; whilst the second claims that there is *nothing* outside of the text, the text outside is nothing), implying by this that any reading that refers the text to some signified outside of textuality is illusory. Within the logocentric epoch, the textual signifier (and writing, inscription, the mark and the trace in general) has always been determined as secondary, as a fallen exteriority preceded by a signified. A deconstructive reading must, therefore, remain within the limits of textuality, hatching its eggs within the flesh of the host.

Thus, the 'methodological' problem for deconstruction becomes one of discovering how a reading can remain internal to the text and within the limits of textuality without merely repeating the text in the manner of a 'commentary'. To borrow the adverbial phrase with which Derrida describes his reading of Husserl, deconstructive reading must move *à travers* the text, *traversing* the space between a repetitive commentary and a metatextual interpretation, '*Traversing [à travers]* Husserl's text, that is to say, in a reading which cannot simply be that of commentary nor that of interpretation' ([13.2], 98; [13.27], 88). By opening up this textual space that is other to 'commentary' or interpretation, a certain distance is created between deconstructive reading and logocentric conceptuality. The signifying structure of a deconstructive reading traverses a space that is other to logocentrism and which attempts eccentrically to exceed the orbit of its conceptual totality. In an important and explicit reference to the 'goal' or 'aim' of deconstruction, Derrida writes, 'We wanted to attain the point of a certain exteriority with respect to the totality of the logocentric epoch. From this point of exteriority a certain deconstruction of this totality... could be broached [*entamée*]' ([13.4], 231; [13.29], 161–2). It is from such a point of exteriority that deconstruction could cut into or penetrate the totality, thereby displacing it. The goal of deconstruction, therefore, is to locate a point of otherness within philosophical or logocentric conceptuality and then to deconstruct this conceptuality from that position of alterity.

It is at this point that the concept of double reading can be properly understood. If the first moment of reading is the rigorous and scholarly reconstruction of the dominant interpretation of a text, its *vouloir-dire*, its intended meaning, in the guise of a commentary, then the second moment of reading, in virtue of which deconstruction obeys a double necessity, is *the destabilization of the stability of the dominant interpretation* ([13.22], 271; [13.44], 147). It is the movement of traversing the text which enables the reading to obtain a position of alterity or exteriority from where the text can be deconstructed. The second moment brings the text into contradiction with itself, opening its intended meaning, its *vouloir-dire*, onto an alterity which goes against what the text wants to say or mean ('ce que le texte veut dire'). Derrida often articulates this double reading around a semantic ambivalence in the usage of a particular word, like *supplément* in Rousseau, *pharmakon* in Plato or *Geist* in Heidegger. It is of absolutely crucial importance that this second moment, that of alterity, should be shown to arise necessarily out of the first moment of repetitive commentary. Derrida ventriloquizes this double structure through the mouth of Heidegger in *De l'esprit*: 'That is why, without opposing myself to that of which I am trying to think the most matinal possibility, without even using words other than those of the tradition, I follow the path of a repetition which crosses the path of the wholly other. The wholly other announces itself within the most rigorous repetition ([13.18], 184).' Thus, by following the path of a repetition, the *Wiederholung* of a text or a tradition, one inevitably crosses the path of something wholly other, something that cannot be reduced to what the text or tradition wants to say. It is at this point that the similarities between Derridian deconstruction and Heideggerian *Destruktion* become apparent. Indeed, Derrida initially employed the term *déconstruction* as an attempt to render into French the Heideggerian notions of *Destruktion* (de-struction, or non-negative de-structuring) and *Abbau* (demolition or, better, dismantling – [13.17], 388). For the Heidegger of *Being and Time*, the working out or elaboration (*Ausarbeitung*) of the question of the meaning of Being does not become truly concrete until the ontological tradition – that is, the tradition that has forgotten the question of

Being, and more precisely the *temporal* dimension of this question –
has been completely repeated (*wiederholen*) and deconstructed.[5] In the
1962 lecture 'Time and Being', *Abbau* is presented (and presented,
moreover, as a synonym for *Destruktion*) as the progressive removal
of the concealing layers that have covered over the first Greek rending
of Being as presence (*Anwesenheit*). The repetition of the metaphysical
tradition is a dismantling that reveals its unsaid *as* unsaid.[6] Returning
to Derrida, it is the belonging together or interlacing of these two
moments or paths of reading – repetition and alterity – that best
describes the double gesture of deconstructive reading: the figure of
the chiasmus.

What takes place in deconstruction is double reading, that is, a
form of reading that obeys the double injunction for both repetition
and the alterity that arises within that repetition. Deconstruction opens
a reading by locating a moment of alterity within a text. In Derrida's
reading of Rousseau, the concept of the supplement is the lever that is
employed to show how Rousseau's discourse is inscribed within the
general text, a domain of textuality irreducible to logocentric conceptuality. In this way one can see how a moment of blindness in a
logocentric text grants insight into an alterity that exceeds logocentrism.
As Derrida remarks in an interview with Richard Kearney, 'deconstruction is not an enclosure in nothingness, but an openness towards the
other'.[7] What takes place in deconstruction is a highly determinate
form of double reading which pursues alterities within texts, primarily
philosophical texts. In this way, deconstruction opens a discourse on
the other to philosophy, an otherness that has been dissimulated or
appropriated by the logocentric tradition. Philosophy, particularly in
its Hegelian moment, has always insisted on thinking its other (art,
religion, nature, etc.) as its *proper* other and thereby appropriating it
and losing sight of its otherness. The philosophical text has always
believed itself to be in control of the margin of its own volume ([13.5],
1; [13.30], x). As Emmanuel Levinas points out in 'Transcendence and
Height', philosophy might be defined as the activity of assimilating all
otherness into the Same.[8] Such a definition would seem to be accurate
in so far as the philosophical tradition has always attempted to understand and *think* the plurality and alterity of a manifold of entities
through a reduction of plurality to unity and alterity to sameness. The
same gesture is repeated throughout the philosophical tradition,
whether it be in Plato, where the plurality of the instances of an entity
(*phainomena*) are understood in relation to a unifying form (*eidos*). Or
whether it be Aristotle, where *philosophia prote* (that is to say, metaphysics) is the attempt to understand the Being of a plurality of entities
in relation to a unifying substance (*ousia*), and, ultimately, a divine
ousia: the god (*to theion*). Or, indeed, whether it be in terms of Kantian

epistemology, where the manifold or plurality of intuitions are brought into unity and sameness by being placed under concepts which are regulated by the categories of the understanding (and other examples could be cited).

The very activity of thinking, which lies at the basis of epistemological, ontological and veridical comprehension, is the reduction of plurality to unity and alterity to sameness. The activity of philosophy, the very task of thinking, is the reduction and domestication of otherness. In seeking to think the other, its otherness is reduced or appropriated to our understanding. To think philosophically is to comprehend – *comprendre*, *comprehendere*, *begreifen*, to comprehend, to include, to seize, to grasp – and master the other, thereby reducing its alterity. As Rodolphe Gasché points out, 'Western philosophy is in essence the attempt to domesticate Otherness, since what we understand by thought is nothing but such a project.'9 As the attempt to attain a point of exteriority to logocentrism, deconstruction may therefore be 'understood' as the desire to keep open a dimension of alterity which can neither be reduced, comprehended, nor, strictly speaking, even *thought* by philosophy. To say that the goal of Derridian deconstruction is not simply the *unthought* of the tradition, but rather 'that-which-cannot-be-thought' is to engage neither in sophistical rhetoric nor negative theology. It is rather to point towards that which philosophy is unable to say.

Derridian deconstruction attempts to situate, 'a non-site, or a non-philosophical site, from which to question philosophy'.10 It seeks a place of exteriority, alterity or marginality irreducible to philosophy. Deconstruction is the writing of a margin that cannot be represented by philosophy. In question is an other to philosophy that has never been and cannot become philosophy's other, but an other within which philosophy becomes inscribed.

However (and this is crucial), the paradox that haunts Derrida's and all deconstructive discourse is that the only language that is available to deconstruction is that of philosophy or logocentrism. Thus to take up a position exterior to logocentrism, if such a thing were possible, would be to risk starving oneself of the very linguistic resources with which one must deconstruct logocentrism. The deconstructive reader is like a tightrope walker who risks 'ceaselessly falling back inside that which he deconstructs' ([13.4], 25; [13.29], 14). Deconstruction is a double reading that operates within a double bind of both belonging to a tradition, a language and a philosophical discourse, and at the same time being unable to belong to the latter. This ambiguous situation of belonging and not-belonging describes the problem of *closure*.

Broadly stated,11 the problem of closure describes the duplicitous historical moment – *now* – when language, conceptuality, institutions and philosophy itself show themselves to belong to a logocentric tradition which is theoretically exhausted whilst at the same time searching for the breakthrough from that tradition. The problem of closure describes the liminal situation of modernity out of which the deconstructive problematic arises and which Derrida inherits from Heidegger. Closure is the double refusal both of remaining within the limits of the tradition and of the possibility of transgressing that limit within philosophical language. At the moment of historical and philosophical closure, deconstructive reading takes place as the disturbance, disruption or interruption of the limit that divides the inside from the outside of the tradition. A deconstructive reading shows how a text is dependent upon the presuppositions of a metaphysics of presence of logocentrism, which that text might attempt either to champion or dissimulate, whilst at the same time showing how that text radically questions the metaphysics it presupposes, entering into contradiction with itself, and pointing the way towards a thinking that would be other to logocentrism. Closure is the hinge that articulates this double and strictly undecidable movement between logocentrism and its other. Deconstruction(s) take(s) place as the articulation of this hinge.

Simon Critchley

➳ PHILOSOPHICAL ROOTS AND ➳ BIBLIOGRAPHICAL HISTORY

Throughout the history of thought new philosophies have unfolded as reactions to or developments of previous ones, and in this way have shown their indebtedness to their forebears. There is no field outside the philosophical tradition from which a completely new thinking could spring into being. Starting from the recognition of this fact, the first part of this section seeks to show how some of Jacques Derrida's central ideas develop out of his encounters with the work of Edmund Husserl. Charting the ground of an individual's thought with any fidelity is always a difficult exercise, the more so in Derrida's case. He has cited and displayed evidence of numerous influences, including Heidegger, Hegel, Levinas, Nietzsche, Freud and Saussure, and his own arguments have cast doubt on the possibility of uncovering simple origins or foundations. All this being said, however, the crucial importance of Husserl's phenomenology can still be clearly demonstrated. Outlining Derrida's readings of Husserl also shows that he has engaged in philosophical argumentation rather than in some esoteric anarchism that is supposedly closed off from all criticism.

The second part of this section attempts to give a concise overview of Derrida's philosophical career within the broad framework of a bibliographical history. Reference will be made to his most important works and to the way in which they follow on from certain questions articulated in the early texts. This is also a difficult task. From the close of the 1950s Derrida has published twenty-six books and innumerable articles, many of them extending into the associated regions of literary criticism, aesthetics and politics. These factors alone militate against the adequacy of short summaries and chronological surveys, quite apart from specifically theoretical objections. Perhaps the best combination of clarity and continuity lies in confining one's attention to those philosophical concerns that stand out most strongly in the Derridian constellation. It is this approach that has been adopted here.

It was as a teenager in Algeria that Derrida first became interested in philosophy. He read Sartre copiously, and was spurred into enrolling for pre-university classes after hearing a radio broadcast by Albert Camus. In 1949 Derrida went to Paris, where he commenced his studies under Jean Hyppolite at the Ecole Normale Supérieure. As far as can be ascertained, Derrida's interest in Sartre waned from the moment he became acquainted with the work of Husserl. The latter's phenomenology, as opposed to the version propounded by Sartre, appeared to Derrida as an inescapable method of analysis. As recently as 1980, Derrida has remarked that he still sees it, although in a different way, as a discipline of incomparable rigour.[12]

Derrida's first article was entitled ' "Genesis and Structure" and Phenomenology'. Published in 1959, this was a development of part of his master's thesis. The problem of genesis or origin and structure had emerged as a result of Husserl's insistence that the meanings of those objects and states of affairs taken as irreducible to what we call the conscious self are never immediately given from outside. There are no transparently intelligible meanings in phenomena which would fall like manna from a heavenly place (*topos ouranios*) and strike the mind ready-made. In all these cases meaning demands not just a subject but a complex subjective contribution. All of the objects or states of affairs that we can entertain must be taken as more than an amorphous fuzz of unceasing mutation. Without at least a relative constancy in phenomena, recognition and discrimination would be impossible. Yet these constancies themselves presuppose a wider horizonal structure within which we ourselves place every appearance. Recognition and discrimination point to a surround of expectations which phenomenology seeks to make explicit. We expect physical objects, for instance, to have currently invisible aspects which can be brought into view, or made present, as we vary our perspective. We also expect physical things to behave in certain ways. On this view everything experienced is implicitly contextualized, whether it pertains to the physical, scientific or cultural worlds.

Unlike the Kantian categories of experience and understanding, Husserl's horizons are not fixed but constantly evolving. Through successive acts of perception we adjust each horizon so that it more comprehensively contextualizes objects or states of affairs. Meaning emerges from a weave made up of changing horizons and their contents. This creative emergence of meaning Husserl calls *constitution*. To explain any constituted phenomenon adequately, we have to give a structural description of this phenomenon and of our present mode of consciousness of it. But we also have to give a genetic or originary description of the evolving horizon which the phenomenon and our mode of consciousness of it presuppose.

According to Derrida, certain insoluble problems ensue from this approach, stemming from the fact that the isolation and description of the objective structures of phenomena and of the horizons through which they are revealed is, on Husserl's premises, an infinite task. Because we must describe ever anew our continually evolving horizons, we will at the same time be altering our correlative characterizations of the objective structures of phenomena. What now appear as foundational structures could well be shown to be derivative in the future. Being caught up in history, we can never claim to encounter closed or finished structures, that is,' structures that would be immune from modification and deposition. Yet another problem is that of discerning where our horizons end and where the objective structures of phenomena begin. There are no sure criteria for distinguishing between the 'productive' and 'revelatory' aspects of certain constituted meanings.

Derrida does not claim any great novelty in this analysis, and he stresses that these difficulties could never have been brought to light were they not built upon Husserl's powers of insight. It is the critical drive in Husserl that foregrounds these problems as he attempts to get back to the things themselves, to describe faithfully the phenomena presented to consciousness.

Derrida does not accept the Husserlian argument that the living present (*lebendige Gegenwart*) of human consciousness is the ultimate locus and ground of meaning. He takes over the structuralist position that meaning depends on sign-systems that transcend the intentional control of individual subjects. There is no self and no other than can be understood apart from signs. The move towards this position is marked in Derrida's first book, *Edmund Husserl's Origin of Geometry, an Introduction* (1962) [13.1; 13.26]. All the problems treated in this early text, according to Derrida, have continued to organize the work he has subsequently embarked upon.[13]

In *The Origin of Geometry* (1936), written shortly before his death and published only posthumously, Husserl was concerned with the communicability of ideal objects, such as geometrical formations, that are initially reached or constituted in an individual human consciousness. Being universal and non-perspectival, geometrical idealities are free from the contingencies of spatio-temporal existence, and in terms of perfection, argues Husserl, they can serve as the model for any object whatsoever. But precisely because of their ideality, they must in principle be accessible to every rational being, capable of being objects for all conscious subjects. One of the core concerns in *The Origin of Geometry* is to explain how a geometrical formation which is initially confined to the solitary psychological life of the first or proto-geometer can become intersubjective, that is, an object for the whole human community.

Husserl's immediate answer is that it is speech which brings ideality into the public realm, allowing the proto-geometer to share his or her discovery with others in the same community. But it is only writing that allows the discovery to be transmitted from generation to generation, thus giving it a history. Through writing or inscription, the geometrical formation is passed down to others, who add corollaries and formulate further theorems and axioms. Through successive generations, new layers are added on top of the original formation. This is the path of scientific progress, and indeed of cultural development in general, and it resembles an elevated rock stratum composed of various sedimented layers. Through encoding the original discovery, the proto-geometer sends it forward in a productive passage through time. The price of productive written transmission, however, is the loss of the conscious intentional states of the proto-geometer's mind that led to his or her discovery. Writing is an autonomous field that can virtualize a discovery, separating a bare formation from the conscious acts of constitution that are communicable through the tone and facial expressions of everyday speech. This loss is itself a condition of progress, for later geometers have to take the bare formation as a ready-made given so as to have the time to improve on it. Quite apart from the comparative shortness of wakeful life, our bodily needs leave us little enough time for research. All the productive arts and sciences, argues Husserl, have to progress in this way. But it is just this element of loss in writing that has led to the contemporary crisis in western civilization. We have lost our roots, our sense of where we came from, of how and why our scientific and cultural traditions began.

Husserl regards this state of crisis as endemic – it can never be overcome. The intentional states of the founders of our traditions are lost for ever, and there is no return-enquiry (*Rückfrage*) that could recover them. But if we cannot reactivate the primordial *archē* of a science in our present age, argues Husserl, we can at least envisage its *telos*, which is that of a complete system of knowledge, of absolutely transparent and univocal understanding. This is not something that can ever be fully actualized; rather it functions as a infinite ideal. The building up of a science on top of an original formation can be understood as a gradual process of approximation towards this ideal. The actual formation can be understood as an essential element within this process that contributes to its determination. In this regard it is described by Husserl as an 'Idea in the Kantian sense'. Only efficacious through writing, the ideal of objective and thorough knowledge and the correlative Idea in the Kantian sense may not constitute a knowledge of origins, but they do show that our scientific and cultural objects are not meaningless when recontextualized.

In his reading of this text, Derrida seeks to show that certain radical conclusions follow from Husserl's premises. These were already touched upon by the latter, but never developed, perhaps because he well understood the problems they would pose for a text that valorized the notion of a unique and transparent origin of geometry and of other traditions in the living present of human consciousness. Derrida is careful to emphasize Husserl's acute awareness of the significance of language, and of writing in particular. Here we see the first direct articulation of the idea that language is more than a material body that receives an already constituted truth. Contributing to the clarification and systematization of a discovery, it is not a passive receptacle of something given ready-made. Constituting ideal objects as definite and repeatable formations, it is a necessary condition of truth, in principle as well as in fact:

> Husserl insists that truth is not fully objective, i.e, ideal, intelligible for everyone and indefinitely perdurable, as long as it cannot be said *and* written. Since this perdurability is truth's very sense, the conditions for its survival are included in its very life . . . freedom is only possible precisely from the *moment* truth *can* in general be said and written, i.e., *on condition* that this *can* be done. Paradoxically, the possibility of being written [*possibilité graphique*] permits the ultimate freeing of ideality . . . the *ability* of sense to be linguistically embodied is the only means by which sense becomes nonspatiotemporal.[14]

This material condition of truth can also jettison what Husserl sees as the original meaning of a truth, its intentional origin. In philosophy and literature, as well as in the natural sciences, Husserl well appreciates the possibilities of loss and misunderstanding brought into play by writing. But what he fails to account for, Derrida goes on to argue, is the possibility of the total loss of a message in the autonomous field of writing. This eventuality is to be distinguished from an empirical catastrophe, such as a worldwide burning of books and defacing of monuments. In this case writing would be materially destroyed and the message consumed. What Derrida is adverting to is the possibility of the complete disappearance of a message in a writing that remains fully intact in the world. The writing that gives life after death to a message can just as well bury that message. As Derrida points out, we can see abundant evidence of this in those prehistoric artefacts and monuments that silently defy all comprehension and translation. That which is the condition of transmission through the ages is not a guarantor of the success of any such transmission.

Derrida rejects Husserl's suggestion that the intentional origin of geometry was unique to one particular person at one time. He maintains that the unpacking of the Idea in the Kantian sense undercuts any such suggestion. This, we may recall, is the notion of an ideal object as an essential element in a process of approximation towards a complete system of objective, univocal knowledge. Derrida's argument is that a person would have no appreciation of the ideality of geometry without possessing this notion, even if they chanced upon a bare geometrical formation in the empirical world. The proto-geometer could never understand the significance of such formations without some awareness of science, of its ultimate end.[15] This awareness would include some of the conditions that a formation would have to fulfill in order to have an essential status in any science. For this reason, the Idea in the Kantian sense is not just the end of geometry – it is its very origin. Anyone who attains to this idea begins in just as original and authentic a fashion as the chronologically first geometer, since it is not specific to any one culture at any one time. Apart from a brute empirical history of ownership and copyrights, Derrida wonders whether we can ever speak of a once-off or unrepeatable origin of geometry. Since the intentional origin of geometry need not be unique to any one factual individual, geometry could in principle have an infinite number of births and birth certificates, each one upstaging its forebears. On this view, it can be difficult to divide intentional acts into ones that are original on the one hand and derivative or parasitic on the other.

Perhaps the most important caveat that Derrida has in connection with *The Origin of Geometry* pertains to Husserl's suggestion that what is lost in writing was a transparent plenitude in its own time. This is the idea that the proto-geometer was adequately aware in the living present of consciousness of what he or she was about in constituting an ideal formation. The fact that the meaning of an ideal object as an Idea in the Kantian sense is universally accessible, notes Derrida, does not entail that this meaning is adequately given in the present. In fact and in principle, the project within which we understand the ideality and objectivity of a formation cannot be realized in the living present of a human subject. The present meaning is given by virtue of an ideal which is deferred *ad infinitum*. The sign that gives the object its meaning is the sign of something for ever absent, because the realization of a complete science within which the significance of an ideal object would be transparently intelligible always recedes as we approach it. We can have the empty idea, but not that of which it is the idea. To comprehend the inability of consciousness to reach such an absolute is to comprehend the structural necessity of deferral, delay, or difference. As a structure of infinite anticipation devoid of final fulfilment, the absolute is a limit, a condition of possibility of meaning that cannot be imagined in itself alone. To make it real one would have to be an omnipotent God untrammelled by perspective and distance, eternally comprehending everything within its absolute gaze. The origin of geometry and of objectivities in general lies in a promised land which even the so-called proto-geometer never saw in the living present of consciousness. Even in its own time the past-present was never an undivided plentitude. The meaning of objectivity presupposed something that could never be brought into view.

Derrida's second book, translated as *Speech and Phenomena* [13.27], was published in 1967. Derrida has described this essay as the one which he likes most, because it raises in a 'juridicially decisive' way the 'privilege of the voice' as it occurs in western metaphysics in general and in Husserl in particular. He also says that this work can be read as the other side, the recto or verso, of the earlier *Introduction* ([13.27], 5). In the later work, Derrida focuses his attention on the Husserlian claim that the living present is based on an undivided immediacy of self-consciousness. In the *Introduction*, Derrida had already argued against the idea that we can ground the meaning of objectivity in an undivided present of consciousness. Now he will argue that this latter notion is a metaphysical illusion in itself. Reflective awareness or subjectivity is also dependent on the representation by the sign of something that cannot be made fully present.

In his account of conscious mental life in the *Logical Investigations* (1900–1), Husserl makes a distinction between a signified meaning that can be fully present to consciousness and one that can be only indirectly present. A meaning of the first type can be described as an expression (*Ausdruck*). A meaning of the second type is anything conveyed through indication (*Anzeichen*). In general terms, the world of indication is composed of those signs referring to things outside direct awareness. The function of an indicative sign is that of standing in for something that is completely or partially absent. Although it has its referent or signified, this type of sign is devoid of intrinsic meaning. To be more than an empty bearer or carrier it must be given meaning by a specific intention, though it may not transmit this in its fullness. When I read a book in which the author indicates something to me, for instance, I can grasp that something without intuiting his or her background intention as well as I could intuit an intention of my own.

In contrast to derivative indications, expressions are inherently meaningful and fully present to the self. They mean something and they express a meaning. Because an expression effectively includes content and object, it is a sign that almost immediately gives way to the actual thing that it signifies. Every expression can subsequently acquire an indicative function, for example when I communicate it to another person via speech. In this case expression is given a phonic material body. It is this vehicle that allows it to enter into the arena of intersubjectivity. I can also communicate through writing, through a graphic material body. This puts expression into the historical field that threatens the perversion and loss of meaning. Writing lacks the immediacy of speech. When I make an utterance I can hear myself speak. I concretely experience and understand an indication that has been permeated by an expression. What I say is present to me, under my intentional control. This immediacy can be lost in writing. When I write something, it can go out beyond my living present. The original immediacy is cast adrift with the indication, and fades into the dead letter on the page. Speech is the only material medium that safeguards the life of expressed intuitions, for it is a reflection of the uncontami-nated immediacy of conscious life. This is why thinking is often described as a form of self-addressed inner speech. In the actual zone of conscious life, however, Husserl does not hold that the solitary mind engages in a silent dialogue with itself. In the interior field of pre-expressive intuition, we can only imagine mercurial messages flit-ting through the galleries of the transcendental ego. We have no need to communicate anything at this level because our meanings are immediately experienced and understood. Not even the blink of an eye can be held to separate an intention and my intuition of it. In the pure self-relation of reflective consciousness, the realm of signs is really quite useless (*ganz zwecklos*).

Derrida rejects Husserl's initial prioritization of speech over writ-ing, which he terms *phonocentrism*. This privilege of the voice is regarded by Derrida as a metaphysical assumption foreign to the rigour of a thoroughgoing phenomenological philosophy. Derrida points to the fact that Husserl characterizes most conscious intentions as imper-fect or unfulfilled. In perception I intend the entire bureau that I am leaning on. Yet it is only partially present to me as a hard and black horizontal surface that I see with my eyes and touch with my elbows. In imagination I intend the cellars of Ludwig of Bavaria's fairytale castle. These are only present to me in so far as they can be envisaged without acquaintance or description. It is linguistic signs that stand in for these absences. We use these to denote objects and states of affairs that are either indirectly given or not given at all. On this description, signs can operate perfectly well in the complete absence of their object, and indeed this is one of their essential functions. But what about cases where the object, so to speak, is the human subject itself? We have to ask whether propositions with reflexive pronouns are properly meaningful in the absence of the subject that communicates them.

Husserl draws back from affirming this. He admits that we can understand the ordinary everyday meaning of a mathematical proposition, for example, quite apart from the circumstances of our use of it. We can read it without thinking of a particular person. But in a statement that uses the word 'I', such as 'I am alive', Husserl states that we can glean its proper meaning only from the individual intentions that permeate it at the time of its utterance or inscription. If we were to read this statement without knowing who wrote it, says Husserl, it might not be meaningless, but it would be alienated from its normal meaning. According to Derrida, however, such a proposition can and does function normally in the absence of a speaker or writer. 'I am alive' retains its normal meaning even when the original subject is dead or fictitious. The meaning borne in the reflexive sign or proposition does not have to be fulfilled by a personal intuition. Language has a life of its own in writing, and there is no good reason to think why the situation is any different in speech. Here also we have to allow for the transmigration of signs that have their own meaning. If the expressed personal intuition that my voice breathes into the sign were to give it its normal meaning, and if this were to stay with the sign, then everyone would have to use my own private language. According to Derrida:

> The absence of intuition – and therefore of the subject of the intuition – is not only *tolerated* by speech; it is *required* by the general structure of signification, when considered *in itself*. It is radically requisite: the total absence of the subject and object of a statement – the death of the writer and/or the disappearance of the objects he was able to describe – does not prevent a text from 'meaning' something. On the contrary, this possibility gives birth to meaning as such, gives it out to be heard and read.
>
> ([13.2], 104; [13.27], 93)

In the world that we actually find, the meaning of each and every sign is independent of whatever momentary intentional fulfilment the speaking or writing subject may give it. Precisely because he recognizes that language has its own life, Husserl tries to limit normal or proper meaning to the here and now of the speaking subject. Yet this subject, implicated in a living medium not under its control, has to stand like a watchguard over its utterances. We often enunciate a statement and immediately qualify it, aware that our intention does not encounter a neutral container. We hang around so as to catch certain 'normal' implications of the sign that we were not sufficiently aware of at the time of speaking or writing. And it could even be argued that writing is better than speaking inasmuch as it focuses the mind and enables greater clarity of expression, though again this is not safeguarded from perversion or loss in either medium.

Derrida is not content with exposing phonocentrism as an unjust-ified prejudice. He wants to show that the conception of an immediate, self-identical consciousness reflected in expression and subsequently cast into an impure world of indication itself falls down. Husserl argues that signs are redundant in the self-relation because we are present to ourselves in an undivided now, though he is very careful to qualify this last idea. This can be seen in a series of lectures which he composed between 1893 and 1917 and later published as *On the Phenomenology of the Consciousness of Internal Time* in 1928. Husserl here rejects out of hand any recourse to the notion of detached atomic instants of consciousness. Our conscious processes are always ongoing and inter-connected, making up a flowing stream. Within this stream every pres-ent moment or immediate now of self-consciousness carries an inheri-tance from the past (retention) and an anticipation of the future (protention).

The past that is held in retention is different from a past that has to be reproduced. Reproduction is the recreation of an event that is completely over, one that lies in the more distant past. It is the reacti-vation of a dead event and it always involves some vagueness and distortion. Retention is the holding of an immediately lapsed past in the present moment of consciousness. It would be analogous to the hum of a dinner-gong that echoes on in my ears. The present-past of retention avoids the inevitable imperfection of reproduction, because there is no significant temporal lapse between the present moment and the immediately past one that makes up the content of the retention. I have to be conscious of the retentional content in the present moment to be conscious of the latter's immediacy. This can only be identified when I have an immediate past against which it can be contrasted.

As stated above, the present moment also involves a protention. This is an anticipation of the next moment of awareness, the one that will immediately follow the now. Implicit in self-consciousness is the expectation that the now will pass into a new moment within which I shall be just as present to myself as I am in this one. I could of course switch attention, be knocked unconscious or drop dead, but the suspension or cessation of self-consciousness cannot be experienced or imagined *per se*. I cannot know what it is like not to be self-aware; since by definition one cannot be cognizant of such a state when one is in it. Barring accidents then, self-consciousness (the ground of human subjectivity) is understood as something ongoing, not as a once-off act. It has an ideal and repeatable character. Every protention is the expression of this understanding, anticipating as it does the repetition of the present moment of self-awareness. Reflective consciousness can be extensive and continuous because each moment contains the 'about to be' as well as the 'just gone'. Through protention and retention, past, present and future are connected in each individual moment of reflective awareness.

On Derrida's reading, Husserl is correct and prescient to recognize that each moment of self-consciousness involves retentions and protentions. But it is this very recognition that opens up a fissure in the claim that the now is something pure, unified and devoid of signification. It has been possible to present the now to consciousness only by setting it against something different, the immediately past now. It has been possible to present it as part of an unbroken unity only by anticipating the moment that will immediately succeed it. Consciousness of the selfsame, the now, always requires consciousness of the other, the not-now. Put another way, that which is different has to be held over and anticipated within the same so as to produce immediacy and continuity, the essential characteristics of a conscious subject. Derrida describes this retentional and protentional process as *auto-affection*. It constitutes rather than being constituted: 'This movement of difference is not something that happens to a transcendental subject; it produces a subject. Auto-affection is not a modality of experience that characterizes a being that would already be itself (*autos*). It produces sameness as self-relation within self-difference; it produces sameness as the nonidentical' ([13.2], 92; [13.27], 82). Derrida is arguing against the idea of a self-identical now and hence of a primordial and self-contained subjectivity. To be itself the now has to point to moments beyond itself. Because they are actual forms of pointing, retention and protention can effectively be understood as signs of what has lapsed and what is pending. But is this admission of signs into the now of reflective consciousness also an invasion by indication? Taking retention on its own, one could argue that since it perfectly captures the past as it was in its own time, it is a fulfilled or expressive sign. In the case of protention, however, the situation seems different. The pending moment which I point to in the now will in turn point to another moment, and the cessation of this process is unimaginable – it could proceed to infinity. What I point to will never fulfil the present sign, because it will not itself be a self-referential plenitude. When one comes to look backwards, one sees that the situation was in fact the same. The present moment was itself anticipated in a previous moment, and that moment was also anticipated, right back to a primal moment of reflection that cannot be isolated because there was no antecedent reflection to identify it against. (The antecedent moment would be an unconscious trace hidden from view.) The most recent protention anticipating the immediate now passed over into a retention on the arrival of this present moment, and from this it can be concluded that both protention and retention (one of which collapses into the other) are condemned to an unfulfilled and indicative function. The present moment cannot fulfil that which pointed to it in the past, and the pending moment will not fulfil that which is pointing to it in the present. Difference doubly contaminates the now. It only allows self-presence through a Janus-faced indication of an indefinite past and future. Presence is always already outside of itself, and so on without a definite end.

Derrida concludes his reading by adverting to a strangely prophetic passage from the first volume of Husserl's *Ideas* (1913). Husserl remembers walking through the Dresden Gallery and seeing a painting by Teniers. This represents a gallery of paintings, each of which represent further paintings in an endless regress. In this passage, as Derrida interprets it, can be glimpsed the fate of phenomenology. This raises the question of whether Husserl in some way reaches deconstruction *avant la lettre*. In the course of *Speech and Phenomena* Derrida speaks of Husserl's 'admirable' analysis of internal time consciousness, an analysis which he further characterizes as one of 'incomparable depth' ([13.2], 94 n. 1; [13.27], 84 n. 9). It seems strange that Husserl failed to see where this analysis was leading. The explanation, for Derrida, lies in the fact that the idea of unmediated or perfect presence is a pervasive and hidden prejudice carried forward from ancient times. The emphasis on the 'now' as an Archimedean point, the ground of immediacy and certainty, is one particular manifestation of this. So powerful is the prejudice that even Husserl, the first to provide the means for its circumscription, none the less remains under its sway. He stands on the very threshold of the deconstruction of the metaphysics of presence.

A brief overview of Derrida's career could well begin with the essays from his formative period in *Writing and Difference* (1967) [13.3; 13.28]. This collection includes the first article on genesis and structure and also 'Force and Signification' and 'Structure, Sign and Play', where the earlier analysis can be seen applied to modern structuralism. Whilst agreeing with the structuralist critique of a subjectivity that would be anterior to the world of signs, Derrida sees the general enterprise as misled in its tendency to construct closed sign-systems that are abstracted from time and change, and, having done this, to characterize these as transcendental realities that determine meaning in general. The dream of unearthing foundational structures centred on some fixed theme is a metaphysical illusion which sustains itself only by concealing the dynamic and ongoing process of constitution through which meanings emerge and mutate. The point at which this strategy is made evident is the point at which structuralism's fabrications begin to tremble and show their cracks. It is here that deconstruction takes its hold.

In 'Violence and Metaphysics', Derrida engages with the thought of Emmanuel Levinas. Characterizing the history of philosophy since Parmenides as a totalitarian wasteland, Levinas calls for an openness to the experience of the other that lies beyond the dominion of reason, whose logos has always been one of violence and power. The only ethical relationship to this other, or others, is one of infinite responsibility and respect. Whilst greatly admiring the approach of Levinas, Derrida argues that he does not pay due attention to Husserl's studies of intersubjectivity or to Heidegger's 'destruction' of those forms of thought that proceed from a determinate precomprehension of Being. Derrida also maintains that ordinary language and the philosophical discourse that proceeds from it cannot be escaped in the way that Levinas would like. Since the other can only be revealed through discourse – the opening of peace as well as of war – the attempt to transcend this risks its suppression, which would result in the worst violence.

In 'Freud and the Scene of Writing', Derrida examines Freud's metaphor of the mystic writing pad, where the unconscious is likened to a text and the structures and layers of this text compared to forms of writing. This text, Derrida will argue, is a weave of signs based on lost traces which involves intervals spaced out in time just as in the world of conscious awareness. It would be one more ruse of reason to see the unconscious text as embodying primordial truths that could be brought to the surface and transcribed, like an original that is somehow reproduced. Even the most radical of critiques run the danger of confirming presence at a deeper level, and metapsychology is no exception. This theme of covertly reinstating what one seeks to reject recurs throughout the remaining essays and through the later Derrida.

Of Grammatology (1967) [13.4; 13.29] is an extended reworking of an article of the same name that Derrida originally published in two parts in 1965. The book incorporates many of the conclusions reached in *Speech and Phenomena*, and its purpose, according to Derrida, is to make enigmatic the concepts of proximity and of the proper that are included in the concept of presence. The deconstruction of these begins with the deconstruction of consciousness. Derrida explicitly generalizes the concept of the indicative sign to include anything that can possibly appear, whether it is 'originally' in consciousness or in the world of sense-experience. All 'present' things are internally constituted by variation of phonic and graphic marks or protentions and retentions. The manifest is what it is through being always ready set against irreducible absences. There is never a thing in itself that could come to glow in the luminosity of its own presence. Derrida rejects the belief that a sign or sign-system can eventually fall away before the naked object, like a veil that would drop from our eyes. This is the myth of the *transcendental signified*, of a terminus to the play of signs somehow outside that play. It recurs in various guises throughout the philosophical tradition, as God, or matter, or absolute knowledge, or the end of history. It remains a myth because it is never realized. In the absence of the transcendental signified we are left with the apparent limitlessness and pervasiveness of the play of signs. In this sense it can be held that everything is writing, with every instantiation of this general writing making up a text. (To give a crude example, the red sky in the morning is a set of signs written on the blank sheet of the sky. This text points to an indeterminate series of other events that will probably include a storm.) All meanings are inscribed in a text and point to other meanings in other texts. The world would be the most general text, though it is never closed or finished. The history of philosophy can be read as a sustained attempt to suppress such a seemingly endless play.

The ideal of the transcendental signified, according to Derrida, is the obverse side of *logocentrism*, which is the affirmation – in whatever form – of a pre-ordained order, of a univocal and proper meaning to all things that merely awaits discovery. Because it poses a threat to the communication of every supposed univocity, graphic writing has traditionally been relegated to the role of a dangerous and accidental supplement, with Rousseau providing the most notable example of such a strategy. Writing has been understood as something subsequent to a pre-given plenitude. But Derrida argues that there is another meaning to supplementarity which has been all but ignored in the philosophical canon. The supplement is also that which is required to make up for a lack. If graphic writing were no longer seen as exterior and accidental, the way would be paved for the recognition of general writing as the weave of differences that inhabit and make possible all forms of presence. It is not by accident that Rousseau conceives of writing as an unhappy mischance, the root of dissemblance and impropriety. Writing has to be suppressed if he is to uphold the logocentric illusion of a prelapsarian state of nature. Rousseau most clearly demonstrates the inevitable violence of metaphysics, which equates propriety with pure presence through the debasement of writing.

The year 1972 saw the publication of three further books by Derrida: *Margins of Philosophy* [13.5; 13.30], *Dissemination* [13.6;

13.31] and *Positions* [13.7; 13.32]. *Margins* is made up of eleven articles written from 1967 on. Most of these are applications of a practice of reading whose theoretical grounding is effectively completed in the second article of the collection, entitled 'Différance'. This piece can also be read as a summary of the earlier works. Derrida presents *différance* as the development of Saussure's insight that in language there are only differences. It is also presented as an outcome of the important Heideggerian notion of ontological difference, the difference between Being and beings considered as such:

> It is the domination of beings that *différance* everywhere comes to solicit, in the sense that *sollicitare*, in old Latin, means to shake as a whole, to make tremble in entirety. Therefore, it is the determination of Being as presence or as beingness that is interrogated by the thought of *différance*. Such a question could not emerge and be understood unless the difference between Being and beings were somewhere to be broached. First consequence: *différance* is not. It is not a present being, however excellent, unique, principal, or transcendent. It governs nothing, reigns over nothing, and nowhere exercises any authority. It is not announced by any capital letter. Not only is there no kingdom of *différance*, but *différance* instigates the subversion of every kingdom. . . . Since Being has never had a 'meaning', has never been thought or said as such, except by dissimulating itself in beings, then *différance*, in a certain and very strange way, (is) 'older' than the ontological difference or than the truth of Being.
>
> ([13.5], 22–3; [13.30], 21–2)

Being is not a meaning that commands from a lofty height. It emerges from beings and they from it. In a similar way the intelligible needs the sensible and the natural the cultural. *Différance* is the productive movement of differing and deferring. Every concept is deferred in signifying a plenitude without realization and differed in gaining identity from that which it is not. *Différance* is not a concept, but that which makes concepts possible. It is not an essence, for it assumes a different form in each relation and does not exist before these.

In the third article, '*Ousia* and *Grammē*', Derrida examines a note by Heidegger concerning Aristotle on time. Aristotle first posed the problem of how Being can be determined as presence without determining time as external to substance, and hence as non-present and non-existent (the no-longer and the not-yet). According to Derrida, Heidegger seriously neglects Aristotle's investigations. Furthermore, Heidegger's own critique of 'vulgar temporality' succumbs – despite its significance – to the *aporia* or perplexity outlined by Aristotle. Authentic existence is characterized as primordial temporality and inauthentic existence as derivative temporality. In this opposition of the primordial and the derivative Derrida observes a covert reintroduction of Being as self-present substance.

'The Ends of Man' addresses the question of humanism, concentrating on Heidegger's critique of the general ideology. Derrida describes this critique as unsurpassed in the 'archeological radicalness' of the questions that it sketches. No metahumanist position can neglect the opening of these questions without being peripheral and secondary ([13.5], 153; [13.30], 128). Heidegger wishes to transcend humanism so as to discover the proper essence and dignity of man, his *humanitas*. He seeks to move towards an understanding of man as an openness to the mystery of Being, one who will shepherd the true meaning of Being in the proximity of the near. Derrida regards this alternative as a subtle variant of traditional humanism. Heidegger's evocations of the proper and of proximity indicate a logocentric ideal, a real meaning of Being and of the self that can be epiphanically revealed to those who attain to the right attitude.

In *Dissemination* [13.6; 13.31] Derrida writes on Sollers, Mallarmé and Plato. In the best-known essay, 'Plato's Pharmacy', phonocentrism is traced back to the *Phaedrus* dialogue, where writing is condemned for endangering the truth of the living voice and reinstated as the inscription of eternal law in the soul. Writing is ambiguously characterized as poison and cure, this being its most charitable characterization in the western tradition.

The extended preface or 'Outwork' to *Dissemination* attacks the historical conception of the book as the best form of encapsulating authorial intentions in the graphic medium, since it has a definite structure of beginning, expanding and ending. Derrida reactivates his claim that the *différance* in all conscious activities usurps transparency and mastery in every form of every medium. The book is a concatenation of irreconcilable elements and forces from which meaning is onanistically disseminated or scattered to the four winds.

Positions [13.7; 13.32] is a series of interviews held with Derrida so as to clarify his own project and its relationship with other intellectual movements. It can lay claim to being one of the more illuminating introductions to his thinking. According to Derrida, deconstruction is not a simple overturning of traditional philosophical prejudices or 'violent hierarchies'. It is best conceived as a double gesture of unseating the privileged motifs within texts (speech, nature, spirit, etc.) and then showing how the opposites on which they depend are sited within a subtext or shadow-text. The so-called master text is always haunted by a double that dislocates it rather than destroying it. *Différance* produces two texts or two ways of looking that are at once together and separate.

Glas (1974) [13.8; 13.33] can be interpreted as a rather jarring example of deconstructive work in progress.[16] Hegel's discourses concerning God, law, religion and the family are presented on one side of each page and Jean Genet's somewhat different treatment of the same topics on the other. Derrida's running commentary oscillates somewhere between the two. The subtlety of this rather inaccessible performance may lie in showing that the reader always becomes a writer to extract sense. It could also be viewed as a once-off experiment in hyper-Joycean equivocity, for Derrida never again presents a work in this precise format.

With *Spurs* (1978) [13.10; 13.35], Derrida moves to a consideration of sexual difference. He focuses his attention on Nietzsche's strange denunciation of woman as the nexus of untruth and subversion, which on first sight might appear as one more rendering of Schopenhauer's misogynism. Derrida draws out of Nietzsche's cryptic remarks an anticipation of some of the themes in modern feminist criticism, since the latter was never noted for his love of the established order or of traditional conceptions of truth.

In *The Post Card* (1980) [13.12; 13.37], Derrida develops at length the theme – already seen at length in his work on the origin of geometry – of messages that fail to reach their destinations. In the course of readings of Freud, Lacan and Heidegger, he compares general writing to a telecommunications service that is quite capable of suffering hitches and breakdowns. The little postcard that is open to all symbolizes the fragility of meanings always already cast into space and time. Even messages that reach their addressees without too much delay can be misunderstood, whether they come from the subconscious, from the mystical contemplation of being, or from 'external' sources.

Most of Derrida's work since the late 1970s has concentrated on literature and its genre distinction with philosophy on the one hand and on matters ethical and political on the other. A good example of the first set of interests can be seen in *Parages* ('Regions') (1986) [13.15], which engages with the work of Maurice Blanchot. Derrida has also written on Ponge, Celan and Joyce.

The increased concern with ethics and politics first emerges in *The Ear of the Other* (1982) [13.1; 13.38], which was based on a colloquium held in Montreal in 1979. Derrida's remarks emerge out of considerations of the philosophical problems of autobiography and translation. He stresses that whilst *différance* undercuts authorial mastery and makes every interpretation a misreading, it does not destroy personal responsibility. The fact that statements and writings immediately take on a life of their own is an argument for eternal vigilance. One should at least attempt to foresee possible misinterpretations of one's works. Though the exercise cannot always succeed, it may minimize certain dangers inherent in inscription. These dangers have been well shown in the use that at least one ideology has made of the work of Nietzsche. We have to proceed as if every part of what we say and write could be taken out of context.

Psyché: Inventions de l'autre ('Psyche: Inventions of the Other') (1987) [13.17] includes articles on deconstructive methodology, sexual difference, racism and nuclear deterrence. In 'Racism's last word', written for an itinerant exhibition of art against apartheid, Derrida scrutinizes this very word. Apartheid is the appellation for one of the world's ultimate forms of racism. It signifies the violence of the talking animal that can make words discriminate rather than discern. Though it claims to represent a state of law derived from a natural or divine right, the day will come when this word will resonate in its own emptiness. Yet the collapse of what it signifies will be credited not just to the triumph of moral standards but to the laws of liberal economics that have come to determine this system as 'inefficient'. These laws of the market are another standard of calculation to be analysed.

In 'No Apocalypse, Not Now', Derrida attacks certain consequentialist assumptions in the logic of nuclear deterrence. The leading idea in the nuclear arms race has been that each advance in destructive capability will so impress the opposition as to make catastrophe more unlikely. Derrida notes that this assumes that the 'best intentions' would always be 'correctly interpreted' by the other side. The seeming success of this strategy has also pleased the military-industrial complex. Expensive contracts can be made without any apparent increase in danger.

In the lengthy afterword to *Limited Inc.* (1988) [13.22; 13.44], the full record of Derrida's critique of the work of J. L. Austin and exchange with John Searle, Derrida tries to clarify questions concerning the aim and extent of the activity of deconstruction. Derrida states that although the themes of full presence and immediacy have been subjected to deconstruction, he has never argued for an untrammelled freeplay of meaning. There can be a relative stability of meaning in texts; the point being made is only that this is not self-sufficient, immutable or indestructible. The double reading revealing a double text shows that the dominant meaning or interpretation of a text cannot live up to all its claims. In undoing conceptual hierarchies deconstruction seeks to achieve a more just balance. It does not suspend or reject the possibility of truth or of communication.

With *Memoires for Paul de Man* (1988) [13.21; 13.43] and *Du droit à la philosophie* (1990) [13.23], Derrida has included essays concerning the responsibilities and position of the intellectual in the modern or post-Enlightenment world.[17] He has maintained that the freedom of the academic world is only an abstract one, since the members of this world are effectively excluded from the fields of ethical and political decision-making. One of the crucial roles of the university in a technocratically managed society, according to Derrida, has been to provide a place where trouble-makers can be properly corralled and the compliant properly funded. As can be imagined, these analyses have not contributed greatly to Derrida's popularity amongst certain academics.

The most intriguing question that the essays in these books have raised – as with much of Derrida's work over the last few years – is that of the future direction of his project. Whilst his concentration on ethics and politics could be read as the unfolding of the hitherto unseen and positive aspects of deconstructive practice, it does not involve a clear advance on the theoretical groundwork already sketched in the 1960s. Furthermore, Derrida has not spoken of any departure from or revision of the existing body of texts. All the comments he has made on his work have been more or less explanatory in nature. It remains to be seen what new paths may be opened in the future by this most controversial of modern thinkers.

Timothy Mooney

 NOTES

1 This section reworks certain arguments from the opening sections of *The Ethics of Deconstruction: Derrida and Levinas* [13.73].

2 This formulation implies, of course, a certain delusion on Rousseau's part, namely that he did not mean to say what he actually said and that what he actually meant to say is in contradiction with what is said in his text. Such a line of thought recalls Paul de Man's objections to Derrida in 'The Rhetoric of Blindness: Jacques Derrida's Reading of Rousseau', in *Blindness and Insight: Essays in the Rhetoric of Contemporary Criticism*, 2nd edn (London: Methuen, 1983), pp. 102–41, where de Man goes so far as to claim that 'Rousseau's text has no blind spots' (p. 139). Consequently, 'there is no need to deconstruct Rousseau' (*ibid.*). However, de Man continues, there is a profound need to deconstruct the established tradition of Rousseau interpretation which has systematically misread his texts. Thus, although de Man claims that Derrida is Rousseau's 'best modern interpreter' (p. 135), one who has restored 'the complexities of reading to the dignity of a philosophical question' (p. 110), Derrida is still blind to the necessarily ambivalent status of Rousseau's *literary* language (p. 136). Derrida fails to read Rousseau as *literature*. *Of Grammatology* is therefore an exemplary case of de Man's thesis on the necessary interaction of blindness and insight in the language of criticism.

   In defence of Derrida, let me briefly say that despite de Man's many insights, *his* blindness to *Of Grammatology* consists in the fact that he reads the latter as a *critique* of Rousseau and not as a double reading. Derrida is no more speaking against Rousseau than he is speaking for him. Indeed, one might go so far as to say that the proper name 'Rousseau', whose texts Derrida comments upon, simply signifies the dominant interpretation (or, for de Man, misreading) of Rousseau; that of the 'époque de Rousseau' ([13.4], 145; [13.29], 97), an interpretation that sees Rousseau simply as a philosopher of presence, and which ascribes to him the fiction of logocentrism, a fiction that extends even to modern anthropologists like Lévi-Strauss, whose structuralism, it must be remembered, is Derrida's real target for so much of part two of *Of Grammatology*.

3 J. Searle, 'Reiterating the Differences: A Reply to Derrida', *Glyph*, 2 (1977): 203.

4 J. Habermas, *The Philosophical Discourse of Modernity*, trans. F. Lawrence (Oxford: Polity Press, 1987), pp. 185–210.

5 Cf. Heidegger, *Sein und Zeit*, 15th edn (Tübingen: Max Niemeyer, 1984), p. 26, trans. J. Macquarrie and E. Robinson as *Being and Time* (Oxford: Blackwell, 1962), p. 49.

6 Cf. Heidegger, *Zur Sache des Denkens* (Tübingen: Max Niemeyer, 1969), p. 9, trans. J. Stambaugh as *Time and Being* (New York: Harper & Row, 1972), p. 9.

7 R. Kearney, *Dialogues with Contemporary Continental Thinkers* (Manchester: Manchester University Press, 1984), 124.

8 Cf. E. Levinas, 'Transcendence et hauteur', *Bulletin de la Société Française de la Philosophie*, 56: 3 (1962): 92.

9 R. Gasché [13.61], 101.

10 *Dialogues with Contemporary Continental Thinkers*, 108.

11 For a detailed discussion of closure in Derrida, see 'The Problem of Closure in Derrida', in [13.73], 59–106.

12 J. Derrida, 'Ponctuations: Le Temps de la thèse', in *Du droit à la philosophie* [13.23], 444, trans. K. McLoughlin, 'The Time of a Thesis: Punctuations', in A. Montefiore (ed.), *Philosophy in France Today* (Cambridge: Cambridge University Press, 1983), p. 38.

13 *Ibid.*, p. 446, trans. pp. 39–40.

14 Derrida, *Introduction à l'origine de la géométrie par Edmund Husserl* [13.1], trans. [13.26], 90. For a detailed outline of Derrida's *Introduction* and its influence on his later work see R. Bernet, 'On Derrida's "Introduction" to Husserl's *Origin of Geometry*' in J. Silverman (ed.) [13.70], 139–53.

15 Neither Derrida nor Husserl would ever deny the bare logical objectivity of a geometrical truth, that the three angles of a triangle make up two right-angles in two-dimensional space, for example. What they are claiming is that a particular objectivity is only philosophically significant when set within a wider context. For a more detailed explanation of this claim, see the *Introduction*, pp. 31–3 (trans. pp. 47–8).

16 Leavey has provided a concordance of references to Hegel in his *Glassary* (Lincoln: University of Nebraska Press, 1986).

17 Derrida's comments on the modern university clearly display the influence of Heidegger, as he would be the first to admit. An interesting comparison can be made between this aspect of Derrida's work and the more recent writings of the Austro-American philosopher Paul Feyerabend. In particular see the latter's *Farewell to Reason* (London and New York: Verso, 1987).

❧ SELECT BIBLIOGRAPHY ❧

The most exhaustive bibliography on the publications of Derrida is by A. Leventure, 'A Jacques Derrida Bibliography: 1962–1990', *Textual Practice*, 5: 1 (spring 1991). Reprinted in amended form in D. Wood, *Derrida: A Critical Reader*. Another useful bibliography is by J. P. Leavey Jr and D. Allison, 'A Derrida Bibliography', *Research in Phenomenology*, 8 (1978): 145–60. Also useful is the list given by P. Kamuf (ed.) in *A Derrida Reader: Between the Blinds* (New York and London: Harvester Wheatsheaf, 1991). Many of Derrida's articles have been published several times in French and English in a bewildering variety of books and journals. I have confined the following list to his published books.

Primary texts

13.1 *Introduction à l'origine de la géométrie par Edmund Husserl*, Paris: Presses Universitaires de France, 1962.

13.2 *La Voix et le phénomène: Introduction au problème du signe dans la phénoménologie de Husserl*, Paris: Presses Universitaries de France, 1967.

13.3 *L'Ecriture et la différence*, Paris: Editions du Seuil, 1967.

13.4 *De la grammatologie*, Paris: Editions de Minuit, 1967.

13.5 *Marges de la philosophie*, Paris: Editions de Minuit, 1972.

13.6 *La Dissémination*, Paris: Editions du Seuil, 1972.

13.7 *Positions*, Paris: Editions de Minuit, 1972.

13.8 *Glas*, Paris: Editions Galilée, 1974.

13.9 *L'Archéologie du frivole: Lire Condillac*, Paris: Denoël-Gonthier, 1976.

13.10 *Eperons: Les Styles de Nietzsche*, Paris: Aubier-Flammarion, 1978.

13.11 *La Vérité en peinture*, Paris: Aubier-Flammarion, 1978.

13.12 *La Carte postale: De Socrate à Freud et au-delà*, Paris: Aubier-Flammarion, 1980.

13.13 *L'Oreille de l'autre: Otobiographies, transferts, traductions: Textes et débats avec Jacques Derrida*, ed. C. Levesque and C. V. McDonald, Montreal: VLB Editions, 1982.

13.14 *D'un ton apocalyptique adopté naguère en philosophie*, Paris: Editions Galilée, 1983.

13.15 *Parages*, Paris: Editions Galilée, 1986. (A collection of essays translated in several English language texts.)

13.16 *Schibboleth, pour Paul Celan*, Paris: Editions Galilée, 1986.

13.17 *Psyché: Inventions de l'autre*, Paris: Editions Galilée, 1987. [A collection of essays translated in several English language texts.]

13.18 *De l'esprit: Heidegger et la question*, Paris: Editions Galilée, 1987.

13.19 *Ulysse Gramophone: Deux mots pour Joyce*, Paris: Editions Galilée, 1987. [Two essays translated in separate English language texts.]

13.20 *Signéponge*, Paris: Editions du Seuil, 1988.

13.21 *Mémoires pour Paul de Man*, Paris: Editions Galilée, 1988.

13.22 *Limited Inc*. Paris: Editions Galilée, 1990.

13.23 *Du droit à la philosophie*, Paris: Editions Galilée, 1990. [A collection of essays translated in several English language texts.]

13.24 *Le Problème de la genèse dans la philosophie de Husserl*, Paris: Presses Universitaries de France, 1990. [A printing of Derrida's master's thesis.]

13.25 *L'Autre Cap*, Paris: Editions de Minuit, 1991.

Translations

13.26 *Edmund Husserl's Origin of Geometry: An Introduction*, trans. J. P. Leavey, Jr, Lincoln: University of Nebraska Press, 1989, rev. edn.

13.27 *Speech and Phenomena and Other Essays on Husserl's Theory of Signs*, trans. D. B. Allison, Evanston: Northwestern University Press, 1973.

13.28 *Writing and Difference*, trans. A. Bass, Chicago: University of Chicago Press, 1978.

13.29 *Of Grammatology*, trans. G. C. Spivak, Baltimore: Johns Hopkins University Press, 1975.

13.30 *Margins of Philosophy*, trans. A. Bass, Chicago: University of Chicago Press, 1982.

13.31 *Dissemination*, trans. B. Johnson, Chicago: University of Chicago Press, 1981.

13.32 *Positions*, trans. A. Bass, Chicago: University of Chicago Press, 1982.

13.33 *Glas*, trans. J. P. Leavey, Jr, and R. Rand, Lincoln: University of Nebraska Press, 1986.

13.34 *The Archeology of the Frivolous: Reading Condillac*, trans. J. P. Leavey, Jr, Lincoln: University of Nebraska Press, 1987.

13.35 *Spurs/Eperons*, trans. B. Harlow, Chicago: University of Chicago Press, 1979, bilingual edn.

13.36 *The Truth in Painting*, trans. G. Bennington and I. McLeod, Chicago: University of Chicago Press, 1987.

13.37 *The Post Card: From Socrates to Freud and Beyond*, trans. A. Bass, Chicago: University of Chicago Press, 1987.

13.38 *The Ear of the Other: Otobiography, Transference, Translation: Texts and Discussions with Jacques Derrida*, trans. P. Kamuf and A. Ronell, Lincoln: University of Nebraska Press, 1988, rev. edn.

13.39 'Of an Apocalyptic Tone Recently Adopted in Philosophy', trans. J. P. Leavey, Jr, *The Oxford Literary Review*, 6: 2 (1984): 3–37.

13.40 'Shibboleth', trans. J. Wilner, in S. Budick and G. Hartman (eds), *Midrash and Literature*, New Haven; Yale University Press, 1986, pp. 307–47.

13.41 *Of Spirit: Heidegger and the Question*, trans. G. Bennington and R. Bowlby, Chicago: University of Chicago Press, 1989.

13.42 *Signéponge/Signsponge*, trans. R. Rand, New York: Columbia University Press, 1984, bilingual edn.

13.43 *Memoires for Paul de Man*, trans. E. Cadava, J. Culler, P. Kamuf, and S. Lindsay, New York: Columbia University Press, 1989, rev. edn.

13.44 *Limited Inc.*, ed. G. Graff and trans. J. Mehlmann and S. Weber, Evanston: Northwestern University Press, 1988.

13.45 *The Other Heading: Reflections on Today's Europe*, trans. P.-A. Brault and M. G. Naas, Bloomington: Indiana University Press, 1992.

13.46 *Acts of Literature*, trans. D. Attridge, London: Routledge, 1992. [A collection of essays by Derrida from several sources.]

Criticism: introductory works

13.47 Atkins, D. G. 'The Sign as a Structure of Difference: Derridean Deconstruction and Some of Its Implications', in R. De George (ed.), *Semiotic Themes*, Lawrence: University of Kansas Press, 1981, pp. 133–47.

13.48 Cascardi, A. J. 'Skepticism and Deconstruction', *Philosophy of Literature*, 8: 1 (1984): 1–14.

13.49 Cousins, M. 'The Logic of Deconstruction', *The Oxford Literary Review*, 3: 2 (1978): 70–7.

13.50 Descombes, V. *Modern French Philosophy*, trans. J. Harding and L. Scott-Fox, Cambridge: Cambridge University Press, 1980.

13.51 Eldridge, R. 'Deconstruction and its Alternatives', *Man and World*, 18 (1985): 147–70.

13.52 Gasché, R. 'Deconstruction as Criticism', *Glyph*, 7 (1979): 177–216.

13.53 Hoy, D. C. 'Deciding Derrida: On the Work (and Play) of the French Philosopher', *London Review of Books* 4: 3: 3–5.

13.54 Kearney, R. *Modern Movements in European Philosophy*, Manchester: Manchester University Press, 1986.

13.55 Norris, C. *Deconstruction: Theory and Practice*, New York and London: Methuen, 1982.

13.56 Norris, C. *Derrida*, London: Fontana, 1987.

13.57 Rorty, R. 'Philosophy as a Kind of Writing: An Essay on Derrida', in *Consequences of Pragmatism*, Minneapolis: University of Minnesota Press, 1982, pp. 89–109.

13.58 Wood, D. 'An Introduction to Derrida', *Radical Philosophy*, 21 (1979): 18–28.

Criticism: more detailed works

13.59 Caputo, J. D. *Radical Hermeneutics: Repetition, Deconstruction, and the Hermeneutic Project*, Bloomington: Indiana University Press, 1987.

13.60 Culler, J. *On Deconstruction: Theory and Criticism after Structuralism*, Ithaca: Cornell University Press, 1982.

13.61 Gasché, R. *The Tain of the Mirror: Derrida and the Philosophy of Reflection*, Cambridge, Mass. and London: Harvard University Press, 1986.

13.62 Giovannangeli, D. *Ecriture et répétition: Approche de Derrida*, Paris: Union Générale d'Editions, 1979.

13.63 Hartman, G. *Saving the Text: Philosophy/Derrida/Literature*, Baltimore, Johns Hopkins University Press, 1982.

13.64 Harvey, I. *Derrida and the Economy of Difference*, Bloomington: Indiana University Press, 1986.

13.65 Kofman, S. *Lectures de Derrida*, Paris: Editions Galilée, 1984.

13.66 Llewelyn, J. *Derrida on the Threshold of Sense*, London: Macmillan, 1986.

13.67 Melville, S. *Philosophy Beside Itself: On Deconstruction and Modernism*, Minneapolis: University of Minnesota Press, 1986.

13.68 Sallis, J. (ed.) *Deconstruction and Philosophy: The Texts of Jacques Derrida*, Chicago: University of Chicago Press, 1987.

13.69 Silverman, H. J. (ed.) *Hermeneutics and Deconstruction*, Albany: State University of New York Press, 1985.

13.70 Silverman, H. J. (ed.) *Derrida and Deconstruction*, New York and London: Routledge, 1989.

13.71 Wood, D. and Bernasconi, R. (eds) *Derrida and 'Différance'*, Evanston: Northwestern University Press, 1988.

Criticism: critical and comparative works

13.72 Altizer, T. J. *et al. Deconstruction and Theology*, New York: Seabury Crossroads, 1982.

13.73 Critchley, S. *The Ethics of Deconstruction: Derrida and Levinas*, Oxford: Basil Blackwell, 1992.

13.74 Dasenbrock, R. W. (ed.) *Redrawing the Lines: Analytic Philosophy, Deconstruction, and Literary Theory*, Minneapolis: University of Minnesota Press, 1989.

13.75 Dews, P. *Logics of Disintegration: Post-structuralist Thought and the Claims of Critical Theory*, New York and London: Verso, 1987.

13.76 Evans, J. C. *Strategies of Deconstruction: Derrida and the Myth of the Voice*, Minneapolis: University of Minnesota Press, 1991.

13.77 Ferry, L. and Renaut, A. *French Philosophy of the Sixties: An Essay on Antihumanism*, trans. M. H. S. Cattani, Amherst: University of Massachusetts Press, 1990.

13.78 Frank. M. *What is Neostructuralism?*, trans. R. Grey and S. Wilke, Minneapolis: University of Minnesota Press, 1989.

13.79 Greisch, J. *Herméneutique et grammatologie*, Paris: Editions du CNRS, 1977.

13.80 Lacoue-Labarthe, P. and Nancy, J. L. (eds) *Les Fins de l'homme: a partir du travail de Jacques Derrida*, Paris: Editions Galilée, 1981.

13.81 Michelfelder, D. and Palmer, R. (eds) *Dialogue and Deconstruction: The Gadamer–Derrida Encounter*, Albany: State University of New York Press, 1989.

13.82 Rapaport, H. *Heidegger and Derrida: Reflections on Time and Language*, Lincoln: University of Nebraska Press, 1989.

13.83 Rose, G. *Dialectic of Nihilism: Post-Structuralism and Law*, Oxford: Basil Blackwell, 1984.

13.84 Ryan, M. *Marxism and Deconstruction: A Critical Articulation*, Baltimore: Johns Hopkins University Press, 1982.

13.85 Staten, H. *Wittgenstein and Derrida*, Lincoln: University of Nebraska Press, 1984.

13.86 Wood, D. (ed.) *Derrida: A Critical Reader*, Oxford, Blackwell, 1992.

CHAPTER 14

Postmodernist theory
Lyotard, Baudrillard and others
Thomas Docherty

❧❁❧

❧ INTRODUCTION ❧

Philosophy has been touched by postmodernism. Philosophy, in the modern academy, is supposed to be the discipline of disciplines: it is philosophy which will be able to gather together, in one over-arching discourse, all the various micro-disciplinary problems and procedures dealt with in the differing and ostensibly unrelated fields of literature, medicine, law, politics and so on; and it is philosophy which will also set itself the task of explaining their necessary separations. Postmodernism has not 'challenged' philosophy; rather it has simply enabled an earthquake under its foundations; for postmodernism is most aptly situated precisely in the moment of the eradication of all foundational thinking. This, of course, makes it a fundamentally paradoxical exercise to 'define' postmodernism, for any definition would at once inherently seek the foundationalist status lexically integral to any description, while it would simultaneously discount in the semantic content of the definition the very possibility of such foundationalism. In what follows, therefore, I shall not so much 'define' postmodernism in philosophy as indicate what is at stake in the debates that have constituted the postmodern moment in our cultures.[1]

The term 'postmodern' was probably first consistently used by Arnold Toynbee in 1939; and it was prefigured in his writings in 1934 (that is, at around the date of the first recorded instance of the term's usage in Spanish, by Federico de Onis).[2] In *A Study of History*, Toynbee suggested that the 'modern' historical period had ended, at a date determined in his studies roughly between 1850 and 1918. Toynbee's historiography was a product of the late nineteenth-century desire to found a synoptic and universal history; and this desire was most easily accommodated in Toynbee's own individual work by the fact that his history approximates to the condition of a Christian theodicy. His task was to redeem humanity by discovering the trajectory of history to be a movement of separation from God and the eternal returns towards a theocentric and universalizing centre of meaning for the world. Secularity – history itself – becomes nothing more or less than a humble interruption in a fundamentally circular narrative structure, whose end is always already somehow contained in its beginning. This, of course, is reflected in much of the artistic literary production of the first decades of the present century in western Europe, where writers such as Eliot, Joyce, Mann, Proust and many others all experimented with the cyclical structures of history. For Toynbee and his kind, the facts of history would make sense in relation to a governing narrative structure which would be given and legitimated in advance, since it is narrated fundamentally from the point of view of a monotheistic God.

Such a notion of history is indebted to conflicts which had their root in Enlightenment. As Hayden White points out, the Enlightenment broadly agreed with Leibniz's monadology in the sense that the philosophers of the Enlightenment subscribed to the view that there was an underlying unity or direction to human history. But the big difference between Leibniz and Enlightenment is that Leibniz thinks that this essential unity of humanity is simply immanent, whereas the philosophers of the Enlightenment view it as an ideal whose realization lies in the future, an ideal which is therefore, at best, imminent, or one which is

> *yet to be realized* in historical time. They could not take it as a *presupposition* of their historical writing, not merely because the data did not bear it out, but because it did not accord with their own experience of their own social worlds. For them the unity of humanity was an *ideal* which they could *project* into the future.[3]

Toynbee's invocation of a postmodern moment can thus be seen to accord with the idealist drive of Leibniz; yet it also acknowledges the necessarily future orientation of history. Toynbee can plainly see that the 'modern' moment is not yet a moment of a universal accord or harmony. In this, he is rather like the literary critic Erich Auerbach, who wrote his great study, *Mimesis*, while living in Turkey in flight from the Nazis. In that study, Auerbach poignantly and desperately attempts to discern, and to validate in the literary history of the western world, the idea of a shared humanity in which, 'below the surface conflicts' which ostensibly wedge us apart, 'the elementary things which our lives have in common come to light'.[4] Both these writers were writing under the sign of the Second World War, in which the ideology of a specific racial difference and disharmony momentarily, but triumphantly, was in the ascendant. Auerbach's answer to his predicament was to find solace in *aesthetic* harmony; Toynbee rather hypothesized a moment in the future, a 'post-modern' *political* moment, when history and humanity can be properly redeemed.

The word 'postmodern' is thus characterized, from its very inception, by an ambiguity. On the one hand, it is seen to describe a historical period; on the other, it simply describes a desire, a mood which looks to the future to redeem the present. This ambiguity is at the core of a tension between postmodernism as an aesthetic style and postmodernity as a political and cultural reality.

This is an instance of one of the dominant philosophical concerns responsible for shaping the question of the postmodern: what is the proper relation in our time between the aesthetic and the political? The particular intimacy of the relation between aesthetics and politics in postmodernism is apparent even from the earliest considerations of the question. Leslie Fiedler characterized the emergence of new aesthetic priorities in the novel during the 1960s as a 'critical point' in which new attitudes to time were developed; and such attitudes, he claimed, 'constitute . . . a politics as well as an esthetics'.[5] In the light of this, it is interesting to note that two of the foremost thinkers in the field of postmodernism, Fredric Jameson and Jean-François Lyotard, both write equally fluently and influentially on aesthetic culture and on political practices; and, more importantly, they have consistently pondered the relation between these hymeneally-linked activities. A deep formative influence lying behind much of the contemporary debate, as is now perhaps obvious, is the legacy of the Frankfurt school, perhaps most especially the work of Adorno, to which I shall return. For present purposes, the single salient fact is that aesthetic postmodernism is always intimately imbricated with the issues of a political postmodernity, even if postmodernism and postmodernity may not always themselves coincide.

As a result of the legacy inherited from Frankfurt, the question of the postmodern is also, tangentially at least, an issue of Marxism. Marxism, in placing the labouring body at the interface between consciousness and material history, is the necessary explanatory and critical correlative of a modern culture whose technology (in the form of an industrial revolution) divides human knowledge or consciousness from human power or material history. But the continuing revolutionary shifts within capitalism itself have necessitated in recent years a marked and vigorous self-reflection on the part of Marxism. In Habermas, for instance, Marxism has taken 'the linguistic turn', in arguments for a continuation of the emancipatory goals of Marxist theory and practice under a revised rubric of 'communicative action'. Habermas's faith in the continuing viability of a vigorously self-revising Marxism is shared

by Jameson, who models his own version of 'late Marxism' to correspond with Mandel's descriptions of 'late capitalism'.[6]

A key date here, of course, is 1968. This is not only a moment
which could be described as the high point of 'grand theory' and of
the emergence of a poststructuralist challenge to what had become by
then the grand structuralist orthodoxies; it is also the moment of a
critical political failure. The seeming availability of a revolution which
brought workers and intellectuals together all across Europe represented a high point for a specific kind of Marxist theoretical practice.
But when these revolutions failed, many began, at precisely that
moment, to rethink their commitments to the fundamental premises of
Marxist theory. Simultaneously, most other erstwhile dominant philosophical trajectories (the phenomenological tradition; the insistence on
the centrality of Hegel via Kojève; the entire 'history of western
thought') came under suspicion and revision.

Rudolph Bahro and André Gorz began, from an economistic
perspective, to rethink issues of growth and sustainable development.
Their emergent ecologism coincided neatly with the 'imaginative'
aspects of 1968, and Cohn-Bendit began his own movement from red
to green. Kant began to assume the same kind of position of centrality
once occupied by Hegel. Feminism and deconstruction both criticized
the monolithic aspects of the institutions of western thinking. These
all coincided neatly with the aftermath of the Algerian and other col-
onial crises, and with the growing awareness of the issues relating to
post-colonialist cultures. The developed countries began to question
not only the desire of the underdeveloped countries for the same levels
of consumerist technology as those enjoyed by the First World, but also
the reliance of that First World upon exhaustible planetary resources.

For many European thinkers who were now coming to question
the fundamental grounds of their intellectual activities and philosophies,
Marxism now began to appear to be part of the problem, especially in
its assumption of the desirability of human mastery over nature. The
emerging Green movement of this period moved closely to a post-
Marxism which was sceptical of Enlightenment: sharing the emancipatory ideals and the desire for the fullest possible enjoyment of human
capacities, but tempering that with the idea of a necessary cohabitation
between humanity and the rest of nature. A postmodern world needed
a post-Marxist politics. Gramsci began to assume a prominent position
in this thinking, and the notion of hegemony replaced that of class as
a fundamental political category. A new political pluralism became
possible precisely at the moment when technology, as Lyotard indicates, had made it possible for the multinational companies to homogenize and unify their forms of control. Yet underneath the increasingly
homogenized capitalist world, the play of local forces continues to pose

the threat of a disruptive pluralism which capitalism must now police if it is to sustain itself. For those forces to be activated, all we require is the release of something inimical to capital, the release of something which cannot be inserted into or accommodated within a capitalist economy. The radical, central philosophers at this moment made their revolutionary investment in the body and in libidinal desire.

Perhaps the most extreme re-thinking of Marx began with the so-called 'philosophy of desire' in texts such as Lyotard's *Economie libidinale* (1974; complete translation not available) or in the work of Deleuze and Guattari in their *Capitalisme et schizophrénie* (1972, 1980; translated 1984, 1987). This work led Lyotard and Deleuze to the position where they favour the supervention of a micropolitics which will attend to the local and the specific without recourse to some grand programme or macropolitical theory such as Marxism, psychoanalysis or evolutionary progress to legitimize actions taken at the local level. Practice is now valid – that is to say, it becomes an 'event' – only when it is unanswerable to, or when it is actually disruptive of, a totalizing 'grand theory'.

The most explicit attack on fundamental Marxist theory, and specifically on its underlying category of 'production' is fully developed in Baudrillard's *Le Miroir de la production* (1973; translated as *The Mirror of Production* 1975), a work which set Baudrillard firmly on a trajectory away from any form of classical Marxism. His work since has increasingly sustained a problematization of the oppositionalist impetus inscribed in Marxist theory. For Baudrillard, opposition to a dominant force is always already inscribed in the structure which holds that dominant force in power. The oppositional energy is diverted and recharged to the account of the dominant force: opposition works like inoculation. Marxism inoculates capital, the better to sustain it: 'critical' or 'oppositional' thinking is, as it were, the last refuge of the bourgeois, who is condemned to go through the motions of theoretical opposition while simultaneously sustaining the historical status quo.

Theory, by which I here mean any critical practice which makes a philosophically foundational claim, enters into crisis itself in the wake of 1968. Not only has knowledge become uncertain, but more importantly the whole question of how to legitimize certain forms of knowledge and certain contents of knowledge is firmly on the agenda. No single satisfactory mode of epistemological legitimation is available. Even if one were, the very Subject of consciousness has, as a result of deconstruction and psychoanalysis, also been thrown into doubt. Postmodernism is shaped and informed by these crises in epistemology, in ontology, in legitimation and in the Subject.

In what follows, I shall firstly outline briefly the intellectual trajectory of two thinkers whose work has shaped much of the debate over postmodernism: Jean-François Lyotard and Jean Baudrillard. I shall then substantively address the issue of the Enlightenment and its contested legacies. This leads into a necessary reconsideration of the question of politics, specifically under the rubric of a theory of justice. In conclusion, I shall draw together the characteristics of postmodern philosophy under the sign of what might be called, in contradistinction to Leibnizian Optimism, a 'new pessimism' distinguished not by sadness but by stoicism.

❧❧ TWO PARADIGMATIC THINKERS ❧❧

Jean-François Lyotard

Lyotard moved to the centre of debates around postmodernism in the late 1970s when he defined *The Postmodern Condition* in terms of an 'incredulity toward metanarratives'.[7] By this, he meant that, in the contemporary world, it had become difficult to subscribe to the great narratives which had previously conditioned existence, be they narratives of salvation as in the various religions, or of emancipation as in Marx, or of therapy as in Freud, and so on. Postmodernism was defined in terms of an anti-foundationalism; it was a mood and not a period; and it was characterized by a pragmatic and experimentalist attitude. Like the artist, the postmodern philosopher was to 'work without rules in order to formulate the rules of what will have been done' *after the event*:[8] that is to say, thinking was to be radically experimental and ostensibly undirected in order to allow for the unpreprogrammed, for the unforeseen, to take place.

This led Lyotard to ponder two key theoretical principles: that of the 'event'; and that of 'justice'.[9] An 'event' occurs when 'it happens' without the 'it' having any specific identity. Such an identification of 'what' happened can only happen when the event is inserted into a determining structure which will assign a meaning to the happening and a substance to it. An 'event' is, as it were, a happening laid bare, devoid of a Subject, devoid of – or, better, prior to – an assigned significance. For Lyotard, the honour of thinking can itself only occur when thinking is 'eventful', when thinking is of the status of an event.

Thought thus has little to do with the accumulation of 'knowledges' whose significance can be arrayed and arranged in hierarchical orders and sequences, initially placed in repositories of knowledge such as libraries and museums, but increasingly in our time stored in ostensibly less material but equally reified form on microchips or on computer discs.

For Lyotard, one effect of this is the necessity to wage war on all forms of totality. He argues that any 'grand narrative' or foundational theory necessarily tends to homogenize the absolute heterogeneity and specificity of singular events, thereby robbing the event of its full ontological or historical status and, more importantly for a philosopher, denying the possibility of genuine thinking. Further, he argues that such totality most often articulates itself under the form simply of consensus. Here, he explicitly set himself apart from a thinker such as Jürgen Habermas, who argues that, given the lack of any prior foundational philosophy upon which to build a rational society, individual Subjects must strive collectively or mutually to attain a rational consensus which will enable the formulation of (at least provisional) values against which individual acts can be judged. In other words, a practical social theory is to be based upon rational discourse and the disinterested pursuit of the better argument by a community. Lyotard argues that the consensus thus reached is illusory, for it is necessarily founded upon a covert violence between the participants in the dialogues, in which the discourse of one Subject will always find itself degraded in and by the discourse of the other. There is no consensus without the covert exercise of an imperialist power, according to Lyotard, who therefore prefers the pursuit of paralogy over consensus.

In order to maintain thinking at the status of the event, it becomes important to bear witness to what Lyotard calls the 'differend'. A differend occurs when, in a dispute between two parties, the rules of conflict which bring them into their opposed positions are made in the idiom of one party while the wrong from which the other suffers simply does not figure and cannot be recognized in that idiom. That is, the fundamental clash is one of language-games; the language-game of each party to the dispute simply cannot accommodate the terms of the wrong suffered by the other; and further, there is no common language to which a 'neutral' appeal can be made to facilitate an adjudication between the two parties.

Here we enter the second specific realm of Lyotard's concern: justice. As with knowledge, justice or judging too must become, for Lyotard, an event rather than a substance. Given that we should abandon the metanarrative, or theory, we now have no grounds upon which to make our judgments, be they aesthetic, ethical, political or whatever. Yet we must judge, as a simple condition of living. For Lyotard, we must bear witness to the differend and learn to judge without criteria. This he relates to the Kant of the third Critique, where a fundamental distinction is made between determining judgment and reflective judgment. Determining judgments are made in conformity to a rule; reflective judgments are those where we lack any formal guiding principle, as in aesthetics. Lyotard urges the prioritization of the latter, for it is only by making judging and thinking reflective – and thereby 'eventful'

– that we will attain to the postmodern mood; and it is only that way that we can avoid the tacit political violence which dominates and informs our modes of philosophy and of social being.

Jean Baudrillard

Baudrillard, like Lyotard, began his career on the political left. But in *The Mirror of Production*, he began his trajectory steadily away from any recognizable Marxism and towards an extremely different position indeed. Fundamentally, Baudrillard began by arguing that Marx was not Marxist enough; that in the attempt to confound political economy, Marx simply could not manage to escape the form 'production' and the form 'representation' which shape political economy. Marxism is thus tainted by a complicity with capitalism, argued Baudrillard. He then began himself to try to find a way out of this by insisting that the world is not 'pro-duced' but 'seduced': seduction, he claimed in *De la séduction*, was logically prior to production. Seduction is not simply sexual: it is rather any mutual interplay of forces of attraction and repulsion. It thus can have no paradigmatic form and veers into a multiplicity of social practices, none of which can assume a position of centrality, normativity or dominance. By this point, Marxism has not been modified as much as entirely abandoned.

Baudrillard began to indicate that Marxism had become part of the problem rather than part of the cure for a society in any case. He suggested that in any given system (such as a capitalist one) which is characterized by efficiency, the possibility of opposition to the system has to be controlled internally if the system is to persist. The single best way of controlling opposition is, of course, by accommodation. Hence, using a medical analogy, Baudrillard argued that every system generates localized 'scandals' which ostensibly throw the system entirely into disrepute – but which operate rather like an inoculation against disease. Thus, for instance, Watergate was a scandal to the office of the President of the USA; but it was a scandal which 'purified' the office by vilifying its temporary occupant; it thus enabled the possibility of that now 'purged', 'incorruptible', office being inhabited very soon after by Ronald Reagan, whose folly, lies and obvious insincerity far outstripped anything of which Nixon seemed capable. Similarly, capitalism needs and thrives on Marxism; masculinism and patriarchy need feminism if they are to strengthen themselves; racism requires anti-racist legislation; and so on.

This somewhat desperate scenario provokes Baudrillard into his most radical claims, and into a position usually described as 'nihilist'. The principle of reality itself, he argues, is defunct. At an early stage in his career, when he concentrated his attention on consumer society, Baudrillard rapidly realized not only that consumption was the new structure of power in the social, but also that something had happened to the very materiality of the object of consumption. He argued that the object as signifier was more important than the object as referent. In other words, classical 'use-value' had been replaced not just by 'exchange-value' but by what might be called 'signifying-value', or the value of the object as a sign. The referent – the 'real' world – began simply to disappear in Baudrillard's theoretical thinking.

When allied to his thinking on negation or criticism as a form of therapeutic inoculation, this has far-reaching consequences. Baudrillard is now able to argue that Disneyland, for example, is there as an arena of fantasy in order to generate the belief that the rest of the USA, everything 'outside' Disneyland, is 'real'. In fact, Baudrillard argues, it is the rest of the USA which is now living entirely at the level of fantasy. Meanwhile 'the real' has disappeared, or has been overtaken by simulacra of the real. Thus he felt able to claim, for instance, that, in a specific sense, the Gulf War of 1990 'did not take place'. Baudrillard indicates that technology has now made it possible for us to reproduce the real in a 'more' real form than the 'original'; and historical events for us now are only real once they have been mediated, usually by television. If we are to make any genuine philosophical or political engagement in this state of affairs, it has to be done by attending not to specific aspects of the real but rather to the very principle of reality itself.

❦ ENLIGHTENMENT AND ITS LEGACIES ❦

A major source for the contemporary debates around the postmodern is to found in the work of the Frankfurt school, and perhaps nowhere more precisely than in the text proposed by Adorno and Horkheimer in 1944, the *Dialectic of Enlightenment*, a work 'written when the end of the Nazi terror was within sight'. This work prefigures some of Lyotard's later scepticism over Enlightenment; and it also seriously engages the issue of mass culture in ways which influence Gorz's thoughts on the 'leisure merchants' of contemporary capitalist societies. It is worth indicating in passing that it is Adorno and Horkheimer, and not Lyotard, who propose that 'Enlightenment is totalitarian':[10] the vulgar characterization which describes contemporary German philosophy as pro-Enlightenment and the French as anti-Enlightenment is simplistic and false.

Enlightenment aimed at human emancipation from myth or super-stition, and from an enthralled enchantment to mysterious powers and forces of nature. Such emancipation was to be effected through the progressive operations of critical reason. According to Peter Gay, 'The Enlightenment may be summed up in two words: criticism and power':[11] criticism would become creative precisely by its capacity for empowering the individual and enabling his or her freedom. Why would Adorno and Horkheimer set themselves in opposition to this ostensibly admirable programme? Why do they argue that 'The fully Enlightened earth radiates disaster triumphant'?[12]

The problem lies not in the theoretical principle of Enlightenment but in its practice. In the desire to contest any form of animistic enchantment by nature, Enlightenment set out to think the world in an abstract form. Consequently, the material content of the world becomes a merely formal conceptual set of categories. As Adorno and Horkheimer put it: 'From now on, matter would at least be mastered without any illusion of ruling or inherent powers, of hidden qualities. For the Enlightenment, whatever does not conform to the rule of computation and utility is suspect'.[13] In a word, reason has been reduced to *mathesis*: that is, it has been reduced to a specific *form* of reason. More importantly, this specific inflection of reason is also now presented as if it were Reason-as-such, as if it were the only valid or legitimate form of rational thinking. But Adorno and Horkheimer share a fear that, in this procedure, reason has itself simply become a formal category, which reduces or translates the specific concepts of material realities into rational concepts, or into a form amenable to mathematization. Reason becomes no more than a discourse, a language of reason (the codes of mathematics), which deals with the 'foreign' matter of reality by translating it into reason's own abstract terms; and something – the 'event', non-conceptual reality itself – gets lost in the translation. As Adorno and Horkheimer have it: 'The multiplicity of forms is reduced to position and arrangement, history to fact, things to matter.'[14] A mathematical consciousness thus produces the world, not surprisingly, as mathematics. So a desired knowledge of the world is reduced to the merest *anamnesis*, in which a consciousness never cognizes the world as it is, but rather *recognizes* the world as the proper image and correlate of the consciousness itself. Enlightenment thus serves only the self-Identity of the Subject of consciousness.

'Emancipatory' knowledge turns out to involve itself firmly with a question of power, which complicates and perhaps even restricts its emancipatory quality. Knowledge, conceived as abstract and utilitarian, as a mastery over a recalcitrant nature, becomes characterized by power; as a result, 'Enlightenment behaves toward things as a dictator toward man. He knows them in so far as he can manipulate them. The man of science knows all things in so far as he can make them.'[15] Knowledge is hereby reduced to technology; and that in nature – the 'event' – which is unamenable to the formal or conceptual categories of such mathematical knowledge simply escapes consciousness. Yet the Subject believes itself to have captured, dominated and conceptually controlled the event; for it can determine the *meaning* of the event. There is thus only the *illusion* of power over nature; and yet there is a more important dividend of power here: the Subject endowed with Enlightenment 'knowledge' has a power over the consciousness of others who may be less fluent in the language of reason. Knowledge is thus caught up in a dialectic of mastery and slavery in which the victim is not a dominated and overcome nature but rather other overwhelmed human individuals. Accordingly, knowledge such as this cannot be purely characterized by disenchantment and emancipation. Enlightenment does not simply produce a disenchanted knowledge of the contents of the material world; rather, it produces a formally empowered Subject of consciousness, a Subject which exerts its power in the discourse of reason, in a language-game. From now on in philosophy – and this is what will be characterized as the 'modern' philosophy from which postmodernism wishes to escape – to know is to be in a position to enslave, or, as Lyotard will argue, 'what was and is at issue is the introduction of the will into reason'.[16]

What is thus at issue is a confusion between the operations of a pure reason on the one hand and a practical reason on the other: a confusion between theory and practice, between *gnosis* and *praxis*. This is an old Aristotelian distinction which has resurfaced precisely at the moment when many thinkers are becoming suspicious precisely of theory itself. Twentieth-century literary criticism, the field in which much of the postmodern debate has been fought out, presents us with a series of attempts to yoke together theory and practice. Language, for instance, is often seen not as something which merely runs alongside and parallel to the 'real' events of material history: rather, it is consistently secularized, realized as itself a historical event. This is so all the way from J. L. Austin's speech-act theories of performative linguistics, through various advocates of the idea of 'language as symbolic action' (Kenneth Burke, R. P. Blackmur and others), and all the way on to the contemporary revival of Jamesian and Deweian pragmatism in the thinking of Rorty, Fish and others.[17] These are all attempts to bring together the epistemological function of language with the ontological event of linguistic activity. And in this regard, twentieth-century literary criticism can be seen to be wrestling with one major and fundamental issue: the perceived rupture between the realm of language and the realm of Being, a rupture articulated most vigorously by those readers of Saussure's *Course in General Linguistics* who prioritize above all else the arbitrariness of the relation between the linguistic signifier and the conceptual signified. By inserting the cognitive activity of a real historical reader between the text and its epistemological content, critics such as Fish, Jauss, Iser and others tried to circumvent the threatened split between, on the one hand, the structure of consciousness (i.e., the conceptual forms in which a consciousness appropriates the world for meaning) and, on the other, history (the material content of a text which may – and indeed, according to Fish, *must* – disturb such formal structures).

In philosophical terms, what is at stake here is an old Kantian question regarding the proper or adequate 'fit' between the noumenal and the phenomenal. Kant was aware that the world outside of consciousness does not necessarily match precisely our perceptual cognitions of that world; and in the *Critique of Pure Reason* he argued that it was erroneous simply to confuse the two. The two elements of signification being confused were distinguished by Frege as 'sense' and 'reference'; and it is a distinction similar to this which was maintained by Paul de Man, who argued that such a confusion is precisely what we know as 'ideology': 'What we call ideology is precisely the confusion of linguistic with natural reality, of reference with phenomenalism.'[18]

De Man's concern was to ensure that literary criticism made no premature assumptions of the absolute validity of reference; and in this he simply followed the deconstructive practice of maintaining a vigilant scepticism about the legitimacy or truth-contents of any linguistic proposition made about those aspects of the real world that could properly be called 'non-linguistic'. He was aware that the premature assumption that the world was available for precise, 'accurate' or truthful linguistic formulation was itself an assumption not only grounded in but fundamentally demonstrative of ideology. But this, of course, is simply a reiteration of Adorno and Horkheimer in their complaint about the assumption made by (mathematical) reason that the world is available for rational comprehension. It should now be clear that the fundamental burden of the *Dialectic of Enlightenment* is that Enlightenment itself is not the great demystifying force which will reveal and unmask ideology; rather, it is precisely the locus of ideology, thoroughly contaminated internally by the ideological assumption that the world can match – indeed, can be encompassed by – our reasoning about it, or by the attendant assumption that the human is not alienated by the very processes of consciousness itself from the material world and events of which it desires knowledge in the first place. Enlightenment, postulated upon reason, is – potentially at least – undone by the form that such reason takes.

For Adorno and Horkheimer, this argument assumed a specific shape recognizable as an abiding question in German philosophy from Kant to Heidegger. What worried Adorno and Horkheimer was that under the sign of Enlightenment, the Subject would be capable of an engagement with the world in a manner which would be 'rational' only in the most purely formal (and thus vacuous) sense of the word. That is, they were anxious that what should be a properly *political* engagement which involves the Subject in a process called intellection or thinking could be reduced to a ritual of thinking, to a merely formal appearance of thinking which would manifest itself as a legitimation not of a perception of the world but of the analytical modes of mathematical reason itself. The political disturbance of the Subject proposed by an engagement with a materially different Other (i.e., the Subject as transformed and transfigured through an 'event') would be reduced to a confirmation of the aesthetic beauty and validity of the process of mathematical reason itself, a reason whose object would thus be not the world in all its alterity but rather the process of reason which confirms the Identity of the Subject as an identity untrammelled by the disturbance of politics, an amorphous identity predicated on a narcissism and uninformed by any real event. In short, the Subject would be reduced to an engagement with and confirmation of its own rational processes rather than being committed to an engagement with the material alterity of an objective world.[19]

The 'aesthetic engagement' with the world might be characterized as follows: the structure of consciousness determines what can be perceived, and processes it in accordance with its own internal logic, its own internal, formal or ritualistic operations of reason. There is thus a ritual or appearance of engagement with the material world only. 'Political engagement' would be characterized by the rupture of such ritual, by the eruption of history into the consciousness in such a way that the aesthetic or formal structures of consciousness must be disturbed, reconfigured, rearranged. Enlightenment's commitment to abstraction is seen as a mode of disengagement of the ideological, opinionated self: abstraction is itself meant to address precisely this problem. But it leads, according to Adorno and Horkheimer, not to a practice of thinking but rather to the ritualistic form of thought; it offers a form without content. Adorno and Horkheimer fear that it is precisely when Enlightenment addresses the political that it in fact most successfully evades the political; that Enlightenment is Idealist precisely when it pretends to be fully materialist.

One twentieth-century legacy of Enlightenment is the so-called 'Copernican revolution' proposed initially by structuralism and semiotics. In the wake of Roland Barthes, the world became an extremely 'noisy' place: signs everywhere announced their presence and demanded to be decoded. Such decoding was often done under the aegis of a presiding formal structure, such as myth in anthropology (Lévi-Strauss), desire in psychoanalysis (Lacan), or grammar in literature (Genette, Greimas, Todorov). In semiotics, it is always important to be able to discover a kind of equivalence between ostensibly different signs: this is, in fact, the very principle of decoding or of translation which is at the basis of semiotic analysis. But as Adorno and Horkheimer indicate: 'Bourgeois society is ruled by equivalence. It makes the dissimilar comparable by reducing it to abstract qualities.'[20] Such abstraction must wilfully disregard the specificity of the material objects or events under its consideration: 'Abstraction, the tool of enlightenment, treats its objects as did fate, the notion of which it rejects: it liquidates them.'[21] The semiotic revolution – a revolution which frequently masqueraded as a political, emancipatory heir of Enlightenment, but a revolution whose content was only at the level of the abstract sign and thus at the level of an aesthetics denuded of politics – is, like Enlightenment, irredeemably bourgeois in the eyes of the postmodernist, for it is irredeemably caught up in a philosophy of identity which negates material and historical reality in the interests of constructing a recognizable Subject of consciousness as a self-identical entity.

When postmodernism rigorously questions the tradition of a self-consciously 'modern' Enlightenment philosophy, it does not do so in the interests of nihilism or irrationality. Postmodernism indicates rather (as did Foucault) that Enlightenment reason may not itself be entirely reasonable.[22] Further, postmodernism returns to the great Kantian questions: how might we know the alterity of a material reality; how might we validate or legitimize that knowledge?

The *Dialectic* was written in a profound awareness of the material and historical realities of fascism and of the Nazi atrocities. It is a text which inserts itself in a specific tradition of philosophical and ethical tracts which ask for an explanation of the presence of evil in the world. This tradition was properly inaugurated in the modern world by the debates around Leibniz and Optimism. Optimism is based on the idea that nature is a Leibnizian monad, and that there is a great unifying chain in nature which links, in a necessary conjunction, all the ostensibly random and diverse elements of a seemingly heterogeneous and pluralistic world. Much more important for our purpose is the observation that Optimism must be based upon a specific idea of *progressive time* which challenges the meaning of events. It argues that what appears 'now' to be a local evil will be revealed 'in the fullness of time' as something which essentially serves the realization of a greater good. As Voltaire's Pangloss has it in *Candide*, 'All is for the best in the best of all possible worlds'; or, as a less comic predecessor, Milton's Satan, has it: 'Evil, be thou my good.'[23] History would reveal the immanent goodness in the most apparently evil acts; under the sign of a homogeneous and monadic eternity, the heterogeneous and secular would be redeemed.

In a sense this philosophy is a precursor of some contemporary theoretical principles; and it foreshadows directly the great (and perhaps final) flowering of a modernist thought in deconstruction. According to Optimistic philosophy, the meaning of an event is not immediately apparent, as if it were never present-to-itself: its final sense – to be revealed as the necessity of goodness – is always deferred (to be revealed under the sign of eternity), and is thus always 'different' (or not what it appears to be to the local eye caught up in the event itself). The major difference between deconstruction and Optimism is that Optimism believes that the final sense lies *immanently* within an event, whereas deconstruction eschews any such 'immanentist' ideas as metaphysical. Yet the trajectory underpinning both is the same in that they share fundamentally and tacitly an investment in the notion of a 'progressive enlightenment': the passage of time is invested with the idea of *progress*.

Optimism was buried, of course, with the buildings under the earthquake in Lisbon on 1 November 1755. But at that time a different idea of progress in history arises. After 1755, progress is characterized as a gradual emancipation from the demands of the sign of eternity. The secularization of consciousness became a necessary precondition for the possibility of an ethics: that is to say, the ethical is increasingly determined by the philosophically rational, or the good is determined by the true. Hans Blumenberg in his *The Legitimacy of the Modern Age*, offers eloquent testimony to the inflection this gives to philosophy and to truth. Traditionally, the pursuit of truth had been pleasurable, eudaemonic; from now on, the absoluteness of truth, and correspondingly its ascetic harshness, becomes a measure of its validity: 'Lack of consideration for happiness becomes the stigma of truth itself, a homage to its absolutism.'[24] Pain legitimizes knowledge.

There arises thus the possibility – and Kantians would argue the necessity – of separating the realm of facts from the realm of values: neither can legitimately be derived from the other, neither facts from values nor values from facts. Optimism has proceeded on the grounds that these were intimately conjoined; and it followed that the progressive movement from evil to good was seen as inevitable. But once epistemology is separated from ethics, the whole idea of historical progress is itself called into question: no longer do we know with any certainty the point towards which history is supposedly progressing. In the wake of this, humanity becomes enslaved not to the enchantments of myth but rather to the necessities of narrative, for humanity has embarked upon a secular movement whose teleology is uncertain, whose plot is not inherently predetermined by values or by an ethical end.[25]

This critique of progress returns in the twentieth century; and is a central component of a postmodernist mood. The paradigmatic example comes in architecture, where there has grown a resistance to the 'modernist' idea that all buildings must be innovative in aim and design. As Jencks and Portoghesi have suggested, it is possible to relearn from the past, to develop a 'new classicism' or simply to engage with an abiding 'presence of the past'.[26] The result is – in principle if not always in practice – a heterogeneous juxtaposition of different styles from different architectural epochs as a putative response to the homogenizing tendency of the so-called 'international style'. This argument leads to two interrelated consequences. The first is that lived space is inhabited by a complicating sense of historical time.[27] More importantly, there grows an awareness in architecture and urban planning in general that the local traditions of a place should be respected in all their specificity, while at the same time these local traditions may be opened to a kind of criticism by their juxtaposition with styles from other localities and from different traditions.[28] This is a localism without parochial insularity: a revalorization of the 'periphery' without the need for a determining 'centre'.

Probably the greatest and most-cited description of the postmodern coincides nicely with this architectural scepticism regarding inexorable progress. In philosophy, Lyotard argued that the postmodern mood was characterized by an 'incredulity towards metanarratives'. In an argument which he subsequently described as 'overstated', Lyotard argued that it was becoming increasingly difficult to subscribe to the great – and therapeutically Optimistic – grand narratives which once organized our lives.[29] What he had in his sights were the great totalizing narratives, great codes which in their degree of abstraction necessarily deny the specificity of the local event and traduce it in the interests of a global homogeneity or a universal history. Such 'master narratives', as they subsequently came to be called, would include the narrative of emancipation via revolution proposed by Marx; the narrative of psychoanalytic therapy elaborated by Freud; or the story of constant development and adaptation advanced under the rubric of evolution by Darwin. Such narratives operate like Enlightenment reason: in order to accommodate widely diverging local histories and traditions, they abstract the meaning of those traditions in a 'translation' into the terms of a master code, thereby violating the specificity of the local and rendering real historical events unrecognizable. As metanarratives, they also become coercive and normative. In the interests of respecting the heterogeneity of the real, and (more importantly for Lyotard) in the interests of maintaining the possibility of thought, of philosophy, we must wage war on such totalizing prescriptive grand narratives. Lyotard's debt to Adornian critical theory is obvious here.

This new pessimism with regard to the idea of historical progress was foreseen by Walter Benjamin, another great source for much postmodern thinking. In his famous seventh thesis on the philosophy of history, he indicates a specific scepticism regarding history which has been picked up and thoroughly developed in postmodernism. His famous words in that thesis – 'There is no document of civilization which is not at the same time a document of barbarism' – prize open the historical document – and, by extension, the event itself – to an internal instability and mutability.[30] Postmodernism has enlarged on this to the extent that it challenges the very notion of there being any universal history at all. It is important to be clear on this: postmodernism does not deny history; rather, it denies that there is only *one* history. For Lyotard, a universal history implies a single transcendent Subject position from which the history might be recuperated, appropriated, recounted or narrated: that is to say, universal history is predicated on monotheism. In place of this, Lyotard advocates the pluralism of paganism: multiple gods, multiple histories, no transcendence.[31] Any singular event can be inserted into any number of histories, each presided over by a different force or power; and its value – its essence – will depend upon the contradictions and incoherence involved in our necessarily considering the event from such a pluralist perspective. In the simpler terms which Benjamin had in mind, the singular event of a battle, say, is different when one is the victim and when one is the victor: postmodernism would ask us to think the narratives proposed by both such positions simultaneously.

'Modernity' itself is increasingly seen as a Benjaminian document of civilization and of barbarism at once. It is a crude banalization of the postmodern position to suggest that it entirely reneges on modernity. Zygmunt Bauman's work is an excellent case in point here. Given the pessimism regarding Enlightenment and subsequent European history, it would be an easy step to consider the twentienth century's greatest disaster, the Nazi atrocities, as a consequence of modernity. But Bauman takes a much more circumspect postmodern attitude to the Holocaust. Citing sociological research into the victims of hijackings and terrorist activity, he indicates that so-called 'personality change' after the traumatic event is in fact illusory. What happens is that historical circumstances after the trauma favour the appearance of traits which were always latent, but which were not appropriate under the historical norms which conditioned the life of the victim before the traumatic event. A different aspect of the personality assumes the normative position: the same person remains. Bauman allegorizes this to consider the Holocaust:

> The unspoken terror permeating our collective memory of the
> Holocaust . . . is the gnawing suspicion that the Holocaust could

be more than an aberration, more than a deviation from an otherwise straight path of progress, more than a cancerous growth on the otherwise healthy body of the civilized society; that, in short, the Holocaust was not the antithesis of modern civilization and everything (or so we like to think) it stands for. We suspect (even if we refuse to admit it) that the Holocaust could merely have uncovered another face of the same modern society whose other, so familiar, face we so admire. And that the two faces are perfectly comfortably attached to the same body.[32]

Modernity does not lead inexorably to the Holocaust; rather, the civilized face of modernity is attended constantly by a barbarism which is its Janus-complement.

The horror at the evil of the Holocaust is, for Bauman, really a horror at the rationality inscribed within the practice of the Holocaust. Enlightenment reason had enabled the development of an extraordinarily complete rationally ordered and self-sustaining social process. Part of the legacy of this is the development of efficiency in productivity, and the (often self-serving) development of technology. The horrifying truth of the matter, according to Bauman, is that 'every "ingredient" of the Holocaust . . . was normal, "normal" not in the sense of the familiar . . . but in the sense of being fully in keeping with everything we know about our civilization, its guiding spirit, its priorities, its immanent vision of the world'.[33] Structurally, the gas chambers are driven by the same presiding principles that were taken for granted as the positive aspects of modernity: rationalized efficiency in industrial production. The barbarism of the Holocaust arises because Enlightenment contained within its drive to reason a carcinogenic drive to rationalism, which can be used as well for fascist as for emancipatory ends. For a postmodern sociologist such as Bauman, it becomes difficult to disintricate the 'rationality of evil' from the 'evil of [modern, instrumental] rationality'. As he indicates, in the world of the death camps, everything was rationalized: 'Each step on the road to death was carefully shaped so as to be calculable in terms of gains and losses, rewards and punishments.'[34] The SS also knew that, in a perversion of Enlightenment, but a perversion made possible precisely *by* Enlightenment, reason was their single best ally in ensuring that their victims would become complicit in their own suffering, betraying their fellows in the reasonable hope of prolonging their own lives thereby: 'to found their order on fear alone, the SS would have needed more troops, arms and money. Rationality was more effective, easier to obtain, and cheaper. And thus to destroy them, the SS men carefully cultivated the rationality of their victims.'[35]

Reason, which was supposed to legitimize the neo-pagan and

emancipatory activities of Enlightenment, is now itself in need of legitimation. It can no longer assume the capacity for self-legitimation without assuming an exclusivity which necessarily victimizes other possible (and equally, if differently) reasonable narratives. Its claims upon universality are supplied by its inherent tendency to fall into the merest rationalism. It produces an administered society, and not a reasonable one; reason is replaced by efficiency and by the aesthetic and formal vacuities of rationalism. As both Derrida and Foucault have argued, though in very different ways, Enlightenment reason is profoundly exclusivist: it can legitimate itself only by first identifying and then stigmatizing its Other. As a result, Enlightenment reason is a potent weapon in the production of social normativity, driving people towards a conformity with a dominant and centred single 'norm' of behaviour. Reason, in short, has to produce the 'scandal' of its Other to keep itself going. Baudrillard has argued that this has an extremely important corollary effect in the twentieth century. In our time, it is not so much reason itself which requires legitimation as the very principle of reality (which, it is assumed, is founded upon rational principles). Society, in a move structurally parallel to Enlightenment reason, thus produces the Other of the real – fantasy – to legitimize the normativity of its own practices. Thus: 'Disneyland is there to conceal the fact that it is the "real" country, all of "real" America, which *is* Disneyland (just as prisons are there to conceal the fact that it is the social, in its entirety, in its banal omnipresence, which is carceral.'[36] The emancipation proposed by Enlightenment brings with it an incarcerating impetus: its 'freedom' turns out to be but the *form* of a freedom, an aesthetics rather than a politics of freedom. The name for this aestheticization of the political is *representation*. In the postmodern, representation, as both a political and an aesthetic category, has come under increasing pressure; and it is to this that we can now turn.

JUSTICE AND REPRESENTATION

Enlightenment reason is self-legitimizing: it takes one historically and culturally specific inflection of reason for the universal form of all Reason; and then adjudges all competing forms of reason to be, *ipso facto*, unreasonable.[37] In crude terms, Enlightenment Europe judged the rest of the cultures of the world in precisely the terms of Enlightenment Europe; and when, not surprisingly, it found the rest of the world to be 'different', it judged it to be inferior, unreasonable, 'underdeveloped'. Hence there arises the legitimation for a racist and imperialist consciousness which underpins some of the most unjust actions of the modern world, culminating perhaps in the Holocaust. Enlightenment's difficulty, it seems, was in accepting the possibility of a plurality of the forms of reason, each specific to particular historical or cultural events in their singularity. That difficulty had its root in the tendency to abstraction, or to theory.

Equally abstract is the idea of a Universal History which, if it is to exist, must disregard the singularities of specific events, reading them as 'signs' or semiotic counters which can be meaningfully inserted into a governing and totalized master narrative. Given that a human culture or society is made possible precisely by the narratives which it tells to itself, then it becomes clear that what is at stake here is a massive political injustice.

The postmodern attack on the notion of a Universal History has important ramifications for the questions of representation and justice. As I indicated earlier, a Universal History is tacitly predicated upon a monotheism which brings in its wake an incipient totalitarianism. It presupposes a single transcendental position ('God') from which the whole of history can be recounted or truthfully narrated. Accordingly, if we subscribe to such notions, then all contradictory ('pagan') human narratives are automatically discarded and deemed to be nothing more than 'fictions'. In pragmatic fact, of course, this has meant that, as Benjamin and others have indicated, all history is told from the point of view of the victor, who, as a 'master narrator', assumes the position of a totalitarian author, or God; and any opposing narratives – such as the narratives which constituted the entire cultural and social history of the victim – are either ignored, denied or brought into line with the dominant narrative of the victor, from whose point of view they appear to be deviant, disjunctive and clearly false. The master narrator simply subsumes other competing narratives within a totalized framework, and assigns the competing narratives to a marginalized position. Those margins have, in modernism, been occupied by various figures such as dissidents, intellectuals, communists, women, lesbian and gay people, 'foreigners', and so on. In contrast to this, the postmodern faces the problematic possibility of a potentially endless and self-contradictory series of re-presentations *without the predication of an implied presence anywhere which would exist to ground or hierarchize the competing representations or narratives.*

In addition to this, and linked to it, is the political complication of the issue of justice. How can we judge an event? In the 'modern' world it is possible to judge according to specific criteria. These criteria are assumed to be shared by a social consensus. But this also implies an instance of presence somewhere, a fundamental ground of truth upon which all judgments can be made. That is to say, both representation and justice require a foundational theory. It is precisely such a theory that postmodernism would challenge, on the grounds that it is a theory which is always tacitly founded upon injustice and upon the covert violence of totalization.

Habermas would agree that no necessary foundation for a social formation exists prior to human beings in community. But he has consistently argued for the necessity of struggling towards the fabrication of a society founded upon a rational consensus. Lyotard challenges this on the grounds that consensus without the prior exercise of power and without covert injustice seems to be impossible; and on the grounds that such a consensus, which would of necessity conceal and act as a cover for the violences and injustices upon which the social is founded, may therefore not even be desirable.

For Lyotard, there is, in any achieved consensus, necessarily repression or, worse, oppression.[38] In order to circumvent this, he advocates that we multiply differences and that we bear witness to the differend, a term taken from legal discourse. A differend arises under specific circumstances: two opposed parties in a dispute are each in the right according to their own terms of reference; the terms of reference of each party cannot accommodate, or refuse to accommodate, the other party; and there is no common ground or third set of terms of reference which will allow an adjudication between the two parties while respecting their own terms of reference. In short, a differend arises when we lack a theory which will encompass radically divergent ('pagan') narratives. This may arise in a court of law; but, for Lyotard, it arises everywhere as an issue of justice and representation.[39]

Neither party to a differend can find an adequate representation of itself in the language-game of the other party. Each therefore feels violated by its insertion into that language-game. Further, we lack a 'neutral' or monotheistic theory which can encompass and adequately represent both parties. In the absence of criteria upon which to make the necessary judgments, how then do we judge?[40]

Judgment and representation are intimately related in the postmodern. The just has always been closely linked to the true; and justice depends upon a revelation of truth. There is a clear structural similarity between this and a Marxist hermeneutic. The project of an ideological demystification starts from the presupposition that a text (or the object of any critical judgment) is always informed by a specific historical and political nexus, and that the text is the site for the covering over (or disappearance) of the contradictions implicit in this historical conjuncture. The task of critical judgment here is in the first instance epistemological: it involves the necessary revelation of a truth lying concealed behind an appearance. But it is precisely the opposition between ideological appearance on one hand and foundational or true reality on the other which the postmodern puts under speculative pressure.

As Baudrillard has argued, the real in our time is no longer what it used to be. Technology has made it possible to confound the separation between the authentic and the fake, between the real and its representation, in ways far more radical than even Benjamin imagined. Yet that separation, of course, is precisely the separation required for a foundational philosophy or for any philosophy which has a strong investment in a univocal and transcendental notion of truth. The postmodern eschews any such simple access to the true or to foundational criteria upon which to base its acts of criticism or of judgment.

We live increasingly in the time of what Debord aptly called 'the society of the spectacle'. Our politics, and our justice, have become increasingly 'spectacular', a matter of 'show trials' and 'live' television courtroom drama. A poignant icon of this state of affairs is to be found in the example, often cited by Paul Virilio, of the women of the Plaza de Maya in Buenos Aires, who congregate in silence at regular intervals simply to bear witness to their relatives who have been made to 'disappear' by a cruel politico-military regime.[41] Political systems – including *soi-disant* 'democratic' systems – increasingly deal with dissident thought by controlling and regulating its appearances; and, on occasion, dissident thinkers themselves are entirely 'disappeared' either directly by force or indirectly by bureaucratic measures. The essence of the political in our time is formulated not upon the old – the 'modernist' – relation between appearance and reality, but rather upon the relation between appearance and disappearance. Increasingly, the real itself is subject to this relation as well, when, for a random instance, the reality of the Gulf War of 1990 was reduced to the status of a video game, death and destruction disappearing until such times as the military decided it was appropriate for their reappearance before the population to be acceptable.[42]

Fundamentally, this shift has affected the status of knowledge upon which judgment and representation are based. The opposition of appearance to reality assumes necessarily that the Object of knowledge is stable, and that there exists a model for the Subject of knowledge which is transcendent. But in the postmodern mood, this has been contaminated by a historicity and mutability which render both Subject and Object unstable. As a result, knowledge itself – predicated upon a stable relation between the Subject and Object of knowledge, upon a moment of anagnorisis or recognition producing the Identity of the Subject – has entered into crisis.

This crisis was foreseen by Kant. In the *Critique of Pure Reason* Kant faced up to the question of the scientificity – by which he meant verifiability – of knowledge about the world; and he argued there for the necessity of a priori judgment in such matters. But more than this, he argued that an a priori knowledge gleaned simply from an analytic methodology would simply tell us a great deal about the methodology, and not necessarily anything new about the world: it would provide only *anamnesis*. That is to say, to perceive the world at all, consciousness needs a form in which to comprehend it; that form – the analytic method of perception – serves primarily the function of self-legitimation. Kant, like the contemporary postmodernist, wanted the world to be able to shock us into new knowledge, into the unforeseen and unpredictable. For Badiou, who makes a clear – and we might now say 'Kantian' – distinction between truth and the accumulation of knowledges, for instance, 'what is clear is that the *origin* of a truth is of the order of an event'.[43] Kant wanted the world to be able to shock us out of the ideological conditioning of our consciousness's structures. He wanted, thus, what he called the *synthetic a priori*, which would exceed the *analytic a priori*. The synthetic would not only confirm the method of epistemological analysis of the world; it would also allow for the structural modification of the very analytic method itself to account for and encompass a new given, the new and therefore unpredictable data of the world. It would thus provide not just anamnesis but what we would now call the event of knowledge, or knowledge as event rather than fact.

In the *Critique of Judgment*, this distinction between analytic and synthetic more or less maps directly on to a distinction between determining and reflective judgments, a distinction made much of by Lyotard in the question of postmodern justice. In a determining judgment, an analytic method determines – predetermines – the result of the judgment: as in mathematics, say, where the structure of arithmetic determines the result of its internally generated problems, such as those of addition or subtraction. In reflective judgment, we have a different state of affairs, for here, as in our judgments about the aesthetically beautiful, there are no predetermining rules in accordance with which we can verify our judgments: we judge 'without criteria', in the phrase made famous by Lyotard. In short, this means that we judge without a predetermining theory. Judgments, we could say, are replaced by acts or by events of judging: the aesthetic *form* of justice is replaced by the political *event* of justice.

In this state of affairs, the operation of reason extends itself beyond its own internally coherent framework and attempts to grasp – or to make – the new. This extension is one in which we can see a shift in emphasis away from scientific knowledge towards what should properly be called narrative knowledge. Rather than knowing the stable essence of a thing, we begin to tell the story of the event of judging it, and to enact the narrative of how it changes consciousness and thus produces a new knowledge. The postmodern prefers the event of knowing to the fact of knowledge, so to speak.

But the central problem remains: how can one legitimize an 'event' of judging? With respect to what can one validate what must effectively be a singular act? For Lyotard, a credulity towards metanarratives (i.e., subscription to a prevailing theory against whose norms single events of judging might themselves be judged and validated) is tantamount to a concession to systems theory. Even Habermas, who is opposed to Lyotard on many counts, opposes this, seeing that in such systems theory 'belief in legitimacy . . . shrinks to a belief in legality'.[44] For Habermas, communicative action can lead to the establishment of consensus, which would provide the necessary – if always provisional – grounds upon which to make our judgments. But Lyotard would see the establishment of consensus as a means of arresting the flow of events, in such a way that truth would be reduced to an accumulation of knowledges. That is to say, in short, that consensus is the means whereby a philosophy of Becoming is reduced to a philosophy of Being. The modernist assumes that it is possible to pass from Becoming to Being; the postmodernist believes that any such move is always necessarily premature and unwarranted, and that its primary victim is truth in the guise of the event.

Politics, as we usually think it, depends upon consensus; most often, such consensus articulates itself under the rubric of 'representation', in which there is first an assumed consensus between representative and represented, and second the possibility of consensus among representatives. This is bourgeois democracy, and, for the postmodernist, hardly a democracy at all. In place of such a politics, the postmodernist makes the demand for a justice. Justice cannot happen under bourgeois democracy, which is always grounded in the tyranny of the many (and even, of course, in many 'democratic' systems, on the tyranny of the few – on the hegemonic control of thought and of mediatic representations, appearances and disappearances, exercised by a few who mediate the norms of a social formation). We may no longer be able to legislate comfortably between opposing or competing political systems, for we can no more subscribe to such totalizing forms; but we can address the instance, the event, of judging and of justice in its singularities.

Here lies the basis of the ethical demand in the postmodern, a demand whose roots lie in the work of a philosopher such as Levinas. We must judge: there is no escape from the necessity of judging in each particular case. Yet we have no grounds upon which to base our judgment. This is profoundly akin to Levinas:

> I have spoken a lot about the face of the Other as being the original site of the sensible . . . . The proximity of the Other is the face's meaning, and it means in a way that goes beyond those plastic forms which forever try to cover the face like a mask of

their presence to perception. But always the face shows through these forms. Prior to any particular expression and beneath all particular expressions, which cover over and protect with an immediately adopted face or countenance, there is the nakedness and destitution of the expression as such, that is to say extreme exposure, defencelessness,vulnerability itself. . . . In its expression, in its mortality, the face before me summons me, calls for me, begs for me, as if the invisible death that must be faced by the Other, pure otherness, separated, in some way, from any whole, were my business.[45]

The 'face-to-face' implicates us in a response, in the necessity of sociality. We must behave justly towards the fact of the Other; but we cannot do that according to a predetermined system of justice or a predetermining political or ethical theory. The Other is itself always other than itself; it is not simply a displaced Identity in which we may once more recognize and reconstitute our self. The demand is for a just relating to alterity, and for a cognition of the event of heterogeneity. In short, therefore, we must discover – produce – justice. Here, for Lyotard and many others is the real political burden of the postmodern: the search for a just politics which will respect the differend that constitutes the event.

❦ THE NEW PESSIMISM ❦

Postmodernism has thrown the very fundamental notion of critique into doubt. It asks two basic questions of critique: first, given that, in order to be consistent internally, critique must have a theoretical foundation, how does it escape the injustice of violence; second, is critique not always accommodated by and within the existing totality of its ostensible object, and thereby rendered at best redundant and at worst complicit with its own defeat? Many conclude, as a consequence, that postmodernism is nihilist through and through, and that it gives succour to a contemporary socio-cultural and political state of affairs in which late capitalism carries on unabated and uncontested.

This view causes a particular concern among critics of culture, who, coincidentally with the rise of postmodernism in philosophy, have striven to validate mass and popular forms of culture, and who therefore see the work of critical philosophy to be thoroughly enmeshed in matters of general political interest. It is a widely held belief that the postmodern has somehow eradicated the boundaries supposed to exist between 'high art' and 'popular culture'. This is largely due to an understanding, deriving largely from Jameson, that the fundamental trope of postmodernism in art is pastiche, a 'parody without purpose'.[46] While modernists would cite or refer intertextually to a wide range of other artistic products (Joyce using Homer, say), they would do so for some specific ends. Postmodernists, it is argued, reiterate the same structural strategy of quotation, partial misrepresentation and so on, but they do this simply for the sake of it. In short, where modernism's strategy of quotation sent the Subject from one signified to another, postmodernism's similar strategy stays defiantly at the level of the signifier. We watch a rock video, in which allusions will be made to Hitchcock, say, and which may use archive cinematic footage; but the point is simply to play with such references and not to assign any governing 'meaning' or intentionality to them.

This is an 'ad hocism' which has seen its counterpart in some forms of contemporary architecture, where some architects have explicitly tried to accommodate their design to the various tastes and demands of a variegated community. Typically, contemporary popular art-forms plunder, and thereby question the 'value' of, the forms of high art, which are often deemed to be obstructively monumental. Modelling themselves on Duchamp, whose 'ready-mades' or 'LHOOQ' derive their power from the questioning of all modes of 'originality', contemporary artists frequently 'sample' or repeat the 'great works' of the past. In fact, as a result of this, much of the popular cultural product which goes under the name of the postmodern in our time is actually simply a continuation of the modern. It is frequently characterized by fragmentation instead of unity, by intertextuality or autoreferentiality instead of reference, by the prioritization of the signifier over the signified, and similar tropes and figures as we found in Joyce, Proust, Mann, Gide, Picasso, Kandinsky, Schoenberg, Stravinsky and others.

There is an important distinction, however. If the allusions and cultural cross-references made in contemporary popular art are not grasped by an audience, then so be it. There is nothing to be gained by such knowledge, which would only allow for the self-satisfying congratulation of narcissistic self-recognition and self-legitimation as a 'connoisseur'. The fundamental argument here is based upon a rather cheerful 'degradation' of knowledge, or at least a degradation of knowledge-as-fact in favour of knowledge-as-event.

Knowledge here has become nothing more than the next 'byte' on the computer screen, the next 30,000 pixel-image, the next software package. It is important to indicate that this is as much an effect of the technology of postmodernity as it is of any philosophical determinants of the cultural practices of postmodernism. For the philosopher or intellectual who assumes that his or her position is to be that of the critic whose criticisms are based upon knowledge, enlightenment, the pursuit of truth or at least of the better arguments in the interests of the construction of a 'rational society', this surely provokes a dismal pessimism.

Yet it would be true to say that this kind of pessimism is, in a sense, rather banal. With this form of pessimism, there yet remains the hope of Enlightenment, of an enlightenment possessed by the critic and therefore available to others. What is at stake in postmodernism is a much more rigorous form of Pessimism, one which will act as a philosophical counter to the Optimism on which Enlightenment and modernity are fundamentally grounded. As I indicated earlier, such Optimism projects into the future a moment of redemption of the present. It suggests the possibility and even the eventual necessity of a coincidence between intellection and material practice, between aesthetics and politics, between 'I' as the Subject of consciousness and 'me' as its Object. Thereby it suggests the immanence as well as the imminence of a moment of self-presence; and fundamentally, therefore, such an Optimism can be seen to be predicated upon a philosophy of Identity. If the postmodern is distinguishable from the modern, the distinction lies in the willingness of postmodernism to countenance and indeed to encourage a philosophy of alterity. The Pessimism of the postmodern lies in a realization that the future will not redeem the present; that the material world may be thoroughly resistant to consciousness and to our determination to master it by signification; that history, in short, does not exist *for* the Subject.

Such a Pessimism, of course, has nothing to do with an emotion of sadness. It is, rather, of the philosophical order of an ethical demand. If the crude formulation of Optimism is that 'all is for the best in the best of all possible worlds', then Pessimism does not strictly speaking simply or simplistically state the reverse, that 'all is for the worst in the worst of all possible worlds'. Rather, it takes as its first step the acknowledgement, even within modernist Optimism, that there are a number of 'possible worlds'. It advances from this that these possible worlds may exist simultaneously (in the form, say, of 'first' world, 'Third' world, 'underdeveloped' world, and so on), and that we should bear witness to the differend which constitutes their mutual relations. We cannot therefore homogenize these worlds, nor can we hierarchize their order of priority or normativity. We are in no position to speak of the 'all', and therefore cannot describe it as being either 'for the best' or 'for the worst': the 'all' is, in fact, precisely the kind of homogenizing semantic trope which postmodernism would counter with 'the local' or, better, the 'singularity of the event'. The singularity of the event always implicates the Subject in an act of judgment, and such judgments, made without criteria, are best faced both stoically and ethically.[47] Postmodern Pessimism derives from the realization that 'the just' can never be formulated; the positive aspect of such Pessimism lies in the realization that the just must be enacted, invented. History may not exist for the Subject; but the Subject must 'just' exist.

 NOTES

1 For a full indication of the scope of these debates, see T. Docherty (ed.), *Postmodernism: A Reader* (Hemel Hampstead: Harvester-Wheatsheaf, 1993), and C. Jencks (ed.), *The Postmodern Reader* (London: Academy Editions, 1992).

2 F. de Onís (ed.), *Antologia de la poesia española e hispanoamericana* (Madrid, 1934); A. Toynbee, *A Study of History*, vol. 1 (1934; 2nd edn, Oxford: Oxford University Press, 1935), p. 1, note 2, and vol. 5 (Oxford: Oxford University Press, 1939), p. 43. For a fuller documentation of the history of the term 'postmodernism', see M. Köhler, ' "Postmodernismus": Ein begriffsgeschichtlicher Überblick', *Amerikastüdien*, 22:1 (1977).

3 H. White, *Metahistory* (Baltimore: Johns Hopkins University Press, 1973; repr. 1987), pp. 61–2.

4 E. Auerbach, *Mimesis* (1946; trans. W. R. Trask; repr. Princeton: Princeton University Press, 1974), p. 552. See my comments on what, theoretically, is at stake in this text in T. Docherty, *After Theory* (London: Routledge, 1990), pp. 122–3.

5 L. A. Fiedler, 'The New Mutants', *Partisan Review*, 32 (1965): 505–6. The distinction between aesthetic postmodernism as mood and political postmodernity as a periodizing term has often been seen as a state of affairs productive of a specific 'schizophrenia'. For more on this, see F. Jameson, *Postmodernism* (London: Verso, 1991), pp. 25ff.; and cf. the work of Deleuze and Guattari and those thinkers usually grouped under the rubric of 'anti-psychiatry', such as Rollo May, David Cooper, R. D. Laing, Norman O. Brown and others.

6 See, e.g., J. Habermas, *Theory of Communicative Action*, 2 vols, trans. T. McCarthy (London: Heinemann, 1984); Habermas, *Philosophical Discourse of Modernity*, trans. F. G. Lawrence (London: Polity, 1985); F. Jameson, *Late Marxism* (London: Verso, 1990); E. Mandel, *Late Capitalism* (London: Verso, 1978).

7 J. Lyotard, *The Postmodern Condition* [14.44], xxiv. Lyotard indicates that such a definition is 'simplifying to extremes'; and later, in *Le Postmoderne expliqué aux enfants* [14.34], 40, he points out that in this text he overstressed the narrative genre.

8 Lyotard, *Postmodern Condition*, [14.44], 81.

9 For more on the event, see Lyotard, 'The Sublime and the avant-garde', in A. Benjamin (ed.) [14.47] and cf. G. Bennington, *Lyotard: Writing the Event* (Manchester: Manchester University Press, 1988). On justice, see Lyotard, *Le Différend* [14.30] and Lyotard and J.-L. Thébaud, *Au juste* [14.41].

10 T. Adorno and M. Horkheimer, *Dialectic of Enlightenment* (1944; trans. J. Cumming, London: Verso, 1986), p. 6.

11 P. Gay, *The Enlightenment*, vol. 1 (Oxford: Oxford University Press, 1966), p. xiii.

12 Adorno and Horkheimer, *Dialectic*, p. 3.

13 *Ibid.*, p. 6.

14 *Ibid.*, p. 7.

15 *Ibid.*, p. 9.

16 Lyotard, 'Svelte Appendix to the Postmodern Question', trans. T. Docherty, in R. Kearney (ed.), *Across the Frontiers* (Dublin: Wolfhound Press, 1988), p. 265.

17 See, for examples, J. L. Austin, *How to do Things with Words* 2nd edn, (Oxford: Oxford University Press, 1975); K. Burke, *Language as Symbolic Action* (Berkeley: University of California Press, 1966); S. Fish, *Self-Consuming Artifacts* (Berkeley: University of California Press, 1972), and *Is there a Text in this Class?* (Cambridge, Mass.: Harvard University Press, 1980); W. J. T. Mitchell (ed.), *Against Theory* (Chicago: University of Chicago Press, 1985), which includes a 'more-pragmatist-than-thou' statement by Richard Rorty, the most explicitly 'New Pragmatist' of current pragmatic theorists.

18 Paul de Man, *The Resistance to Theory* (Manchester: Manchester University Press, 1986), p. 11. See also G. Frege, 'On Sense and Meaning', in M. Black and P. T. Geach (eds), *Translations from the Philosophical Writings of Gottlob Frege* (Oxford: Blackwell, 1952).

19 On the philosophical deconstruction of such identity, see, e.g., V. Descombes, *Modern French Philosophy*, trans. L. Scott-Fox and J. M. Harding (Cambridge: Cambridge University Press, 1980), p. 38.

20 Adorno and Horkheimer, *Dialectic*, p. 7.

21 *Ibid.*, p. 13.

22 See M. Foucault, *Folie et déraison* (Paris: Plon, 1961).

23 Voltaire, *Candide* (Oxford: Oxford University Press, 1968), passim; John Milton, 'Paradise Lost', in B. A. Wright (ed.), *Milton: Poems* (London: Dent, 1956), p. 218 (Bk iv, line 112) and p. 164 (Bk i, line 253). Cf. my comments on this in Docherty, *On Modern Authority* (Brighton: Harvester Press, 1986), ch. 7.

24 H. Blumenberg, *The Legitimacy of the Modern Age* (1966), trans. R. M. Wallace (Cambridge, Mass.: MIT Press, 1983), p. 404.

25 The indebtedness of this mode of thinking to the proto-existentialist Kierkegaard should be clear: the sense that one was always 'embarked' and that the grounds upon which one makes judgments are constantly shifting was always close to the centre of Kierkegaardian thinking.

26 See, e.g., C. Jencks, *Postmodernism* (London: Academy Editions, 1987), and P. Portoghesi, *Postmodern* (New York: Rizzoli, 1983).

27 See D. Harvey, *The Condition of Postmodernity* (Oxford: Blackwell, 1989).

28 See K. Frampton, 'Towards a Critical Regionalism', in H. Foster (ed.), *Postmodern Culture* (London: Pluto Press, 1983).

29 J.-F. Lyotard, *The Postmodern Condition* [14.44], xxiv. For the suggestion that this is over stated, see Lyotard, *Le Postmoderne expliqué aux enfants* [14.34], 40.

30 W. Benjamin, *Illuminations*, ed. Hannah Arendt, trans. H. Zohn (Glasgow: Fontana, 1973), p. 258.

31 See, e.g., Lyotard, *Rudiments païens* [14.27] and *Instructions païennes* [14.26].

32 Z. Bauman, *Modernity and the Holocaust* (Oxford: Polity Press, 1979), p. 7.

33 *Ibid.*, p. 8.

34 *Ibid.*, pp 202–3.

35 *Ibid.*, p. 203.

36 J. Baudrillard, *Simulations* [14.19], 25.

37 See J. Derrida, *Margins of Philosophy*, trans. A. Bass (Brighton: Harvester, 1982), p. 213.

38 Lyotard and R. Rorty, 'Discussion' [14.49], 581–4.

39 See Lyotard, *Le Différend* [14.30].

40 For a full exploration of this notion of 'judging without criteria', see Lyotard and Thébaud, *Au juste* [14.41].

41 See G. Debord, *La Société du spectacle* (Paris: Buchet-Chastel, 1968); P. Virilio, *L'Horizon négatif* (Paris: Galilée, 1984), esp. cinquième partie.

42 See J. Baudrillard, *La Guerre du golfe n'a pas eu lieu* [14.15], and C. Norris, *Intellectuals and the Gulf War* (London: Lawrence & Wishart, 1991).

43 A. Badiou, *Manifeste pour la philosophie* (Paris: Seuil, 1989), p. 17 (trans. T. Docherty).

44 J. Habermas, *Legitimation Crisis*, trans. T. MacCarthy (London: Heinemann, 1976).

45 E. Levinas, *The Levinas Reader*, ed. Séan Hand (Oxford: Blackwell, 1989), pp. 82, 83.

46 See F. Jameson, 'Postmodernism; or, the Cultural Logic of Late Capitalism', in his *Postmodernism* (London: Verso, 1991); and see also the various earlier, and more influential, forms of Jameson's essay in Foster (ed.), *Postmodern Culture* (where it appears as 'Postmodernism and Consumer Society') and in *New Left Review*, 146 (1984): 56–93.

47 On such stoicism, see G. Deleuze, *Logique du sens* (Paris: Minuit, 1969).

❧ SELECT BIBLIOGRAPHY ❧

What follows here is a list of titles by Lyotard and by Baudrillard which are relevant to the theme, concept, practices or philosophies of postmodernism. Given the fact that postmodernism is explicitly eclectic, it does not comprise a representative selection of the writings available on postmodernism. For a more detailed bibliography of postmodernism, as opposed to a list of the writings of Lyotard and Baudrillard, the reader should consult the following texts: S. Connor, *Postmodernist Culture* (Oxford: Basil Blackwell, 1989); T. Docherty, *Postmodernism: A Reader* (London: Harvester-Wheatsheaf; New York: Columbia University Press, 1993); L. Hutcheon, *A Poetics of Postmodernism* (London: Routledge, 1988).

Baudrillard

Primary texts

14.1 *Le Système des objets*, Paris: Gallimard, 1968.
14.2 *La Société de consommation*, Paris: Gallimard, 1970.
14.3 *Pour une critique de l'économie politique du signe*, Paris: Gallimard, 1972.
14.4 *Le Miroir de la production*, Tournail: Casterman, 1973.
14.5 *L'Echange symbolique et la mort*, Paris: Gallimard, 1976.
14.6 *L'Effet Beaubourg*, Paris: Galilée, 1977.
14.7 *Oublier Foucault*, Paris: Galilée, 1977.
14.8 *De la séduction*, Paris: Denoël, 1979.
14.9 *Simulacres et simulation*, Paris: Galilée, 1981.
14.10 *Les Stratégies fatales*, Paris: Grasset, 1983.
14.11 *La Gauche divine*, Paris: Grasset, 1985.
14.12 *Amérique*, Paris: Grasset, 1986.
14.13 *L'Autre par lui-même*, Paris: Galilée, 1987.
14.14 *Cool Memories*, Paris: Galilée, 1987.
14.15 *La Guerre du golfe n'a pas eu lieu*, Paris: Galilée, 1991.

Translations

14.16 *The Mirror of Production*, trans. M. Poster, St Louis: Telos Press, 1975.
14.17 *For a Critique of the Political Economy of the Sign*, trans. C. Levin, St Louis: Telos Press, 1981.
14.18 *In the Shadow of the Silent Majorities*, trans. P. Foss, P. Patton, and J. Johnston, New York: Semiotext(e), 1983.
14.19 *Simulations*, trans. P. Foss, P. Patton, and P. Beitchman, New York: Semiotext(e), 1983.
14.20 *The Evil Demon of Images*, Sydney: Power Institute Publications, 1987.
14.21 *Selected Writings*, ed. M. Poster, Cambridge: Polity Press, 1988.

Lyotard

Primary texts

14.22 *La Phénoménologie*, Paris: PUF, 1954.
14.23 *Dérives à partir de Marx et Freud*, Paris: Union Générale d'Editions, 10/18, 1970.
14.24 *Discours, figure*, Paris: Klincksieck, 1971.
14.25 *L'Economie libidinale*, Paris: Minuit, 1974.
14.26 *Instructions païennes*, Paris: Galilée, 1977.
14.27 *Rudiments païens*, Paris: Union Générale d'Editions, 1977.
14.28 *La Condition postmoderne*, Paris: Minuit, 1979.
14.29 *Le Mur du pacifique*, Paris: Galilée, 1979.

14.30 *Le Différend*, Paris: Minuit, 1983

14.31 *L'Assassinat de l'expérience par la peinture: Monory*, Paris: Le Castor Astral, 1984.

14.32 *Le Tombeau de l'intellectuel*, Paris: Galilée, 1984.

14.33 *L'Enthousiasme: la critique kantienne de l'histoire*, Paris: Galilée, 1986.

14.34 *Le Postmoderne expliqué aux enfants*, Paris: Galilée, 1986.

14.35 'Sensus Communis', *Le Cahier du Collége International de Philosophie*, 3 (1987): 67–87.

14.36 *L'Inhumain*, Paris: Galilée, 1988.

14.37 *Leçons sur l'analytique du sublime*, Paris: Galilée, 1991.

14.38 Lyotard, J.-F. and Chaput, T., *Less Immatériaux*, Paris: Centre Georges Pompidou, 1985.

14.39 Lyotard, J.-F. and Francken, R., *L'Histoire de Ruth*, Paris: Le Castor Astral, 1983.

14.40 Lyotard, J.-F. and Monory, J., *Récits tremblants*, Paris: Galilée, 1977.

14.41 Lyotard, J.-F. and Thébaud, J.-L., *Au juste*, Paris: Christian Bourgois, 1979.

14.42 Lyotard, J.-F. et al., *La Faculté de juger*, Paris: Minuit, 1983.

Translations

14.43 'One of the Things at Stake in Women's Struggles', *SubStance*, 20 (1978): 9–17.

14.44 *The Postmodern Condition: A Report on Knowledge*, trans. G. Bennington and B. Massumi, Manchester: Manchester University Press, 1984.

14.45 *The Differend*, trans. G. van den Abbeele, Manchester: Manchester University Press, 1990.

14.46 *Peregrinations*, New York: Columbia University Press, 1988.

14.47 *The Lyotard Reader*, ed. A. Benjamin, Oxford: Blackwell, 1989.

14.48 *Just Gaming*, trans. W. Godzich, Manchester: Manchester University Press, 1985.

14.49 Lyotard, J.-F. and Rorty, R, 'Discussion', *Critique*, 41 (1985): 581–4.

Glossary

✦

alterity – a perspective on otherness that goes beyond mere binary opposition. In the work of Emmanuel Levinas, the other is ethically prior to any projection of self.

apodictic – a term used to refer to that which is absolutely certain and necessarily true. Husserl introduced the phenomenological method in order to make philosophy a 'rigorous' science based on apodictic grounds.

aporia – from the Greek *apeiron* (boundless, infinite). Term used for a puzzling question or theme that generates other questions, but has no clear and simple resolution.

apperception – a primary tenet of the philosophy of reflective consciousness that refers to an awareness of one's own changing mental states. For Kant transcendental apperception describes the unity of consciousness (pure ego) that precedes and synthesizes our perceptions, thus grounding any possibility of experience at all.

binary opposition – a principle first explored in the theory of Ferdinand de Saussure, the Swiss linguist whose *Cours de linguistique générale* (1916) pointed out the relational features of language that later influenced the development of structuralism. It identifies the 'phonemic' differences that allow us to recognize significant contrasts between words as spoken (e.g., *b*at/*c*at), while at the same time ignoring phonemic differences that are not used to distribute meaning in a particular language (e.g., *c*oat/*c*aught).

categorical imperative – Kant's 'moral law' which is universally binding by self-legislating reason. One formulation would be: 'Act only on that maxim through which you can at the same time will that it should become a universal law.'

critical theory – in its most general application, designates the activity of cultural critique as philosophical *praxis*. This would include *Kulturkritik* as practised by members of the Frankfurt school (Horkheimer, Marcuse, Adorno, Benjamin and Habermas), as well as by French and Italian social philosophy represented by Gramsci, Foucault, Althusser and Lyotard. A broad category encompassing studies using Marxist and Freudian methods of analysis, as well as works focusing on aesthetics and mass culture.

Dasein – Heidegger's term to designate 'that being for whom Being is an issue', a concept most fully developed in *Being and Time*. Originally a word in German simply meaning 'existence', it takes on a contextualized resonance, and Heidegger stressed that *Dasein* was never to be understood simply as the Cartesian 'subject'.

deconstruction – a term used by Jacques Derrida to describe the strategies and tactics which can be used to re-examine the presuppositions of texts which are usually read from a logocentric perspective. It represents a philosophical challenge to the 'metaphysics of presence' by including attention to the negative term which is always left as a trace of supplementary meanings.

différance – more than just the difference (*différence*) that stands in opposition to identity, this term is used by Derrida to describe the prior ground upon which such oppositions are constructed. As such, it always resists binary categories by going beyond them.

differend (*différend*) – a term used by Jean-François Lyotard to emphasize the incommensurability of different 'language games' that usually results in the silencing of the weaker participant. A persistent heterogeneity that can never be reduced to sameness.

discourse ethics – a term used by Jürgen Habermas to refer to the linguistic dimension of his project for communicative action. All speakers have the right to freely argue for normative claims that possess universal validity.

eidos – Greek term which has been used in various ways to convey the sense of form, shape, appearance, image or idea. Plato uses this term for his abstract Forms or Ideas reflecting universal essences. For Husserl *eidos* is the essence of a noematic content revealed by the phenomenological method of inquiry. (See also *phenomenology*.)

epochē – the bracketing or suspension of empirical and metaphysical presuppositions of the 'natural attitude'. Husserl proposed such bracketing as the first methodological move of his phenomenology.

être-en-soi – Sartre's term for 'being-in-itself', a mere thing which is acted upon and remains passive. For Sartre this entails inauthentic existence, which evades the responsibility for making choices. Opposed to être-*pour*-soi, being-*for*-itself, which actively makes choices and takes responsibility in living authentically.

existentialism – in the twentieth century, the philosophy of existence developed ideas of both Kierkegaard (1813–55) and Nietzsche (1844–1900) that stressed the primacy of individual freedom, choice and responsibility in a world devoid of absolute values. Significant contributors would be Jean-Paul Sartre, Albert Camus and Simone de Beauvoir.

Frankfurt school – founded in 1923, the major centre for critical theory during the 1930s, and re-established after the Second World War, when many of its members were forced to flee to America. (See also *critical theory*.)

fusion of horizons – a concept used by Hans-Georg Gadamer (*Horizontverschmelzung*) to indicate the importance of recognizing historical distance in the activity of philosophical hermeneutics. Approaching any text necessarily brings together the historical horizon of the interpreter, which must be taken into account, with that of an historically distant tradition.

genealogy – a term used first by Nietzsche and later by Foucault to describe the historical interrogation of discursive practices that produce knowledge and shape institutions. Neither predictably evolving nor continuous, these discourses reveal the ultimate locus of power relations that construct the subject.

grammatology – the science of the written sign proposed by Derrida that challenged the dominance of spoken (phonocentric) discourse which privileges presence. The written sign is thus left open to alternative interpretations and meanings.

hegemony – a concept developed by Antonio Gramsci that stresses the ideological importance of cultural institutions in protecting the interests of a dominant class. Apparent consensus is achieved by a political and cultural leadership that transmits and legitimates its own values, which remain unexamined as ideologically neutral. The concept changed the focus of much Marxist theory from the economic base to superstructure.

hermeneutics – a term broadly defined by Paul Ricoeur as 'the art of deciphering indirect meaning'. This philosophical task of interpretation proceeds via the mediations of symbol, myth, dream, image, narrative, text and ideology. For Gadamer as well, all encounters with tradition must be viewed through this structure of interpretation.

hermeneutics of suspicion – the practice of critical or 'depth' hermeneutics that reveals the hidden and often ideological nature of texts, events and social practices. Ricoeur identifies three 'masters of suspicion': Marx, Nietzsche and Freud.

ideal speech situation – a concept suggested by Habermas to describe the required conditions of equality and free, unencumbered speech for participants to reach a universally binding consensus in rational discourse.

ideology – For Marx this meant 'false consciousness', that is, the complex of abstract beliefs that ignore historical and material existence by distorting and concealing social contradictions. The Marxist critiques of religion and German idealism aim to highlight this contradiction. Expanded by the work of Gramsci who recognized the importance of the 'superstructure' in supporting ideological hegemony through cultural institutions. Less negatively, for Ricoeur, the natural inclination within any social grouping to bind itself through foundational myths that appeal to tradition and resist change.

instrumental rationality – a translation of Max Weber's concept *Zweckrationalität*, which identifies goal-oriented rationality as 'the iron cage' from which we cannot escape. It permeates our lives in the form of increasing bureaucracy and narrowing expertise. It greatly influenced Horkheimer's and Adorno's critique of Enlightenment rationality, *Dialectic of Enlightenment*.

intentionality – a concept revived by Franz Brentano from medieval philosophy and later more fully developed by Edmund Husserl in his phenomenology. His emphasis on consciousness as always 'consciousness-of-something' is the foundation for his noetic–noematic structure of the intentional act. Consideration must be given to both the noetic act itself (willing, believing, etc.), as well as to the noematic 'content' of this act. Only in this way is the essence or *eidos* of what is intended revealed. For Husserl, the three modes of intentionality (perception, imagination, and signification) are fully interrelated.

jouissance – While this term is usually translated from the French as 'pleasure', it connotes an orgasmic joy and release that engages the whole body.

life-world (*Lebenswelt*) – a term used in the late work of Husserl (*The Crisis of the European Sciences*, 1937), referring to a shared background of culture, tradition and language that contextualizes subjective experience. The prototype of the life-world can be found in the life-philosophy and hermeneutic work of Wilhelm Dilthey who developed Hegel's concept of life and its domain of internal relations. Dilthey also greatly influenced Heidegger's focus on lived, historical experience in *Being and Time* (1927). Most recently, the term re-emerges in Habermas's theory of communicative action.

logocentrism – philosophical thinking that privileges 'presence' and attempts to define reality, truth, and knowledge with a concept of 'being' which is rooted in identifiable binary oppositions.

mauvaise-foi – a term used by Sartre that literally means 'bad faith', a mode of living inauthentically and passively. A refusal to acknowledge that one always has the freedom to choose.

Naturwissenschaft – the German for 'natural philosophy', the study of nature in general. Originally used to refer specifically to the science of investigating mechanistic principles and laws within the field of physics. Opposed to *Geisteswissenschaften* (human sciences) in the work of early hermeneutic theorists such as Dilthey.

noema – see *phenomenology*.

norms – a term referring to the standards or rules invoked to guide human conduct in determining what *ought* to be done, or what one is obliged to do, in an ideal and regulative sense.

ontological difference – for Heidegger, the distinction between 'Being' (*Sein*) and 'beings' (*Seiende*), which emphasizes that merely cataloguing existing beings or 'entities' ignores the ontological priority of Being-*qua*-Being.

ontology – a branch of philosophy that investigates 'being-as-being'. Questions are raised regarding topics in the metaphysical domain, such as the nature of reality, existence, essence and necessity.

ousia – from the Greek for 'substance'. The term used by Aristotle to indicate the most important and permanent of his ten categories.

phallocentrism – a form of logocentric thinking in which the phallus takes on the identity of *logos* or reason. Women are thereby defined within the context of patriarchal relations which represents them exclusively from a male perspective.

phenomenology – one of the most influential philosophies of the twentieth century, developed by Edmund Husserl. He attempted to secure a rigorous method for describing the vital role of human consciousness in constituting meaning. His project to go 'back to the things themselves' ('zu den Sachen selbst'), first announced in *Logical Investigations* (1900), required a step back from 'the natural attitude' of common sense in an effort to describe the essential contents (*noema*) of our intending acts (*noesis*). Husserl's 'eidetic phenomenology' was later revised by Heidegger into a 'hermeneutic' and 'existential' phenomenology (*Being and Time*, 1927), which in turn influenced numerous philosophers, such as Gadamer, Ricoeur, Merleau-Ponty and Sartre. (See also *intentionality*.)

positivism – the view of scientific methodology that privileges 'neutral' observation and control in experimental procedures. First envisioned by Auguste Comte (1798–1857) as the most developed stage of human development, it is now associated with technological rationalization and control.

postmodernism – a term used by Jean-François Lyotard (*The Postmodern Condition*, 1979) to refer to the radical and constant mutability contained within the concept of modernism itself; not to be understood simply as a 'stage' that comes after or replaces modernism. An influential challenge to the notion of the autonomous subject guided by the metanarratives of historical consciousness, postmodernism has affected varied intellectual domains, such as philosophy, literature and art.

poststructuralism – shares with structuralism the rejection of the paradigm of the human subject as the self-contained *cogito* or consciousness found in phenomenology and existentialism. However, it also rejects the static internal relations of the structuralist model, opting instead for multiple possibilities within the signifier–signified combinations. The later work of some French philosophers who began as 'structuralists' (e.g., Lacan, Barthes) most closely fits this stance. (See also *semiotics*.)

readiness-to-hand (*Zuhandenheit*) – for Heidegger, *Dasein*'s relationship to entities as practical comportment and everyday involvement, e.g., just *using* the hammer and not consciously articulating the process. Contrasts with the concept of 'Presence-at-Hand' (*Vorhandenheit*), whereby *Dasein* regards an 'object' with abstract (circumspective) comportment.

reification – a concept (*Verdinglichung*) used by Marx to describe the reduction of human beings and human relations to 'thing-like' objects, as well as the alienation of human labour from the material objects produced by its own work. Later much developed by Lukács in the longest chapter of *History and Class Consciousness*.

semiotics – a 'science of signs', also known as semiology, developed by Ferdinand de Saussure in Europe and C. S. Peirce in America. Studies the constitutive-relational nature of signs and their communicative properties in society. The linguistic sign is a structural relationship between an acoustic 'signifier' and the concept or 'signified' it refers to. Much extended by Roland Barthes in his analyses of social semiotics where signification is heavily dependent on the connotation or associative powers of the sign, in popular culture and advertising especially.

signifier, signified – see *semiotics*.

social imaginary – for Ricoeur, the symbolic discourses which permit the formation of complex socio-political groupings. Foundational symbols and myths provide the ideological basis for this identity, which is constantly tested by the potential for change and the need for change (utopian possibilities).

structuralism – a movement focusing on internal structural relations rather than content, based on the linguistic method of analysis developed by Ferdinand de Saussure. He suggested that language constituted a self-contained system, wherein meaning was generated within language itself rather than merely reflecting a 'given' reality. This revolutionary claim, and the methodology it entailed, attracted immense interest across a spectrum of intellectual disciplines. Lévi-Strauss applied de Saussure's insights to anthropology, Lacan to psychoanalysis, Althusser to Marxism and Foucault to his wide-ranging social critique. The exponents of structuralism maintained an adversarial relation with existentialists and phenomenologists, whose belief in a transcendentally free human subject was rejected. (See also *poststructuralism*.)

technē – from the Greek for skill, art, or craft. For Aristotle anything created by humans, as opposed to *physis* (nature) which is anything not humanly crafted. This knowledge of *how* to reach a desired end can be procedural as well, and would include not only the fine arts of music, dance, poetry, drama, etc., but also such special skills as rhetoric and medicine.

Mara Rainwater, University College Dublin

Index